Grace Livingston Hill Collection #1

Grace Livingston Hill (1865–1947) remains popular more than fifty years after her death. She wrote dozens of books that carry her unique style for combining Christian faith with tasteful and exciting romance.

Isabella Alden (1841–1930), an aunt of Grace Livingston Hill, was a prolific author as well, using her writing to teach lessons espoused by her husband Gustavus, a minister.

Aunt Crete's Emancipation, Grace Livingston Hill

Aunt Crete stays at home to do the chores while her sister and niece, Luella, take off for a posh summer resort. Luella insists on leaving sooner than planned to avoid a "backwoods cousin" coming from the West. Moments after their hasty departure, Donald Grant arrives and soon learns the truth of his aunt's Cinderella circumstances. True love and a generous heart set to work to free a tired old woman.

A Daily Rate, Grace Livingston Hill

Celia Murray finds her purpose in moving to the city somewhat altered when the needs of others become apparent. The woman who runs her boardinghouse falls ill and in debt; young boarders need guidance; and her favorite aunt is unwelcome in a neice's home. But a reversal of fortune and a benevolent spirit transform Celia's life as well as those around her.

The Girl From Montana, Grace Livingston Hill

Elizabeth Bailey was raised in the wilderness of Montana and is now alone in the world with nothing but a budding faith in God to cling to. After her last remaining brother is murdered, she escapes her brother's killer and heads east to find her only relatives. Enroute to Pennsylvania, she meets George, a man who is trying to escape a different kind of torment and who saves her life. She is drawn to him, and he to her— but an emergency at home forces him to leave her behind. As Elizabeth journeys onward, she wonders: Will they ever meet again?

Mara, Isabella Alden

Isabella Alden weaves her compelling story around the lives of four very different young women who befriend one another in school. Going their separate ways they encounter diverse lifestyles and disappointed hopes. Revelation of the truth—that she has unwittingly married a man with a dark secret—nearly destroys Naomi, one of the young women, but an unexpected reunion marks a turning point in her life.

Grace Livingston Hill

COLLECTION NO. 1

FOUR COMPLETE NOVELS

Updated for today's readers

BARBOUR
PUBLISHING, INC.
Uhrichsville, Ohio

Edited and updated for today's readers by Deborah Cole

© MCMXCIX by R. L. Munce Publishing Co., Inc.

ISBN 1-57748-443-6

Published by Barbour Publishing, Inc., P.O. Box 719, Uhrichsville, Ohio 44683
http://www.barbourbooks.com

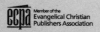 Member of the
Evangelical Christian
Publishers Association

Printed in the United States of America.

Aunt Crete's Emancipation

Chapter 1

W ho's at the front door?" asked Luella's mother, coming in from the kitchen with a dish towel in her hand. "I thought I heard the doorbell."

"Luella's gone to the door," said her sister from her vantage point at the crack of the sitting room door. "It looks to me like a telegraph boy."

"It couldn't be, Crete," said Luella's mother impatiently, coming to see for herself. "Who would telegraph now that Hannah's dead?"

Lucretia was short and dumpy, with the comfortable, patient look of the maiden aunt who knows she's indispensable because she'll meekly take the burdens no one else wants to bear. Her sister could easily look over her head into the hall, and her gaze was penetrative and alert.

"I'm sure I don't know, Carrie," said Lucretia apprehensively, "but I'm all a tremble. Telegrams are dreadful things."

"Nonsense, Crete, you always act like such a baby. Hurry up, Luella. Don't stop to read it. Your aunt Crete will have a fit. Wasn't there anything to pay? Who's it for?"

Luella, a rather stout young woman in stylish attire, with her mother's keen features unsoftened by sentiment, advanced, irreverently tearing open her mother's telegram and reading it as she came. It was one of the family grievances that Luella was stout like her aunt instead of tall and slender like her mother. The aunt always felt secretly that they somehow blamed her for being that type.

"It makes one so hard to fit," Luella's mother remarked frequently. Then she added with a disparaging glance at her sister's dumpy form, "So impossible!"

At such times the aunt always wrinkled up her pleasant little forehead into an upside-down V and trotted off to her kitchen or her buttonholes or whatever was the present task, sighing helplessly. She tried to be the best she could always. But one couldn't help one's figure, especially when one was partly dependent on one's family for support, and dressmakers and tailors took so much money. It was bad enough having one stout figure to fit in the family without two. And the aunt always felt called upon to have as little dressmaking done as possible, in order that Luella's figure might be improved from the slender treasury.

"Clothes do make a big difference," she reflected.

And sometimes when she was all alone in the twilight, and there was really nothing her alert conscience could possibly put her hand to doing for the moment, she amused herself by thinking what kind of dress she would buy, and who should make it, if she suddenly attained a fortune. But this was a harmless amusement, inasmuch as she never let it make her discontented with her lot or ruffle her placid brow for an instant.

But just now she was "all a tremble," and the V in her forehead was rapidly becoming a double V. She watched Luella's dismayed face with growing alarm.

"For goodness' sake alive!" said Luella, flinging herself into the most comfortable rocker and throwing her mother's telegram on the table. "That's not to be tolerated! Something will have to be done. We'll have to go to the shore at once, Mother. I'd die of mortification to have a country cousin come around just now. What would the Grandons think if they saw him? I can't afford to ruin all my chances for a cousin I've never seen. Mother, you simply must do something. I won't stand it!"

"What in the world are you talking about, Luella?" said her mother impatiently. "Why didn't you read the telegram aloud, or why didn't you give it to me at once? Where are my glasses?"

The aunt waited meekly while her sister found her glasses and read the telegram.

"Well, I declare! That is provoking to have him turn up just now of all times. Something must be done, of course. We can't have a gawky Westerner around in the way. And, as you say, we've never seen him. It can't make much difference to him whether he sees us or not. We can hurry off and be conveniently out of the way. It's probably only a duty visit he's paying anyway. Hannah's been dead ten years, and I always heard the child was more like his father than his mother. Besides, Hannah married and went away to live when I was only a little girl. I really don't think Donald has much claim on us. What a long telegram! It must have cost a lot. Was it paid for? It shows he knows nothing of the world, or he'd have put it in a few words. Well, we'll have to get away at once."

She crumpled the telegram into a ball and flung it to the table again. But it fell wide of its mark and dropped to the floor instead. The aunt patiently stooped and picked it up, smoothing out the crushed yellow paper.

"Hannah's boy!" she said gently, and she touched the yellow paper as if it were sacred.

Am taking a trip east and shall make you a little visit if convenient. Will be with you sometime on Thursday.

Donald Grant.

She sat down suddenly in the nearest chair. Somehow the relief from anxiety made her knees weak. "Hannah's boy!" she murmured again and laid her hand caressingly over the telegram, smoothing down a torn place in the edge of the paper.

Luella and her mother were discussing plans. They decided they must leave on the early train the next morning, before there was any chance of the Western visitor arriving.

"Goodness! Look at Aunt Crete," said Luella, laughing. "She looks as if she's seen a ghost. Her lips are all white."

"Crete, you oughtn't to be such a fool. As if a telegram would hurt you! There's nobody left to be worried about like that. Why don't you use your reason a little?"

"Hannah's boy is really coming!" beamed Aunt Crete, ignoring their scorn of her.

"Upon my word! Aunt Crete, you look as if it were something to be glad about, instead of a downright calamity."

"Glad, of course I'm glad, Luella. Wouldn't you be glad to see your oldest sister's child? Hannah was always very dear to me. I can see her now the way she looked when she went away, so tall and slim and pretty—"

"Not if she'd been dead for a century or so, and I'd never seen the child, and he was a gawky, embarrassing creature who would spoil the prospects of the people I was supposed to love," retorted Luella. "Aunt Crete, don't you care the least bit for my happiness? Do you want it spoiled?"

"Why, of course not, dearie," beamed Aunt Crete, "but I don't see how it will spoil your happiness. I should think you'd want to see him yourself."

"Aunt Crete! The idea! He's nothing to me. You know he's lived away out in the wild West all his life. He probably never had much schooling and doesn't know how to dress or behave in polite society. I heard he went away off up in the Klondike somewhere and worked in a mine. You can imagine just what a wild, ignorant creature he'll be. If Clarence Grandon should see him, he might think my whole family's like that, and then where would I be?"

"Yes, Crete, I'm surprised at you. You've been so anxious all along for Luella to shine in society, and now you talk just as if you didn't care in the least what happened," put in Luella's mother.

"But what can you do?" asked Aunt Crete. "You can't tell him not to come—your own sister's child!"

"Oh, how silly you are, Crete!" said her sister. "No, of course we can't very well tell him not to come, as he hasn't given us a chance; for this telegram is evidently sent on the way. It's dated Chicago, and he hasn't given us a trace of an address. He doesn't live in Chicago. He's very likely almost here and may arrive anytime tomorrow. Now you know we've simply got to go to the shore next week. The rooms are reserved at the hotel and paid for, and we might as well hurry up and get off tonight or early in the morning and escape him. Luella would die of mortification if she had to visit with that fellow and give up her trip to the shore. As you weren't going anyway, you can receive him. It will keep him quietly at home. He won't expect an old woman to go out with him and show him the sights, so nobody will notice him much, and there won't be a lot of talk. If he looks very ridiculous, and that prying Mrs. Brown next door speaks of it, you might explain he's the son of an old school friend who went out west to live years ago—"

"Oh, Carrie!" exclaimed Aunt Crete. "That wouldn't be true. And, besides, he can't be so very bad as that. And even if he is, I shall love him—for he's Hannah's boy."

"Love him all you want to," sniffed her sister. "But for pity's sake don't let the neighbors know what relation he is."

"That's just like you, Aunt Crete," said Luella in a hurt tone. "You've known me and pretended to love me all your life. I'm almost like your own child, and yet you take up with this unknown nephew and say you'll love him in spite of all the trouble he's making me."

Aunt Crete doubled the V in her forehead and wiped away the beads of perspiration. Somehow it always seemed she was in the wrong. Would she be understood in heaven? she wondered.

Luella and her mother went on planning. They advised what Aunt Crete was to do after they left.

"There're the raspberries and blackberries not done up yet, Crete, but I guess you can manage alone. You always do the biggest part of the canning anyway. I'm awfully sorry about your sewing, Crete. I meant to fit your two thin dresses before we went away, but the dressmaker made Luella's things so much more elaborate than I expected that we really haven't had a minute's time, what with all the lace insertion she left for us to sew on. Perhaps you better run down to Miss Mason and see if she had time to fit them, if you think you can't wait till we get back. You'll hardly be going out much while we're gone, you know."

"Oh, I'll be all right," said Aunt Crete happily. "I guess I can fix up my gray lawn for while Donald's here."

"Donald! Nonsense! It won't matter what you wear while he's here. He'll never know a calico from a silk. Now look here, Crete. You've got to be awfully careful, or you'll let out when we went off. There's no use in his finding out we didn't want to see him. You wouldn't want to hurt his feelings, you know. Your own sister's child!"

"No, of course not," agreed Aunt Crete, though there was a troubled look in her eyes. She never liked prevarication. And when she was left with some polite fabrication to excuse her relatives out of something they wanted to shirk, she nearly always got it twisted so that it was either an out-and-out lie, which horrified her, or else let the whole thing "out of the bag," as Luella said.

But there was little time for discussion, for Luella and her mother had a great deal of packing to do. And Aunt Crete had the dinner to get and the house to set in order, surreptitiously, for the expected guest.

They hurried away the next morning in a whirl of bags and suitcases and parasols and umbrellas. They had baggage enough for a year in Europe, although they expected to stay only two or three weeks at the shore at most. Aunt Crete helped them into the station cab, ran back to the house for Luella's new raincoat, back again for the veil and her sister's gloves, and still a third time to bring the new books, which had been set aside for reading on the journey. Then at last they were gone. And with one brief sigh of satisfaction Aunt Crete permitted herself to reflect that she was actually left alone to receive a dear guest all her own.

Never in all her maiden existence had she had this pleasure before. She might use the best china and have three kinds of pie at once, yes, and plum cake if she chose. Boys like pie and cake. Donald would be a big, nice boy.

What did it matter to her if he was awkward and from the West? He was in a large sense her own. Hannah was gone, and there was no one else to take a closer place. Who but his mother's sister should have the right to mother him for a while? He would be her own as Luella never had been, because there was always Luella's mother to take the first place. Besides, Luella had been a disappointing baby. Even in her infancy she developed an independence that scorned kissing and cuddling. Luella always had too many selfish interests on hand to have time for breathing out love and baby graces to admiring subjects. Her frown was always quicker than her smile. But somehow Aunt Crete felt that it would be different with this boy, and her heart swelled within her as she hurried into the house to make ready for his coming.

The front hall was littered with rose leaves. Luella had shaken a bunch of roses to get rid of the loose leaves and found they were all loose leaves. Therefore she flung them down on the floor. She'd meant to wear them with her new pongee traveling suit. It looked nice to wear roses on a journey, for it suggested a possible admirer. But the roses hadn't held out, and now Aunt Crete must sweep them up.

A glance into the parlor showed peanut shells scattered over the floor and on the table. A few of Luella's friends had come in for a few minutes the evening before, and they'd indulged in peanuts, finishing up by throwing the shells at one another amid shouts of hilarious laughter. Aunt Crete went for the broom and dustpan. If he came early, the hall and parlor must be in order first.

⚬⚬

Luella and her mother had little time to waste, for the tickets were barely bought and the trunks checked before the train thundered up. It was a through vestibuled train. As Luella struggled up the steps of one car with her heavy suitcase, a tall young man with dark, handsome eyes and a distinguished manner swung himself down the steps of the next car.

"Hello, Luella!" called a voice from a pony cart by the platform. "You're not going away today, are you? Thought you said you weren't going till next week."

"Circumstances made it necessary," called Luella from the top step of the car while the porter held up the suitcase for her to take. "I'm running away from a backwoods cousin who's coming to visit. I'll write and tell you all about it. Good-bye. Sorry I can't be at your house tomorrow night, but it couldn't be helped."

Then Luella turned another gaze upon the handsome stranger, who was standing on the platform just below her, looking about interestedly. She thought he'd looked at her pongee traveling suit consciously, feeling that he could only have thought she looked well.

He was still standing on the platform as the train moved out, and Luella could see the girl in the pony cart, too. It would be interesting to find out who he was. Luella preened herself and settled her large hat in front of the strip of mirror between the windows and then looked around the car to see who her fellow passengers were.

"Well, I'm glad we're off," said her mother nervously. "I was as afraid as could be your cousin might come in on that early through train before we got started. It would have been trying if he'd come just as we were getting away. I don't know how we could have explained it."

"Yes," said Luella. "I'm glad we're safely off. He'll never suspect now."

Just at that moment the grocery boy arrived at the back door with a crate of red raspberries.

"Land alive!" said Crete disappointedly. "I hoped those wouldn't come till tomorrow." She bustled about, taking the boxes out of the crate so the boy might take it back. Before she was finished the doorbell rang.

"Land alive!" said Crete again as she wiped her hands on the kitchen towel and hurried to the front door, taking off her apron as she went. "I do hope he hasn't come yet. I haven't cleared off that breakfast table. If he happens to come out, there are three plates standing."

But the thought had come too late. The dining room door was stretched wide open and the table in full view. The front door was guarded only by the wire screen. The visitor could take full notes, if he so desired.

Chapter 2

Miss Lucretia opened the screen and noticed the fine appearance of the young man standing there. He wasn't shabby enough for an agent. Someone had made a mistake, she supposed. She waited pleasantly for him to tell his errand.

"Is this where Mrs. Carrie Burton lives?" he asked, removing his hat courteously.

When she answered yes, his whole face broke into dancing eagerness.

"Is this my Aunt Carrie?" he asked and held out a tentative, appealing hand for welcome. "I'm Donald Grant."

"Oh!" said Miss Lucretia delightedly. "Oh!" She took his hand in both her own. "No, I ain't your Aunt Carrie; I'm your Aunt Crete. But I'm just as glad to see you. I didn't think you'd be so big and handsome. Your Aunt Carrie isn't home. They've just—why—that is—they are—they'd planned to be at the shore for three weeks, and they'll be real sorry when they know—" This last sentence was added with extra zeal, for Aunt Crete exulted in the fact that Carrie and Luella would indeed be sorry if they could look into their home for one instant and see the guest they'd run away from. She felt sure that if they'd known how fine-looking a young man he was, they would have stayed and been proud of him.

"I'm sorry they're away," said the young man, stooping to kiss Aunt Crete's plump, comfortable cheek. "But I'm mighty glad you're at home, Aunt Crete," he said with genuine pleasure. "I'm going to like you for all I'm worth to make up for the absence of my aunt and cousin. You say they've gone to the shore. When will they be at home? Is their stay there almost up?"

"Why, no," said Aunt Crete, flushing uncomfortably. "They haven't been gone long. And they've engaged their rooms there for three weeks at a big hotel. Luella, she's always been bound to go to one of those big places where rich people go, the Traymore. It's advertised in all the papers. I expect you've seen it sometimes. It's one of the most expensive places at the shore. I've almost a notion to write and tell them to come home, for I'm sure they'll be sorry when they hear about you, but you see it's this way. There's a young man been paying Luella some attention, and he's going down there soon. I don't know but he's there already, and his mother and sister are spending the whole season there, so Luella had her heart set on going down and boarding at the same hotel."

"Ah, I see," said the nephew. "Well, it wouldn't do to spoil my cousin's good time. Perhaps we can run down to the shore for a few days ourselves after we get acquainted. Say, Aunt Crete, am I too late for a bite of breakfast? I was so tired of the stuff they had on the dining car I thought I'd save up my appetite till I got here, for I was sure you'd have a bit of bread and butter anyway."

"Bless your dear heart, yes," said Aunt Crete, delighted to have the subject turned. She had a terrible fear she would yet tell a lie about the departure of her sister and niece, and a lie was a calamity not always easily avoided in a position like hers. "You just sit down here, you dear boy, and wait about two minutes till I set the coffeepot over the fire and cut some more bread. It isn't a mite of trouble, for I hadn't cleared off the breakfast table yet. In fact, I hadn't rightly finished my own breakfast because I was so busy getting to rights. The grocery boy came, and—well, I never can eat much when folks are going—I mean when I'm alone," she finished triumphantly.

She hurried out into the dining room to get the table cleared off, but Donald followed her. She tried to scuttle the plates together and remove all traces of the number of guests at the meal just past, but she couldn't be sure whether he noticed the table or not.

"May I help you?" asked the young man, grabbing Luella's plate and cup, and following his aunt into the kitchen. "It's so good to get into a real home again with somebody who belongs to me. You know Father is in Mexico, and I've been in the university for the last four years."

"The university!" Aunt Crete's eyes shone. "So you have universities out west? My! Won't Luella be astonished? I guess she thinks out west is all woods."

Donald's eyes danced.

"We have a few good schools out there," he said quietly.

While they were eating the breakfast Aunt Crete prepared in an incredibly short space of time, Donald asked a great many questions. What did his aunt and cousin look like? Was Aunt Carrie like her or like his mother? And Luella, had she been to college? And what did she look like?

Aunt Crete told him mournfully that Luella was more like her than like her mother. "And it seems sometimes as if she blamed me for it," said the patient aunt. "It makes it hard, her being a sort of society girl and wanting to look so fine. Dumpy figures like mine don't dress up pretty, you know. No, Luella never went to college. She didn't take much to books. She liked having a good time with young folks better.

"She's been wanting to go down to the shore and be at a real big hotel for three summers now, but Carrie never felt able to afford it before. We've been saving up all winter for Luella to have this treat, and I do hope she'll have a good time. It's real hard on her, having to stay right home all the time when all her girlfriends go off to the shore. But you see she's got in with some real wealthy people who stay at expensive places, and she isn't satisfied to go to a common boardinghouse. It must be nice to have money and go to a big hotel. I've never been in one myself, but Luella has, and she's told all about it. I'd think it would be grand to live that way awhile without a thing to do."

"They should have taken you along, Aunt Crete," said the young man. "I do hope I didn't keep you at home to entertain me."

"Oh, no, bless your heart," said the aunt. "I wasn't going. I never go anywhere. Why, what kind of a figure would I cut there? It would spoil Luella's good time to have me around. I'm so short-waisted. She always wants me to wear a coat when I go anywhere with her, so people won't see how short-waisted I am."

"Nonsense," said Donald. "I think you're lovely, Aunt Crete. You've got such pretty white hair, all wavy like Mother's. And you've got a fine face. Luella ought to be proud to have you."

Aunt Crete blushed over the compliment, and choking tears of joy throbbed for a minute in her throat.

"Now hear the boy!" she exclaimed. "Donald, do have another cup of coffee."

After breakfast Aunt Crete showed her guest to his room and then hurried down to get the stack of dishes out of the way before he came down again. But he appeared in the kitchen door in a few minutes.

"Give me a dish and some berries," he demanded. "I'm going to help you."

And despite all her protests he helped her with such vigor that by twelve o'clock twenty-one jars of crimson berries stood in a shining row on the kitchen table, and Aunt Crete was dishing up a savory dinner for two. Her face was shining as brightly as if she'd done nothing but play the whole morning.

"We did well, didn't we?" said Donald as he ate his dinner. "I haven't had such a good time since I went camping in the Klondike. Now after we get these dishes washed you're going to take a nice long nap. You look tired and warm."

Aunt Crete protested that she wasn't tired, but Donald insisted. "I want you to get nice and rested up, because tomorrow we're going shopping. By the way, I've brought you a present." He sprang up from the table and went to his suitcase to get it.

Aunt Crete's heart beat with anticipation as he handed her a little white box. What if it should be a breastpin? How she would like that! She'd worn her mother's, a braid of hair under a glass with a gold band under it, ever since she was grown up, and sometimes she felt as if it was a little old-fashioned. Luella openly scoffed at it and laughed at her for wearing it, but no one ever suggested getting her a new one. If she'd bought one for herself, she knew they'd have thought her extravagant.

She opened the box with excited fingers, and there inside was a little leather case. Donald touched a spring, and it flew open and disclosed a lovely star made of seed pearls, reposing on white velvet. It was a breastpin indeed, and one fit for a queen. Fortunately Aunt Crete didn't know enough about jewelry to realize what it cost, or her breath might have been taken away. As it was, she was stunned for the moment. Such a beautiful pin—and for her! She could scarcely believe it. She gazed and gazed and then, laying the box on the table, rose up and took Donald's face in her two toilworn hands and kissed him.

"I'm glad you like it," he said with a pleased smile. "I wasn't quite sure what to get, but the salesman told me these were always nice. Now let's get at these dishes."

In a daze of happiness Aunt Crete washed the dishes while Donald wiped them, and then despite her protest he made her go upstairs and lie down.

When had she ever taken a nap in the daytime before? Not since she was a little girl and fell from the second-story window. The frightened family had rushed around her and put her to bed in the daytime, and for one whole day she'd been waited upon and cared for tenderly. Then she was able to get up, and the hard, careless, toilsome world had rushed on again for her. But the memory of that blessed day of rest, touched by gentleness, had lingered forever a bright spot in her memory. She was always the one who did the hard things in her family, even when she was quite young.

Aunt Crete lay cautiously down upon her neatly made bed after she put on her best gown, a rusty black and white silk made over from one Luella had tired of, and clasped her hands blissfully on her breast, resting with her eyes wide open and a light of joy upon her face. She hardly felt it right to relax entirely, lest Donald might call her. But finally the unaccustomed position in the middle of the day sent her off into a real doze. Just about that time the telephone bell rang.

The telephone was in the sitting room downstairs. It was put in at the time when the telephone company was installing them free to introduce them in that suburb. It was ordinarily a source of great interest to the whole family, though it seldom rang except for Luella. Luella and her mother were exceedingly proud of its possession.

Donald was in the sitting room reading. He looked up from his paper, hesitated a moment and then took down the receiver. Perhaps his aunt was asleep already, and he could attend to this without waking her.

"Hello. Is this 53 M?"

Donald glanced at the number on the telephone and answered, "Yes."

"Here you are, Atlantic. Here is Midvale," went on the voice of the operator at Central.

"Hello! Is that you, Aunt Crete? This is Luella," came another girl's strident voice in hasty impatience. "What in the world were you so long about answering the phone for? I've been waiting here an age. Now, listen, Aunt Crete. For heaven's sake don't you tell that crazy cousin of ours where to find us, or like as not he'll take a notion to run down here to see us, and I'd simply die of mortification if he did. This is a very fine hotel, and it would be terrible to have a backwoods relation appear on the scene. Now be sure you keep quiet. I'll never forgive you if you don't.

"And say, Aunt Crete, won't you please sew on the rest of that Val edging down the ruffles of the waist and on the skirt of my new lavender organdie, and do it up and send it by mail? I forgot all about it. It's on the bed in the spare room, and the edging is started. You sew it on the way it's begun. You'll see. Now don't sew it on in the old way because it's quicker. It doesn't look a bit pretty, and you've nothing much else to do, now that we're gone anyway.

"And say, Aunt Crete, would you mind going down to Peter's today and telling Jennie I forgot all about getting those aprons to finish for the fair, and tell her you'll finish them for her? Do it today, because she has to send the box off by the end of the week. And Mother says you better clean the cellar right away, and she wondered if you'd feel equal to whitewashing it. I should think you'd like to do that; it's so cool this warm weather to be down cellar. And, oh, yes, if you get lonesome and want something to do, I forgot to tell you I left those three flannel shirtwaists cut out and ready to be made—in the upper bureau drawer of the spare room.

"Now don't read your eyes out the way you did the last time we went off and left you and have to wear dark glasses for a week, because I have lots of things planned to do when I get home. I'm going to have Helena Bates for a week, and there'll be several lunches and picnics doing.

"Oh, say, Aunt Crete, Mother says, if there're any more pie cherries to be had, you better put up some, and be sure and stone them all. I just hate them with the seeds in. And I guess that's all. Only don't forget you promised to have all those buttonholes worked for me in those underclothes I'm making, before I get back. Are you all right? Let me see. There was something else.

"Oh, yes, Mother says you don't need to get out the best china and make a great fuss as if you had grand company; he's only a country boy, you know. Say, Aunt Crete. Are you there? Why don't you answer? Aunt Crete! Hello! For pity's sake, what's the matter with this phone? Hello, Central! Oh, dear! I suppose she's gone away. That's the way Aunt Crete always does!"

Donald, with a strange, amused expression on his face, stood listening and hesitating. He didn't know exactly what to do. Without any intention at all he had listened to a conversation not intended for his ears. Should he answer and tell who he was? No, for that would only embarrass Luella. Neither would it do to call Aunt Crete now, for they'd be sure to find out he heard. Perhaps it was better to keep entirely still. There seemed to be nothing serious at stake.

Ruffles and shirtwaists and gingham aprons for a guild and whitewashing the cellar! Nobody would die if those things weren't done. His blood boiled over the tone in which the invisible cousin at the other end of the wire had ordered Aunt Crete about. He could read the whole life story of her patient self-sacrifice on the one hand and imposition on the other. He felt strongly impelled to do something in the matter. A rebuke of some sort should be administered. How could it best be done?

Meantime Luella was fuming with the telephone girl, and the girl was declaring that she could get no answer from Midvale anymore. Donald stood wickedly enjoying their discomfiture and was at last rewarded by hearing Luella say: "Well, I guess I've said all I want to say anyway, so you needn't ring them up again. I've got to go out boating now." The receiver at the shore clicked into place, and the connection was cut off.

Then the young man hung up the receiver at the Midvale end of the line and sat down to think. Bit by bit he pieced together the story until he'd very nearly made out the true state of affairs. So they were ashamed of him and were trying to get away. Could they have been the people who got on the train as he got off? Was that girl with the loud voice and the pongee suit his cousin? The voice over the telephone seemed like the one that called to the girl in the pony cart. And had his eyes deceived him, or were there three plates on the breakfast table that morning? Poor Aunt Crete! He would give her the best time he knew how, and perhaps it was also set for him to give his cousin a lesson.

Chapter 3

Aunt Crete woke up at last from an uncomfortable dream. She thought Carrie and Luella had come back and were about to snatch Donald away from her and bear him off to the shore.

She rose in haste and smoothed her hair, astonished at the freshness of her own face in the glass. She was afraid she had overslept and lost some of the precious time with Donald. There was so much to ask him, and he was so good to look at. She hurried down and was received warmly. Donald's meditations had culminated in a plan.

"Sit down, Aunt Crete. Are you sure you're rested? Then I want to talk. Suppose we run down to the shore and surprise the folks. How soon could you be ready?"

"Oh, dear heart! I couldn't do that!" exclaimed Aunt Crete, her face nevertheless alight with pleasure at the very thought.

"Why not? What's to hinder?"

"Oh, I never go. I always stay at home and attend to things."

"But that's no reason. Why couldn't things attend to themselves?"

"Why, I couldn't leave the house alone."

"Now, what in the world could possibly happen to the house that you could prevent by staying in it? Be reasonable, dear aunt. You know the house won't run away while you're gone, and, if it does, I'll get you another one. You don't mean to tell me you never go off on a vacation. Then it's high time you went, and you'll have to stay longer to make up for lost time. Besides, I want your company. I've never seen the East Coast and expect to enjoy it hugely, but I need somebody to enjoy it with me. I can't half take things in alone. I want somebody my very own to go with me. That's what I came here for. I thought of inviting you all to go down for a little trip, but, since the others are down there, why, we can join them."

Aunt Crete's face clouded. What would Luella say at having them appear on her horizon? The young man was all right, apparently, but there was no telling how angry Luella might be if her aunt came. She knew Luella preferred to keep her in the background.

"I really couldn't go, dear," she said wistfully. "I'd like it with all my heart. And it would be especially nice to go with you, for I never had anybody to go round with me, not since your mother was a girl and used to take me with her wherever she went. I missed her dreadfully after she was married and went out West. She was always so good to me."

The young man's face softened, and he reached his hand impulsively across the table and grasped the worn hand of his aunt.

"Well, you shall have somebody to go round with you now, Auntie—that is, if you'll let me. I'm not going to take no for an answer. You just must go. We'll have a vacation all by ourselves and do just as we please, and we'll show up at the hotel where Aunt Carrie and Luella are and surprise them."

"But, child, I can't!" said Aunt Crete in dismay, seeing his determination. "Why, I haven't any clothes suitable to wear away from home. We were all so busy getting Luella fixed out that there wasn't any time left for mine, and it didn't really matter about me anyway. I never go anywhere."

"But you're going now, Aunt Lucretia," he said, "and it does matter, you see. Clothes are easily bought. We'll go shopping after breakfast tomorrow morning."

"But I really can't afford it, Donald," said his aunt with an air of finality. "You know I'm not rich. If Carrie weren't good enough to give me a home here, I shouldn't know how to make two ends meet."

"Never mind that, Aunt Crete. This is my layout, and I'm paying for it. We'll go shopping tomorrow morning. I've got some money in my pocket that I'm just aching to spend. The fact is, Aunt Crete, I struck gold up there in the Klondike, and I've got more money than I know what to do with."

"Oh!" said Aunt Crete with awe in her voice at the thought of having more money than one knew what to do with. Then shyly, "But—"

"But what, Aunt Lucretia?" asked Donald as she hesitated and flushed till the double V came into her forehead in the old helpless, worried way.

"Why, there's a lot of canning and housecleaning that has to be done, and I don't really think Carrie would like for me to leave it all and run away on a pleasure excursion."

Righteous indignation filled the nephew's heart. "Well, I'd like to know why she wouldn't like it!" he exclaimed impulsively. "Has she any better right to have a vacation than you? I'm sure you've earned it. You blessed little woman, you're going to have a vacation now, in spite of yourself. Just put your conscience away in pink cotton till we get back—though I don't know whether I'll let you come back to stay. I may spirit you off with me somewhere if I don't like the looks of my cousin. I'll take all the responsibility for this trip. If Aunt Carrie doesn't like it, she may visit her wrath upon me, and I'll tell her just what I think of her. Anyhow, to the shore you are going right speedily—that is, if you want to go. If there's some other place you'd rather go besides to the Traymore, speak the word, and there we'll go. I want you to have a good time."

Aunt Crete gasped with joy. The thought of the ocean, the real ocean, was wonderful. She'd dreamed of it many times but never had seen it, because she was always the one who could just as well stay at home as not. She never got rundown or nervous or cross and was ordered to go away for her health, and she never insisted upon going when the rest went. Her heart was bounding as it hadn't bounded since the morning of the last Sunday school picnic she'd attended when she was a girl.

"Indeed, dear boy, I do want to go with all my heart if I really ought. I've always wanted to see the ocean, and I can't imagine anyplace I'd rather go than the Traymore. Luella's talked so much about it."

"All right. Then it's settled that we go. How soon can we get ready? We'll go shopping tomorrow morning bright and early and get a trunkful of new clothes. It's always nice to have new things when you go off. You feel like another person and don't have to be sewing on buttons all the time," laughed Donald, as if he was enjoying the whole thing as much as his aunt. "I meant to have a good time getting presents for the whole family, but, since they aren't here, I'm going to get them all for you. You're not to say a word. Do you have a trunk?"

"Trunk? No, child, I've never needed a trunk. The time I went to Uncle Hiram's funeral I took Carrie's old haircloth one, but I don't know as that's fit to travel again. Carrie's got her flannels packed away in camphor in it now, and I shouldn't like to disturb it."

"Then we'll get a trunk."

"Oh, no," protested Aunt Crete, "that would be a foolish expense. There're some pasteboard boxes upstairs. I can make out with them in a shawl strap. I won't need much for a few days."

"Enlarge your scale of things, Aunt Crete. You're going to stay more than a few days. You're going to stay till you're tired and just want to come back. As we're going to a 'fine' hotel"—Donald reflected that Aunt Crete couldn't understand his reference to Luella's description of the Traymore—"we can't think of shawl straps and boxes. You shall have a big trunk. I saw an advertisement for one that has drawers and a hatbox in it, like a bureau. We'll see if we can find one to suit."

"It sounds just like the fairy tales I used to read to Luella when she was a little girl," beamed Aunt Crete. "It doesn't seem as if it's I. I can't make it true."

"Now let's write down a list of things you need," said the eager planner. "We'll have to hurry up things and get off this week if possible. I've been reading the paper, and they say there's a hot wave coming. I need to get you to the shore before it arrives, if possible. Come, what shall I put down first? What have you always thought you'd like, Aunt Crete? Don't you need some silk dresses?"

"Oh, dear heart! Hear him! Silk dresses aren't for me. Of course I've always had a sort of hankering after one, but nothing looks very nice on me. Carrie says my figure is dumpy. I guess, if you're a mind to, you can get me a lace collar. It'll please me as well as anything. Luella saw some for a quarter that were real pretty. She bought one for herself. I think it would do to wear with my new pin, and all my collars are pretty much worn out."

"Now look here, Aunt Crete! Can't I make you understand? I mean business, and no collars for a quarter are going to do. You can have a few cheap ones for morning if you want them, but we'll buy some real lace ones to wear with the pin. And you shall have the silk dress, two or three of them, and a lot of other things. What kind do you want?"

"Oh, my dear boy! You just take my breath away. I with two or three silk dresses! The idea! Carrie would think me extravagant, and Luella wouldn't like it a bit. She always tells me I'm too lively for my years."

Donald set his lips and wished he could have speech for a few minutes with the absent Luella. He felt that he'd like to express his contempt for her treatment of their aunt.

"I've always thought I'd like a gray silk," mused Aunt Crete with a dreamy look in her eyes. "But I just know Luella would think it was too dressy for me. I suppose black would be better. I can't deny I'd like black silk, too."

"We'll have both," said Donald decidedly. "I saw a woman in a silver-gray silk once. She had white hair like yours, and the effect was beautiful. Then you'll need some other things. White dresses, I guess. That's what my chum's grandmother used to wear when I went there visiting in the summer."

"White for me!" exclaimed the aunt. "Oh, Luella would be real angry at me getting white. She says it's too conspicuous for old women to dress in light colors."

"Never mind Luella. We're doing this, and whatever we want goes. If Luella doesn't like it, she needn't look at it."

Aunt Crete was all in a flutter that night. She could hardly sleep. She didn't often go to town. Luella did all the shopping. Sometimes she suggested going, but Carrie always said it was a needless expense. Besides, Luella knew how to buy at a better bargain. It was a great delight to go with Donald. Her face shone, and all the weariness of the day's work, and all the toilsome yesterdays, disappeared from her brow.

She looked over her meager wardrobe, most of it castoffs from Carrie's or Luella's half-worn clothing, and wrote down in a cramped hand a few absolute necessities. The next morning they had an early breakfast and started at once on their shopping expedition. Aunt Crete felt like a little child being taken to the circus. The idea of getting a lot of new clothes all for herself seemed too serious a business to be true. She was dazed when she thought of it. So when Donald asked what they should look at first, she showed plainly that she would be little help in getting herself fitted out. She was far too happy to bring her mind down to practical things, and, besides, she couldn't adjust herself to the vast scale of expenditure Donald had set.

"Here are some collars," said Donald. "We might as well begin on these."

Aunt Crete examined them with enthusiasm and finally picked out two at twenty-five cents apiece.

"Are those the best you have?" questioned Donald.

"Oh, no," said the saleswoman, quick to identify the customer who didn't stop at price. "Did you want real or imitation?"

"Real, by all means," he answered promptly.

"Oh, Donald," breathed Aunt Crete in a warning whisper, "real lace comes dreadful high. I've heard Luella say so. Besides, I shouldn't have anything to wear it with or anyplace to go fixed up like that."

"Have you forgotten you're going to the Traymore in a few days?" he asked her with a twinkle in his eye. "And what about the gray silk? Won't it go with that? If not, we'll get something better."

Assisted by the saleswoman, they selected two beautiful collars of real lace and half a dozen plain ones for everyday wear.

"Couldn't you go with us?" asked Donald of the saleswoman as the purchase was concluded. "My aunt wishes to get a good many things, and neither she nor I is much used to shopping. We'd like to have your advice."

"I'm sorry. I'd like to, but I'm not allowed to leave this counter," said the woman with a kindly smile. "I'm head of this department, and they can't get along without me this morning. But they have buyers in the office just for that purpose. You go up to the desk over on the east side just beyond the rotunda and ask for a buyer to go around with you. Get Miss Brower if you can, and tell her the head of the lace department told you to call for her. She'll tell you just what to get," and she smiled again at Aunt Crete's kindly, beaming face.

They went to the desk and found Miss Brower, who, when she heard the message, took them smilingly under her wing. She knew that meant a good sale had been made, and there would be something in it for her. Besides, she had a kindly disposition and didn't turn up a haughty nose at Aunt Crete's dumpy little figure.

"Now just what do you want first?" she asked brightly.

"Everything," said Donald helplessly. "We've only bought a lace collar so far, and now we want all the rest of the things to go with it. The only things we've decided on so far are two silk dresses, a black one and silver-gray. How do we go about getting them? Do they have them ready-made?"

"Nothing that would be quite suitable, I'm afraid, in silks. But we'll go and see what's in stock," said the assistant with a skillful eye, taking in Aunt Crete's smiling, helpless face, lovely white hair, dumpy, ill-fitted figure and all. "There might be a gray voile that would suit her. In fact, I saw one this morning, very simple and elegant, lined with gray silk and trimmed with lace dyed to match. It's a beauty and just reduced this morning to thirty dollars from sixty. I believe it will fit her."

Aunt Crete gasped at the price and looked at Donald. But he seemed pleased and said, "That sounds good. Let's go and see it. We'll have a gray—what was it you called it—voile? Remember that name, Aunt Crete. You're going to have a gray voile. But we want the silk, too. Do they make things here? We want to go away in a few days and would like to take them with us."

"Oh, yes, they'll make anything to order, and this time of year we're not so busy. I guess you could get a 'hurry-up' order on it and have it ready in a couple of days. Or it could be forwarded to you if it wasn't quite finished when you left."

They stepped into the elevator and in a moment were ushered into the presence of the rare and the imported. Aunt Crete stood in a maze of delight and wonder. All this was on exhibition just for her benefit, and she was Alice in Wonderland for the hour. Donald stood back with his arms folded and watched her with satisfaction. One thing alone was wanted to complete it. He wished Luella were up in the gallery somewhere watching also. But that he held in anticipation. Luella should be made to understand she did wrong in underrating this sweet, patient soul.

The gray voile was entirely satisfactory to the two shoppers. Donald recognized it as the thing many women of his acquaintance wore at the receptions he'd attended in university circles. Aunt Crete fingered it wistfully and had her inward doubts whether anything so frail and lovely, like a delicate veil, would wear. But looking at Donald's happy face, she decided not to mention it. The dress was more beautiful than anything she ever dreamed of possessing.

"But it won't fit me," she sighed as she and Miss Brower were on the way to the trying-on room where the garment was to be fitted to her. "I'm so dumpy, you know, and Luella always says it's no use to get me anything ready-made."

"Oh, the fitter will make it fit," said Miss Brower convincingly. Then, glancing at the ample waist, whose old-fashioned lines lay meekly awry as if they were used to being put on that way and were beyond even discouragement, she added, "Why don't you wear one of those stiffened waists? There's a new one on sale, has soft bones all around and is real comfortable. It would make your dresses sit a great deal better. If you like, I'll go get one, and you can be fitted over it. You don't like anything very tight, do you?"

"No," said Aunt Crete in a deprecatory tone, "I never could bear anything real tight. That's what puts Luella out so about me. But if you say there's a waist that's comfortable, I should be so obliged if you'd get it. I'd be willing to pay any price not to look so dumpy."

If it took the last cent she possessed and made all her relatives angry with her, she felt she must have something to fit her once.

Miss Brower, thus commissioned, went away and returned very soon with the magical waist that was to transform Miss Lucretia's "figger." If Donald could have seen his aunt's face when she was finally arrayed in the soft folds of the gray voile and was being pinned up and pinned down and pinned in and pinned out, he would have been fully repaid. Aunt Crete's ecstasy was marred only by the fact that Luella couldn't see her grandeur. Actually being fitted in a department store to a real imported dress! Could mortal attain higher in this mundane sphere?

When the fitting was pronounced finished and Aunt Crete was about to don her discouraged shirtwaist once more, Miss Brower appeared in the doorway with a coat and skirt suit over her arm, made of fine soft black taffeta.

"Just put this on and let the gentleman see how he likes it," she said. She had been out to talk over matters with Donald and understand what was wanted. She advised the taffeta coat and skirt for traveling, with an extra cloth coat for cool days. Aunt Crete, with the new dignity that consciousness of her improved figure gave her, rustled out to her nephew looking like a new woman, her face beaming.

That was a wonderful day. Aunt Crete retired again for the black taffeta to be altered a little, and yet again for a black and white dotted swiss and a white linen suit and a handsome black crepe de chine; then she was measured for the silver-gray silk, which the head dressmaker promised could be hurried through. They bought a black chiffon waist and some filmy, dreamy white shirtwaists, simple and plain in design, and exquisite lace simply applied, fine handmade tucks and finer material.

Miss Brower advised white linen and white lawn for morning wear at the seashore and gave Aunt Crete confidence, telling how she had a customer, "a woman about as old as you, with just such lovely hair," who but yesterday purchased a set of white dresses for morning wear at the seashore. This silenced the thoughts of her sister's horror at "White for you, Crete! What are you thinking of?" Never mind, she was going to have one good time, even if she had to put all her lovely finery away in a trunk afterward and never bring it out again, or—dreary thought—were made to cut it over for Luella sometime. Well, it might come to that, but at least she'd enjoy it while it was hers.

Two white linen skirts, a handsome black cloth coat, several pairs of silk gloves, black and white, some undergarments dainty enough for a bride, a whole dozen pairs of stockings! How Aunt Crete rejoiced in those! She'd been wearing stockings whose feet were cut out of old stocking legs for fifteen years. She couldn't remember when she'd had a whole new pair of stockings all her own. And then two new bonnets.

All these things were acquired little by little. While they were in the millinery department, and Miss Brower had just set a charming black lace bonnet made on a foundation of white roses on the white hair, Donald decided she was one of the most beautiful old ladies he'd ever seen. The drapery was a fine black lace scarf, which swept around the roses and tied loosely on the breast, and it gave the quiet little woman a queenly air. She was getting used to seeing her own face in strange adornments, but it startled her to see that she really looked handsome in this bonnet. She stood before the transformation in the mirror almost in awe and never heard what Miss Brower was saying.

"That's just the thing for best, and there's a lovely lace wrap in the cloak department she ought to have to go with it. It would be charming."

"Get it," said Donald with respectful brevity. He was astonished himself at the difference mere clothes made. Aunt Crete was fairly impressive in her new bonnet. And the lace wrap proved indeed to be the very mate to the bonnet, hiding the comfortable figure and making her look "just like other people," as she breathlessly expressed it after one glance at herself in the lace wrap.

They bought a plain black bonnet, a sweet little gray one, a fine silk umbrella, a lot of pretty belts and handkerchiefs, some shoes and rubbers, a handbag of cut steel, for which Luella would have bartered her conscience— what there was left of it. And then they smiled good-bye at Miss Brower, left her for a little while and went to lunch.

Such a lunch! Soup and fish and spring lamb and fresh peas and new potatoes and two kinds of ice cream in little hard sugar cases that looked like baked snowballs. Aunt Crete's hand trembled as she took the first spoonful. The wonders of the day were so great that she was fairly worn out, and two little bright red spots of excitement had appeared in her cheeks. But she was happy! Happier than she remembered ever being in her life. Her dear old conscience had a moment of sighing that Luella couldn't have been there to enjoy it too, and then her heart bounded in wicked gleefulness that Luella wasn't there to stop her nice time.

They walked into a great hall in the same store and sat among the palms and coolness made by electric fans, while a wonderful organ played exquisite music. Aunt Crete felt she certainly was in heaven without the trouble of dying. She never dreamed, dear soul, that she had been dying all her life that others might live and that to such the reward is promised.

They went back to Miss Brower later. Behold! The silver-gray silk was cut out and ready to fit. Aunt Crete felt it was dainty work, the whole of it, and she touched the fabric as if it had been made by magic.

Then they went and bought a trunk and a handsome leather satchel, and Donald took a notion that his aunt must have a set of silver combs for her hair such as he saw in the hair of another old lady.

"Now," said Donald reflectively, "we'll go home and get rested, and tomorrow we'll come down and buy any things we've forgotten."

"And I'm sure I don't see what more a body could possibly need," said Aunt Crete, as, tired and contented, she climbed into the train and sat down in the hot plush seat.

The one bitter drop in the cup of bliss came the next morning—or rather two drops—in the shape of letters. One from Aunt Carrie for Donald was couched in stiffest terms, in which she professed to have just heard of his coming and to be exceedingly sorry she wasn't at home; she was kept from returning only by a sprained ankle, for the doctor told her she mustn't put her foot to the ground for two or three weeks yet, or she would suffer for it.

The other letter was for Aunt Crete and was a rehash of the telephone message, with a good sound scolding for having left the telephone before she finished speaking. Luella wrote it herself because she felt like venting her temper on someone. The young man who was so attentive to her in town had promenaded the piazza with another young woman all the evening before. Luella hoped Aunt Crete would put up plenty of gooseberry jam. Aunt Crete put on her double V as she read and sighed for a full minute before Donald looked up amused from his letter.

"Now, Aunt Crete, you look as if a mountain had rolled down upon you. What's the matter?"

"Oh, I'm just afraid, Donald, that I'm doing wrong going off this way, when Carrie expects me to do all this canning and sewing and cleaning. I'm afraid she'll never forgive me."

"Now, Aunt Crete, don't you love me? Didn't I tell you I'd stand between you and the whole world? Please put that letter up, and come and help me pack your new trunk. Do you want that gray silk put in first, or shall I put the shoes at the bottom? Don't you know you and I are going to have the times of our lives? We're going to run away from every care. Do you suppose your own sister would want you to stay here roasting in the city if she knew you had a nephew just aching to carry you off to the ocean? Come, forget it. Cut it out, Aunt Crete, and let's pack the trunk. I'm longing to be off to smell the briny deep." And laughingly he carried her away and plunged her into thoughts of her journey, giving her no time the rest of the day to think of anything else.

Chapter 4

They locked the house early one morning when even the dusty bricks had a smell of freshness to them before the hot sun baked them for another day. The closed blinds seemed sullen like a conquered tyrant, and the front door looked reproachfully at Aunt Crete as she turned the key carefully and tried it twice to be sure it was locked.

The lonesome look of the house gave the poor lady a pang as she turned the corner in her softly rustling silk coat and skirt. She felt it had hardly been right to put on a new black silk in the morning and go off from all the cares of the world, just leave them, boldly ignore them, like any giddy girl, and take a vacation. She regarded herself with awe and a rising self-respect in every window she passed. Somehow the dumpy look had passed away mysteriously. It wasn't her old self that was passing along the street to the station bearing a cut-steel handbag, while Donald carried her new satchel, and her new trunk bumped on a square ahead in the expressman's wagon.

It was a hot morning, and the great city station seemed close and stuffy, but Aunt Crete mingled with the steaming crowd blissfully. To be one with the world, attired irreproachably; to be on her way to a great hotel by the sea, with new clothes, and escorted devotedly by someone who was her very own, this indeed was happiness. Could anyone desire more upon the earth?

Donald put her into a cab at the station, and she beamed happily out at the frightful streets that always made her heart come into her mouth on the rare occasions when she had to cross them. The ride across the city seemed a brief and distinguished experience. It was as if everybody else was walking and they only had the grandeur of a carriage. Then the ferry boat was delightful to the new traveler, with its long, white-ceiled passages and its smell of wet timbers and tarred ropes. They had a seat close to the front, where they could look out and watch their own progress and see the many puffing monsters laboriously plying back and forth, and the horizon line of many masts like fine brown lines against the sky. Aunt Crete felt that at last she was out in the world. She couldn't have felt it more if she'd been starting for Europe.

The seashore train, with its bamboo seats and its excited groups of children bearing tin pails and shovels and tennis rackets, filled her with a fine exhilaration. At last, at last, her soul had escaped the bounds of red brick walls that she'd expected would surround her as long as she lived. She drew deep breaths and beamed upon the whole trainful of people, yelling baby and all. She gazed and gazed at the fast-flying Jersey scenery, grown so monotonous to some of the travelers, and admired every little white and green town at which they paused.

Donald put her into a carriage when they reached the shore. Half an hour off they began to smell the sea and to catch glimpses of low-flying marshes and a misty blueness against the sky. Now every friendly hackman at the station seemed a part of the great day to Aunt Crete. So pretty a carriage, with low steps and gray cushions and a fringe all around the canopy, and a white speckled horse with long, gentle, white eyelashes. Aunt Crete leaned back self-consciously on the gray cushions and enjoyed the creak of her silk jacket as she settled into place.

She felt as if this was a play that would soon be over. But she would enjoy it to the very end and then go back to her dishwashing and cellar-cleaning and being blamed, and bear them all in happy remembrance of what she'd had for one blissful vacation.

She didn't know that Donald had telephoned ahead for the best apartments in the hotel. She was watching for the first blue line of the great mysterious ocean. When it came into sight, billowing suddenly above the line of board-walk as they turned a corner, her heart stood still for one moment and then bounded onward set to the time of wonder.

Two obsequious porters jumped to assist Aunt Crete from the carriage. The hand baggage drifted up the steps as if by magic and awaited them in the apartments to which they arose in a luxurious elevator. Aunt Crete noticed several old ladies with pink and blue wool knitting, sitting in a row of large rocking chairs, as she glided up to the second floor. It gave her rest on one point, for they all wore white dresses. She'd been a little dubious about those white dresses Donald insisted upon. But now she might enjoy them unashamed. Oh, what would Luella say?

She glanced around the room, half-fearfully expecting to find Luella waiting there. Somehow, now she was there, she wanted to get used to it and enjoy it all before Luella came. For Luella was an uncertain quantity. Luella mightn't like it, after all! Dreadful thought! And after Donald had taken so much trouble and spent so much money all to surprise them!

The smiling porter absorbed the good tip Donald handed him and went his way. Aunt Crete and Donald were left alone. They looked at each other and smiled.

"Let's look around and see where they've put us," said Donald, pushing the swaying curtains aside. There before them rolled the blue tide of the ocean.

Aunt Crete sank into a chair and was silent for awhile. Then she said, "It's just as big as I thought it would be. I was so afraid it wouldn't be. Some folks next door went down to the shore last year, and they said it didn't look big enough to what they'd expected, and I've been afraid ever since."

Donald's eyes filled with a tender light that was beautiful to see. He was enjoying the spending of his money, and it was yielding him a rich reward already.

The apartments assigned to them consisted of a parlor and two large bedrooms with private baths. Donald discovered a few moments later, when he went down to the office to investigate, that Luella and his aunt occupied a single room on the fourth floor back, overlooking the kitchen court. It wasn't where he'd have placed them, had they chosen to await his coming and be taken down to the shore in style. But now that they'd run away from him and were too evidently ashamed of him, perhaps it was as well to let them remain where they were, he reflected.

"Aunt Carrie and Luella have gone out with a party in a carriage for an all-day drive to Pleasure Bay," announced Donald when he came up. "Aunt Carrie's ankle must be better."

"Well, that's real nice!" exclaimed Aunt Crete with a smile, turning from her view of the sea, where she'd been ever since he left her. "I'm glad Luella is having a good time, and we won't miss her a mite. You and I'll have the ocean all to ourselves today."

Donald smiled approvingly. He wasn't altogether sure he cared to meet the other aunt and cousin at all. He wasn't sure he wouldn't like to run away from them and carry Aunt Crete with him.

"Very well," he said, "I'm glad you're not disappointed. We'll do just whatever we want to. Would you like to go in bathing?"

"Oh, my! Could I! I've always thought I'd like to see how it would feel, but I guess I'm too old. Besides, there's my figger. It wouldn't look nice in a bathing suit. Luella wouldn't like it a bit, and I don't want to disgrace her, now I'm here. She always makes a lot of fun of old people going in and sitting right on the edge of the water. I guess it won't do."

"Yes, it will do, if you want to. Didn't I tell you this was my party, and Luella isn't in it? That's ridiculous. I'll take you in myself, Aunt Crete, and we'll have the best time out. And you won't be scared either. I can swim like a fish. You shall go in every day. Would you like to begin at once?"

"I would," said Aunt Crete, rising with a look of resolution in her face. She felt that Luella would condemn the amusement for her. So, if she was to dare it, it must be done before her niece appeared.

They went down to the beach and for a few minutes surveyed the bathers as they came out to the water. Then with joy and daring in her face Aunt Crete went into the little bathhouse with wildly beating heart, arrayed herself in the bright blue flannel garb provided for her use and came timidly out to meet Donald, tall and smiling in his blue jerseys.

They had a wonderful time. It was almost better than shopping. Donald led her down to the water and gently accustomed her to it until he'd led her out beyond the roughness, where his strong arms lifted her well above the swells until she felt as if she were a bird. It was marvelous that she wasn't afraid, but she wasn't. It was as if she had that morning been transferred back over forty years to her youth again and was having the good times she'd longed for, such as other girls had—the swings and the rides and the skatings and bicyclings. How many such things she'd watched through the years, with her heart palpitating with daring to do it all herself! Her petulant sister and the logy Luella never dreamed that Aunt Crete desired such unauntly indulgences. If they had, they would have taken it out of her, scorched out with scorn.

The white hair with its natural waves fluffed out beautifully, like a canary's feathers, after the bath, and Aunt Crete was smiling and charming at lunch in one of her fine new white dresses. She'd hurried to put it on before Luella appeared, lest they might all be spirited away from her if Luella discovered them. She reflected with a sigh that they would likely fit Luella beautifully and that that would probably be their final destination, just as Luella's discarded garments came to her.

But nothing marred the lunchtime and the beautiful afternoon. After a delicious nap to the accompaniment of the music of the waves, she was taken to ride in the fringed carriage again, while a bunch of handsome ladies, old and young, sat on the hotel piazza in more of those abundant rockers and watched her approvingly. She felt she was of some importance in their eyes. She had suddenly blossomed out of her insignificance and was worth looking at. It warmed her heart with humble pleasure. She felt she'd won approval, not through any merit of her own, but through Donald's loving-kindness. It was wonderful what a charm clothes could work.

"Put on your gray silk for dinner," said Donald with deliberate malice in his heart.

"Oh," gasped Aunt Crete, "I think I ought to keep that for parties, don't you?"

"If ever there was a party, it's going to be tonight," said Donald. "It's going to be a surprise party. You want to see if Aunt Carrie and Luella will know you, you know."

So with trembling fingers Aunt Crete arrayed herself in her gray silk and fine linen, very materially assisted by a quiet maid, whom Donald ordered sent to the room and who persuaded Aunt Crete to let her arrange the pretty white hair.

It was surprising to see, when the coiffure was complete, that she looked quite like the other old ladies, who weren't old at all, only playing old.

"I don't believe they'll know me," whispered Aunt Crete to herself as she stood before the full-length mirror and surveyed the effect. "And I didn't think I could ever look like that!" she murmured after a more prolonged gaze, during which she made the acquaintance of her new self. Then she added half wistfully, "I wish I'd known it before. I think perhaps they'd have—liked me—more if I'd looked that way all the time."

She sighed half regretfully, as if she were bidding good-bye to this new vision, and went out to Donald, who awaited her. She felt that the picnic part of her vacation was almost over now, for Carrie and Luella would be sure to spoil it somehow.

Donald looked up from his paper with a welcome in his eyes. It was the first time she'd seen him in evening dress, and she thought him handsome as a king.

"You're a very beautiful woman, Aunt Crete. Do you know it?" said Donald with satisfaction.

He'd felt that the French maid would know how to put just the right touch to Aunt Crete's pretty hair to take away her odd "unused" appearance. Now she was completely in fashion, and she looked every inch a lady. She somehow seemed to have natural intuition for gentle manners. Perhaps her kindly heart dictated them, for surely there can be no better manners than come wrapped up with the Golden Rule, and Aunt Crete had lived by that all her life.

They entered the great dining hall and made their way among the palms in a blaze of electric light, with the headwaiter bowing obsequiously before them. They had a table to themselves, and Aunt Crete rejoiced in the tiny shaded candles and the hothouse roses in the center, lifting the handsome napkins and silver forks with awe. Sometimes it seemed as if she were still dreaming.

∽◌◠

The party from Pleasure Bay reached home rather late in the afternoon, after a tedious time in the hot sun at a place full of peanut stands and merry-go-rounds and moving picture shows. Luella didn't have a good time. She was disappointed that none of the young men in the party paid her special attention. In fact, the special young man for whose sake she prodded her mother into going didn't accompany them at all. Luella was thoroughly cross.

"Mercy, how you've burned your nose, Luella!" said her mother sharply. "It's so unbecoming. The skin is all peeling off. I do wish you'd wear a veil. You can't afford to lose your complexion, with such a figure as you have."

"Oh, fiddlesticks! I wish you'd let up on that, Ma," snapped Luella. "Didn't you get a letter from Aunt Crete? I wonder what she's thinking about not to send that lavender organdie. I wanted to wear it tonight. There's to be a hop in the ballroom, and that would be just the thing. She ought to have done it; she's had time enough since I telephoned. I suppose she's gone to reading again. I do wish I'd remembered to lock up the bookcase. She's crazy for novels."

All this time Luella was being buttoned into a pink silk muslin heavily decorated with cheap lace. There were twenty-six tiny elusive buttons, and Luella's mother was tired.

"What on earth takes you so long, Ma?" snarled Luella, twisting her neck to try to see her back. "We'll be so late we won't get served, and I'm hungry as a bear."

They hurried down, arriving at the door just as Aunt Crete and Donald were being settled into their chairs by the smiling headwaiter.

"For goodness' sake! Those must be swells," said Luella in a low tone. "Did you see how that waiter bowed and smiled? He never does that to us. I expect he got a big tip. See, they're sitting right next to our table. Goodness, Ma, your hair is all slipped to one side. Put it up quick. No, the other side. Say, he's an awfully handsome young man. I wonder if we can get introduced. I just know he dances gracefully. Say, Mother, I'd like to get him for a partner tonight. I guess those stuck-up Grandons would open their eyes then."

"Hush, Luella. He'll hear you."

They settled into their places unassisted by the dilatory waiter, who came languidly up a moment later to take their order.

Aunt Crete's back was happily toward her relatives, so she ate her dinner in comfort. The palms were all about, along with the gentle clink of silver and glass and the sound of refined voices. The soft strains of an orchestra hidden in a balcony of ferns and palms drowned Luella's strident voice when it was raised in discontented strain, so Aunt Crete failed to recognize it.

But Donald had been on the alert. In the first place, he asked a question or two, knew about where his relatives usually sat and purposely asked to be placed near them. He studied Luella when she came in and felt pretty sure she was the girl he saw on the train platform the morning he arrived in Midvale. Finally, in a break in the music, he distinctly caught the name "Luella" from the lips of the sour woman in the purple satin with white question marks all over it and plasters of white lace.

Aunt Carrie was tall and thin, with a discontented droop to her lips and premature wrinkles. She wore an affected air of abnormal politeness and disapproval of everything. She was studying the silver-gray silk back in front of her, wondering what there was about that elegant-looking woman with the lovely white-waved pompadour and puffs and that exquisite real lace collar to remind her of her poor sister Lucretia. She always coupled the adjective *poor* with her sister's name when she thought of all her shortcomings.

Luella's discontent was somewhat enlivened by the sight of the young man who didn't go on the drive to Pleasure Bay. He stood in the doorway, searching the room with keen, interested eyes. Could he be looking for her? Luella's heart leaped in a moment's triumph. Yes, he seemed to be looking that way as if he'd found the object of his search, and he was surely coming down toward them with a real smile on his face. Luella's face broke into preparatory smiles. She would be coy and pretend not to see him, so she began a voluble and animated conversation with her mother about the charming time they had that day. It might have surprised the worthy woman if she weren't accustomed to her daughter's wiles. She knew it to be a warning of the proximity of someone Luella wished to charm.

The young man came on straight by the solicitous waiters, who waved him frantically to various tables. Luella cast a rapid side glance and talked on cheerfully with drooping head and averted gaze. Her mother looked up, wondering, to see the cause of Luella's animation. He was quite near now, and in a moment more he would speak. The girl felt excited thrills creeping up her back, and the color rushed into her cheeks, which were already red enough from the wind and sun of the day.

"Well, well," said the young man's voice in a hearty eagerness Luella had never hoped to hear addressed to her, "this is too good to be true. Don, old man, where did you drop from? I saw your name in the register and rushed right into the dining room—"

"Clarence Grandon, as true as I live!" said a pleasant voice behind Luella. "I thought you were in Europe. This is the best thing that could have happened. Let me introduce my aunt—"

Some seconds before this Luella's thrills changed to chills. Mortification stole over her face and up to the roots of her hair. Even the back of her neck, where her bathing suit was cut low and square, turned angry looking. The pink muslin had a round neck and showed a half-circle of whiter neck below the bathing suit square. But Luella had the presence of mind to smile on to her mother in mild pretense that she just noticed the advent of the young man.

A waiter was bringing an extra chair for Mr. Grandon, and he was to be seated so that he could look toward their table. Perhaps he would recognize her yet, and there might be a chance of introduction to the handsome stranger. Luella dallied with her dinner in fond hope, and her mother aided and abetted her.

The lovely old lady with the silver-gray silk and the real lace collar and beautiful hair had her back squarely toward the table where Luella and her mother sat. They couldn't see her face. They could only notice how interested both the young men were in her and how courteous they were to her, and they decided she must be some very great personage indeed. They watched her half enviously and began to plan some way to scrape an acquaintance with her.

They had one glimpse of her face as the headwaiter rushed to draw back her chair when she finished her dinner. It was a fine, handsome face, younger than they expected to see, with beautiful sparkling eyes full of mirth and contentment. What was there in the face that reminded them of something? Had they ever met that old lady before?

Luella and her mother brought their dallied dessert to a sudden ending and followed hard upon the footsteps of the three down the length of the dining hall. But the lady in gray with her two attendants had disappeared already. Disconsolately they lingered about, looking up and down the length of piazzas in vain hope of seeing them sitting in one of the great rows of rockers, watching the many-tinted waves in the dying evening light. But there was no sign of them anywhere.

As they stood thus leaning over the balcony, a large gray automobile with white cushions, like a great gliding dove, slipped silently up to the entrance below them in the well-bred silence an expensive machine knows how to assume under dignified owners.

Luella twitched her mother's sleeve. "That's Grandon's car," she whispered. "P'raps I'll get asked to go. Let's sit down here and wait."

The mother obediently sat down.

Chapter 5

They hadn't long to wait. They heard the elevator door slide softly open and then the gentle swish of silken skirts. Luella looked around just in time to be recognized by young Mr. Grandon if he hadn't at that moment been placing a long white broadcloth coat about his mother's shoulders. There were four in the party, and Luella's heart sank. He wouldn't be likely to ask another one. The young man and the gray-silk, thread-lace woman from the other dining table were going with them, it appeared. Young Mr. Grandon helped the gray-silk lady down the steps while the handsome stranger walked by Mrs. Grandon. They didn't look around at the people on the piazza at all. Luella bit her lips in vexation.

"For pity's sake, Luella, don't scowl so," whispered her mother. "They might look up yet and see you."

This warning came just in time. Just as he was about to start the car, young Mr. Grandon glanced up and, catching Luella's fixed gaze, gave her a distant bow, which was followed by a courteous lifting of the stranger's hat.

Aunt Crete was seated beside Mrs. Grandon in the backseat and beaming her joy quietly. She was secretly exulting that Luella and Carrie hadn't been in evidence yet. She felt that her joy was being lengthened by a few minutes more, for she couldn't get away from the fear that her sister and niece would spoil it all as soon as they appeared on the scene.

"I thought Aunt Carrie and Luella would be tired after their all-day trip, and we wouldn't disturb them tonight," said Donald in a low tone, looking back to Aunt Crete as the car glided smoothly out from the shelter of the wide piazza.

Aunt Crete smiled happily back to Donald and raised her eyes with a relieved glance toward the rows of people on the piazza. She was afraid to look her fill before, lest she should see Luella frowning at her somewhere. But apparently they weren't back yet or perhaps hadn't finished their dinner.

As Aunt Crete raised her eyes, Luella and her mother looked down into her upturned face enviously. But Aunt Crete's gaze just grazed them and fell upon an old lady of stately mien with white, fluffy hair like her own and a white crepe de chine gown trimmed with much white lace. In deep satisfaction Aunt Crete reflected that, if Luella had anything to say against her aunt's wearing modest white morning gowns, she would cite this model, who seemed to be an old aristocrat if one judged by her jewels and her general makeup.

"Somewhere I've seen that woman with the gray silk!" exclaimed Luella's mother suddenly as Aunt Crete swept by. "There's something real familiar about the set of her shoulders. Look at the way she raises her hand to her face.

My land! I believe she reminds me of your Aunt Crete!"

"Now, Mother!" scoffed Luella. "As if Aunt Crete could ever look like that! You must be crazy to see anything in such an elegant lady to remind you of poor old Aunt Crete. Why, Ma, this woman is the real thing! Just see how her hair's put up. Nobody but a French maid could get it like that. Imagine Aunt Crete with a French maid. Oh, I'd die laughing. She's probably washing our country cousin's supper dishes at this very minute. I wonder if her conscience doesn't hurt her about my lavender organdie. Say, Ma, did you notice how easily that handsome stranger handed the ladies into the car? My, but I'd like to know him. I think Clarence Grandon is just a stuck-up prig."

Her mother looked at her sharply.

"Luella, seems to me you change your mind a good deal. If I don't make any mistake, you came down here so's to be near him. What's made you change your mind? He doesn't seem to go with any other girls."

"No, he just sticks by his mother every living minute," sighed Luella unhappily. "I do wish I had that lavender organdie. I look better in that than anything else I've got. I declare I think Aunt Crete is real mean and selfish not to send it. I'm going in to see if the mail has come. If the organdie isn't here or any word from Aunt Crete, I'm going to call her up on the telephone again."

Luella vanished into the hotel office, and her mother sat and rocked with puckered brows. She very much desired a place in high society for Luella, but how to attain it was the problem. She hadn't been born for social climbing and found it difficult to do.

Meantime the motorcar rolled smoothly over the perfect roads, keeping always that wonderful gleaming sea in sight. And Aunt Crete, serenely happy, beamed and nodded to the pleasant chat of Mrs. Grandon and was so overpowered by her surroundings that she forgot to be overpowered by the grand Mrs. Grandon. As in a dream she heard the kind tone and responded mechanically to the questions about her journey and the weather in the city and how lovely the sea was tonight. But as she spoke the few words with her lips, her soul was singing, and the words of its song were these:

> Must I be carried to the skies
>   On flowery beds of ease,
> While others fought to win the prize
>   And sailed through bloody seas?

As they glided along the palace-lined shore, with the rolling sea on one hand and the beautiful people in their beautiful raiment at ease and happy on the other hand, it seemed as if she was picked right up out of the hot little brick house in the narrow street, put on a wonderful flowery bed of ease and was floating right into a heaven of which her precious Donald was a bright, particular angel. She forgot all about Luella and what she might say and just enjoyed herself.

She even found herself telling the elegant Mrs. Grandon exactly how she made piccalilli, and her heart warmed to the other woman as she saw that she was really interested. She never supposed, from the way Luella spoke of the Grandons, that they would even deign to eat such a common thing as a pickle, let alone know anything about it. Aunt Crete decided Mrs. Grandon wasn't stuck-up in the least, but just a nice, common lady like anyone. As she went up in the elevator beside her and said good night, she felt as if she'd known her all her life.

When she turned out her light and crept into the great hotel bed, it came to her to wonder whether Luella and Carrie could be meant by the ones in the hymn,

> While others fought to win the prize
> And sailed through bloody seas.

She couldn't help feeling that perhaps she was selfish in enjoying her day so much when for all she knew Luella might not be having a good time. For Luella not to have a good time meant blame for her aunt generally. Ever since Luella was born it was borne in upon Aunt Crete that she was morally obligated to make Luella have a good time. And now Aunt Crete was having a good time, the time of her life. She was so happy over it that she hugged herself and thought of the dear stars out there in the deep, dark blue of the arching sky and the cool dark roll of the white-tipped waves and was thankful.

Luella and her mother gloomily watched the dancing through the open windows of the ballroom. But since they knew no one inside, they didn't venture in. Luella kept one eye out for the return of the car. But she somehow missed it and finally retired to the solace of cold cream and the comforts of the fourth floor back, where lingered in the atmosphere a reminder of the dinner past and a hint of the breakfast that was to come.

As the elevator ascended past the second floor, the door of one of the special apartments stood wide, revealing a glimpse of the handsome young stranger standing under the chandelier reading a letter, his face alive with pleasure. Luella sighed enviously and in her dreams strove vainly to enter into the charmed circle where these favored beings moved. She didn't know that of her own free will she had closed the door to that very special apartment, which might have been hers except for her own action.

The next morning Luella was twisting her neck in a vain endeavor to set the string of artificial puffs straight upon the enormous cushion of her hair, till they looked for all the world like a pan of rolls just out of the oven. She had jerked them off four separate times and pulled the rest of her hair down twice in a vain attempt to get just the desired effect. Her patience, never very great at any time, was well-nigh exhausted. Her mother was fretting because the best pieces of fish and all the hot rolls would be gone before they got down to breakfast, and Luella was snapping back in most undaughterly fashion, when a noticeable tap came on the door.

It wasn't the tap of the chambermaid of the fourth floor back or of the elevator boy, who knew how to modulate his knock for every grade of room from the second story, ocean front, up and back. It was a knock of rare condescension, mingled with a call to attention. It warned these favored occupants of room 410 to sit up and take notice, not that they were worthy of any such consideration as was about to fall upon them.

Luella drove the last hairpin into the puffs and sprang to the door just as her mother opened it. She felt something was about to happen. Was she to be invited to ride in that automobile at last, or what?

There in the hall, looking very much out of place, stood the uniformed functionary who usually confined his activities to the second floor front, where the tips were large and the guests of unquestioned wealth, to say nothing of culture, stayed. He held in his hand a shining silver tray on which lay two cards. And he delivered his message in a tone that not only showed the deference he felt for the one who had sent him, but compelled such deference also on the part of those to whom he spoke.

"The lady and gen'leman say, Will the ladies come down to the private pahlah as soon aftah breakfus' as is convenient, room number 2, second floor front?" He bowed to signify that his mission was completed and that if it didn't carry through, it was entirely beyond his sphere to do more.

Luella grasped the cards and smothered an exclamation of delight. "Second floor front," gasped her mother. "The private parlor! Did you hear, Luella?"

But Luella was standing by the one window, frowning over the cards. One was written and one was engraved, a lady's and a gentleman's cards. "Miss Ward." "Mr. Donald Ward Grant."

"For the land's sake, Ma! Who in life are they? Do you know any Miss Ward? You don't s'pose it's that lovely gray-silk woman. Miss Ward. Donald Ward Grant. Who can they be, and what do you suppose they want? Grant. Donald Grant. Where have I, why—! Oh, horrors, Ma! It can't be that dreadful cousin has followed us up, can it? Donald Grant is his name, of course—yes, Donald Ward Grant. It was the Ward that threw me off. But who is the other? Miss Ward. Ma! You don't—"

"Luella Burton, that's just what it is! It's your Aunt Crete and that dreadful cousin. Crete never did have any sense, if she is my sister. But just let me get hold of her! If I don't make her writhe. I think I'll find a way to make her understand—"

Luella's expansive bravery beneath the row of biscuit puffs seemed to shrink and cringe as she took in the thought.

"Oh, Ma!" she groaned. "How could she? And here of all places? To come here and mortify me! It's just too dreadful. Ma, it can't be true. Aunt Crete would never dare, And where would she get the money? She hasn't a cent of her own, has she? You didn't go and leave her money, did you?"

"No, only a little change in my old pocketbook. It wouldn't have been enough to come down here on, unless she bought a day excursion. Wait. I did leave five dollars to pay the grocery bill with. But Crete surely wouldn't take that. Still, there's no telling. She always was kind of a child. Oh, dear! What shall we do?" The mother sat down on the tumbled bed beside the tray of Luella's cheap trunk.

"Well, we must do something, that's certain—if we have to run away again. It would never do to have those two appear here now. Mercy! Think of Aunt Crete in her old black and white silk sitting at the next table to that lovely lady in gray. I'd simply sink through the floor."

"We can't run away, Luella," snapped the practical mother. "We've paid for our room two weeks ahead. I didn't want to do that. But you thought if Aunt Crete should get any nonsense into her head about our coming home, we'd tell her we'd paid for the room, and that would settle it with her. So now it's done, and we can't afford not to abide by it. Besides, what good would that do? We couldn't afford to go anywhere but home, and that would be as bad as it was in the first place. We've got to think it out. If I just had hold of Crete a minute, I'd make her fix it up. She'd have to think of some way out of it herself without any of my help, to pay her for her stupidity in coming. I can't understand how she'd do it."

"I didn't think she'd dare!" glared Luella with no pleasant expression on her face.

"I'll tell you what we'll have to do, Luella," said her mother. "We'll slip down those stairs in the back hall. I went down one day, and they go right out on the piazza that runs in front of the dining room. We'll just slip in the back door and get our breakfast right away. It's getting pretty late. You better hurry. They've likely come up from town on that very early train, and they'll sit and wait for us.

"We'll ring for a messenger bellboy and send down a note that my ankle is so much worse I can't come downstairs, and you can't leave me. We'll say: 'Mrs. Burton and Miss Burton regret that they cannot come down as requested. Mrs. Burton is confined to her bed by a sprained ankle, and her daughter cannot leave her. Miss Ward will have to come up.' You write it on one of your visiting cards, Luella, and we'll send it down as quick as we get back from breakfast.

"Hurry up. The only thing about it will be that climb up three flights after breakfast, but it won't do for us to risk the elevator. Crete might recognize us, for the elevator goes right by that second floor front parlor. What I don't understand is how they got in there. Only rich people can afford that. But, land! Crete's just like a baby. She hasn't been out in the world ever, and very likely she never asked how much the rooms were but just took the best she could lay her eyes on. Or more likely it's a mistake, and she's sitting in that little reception room down on the office floor and thinks it the second floor because she came up such a long flight of steps from the sidewalk.

"We'll have to tell the bellboy to hunt up the fellow that brought their cards and take it to the same folks. Come on now, Luella, and go slow when you turn corners. There's no telling but they might be prowling round trying to hunt us. So keep a lookout."

Thus by devious and back ways they descended to a late breakfast and scuttled up again without being bothered.

Luella wrote the note on her card as her mother dictated, and a small boy all brass buttoned was dispatched with careful directions. Then the two retired behind their ramparts and waited.

Time went by, until half an hour elapsed since they came back from breakfast. They listened anxiously to every footfall in the hall, and part of the time Luella kept the door open a crack with her ear to it. Their nerves were in a quiver. When the chambermaid arrived, they were fairly feverish to get her out of the way. If Aunt Crete should come while she was in the room, it might get all over the hotel what kind of relatives they had.

Mrs. Burton suggested to the chambermaid that she leave their room till last, as they wanted to write some letters before going out. But the maid declared she must do the room at once or not at all. The elevator slid up and down around the corner in the next hall. They heard a footfall now and then, but none that sounded like Aunt Crete's. They rang again for the office boy, who declared he delivered the message in the second floor front and that the lady and gentleman were both in and said, "All right." He vanished impudently without waiting for Luella's probing questions, and they looked at each other in anxiety and indignation.

"It's too mean, Ma, to lose this whole morning. I wanted to go in bathing," complained Luella, "and now no telling how long I'll have to stick in this dull room. I wish Aunt Crete was in Halifax. Why couldn't I have had some nice relatives like that lovely old gray-silk lady and her son?"

Just then the elevator clanged open and shut, and steps came down the hall. It certainly wasn't Aunt Crete. Luella flew to the door at the first tap. There, submerged in a sheaf of American Beauty roses, stood the functionary from the lower floor, with a less pompous manner than he'd worn before. The roses raised by several degrees his respect for the occupants of the fourth floor back.

Luella stood speechless in wonder, looking first at the roses and then at the servant. Such roses never came into her life before. Could it be—must it be—a miserable mistake?

Then the servant spoke.

"Miss Ward sends the flowers an' is sorry the ladies aren't well. She sends her regrets an' says she can't come to see the ladies 'count of a drive she promised to take today, in which she hoped to have the ladies' comp'ny. She hopes the ladies are better this even'n."

He was gone, and the mother and daughter faced each other over the roses, bewilderment and awe in their faces.

"*What* did he say, Luella? *Who* sent those roses? Miss *Ward?* Luella, there's a mistake. Aunt Crete couldn't have sent them. She wouldn't *dare!* Besides, where would she get the money? It's perfectly impossible. It can't be Aunt Crete, after all. It must be someone else with the same name. Perhaps Donald has picked up someone here in the hotel. You can't tell. Or perhaps it isn't our Donald at all. It's likely there are other Donald Grants in the world. We should have gone down at once to find out and not skulked in a corner. But you're always in such a hurry to do something, Luella. There's no telling at all who this is now. It might be those folks you admired so much, though what on earth they should have sent their cards to us for—and those lovely roses—I'm sure I don't know."

"Now, Ma, you needn't blame me. It was you proposed sending that note down. You know it was, Mother. And of course I had to do what you said. I was so upset anyway that I didn't know what was what. But now, you see, perhaps you've cut me out of a lovely day. We might have gone on a ride with them."

"Luella," her mother broke in sharply, "if you talk another word like that, I'll take the next train back home. You don't know what you're talking about. It may be Aunt Crete, after all, and a country cousin for all you know. If it is, would you have wanted to go driving in the face of the whole hotel, with like as not some old shin-and-bones horse and broken-down carriage?"

Luella was silenced for the time, and the room settled into gloomy meditation.

Chapter 6

Meanwhile Aunt Crete in the whitest of her white was settling herself comfortably on the gray cushions of the fringed phaeton again, relief and joy mingled in her countenance. It wasn't that she was glad Carrie's ankle was so bad but just that she was to have another short reprieve before her pleasure was cut off. Soon enough, she thought, she'd be destined to sit in the darkened room and minister to her fussy sister. And Luella would take her place in the carriages and automobiles with her handsome young cousin, as young folks should do, of course. But, oh, it was good, good, that a tired old lady, who had worked hard all her life, could yet have had this glimpse of the brighter side of life before she died.

It would be something to sit and think over as she scraped potatoes for dinner or picked over blackberries for jam or patiently sewed on Val lace for Luella. It would be an event to date from, and she could fancy herself mildly saying to Mrs. Judge Waters, when she sat beside her sometime at missionary meeting, if she ever did again, "When my nephew took me down to the shore," and so forth. She never knew just what to talk about when she sat beside Mrs. Judge Waters, but here was a topic worth laying before such a great lady.

Well, it was something to be thankful for, and she resolved not to think of poor Carrie and Luella until her beautiful morning was over. Then she would show such patience and gratitude as would fully make up to them for her one more day of pleasure.

It was Donald, of course, who suggested the roses. When the message came from the fourth floor back, Aunt Crete turned white about the mouth, and her eyes took on a frightened, hunted look. The double V in her forehead flashed into sight for the first time since they reached the Atlantic coast. He saw at once in what terror Aunt Crete held her sister and niece, and his indignation rose in true Christian fashion. He resolved to place some nice hot coals on the heads of his unpleasant relatives and run away with dear Aunt Crete again—hence the roses and the message. Aunt Crete was fairly childish with pleasure over them when he finally persuaded her it would be all right to send these in place of going up herself as she was bidden.

She listened eagerly as Donald gave careful directions for the message, and the stately functionary respectfully repeated the words with his own high-sounding inflection. It made the pink come and go again in Aunt Crete's cheeks. She felt that Luella and Carrie couldn't be angry with her after these roses, especially when everything was done up in such a nice, stylish manner.

The drive was one long dream of bliss to Aunt Crete. They rode miles up the coast and took lunch at a hotel much grander than the one they left. When they returned in the afternoon Aunt Crete felt much less in awe of the Traymore, since her experience in hotels had broadened. They also met some friends of Donald's, a professor from his alma mater, who with his wife was just returning from a trip to Europe.

The bathers were making merry in the waves as they returned, and Aunt Crete's wistful look made Donald ask whether she felt too tired to take another dip. But she declared she wasn't one bit tired.

She came from her bathing with shining eyes and triumphant mien. Whatever happened now, she'd been in bathing twice. She felt like quite an experienced bather, and she could dream of that wonderful experience of being lifted high above the swells in Donald's strong young arms.

She obediently took her nap and surrendered herself to the hands of the maid to have the finishing touches put to her grooming. It was the soft gray voile she elected to wear tonight, and Donald admired her when she emerged from her room in the dress, looking every inch a lady.

A knock sounded at the door before he had time to admire Aunt Crete. But his eyes said enough, and she felt a flow of humble pride in her new self, the self he created out of what she always considered an unusually plain old woman. With the consciousness of her becoming attire upon her she turned with mild curiosity to see who knocked, and, behold, her sister and niece stood before her!

They had passed the day in melancholy speculations and the making and abandoning of many plans. After careful deliberation they at last concluded there was nothing to be done but go down and find out who these people really were, and if possible allay the ghost of their fears and set themselves free from their dull little room.

"If it should be Aunt Crete and Donald, we'll just settle them up and send them off at once, won't we, Mother?"

"Certainly," said Mrs. Burton with an angry snap to her eyes. "Trust me to settle with your aunt Crete if it's really her. But I can't think it is. It isn't like Crete one bit to leave her duty. She's got a lot of work to do, and she never leaves her work till it's done. It must be someone else. What if it should be those folks you admire so much? I've been thinking. We had some New York cousins by the name of Ward. It might be one of them, and Donald might have gone to them first, and they've brought him down here. I can't think he's very much, though. But we'll just hope for the best anyway, till we find out. If it's Aunt Crete, I'll simply talk to her till she's brought to her senses and make her understand she's got to go right home. I'll tell her how she's mortifying you and spoiling your chances of a good match, perhaps—"

"Oh, Ma!" giggled Luella in admiration.

"I'll tell her she must tell Donald she's got to go right home, that the sea air don't agree with her one bit—it goes to her head or something like that, and then we'll make him feel it wouldn't be gallant in him not to take her home.

That's easy enough, if 'tis them."

"But, Ma, have you thought about your sprained ankle? How'll they think you got over it so quick? S'posing it shouldn't be Aunt Crete."

"Well, I'll tell her the swelling's gone down, and all of a sudden something seemed to slip back into place again, and I'm all right."

This was while they were buttoning and hooking each other into their best and most elaborate garments in case the people they were to meet might prove to be of patrician class.

They were somewhat puzzled how to find their possible relatives after they were attired for the advance on the enemy. But consultation with the functionary in the office showed them that, whoever Miss Ward and Donald Grant might be, they surely were at present occupying the apartments on the second floor front.

For one strenuous moment after the elevator left them before the door of the private parlor, they carefully surveyed each other, fastening a stubborn hook here, putting up a stray rebellious lock there, patting a puff into subordination. Mrs. Burton was arrayed in an elaborate tucked and puffed and belaced lavender muslin whose laborious design was attained through hours of the long winter evenings past.

Luella wore what she considered her most fetching garment, a long, scant, high-waisted robe of fire-red crepe, with nothing to relieve its glare, reflected in staring hues in her already much-burned nose and cheeks. Her hair was in preparation all afternoon and looked as if it were carved in waves and puffs out of black walnut, so closely was it surrounded with that most noticeable of all invisible devices, an invisible net.

They entered and stood face-to-face with the wonderful lady in the gray gown, whose every line and graceful fold spoke of the skill of a foreign tailor. And then, strange to say, it was Aunt Crete who came to herself first.

She was perfectly conscious of her comely array and strong in the strength of her handsome nephew who stood near to protect. Suddenly she lost all fear of her fretful sister and bullying niece and stepped forward with an unconscious welcoming grace that must have been hers all the time, or it never would have come to the front in this crisis.

"Why, here you are at last, Luella! How nice you look in your red crepe! Why, Carrie, I'm real glad you've got better so you could come down. How is your ankle? And here is Donald. Carrie, can't you see Hannah's looks in him?"

Amazement and embarrassment struggled in the faces of mother and daughter. They looked at Aunt Crete, and they looked at Donald, and then they looked at Aunt Crete again. It couldn't be, it wasn't, yet it was, the voice of Aunt Crete, kind and forgiving, and always thoughtful for everyone, yet with a new something in it. Or was it rather the lack of something? Yes, that was it, the lack of a certain servile something that neither Luella nor her mother could name, yet which made them feel strangely ill at ease with this new-old Aunt Crete.

They looked at each other bewildered and then back at Aunt Crete again. They traced line by line the familiar features in their new radiance of happiness and tried to conjure back the worried V in her forehead and the slinky sag of her old gowns. Was the world turned upside down? What had happened to Aunt Crete?

"Upon my word, Lucretia Ward, is it really you?" exclaimed her sister, making a wild dash into the conversation, determined to right herself and everything else if possible. She felt like a person suddenly upset in a canoe; she struggled wildly to get her footing once more if there was any solid footing anywhere, with her sister Crete standing there calmly in an imported gown, her hair done up like a fashion plate and a millionaire's smile on her pleasant face.

But Luella was growing angry. What did Aunt Crete mean by masquerading round in that fashion and making them ashamed before this handsome young man? And was he really their western cousin? Luella felt that a joke was being played on her, and she always resented jokes—at least, unless she played them herself.

Then Donald came to the front, for he feared for Aunt Crete's poise. She mustn't lose her calm dignity and get frightened. There was a sharp ring in the other aunt's voice, and the new cousin looked unpromising.

"And is this my aunt Carrie? And my cousin Luella?" He stepped forward and shook hands pleasantly.

"I'm glad to speak with you at last," he said as he dropped Luella's hand, "though it's not the first time I've seen you or heard your voice, either, you know."

Luella looked up puzzled and tried to muster her scattered graces and respond with her ravishing society air. But somehow the ease and grace of the man before her overpowered her. And was he really her cousin? She tried to think what he could mean by having seen and talked with her before. Surely he must be mistaken, or—perhaps he was referring to the glimpse he had of her when Mr. Grandon bowed the evening before. She tossed her head with a kittenish movement and arched her poorly penciled eyebrows.

"Oh, how is that?" she asked, wishing he hadn't been quite so quick to drop her hand. It would have been more impressive to have had him hold it just a second longer.

"Why, I saw you the morning you left your home, as I was getting out of the train. You were just entering, and you called out of the window to a young lady in a pony cart. You wore a light kind of a yellowish suit, didn't you? Yes, I was very sure it was you."

He was studying her face closely, a curious twinkle in his eyes, which might or might not have been complimentary. Luella couldn't be sure. The color rose in her cheeks and neck and up to her black-walnut hair till the red dress and the red face looked all aflame. She suddenly remembered what she called out to the young lady in the pony cart, and she wondered whether he had heard or noticed.

"And then," went on her handsome persecutor, "I had quite a long talk with you over the telephone, you know—"

"What!" gasped Luella. "Was that you? Why, you must be mistaken. I never telephoned to you—that is, I couldn't get anyone on the phone."

"What's all this about, Luella?" questioned her mother sharply, but Donald interposed.

"Sit down, Aunt Carrie. We're so excited over meeting you at last that we're forgetting to be courteous."

He shoved forward a comfortable chair for his aunt and one for the blushing, overwhelmed Luella. Then he took Aunt Crete's hands lovingly and pushed her gently backward into the most comfortable rocker in the room.

"It's just as easy to sit down, dear aunt," he said, smiling. "And you know you've had a pretty full day and mustn't get tired for tonight's concert. Now, Aunt Carrie, tell us about your ankle. How did you come to sprain it so badly, and how did it get well so fast? We were quite alarmed about you. Is it really better? I'm afraid you've taxed it too much coming down this evening. Much as we wanted to see you, we could have waited until it was quite safe for you to use it, rather than have you run any risks."

Then it was the mother's turn to blush, and her thin, somewhat colorless face grew crimson with embarrassment.

"Why, I—," she began, "that is, Luella was working over it, rubbing it with liniment. All of a sudden she gave it a sort of a little pull, and something seemed to give way with a sharp pain, and then it came all right as good as ever. It feels a little weak, but I think by morning it'll be all right. I think some little bone got out of place, and Luella pulled it back in again. My ankles have always been weak anyway. I suffer a great deal with them in going about my work at home."

"Why, Carrie," said Aunt Crete, leaning forward with troubled reproach in her face, "you never complained about it."

A dull red rolled over Mrs. Burton's thin features again and receded, leaving her face pinched and haggard-looking. She felt as if she were seeing visions. This couldn't be her own sister, all dressed up so and yet speaking in the old sympathetic tone.

"Oh, I never complain, of course. It don't do any good."

The conversation was interrupted by another tap on the door. Donald opened it and received a large express package.

While he was giving some orders to the servant, Mrs. Burton leaned forward and said in a low tone to her sister: "For goodness' sake, Lucretia Ward, what does all this mean? How ever did you get decked out like that?"

Then Donald's clear voice broke in upon them as the door closed once more, and Luella watched him curiously cutting with eager, boyish haste the cords of the express package.

"Aunt Crete, your cloak has come. Now we'll all see if it's becoming."

"Bless the boy," said Aunt Crete, looking up with delighted eyes. "Cloak—what cloak? I'm sure I've got wraps enough now. There's the cloth coat and the silk one and that elegant black lace—"

"No, you haven't. I saw right off what you needed when we went out in the auto last night, and I telephoned to that Miss Brower up in the city this morning. She's fixed it all up. I hope you'll like it."

With that he pulled the cover off the box and brought into view a long, full evening cloak of pale pearl-colored broadcloth lined with white silk and a touch about the neck of black velvet and handsome creamy lace.

He held it up at arm's length admiringly.

"It's all right, Aunt Crete. It looks just like you. I knew that woman would understand. Stand up, and let's see how you look in it. Then after dinner we'll take a little spin around the streets to try you in it."

Aunt Crete, blushing like a pretty girl, stood up, and he folded the soft garment about her in all its elegant richness. She stood just in front of the full-length mirror and couldn't deny to herself that it was becoming. But she was getting used to seeing herself look nice and wasn't so much overpowered with the sight as she was with the tender thought of the boy who got it for her. She forgot Carrie and Luella and everything except that Donald had gone to great trouble and expense to please her. She turned around and put her two hands, one on each of his cheeks, standing on her tiptoes to reach him, and kissed him.

He bent and returned the kiss laughingly.

"It's a lot of fun to get you things, Aunt Crete," he said. "You always like them so much."

"It's beautiful, beautiful," she said, looking down and smoothing the cloth tenderly as if it were his cheek. "It's much too beautiful for me. Donald, you'll spoil me."

"Yes, I should think so," sniffed Luella, as if offering an apology in some sort for her childish aunt.

"A little spoiling won't hurt you, dear aunt," said Donald seriously. "I don't believe you've had your share of spoiling yet, and I mean to give it to you if I can. Doesn't she look pretty in it, Cousin Luella? Come now, Aunt Carrie. I suppose it's time to go down to dinner, or we won't get through in time for the fun. Are you sure your ankle is quite well? Are you able to go to the concert tonight? I've tickets for us all. Sousa's orchestra is to be there, and the program is an unusually fine one."

Luella was mortified and angry beyond words, but a chance to go to the concert, in company with Clarence Grandon and his mother, wasn't to be lightly thrown away. She crushed down her mortification, contenting herself with darting an angry glance and a hateful curl of her lip at Aunt Crete as they went out the door together. This, however, was altogether lost on that little woman, for she was watching her nephew's face and wondering how it came that such joy had fallen to her lot.

The mortified mother and daughter had no chance to exchange a word as they went down in the elevator or followed in the wake of their relatives, before whom all porters and office boys and even headwaiters bowed and jumped to offer assistance. They were having their wish, to be sure, entering the dining hall behind the handsome young man and the elegant, gray-clad, fashionably coiffured old lady, a part of the train, with the full consciousness of "belonging," yet in what a way! Both were having ample opportunity for reflection, for they could see at a glance that no one noticed them, and all attention was for those ahead of them.

Luella bit her lip angrily and looked in wonder. Her aunt had somehow lost her dumpiness and walked as gracefully beside her tall young nephew as if she were accustomed to walk in the eyes of the world thus for years. The true secret of her grace, if Luella had known it, was that she wasn't thinking in the least of herself. Her conscience was at rest now, for the meeting between the cousins was over, and Luella was to have a good time, too. Aunt Crete was never the least bit selfish. It seemed to her that her good time was only blooming into yet larger things, after all.

Behind her walked her sister and niece in mortified humiliation. Luella was trying to recall just what she had said about "country cousins" over the telephone and exactly what she had said to the girl in the pony cart the morning she left home. The memory didn't cool her already heated complexion. It was dawning upon her that she'd made a mighty mistake in running away from such a cousin and in such a manner.

All her life, in such a case, Luella was accustomed to blaming someone else for her disappointments and vent, as it were, her spite upon that one. Now, in looking about to find such an object of blame her eyes naturally fell upon the one who had borne the greater part of all blame for her. But, try as she would to pour out blame and scorn from her large, bold eyes upon poor Aunt Crete, somehow the blame slipped off from the sweet gray garments and left Aunt Crete as serene as ever, with her eyes turned trustingly toward her dear Donald. Luella was brought to the verge of vexation by this and could scarcely eat any dinner.

The dessert was just being served when the waiter brought Aunt Crete a dainty note from which a faint perfume of violets stole across the table to the knowing nostrils of Luella.

With the happy abandonment of a child Aunt Crete opened it joyously.

"Who in the world can be writing me?" she said wonderingly. "You'll have to read it for me, Donald. I left my glasses up in my room."

Luella reached out her hand for the note, but Donald had it first, as if he hadn't seen her impatient hand claiming her right to read Aunt Crete's notes.

"It's from Mrs. Grandon, Auntie," he said.

"Dear Miss Ward," he read, "I'm sorry that I'm feeling too weary to go to the concert this evening as we planned. My son makes such a baby of me that he thinks he can't leave me alone. But I do hope we can have the pleasure of the company of you and your nephew on a little auto trip tomorrow afternoon. My brother has a villa a few miles up the shore, and he telephoned us this morning to dine with them tonight. When he heard of your being here, he said by all means to bring you with us. My brother knows of your nephew's friendship with Clarence and is anxious to meet him, as are the rest of his family. I do hope you'll feel able to go with us.

With sincere regrets that I cannot go with you to the concert this evening,

Helen Grandon.

For the moment Luella forgot everything else in her amazement at this letter. Aunt Crete receiving notes from Mrs. Grandon, from whom she and her mother could scarcely get a frigid bow! Aunt Crete invited on automobile trips and dinners in villas! Donald, an intimate friend of Clarence Grandon's! Oh, foolish and blind! What had she done! Or what had she undone?

She studied the handsome, keen face of her cousin as he bent over the letter and agonized to think of her own words, "I'm running away from a backwoods cousin"! She could hear it shouted from one end of the great dining hall to the other, and her face blazed redder and redder till she thought it would burst. Her mother turned from her in mortified silence and wondered why Luella couldn't have had a good complexion.

Studied politeness was the part Donald had set for himself this evening. He saw that his victims were sufficiently unhappy. He had no wish to see them writhe under further tortures. Though when he looked upon Aunt Crete's happy face and thought how white it turned at dread of them, he felt he must let the thorns he planted in their hearts remain long enough to bring forth a true repentance. But he said nothing further to distress them. They began to wonder whether, after all, he really had seen through their plan of running away from him.

It was all Aunt Crete's fault. She should have arranged it in some way to get them quietly home as soon as she found out what kind of cousin had come to see them. It never occurred to Luella that nothing her poor, abused aunt could have said would have convinced her that her cousin was worthy of her homecoming.

As the concert neared its close, Luella and her mother prepared for a time of reckoning for Aunt Crete. When she was safely in her room, what would hinder them from going to her alone and having it out? The sister's face hardened, and the niece's eyes glittered as she stonily thought of the scornful sentences she would hurl after her aunt.

Donald looked at her menacing face and read its thoughts. He resolved to protect Aunt Crete, whatever came. So at the door, when he saw his aunt Crete pause, he said gently: "Aunt Crete, I guess we'll have to say good night now, for you've had a hard day of it, and I want you to be bright and fresh for morning. We want to take an early dip in the ocean. The bathing hours are early tomorrow, I see."

He bowed good night in his pleasantest manner, and the ladies from the fourth floor reluctantly withdrew to the elevator. But fifteen minutes later they surreptitiously tapped at the private door of the room they understood to be Aunt Crete's.

Chapter 7

The door was opened cautiously by the maid. She was doing Aunt Crete's hair, after finishing a refreshing facial massage given at Donald's express orders.

Aunt Crete looked round upon her visitors with a rested, rosy countenance, which bloomed out under her fluff of soft, white hair and quite startled her sister with its freshness and youth. Was this really her sister Crete, or had she made a terrible mistake and entered the wrong apartment?

But suddenly a change came over Aunt Crete's ruddy countenance as over the face of a child who in the midst of happy play sees a trouble descending upon it. A look almost of terror came over her, and she caught her breath and waited to see what was coming.

"Why, Carrie, Luella!" she gasped weakly. "I thought you'd gone to bed. Marie's just doing up my hair for the night. She's been giving me a face massage. You ought to try one. It makes you feel young again."

"H'm!" said her affronted sister. "I shouldn't care for one."

Marie looked over Luella and her mother, beginning with the painfully elaborate hair arrangement and going down to the tips of their boots. Luella's face burned with mortification as she read the withering disapproval in the French woman's countenance.

"Let's sit down till she's done," said Luella, dropping promptly on the foot of Aunt Crete's bed and gazing around in frank surprise over the spaciousness of the apartment.

Thereupon the maid ignored them and went about her work, brushing out and deftly manipulating the wavy white hair and chattering pleasantly meanwhile, just as if no one else were in the room.

Aunt Crete tried to forget what was before her or, rather, behind her. But her hands trembled a little as they lay in her lap in the folds of the pretty pink and gray challis kimono she wore. All of a sudden she remembered the unwhitewashed cellar and the uncooked jam and the unmade shirtwaists and the little hot brick house gazing at her reproachfully from the distant home. And here she was in this fine array, forgetting it all and being waited upon by a maid—a lazy truant from her duty.

Did the heart of the maid divine the state of things? Or was it only her natural instinct that made her turn to protect the pleasant little woman, in whose service she was always well paid, against the two women who were so evidently of the common walks of life and were trying to ape those that in the maid's eyes were their betters? However it was, Marie prolonged her duties a good half hour. Luella's impatience waxed furious, so that she lost her fear of the maid gradually and yawned loudly, declaring that Aunt Crete had surely had enough fussing over for one evening.

They held in their more personal remarks until the door finally closed upon Marie. But they burst forth so immediately that she heard the opening sentences through the transom. She therefore thought it wise to step to the young gentleman's door and warn him that his elderly relative he seemed so careful of was likely to be disturbed beyond a reasonable hour for retiring. Then she withdrew discreetly, having not only added to her generous income by a good bit of silver, but also followed the dictates of her heart, which had taken kindly to the gentlewoman of the handsome clothes and few pretensions.

"Well, upon my word! I should think you'd be ashamed, Aunt Crete!" burst forth Luella, rising from the bed in a majesty of wrath. "Sitting there, being waited on like a baby, when you ought to be at home this minute earning your living. What do you think of yourself anyway, living in this kind of luxury when you haven't a cent in the world of your own, and your own sister, who has supported you for years, up in a little dark fourth-floor room? Such selfishness I never saw in all my life. I wouldn't have believed it of you, though we might have suspected it long ago from the foolish things you were always doing. Aunt Crete, have you any idea how much all this costs?"

She waved her hand tragically over the handsome room, including the trunk standing open and the gleam of silver-gray silk that peeped through the half-open closet door. Aunt Crete fairly cringed under Luella's scornful eyes.

"And you, nothing in the world but a beggar, a *beggar!* That's what you are—a beggar depending upon *us*—and you swelling around as if you owned the earth and wearing silk dresses and real lace collars and expensive jewelry, even having a maid and shaming your own relatives and getting in ahead of us, who've always been good to you, and taking away our friends and making us appear like two cents! It's just fierce, Aunt Crete! It's—it's *heathenish!*" Luella paused in her anger for a fitting word and then took the first one that came.

Aunt Crete winced. She was devoted to the Woman's Missionary Society, and it was terrible to be likened to a heathen. She wished Luella had chosen some other word.

"I'd think you'd be so ashamed you couldn't hold your head up before your honest relatives," went on the shameless girl. "Taking money from a stranger—that's what he is, a *stranger*—and you whining round and lowering yourself to let him buy you clothes and things, as if you didn't have proper clothes suited to your age and station. He's a young upstart coming along and buying you any—and such clothes! Do you know you're a laughingstock? What would Mrs. Grandon say if she knew whom she was inviting to her automobile rides and dinners? Think of you in your old purple calico washing the dishes at home and scrubbing the kitchen, and ask yourself what you'd say if

Mrs. Grandon called on you and found you that way. You're a hypocrite, Aunt Crete, an awful hypocrite!"

Luella towered over Aunt Crete, and the little old lady looked into her eyes with a horrible fascination, while her great grief and horror poured down her sweet face in anguished tears that wouldn't be stayed. Her kindly lips were quivering, and her eyes were wide with tears.

Luella saw she was making an impression and went on more wildly than before, her fury growing with every word and not realizing how loud her voice was.

"And it isn't enough that you'd do all that, but now you're going to spoil my prospects with Clarence Grandon. You can't keep up this masquerade long, and when they find out what you really are, what will they think of *me?* It'll be all over with me, and it'll be your fault, Aunt Crete, your fault, and you'll never have a happy moment afterward, thinking of how you spoiled my life."

"Now, Luella," broke in Aunt Crete solemnly through her tears, "you're mistaken about one thing. It won't be my fault there, for it wouldn't have made a bit of difference, poor child. I'm real sorry for you, and I meant to tell you just as soon as we got home, for I couldn't bear to spoil your pleasure while we were here, but that Clarence Grandon belongs to someone else. He isn't for you, Luella, and there must have been some mistake about it. Perhaps he was just being kind to you. For Donald knows him real well, and he says he's engaged to a girl out west, and they're going to be married this fall, and Donald says she's real sweet and—"

But Aunt Crete's quivering voice stopped suddenly in mild affright, for Luella sprang toward her like some mad creature, shaking her finger in her aunt's face and screaming at the top of her voice: "It's a lie! I say it's a lie! Aunt Crete, you're a liar. That's what you are with all the rest."

And the high-strung, uncontrolled girl burst into angry sobs.

No one heard the gentle knock that was twice repeated during the scene, and no one saw the door open until they all suddenly became aware that Donald stood in the room, looking from one face to another in angry surprise.

Donald didn't retire at once after bidding Aunt Crete good night. He found letters and telegrams awaiting his attention, and he was busy writing a letter of great importance when the maid gave him the hint of Aunt Crete's late callers. Laying down his pen, he stepped quietly across the private parlor that separated his room from his aunt's and stopped a moment before the door to make sure he heard voices. Then he knocked and knocked again, unable to keep from hearing most of Luella's tirade.

His indignation knew no bounds, and he concluded his time had come to interfere, so he opened the door and went in.

"What does all this mean?" he asked in a tone that frightened his aunt Carrie and made Luella stop her angry sobs in sudden awe.

No one spoke, and Aunt Crete looked a mute appeal through her eyes. "What is it, dear aunt?" he said, stepping over by her side. He placed his arm protectingly around the poor, shrinking figure, who somehow in her sorrow and helplessness reminded him strongly of his own lost mother. He couldn't remember at that moment that the other woman, standing hard and cold and angry across the room, was also his mother's sister. She didn't look like his mother or act like her.

Aunt Crete put her little curled white head in its crisping-pins down on Donald's coat sleeve and shrank into the pink and gray kimono appealingly as she tried to speak.

"It's just as I told you, Donald, you dear boy," she sobbed out. "I— shouldn't have come. I knew it, but it wasn't your fault. It was all mine. I should have stayed at home and not dressed up and come off here. I've had a beautiful time, but it wasn't for me, and I shouldn't have taken it. It's just spoiled Luella's nice time, and she's blaming me, just as I knew she would."

"What does my cousin mean by using that terrible word to you, which I heard as I entered the room?"

Donald's voice was keen and scathing, and his eyes fairly piercing as he asked the question and looked straight at Luella, who answered not a word.

"That wasn't what she meant, Donald," said Aunt Crete apologetically. "She was most out of her mind with trouble. You see I had to tell her what you told me about Clarence Grandon being engaged to another girl—"

"Aunt Crete, don't say another word about that!" burst out Luella with flashing eyes and crimson face.

"For mercy's sake, Crete, can't you hold your tongue?" said Luella's mother sharply.

"Go on, Aunt Crete. Did my cousin call you a liar for saying that? Yet it was entirely true. If she's not disposed to believe me either, I can call Mr. Grandon in to testify in the matter. He'll come if I send for him. But I feel sure, after all, that it won't be necessary. It's probably true, as Aunt Crete says, that you were excited, Luella, and didn't mean what you said. After a good night's sleep you'll be prepared to apologize to Aunt Crete and be sorry enough for worrying her. I'm going to ask you to leave Aunt Crete now and let her rest. She's had a wearying day and needs to be quiet at once. She's my mother's sister, you know, and I feel as if I must take care of her."

"You seem to forget that I'm your mother's sister, too," said Aunt Carrie coldly, as she stood stiff and disapproving beside the door, ready to leave.

"If I do, Aunt Carrie, forgive me," said Donald courteously. "It isn't strange when you remember that you forgot I was your sister's child and ran away from me. But never mind—we'll put that aside and try to forget it. Good night, Aunt Carrie. Good night, Cousin Luella. We'll all feel better about it in the morning."

They bowed their belittled heads and went with shame and confusion to the fourth floor back. When the door was closed upon them, they burst into angry talk, each blaming the other, until at last Luella sank in a piteous heap upon the bed and gave herself over to helpless tears.

"Luella," said her mother in a businesslike tone, "you stop that bawling and sit up here and answer me some questions. Did you or did you not go riding with Mr. Clarence Grandon last winter in his automobile?"

Luella paused in her grief and nodded hopelessly.

"Well, how'd it come about? There's no use sniffing. Tell me exactly."

"Why, it was a rainy day," sobbed out the girl, "and I met him on the street in front of the public library the day I took back *The Legacy of Earl Crafton* and that other book by the same author—"

"Never mind what books. Tell me what happened," said the exasperated mother.

"Well, if you're going to be cross, I won't tell you anything," was the final reply. For a moment nothing was heard in the room but sobs.

Luella recovered the thread of her story, however, and went on to relate how in company with a lot of other girls she met Mr. Grandon the day before at the golf links, where a championship game was being played. She didn't explain the various maneuvers by which she contrived to be introduced to him or that he didn't seem to know her at first when she bowed in front of the library building. She'd called out, "It's a fine day for ducks, Mr. Grandon. Isn't it good the game was yesterday instead of today?" And he'd asked her to ride home with him.

That was her version. Through careful questioning her mother finally arrived at the fact that the girl more than hinted to be taken home, having loudly announced her lack of rubbers and umbrella, though she seldom wore rubbers and had on a raincoat and an old hat.

"But how about that big box of chocolates he sent you, Luella? That showed special attention if he was engaged."

"Oh," pouted Luella, "I don't suppose that meant anything either, for I caught him in a word game on the way home that day. We said the same words at the same time, something like 'It's going to clear off.' I told him, when we girls did that, the one that spoke first had to give the other a box of chocolates. So the next day he sent them."

"Luella, I never brought you up to do things like that. I don't think that was very nice."

"Oh, now, Ma, don't you preach. I guess you weren't a saint when you were a girl. Besides, I don't think you're very sympathetic." She mopped her swollen eyes.

"Luella, didn't he ever pay you any more attention after that? I kind of thought you thought he liked you, by the way you talked."

"No, he never even looked at me," sobbed the girl, her grief breaking out afresh. "He didn't even know me the next time we met but stared straight at me till I bowed, and then he gave me a cold little touch of his hat. And down here he hasn't even recognized me really. I suppose that lady mother of his didn't like my looks."

"Look here, Luella. I wish you'd act sensible. This has been pretty expensive trying to run around after the Grandons. What with the hotel bills and all that dressmaking, and now there's no telling how Aunt Crete will act after we get home. Like as not she'll think she's got to have a maid and dress in silks and satins. There's one comfort—probably some of her clothes will fix over for you when she gets off her high horse and comes down to everyday living again. But I wish you'd brace up and forget these Grandons. It's no use trying to get up in the world higher than you belong. There's that nice John Peters who would have been real devoted to you if you'd just let him. And he owns a house of his own already and has the name of being the best plumber in Midvale."

Luella sighed.

"He's only a plumber, Ma, and his hands are all red and rough."

"Well, what's that?" snapped her practical mother. "He may have his own automobile before long, for all that. Now dry up your eyes and go to sleep. In the morning you go down real early and apologize to your silly aunt Crete. And make her understand she's not to disgrace us by going bathing while she's here. My land! I expect to see her riding round on one of those saddle ponies on the beach next or maybe driving that team of goats we saw today, with pink ribbon reins. Come now, Luella. Don't you worry. Set out to show your cousin Donald how nice you can be, and maybe some of the silk dresses will come your way. Anyhow, this can't last forever, and John Peters is at home when we get there."

So Luella, soothed in spirit, went to bed and arose early the next morning, descending upon poor Aunt Crete while dreams of sailing with Donald on a moonlit sea were still mingling with her waking thoughts.

Chapter 8

L uella did her work quietly, firmly, and thoroughly. She vanished before Marie thought of coming to her morning duties.

At breakfast Donald found a sad, cowed little woman waiting for him to go down to the dining room. He tried to cheer her up by telling her how nice a time they were to have in bathing that morning, for the water was sure to be delightful. But Aunt Crete shook her head sadly and said she guessed she'd better not go in bathing anymore. Then she sighed and looked wistfully out on the blue waves dancing in the sunshine.

"Don't you feel well, Aunt Crete?" asked Donald anxiously.

"Oh, yes, real well," she answered.

"Did it hurt you to go in yesterday, do you think?"

"No, not a mite," she responded promptly.

"Then why in the name of common sense don't you want to go in today? Has Luella been trying to talk some of her nonsense?"

"Well, Luella thinks my figger looks so bad in a bathing suit. She says of course you want to be polite to me, but you don't really know how folks'll laugh at me and make her ashamed of belonging to me."

"Well, I like that!" said Donald. "You just tell Miss Luella we're not running this vacation for her sole benefit. Now, Aunt Crete, you're going in bathing, or else I won't go, and you wouldn't like to deprive me of that pleasure, would you? Well, I thought not. Now come on down to breakfast, and we'll have the best day yet. Don't you let Luella worry you. And, by the way, Aunt Crete, I'm thinking of running up to Cape Cod and perhaps getting a glimpse of the Maine coast before I get through. How would you like to go with me?"

"Oh!" gasped Aunt Crete in a daze of delight. "Could I?" Then, mindful of Luella's mocking words the night before, she added: "But I mustn't be an expense to you. I'd just be a burden. You know I haven't a cent of my own in the world, so I couldn't pay my way, and you've done a great deal more than I should have let you do."

"Now, Aunt Crete, once for all you must get that idea out of your head. You could never be a burden to me. I want you for a companion. If my mother were here, shouldn't I just love to take her on a journey with me and spend every cent I had to make her happy? Well, I haven't Mother here. But you're the nearest to Mother I can find, and I somehow feel she'd like me to have you in her place. Will you come? Or is it asking too much to ask you to leave Aunt Carrie and Cousin Luella? They've got each other, and they never really needed you as I do.

"I've got plenty of money for us to do as we please, and I mean it with all my heart. Will you come and stay with me? I may have to take a flying trip to Europe before the summer's over, and, if I do, it would be dreadfully lonesome to go alone. I think you'd like a trip on the ocean, wouldn't you? And a peep at London, and perhaps Paris and Vienna and old Rome for a few days? And in the fall I'm booked for work in my old university. It's only an assistant professorship yet, but it means a big thing for a young fellow like me. And I want you to come with me and make a cozy little home for me between times and a place where I can bring my friends when they get homesick."

He paused and looked down for an answer and was almost startled by the glory of joy in Aunt Crete's face.

"Oh, Donald, could I do that? Could I be that to you? Do you really think I could be of use enough to you to earn my living?"

He stooped and kissed her forehead reverently to hide the tears that came unbidden to his eyes. It touched him beyond measure that this sweet life had been so empty of love and so full of drudgery that she would speak that way about such a simple matter. It filled him with indignation against those who took the sweetness from her and gave her the dregs of life instead.

"Dear aunt," he said, "you could be of great use to me and more than earn anything I could do for you many times over, just by being yourself and mothering me. But as for work, there isn't to be one stroke except just what you want to do for amusement. We'll have servants to do all the work, and you shall manage them. I want you for an ornament in my home, and you're going to have a good rest and a continual vacation the rest of your life, if I know anything about it.

"Now come down to breakfast, so we can go in bathing early, and don't you worry another wrinkle about Luella. You don't belong to her anymore. We'll send her a parasol from New York and a party gown from Paris, and she won't bother her pompadour anymore about you—you may be sure."

In a maze of delight Aunt Crete went down to breakfast and dawned upon the astonished vision of her sister and niece in all the beauty of her dainty white morning costume. They were fairly startled at the vision she was in white, with her pretty white hair to match it. Luella gasped and held her disapproving breath. But Aunt Crete was too absorbed in the vision of joy that had opened before her to know or care what they thought of her in a white dress.

No girl in the new joy of her first love was ever in a sweeter dream of bliss than was Aunt Crete as she beamed through her breakfast. Luella's looks of scorn and Luella's mother's sour visage had no effect upon her whatever. She smiled happily and ate her breakfast in peace. Hadn't she just been set free forever from the things that made her life a burden before this, and hadn't she been shown into a large place of new joys where her heart might find rest?

After breakfast Donald made them all walk down the boardwalk to the various shops filled with curios, where he bought everything Luella looked at and lavished several gifts also upon her mother, including a small Oriental rug she admired. They returned to the hotel in a good humor, and Luella began to have visions of luxurious days to come. She felt sure she could keep Aunt Crete down about where she wanted her, and her eyes gloated over the beautiful white dress she hoped to claim for her own when they all went home and she convinced Aunt Crete how unsuitable white was for old ladies.

She was quite astonished, after her morning talk with her aunt, to hear Donald say as he looked at his watch, "Come, Aunt Crete. It's time to go in bathing." She was equally shocked to see her aunt walk smiling off toward the bathhouses, utterly regardless of her wrathful warning glances. It was rather disconcerting to have Aunt Crete become unmanageable right at the beginning this way. In view of the fact, however, that her hands were filled with pretty trifles her cousin bought she didn't feel like making any protest beyond threatening glances. But the dear soul whose mind was in Europe and whose heart was in a cozy little home all her own and Donald's, didn't see at all.

Aunt Crete was happy. She felt it in every nerve of her body as she stepped into the crisp waves and bounded out to meet them with the elasticity of a girl.

Luella, following a moment later in her flashy bathing suit of scarlet and white, watched her aunt in amazement and somehow felt that Aunt Crete was drifting away from her, separated by something more than a few yards of blue saltwater.

Donald kept up a continual flow of bright conversation during the noon meal. He even engaged Luella and her mother on the long piazza in looking through the marine glass at a great ship that floated lazily by, while Aunt Crete was getting ready to go on the ride. And before Luella and her mother were quite aware of what was happening they stood on the piazza watching Aunt Crete. Dressed in her handsome black crepe de chine, which even boasted a modest train, and her black lace wrap and bonnet, she was being handed into the Grandon motorcar, while Donald carried her long new gray cloak on his arm. The gray car moved smoothly away out of sight, and Luella and her mother were left staring at the sea with their own bitter reflections.

The automobile party didn't return until late that night, for the moon was full and the roads were fine, and Donald saw to it that Aunt Crete was guarded against any intrusion.

At breakfast the next morning Donald told them, and Aunt Crete was listening with the rapt smile that a slave might have worn as he listened to the reading of the proclamation of emancipation.

"Aunt Carrie," he began as pleasantly as if he were about to propose that they all go rowing, "Aunt Crete and I have decided to set up a permanent partnership. She has consented to come and mother me. I've accepted a position in my old university, and I'm very tired of boarding. I think we'll have a cozy, pleasant home. We'll be glad for you and Luella to come and visit us sometimes after we get settled and have some good servants. So Aunt Crete will have plenty of time to take you around and show you the sights.

"In the meantime, I may have to take a brief trip abroad for the university. If so, I'll probably start in about a week, and before that I want to get a glimpse of the New England coast. I've decided to take Aunt Crete and run away from you today. We leave on the noon train, so there's time for a little frolic yet. Suppose we go down to the boardwalk and eat an ice cream cone. I saw some delicious ones last night that made my mouth water, and we haven't had that experience yet. We'll get some rolling chairs so Aunt Crete won't be too tired for her journey.

"Come, Aunt Crete. You won't need to go upstairs again, will you? I told Marie about the packing. It won't be necessary for you to go back until it's time for you to change to your traveling clothes."

In a daze of anger and humiliation Luella and her mother climbed into their double rolling chair and ate their ice cream cones sullenly, propelled by a large boy. But Aunt Crete had a chair to herself and was attended by Donald. He kept up a constant stream of delightfully funny conversation about the people and things they passed, making Aunt Crete laugh until the tears came into her happy eyes.

Luella and her mother had no opportunity to talk to Aunt Crete alone, even after they returned to the hotel, for Donald kept himself in evidence everywhere. At last Luella declared that she didn't see why Donald thought he had a right to come and take Aunt Crete away from them, when they'd always taken care of her.

Her mother added in an injured tone: "Yes, you don't seem to realize what a burden it's been all these years, having to support Crete, and her so childish and unreasonable in a great many ways and not having any idea of the value of money. I've spent a good deal on Crete, considering everything. And now, when Luella's going out and has to have clothes and company, it's rather hard to have her leave us in the lurch this way, and me with all the work to do."

"That being the case, Aunt Carrie," said Donald pleasantly, "I suppose you'd be glad for me to relieve you of the burden of Aunt Crete's support, for it'll be nothing but a pleasure to me to care for her the rest of her life. As for what you've spent for her, just run it over in your mind, and I'll be quite glad to reimburse you. Aunt Crete is really too frail and sweet to have to work any longer. I'd think my cousin was almost old enough to be a help to you now, and she looks perfectly strong and able to work."

Luella flashed a vindictive glance at her cousin and turned haughtily toward the window. Then the porter came for the trunks, and the travelers said a hasty good-bye and left.

As Donald shook hands with Luella in parting, he looked merrily into her angry eyes and said, "I do hope, Luella, that it hasn't been too much of a trial to have your 'backwoods cousin' spend a few days here. You'll find a box of bonbons up in your room, if the porter did his duty, which may sweeten your bitter thoughts of me. We hope you'll have a delightful time the remainder of your stay here. Good-bye."

∽

About three months after Donald returned from Europe and settled into his western university life, Aunt Crete received a letter from her sister. It was brief and to the point, and Aunt Crete could read between the lines. It read:

> *Dear Crete,*
> *Aren't you about sick of that nonsense and ready to come home? Luella has decided that she can't do better than take John Peters. He's promised to buy an auto next year, if the plumbing business keeps up. I think at least you might come home and help get her things ready. There's a great deal of sewing to do, and you know I can't afford to hire it, and Luella's out so much, now that she's engaged. Do come soon.*
>
> *Your sister,*
> *Carrie.*

Aunt Crete looked sober. But Donald, looking over her shoulder, read and then went to his desk for a moment. Coming back, he dropped a check for five hundred dollars into his aunt's lap.

"Send her that from me, Aunt Crete, and another from yourself, if you like, and let her hire the sewing done. They don't want you, and I do."

Aunt Crete had her own bank account now, thanks to her thoughtful nephew. And she smiled back a delighted "I will" and went off to write the letter, for Aunt Crete was at last emancipated.

A Daily Rate

Chapter 1

The world wouldn't have looked so dreary perhaps, if it hadn't been her birthday. Many people expect something unusual to happen on a birthday, no matter how many times they're disappointed. Not that Celia Murray was expecting anything, even a letter, on this birthday. She stood shivering, nevertheless, in the dim front room of Mrs. Morris's boardinghouse, watching for the postman to reach their door. She did it merely because she wished to be close enough to get the letter at once—provided there was a letter—and not because she really hoped for one.

It was Saturday evening and the end of a half holiday in the store in which she usually stood all day as saleswoman. The unusual half day off was because of some parade in the city. Celia didn't spend her afternoon at the parade. Instead, she was in her small, cold, back bedroom on the third floor, mending worn garments. They were spread out on the bed in a row, and she went steadily down the line putting a few stitches here and a button there, and setting a patch in another. She counted every minute of daylight hoping to finish her work before it faded; the gas in her room was faint since the burner was old and worn out. She tried to be cheerful over the work. She called it her "dress parade." She knew it was the best way to accomplish as much as she wished to do.

Now it was six o'clock. She turned down the flickering light in her room and descended to the parlor to watch for the postman.

He was late tonight, probably because of the parade. She leaned her forehead against the cold glass and looked out into the misty darkness. Everything was murky and smoky. The passersby seemed tired and in a hurry. Some had their collars turned up.

She wondered where they were going and if pleasant homes awaited them: a young workingman hurrying along with breezy step and swinging a dinner pail, perhaps with a laughing baby and a tidy wife waiting for him at home; a strong old German, a day laborer perhaps, with a table full of noisy children and set with sauerkraut, cheese, coffee, and other viands; a stream of girls, some clerks like her and some mill girls. On other evenings these girls would look different, but many of them tonight were in holiday attire because of the half holiday which was generally given throughout the city. Some of these girls had homes of more or less attractiveness, and others, like her, lived in boardinghouses.

Celia sat down on one of the hard haircloth chairs and looked around the parlor. In the dimness of the turned-down gas, the room appeared more forlorn than usual. The ingrain carpet had long ago lost any claims to respectability, with its sodden appearance and unmistakable holes. These had been turned so as to come mostly under the tables and sofa, but they were generally visible to the casual observer. The parlor suite of haircloth had lost its spring from being much sat upon, and several of the chairs and one end of the sofa looked like fallen cake.

An asthmatic cabinet organ sat at the end of the room; a departing boarder, under compulsion, left it in lieu of his board. A few worn pieces of music were scattered upon it. The piece now open on the top was that choice selection "The Cat Came Back," a favorite with a young railroad brakeman who had a metallic tenor voice and good lungs. He was one of the boarders and considered quite a singer in the house. At the doorway stood a red, bedraggled chenille portiere, bordered with large pink cabbage roses.

The mantel had a worn plush scarf embroidered in an ugly, out-of-date style. On it was a large glass case of wax flowers, several cheap vases, and a match safe. Over it hung a portrait of the landlady's departed husband, and another of her adorned the opposite wall, both done in staring crayon work from ancient tintypes, heavily and cheaply framed. These with a marriage certificate, framed in gilt, made up the room's decorations.

Celia sighed as she looked about and took it all in once more. She'd been in it a week. Would she ever get used to it? She didn't curl her lip in scorn as other girls might have over the room and its furnishings. Neither did she feel the utter distaste that's like hatred. Instead she felt pity for it all and for the poor lonely creatures who had no other place to call home. Where such pity is, sometimes love isn't far away. She even rose, went to the doorway and looped the loose, drooping folds of the chenille curtain in a more graceful fashion. Somehow her fingers couldn't help doing a little toward making that room different.

Then she sighed and walked to the window again. She could see the belated postman across the street, flitting back and forth, ringing this bell and that, and searching in the great leather bag for papers or packages. His breath showed white against the dark grayish-blue of the misty evening air. His gray uniform seemed to be part of the mist. The yellow glare of the streetlight touched the gilt buttons and made a bright spot of the letters on his cap as he paused to study an address before coming to their door.

Celia opened the door before he could ring and took the few letters from his hand. The boarders in that house didn't have many correspondents. She stepped into the parlor once more and turned up the gas for a moment to see if she had any.

Strange to say, there were two, rather thin and unpromising, but they gave an unusual touch to the dull day. One bore a familiar postmark and was in her aunt's handwriting. The other held the city mark and seemed to be from a law firm. She didn't feel much curiosity about it. It was probably a circular and didn't look in the least interesting. She pushed them both quickly into her pocket as the front door opened letting in several noisy boarders. She didn't wish to read her letters in public. They'd keep till after supper.

The bell was already ringing. It wouldn't be worthwhile to go upstairs before going to the dining room. Experience taught her that the supper was at its very worst the minute after the bell rang. The consequences of waiting were undesirable. The meals in that house weren't too tempting at any time. Not that she cared much for her supper; she was too weary. But one must eat to live.

In the dining room the gas was turned to its highest. The coarse tablecloth wasn't the cleanest, for it was reminiscent of former breakfasts and dinners. The thick white dishes, nicked and cracked, bore marks of hard usage. At either end of the table were plates of heavy, sour-looking bread. The butter looked messy and uninviting.

The inevitable, scanty supply of prunes stood before the plate of the young German clerk, who was already helping himself to a liberal dish. The clerk was fond of prunes and always got to the table before anyone else. Some of the others good-naturedly called him selfish and passed meaningful remarks veiled in thin jokes concerning his habit. But if he understood he kept the matter to himself and didn't seem thin-skinned.

A stew was served for dinner that night. Celia dreaded stews since her first night when she found a long curly hair in the gravy on her plate. The stew was brought out in little thick white dishes, doled out in exact portions. Fat green pickles, suggesting copper in their pickling, and a plate of cheese and another of crackers were also served. A girl brought each one a small spoonful of canned corn, but it was cold and scarcely cooked at all, and the kernels were large and whole. Celia tasted the stew, pushed her dish back and didn't touch it again. On the side table was a row of plates; each contained a thin piece of pale-crusted pie, with a dark interior and an undefined character.

Celia tried to eat. The dishes weren't all clean. Both her spoon and fork had sticky handles. The silver was worn off the blade of her knife, and she couldn't help thinking that perhaps it had constantly been used to convey food to the mouth of the brakeman with the tenor voice.

One by one the boarders drifted in. It was surprising how quickly they gathered after that bell rang. They knew what they had to depend on for bread and butter, and it was first come, first served. Little Miss Burns sat across the table from Celia. She was thin and nervous and laughed excitedly a good deal. Tired little lines were around her eyes, and her mouth still wore a baby droop, though she was well along in years.

Celia noticed she drank only a cup of tea and nibbled a cracker. She didn't look well. The dinner was no more appetizing to her than to the young girl who so recently came there to board. She should have some delicate slices of nicely browned toast, a cup of tea with real cream in it, and a fresh egg poached just right, or a tiny cup of good strong beef bouillon, Celia said to herself. She amused herself by thinking how she'd like to slip out to the kitchen and get them for her, only—and she almost smiled at the thought—she'd hardly find the necessary articles for making all that in the Morris kitchen.

Next to Miss Burns sat two young girls, clerks in a three-cent store. They carried a good deal of would-be style and wore many bright rings on their grimy fingers, whose nails were never cleaned nor cut apparently—except by their teeth. These girls were rather pretty in a coarse way, laughing and talking a good deal in loud tones with the tenor brakeman, whose name was Bob Yates, and with the other young men boarders.

These young men were respectively a clerk in a department store, a student in the university, and a young teacher in the public schools. Celia noticed that neither the students nor the schoolteacher ate heartily and that the young dry goods salesman had a hollow cough. How nice it would be if they could have a good dinner just once—soup and roast beef, and good bread and vegetables, with a delicious old-fashioned apple dumpling smoking hot, such as her aunt Hannah could make. How she would enjoy giving it to them all. How she would like to eat some of it herself!

She sighed as she pushed back her plate with a good half of the stew untouched and felt it was impossible to eat another mouthful. Then she felt ashamed to think she cared so much for mere eating and tried to talk pleasantly to the little old lady beside her, who occupied a small dismal room on the third floor and seemed to stay in it most of the time. Celia hadn't yet found out her occupation or her standing in society. But she noticed that she trembled when she tried to cut her meat, and she was shabbily clothed in rusty black that looked as if it had served its time out several times over.

Mrs. Morris came into the dining room when the pie was being served. She was large and anxious-looking and wore a soiled calico wrapper without a collar. Her hair hadn't been combed since morning, and some locks had escaped on her neck and forehead and added to her generally dejected appearance. She sat down wearily at the head of the table and added her spiritless voice to the conversation. She asked them all how they enjoyed the parade and declared it would have been enough parade for her if she could have "set down for a couple of hours." Then she sighed and drank a cup of tea from her saucer, holding the saucer on the palm of her hand.

Here Celia expected to spend the home part of her life for several years at least, or if not here, in some place equally dreary and destitute of anything constituting a home.

Except for her brief conversation with the old lady on her right and a few words to Miss Burns, she spoke to no one during the meal. As soon as she excused herself from the pie and folded her napkin, she slipped upstairs to her room, for the thought of the two letters in her pocket seemed more inviting than the pie. She turned the gas to its highest and drew them forth.

Her aunt Hannah's came first. Only one sheet and not much written on it. Aunt Hannah was well but very busy, for Nettie's children were all down with whooping cough and the baby had been quite sick, poor little thing, and she had no time to write. Hiram, Nettie's husband, too, had been ill and laid up for a week, so Aunt Hannah had been nursing night and day. She enclosed a little bookmark to remember Celia's birthday. She wished she could send her something nice, but times were hard and Celia knew she had no money, so she must take it out in love.

Hiram's sickness and the doctor's bills made things tight for Nettie or she'd have remembered the birthday, too, perhaps. It was hard being a burden on Nettie, now when the children were young and she and Hiram needed every cent he could earn, but what else could she do? She sent her love to her dear girl, however, and wanted her to read the verse on the little ribbon enclosed, and perhaps it would do her good. She hoped Celia had a nice comfortable "homey" place to board and would write soon.

That was all. The white ribbon bookmark was satin and bore these words, "His allowance was a continual allowance. . .a daily rate. . .2 Kings 25:30," and beneath in small letters:

Charge not thyself with the weight of a year,
　　Child of the Master, faithful and dear,
Choose not the cross for the coming week,
　　For that is more than he bids thee seek.
Bend not thine arms for tomorrow's load,
　　Thou mayest leave that to thy gracious God,
Daily, only, he says to thee,
　　"Take up thy cross and follow me."

Chapter 2

Celia read the words over mechanically. She wasn't thinking so much of what they said, as she was of what her aunt wrote, or rather didn't write, and what could be read between the lines, from knowing that aunt and her surroundings. In other words Celia Murray was doing exactly what the words on the white ribbon told her not to do. She was charging herself "with the weight of a year." She'd picked up the cross of the coming months and was bending under it already.

Her trouble was Aunt Hannah. Oh, if she could only do something for her. She knew very well that that little sentence about being a burden on Nettie meant more than Aunt Hannah would have her know. She knew Aunt Hannah would never feel herself a burden on her niece Nettie—for whom she'd slaved half her life and was still slaving—unless something had been said or done to make her feel that way. And Celia, who never liked her cousin-in-law, Hiram, for more reasons than mere prejudice, knew pretty well who'd made good, faithful, untiring Aunt Hannah feel she was a burden.

Celia's eyes flashed, and she clasped her hands together suddenly. "Oh, if I could only do something to get Aunt Hannah out of that and have her with me!" she exclaimed aloud. "But here I am with six and a half dollars a week and paying out four and a quarter for this miserable hole they call a home. My clothes are wearing out as fast as they can, and the possibility hangs over me that I may not suit and may be discharged anytime. How can I ever get ahead enough to do anything?"

She sat there thinking over her life and Aunt Hannah's. Her own mother and Nettie's mother had died within a year of each other. They were both Aunt Hannah's sisters. Celia's father died soon after his wife, and Celia went to live with her cousins who were being mothered by Aunt Hannah, then a young, strong, sweet woman. Her uncle, Mr. Harmon, Nettie's father, was a hard-working, silent man, who supplied the wants of his family as well as he could. But that wasn't always luxuriously, for he was never a successful man.

The children grew fast and required many things. There were five of his own and Celia, who shared with the rest; she never really got her share, because she was ready to give up and the others were ready to take. Somehow the Harmon children had a streak of selfishness in them, and they always seemed willing for Aunt Hannah and Celia to take a backseat whenever anyone had to, which was nearly all the time.

Celia never resented this for herself, even in her heart; but for her aunt she often did. That faithful woman spent the best years of her life, doing for her sisters' children as if they were her own, and yet without the honor of being their mother and feeling the home was her own. She never married; she was simply Aunt Hannah, an excellent housekeeper, and the best substitute for a mother one could imagine.

As the children grew up they brought all their burdens to Aunt Hannah to bear. When there were more than she could conveniently carry, they would broadly hint that it was Celia's place to help her, for Celia was the outsider, the dependent, the moneyless one. It fell to her lot to tend the babies till they grew into boys, and then to follow after and pick up the things they left in disorder in their wake. She altered the girls' dresses to suit the style and fashioned dainty hats from odds and ends, turning and pressing them over to make them as good as new for some special occasion. And when it came her turn, she stayed at home, because she had nothing to wear, no time to make it over and nothing left to make over, because she'd given it all to the others.

Then came the day, not so many weeks ago. Celia remembered it as vividly as though it were yesterday; she'd gone over the details so many times they were burned upon her brain. Yet how long the time really had been and how many changes had come! The boy came up from the office with a scared face to say that something happened to Mr. Harmon, and then they brought him home and the family too soon learned there was no use in trying to resuscitate him—all hope was gone before he was taken from the office. Heart failure, they said!

Instantly following this came that other phrase "financial failure," and soon the orphans found they were penniless. This wasn't so bad for the orphans, for they were fully grown and the girls were both married. The three boys had good positions and could support themselves. But what of Aunt Hannah and Celia? Nettie and Hiram took Aunt Hannah into their family, ill-disguising the fact she was asked because of the help she could give in bringing up and caring for the children. But Celia understood from the first that there was no place for her.

She was given a good education with the others—that is, a common school course followed by a couple of years in the high school. She had her two hands and her bright wits and nothing else. A neighbor offered to use her influence with a friend of a friend of a partner in a city store, and the result was her position.

She learned since coming that it was a good one as such things went. She had regular hours for meals and occasional holidays, and her work wasn't heavy. She felt she should be thankful. She accepted it, of course, for there was nothing else. But she looked at Aunt Hannah with a heavy heart and knew her aunt felt it as keenly. These two had been very close to each other, separated from the others in a sense and with burdens to bear. Perhaps their sense of loneliness in the world made them cling to each other more.

Celia wished she could have said, "Aunt Hannah, come with me. I can take care of you now. You've cared for me all my life; now I'll give you a home and rest."

Ah! If that could have been! Celia drew her breath quickly, and the tears came between the closed lids. She knew if she once allowed the tears full sway, they wouldn't stop; she'd be left in no fit state to appear before those inquisitive boarders or perhaps even to sell ribbons in Dobson and Co.'s on Monday. No, she mustn't give way. She'd read that other letter and take her mind off these things. She could do nothing more now, except to write Aunt Hannah a cheering letter, which she couldn't do unless she grew cheerful herself.

So she opened the other letter.

It was from Rawley and Brown, a firm of lawyers on Fifth Street, desiring to know if she was Celia Murray, daughter of Henry Dean Murray of so forth and so on. If she was, would she please either write or call on them at her earliest convenience and produce evidence of her identity?

The girl laughed as she read it over again. "The idea!" she said, talking aloud to herself again as she'd grown into the habit of doing since she was alone, just to feel as if she were talking to someone. "If they want to identify me, let them. I'm not asking anything of them. If I'm I, prove it! How funny! Why? There can't be a fortune, for Father didn't have a cent. I'm sure I've had that drummed into my head enough by Nettie, and even Uncle Joseph took pains to tell me that occasionally. Well, it's mysterious."

She stood up and walked around the room singing the old nursery rhyme:

"If it be me, as I suppose it be,
    I've a little dog at home and he'll know me;
If it be *I*, he'll wag his little tail,
    And if it be *not* I, he'll bark, and he'll wail."

"Dear me!" said Celia. "I'm worse off than the poor old woman who fell asleep on the king's highway. I don't even have a little dog at home who'll know me." She sighed and sat down, picking up the white ribbon that had fallen to the floor. Then she read it over again carefully.

"How like Aunt Hannah that sounds!" she said to herself, as she read the poem slowly over. " 'Child of the Master, faithful and dear,' I can hear Aunt Hannah saying that to me. She was always one to hunt out beautiful things and say them to me as if they were written for me. If Aunt Hannah had ever had time, she would have been a poet. She has it in her.

"I've been doing exactly what this poem says I mustn't do: choosing my cross for the coming week. Yes, and bending my arm for tomorrow's load. I've been thinking what a dreary Sunday I'd have and wondering how I could endure it all day long in this ugly, cold room. And I won't stay down in that mean parlor and listen to their horrible singing. It wouldn't be right anyway, for they haven't the slightest idea of Sabbath keeping. Last Sunday was one hurrah all day long. I wonder what that verse at the top is—'His allowance was a continual allowance.' I don't remember ever reading it before. But trust Aunt Hannah to ferret out the unusual verses. I must look it up. Second Kings: Who was it about, anyway? The twenty-fifth chapter. Oh, here it is!" She read:

"And it came to pass in the seven and thirtieth year of the captivity of Jehoiachin king of Judah, in the twelfth month, on the seven and twentieth day of the month, that Evil-Merodach king of Babylon in the year that he began to reign did lift up the head of Jehoiachin king of Judah out of prison; and he spake kindly to him, and set his throne above the throne of the kings that were with him in Babylon; and changed his prison garments: and he did eat bread continually before him all the days of his life. And his allowance was a continual allowance given him of the king, a daily rate for every day, all the days of his life."

Celia paused and read the verses over again.

She began to see why her aunt sent it to her and, even more, why her heavenly Father sent it to her. It was the same thought in the bit of a poem. God was taking care of her. He was a king and could lift her head up out of prison, if this was a prison. He could even set her on a throne, change her prison garments and give her an allowance of grace to meet all her daily needs. A continual allowance: she didn't need to worry that it would give out. It was "all the days of her life."

And Aunt Hannah was His also. He would care for her in the same way. She could only trust and do what He gave her to do. It was hard for her to do that. She was so used to looking ahead and bearing burdens for others and planning for them. She recognized her fault and resolved to think more about it.

Meanwhile, she must write a long cheery letter to Aunt Hannah, whom she could easily see was homesick for her already, though only a week had passed since they separated. She gathered her writing materials, pulled her chair a little nearer the poor light and put on her heavy outdoor coat; the room was chilly, though it was only the latter part of October. Then she began to write. At the same time she was thinking she could make a pleasant Sabbath afternoon for herself by studying Jehoiachin. He was so much a stranger to her that she hardly remembered such a person in the Bible.

The letter she wrote was long and cheerful. She penned pictures of the places and things she'd seen and described in detail the different boarders. She tried not to tell the disagreeable things. She knew Aunt Hannah would be quick to understand how hard it was for her to bear, and she wouldn't lay a feather's burden upon those dear hardworked shoulders. So she wrote of lively conversations and made light of the poor fare. She said she had a good, cheap place, so they told her, and she guessed they were right.

She also used her imagination and described the dear little home she was going to make for Aunt Hannah to come and rest in and spend her later years. And she told her she was going to begin right away to save up for it. She made it all so real that tears came to her eyes for longing for it, and one dropped down on the paper and blotted a word. She hastily wiped it out and then took a fresh page, for Aunt Hannah had keen eyes. She would know what made that blot.

She paused a minute with her pen in the air before she closed the letter. Should she, or shouldn't she, tell Aunt Hannah of that letter from the lawyers? No, she wouldn't until she saw whether it came to anything and, if so, what. It might only worry her aunt. There were worries enough at Hiram's without her putting any more in the way. So she finished her letter, sealed and addressed it, and then ran down to put it in the box.

As she closed the door on the misty, outside world behind her, she met the tall, lanky cook in an untidy work dress and unkempt hair. Celia noticed that her hair was black and curled, like the one she found in the stew her first night there. She was going upstairs, but the cook reached out her hand to detain her.

"Say," she said in a familiar tone, "I wish you'd jes' step into Mis' Morris's room and stay a spell. She's took dreadful sick this evenin', and I've been with her off an' on most all the time. I've got pies to bake fer tomorrow, an' I can't spend no more time up there now. She ought to have someone, an' the rest seems all to be gone out 'cept that ol' lady up there, an' she's gone to bed by this time, I reckon."

Celia could only go, of course, though the task looked anything but pleasant. Mrs. Morris had never seemed pleasant. She inquired about the sickness, but the cook didn't know. No, no physician was sent for.

"There wan't no one to go in the first place, and, second, doctors is expensive things, take 'em anyway you will, medicine and all. Mrs. Morris can't afford no doctors. She's most killed with debt now."

Celia turned on the stairs and followed the woman's directions to Mrs. Morris's room. She thought of the words she read a little while ago.

> Daily, only, He says to thee,
>   "Take up thy cross and follow Me."

She smiled and thought how soon a cross came to her after she laid down the wrong one of a week ahead. Tapping softly on Mrs. Morris's door, she lifted up her heart in prayer to be shown how to do or say the right thing if the need arose. Then she heard a strained voice, like someone in pain, call, "Come in," and she opened the door.

Chapter 3

Mrs. Morris lay on her unmade bed, still in a soiled wrapper. Her expansive face was drawn in agony, and she looked pale and sick. She seemed surprised to see Celia and supposed she came to request another towel or make some complaint.

"You'll have to ask Maggie," she said, without waiting to hear what the girl had to say. "I can't talk now—I'm suffering so. It's just terrible. I never was so sick in my life."

"But I've come to help you," explained Celia. "Maggie told me you were sick. Tell me what's the matter. Perhaps I can do something for you. I know a little about sickness and nursing."

"Oh, such awful pain!" said the woman, writhing in agony. "I suppose it's something I've et. Though I never et a thing, all day long, but a little piece of pie at dinner tonight and me tea. Me nerves is all used up with worrying anyway, and me stomach won't stand anything anymore."

Celia asked a few practical questions and then told her she'd return in a minute. She hurried to the kitchen, though she'd never penetrated to that realm of darkness—and dirt. She ordered Maggie to bring her a large quantity of very hot water as soon as she could and send someone for a doctor. Then she went up to her own room and picked up a bottle or two from her small supply of medicines and a piece of an old blanket she'd brought from home.

She hesitated a moment. She should have another flannel. The woman was too sick to find anything and said she didn't know where there were any old flannels. She must take up this cross to save that poor woman from her suffering and perhaps save her life, for she was evidently very sick. She quickly took out her own clean flannel petticoat. It wasn't very fine and was somewhat old, but it was a sacrifice to use her personal clothing in that dirty room and for the woman who didn't seem to be clean herself. But there was no help for it, and she hurried back as fast as she could.

She gave the woman a little medicine that she thought might help her and knew wouldn't harm her till the doctor came. Then plunging the cherished blanket into the hot water, she wrung it as dry as she could and applied it to the seat of pain, covering it with the flannel skirt. She knew there was nothing like hot applications to relieve severe pain. She saw by the look of relief on the sick woman's face that the pain had relaxed to some extent.

After a moment, Mrs. Morris said: "I don't know as you'd a needed to send for a doctor; this might have helped me without him. I can't bear to think of his bill. Bills'll be the death of me yet, I'm afraid."

But a spasm of pain stopped her speech, and Celia repeated the applications.

It was some time before the arrival of the doctor, who evidently thought the patient a very sick woman. Mrs. Morris realized this, too. After he was gone and Celia was left alone with her, she asked if the doctor thought she was going to die.

"Though I ain't got much to live for, the land knows—nor to die for either, for that matter."

"Oh, you forget!" said Celia reverently, yet aghast that she'd speak so of dying. "There's Jesus! Don't you know Him?"

The woman looked at her as if she'd spoken the name of some heathen deity and then turned her head wearily.

"No," she said, "I don't suppose I'm a Christian. I never had any time. When I was a girl there was always plenty of fun, and I never thought about it. After I got married there wasn't time. I told the minister I'd think about joining church at the time of my daughter's funeral, but I never did. I kind of wish I had now. One never is ready to die, I s'pose. But then living isn't easy either, the land knows."

An ashen look spread over her face. Celia wondered if perhaps she might be dying even now. She shuddered. It seemed so terrible for anyone to die that way. She'd never been with a sick person close to death, and she didn't know the signs well enough to judge how much danger there might be. The woman must have some thread of hope, if she was really dying. She came close to her and took her hand tenderly.

"Dear Mrs. Morris! Don't talk that way. Dying isn't hard, I'm sure, if you have Jesus. He's always near and ready, if you'll only take Him now. I know He helps a person die, for I can remember my own dear mother, though I was only a little girl. She had a beautiful look on her face when she bid me good-bye and told me she was going to be with Jesus. And she said I must get ready to come to her. She looked very happy about it."

Mrs. Morris opened her eyes and gave her a searching look. Then she said in a voice halfway between a groan and a frightened shout: "Why do you talk like that? You don't think I'm dying, do you? Tell me quick! Did the doctor say I was going to die? Why did he go away if that was so? Send for him quick!"

Then the inexperienced girl realized she'd made a mistake and was too earnest. The woman might make herself much worse by such excitement. To talk to her that way wouldn't do any good; she must wait until a suitable season.

"No, Mrs. Morris," she said, rising and speaking calmly, "he didn't say so, and I don't believe you're going to die. You mustn't get so excited, or you'll make yourself worse. Here, take your medicine now, for it's time. I didn't mean I thought you were dying, and I'm sorry I spoke about my mother's death; it was foolish of me. Please forget it now. I only wanted to tell you how Jesus was standing near, ready to comfort you always, whether you lived or died. But now you should go to sleep. Would you like me to sing to you? Is the pain a little easier? The doctor said you must lie very quiet. Can I get you anything?"

By degrees she calmed the woman again and then sat down to watch and give her the medicine. Maggie put her head in the room about midnight to say she was going to bed now and had left a fire, if more hot water was needed. Celia sat there gradually realizing she was left to sit up all night with this sick woman, an utter stranger to her. Once again she reminded herself that it was the cross the Master laid upon her with His own hand, and she felt a sweetness in performing this duty which she wouldn't have otherwise chosen.

Celia was glad it was Saturday night instead of some other, for she could ill afford to sit up and lose all her sleep when she had to stand at the counter the next day. She smiled to herself in the dim light and thought this must be part of the Master's plan so she could do this duty and her others also. He asked her to do only what she had strength for. He gave her the daily allowance of that. But what if she must sit up tomorrow night?

"Daily, only, he says to thee," and "Thou mayest leave that to thy gracious Lord, " came the answering words, for now she knew the little poem by heart. She went upstairs, changed her dress for a loose wrapper and picked up her Bible and one or two articles she thought might be useful in caring for the sick woman. When she came down again Mrs. Morris seemed to be asleep, and Celia settled herself by the dim light with her Bible. She felt she needed some help and strength.

She hadn't read long when Mrs. Morris said in a low voice, "Is that the Bible you've got? Read a little piece to me."

Celia hardly knew where to turn for the right words just now, but her Bible opened by itself to the Twenty-third Psalm. She read the words in a low, musical voice, praying all the while that the Spirit might reach the sick woman's heart with them. When she stopped reading, Mrs. Morris seemed to be asleep again, and Celia settled herself in the least uncomfortable chair in the room and began to think.

But she didn't have long for this occupation, for this was to be a night of action. The terrible pain had been held in check by a powerful opiate the doctor gave when he first came in. But it returned in full force, and the patient soon was writhing in mortal agony once more. Celia immediately called Maggie and sent for hot water and the doctor again. At last, when morning was staining the sky with crimson, she sat down to breathe and realized Mrs. Morris was still alive. It seemed almost a miracle she was, for the doctor said when he arrived that he doubted if he could save her.

Early in the morning Miss Burns came in to relieve her watch, and Celia snatched a little sleep. But on awakening she was needed again; Mrs. Morris had asked for her.

She went down to the breakfast table and found what she hadn't imagined possible: Breakfast was so much worse than usual, since the mistress was sick, that she couldn't eat it at all. Mrs. Morris made some difference in things, though Celia thought the night before that they couldn't be much worse. She had yet to discover that there were many grades below even this in boardinghouses.

The Sabbath wasn't spent in studying Jehoiachin. It was full, but not with attending church services. She didn't stay in her cold little room. She'd have been glad to flee to that refuge. Instead, she made her headquarters in Mrs. Morris's room. From there she began to order things about her, for Mrs. Morris seemed to depend entirely on her. She answered Maggie's questions about this thing and that and kept the boarders from coming in to commiserate with Mrs. Morris. She also cleaned up the room and gave a touch of decent care to the sick woman and her surroundings.

Once or twice the patient opened her eyes, looked around, seemed to notice the subtle difference, and then closed her eyes again. Celia couldn't tell if she was pleased or indifferent. But it wasn't in Celia's nature to stay in a room and not pick up a shoe or straighten a quilt or hang clothes out of sight. She did it as a matter of course.

Sometimes she wondered what Aunt Hannah would think if she could see her now, and she smiled at the fact that this was just what she had had to do all her life—give up to help other people. Then she thought perhaps it was the most blessed thing that could happen to her. Other times she remembered the letter from the lawyers and wondered what it meant and how she could find out.

Sunday evening she sat with Mrs. Morris for a few hours. The pain had eased, though she'd spent an intensely trying day. She seemed worried and inclined to talk. Celia tried to calm her before sleeping, but it was no use.

"How can I sleep," answered the woman impatiently, "with so many things to worry about? Here I am on me back for the land knows how long, and the doctor wanting me to go to the hospital. How can I go to the hospital? What will become of me house and me business if I up and go off that way? And then when I get well, if I ever do, what's to become of me? Me house would be empty, or me goods sold for grocery debts and other things, and I'd starve. I might as well chance dying outright now as that. I know I'd die in the hospital anyway, worrying about things.

"Maggie couldn't carry on, even if I was gone only two days. She never remembers to salt anything. Those two girls from that three-cent store have been complaining about the soup today already. They say it was just like dishwater. And that German fellow came and told me tonight, with me lying here sick, that he'd have to leave if things didn't improve. He said I ought to get better help! Think of it! How am I going to get help and me on me back not able to stir? I don't much care if he does leave; he always ate more than all the rest put together.

"But, land, if I get well right away and keep on, I don't see where I'm coming to—with bills everywhere, milk and meat and groceries and dry goods. I don't know how I'm ever to pay 'em. It'll be just pay a little and get deeper into debt, then pay a little of that and make more debt, till I come to the end sometime. I s'pose it might as well be now as anytime."

Poor Celia! She had no words for this kind of trouble. Debt was always an awful thing to her, a great sin never to be committed. She never realized debt was normal, day-to-day living for some people. She tried to think of something comforting to say, for how could a woman get well with a weight like this on her mind? It wouldn't do any good to quote Scripture verses about taking no thought for tomorrow or her sweet poem about not bearing next week's crosses. The poor woman wouldn't understand. She didn't know how to claim the promise of being cared for. She'd scarcely understand if Celia tried to tell her Jesus would help her somehow if she cast her care on Him. This was what she longed to say, but after the previous night's experience she was afraid to say anything that might excite the nervous woman.

"How much money do you need to pay all your debts and set you straight again?" she asked, thinking an opportunity to go over her troubles might quiet her.

"Oh, I don't know," said the woman, almost in tears. "If I had a thousand dollars, I'd sell out me business and go somewhere and get out of it. Things are so bad." Then she burst into tears.

Celia was at her wit's end. Everything she said seemed to make matters worse. Suddenly she began to sing quietly,

"Jesus, Savior, pilot me,
    Over life's tempestuous sea."

Her voice was sweet and pure, and the woman listened while Celia sang, until she fell asleep.

Chapter 4

Celia discovered that the lawyers who wrote to her were in a building not many blocks from Dobson and Co.'s store. She felt anxious to learn what they wanted of her. So the next morning she obtained permission for a few minutes' extra time at lunch and hurried there.

She reached the number at last and searched the weathered sign for the names "Rawley and Brown." There it was, almost the last one on the list, "Fourth floor, back." She climbed up the four flights of stairs—the elevator was out of order—and arrived out of breath at the office door.

She entered the room and found two elderly men sitting at desks covered with papers. Each man was talking with a client near his desk. After Celia stood for some minutes by the door, the elder of the two finally looked over his glasses at her inquiringly. She was Miss Murray responding to their letter, she told him. He pointed to a chair and asked her to wait until Mr. Rawley was available. Over in the corner behind a screen she could hear the click of a typewriter and see the top of a frizzy head belonging most likely to a secretary. Soon both clients departed, and she was left with the two lawyers.

Mr. Rawley at last turned to her and began a list of questions. Celia answered everything she could, including the names of her different living relatives, and wondered when the mystery would be explained. Finally he cleared his throat and looked at her sharply, yet thoughtfully.

"Miss Murray," he said, "did you ever hear your father speak of having a great-uncle?"

Celia thought for a moment. She was only ten years old when her father died. She could remember some conversation between her father and mother about relatives she'd never seen.

"I'm not sure about the *'great'* part of it. He might have been a great-uncle, but I know Father called him Uncle Abner. He must have died long ago. He was a very old man then. I can remember Father saying laughingly to Mother one day that he'd never see anybody prettier than she was, not if he lived to be as old as Uncle Abner."

"A-ahem!" said Mr. Rawley. He uncrossed his feet and crossed them again and put his two thumbs together as he peered at them from under his bushy eyebrows. "Yes, ah! Well, and did that uncle have any—ah—heirs?"

Celia wanted to laugh. She was already planning how to write a funny letter to Aunt Hannah describing this interview with the lawyers, but she kept her face straight and answered steadily.

"I don't know."

"Well, I must say, my dear young lady," remarked Mr. Rawley, after a somewhat prolonged pause, "that your evidence is somewhat—that is to say—inadequate. You could hardly expect us, with so little to go on—that is to say, without more investigation, you could hardly expect us—"

"You forget, sir," said Celia, really laughing now, "that I haven't the slightest idea what all this is about. I expect nothing. I came here to be informed."

The old lawyer gave her another searching look and then seemed to conclude that she was honest.

"Well, young lady, I think I may safely tell you this much. Mr. Abner Murray had property which naturally descended to his only son. That son was in India for years. He didn't return at his father's death, and in fact his whereabouts weren't known until a short time ago, when positive information of his death without heirs was received. The property would then revert to Mr. Murray's next of kin and his heirs. Abner Murray had a brother, who is supposedly your father's father. If this should prove to be the case, through his death and your father's, his only heir, the property would naturally fall to you since you're the only living child of your father. Do you follow me closely?"

Celia looked at Mr. Rawley respectfully now and seriously. The matter had taken on a different aspect. It was a complete surprise. She hadn't even in her wildest dreams allowed herself to hope for any such thing. Fortunes fell to girls in books, not to flesh-and-blood, hardworking, everyday girls.

She looked at the lawyer in silence a minute, then smiled faintly and said: "That would be very nice if it's true. I wish it might be. And now I suppose you're finished with me for the present, until you've investigated the truth of my statements."

Mr. Rawley seemed surprised she took it so coolly and asked no more questions.

The truth was, she'd caught a glimpse of the clock and saw she barely had time to reach her counter, and she hadn't eaten lunch. She might lose her position if she exceeded the time. At present this was worth all the mythical fortunes the future might hold for her. So, without further discussion, she hurried away. Not stopping to eat, she laid aside her wraps and was in her place behind the counter when the hand pointed just one minute after the time allotted her.

It was a busy afternoon, and she didn't have much time to think. Everybody seemed to want ribbons. "Perhaps I'll be in a position sometime to buy some of these yards myself, instead of measuring them off for other people, if that old Mr. Rawley ever finds out whether *I* am *I*," she thought as she clipped off two yards of blue satin and three yards of pink taffeta.

Property, he'd said. What did he mean by property? Did her great-uncle Abner leave an old house standing somewhere, that would be of no earthly use to anybody unless sold and bring nothing then? Or perhaps it was some musty old library. She had no faith that there was much money. Such things didn't run in their family.

But, oh, what if it should be something worthwhile? What, for instance, if it should be a thousand dollars? What mightn't she do? Why, a thousand dollars would enable her to do some of the nice things she longed to do.

She could bring Aunt Hannah here to the city and set up a tiny house with her in it somewhere. With that much money to start on, they could surely make their living, she in the store and Aunt Hannah at home sewing. It flashed across her mind that that was the sum Mrs. Morris wished for. She said if she only had a thousand dollars she could pay her debts and have enough left to start on and get out of her uncomfortable life.

How nice it would be if she, Celia, could have enough money to say, "I have the thousand dollars, Mrs. Morris, and I'll give it to you. You may pay those people and go away to some more quiet, restful life." Then how delightful it would be to take that poor miserable boardinghouse and make it over. Make the boarders' lives cheerful and pleasant, and give them healthful food and clean, inviting rooms to live in! What a work that would be for a lifetime! If she ever did get rich, she believed she would do just that thing: Hunt up the most wretched boardinghouse she could find and take it, boarders and all, and make it over.

She could do it with Aunt Hannah's help. Aunt Hannah could cook and plan, and she could execute and beautify. The thought pleased her so well that she worked it out in details during the long walk back to her boardinghouse that night. She even went so far as to plan what she would give them for dinner the first night and how the dining room would appear—and how their faces would look when they saw it all. What fun it would be!

Miss Burns would have something every night that would tempt her appetite. And the poor old woman on the third floor would be given the most tender cut in the whole steak, so she didn't need to tremble when she cut it. And there was that young schoolteacher who needed rich creamy milk. She heard him decline the muddy coffee several times, and once he asked if he might have a glass of milk; but Maggie told him they were out of milk.

She debated whether she would retain her position in the store and decided she would for a time. That would give her a chance to carry out some plans without letting the boarders know who was at the bottom of it all. Things shouldn't be changed much at first, except that everything should be clean and wholesome. Then gradually they would beautify.

Perhaps the others would help in it. Perhaps she could lure the young man from the dry goods store into spending an evening at home and helping her. She suspected he spent his evenings out and remained late in places that did him no good, to say the least. It would do no harm for her to try to get acquainted with him and help him, even if she never got a fortune to help raise her neighbors into better things. She would begin the reformation of young Mr. Knowles that very evening, if an opportunity came. With these plans she completed her long walk in much shorter time than usual and with a lighter heart. It did her good to be interested in life beyond the mere duties of the hour.

She found Mrs. Morris in much the same state of depression as the day before. The doctor had urged again that she go to the hospital for regular treatment. She was as determined as ever that she would not, or rather *could* not. She wanted Celia to come and sit with her. She had taken a liking to her new boarder, and she didn't hesitate to say so and to declare that the others were an unfeeling set who bothered her and didn't care if she was sick.

Celia tried to cheer her up. She gave her a flower one of the other workers in the store gave her and told her she'd come up after dinner was over. Then she went down to the table and found Mr. Knowles seated to her left and coughing. They exchanged remarks about the weather, and Celia told him he seemed to have a bad cold. He told her that was a chronic state with him and then coughed again as he tried to laugh. She entered into his mock joking and told him that if his mother were there she'd tell him not to go out that evening, in such damp weather and with that cough.

His face grew sober, and he said very earnestly: "I suppose she would."

"Well, then, I suppose you'll stay in, won't you?" said the girl. "It isn't right not to take care of yourself. The wind is raw tonight. Your cough will be much worse tomorrow if you go out in it. You ought to stay in for your mother's sake, you know."

It was a bow drawn at a venture. Celia stole a glance at him. He looked up at her quickly, his handsome face sober and almost startled.

"But Mother isn't here," he said, his voice husky. "She died a year ago."

"But don't you think mothers care for their sons even after they've gone to heaven? I believe they do. I believe in some way God lets them know when they're doing right. You should take care of yourself just the same, even if she isn't here, for you know she'd tell you to do it, now, wouldn't she?"

"Yes, I know she would," he answered and then, after pausing, added, "but it's so hard to stay in here. There's no place to sit and nothing to do all evening. Mother used to have things different."

"It *is* hard," said Celia, with sympathy in her voice, "and this is a dreary place. I've thought so myself ever since I came. I wonder if you and I couldn't make things a little pleasanter, if we tried."

"How? I never thought I could do anything along those lines. How would you go about it?"

"Well, I'm not just sure," said Celia, thinking rapidly and bringing forth some of her half-made plans to select one for this emergency. "But I think we ought to have a good light first. The gas is miserable."

"You're right. It's that," responded Mr. Knowles.

"Didn't I see the big lamp on the parlor table?"

"Yes, I think there's a lamp there. But it smokes like an engine and gives a wicked flare of a light that stares at you enough to put your eyes out."

"Well, I wonder if we couldn't do something to cure that lamp of smoking. I'm somewhat of a doctor of lamps, after serving a long apprenticeship at them, and if you'll help me I'll try. I have some lovely pink crepe paper upstairs for a shade in my room, but I'll sacrifice that to the house if you can get me a new wick. What do you say? Shall we try it? I'm sure Mrs. Morris won't object, for it will save gas, besides making things pleasanter for the boarders. I have a book I think you'll enjoy, after the lamp is fixed for reading. If you're going to stay at home tonight, I'll bring it down."

The young man entered into the scheme enthusiastically. He was very young, not more than nineteen, or Celia wouldn't have cared or dared to speak to him in this half-commanding way. But she was used to boys and to winning them to do what she wished, and she won her way this time surely. The young man was only too glad to have something to keep him in, and his heart was still very tender toward his lost mother. Celia saw he wouldn't be hard to influence. She wished she were wise and able to help him.

She felt burdened for the other souls in the house and wished to be strong enough to lift them up. How strange it was that daily the way kept opening for her to help others. She seemed to be the only Christian there. What a weight of responsibility rested upon her if that was so. She must pray for guidance so she might be wise as a serpent and harmless as a dove; that she might, if possible, bring each of them to know Jesus Christ. And what was *she* to do all this? A mere weak girl, who was discouraged and homesick and couldn't get enough money together to keep herself from need, perhaps, or enough grace to keep her own heart from failing or her feet from falling. What was *she* to think of guiding others? How could she do all this work? She couldn't do it. It was too much.

Ah! She might leave all that to her gracious Lord. She forgot that He wanted her simply to take the duty of the hour or the minute and do it for Him. What did it matter if the results showed or not, as long as He was obeyed? When she slipped up to her room for the pink crepe paper she knelt down and asked that it, the book, the lamp, and her little effort for the evening might be blessed. Then she went down to conquer the lamp.

Chapter 5

For the land sake! Yes," said Mrs. Morris, turning wearily on her pillow, "do what you please with it. I wish it was a good one. I'd like to afford a real good one with a silk shade with lace on it, but I can't. There's lots ought to be done here, but there's no use talking about it. I'm clean discouraged anyway. I wish I could sell out, bag and baggage, and go to the poorhouse."

"Oh, Mrs. Morris, don't talk that way!" said Celia brightly. "You'll get well pretty soon. Don't think about that now. We'll try to keep things in order till you can see to them yourself. And, meanwhile, I believe I can make that lamp work beautifully. I'll come back soon and report the progress. Now eat that porridge. The doctor told me it would be good for you. I made it myself, and it's what Aunt Hannah used to make for sick people. There's nothing like twice-boiled flour porridge. Is it seasoned right? There's the salt."

Then she hurried downstairs to the lamp.

Young Mr. Knowles was already there with the new wick he purchased at the corner grocery. And Celia soon had the lamp burning brightly. Frank Hartley, the university student, was attracted by the unusual light and declared he'd bring his books down to the parlor for awhile. It was cold as a barn in his room anyway. He and Harry Knowles watched with admiration as Celia's fingers manipulated the pretty rose-colored paper into a shade with a gathering string, a smoothing out on the edges and a pucker and twist here and there, and then a band and bow of the crepe paper. It looked so simple that they were amazed at its beauty and resemblance to the petals of a flower.

She put the promised book, a paper-covered copy of *In His Steps,* in Harry Knowles's hand and said she'd come down later to see what he thought of the story. Then she slipped away to Mrs. Morris's room. She must write to Aunt Hannah sometime tonight about her visit to the lawyers, for her aunt might have some evidence on her behalf; but the duty to the sick woman came first.

She turned her head as she left the room and saw the two young men settling themselves comfortably around the bright lamp. The schoolteacher, George Osborn, came in the front door just then. Catching the rosy light from the room, he stepped in, looked around surprised, then hung up his hat and stood a minute before the register to warm his hands. It was a touch of cheer he hadn't expected. Presently he went upstairs and brought down a pile of reports to work on and seated himself with the other two around the light.

Celia was upstairs telling Mrs. Morris about the lamp and how well it burned, and gave an account of the three young men seated around it. Mrs. Morris listened astonished.

"Well, I've told them boys time an' again they ought to stay at home, but they never would before. You must've worked a spell on them. Of course, that teacher stays up in his room a lot. But he's trying to support his mother and put his brother through college, and you can't expect much of him. He'll just give himself up entirely to them, and that'll be the end of his life. Some folks in this world always have to be sacrificed to a few others. I'm one of those meself, though the land knows who's the better for me being sacrificed. It does seem as if I've had to give up every blessed thing I ever tried for in me life.

"Just set down awhile. I feel a little easier this evening, and I've been doing a powerful lot of worrying all day. I haven't a soul to advise me that knows anything. You seem to be made out of good stuff, and you've been real good to me, and I just wish you'd tell me what you think I ought to do."

Celia sat down, thinking it was strange to be asked for advice this way. Coming out into the world alone to earn one's living placed a great many responsibilities upon a person sometimes. She felt inadequate to advise. She didn't think she had wisdom to settle her own life, let alone another's and one so much older who, it would seem, would have learned a great deal from experience. But she tried to be sympathetic and asked Mrs. Morris to tell her all about it, and she would do the best she could. In her heart she asked the Father to give her the wisdom to answer wisely.

"Well, you see, it's this way. I'm deep in debt as I told you before. It's been getting worse every year, and every year I hoped by the next to make the two ends meet somehow. But they never did. I've cut down and cut down. And then boarders went off without paying two or three times after I trusted them. That Mr. Perry left that old rickety organ. It was nice enough to have an organ for the boarders, but you see I can't afford to have one. If I could have, I'd have bought a new one, you know. Well, things like that have happened time and again.

"Once a woman who recited pieces for a living came into the house. She had a lot of dirty satin clothes, and afterward she left quite suddenly. I never knew she was gone till a man came for her trunk. Of course I got the trunk for her board. She was here two months and paid only one week's board—kept putting me off. When I had that trunk sold at auction it brought me just one dollar and sixty-two cents. What do you think of that? And she had the second-story front alone, too. And *airs!* Why, she'd have her breakfast sent up every morning about ten o'clock. She made me think she was a great woman. Well, I learned better.

"But it does seem as though I've had more trouble with folks. One time a woman was here with her little girl, and the child took scarlet fever. The board of health came in and sent everybody off and scared them so 'twas a long time before I could get them back. Well, there's been a plenty of other things just like that.

"You don't wonder, do you, that I'm in debt? The worst of it is it's been getting worse and worse. That Maggie just wastes everything she lays her hands on, and I don't know's I'd better myself any if I tried to get somebody else. There's always changes and new things to buy.

"Now what would you do? You see it's this way. I've got a sister out west that lives by herself in a little village. She's a widow and has enough to live on, and she's written to me to come out and live with her. She thinks I could get a little sewing now and then, and I could help her in her house. I can't ask her for money, for I haven't got the face to, having asked her once before. Besides, she's not one to give out and out that way, even if she could afford to, which I guess she can't, though she'd be glad to give me a home with her. I'm too proud to borrow what I know I never could pay, and I won't skip out here as some would and leave me debts behind me. I'm honest, whatever else I ain't. Now what would you do?

"No, I don't own this house; if I did I'd have been bankrupt long ago with the repairs it needs that I couldn't get out of the landlord. But I took it for the rest of the year, and the lease won't run out till April, so you see I'm in for that. It's just the same old story. 'A little more money to buy more land, to plant more corn, to feed more hogs, to get more money, to buy more land, to feed more hogs.' Only I always had a little less of everything each time. Now, Miss Murray, what would you do if it was you?"

"Haven't you anything at all to pay with? No"—she hesitated for a word, and the one she heard that day came to her—"property? Don't you have any property? Nothing you could sell?"

Celia was always practical. She wanted to know where she stood before she gave advice. Mrs. Morris looked at her a moment in a dazed way, trying to think if there was anything at all.

"No, not a thing except my husband's watch and this old furniture. I suppose I might sell out me business, but nobody would buy it, and I'd pity 'em, poor things, if they did."

She talked a long time with the woman, trying to find out about boarding-houses and how they were run. Before she was finished she had an inkling why Mrs. Morris had failed in business and was so deeply in debt. She was young and inexperienced, but she felt sure she could have avoided some of the mistakes that caused Mrs. Morris's trouble.

Finally she said in answer to the repeated, "What would you do if you was me?": "Mrs. Morris, I don't quite know till I've thought about it. I'll tell you tomorrow, perhaps, or the next day. It seems to me, though, that I'd stop right now and not get more deeply in debt. That can't better matters. I think somebody might buy your things, and some way might be found for you to pay your debts. But first you must get well, and we'll do the very best we can to get on here till you're well enough to know what you'll do. Now may I read to you just a few words? And then you should go to sleep. Just rest your mind about all those things, and I promise you I'll try to think of something that will help you."

She turned to the Bible she'd brought in with her and read a few verses in the fourteenth chapter of John: "Let not your heart be troubled; ye believe in God, believe also in me."

She was very tired when she reached her room that night. The letter she intended to write to Aunt Hannah was still unwritten. The book she took from the public library to read was lying on her bureau untouched. She'd been bearing the burdens of other people, and the day had been full of excitement and hard work. She threw herself on her bed, so weary that she felt convulsive sobs rising in her throat.

What had she done? She had promised to think up some way to help Mrs. Morris. Mrs. Morris was nothing to her; why should she take this upon herself? Yet she knew God called her to help that woman as surely as He called her to sell ribbons for Dobson and Co. or to help Aunt Hannah with the mending.

She didn't want to do it, either. It was unpleasant in many ways and required sacrifices she hadn't dreamed of when she began. She gave up the pretty lampshade for the general good of the house. Now, when she bought a lamp at a cheap sale somewhere, she'd have to wait till she could afford more paper and a frame for her shade. Well, never mind! She certainly was repaid for that act, for those young men enjoyed it.

How much pleasure a little thing can give! And how many things might be easily done to make the house brighter and more pleasant and how much she'd enjoy doing them—if Aunt Hannah were only here! How nice it would be if she had some money and could buy Mrs. Morris out and help her get off to her relatives. Then she could get to work and make that house cheerful and beautiful and a true home for its present inmates. How Aunt Hannah would enjoy that work, too! It was just such work that would fulfill that good woman's highest dreams of a beautiful vocation in life.

Suddenly Celia sat up on the hard little bed and stared at the opposite wall with a thoughtful, energetic look on her face.

"What if I should!" she said aloud. "What if there's some money, say as much as a thousand dollars and maybe a little over so we don't run behind. Wouldn't that be grand! Oh, you dear Uncle Abner! If it proves true, and if you can see from heaven, I hope you know how happy you'll make several people. I'll do it! And Aunt Hannah shall come and run the house and be the housekeeper. And maybe we can get old Molly. I'm certain we never could do a thing with that Maggie; she's so terribly dirty. Molly would leave anywhere to be with Aunt Hannah.

"I'm talking as if I were a millionairess and could spend my millions. I shouldn't have thought of this, for it will turn my head. I'll be so disappointed when Mr. Rawley tells me, tomorrow or the next day, that I'm not myself or that the property is some old henhouse and a family cat. I'm afraid I won't be properly thankful for the cat. I wonder if it isn't just as bad to take up the happy crosses for the coming year as the uncomfortable ones. But I must write to Aunt Hannah. Mr. Rawley wanted some marriage certificates she has. I'm so excited!"

Writing to her aunt sobered her somewhat and brought forth an unwelcome voice. "Celia Murray, do you know what you're doing?" This was what she heard whispered to her from behind. "You've come to the city to earn your living, and you've come here to board, not to nurse sick landladies or become a guardian angel for stray young men or exercise the virtue of benevolence. You must think of yourself. How will you ever be fit for your work if you spend so much time and energy working for other people and staying up nights?

"Shouldn't you seek another boardinghouse? If you looked about a little you might find one where you'd have more conveniences and a better room and board. Let Mrs. Morris get along the best she can. You're not responsible for her. She's a grown woman and should know enough to take care of herself. Anyway, she's only suffering the consequences of her foolishness. Better try tomorrow to find another boardinghouse."

Even as Celia heard these words spoken in a tempting voice, she knew she wouldn't go. She wasn't made of that kind of stuff. Besides she was interested. Whatever her cross for the coming week was to be, it wouldn't be a burden to remain here and help work out God's plans, if she might be permitted to do so.

"And if my King is pleased only to lift my head out of prison and set me where I might help others in this boardinghouse, I'd try to make as good use of my freedom and my allowance as Jehoiachin did. I wonder what he did with his allowance anyway. And it must have been such a pleasant thing to know his allowance wouldn't fail the rest of his life. I wonder if he got downhearted sometimes and feared that Evil-Merodach might die and leave him in the lurch or turn against him.

"Now with me it's different. My King is all-powerful. What He's promised, I *know* He'll do. I don't ever need to dread His dying, for He's everlasting. I can trust Him perfectly to give me an allowance of whatever I need the rest of my life. Yet why do I distrust and fear I might be left hungry someday? What a strange contradiction. I'm a child of the King—I must trust Him!"

Then she turned out her light and knelt to pray.

Chapter 6

It's said that Satan trembles when he sees the weakest saint upon his knees. Then he no doubt consults with his evil angels and sends them to overcome that saint in his resolutions and endeavors. Indeed, it certainly seemed to Celia the next morning as if everything had conspired to make her life hard.

First, it was raining—a cold, steady drizzle that promised to continue all day and for several days, if it didn't turn into snow. The furnace, not too good at any time, was poorly managed. Mrs. Morris usually regulated it herself, but Maggie made a poor hand at it. She chose this morning to forget to see to it at all until the fire had gone out. She had no time to build it up then, for she had to get breakfast for the boarders who must be off to work at their appointed hours.

Celia dressed quickly, for her room was too cold to linger. Her fingers were blue as she turned the pages of her Bible to read a few words while combing her hair. But she was so cold that she finally gave up. She was tired, too, for she'd lost sleep lately; and it was hard to get up before light and hurry around in the cold.

She thought of Aunt Hannah getting breakfast for Nettie's family and buttoning the children's clothes between times. For some reason the thought of her aunt weighed heavily upon her this morning. She couldn't get away from it. Why did they have to separate? She felt a tightness in her throat as the tears came to her eyes.

Then trying to pull a knot out of her hair she broke two teeth off her comb. She hated to use a comb with the teeth out, and she couldn't afford a new one now. She glanced at her watch and saw it was later than usual. She finished getting ready quickly and ran downstairs to the dining room.

The clerk stood at the dining room door with a scowl on his face. He filled up the door so completely that Celia was obliged to ask him to let her pass before he moved. She was indignant at him for this. She compared him to a condemned animal in the Bible. It wasn't kind, but Celia didn't possess her usual sweet spirit this morning. He looked like an impossible man to please anyway. But then she discovered breakfast wasn't served.

In a moment Mr. Knowles came down, greeted her pleasantly, looked at the empty table and the clock, filled his pocket with some crackers from a plate and said he guessed he'd skip breakfast. If he didn't get to the store on time, his place wasn't worth anything; it was so late now that he'd have to run all the way to the car to make it. Celia was indignant that he had to go to a hard day's work unfed. It was the hard fate of the wage earner. He must be on time, even if the house fell in.

She peered into the kitchen and saw Maggie stomping about the room, slamming this and pounding that. She glimpsed unbaked biscuits through the oven door when Maggie opened and shut it. And on the top of the stove stood a pot of greasy-looking hash cooking slowly. The stove looked sulky, and the ashes weren't taken up.

"Maggie," she said, "may I help you get something on the table? These people have to go to work, and so do I. If we can't eat in five minutes we'll have to go without."

"Well, then, go without!" exclaimed Maggie with her hands on her hips. "I'm sure it won't hurt you fine folks once in awhile. I never hired out to do everything, and I ain't responsible. I'll get the breakfast as soon as I can and not a bit sooner, and you can get out of my kitchen. I don't want you bothering me. I get all flustered with so many folks coming after me. Go on out now, and wait till yer breakfast's ready. And tell the rest I won't cook any dinner fer 'em, if a soul comes in this kitchen again."

Celia retreated, outraged. To be spoken to in such a manner when she was offering help was insulting. Whenever she felt angry, tears would come to her eyes, and they came now. She walked quickly to the window to hide them, looked out in the dim alley that ran between the houses and watched the rain fall on the bricks of the house opposite her. Toward the front she could see a window and someone standing at it. She turned quickly away again. There was no refuge there.

Glancing at the table with its unbrushed crumbs and the dishes of uncooked hash and underdone biscuits Maggie was just bringing in, she decided to follow Mr. Knowles's example and take some crackers. Then seizing her hat and coat from the hall rack, she left for the store. It was a long walk, and she was cold and wet; but she didn't feel justified in spending the five cents to ride.

In her present mood she had no faith in Uncle Abner's fortune. It would probably turn out to be some poor land somewhere that would never be worth a cent. That was the kind of inheritance that usually came to their family. There was the lot in a new town out west that was left to Aunt Hannah by her oldest brother; the city authorities compelled property holders to pave the streets and pay large taxes, and there were no purchasers. Such inheritances one was better off without.

As she trudged on in the rain, she realized she'd forgotten to kneel by her bed before she left her room that morning, because of how cold and late it was. That must be why she felt so cross and unreasonable, so she tried to pray as she walked. But other thoughts distracted her, and she had to avoid running into someone with her umbrella turned down in front of her to keep off the driving rain. She thought of Aunt Hannah again, now probably washing the breakfast dishes or sewing or ironing, and she sighed and felt that life was wet and cold and dreary.

Halfway to the store, she encountered a little newsboy who followed her and begged her to buy a paper. He looked hungry. His feet were out at the toes of his oversized shoes. Celia had no money to buy a paper and gave a sharp no to the boy, who turned sadly away. It made her cross to see his need, when she couldn't help him. And when she realized how cross her voice had been, she was even more vexed. Then, without noticing, she stepped into a mud puddle and shivered as she felt the dampness through the thin leather of her boots. She wondered what she would do when the inevitable sore throat arrived from getting her feet wet.

And so she hurried on, carrying the heavy cross she'd fashioned that morning out of bits of her own and other people's troubles. It spoiled the sweet peace God had sent her. Indeed, her guardian angel wished she hadn't so soon forgotten her heavenly Father and His love.

Matters were no better when she reached the store. One of the girls who worked at the ribbon counter with her was sick, so Celia had to do her own duty and the girl's also. This wouldn't have been so bad if she'd been left to herself. But the department head, a young woman, was also in a bad mood and ordered her about in a very disagreeable manner. She found fault and demanded of Celia more than she could accomplish in a reasonable time.

Furthermore, it was busier than usual, despite the rain, for every woman in town seemed to need ribbon on that particular morning; no doubt each one thought the others would stay at home out of the rain. At the noon hour Celia's time was cut in half because of the rush. Then she spent a few precious minutes of that putting up some ribbons left carelessly on the counter by another saleswoman who went to lunch.

To the young girl new to her work, and fresh from a home where every necessary comfort at least had been hers, it was a long, hard day. She looked forward with no hope of a letup to the evening. As the day waned she grew more cross and hungry, then faint, and then she lost both those feelings and settled down to a violent headache.

Her imagination got the best of her. What if she got sick? Who would take care of her and how would she live? Aunt Hannah would have to come, and what an expense that would be! No, Aunt Hannah couldn't come. No one had money to pay her fare or her board when she got there, and she was bound to stay with Nettie and Hiram as long as they were supporting her. She'd have to get along without telling Aunt Hannah. What would become of her? Oh, why, of course, she'd have to go to the hospital among strangers and be nursed and perhaps die. And Aunt Hannah would never hear and then worry, and no one would tell her.

In the midst of these thoughts she heard the clear voice of the floorwalker: "Miss Murray, will you step to the office a moment? There's a message for you, a special delivery letter, I believe."

With her heart throbbing at the possibilities in a special delivery letter, she walked the length of the long store. Her aunt must be sick, and they'd sent for her. Surely they'd do that if she became so ill she needed care, for Nettie would never care for her; she was no nurse and hated sickrooms. Besides, Nettie would have enough to do in caring for her home and children, and Hiram wouldn't want to pay for someone else to come. All this occupied her mind, as she walked swiftly toward the office.

She signed the receipt with a trembling hand, then retired to the cloak-room to read the letter. She was so nervous she could scarcely open the envelope or notice Rawley and Brown's printed heading on the paper. The letter asked simply for her to call on them again and as soon as possible. She returned to her place among the ribbons, almost angry with Rawley and Brown for frightening her, yet relieved nothing was the matter with her aunt.

It was nearly five o'clock, and the crowd of women had finished shopping. The rain was pouring down harder than ever. The store was relatively empty. Perhaps she might leave for a few moments now. Permission was granted, since she used only half her noon hour, and she hurried up to the dark little office again.

Mr. Rawley hadn't gone home yet, though he had his overcoat on and was ready to leave. He asked a few more questions to establish certain facts, and Celia answered them as best she could.

When he seemed to be through and was walking her to the door, she turned and asked timidly: "Would you be so kind as to tell me what this is all about? You said there was property. If it should turn out to be mine, what would it be? I suppose you don't mind giving me a general idea of that, do you?"

He looked at her almost kindly under his shaggy brows. "Why, no, child!" he said. "That's perfectly proper, of course. Why, I haven't the exact figures in my head, but it's several thousand, well invested, and an old farm up in New York State that's rented. It would be enough to provide a pretty good income every year; and if you left the investments as they are, it would be a continuous one, for they're not likely to fail or fall through. Then, too, there's a considerable accumulation because of the doubt about the heir. I hope you'll turn out to be that heir, and I have no doubt you will. Good afternoon."

Celia tripped down the dark old staircase as if it were covered with the softest carpet ever made. Several thousand! What wealth! She wished for one single thousand, and her Father sent her not one, but many—for she started to believe now that the money was hers. All the evidence seemed to point that way. The lawyer seemed convinced, and only a few documents from her uncle Joseph's old lawyer were needed to corroborate what she told him. She felt pretty sure it was all true.

And here she was cross and growling all day. Furthermore she'd carried crosses not meant for her shoulders and may have missed doing some things

God had laid out for her to do. Only last night she knelt in earnest consecration, and now today she almost forgot she had a Father whose dear child she was and who was caring for her. Couldn't she retrieve some of the lost day? She had only one hour left in the store. She would try what she could.

She smiled on the beggar child who stood looking wistfully in at the pretty things in the store window as she went to her work. When she reached the ribbon counter again, she found the department head tired and complaining of a headache. She could bear other burdens besides her own. She might offer to do her work for her and let her rest, and she could bring her a glass of water. It wasn't her job to put up certain ribbons not in her own case, but she could do it for the other girl who was absent and save the head girl.

As her fingers flew among the bright silks and satins, she wondered if she'd have more burdens to bear for others when she reached the boarding-house. Perhaps Mrs. Morris would be better tonight and able to sit up and direct things a little. And she hoped that soon she'd have the means to make that house permanently better in some ways and help its residents. How light her heart and her shoulders felt now that she lay down that heavy self-imposed cross! It was wonderful! Oh, why couldn't she learn to trust her Master? The verse of a beloved hymn came and hummed itself over in her mind.

> Fearest sometimes that thy Father
>   Hath forgot?
> When the clouds around thee gather,
>   Doubt Him not!
> Always hath the daylight broken—
>   Always hath He comfort spoken—
> Better hath He been for years,
>   Than thy fears.

Chapter 7

Miss Hannah Grant sat in her room under the eaves darning little Johnny's sock. Her hair was gray and rippled smoothly over her finely shaped head. Her sweet face wore the sad, faraway expression that was habitual since she came to live with her niece Nettie. Perhaps a close observer would see that the sadness was a shade deeper this afternoon. Her eyes were deep gray and went well with her hair. She gave one the impression of being able to see further with them than most people, and they held a luminousness that lit up her otherwise plain face and made her truly beautiful.

Her gown was plain, old, and gray. She always wore gray dresses. They were becoming long ago in the days when it mattered whether she wore becoming things. Now that she cared no more about the becomingness, she wore them for sweet association's sake and for the sake of one long gone who used to admire them when she wore them. She didn't seem to know that they still suited her better than any other color.

The hole was large and ill-shaped, for Johnny was hard on his socks. But she darned it patiently back and forth. Once she laid it down and walked to the closet for her little gray worsted shawl to throw around her shoulders; the room was heated only by a drum from the stove downstairs, and she felt chilly.

She usually sat in the sitting room in the afternoon to sew or mend, but there was a reason for coming up here today. She'd settled herself as usual by the west window downstairs to get a good light on her work, with a large peach basket full of socks by her side and her workbasket on the window. The baby, creeping about the floor, had upset the peach basket and scattered its contents around. Nettie came down just then in a new red cashmere shirtwaist her aunt had finished the day before and jerked him unceremoniously away from the socks. She hastily bundled them all into the basket and shoved it behind Aunt Hannah's chair and out of her reach.

"I wish you wouldn't bring that old thing into the sitting room," Nettie told her aunt sharply. "Can't you bring one pair of socks at a time and not litter up the whole room? I'm expecting Mrs. Morgan and her sister to come over with their embroidery and crocheting, and I'd like things to look a little nice."

Aunt Hannah meekly disposed of the sock basket behind her ample apron, and silence fell in the room for a few minutes.

"Aunt Hannah, you'd better go and change your dress, if you're going to sit here," Nettie added in the same disagreeable tone. "That old gray thing doesn't look nice. I wish to goodness you had a black silk, or something, like other folks. You always waste your money on gray things when you buy anything. It's a dreadfully gloomy color. It makes you look sallow, too, now that you're getting older."

Nettie went out in the kitchen then for a minute and returned just as Aunt Hannah was starting upstairs with the darning basket.

"Aunt Hannah!" she called. "Take your shawl and bonnet up with you, won't you? I s'pose you'd just as soon keep them up there, wouldn't you? Hiram says he hates to see the hall rack cluttered up so."

Aunt Hannah put the basket on the stairs, descended swiftly, gathered her shawl and bonnet and one or two other belongings which were downstairs, in inconspicuous places, and carried them all upstairs. She wasn't in the habit of leaving her bonnet and shawl on the rack; she did so last night when she came in from prayer meeting because she had buckwheat cakes to set before going to bed. When she finished that and started to pick them up, Nettie asked her to carry a lamp and two comfortables up for her; in doing so, the shawl and bonnet escaped her notice. It was a little thing, and she realized the hall rack looked better without her shawl and bonnet. But it was one of the many things that made her feel she had no home. She put them all away and sat down in her little cold room near the drum to darn.

She did what she was asked to do with one exception. She didn't change her dress and go down again. She saw that Nettie would like to have her out of the way for the afternoon, and she didn't wish to remain where she wasn't wanted. She didn't sigh as some women would have. Instead, her eyes took on that faraway look. She was beginning to long sorely for the open gates of her home above where she never needed to feel that desolation of not belonging; there she would meet loved ones and, above all, her Father, face-to-face. Yet she knew her heavenly Father was with her, even in this home where she was treated as a burden. She could thus be content to stay and do His bidding. But sometimes that great longing to see Him face-to-face grew upon her till her heart ached with the desire to go.

In her bureau drawer, safely hidden in tissue paper in a white box smelling of rose leaves, were some letters and an old daguerreotype. The picture was in an old-fashioned leather frame that was closed with a little brass hook and lined with stamped purple velvet. The face inside was of a young man with sweet, serious eyes; a handsome face, smoothly shaven; heavy, dark hair tossed back from a high forehead; and the attire of an earlier time—a high rolling collar and stock.

This man had written the letters to Hannah Grant when he was a student at the theological seminary, and they contained important plans for the future, Hannah's and his. They mightn't have seemed important to some women, for they were planning, as soon as he finished his ministerial training, to go to the foreign mission field and work together for the Master they both loved better than anything else. And next to Him they loved each other.

How bright her life seemed to her then as she did her daily duties; sang about them; thought of the future and wrote her happy letters; and thanked the Lord daily that she was to do His work in this honorable way. The time passed rapidly then, and the years of study were completed. Hannah's wedding day was set; her simple lovely wedding gown was finished, and it was gray. He loved gray. It had little touches of soft white about the throat and wrists, just enough to bring out the coloring of Hannah's delicately cut face.

Then, suddenly, one of those mysteries of the kingdom happened that we'll understand someday and to which now we can only say, "It is the Lord—let Him do what seems best to Him," and trust. The earnest young missionary was taken up higher, to receive his reward there. His bride, when she rallied from the shock of her life joy's sudden end, bowed to the will of Him to whose keeping she long ago gave her will and her life. She was able to say with tears of triumph that, in some way like that earlier man of God, her beloved "walked with God and was not, for God took him."

She thought even then to go alone and take the message of Jesus to those who didn't know Him. She thought she could bear her sorrow more easily if she could do some of the work they would have done together. But God opened another door for her and showed her plainly that He called her to a duty at home. So she took her saddened heart, her sweet face, and her tender ways to her sisters' motherless children and had lived there ever since.

Sometimes now, when she thought how she wasn't wanted in this home, yet couldn't go anywhere else because of circumstances, she'd take out that pictured face. She wondered if James could know how she was being treated and what he'd think and feel about it, and she thought about how he would guard her from the world and shield her if he were only here. And then she was glad he couldn't know, or that if he could, he was where he knew it wouldn't be too long before she would come home to be with Jesus and with him forever. Time was only a brief space to him. Her eyes would take on their faraway look then.

So she sat and worked and thought. After awhile the expected visitors arrived. She heard their voices, and presently they drew closer to the stove in the sitting room. From upstairs their talk could be heard distinctly now. But Hannah was absorbed in her own thoughts, and she paid no attention as they gossiped about this one and that, with a "You don't say so," and a "Well, I always thought as much," and a "Did she say that?"

Finally she heard Nettie say, "Yes, she'll stay with us this winter anyway. No, it isn't quite as pleasant as being alone, you know, but then what could we do? She had no home to go to. My husband wanted my cousin to come, too, though it was more than we really could afford to feed and clothe two more. But she was very ungrateful and wanted to have her own way and see the world a little. I expect she'll come back humbly enough when she's been away a couple of weeks longer. If she does I'm sure I don't know what in the world we'll do with her.

"Oh, yes, Aunt Hannah helps me a little here and there, but you can't ask much of people who are getting on in years. [Aunt Hannah was forty-nine.] My father always kept her in luxury since she was my mother's only sister. Yes, people get spoiled sometimes that way. But, dear me, all she can do wouldn't make up for the outgo. Yes, she was sort of acting as housekeeper in our home after Mother died, but you know no one can ever take a mother's place. (Johnny, shut that door and go away and stop your coaxing, or I'll take you upstairs and give you a good spanking. No, you *can't* go down by the pond to play today.) No, I never had so much to do with her as the younger children. I was the older daughter, you know."

Aunt Hannah quickly and noiselessly moved away from her position by the drum to the other side of the room. And this from the little girl she so carefully mothered and tended and tried to train! And loved, too, for Hannah Grant loved all God loved and placed in her way. Ah, this was hard! And must she go on living here and knowing she wasn't wanted, that she was a burden, and that lies—yes, lies, for there was no use calling them by a softer name—were being told to the people in the village about her? How could she?

She could see how it would go from year to year. Hiram would come in cross at night and either ignore her altogether or contradict every word she spoke. He'd find fault with anything he knew she did, in a surly, impersonal way, which they both knew he meant for her. The children would grow up to disrespect her, as they were beginning to do already.

And her dear Celia! She was working bravely far away from her! There was no prospect of anything better for years to come, perhaps never.

She knelt down by her bed and prayed for a long time. Then she arose quietly and returned to her window, a chastened look on her face. He'd helped her bear more than this before. Indeed, people despised and rejected Jesus.

She darned on till the room grew dark, and then she sat in the twilight. She couldn't bring herself to go downstairs yet, not till she must get supper. She thanked the Lord she had a room to herself where she might take refuge and think of Him. Seldom did Aunt Hannah have even this privilege in the daytime since coming to live with Nettie; there was always so much to be done, and Nettie expected it done quickly.

The company below departed, but Hannah took no heed. She sat and watched the gray sky grow into night. There was no sunset, for the day was gray, without even a point of light to make the sky lovely. It sank into darkness, quietly, soberly, unnoticed, and unlovely. She thought it was like her. But then God had some reason for not making a bright sunset tonight, and surely He had some reason for wanting her life gray instead of rose-colored. She sighed a little and, now that the darkness had stolen softly upon her, let a tear have its way down her cheek.

Downstairs Nettie was growing restless. Hiram came in a little earlier than usual with a sour look and asked how long it would be before supper. Nettie said it wouldn't be long and wondered why Aunt Hannah didn't come downstairs. Hiram remarked that if the old woman was getting lazy and taking on fine-lady airs they'd better give her a warning, for he couldn't support her for nothing. He threw a letter for her on the table while Nettie was lighting the lamp. Nettie glanced at the writing. Then she sent Johnny up with it and told him to tell Aunt Hannah his father had come and wanted his supper right away.

"It's from Celia again," she said in a contemptuous tone. "She wastes more money on postage. I don't think it's right to do that in her position. If she has any extra money she better save it up and help with supporting Aunt Hannah. A fat letter, too. I don't see what she finds to write about. This is the third one this week. It's perfectly absurd!"

But Aunt Hannah didn't hear what they said; she wasn't sitting near the drum and wouldn't again, even if she was cold.

Johnny came down and reported that Aunt Hannah had a light in her room. Nettie rattled the stove and slammed the dishes around. But still her aunt didn't come. Finally Nettie began to get supper herself. She sent Johnny up again pretty soon to tell Hannah she wished she'd come downstairs, that she needed her. Johnny came back and said Aunt Hannah told him to tell Mama she'd be down pretty soon; she couldn't come just now.

"Well, really!" said Hiram, looking up from his paper. "Seems to me she's putting on airs at a great rate. If I were you, Nettie, I'd just sit down and wait till she comes. I wouldn't get supper at all. If you haven't the grit to tell her to come down now when you send for her, I'll do it for you."

But Nettie rattled the stove and the dishes and managed to get supper ready pretty soon. She didn't quite understand her aunt. This was a new development. Never in all the years she'd known her and been cared for by her had her aunt ever refused a request for help. It must be something serious. Was she sick? Nettie had a little heart left in her, and it irritated her to hear her husband speak that way about her relatives. So she bristled at him while she made the coffee.

"You'll not do any such thing, Hiram Bartlett. I guess she has a right to stay in her room once in awhile. I never knew her to do anything like this in her whole life. If she was your aunt, you wouldn't speak about her that way. I think you ought to be a little grateful for the way she took care of you last week when you were so sick, and me with the baby sick, too. If she hadn't been here I'd have had my hands more than full. I don't know what I'd have done.

"Johnny, make that baby stop crying! Lillie, pick that doll up off the floor! I keep walking over your things.

"I s'pose Celia's got into some trouble and Aunt Hannah's worried about her. I expected as much. That girl doesn't have enough experience of the world to go off to the city alone. Somebody should have taken her home to live. If one of the boys had been married she could've gone with them, but the boys are so selfish they never think of other people. If you had any sense of the fitness of things you'd have done it yourself."

They talked on in a wrangling way till supper was ready, but not until they'd nearly finished the evening meal did the hall door open and Aunt Hannah walk in.

Chapter 8

Aunt Hannah lit her lamp a few minutes after daylight faded, to get a little comfort from her Bible before facing her trials. To go downstairs that night and face Hiram and Nettie calmly after the words she had heard her niece speak was the heaviest cross she'd had to bear in many years. She tried to think of all the comfort in the Bible as she sat in the twilight. She had a great store of precious words to draw from, for her Bible had always been a delight to her, and she knew just where to turn in her memory for the right help.

"Fear thou not; for I am with thee: be not dismayed; for I am thy God: I will strengthen thee; yea, I will help thee; yea, I will uphold thee with the right hand of my righteousness. . . When thou walkest through the fire, thou shalt not be burned. . . God is faithful, who will not suffer you to be tempted above that ye are able; but will with the temptation also make a way to escape, that ye may be able to bear it. . . Blessed is the man that endureth temptation: for when he is tried, he shall receive the crown of life, which the Lord hath promised to them that love him. . . .

"For I reckon that the sufferings of this present time are not worthy to be compared with the glory which shall be revealed in us. . . All things work together for good to them that love God. . . To be conformed to the image of his Son. . . If God be for us, who can be against us? . . . Nay, in all these things we are more than conquerors through him that loved us."

Then she lit the lamp to search out another promise. Just looking at the words, she thought, would somehow help her. At that moment Johnny brought up Celia's letter. She opened it quickly, anticipating another trouble. What could have happened to Celia since her last letter?

It was a thick letter, and she read it slowly. She forgot about time because the letter's contents absorbed her mind so completely. When Johnny came upstairs the second time, she had something new to think about that demanded immediate attention and had prior claims to any downstairs. The letter read:

Dear Aunt Hannah,

Do you remember the words on the little bookmark you sent me for my birthday? I know you do, for you have a way of hiding all such words away in that wonderful memory of yours. The heading was about an allowance from the king, a continual allowance. When I read it I knew just what you meant by sending it to me. You wanted to remind me that my King had plenty of extra strength to give me and that He'd promised to furnish me with enough for each day of my life to bear that day's trials. It helped me, for I knew I was trying to bear some of the trials by myself. I often forget that I don't have to take up next year's crosses and worry about them.

But I remember, when I first read the words, that I couldn't help longing deep in my heart that I could have a real earthly allowance of money—just solid, hard, dirty money, coming in every week, every month, every year. I longed for enough to supply the needs so I might live with you and work for you and have you all to myself.

Then I felt that my head would be lifted up out of prison forever—for I read the chapter about Jehoiachin as you intended, you dear auntie—and it helped me, too. You see, I was taking up a big heavy cross for you for the coming year. I didn't feel happy about you there at Hiram's. In spite of me I can't like Hiram's ways, and I don't believe you do.

I know for one thing, a very small thing, that you hate tobacco smoke and have never been used to it. Yet Hiram smokes all over the house whenever he pleases, without even caring whether it's repulsive to you or not. In fact, I'm wicked enough to suspect he might do it more, just because you don't like it, to show you he's master of his own house. I'm so sorry to feel that way about my cousin-in-law, but I can't help it. There's some comfort about it—I don't believe Nettie minds. Since she's his wife and must go through life with him, it's a relief to think she doesn't.

But there! This is all out of the way and unchristian, and I've been too much blessed to allow myself to say anything unchristian about anyone. Only I wanted you to understand that I appreciated how hard it was for you to accept Nettie's proposal cheerfully and go to live with her for a few years. I didn't say so then because I thought any words would only make it harder to bear. I know my dear auntie finds a thing easier to bear if other people think she's perfectly happy. That's just one way you do so and the only way you're ever the least bit dishonest.

But I must hurry on with my main theme which I haven't even hinted at yet. And I have a great deal to write and must get it in tonight. I can't bear to have you wait a minute longer than necessary to hear the good news.

In the first place, you're not to stay at Nettie's another day—not unless you prefer to, of course. You're to pack up every scrap that belongs to you and take the first train to Philadelphia, sending me a telegram (at my expense) to say what train you start on. You must come to the Broad Street station—have your trunks checked

there, too, and don't leave any of your things behind. There's plenty
of room to put all your things here, and you're not to go back to
Nettie's unless you go on a pleasure visit.

Aunt Hannah glanced up to see if the little room with its old ingrain carpet
and cheap furniture was still about her. She was almost breathless with the letter's proposal. Things seemed whirling around her. She wanted to get something
to steady herself before she read on. She saw the black side of the sheet-iron
drum and remembered this afternoon, and a glance toward her open Bible
showed her the lines "God is faithful. . .will with the temptation also make a way
to escape, that ye may be able to bear it." She drew a long breath and closed her
eyes for a minute to lift her heart to God. He was going to make the way to
escape. She didn't yet understand how it was to be done, but her faith caught at
the fact that it was to be done. Then she went back to the letter.

You're to give your checks to the porter on the car—and
you're to take a sleeper if you come at night, or a parlor car if you
choose to come in the daytime. I enclose your ticket.

Aunt Hannah noticed then that a small pink and white paper had fallen
from the letter and slipped to the floor. She stooped and picked it up in a dazed
way. Good for one trip to Philadelphia, it certainly was. This was something
tangible and brought her back to everyday life. She really was to go, for here
was the ticket. She went on with the letter eagerly now.

You're to have the porter carry your satchel into the station for
you, and I'll meet you at the gate and take you home. Yes, HOME,
Aunt Hannah, yours and mine, do you hear that? It isn't very pretty
or inviting yet, but it's ours for awhile, for as long as we want it,
and we'll fix it into a charming home. And now you want to know
how it all happened and what it means.

Well, this morning I was asked again to come to Rawley and
Brown's office on very important business. Since they told me it
might keep me some time I asked for the day off at the store. I
couldn't have had that, if I hadn't done double duty for the last
week in place of a girl who was sick. Mr. Dobson was very nice
and said certainly in such a case he'd give me permission. Of
course, I suppose I'll lose my pay for that day, but it had to be
done, and it doesn't matter now anyway.

Well, Mr. Rawley hemmed and hawed a good deal and finally
told me everything was satisfactorily settled at last. I was duly
declared by the court to be Uncle Abner's heir, without any question

or doubt anywhere. He wished to go over the papers with me and place the property in my hands. There was some red tape to go through which I needn't stop now to tell you about. It was all very interesting to me, the number of times I had to sign my name and all the witnesses. I felt just like a girl in a book, but I haven't time for that. There's more to come.

It seems Uncle Abner had a farm where he lived after he got old and his wife died and his son went to India. A young farmer and his family lived there and took care of him, and they've rented the house ever since. They still live there. The farm is pretty good, way up in New York somewhere, I think; I didn't pay much attention to it.

Then he owned an interest in a coal mine near Scranton and a few government bonds, not many of those. But the whole is well invested and brings in a nice little income every year. I couldn't help thinking of Jehoiachin when Mr. Rawley was telling me about it. He said it was so well invested that it was, as near as anything earthly could be, a continual 'income as long as I lived' if I kept things in their present shape. Uncle Abner was a very careful man and always invested in pretty safe things with what little he had. I didn't tell him I considered it much instead of little, though. It seemed a fortune to me. I suppose I'll learn better hereafter, but I'm going to try to be very wise with it anyway, with God's help.

Now you want to know how much it is. Well, it amounts to about nine hundred dollars a year at the lowest calculation, besides several years of accumulated interest not invested yet. Isn't it riches? Why, you've often told me that not many ministers and few missionaries get more than that. Now why shouldn't you and I be missionaries? I know it's been your dear desire all your life, and I don't know of anything that would be grander work. And since we can't go as foreign missionaries just now, what if we should be home missionaries?

Of course, two lone women couldn't take mortar and bricks and build a church and preach. At least I shouldn't like to try it, though I'm not at all sure I couldn't do it. You know we always thought, if we had the time and material and pattern, you and I could do almost anything anybody else could if we tried. Well, I began to think about a mission for us, and before I was halfway home to write to you it came to me just what I'd like to do.

Why shouldn't you and I make a real home mission for ourselves right here in the city of Philadelphia, by making a good home for a few people who don't have one of their own? It seems to me there's as much gospel sometimes in a good sweet loaf of bread *like the ones you make, as there is in—well—some sermons. Don't you think so? Then we could help the people who ate the bread to go to the churches and try to help them in their everyday lives.*

Why, some of the young men here would stay at home evenings occasionally, perhaps regularly, if they had a pleasant, warm, light place to stay in. Instead they probably go to the saloons. Anyway, auntie dear, they don't look rested in the morning when they come down to breakfast. And, oh, what a breakfast we had this morning! I don't think I'll ever like hash again, though I always used to enjoy ours so much when you made it. But hash in Mrs. Morris's boarding-house is very different indeed.

When I got home I went straight to Mrs. Morris's room. She's not completely well from being so sick a few weeks ago, though she goes around and directs things. But she seems so worried all the time. You know I told you how many bills she has unpaid and how hard times have been for her. You wouldn't wonder a bit if you could be here and watch the way things go a little while. She was lying on her bed when I went in, looking as if she'd like to cry, if she only were young enough and had the energy.

She told me right away that she was in trouble again. She was a month behind in her rent. The agent had been around and said it must be paid in advance after this, and he couldn't wait longer than five o'clock. She only pays twenty-five dollars a month, and with all her boarders you'd think she could pay it. But she doesn't, that's all.

While she was talking I made my plans quickly. I didn't want to act too rashly, for you know you always tell me that's one of my great faults. But I knew if I did anything it ought to be done very soon. Probably it would have been wiser to ask Mr. Rawley's advice, and perhaps some of my relatives, but I had an innate suspicion that I wouldn't be allowed to do it at all, if I asked. And why shouldn't I? The money is mine, and I'm of age if I'm not very experienced. I knew you'd like it—at least I felt very sure you would—and if you and God like a thing I don't care what the rest of the world thinks. So I asked Mrs. Morris a lot of questions, some I hadn't asked her before.

You see, I had a whole two hundred dollars in my pocketbook that Mr. Rawley gave me. He said it was mine, and I might as well take it to begin on. So I took it. I knew I'd want to do a lot of things right away and that the first one would be to buy your ticket and get you here at once. I was just aching to spend some money, for it was the first time in my life I had much to spend.

I asked Mrs. Morris about her butcher's bill and her grocery bill, and I found they weren't as big as she made me think at first. Then I asked her point blank how she'd like to let a woman come in here in her place for three months or so; she'd take the boarding-house off her hands, pay the bills for the present and let her pay them later, if she chose, or, if not, hold the furniture as collateral. She didn't know what I meant by collateral, but she soon under-stood and said she'd be only too glad; only she never could find any woman who'd be so foolish. She said, too, that she was afraid if she once got away she'd never come back but just stay and leave the old furniture to make it right with her debts. Then she sighed and returned to her trouble and cried.

I couldn't stand it any longer. I told her I thought I knew the right one for her, and I'd write to her at once and attend to it all if she was sure she agreed to it. It didn't take her long to decide what to do after she was convinced I meant what I said. She began to pack up her clothes right away and talk about what she'd take with her. She hasn't much worthwhile, I guess. She'll want those horrid crayon portraits of her family and herself, I hope, and a few other decorations.

When we reached this point, it was five o'clock, and the doorbell reminded Mrs. Morris of the rent agent. Sure enough, he'd come, and Maggie came up to call Mrs. Morris. She looked at me blankly as if to say, 'What shall I do?' She'd forgotten all about him.

I thought a minute and then told her I had some money—enough, I thought, to pay the agent. So I went downstairs and put on my most dignified air. He bristled at me and demanded Mrs. Morris.

"Mrs. Morris isn't well and is lying down," I said, "and I've come down in her place. Is there anything I can do for you?"

"Well, I've got to see her even if she is lying down," he said in a loud voice and walked toward the stairs as if he'd go up to her at once. "She's got to pay her rent. She'll be put out if she don't do it at once. This thing has gone—"

"Oh," I said, "it isn't in the least necessary for you to get excited, if that's all. I can attend to the rent as well as anything else. Are you the agent?"

"Yes, I am," he said, "and I won't have any more talk either. I want my money."

I had my pocketbook in my hand and tried to freeze him with a look as I opened it. When he saw me bring out a big roll of bills he almost looked faint—he was so astonished.

"How much is back?" I asked.

"Two and a half months," he snarled.

I began to count out the money. Then I remembered my own experience with Rawley and Brown and thought I'd give him a little taste of it. I drew back and said, "You're sure you're the agent and fully entitled to receive this money? Can you give me any credentials?"

He was very much taken aback and got red and embarrassed. At last he remembered that Mrs. Morris knew him. Then he grew angry again and demanded to see her. I sent a message up to Mrs. Morris that if she was able we'd like for her to come down, and she came. When it was finally all settled and the receipt signed, I told the young man that he might tell the owner that the rent hereafter would be paid in advance and on time; also a few repairs needed immediate attention, and we'd like to have him call at his earliest convenience. He went away crestfallen, and I began to feel like a householder.

The only thing that troubles me is Mrs. Morris's extreme gratitude, because, dear auntie, I'm afraid I haven't loved her as much as I ought to for Christ's sake. So I can't take the credit she'd give me. It's all very selfish in me.

Now the matter stands this way. If you can come this week, do so. Mrs. Morris will be ready to leave on your arrival. She'll go to her sister out west, and I doubt if she ever returns. I've given her some money to go with. You can't always buy a full-fledged boarding-house, boarders and all, so cheap. I suppose someone would call it dear, but I'm happy in my purchase.

I'll keep my place in the store till you come anyway, for I don't care to have the boarders find out my connection with the business, till they see some of the improvements I want to make.

The only servant here is worse than none. She's so dirty and saucy you never could stand her. If you possibly can induce Molly to come with you, bring her. I enclose a New York draft which I think will be all the money you'll want to bring here and pay any little bills till you get here.

And now, dear auntie, I do hope and pray you'll say yes and come at once and not find any "oughts and ought nots" in the way, as you sometimes do. You see, I've burned my bridges behind me, because I felt that you "ought" whether you think so or not. I mean to take care of you now myself, and you're working too hard there. Here we'll keep you in pink cotton and only let you direct. I'll keep good servants, and if I don't always make the two ends meet, why, my King shall give me "a continual allowance" to draw upon.

Your loving, eager,
Celia.

Chapter 9

Hannah's face radiated such a calm light as she entered the dining room that the people around the table didn't understand. In fact it rather angered them. She walked quietly to her usual chair and sat down. Nobody spoke, but she'd so far forgotten her afternoon's troubles that she was oblivious of this. Hiram was trying to think of the most sarcastic thing he could say and so failed to say anything, while Nettie in her various revulsions of feeling didn't know how to begin. Aunt Hannah herself opened the conversation in the calmest, most self-contained tone possible, as if she often asked the question of her nephew.

"Hiram, can you tell me what time the through Philadelphia trains go?"

Hiram raised his cold, black eyes to her face in astonishment and stared at her as if to say, "What possible concern of yours is that?" Then he dropped them to his plate again and went on eating. After a suitable pause he said freezingly, "No."

Aunt Hannah tried again. "Isn't there a timetable in the paper? Could you find out for me?"

"I don't know," said Hiram, this time without looking up. "I suppose if it's there you can find it as well as I can."

"What in the world do you want with the timetable, Aunt Hannah?" asked Nettie crossly, with an undertone of anxiety. "Is anything wrong with Celia? I presume she's lost her place and is coming back on us. I always supposed that was how her venture would turn out. She should have tried to get a place in the country for housework. It was all she was ever trained to do. Anybody might know she couldn't get on in the city."

"Nothing's the matter with Celia, Nettie," answered her aunt, "except that she's written for me to come to Philadelphia. She's found something there for me to do, and I've decided it'll be best for me to go at once. I'll have to start tomorrow, if possible, because I'm being waited for."

"You go to Philadelphia!" exclaimed Nettie, dropping her fork. "The perfect idea! Has Celia gone crazy? Why, Aunt Hannah, you couldn't get along in the city. Why, you—you—wouldn't know how to get anywhere. You don't understand. Philadelphia is a large city, and you couldn't get across the street alone. And what could you do? You're not going to start as a store clerk, I hope. You'd break down at once, and then we'd have you both to care for. And you know, Aunt Hannah, willing as we are, we're not able to do that." Nettie paused for breath.

Then Hiram turned his little black eyes on her and asked contemptuously, "And who's going to pay your fare on this pleasure excursion you're taking?

You certainly can't expect me to do it. I think I've done all I'm called upon to do. I understood the bargain was that you were to work for your board here."

Hiram had never been so openly insolent before. If he had, Hannah would have left long ago, even if she were obliged to walk the streets in search of work for her living.

She turned her clear eyes upon him and said quietly with the grace the Father gave her from her communings with Him: "Yes, Hiram, that was the bargain, and I certainly have worked. I've fully earned all I've eaten and the amount of shelter that's been given to me. As for any further assistance, I've never asked for it yet, and I hope I may never be obliged to do so. Celia has sent me money and a ticket—and I'll not be obliged to ask any favors of anyone."

"Celia sent you money!" Nettie fairly screamed it. "Where in the world did she get money?"

"Yes, where did Celia get money?" asked Hiram sharply. "It seems to me there's something pretty shady about this business. Miss Celia'll get into serious trouble and bring no credit to her family, if she keeps on."

Aunt Hannah arose from her untouched supper, drew herself up to her full height and looked down upon Hiram Bartlett till he seemed to shrink beneath her gaze. There comes a time when a strong sweet nature like Hannah Grant's can be roused to such righteous indignation that it will tower over smaller natures and make them cower and cringe in their smallness and meanness. She had reached one of those places. As Nettie watched her, she thought her aunt must have been almost handsome when she was young.

"Hiram," said Hannah, and her voice was controlled and steady, "don't you ever dare to breathe such a thought again about that pure-souled girl. You know in your inmost being that what you said would be impossible. Sometime, when you stand before God, you'll be ashamed of a good many of your other words and actions."

That was all she said to him. She didn't lose her temper or say anything she didn't feel she should say or would have taken back afterward.

Then she turned to Nettie and said quietly: "Celia has had a little estate left her from her father's great-uncle Abner. She's not quite independent regarding money and wishes to have me with her as soon as possible. I intend to go tomorrow evening, if I can get ready."

She left the room then and went upstairs. When she got there, though, instead of packing, she turned the key in the lock and knelt down by her bed. She prayed first for Hiram, and second, that God might overrule anything she said amiss.

Meanwhile, astonishment and confusion reigned downstairs. Celia as a poor shop girl and Celia with money were two very different people. Even Hiram felt that. He retired behind his paper till a suitable time elapsed for his wife to talk out her anger, amazement, and humiliation. Then he reflected that it would be very convenient to manage Celia's money, even though it wasn't much; he was just starting business for himself, and every little bit helped in the matter of capital.

"It would just serve you right, Hiram Bartlett, if Celia should turn out to be rich," said his wife angrily. "The way you've treated her and Aunt Hannah should make you ashamed, but I don't suppose it will. Now what am I to do? Three children and one a fretful baby and all my housework to do all alone. If you'd treated Aunt Hannah nicely, she would have stayed anyway. Maybe Celia would have come here to live and taught the children. She's real good at teaching little children. I remember she used to be so patient with the boys at home. It would be awfully convenient to have somebody around with money."

In the course of the evening, while Hannah quickly gathered her possessions for packing, Nettie knocked at her door. She asked a great many questions and wanted to argue with her aunt to show her the inadvisability and impossibility of her going to Philadelphia to live with Celia. Her plain duty was here with Nettie and her family. When she saw she was making no headway, she worked on her aunt's strong sense of duty. She finally cried and told her she never thought Aunt Hannah would leave her that way, with all those children and no help. Further, she always knew her aunt cared more for Celia than for any of them. It wasn't fair when they offered her a home and did everything for her, and she came there with the understanding that she'd stay several years anyway. It wasn't fair to Hiram.

After she talked this way for some time, her aunt turned to her almost desperately. She didn't want to say anything rash. But Nettie must be shown how inconsistent she was.

"Nettie," she said, as calmly as she talked to Hiram, "you know that you and Hiram never wanted either me or Celia with you. You consider me in the way and only good to work. I don't say anything against that, for that may be true. But you grudge me my home here, and you're telling your friends you're doing a great deal for me in my helpless old age and that I'm a burden. You know yourself whether that's quite fair and whether I haven't worked as hard as any woman could for my board and lodging. But that isn't to the point. You have a perfect right to think so about me. It may be all true, and I can't stop you from saying such things to outsiders.

"But I have a right to say whether I'll be taken and disposed of as if I was a piece of goods and cared for as if I was a baby. I'm not quite so infirm yet but that I can earn my living where I'll be more welcome. I thank the Lord a way has opened for me to go where I'm wanted. But I must honestly tell you, Nettie, that I should have gone just the same if I'd known that you felt so, for I feel that my place is with Celia, if I can be with her. She's alone in the world. You have your husband and children. She has nobody but me. I bear you no grudge, Nettie, and I think you'll be happier with me away."

Then she went on packing, and Nettie retreated to talk with her husband.

The result was a proposition to coax Celia to come home and live with them, and Nettie said a few nice things she hoped would patch up her aunt's feelings. But Aunt Hannah was firm and wouldn't even delay to write to Celia. She went diligently on with her preparations.

Gradually they settled down to the inevitable and by the next noon had so far calmed down as to ask some questions about the more definite details. Hannah had started out early in the morning without telling them where she was going or seeming to remember breakfast was to be gotten and cleared away. She was living by faith. She ate nothing that morning.

She visited a little house on a side street where Molly, an old servant, lived. Molly had declined Nettie's earnest solicitation to live with her at very small pay; she preferred to earn her living by doing fine ironing. Hannah also visited the station, the telegraph office, the bank, and the expressman's office, and then returned to her packing again. Later in the afternoon she went out again and called on the minister's wife, the doctor's wife, and a few very dear friends, bidding them a quiet good-bye. She wished to slip away without causing any unnecessary talk.

But at the dinner table Nettie ferreted out Celia's whole plan.

"Celia has bought a boardinghouse!" exclaimed Nettie. "What an absurd idea! What does either one of you know about keeping boarders? You'll both let them run right over you. You'll get in debt the very first week. Why, Aunt Hannah, you have no right to encourage Celia in such a scheme. She's too young, anyway, to be in a city without a guardian. She should be here. Hiram could manage her money and double it in time. And if she really has as much as you say, she has plenty to live quite comfortably without doing anything. You should tell her so."

But Aunt Hannah wasn't intimidated. Nettie tried again.

"And then think how plebeian it will be! It was bad enough to work in a store, but a boardinghouse keeper, and for one who has money of her own. It's simply unheard of. I'll be ashamed to death for Mrs. Logan to know about it. I've had enough trouble without being ashamed of my family. Celia always did do odd things, anyway. Don't you think it's very impractical, Hiram?"

Nettie asked his opinion as if that would settle the matter for everybody concerned, and he answered in the same manner.

"I certainly do think it's the wildest, most impossible scheme I ever heard of, and one that shouldn't be permitted. It'll ruin Celia's property. And when that's all gone, and you and Celia are in trouble, I suppose I'll be called upon to help you. Of course I'll do the best I can, but you must remember I haven't very much money to throw away on wild childish schemes." He spoke with the air of a martyr.

Hannah answered him cheerily. She'd recovered her spirits since she sent her telegram. "You needn't worry, Hiram. I don't believe Celia or I will ever need your help. But if we do, I don't think we'll trouble you. They have a good many charitable institutions in the City of Brotherly Love, and we'll surely be well cared for if the improbable happens."

Then she placed her nicely prepared little coals of fire in the hands of her two grand-nephews and her grand-niece and went smiling upstairs. The coals were tiny paper parcels, each containing a bright five-dollar gold piece. She lay awake the previous night, worried about the sharp words she felt obliged to speak and the sentence Nettie flung out about her leaving her without help. She wanted to show she bore no grudge for what they said. Celia sent her the money to spend as she thought best, and Hannah knew her girl well enough to feel she'd say this was a good way to spend it. Besides, she felt sure she could run a boardinghouse successfully in a financial way, as well as some others, if she had the chance, so she might in time have more five-dollar gold pieces to do with as she chose.

She was becoming very happy, as she packed and strapped the last trunk, smoothed her hair and tied on her gray bonnet and veil. At the last Hiram and Nettie behaved quite well. Those five-dollar gold pieces went a long way toward making the bereavement of Aunt Hannah's departure felt. Hiram took her satchel down, and Nettie walked beside her carrying her umbrella and wheeling the baby, while Johnny and Lily trotted on ahead. A special importance was attached to a sudden and first-class departure such as Aunt Hannah's was turning out to be, and it couldn't be neglected.

They made an interesting procession down the street. More than one neighbor looked out of her window, and a few knew Hannah was going away. But they'd said good-bye and only turned their heads the other way to wipe away a tear of regret, or sigh because their good friend wouldn't be nearby with her cheery face and comforting words.

One or two observed Molly Poppleton also passing down the street accompanied by an old man wheeling her ancient trunk on a wheelbarrow and carrying a good-sized bundle.

Several of the women came to their gates to look down the street and wait till Nettie returned to ask what it meant.

And Nettie enjoyed a triumphal march back to her home. "Yes, she's gone. We'll miss her very much." Her nose was red with being rubbed, and her eyes had a suspicious redness about them. "No, Celia isn't ill, but she couldn't stand it any longer without Aunt Hannah. You know Celia's had a fortune left her? Oh, yes, she'll have plenty now. Yes, Aunt Hannah has to go and be her chaperone. I suppose she'll come out in society now that she has enough money to do as she pleases. Oh, yes, she's very generous; she always was. She sent the children each handsome presents in gold. Yes, Aunt Hannah has taken old Molly for a maid. She'll be obliged to have a maid there, you know. Funny, isn't it, that a woman who knows how to work should need a maid? I wouldn't like it myself, but then one has to do as other people do."

Finally Nettie went home and got supper and washed up her dishes and put her three babies to bed. Then she sat down wearily and wished for Aunt Hannah.

But Aunt Hannah sat serenely in the sleeper, waiting for her berth to be made up, and thought that she too, like Jehoiachin, had had her head lifted up out of prison.

Chapter 10

It was perhaps one of the happiest nights Hannah Grant ever spent. She slept like a little child, for she was tired after her day and night of excitement. But in the early dawn she awoke and lay there listening to the regular cadence of the moving train. It was music to her. Her life had for years been monotonous, and every detail of the journey was delightful to her. The turning wheels seemed to sing to her, "Now hath mine head been lifted up above mine enemies round about me." She tried to turn that thought out of her mind as soon as she discovered its significance; she didn't like to think that even in her heart was hidden a feeling that Hiram and Nettie were her enemies. But somehow the rejoicing stayed anyway.

She looked forward to the morning and the next day and the opening of her new life. What would it hold for her? Would there be trials? Yes, but she'd had trials before. She would have "His strength to bear them, with His might her feet could be shod. She could find her resting places in the promises of her God." She'd done so before. And it was such delightful work before her, the prospect of making a home pleasant.

Hannah rested, too, in the thought of experienced Molly Poppleton now reposing in the berth above her. She was going on a mission at last. How good God was to her! He'd tried her for a little while, but He was bringing her into a new place. She could see that, even though she couldn't know the trials before her. Of course the earth was full of trials. But she didn't need to carry them; Christ bore them all for her long ago. She would trust, and He'd bring her safely through as He'd done before and was doing now.

Then she reflected upon the Savior she loved so much and communed with Him. She promised to try to help every person who came in that house she was to make pleasant for Him and His children and to try to live for Him before them every day. And that crowded, rushing car became a holy place, because God met her there and blessed her.

The train reached the Broad Street station at a very early hour. Celia was glad, for it gave her plenty of time to meet her aunt and go back with her to the house, without being late at the store. She hadn't decided yet if she'd give up her position. She might do more good if she retained it for now, at least until she found someone else who needed it. Then she could give it to someone with profit, both to that person and to her employers who'd been very kind to her.

At exactly half past five she arrived at the Broad Street station. It was an early hour for her to be out alone, and it was still dark except for the electric lights that glared everywhere as if trying to keep off the day. But the train would come in at five minutes to six. Celia was too eager and happy to sleep longer, so she paced up and down in the ladies' room until the train was almost due. As the time drew near for the train she went out and stood behind the gates watching the trains moving back and forth.

"Oh, what if she shouldn't come?" she asked herself. "What if something happened to the train? Or what if Nettie and Hiram persuaded her at the last minute not to come? Or what if she missed the train? No, she would have telegraphed. 'Charge not thyself'—dear me! How much I do that. I must stop worrying ahead about everything. Aunt Hannah must have seen that fault in me very clearly. I never realized how much I do it."

Then the train whistled and rolled into the station, and the passengers began to alight and stream into the gates, looking sleepy and cold. Celia stood in the grayness of the foggy morning and trembled with the excitement and joy of looking for her aunt. Suddenly she saw the ample form of Molly Poppleton looming up behind the gilt-buttoned porter, and she caught a glimpse of a little gray bonnet just beyond and knew Aunt Hannah was come.

She took them home in the streetcar and then escorted them up to her little third-story back room. She had risen early and put it in order. Molly looked around in disdain.

"Well, Miss Celia, you don't have things as fine in the city as I expected," she said. "The idea of their putting you up in a room like this! Why, it ain't as good as the kitchen chamber at Cloverdale. I always heard a city was a dreadful place to live, but I never thought it was this bad. The wonder to me is anybody that don't have to, stays in 'em. But we'll have it *clean* pretty soon anyway—don't you worry."

And she walked to the window and surveyed the narrow court below, where she surmised she'd have to dry her clothes. She sniffed to herself, but Celia could see her practical eye already planning how she'd change the position of the ash bucket and the garbage pail. She gave a sigh of relief at the thought of Molly Poppleton's ability and turned to her aunt, fairly smothering her in kisses. Then she put a hand on each soft cheek, held her at arm's length and looked into her face.

"Now, you dear auntie, tell me just what you think of me. Am I a wild, impractical girl, full of crazy schemes? Tell me right away."

"Well," said Aunt Hannah with a twinkle in her eyes, "that's what Hiram thinks."

"Oh, he does, does he? Well, I don't really suppose it will matter much, do you? But I mustn't stop now to talk. I have to be at that store in an hour, and it takes half of that to get there. We must talk business. Do you think you and Molly can get along today by yourselves? I mean, without my worthy assistance? Of course I'll be home at half past six. I'll turn in my resignation there if you think best, but I hardly like to do it quite so soon after Mrs. Green was so kind to get it for me. It doesn't seem quite fair to the firm either to stop now, after they've taken the trouble of teaching me.

"Mrs. Morris is leaving on the noon train. She's ready, except that her faith hasn't been quite equal to believing you were really coming to take her place. She told the boarders this morning that she was going away for her health and secured a woman to take her place for awhile. She guessed they'd like it just as well. She wasn't sure when she'd return. The clerk promptly gave notice he'd leave, and I'm glad of it. Some of the others said if things didn't go better they'd follow his example. But I think they'll change their minds when they see the difference.

"I went to the market last evening and bought a great big roast, one of the finest cuts, and some fine potatoes and apples and yeast and flour. I know Mrs. Morris's flour isn't good, for she can't make anything out of it fit to eat. I also got some spinach and celery and sweet potatoes, canned tomatoes, and a few other things. I want to have a regular treat the first night regardless of the cost. You can figure things down afterward, but I thought we'd have enough for once to make up for the days of starvation.

"That Maggie, down in the kitchen, is a slouch and a bear. She gets in a towering rage whenever you go near her. I haven't said anything about her, except to ask what contract Mrs. Morris had with her. It's on a day-to-day basis, so you can do as you please. If you and Molly want her and can get the right kind of help out of her, keep her. If not, get rid of her, and we'll find a second girl who knows how to do things right.

"Now, shall we go down and see Mrs. Morris? Are you sure you're up to this and not too tired to begin today? I suppose Mrs. Morris would wait till you're rested, if you want her to."

But Aunt Hannah smiled and said no, she was eager to begin. Then she took off her bonnet, smoothed her gray hair, and went down.

Mrs. Morris had on the inevitable old calico wrapper. Celia wondered if she meant to travel in it. Her hair wasn't combed that morning, only twisted in a knot. She seemed embarrassed by Aunt Hannah in her trim gray traveling dress and hardly knew on what footing to meet her.

"For the land sake!" she exclaimed, wiping her hands, from custom perhaps, on the side of her wrapper before shaking hands. "So you've come! And you're really willing to undertake it and think you can succeed? I'm afraid you'll be disappointed. It's a hard life! You look too good for such a life. Boarders are an awful torment! Me heart has just been broke time an' again with the troubles I've been through with them. I'll show you all around, and if you feel you can't do it, I shouldn't feel you was bound in any way to stick to your bargain. Miss Murray seemed to be so sure, but I wouldn't want you to be took at no disadvantage. You see, I'm afraid, if I get away, I won't want to come back again, and I don't want to go off and feel I left you dissatisfied."

They went down to breakfast soon, and Celia saw her aunt seated before the uninviting meal. She felt sorry for her, and yet she thought she'd enjoy the meal with the prospect of the one she'd give the boarders later in the day. But she was scarcely prepared for the look of horror that gradually spread over the good woman's face, as she tasted dish after dish and found them equally unpalatable.

The oatmeal that morning was thick and lumpy and only half cooked. Besides, the salt had been forgotten. The pork and greasy fried potatoes were cold and unseasoned. The coffee was weak and muddy. Celia swallowed a few bites. She felt that she could go hungry for one day. Then she said a quiet good-bye to her aunt, squeezing her hand under her napkin so the boarders wouldn't see, and slipped away.

Aunt Hannah finished all she cared to of her meal and went back to Mrs. Morris.

Molly sat down to her breakfast in undisguised disgust. Nothing but the prospect of the power that was to be hers held her tongue from expressing her mind about good food cooked decently. She didn't even pretend to eat much and looked with animosity at the slatternly form of Maggie as she sauntered in to gather some plates. Molly spent most of her time in the dining room counting the flyspecks and fingerprints on the wall and windows. She made up her mind to get time for those windows somehow before dinner, if possible. If not, they'd be done before another dawn of light and breakfast anyway.

Meanwhile Mrs. Morris was showing Aunt Hannah the house. This room brought so much a week and that one only so much, and so on. At each room she told a tale of its various residents during the years she kept a boarding-house. Aunt Hannah listened quietly, mentally making notes of what she would and wouldn't do. She saw, without seeming to, the worn furniture, the need of a patch on a carpet or a turning of furniture to hide it, the need of a wardrobe or bureau in some cases. She set down in her mind the number of window shades torn, worn-out or lacking, and thought how much some cheap muslin curtains would improve things. She felt like a rich princess, as she went from room to room seeing its needs, and knowing she could change it all.

Sometimes the bareness or the boarder's attempt at decoration was pitiful. She paused a moment before a picture of a quiet sweet-faced woman, in a dark velvet frame on Harry Knowles's bureau. She wondered who she was and if the young man Mrs. Morris said roomed there was worthy of a mother with such a face as that.

Then she followed Mrs. Morris to her room and sat there during an hour of conversation in which Mrs. Morris, with many sighs and tears, detailed her entire life and troubles. Aunt Hannah's quiet, respectful attention and sympathy led her on until she unburdened her heart. Then came the Christian woman's opportunity. She spoke the word in season to the other woman, that word which bears fruit in due time.

Mrs. Morris, with her empty life and joyless spirit, received the words with tears and some gratitude. But she gave no outward sign that they more than touched the surface of her life. Yet she recalled what was said to her. And she sat in the train that afternoon, speeding far away from her disappointments, with her fare paid by one Christian, and her house taken and managed by another whom she saw must be a true saint. And she pondered these things in her heart.

Mrs. Morris was gone, and Hannah Grant descended to the kitchen, bidding the impatient Molly Poppleton wait until she called her.

Just before Mrs. Morris left, she informed the sullen-looking Maggie that Miss Grant was taking her place. Maggie responded with a significant look, which didn't appear promising for the new mistress. She met Miss Grant in the middle of the dining room on her way to the kitchen. Her hair was frowsy, her dress soiled and torn, and her arms akimbo. Altogether she would have furnished a formidable encounter to a woman who wasn't used to managing servants and holding the reins of her household well in her own hands.

"I just came to see what you wanted fer dinner," she announced. "There's some things come from a new place where we never deal. I thought I'd let you know."

Aunt Hannah thought a minute. Then she said, "Yes, Maggie, I'll be out in the kitchen soon to attend to dinner. Meanwhile it's only one o'clock, and there's enough time to get this room in order first. I think you'd better wash those windows."

Maggie stood aghast.

"And what's the matter with this room, I'd like to know?" she said in a loud, belligerent tone. "It's just the same as it always is, and what's good enough fer Mis' Morris ought to be good enough fer you. Indeed I'll wash no windows today. I've got me afternoon's work all planned out. This room'll be swep' when I sets the table fer dinner, an' that's all it'll get today. And you needn't trouble yourself about comin' in the kitchen. I never like to have the missus in the kitchen—it flusters me. I know me business and I 'tend to it. And I likes to have them as I live with attend to theirs. If you've got any orders, give 'em, and I'll get dinner on time—you needn't worry about that."

Maggie had backed up against the kitchen door, her arms still akimbo, and stood as if to defend the fortress of her domain.

Aunt Hannah waited till she'd drawn down a crooked shade and rolled it straight again, pinning the torn edge, before she answered. Then she turned and faced the irate Maggie calmly.

"I always manage my own kitchen, Maggie," she said in a quiet voice, "and I intend to do so still. I want this dining room put in order first, before anything else is attended to. Get some cloths and hot water right away, please."

Hannah Grant possessed a dignity that was new in Maggie's experience. She was used to intimidating Mrs. Morris with such a conversation as she just used, and she supposed she could do the same with her new mistress. She never expected to have it treated with such calm indifference. She was forced to her last resort.

"I can't stay in a house where things are managed that way. No lady goes into the kitchen. I know me business, and I don't like to be interfered with. If you ain't suited with me doing as I think best, I can find plenty of places."

"Oh, certainly, if you prefer," said Hannah, pulling down the other shade and fixing it neatly.

"Well, if I do, I'll go right away, and then what'll you do?" burst out the astonished Maggie. "There's all them boarders got to have their dinner. You can't fool with boarders, you know. They'll all leave you."

"I shall do very well," answered Hannah. "I brought one of my own helpers with me, and I can get others very easily. If you choose to stay and do as I say, I'd like to have those windows washed at once; otherwise you may go."

Poor Maggie was crestfallen. This was new treatment. She was used to mistresses who had to cater to her desires. She did a great deal of work and preferred to do it her way. But Hannah was firm. At that moment Molly, too impatient to wait any longer, put her head in at the door and asked if Miss Hannah was ready for her. That was enough. Maggie tossed her head and declared she wouldn't do another stroke of work in that house and demanded back pay. Miss Hannah settled up with her, and she departed, leaving Molly monarch of the kitchen and surveying her new realm scornfully.

Chapter 11

I t's just a pigpen! That's what it is!" Molly declared, holding up her ample calico skirts and clean gingham apron in a gingerly way. "I don't know where to begin. I didn't suppose a human being could be so dirty!"

Then she plunged into working. The range got such a cleaning as it hadn't had in years. The ashes were cleaned out and the soot removed from all its little doors and traps and openings. Molly wasn't used to a city range with all its numerous appliances, but she had keen common sense and used it. She knew dirt and ashes couldn't help a fire burn, so she removed them. And she scrubbed it inside and out, for she found the oven encrusted with burned sugar and juice of some sort and the top covered with grease. Then she started a fire. Before long it was glowing, and the water in the old tank was steaming hot.

There wasn't time for the dining room windows that day, after all. With skirts tucked together and sleeves rolled high Molly generously used the hot water and soap in the kitchen. She scoured with the old ragged cloths Maggie must have used as wiping towels, trusting to Miss Hannah's sense of the fitness of things to provide others somehow. The kitchen table and shelves and windows and paint and sink were scrubbed, and even the floor. Then Molly stood back and surveyed the room now pervaded with a damp atmosphere smelling of soap.

"There! I guess it'll do for overnight, and the first chance I get I'll give it a good cleaning. I never saw the like in my life! How them poor boarders stood it eating out of a dirty hole like this I don't see. Now what's to do? That sink was a caution! The water and dust was all in a mess underneath, and the top was slimy! I wonder what the creature calling herself Maggie thought she was to do."

Meanwhile Hannah went to her trunk and arrayed herself in an old gray gingham and a dark apron that enveloped her completely. She discovered they must begin at the very foundation before they could hope to do anything toward getting dinner. She investigated Celia's supplies and found they were sufficient for their present needs. Celia's training hadn't been for nothing. She knew by intuition that her aunt would ask for soap and yeast and baking powder among the first things. She thought of the little things that might not be in stock in Mrs. Morris's kitchen and had provisions for the present. The pantry wasn't very full. A plate held a pile of sour white-looking pancakes, another with some lumpy oatmeal, then a few boiled potatoes, a bowl of watery soup, and two or three ends of bakers' loaves. Hannah sniffed one of these, then laid it down again and said, "Bah!"

After studying the array, she gathered them all into a pan and dumped them into the garbage pail. A heavy, lifeless pie on a higher shelf also met the same fate. Then she got the dishpan and some clean hot water and washed a few dishes for her immediate use. Next she prepared some bread. It was late in the day, but it wouldn't take long; it could rise while she was doing other things and bake after dinner was cooked. She could even make part of it into pulled rolls for dinner.

Then she hunted for bread cloths and clean rags. She couldn't work without tools. In one of her trunks was a roll of old rags and linen; with Molly's help she unstrapped the trunk and searched it out. It gave her great satisfaction to cover the bread with a clean cloth and feel that so much of her work was going on right. She decided that all the dishes must be washed. She and Molly both worked at this, Molly washing off the shelves while she wiped the dishes. By that time it was four o'clock.

"It's high time we was seeing about dinner," said Molly, as she thumped the last pile of plates on the clean shelf. "What are you going to do for a tablecloth? That one in there ain't fit, an' there ain't a clean one about the drawer anywhere. There's a pile of dirty ones behind the door in the back stairway. I reckon I'll have to wash one. As for napkins I suppose they didn't use 'em. I can't find any."

Hannah hunted again and discovered more soiled tablecloths and a stack of soiled napkins. Molly already had the washtub going and was working as if her life depended upon it. It was well for Hannah's plans and Celia's hopes that Molly was equal to emergencies, indeed delighted in them, and was a swift worker. By the time Hannah had the tablecloth and dishes off the table and the dining room swept and dusted, that linen was swinging in a brisk breeze in the backyard, and the irons were growing hot on the range.

"Five o'clock and the table not set!" exclaimed Molly. She was working on time, and the pleasure of the race depended upon her finishing before Miss Celia arrived and ringing that dinner bell exactly on time. "Well, I reckon we'll get through somehow. You can't turn a pigpen into a parlor in one day. I declare, Miss Hannah, it was a pity to turn that girl loose on the community. We should have kept her by force and taught her how to scrub before we let her go. The things that wasn't too filthy to be burned or rusted is burned and rusted, and the things that had anything about them to get lost and broken has that the matter. I reckon we'll have a few things to buy 'fore we get fixed out for comfort."

But Molly was working swiftly while she talked; she'd filled the little salts and peppers and rubbed up the knives. Celia hadn't forgotten bath brick or silver polish, though very little had any claim to being silver.

The dishes and table appointments were plain. Many would have said it was impossible to make any difference in that table without spending a lot of money. Hannah didn't think so. She knew the subtle difference between order and disorder, and the startling contrast between cleanliness and dirt. Cleanliness was next to godliness, she thought, and she was practicing that today. The godliness, she hoped, would follow soon after. While she pulled the little cushions of velvety dough for the rolls, she prayed a rich blessing on that first meal in the house under her care.

Then she let her mind wander for a moment to the home she had left; it was no more of a home to her than this was to its inmates. She wondered how they were getting on and if the baby was well. The only drawback to leaving Nettie's was the baby. Aunt Hannah couldn't help loving babies and enjoying their soft dimpling arms clinging about her neck and their apple blossom breath on her cheek. Babies always loved Aunt Hannah. Only after they grew older and imitated grown-ups did they become impertinent and unloving. Even then, Johnny and Lily always came to their aunt with a burn or a bump, for somehow her motherly arms knew how to comfort the troubled little ones.

But Hannah didn't have time to think of past duties and troubles. She gave the last little jerk to the puffy roll, tucked it in the pan to rise for the last time and then hurried in to set the table. Molly had laid on the table the crisp tablecloth she forced to dry with her hot irons and was now ironing away at the napkins. Molly and Hannah had high ideals, brought from comfortable private homes, and they wished to make this house a home in the best sense of the word. They worked faster now, for the clock warned them it was getting late.

The well-seared roast beef was roasting in the oven with a good supply of sweet and Irish potatoes on the grate below, grouped about a huge baked apple dumpling Molly had hastily concocted. Molly was straining the spinach and rubbing it through the colander, after which it returned to the stove to keep hot before adding butter and more pepper. She looked doubtfully at the water the spinach was cooked in and, glancing at the clock, rushed about to carry out another resolution.

"You can put on the soup plates ef you're a mind to," she called out to Aunt Hannah. "I can make a taste of spinach soup with the water and some milk and flour and butter. It'll make things seem nicer for the first night and don't take a minute. That'll give the rolls time to get a little browner before they're needed."

Then she began to sing at the top of her voice: "Am I a soldier of the cross—"

Molly always sang at the top of her lungs when she had some important work to do or was in an unusual hurry with her work. Having hard work to do made her happy.

Opening the front door with her latchkey, Celia heard singing and rejoiced. It was the old Molly. She hadn't become discouraged and gone home but was working with heart and voice as she did in their old kitchen at home. She ran out into the dining room to check on things before going upstairs. But she stopped in the doorway astounded.

Even her highest hopes hadn't visualized this change. What made it? Was it the shining tablecloth, the glistening glasses, the knives and forks laid straight, or what? A nice square cake of butter was in each butter plate at the ends of the table. The salts were smoothed off and stamped with the bottom of the saltcellars. The plates were stacked at one end of the table instead of upside down on the napkins at each place. Where were the crackers and gingersnaps that never failed to appear at every dinner since she'd boarded there? Where was the inevitable dish of prunes? Gone, and in its place a dish of translucent cranberry jelly Molly found time somehow to fix. Even the gas had a clean globe on it.

Celia wondered how so much was accomplished in one short afternoon. She heard the front door opening from the outside and hurried into the kitchen, closing the dining room door behind her first. This must burst upon them all at once when they entered the dining room.

Aunt Hannah was taking the brown balls from the roll pan and piling them on a plate when her niece entered the kitchen.

"Celia, go upstairs," she greeted her, "and wash your hands and then come down and fix the celery. Molly and I haven't a second to do it, and in five minutes it's time to ring the bell. Have the boarders come yet?"

Celia rushed away and was back quickly, bringing Aunt Hannah's white apron and a brush to smooth her hair so she wouldn't be delayed from coming to dinner on account of her appearance. At last the dinner was ready, and it was time to ring the bell. She put the two glasses of celery on the table and, handing Molly the bell, went into the parlor. She didn't wish anyone to know yet that she had a right in the kitchen. For now she was just the ribbon girl from Dobson and Co.'s. She wanted to accomplish some things first.

The bell rang, and the boarders trooped down. The little old lady from upstairs was first and slowed the others for a moment. She walked into the dining room with Miss Burns. Both stopped in the doorway, blinking, before they walked slowly, as in a daze, to their respective places. The two girls from the three-cent store stood back awkwardly against the wall, staring openly. The three young men followed, with Harry Knowles first.

He whistled and, turning around, headed back into the hall. "Whew! This is great!" he said. "I'm going to wash my hands and comb my hair. I don't fit in here."

Aunt Hannah with her gray hair, placid face, and gray dress with its white apron presided well over that table. The dishes might be thick and the tablecloth coarse, but no dinner on any rich man's table was ever cooked or served better, or more thoroughly enjoyed.

After they were seated Miss Burns giggled nervously: "Oh, really, now, this is simply—simply—*fine,* don't you know. This is quite a change, isn't it, dear?"

She looked across the table at Celia who was passing celery and handing soup plates as Aunt Hannah ladled out the pale-green tempting soup. Her guests ate it in wonder. They weren't acquainted with puree of spinach. They wondered how it got colored and what it was; most finished every drop, with some tilting their plates to do so. The three-cent store girls and the university student asked for seconds and got it.

Then Molly, with her sleeves rolled down and a white apron over her dark one, took out the soup and brought in the platter with that great brown perfectly cooked roast. With it she brought potatoes and spinach and hot plates. And Aunt Hannah, using the knife she sharpened herself, cut large juicy slices of roast and filled the plates.

They were rather silent that first night. Their surroundings, familiar and yet unfamiliar, embarrassed them. And the dinner absorbed their thoughts while they absorbed it.

When it was time for dessert they sat back satisfied. Perhaps it was as well that the inevitable pie didn't come to spoil this ideal repast. But they forgot that feeling when the great pudding was brought in. Its crust was browned nicely on the top, and it was light as a feather when cut, with luscious amber apple quarters in the bottom and a dressing of sweet transparent syrup with a dash of cinnamon.

"I tell you what!" said Harry Knowles, leaning back in his chair to fold his napkin and talking in an aside to Celia. "That was the best dinner I've tasted since I left home. I feel as if I'd been invited out, don't you? I don't know what it means, do you? She certainly can't keep it up. I suppose she's just treating us the first night. But I declare, if I could have meals like that, I might be a different fellow and amount to something. How's our lamp getting on? I thought of a way to fix the spring in that sofa the other night. I believe I'll stay in and try it tonight."

As the boarders were leaving the table, Aunt Hannah apologized for not putting the rooms in order that day. She'd only been in power, she said, since one o'clock, and she hadn't had time to do everything. She hoped to have things in better shape very soon if they would all be patient. Then the boarders went into the parlor to whisper with one another about that good dinner, and Celia slipped unseen out to the kitchen to exult and to help.

Chapter 12

O ut on the street, not far from that boardinghouse, two young men met. "How are you, Horace? Glad to see you, old fellow! You look as thin as a rail. What do they feed you down in that miserable hole where you hide yourself? I say, you need either a new boardingplace or a wife."

"I'm hunting for one," the other man said, laughing. "A new boardinghouse, that is, not a wife."

"Well, you may find one while searching for the other. They always used to say, when we were children, that if you lost a thing you never could find it till you lost something else and hunted for that. You haven't exactly lost a wife, because you never had one, so that's just as bad. But maybe you'll find her. I'm afraid, though, that anyone you'd find in hunting a boardinghouse wouldn't be worth her salt. That's my experience. Say, old fellow, why don't you come up our way and live? It isn't much farther, and you're a good walker. You could even walk to that blessed church of yours. Now the place Royce boards would be first-rate, and I happen to know there's a vacant room there now, second-story front, fine sunny room, all conveniences, and splendid board."

"But I can't afford second-story fronts, Roger. I have to pay most of my own salary. You know we're building, and the church is just struggling to live. It's all made up of poor people."

"Well, why in the world did you go down there? You might have had a church in Germantown if you'd taken it, and you also had a chance out in West Philadelphia, I heard. Why, you have enough friends to get you hearings in several big churches in the heart of the city where they pay big salaries. I'm sure I don't see any virtue in hiding your light under a bushel. For my part, I think you're as good, if not better, than any preacher I've heard in the city—if you'd only let go of a few impossible views you have about social equality. But that's neither here nor there. You're here, and the churches are there. I'll just have to tend you in your last sickness and pay the funeral expenses, if you keep it up. I must see what I can do about getting our church to help that mission of yours, if you stay with it."

"I wish you would, Roger, for they need help. A church in this neighborhood is needed more than in the quarters you've mentioned, where there's a church almost every two blocks. But I need to go. I have a meeting this evening and want to stop one more place before I go to church."

They parted, with the young man Roger wishing the other would reconsider and come up higher in town to board and thus be near his friends. Then Horace Stafford consulted a list of addresses in his notebook. A moment later he paused at a house and rang the doorbell, and the door was opened by Celia.

Now Celia was very happy about the dinner. She lingered in the halls catching the boarders' words, and she knew they were intensely pleased and surprised. When she was happy or excited a clear red color came into her cheeks and a brightness into her deep, gray-blue eyes which made her very beautiful. She wasn't always beautiful, but she was always pleasant to look at. Certain conditions, however, had the power of making this charm bloom into beauty.

Tonight the color and shine were there, and she presented a charming picture to the young man. He'd spent the afternoon calling at boardinghouses and knew what to expect when the door opened. He was agreeably surprised, therefore, as he stepped into the hall and waited while Celia called Aunt Hannah. He'd asked for Mrs. Morris, having been directed there for board. He glanced into the parlor and sighed—the same dreary sort of parlor he'd come to expect. But he didn't know what was the matter with it, and since he'd spend little time in it, it didn't make much difference.

He heard a quiet, cultured voice upstairs saying, "Tell Molly I'll send her some in a moment." Then Miss Grant appeared before him.

She didn't know much about taking new boarders, but she did the best she could. She told him one room was left vacant that day, but it wasn't in order yet. If he cared to see it, though, he might come upstairs and do so. He followed her to the room, which happened to be the second-story front. It wasn't large, for economy of space was exercised in building the house. But it had a sunny exposure, and the young man knew from experience in a dark room that it was a great advantage.

The bed didn't look soft or inviting, and the two chairs were dilapidated. The bureau was cheap, with a rheumatic castor that gave it a reeling appearance. The linens were tumbled in a heap on the bed, as the clerk left it. It wasn't what one would call luxury, but it was so much better than some he'd seen.

"Could I have a table to write on?" he asked.

Miss Grant considered it a moment and told him she thought he could. He asked the price; it wasn't much more than he was paying now. After a little reflection he said he'd take it.

Later, when he went downstairs to wait for the supper she said he might have—he'd asked if it was too late for the evening meal—he wondered why he'd taken it. What power was upon him upstairs to influence him to cast his lot here? It wasn't that room, even though it was a second-story front, for it was forlorn in the dim flickering gaslight. Nor was it the general look of the house, for it certainly wasn't attractive.

As he sat in the shadow of the front window and studied some of the boarders at the other end of the room, he felt that same sense of desolation he'd felt in so many boardinghouses that afternoon. He couldn't hope to find many congenial spirits here. He sighed. It was hard not to have pleasant friends around to talk of the things he knew and loved, when he came in at night after work.

Miss Grant came back through the hall then and in her quiet sweet voice told him he could come to the dining room now. He knew then it was his landlady who'd drawn him to make this his temporary home. She seated him, poured his coffee, and then excused herself and left.

He bowed his head a moment, more in supplication that the Lord would give him rest and strength for his work than in thankfulness for his food; he'd learned that some food was as hard to eat as it was to digest. With pleased surprise he saw the tablecloth was clean and free from crumbs. The plate before him held food as appetizing as any he could remember. Of course the potatoes were reheated and not as nice as when first served. But the meat was tender and juicy, and he ate it eagerly. The delicious rolls and coffee were enough to satisfy a hungry man, and he began to feel he hadn't chosen his home amiss.

Then the kitchen door opened, and Celia brought in a large dish of apple dumpling covered with plenty of sauce. She put it down beside his place and started removing the empty dishes, asking if he'd have anything more.

"Thank you," he said, smiling. "I've had plenty, and it's been so good. I've been boarding where they had miserable fare, and I didn't know how hungry I was. This meal tasted like my mother's cooking."

Celia's eyes danced as she told him quietly she was glad. She returned to the kitchen and the dishes, but she couldn't help thinking what handsome eyes and bright smile that man had. He was tall and thin with an intellectual face many people would have called homely, but it was the kind Celia and her aunt called "homely handsome."

The new boarder left the house after finishing his meal. He told his new landlady he'd bring his belongings when he returned later in the evening, and she promised to have his room ready.

Celia went upstairs to see if she could do anything. She was thrilled with the house and its residents and all she wished to do. No child in a fairy tale ever had such delightful possibilities put into her hands, she thought, as had been given to her.

"Now," said Aunt Hannah, "that room must be fixed for that man, for he'll come back soon. How shall we make it more habitable? Poor fellow! He must have been hard put for shelter to take it looking like that, or perhaps he doesn't know any better. It looked so desolate that I could scarcely bear to take him to it."

"Yes, he knows better, Aunt Hannah," said Celia, laughing. "I know he does. He has a mother, and—," she added, pink stealing into her cheeks, "he has a smile."

"Well, I'm glad he has that," said Aunt Hannah, pulling the linens off gingerly and extracting the sheets and pillowcases from the mass. "He'll need it to keep cheerful in this room tonight. Celia, I wish I could get into my grandmother's linen and blanket closet for a little while tonight. I'd like to burn this quilt." She held it out by her finger and thumb and examined it carefully.

"Burn it then," said Celia. "Don't we have an allowance? We'll buy another."

The bed was made up with the cleanest things Hannah could find, and the washbowl and pitcher and soap dish were immaculate. Two copies of those flaring chromos called "Wide Awake" and "Fast Asleep" framed in varnished coffee berries were removed from the walls. Not much was left to do. It was too late to do more with the paint than wipe it off with a damp cloth, and the floor needed only brushing up.

Hannah found a kitchen table which had served as a dressing table in Mrs. Morris's room, and Molly carried it upstairs for a writing table. Hannah sighed because it had no cover. Celia remembered something, went up to her room and took the embroidered denim cover from her trunk; she'd made it for her aunt for Christmas. It was a little sacrifice, but the table needed it. And it would make the bare room look more habitable.

"There, Aunt Hannah," she said, "I made it for you, but you may do what you like with it."

Then Aunt Hannah took Celia's face in her hands and kissed her. "My dear girl!" she said and put the pretty cover on the table.

"I'm not sure I'd have done that," thought Celia later, "if it hadn't been for that smile and his speaking about his mother."

She glanced around the room again. Aunt Hannah had gone down to the kitchen to help Molly prepare for breakfast. Her eyes fell on the two rickety chairs. She thought of Harry Knowles. Then she ran down to the parlor and beckoned him to come into the hall.

"Harry," she said in a pleasant sisterly way, "did you know there's a new boarder? I was passing the room just now. It looked awfully dreary before it was fixed up. The worst thing is the chairs. I wonder if you couldn't bring up your hammer and fix them a little. It seems too bad for a new boarder to find things all run-down on the first night he comes."

"All right, I'm with you, Miss Murray," said Harry, interested at once. "I know how it feels myself. Besides, that good dinner has given me a longing to do something for somebody else."

They went upstairs to the chairs. As they went Harry said quietly, "Say, Miss Murray, that Miss Grant is going to be great, don't you think? She makes me think of my mother just a little."

Celia smiled and said she thought so, and they went to work.

At last the front room was in order, and buckwheat cakes were set rising in the yellow bowl downstairs for the morning breakfast. And the lights were out and everything quiet, when Celia, still awake, suddenly realized her aunt was awake too and asked her why.

"Well, Celia, I suppose I am rather tired tonight, though I don't feel it one bit, because I've been so interested in it all. But I'm beginning to think maybe I oughtn't to have let you undertake this scheme. It's all very nice and benevolent, but what if it doesn't succeed? If it runs behind and takes a good deal of your money and you have to work hard for your living again, I'd never stop blaming myself.

"Then, too, I'm a little worried about that new man. I don't know if I should have rented a room to him without knowing anything about him, and I've always heard a city was an awful place to get taken in. He may be a robber or some dreadful kind of a man, though to be sure he didn't look it. I must confess I liked his looks very much. But you know, dear, Satan sometimes appears as an angel of light. I've heard gamblers are often mistaken for ministers. I know perfectly well that I'm 'green,' as the boys used to say, and perhaps I've been deceived. He was very late getting in and looked pale. He may be dissipated, though I can't really think that."

"Now, auntie dear," laughed Celia, putting her arms about her, "that isn't a bit like you. You must be too tired, or you'd never talk like that. Remember your words to me: 'Charge not thyself with the weight of a year,' and 'Bend not thine arm for tomorrow's load. Thou mayst leave that to thy gracious Lord.' Don't you fret one bit. What if he's a gambler or a robber? He can't do us any harm. We've nothing to gamble and nothing to rob. Perhaps we'll do him some good. Anyway, I don't believe he's anything but good—he talked to me—that is, he said he has a mother and she cooked like that, and then he smiled."

Then they both laughed, and Hannah kissed her niece and thanked her for the reminder that she didn't need to bear burdens. After that they fell asleep.

Chapter 13

The minister was weary when he went up to his new room that night. He put down his satchel and looked around, hoping the bed would be more inviting than when he saw it last. He sighed with relief. It looked clean anyway. He turned down the covering and smoothed the sheets. They didn't appear to have been slept in. He sighed again. That was one fear off his mind.

Then he noticed the table with its pretty cover. He wasn't used to fancy work and didn't know if this was done by hand or machinery. He only knew it was a touch of beauty in his dreary room, and it cheered him. He went over to the table and awkwardly felt of the material, passed his hand over the embroidery and smiled. He told himself he'd write to his mother about it, and she'd be pleased.

Finally he knelt down beside the table and bowed his head in prayer. He asked to receive and give a blessing in the house and, if possible, that it might be right and best for him to remain for a time.

About that same time Harry Knowles stood before the bureau in his room and looked at his mother's picture. His face was serious. He looked into her eyes, longing to have her with him again to ask her advice, until tears formed in his own eyes. He let them drop unheeded on the bureau and on the little velvet frame. She seemed to be gazing into his life, asking him what he'd done with his time since she left him.

At last he turned away and said aloud, "Well, I'm glad I didn't go tonight. I s'pose the boys'll give me no end of chaff about backing out, but I've proved to myself that I can stay at home *once* when I say so. I wish Mother *was* here. I'd tell her all about it, I believe, and promise her to start over again. I wonder if it'd be any use! If a fellow only had someone to help him!" And he sighed and went to bed.

It isn't certain what time Molly arose the next morning. If she'd gotten up a little earlier, Celia told her, she might have met herself going to bed. The range, unused to such treatment, brightened up early too and was soon baking and boiling away. The oatmeal was cooked slowly all night and was about to become a delicious porridge, like that found in its perfection only in Scotland. Molly coaxed the milk till it produced a thin yellow cream for the oatmeal. True, she scoffed at it and said it wasn't as rich as skim milk in Cloverdale. But then the boarders weren't used to Cloverdale milk, and they called this cream.

She picked and shredded the codfish so fine that the departed Maggie would have stood amazed at such wasted labor. Then with skill she mixed the right proportion of potatoes for the most delectable codfish balls, when browned to a crisp, that anyone ever tasted.

"Codfish balls are good, and anybody that doesn't like 'em when they're made just right doesn't know, that's all. Besides, a person can't have beefsteak everyday, and there's plenty else to eat." So Molly said.

She tested the buckwheat cakes to be sure they had the right amount of soda and enough milk to brown them on both sides, set the coffee where it would finish, and rang the bell—one minute early. Molly Poppleton loved to be ahead, even by one minute.

"I say," said Harry Knowles, holding a golden-brown fish ball on his fork and admiring it, "if that's a fish ball, then I never saw one before. It's a libel on that pretty thing to call it that, or else all the ones I ever tried to eat were poor imitations."

Molly came in just then with a generous supply of hot buckwheats and heard his remark. She swelled with joy and pride, and after that Harry Knowles was her favorite among the boarders, except for the minister who grew into her good graces another way not long afterward.

Horace Stafford had come in shortly before and was enjoying his dish of oatmeal. He wondered what made the difference between it and other oatmeal he tried to eat in the weeks since he'd moved to Philadelphia. Had he found a place where things were really good to eat, or was he acquiring a good appetite from working so hard? He resolved to ask the cook, when they were better acquainted, if he might take a dish of this to the old Scottish woman lying sick in an attic and longing for her dear home across the seas.

⬯

That breakfast was a pleasant surprise to more than one of the boarders. The brakeman, coming in a little late from his all-night run, had taken his dinner the night before at the other end of his line. Therefore he wasn't prepared for any changes other than Mrs. Morris's departure and someone else's arrival to take her place. He was dumbfounded. He pulled his chair to the table with his usual familiar assurance and then looked around uncomfortably. He wasn't quite sure what made him feel that way.

Was it the pleasant-faced, white-haired woman at the head of the table? She smiled good morning to him cordially; yet at the same time he felt as if she was from a different world other than his. Or was it the few flowers in the tiny vase in the center of the table? Or—? But he couldn't detail the rest of the changes, for they seemed so subtle. He turned his attention to the good breakfast. Maggie had evidently improved.

In short, those boarders went to their day's work well fed and comfortable for the first time in many weeks. They were thus better workers and better human beings in every way, because they weren't troubled all day with nature's demands and complaints as a result of what they'd eaten or not eaten.

Just as Celia was going out the door, her aunt, who had followed her, drew her into the parlor for a moment.

"Celia, dear," she said, "we must talk tonight as soon after dinner as possible and find out how to run this house and make some decisions. You know we can't go ahead blindly and get into debt as Mrs. Morris did."

"I'll risk you, dear auntie," Celia said. "But we'll have our talk, and I'll get home as early as I can to help, if you need me. Then after dinner we'll have a cozy time and do a lot of figuring. I've done some already. Good-bye. Don't try to reform everything today; leave a little for tomorrow. Do you want me to stop at an employment office and get more help?"

"No, not yet, dear. There's too much to be done before we introduce any new elements, and besides we don't know yet whether we can afford anyone else. We mustn't run behind, you know."

Then they parted with an understanding smile, and Aunt Hannah went to her new duties with enthusiasm. She meant to make a few radical changes in some of her guests' sleeping rooms before that day ended, and there was much planning and marketing to do.

Molly was in her element in the kitchen. Hannah could hear her voice singing above the clatter of pots and pans.

> "What though the spicy breezes
>   Blow soft o'er Ceylon's isle;
> Though every prospect pleases,
>   And only man is vile—"

She was cleaning out the departed Maggie's kettle closet under the back stairs and stopped occasionally to express her mind about some dirty corner, then continued:

> "In vain with lavish kindness
>   The gifts of God are strewn:
> The heathen in his blindness,
>   Bows down to wood and stone!"

Hannah smiled as she went upstairs. She knew the good-hearted Molly was mingling the theme of her song with her thoughts about the dirty house and the boarders' needs and would work it out in time.

> "Shall we whose souls are lighted
>   With wisdom from on high—
> Shall we to men benighted,
>   The lamp of life deny?"

The singer went on, and Hannah knew Molly's intent was to make a cheerful, clean house and good food and give the others a chance to help save the poor city heathen boarders. Molly thought all native city boarders were heathens in the truest sense of the word. Thus she received with joy the few words Miss Hannah spoke to her about the mission they were going to start— the mission of making one bright little clean home spot for a few people who were in discomfort.

The dining room windows and several other windows were washed that morning. Molly sang a great many Isaac Watts hymns through before she prepared lunch for herself and Miss Hannah. She didn't remember when she was so happy. Neither, indeed, did Miss Hannah.

Sometime after Hannah Grant lost the love of her youth, she saw she wasn't to go on a great salvation mission to the heathen of other nations. Since then, it had been her one great ambition to call some spot her own and help people there. Now it seemed as if she was to have the opportunity. She thanked her heavenly Father every hour, even for the privilege of brightening a place that before this was dark.

After dinner the minister was in his room writing to his mother, before he left for a meeting at the mission. Down in the parlor the brakeman sat at the organ accompanying himself as he sang in stentorian voice and touching ballad of "Granny's only left to me her old armchair."

Celia smiled as she ran upstairs where her aunt was waiting for the conference.

"Just listen, Aunt Hannah. Did you ever hear the like?" she asked, putting her head in at the door. The words of the chorus in decided nasal twang floated up the two flights of stairs.

> "How they tittered, how they chaffed,
>   How my brothers and my sisters laughed,
> When they heard the lawyers declare,
>   Granny's only left to me her old armchair."

"Do you really think it's any use to try to help people who like that music, even if you try through buckwheat cakes?"

Celia was cheerful as she spoke, but her aunt detected an undertone of trouble in her voice and understood it.

"Dear, Christ died for him, even if he doesn't understand the little refining influences you're trying to bring around him. Yes, of course it's worthwhile. You can't expect him to turn into a person with the tastes of Beethoven. You're not that yourself, remember, and it's all in the scale of life. But I know what you mean, and I do think it's worthwhile to try. If it wasn't, God wouldn't have put him here for us to try on. You mustn't expect the same result as you would from—"

"From your new boarder, auntie? The gambler with the smile, you mean!"

Celia was laughing now, for both saw with the morning light that whatever else their new boarder was, he was a man to be trusted.

"Yes," said Aunt Hannah. "You mustn't expect the same results from trying to help this man that you would the other. But you'll find a depth to his nature that you don't suspect, if you look for it. Listen! He's singing something else. It may give you a clue."

Again the voice rang out deeply, pathetically, and nasally,

"Lost on the Lady Elgin.
    Slumbering to wake no more,
Numbering about three hundred—
    Who failed to reach the shore."

"Oh, auntie, I can't stand another line," said Celia, rushing into the room and throwing herself on the bed in a paroxysm of laughter. "To have those words in that ludicrous song roared out in that dramatic way is *too* funny. And he asked me if I'd sing 'Where is my wandering boy tonight?' with him. How *could* I?"

"Now, dear girl," said Aunt Hannah, sitting down on the bed beside her, "perhaps that's just your chance. Sing 'Where is my wandering boy tonight?' with him sometime. You may be able to help him to higher things, even if he continues to amuse you with his music. If you want to help all the people, you'll have to do as Paul did and be all things to all men, that you may by all means save some."

Celia sobered at once. "Yes, I know, Aunt Hannah, but I'm not sure I could ever be that, unless I was interested in all people. It troubles me sometimes, but this dark-browed, smiling, conceited brakeman isn't in the least attractive. Now that boy Harry Knowles is. I feel sorry for him. He misses his mother, and I'm afraid he goes with a wild set. I got him to fix some chairs last night, and he seemed interested and stayed at home. But tonight he slipped out just before I came up and looked the other way when I came down the hall, as if he didn't want me to see him and ask him to stay in. At least I guess that was the reason, because I've asked him to stay once or twice.

"It worries me to think he's going wrong. I feel as if I could pray all night that God would save him. I can't get away from that look in his mother's picture. He brought it down to the parlor one night and showed it to me. And he's so young, only just eighteen. Auntie, I want to do so much. Do you suppose God will let me do something at least?"

"Dear child," said Aunt Hannah as she bent over and kissed her, "I feel sure He will, and He'll hear your prayers and help you to work in the right way and be interested in the uninteresting, too. Now get your pencil and paper and let's go to work."

Celia sprang up, and soon they were hard at work.

"What I want to do is this, Aunt Hannah," said Celia. "I want to make this a pleasant home for us all, on the money we pay in for our board. You and I will pay ours, too, if it can't be run without that, and then we'll have things as nice as we can on that. If we need anything extra, then we can count that a gift from our allowance. But to be strictly honest as a boardinghouse, and not a charitable institution, we should run it on what's paid in, shouldn't we? I'd like to prove that a boardinghouse can be comfortable as well as cheap. Do you think it can be done?"

"I do," said the elder woman thoughtfully. "I've done some careful thinking myself, and I think I can. I'll enjoy trying anyway."

"And, Aunt Hannah, there's another thing. My allowance is half yours, you know. I won't have it any other way. You and I have nine hundred dollars a year to live on, besides what isn't in the bank in cash, and we can do what we please with it, even give it away if we want to. If we can make this house pay our board, then we'll have the rest to live on. But if we can't we'll run the house up to the full extent of what we can afford to put into it, for a few months at least, just to give these poor souls a taste of something like home. I'd rather do that than give my money somewhere else, for I think they all need it. Do you think we have enough money to start on to make things go nicely at the beginning? Nine hundred dollars a year seems to me a great deal of money, but people say money doesn't go far in the city."

Celia's brow was clouded as she spoke.

"There goes my girl down into the cellar of despair over a thought," said Aunt Hannah, leaning over to smooth the pucker out of her niece's brow. "I wish you'd get just a little more trust in your heavenly Father, that He'll take care of the work He's put into your hands and see that it prospers in spite of your worries. Now tell me everything you know about this house and the way it's run."

Chapter 14

Aunt Hannah and Celia finished the last puzzling question, added up the final row of figures and were sleeping peacefully in their beds. The lights in the house were out. Suddenly a loud noise was heard at the street door, as if someone was thrown, or threw himself, several times heavily against it. This was followed by loud voices talking excitedly, then in more muffled tones. The doorknob was turned and rattled, and a latchkey clicked and half turned in the lock by clumsy fingers.

The minister heard the noise first, since his room was over the front of the house. He opened his window and spoke a few calming words to quiet the disturbance. But he received only curses for his interference. He thought he recognized in one of the midnight revelers the form of one of the boarders. Closing his window, he dressed quickly to go down and help if needed.

By the time he was halfway down the stairs and striking a match, the fumbling latchkey turned, and the door burst open. Three young men tumbled into the hall at Horace Stafford's feet. Aunt Hannah and Celia had already reached the stair landing from the third floor and stood at the head of the stairs just above Mr. Stafford, as he struck the light.

"What does this mean?" said Aunt Hannah, in as stern a voice as she could muster. Celia, bewildered and trembling, clung to her arm and begged her to come back.

But there was too much disturbance below for her to be heard, and she and Celia could only stand and watch.

The new boarder seemed to know what to do. He lit the gas, turned it up to its full strength and then extricated the three young men, who were tangled on the floor at his feet. Two of them were promptly withdrawn from the hall by their comrades outside, and the remaining one stood miserably against the wall and looked about him.

It was hard to recognize in this dirty, rough fellow with bloodshot eyes and white face the bright young man who always looked so neat and whom everybody liked and called Harry.

"Oh, no, that's Harry Knowles," said Celia, in horrified tones.

Then the young man looked up. "Hulloa, Celia," he called, in a pitifully bright voice, "is that you? Yes, I'm here all right. But I've been out on a lark, and the lark's gone to my head. Come down and talk to a fellow awhile, just for a change."

Celia shrank back in dismay, as she saw the poor fellow stagger toward the stairs and heard him say, "Can't you get down? Well, I'll come up and get you. Awful shaky stairs, I know, but I'll manage 'em—don't you be afraid."

And then a strong hand grasped his arm, and a clear, commanding voice said, "Stand right where you are! Don't stir a step, and don't speak another word to those ladies."

Then the minister turned to the frightened women and said in low tones, "Don't be afraid. Go to your rooms, and I'll take care of him."

Harry had sat stupidly down on the stairs saying meekly, "All right, cap'n, jes's you say. You're the boss, an' I'm sleepy."

Hannah took assurance from the calm face and powerful frame of her new boarder and led Celia away. Meanwhile, the minister carefully and even gently helped the young man to his room and took care of him as if he were his own brother.

Aunt Hannah had her hands full with Celia. The young girl threw herself on the bed weeping, and it required all her aunt's persuasive powers to quiet her. Celia wasn't used to young men who drank. Her cousins had been steady, whatever else they might not have been. She'd never seen a man come home at night drunk, and she'd never been spoken to by one.

The familiar tone and the vacant, silly stare of the young man as he looked up at her gave her a shock she couldn't forget. Whenever she tried to be quiet and sit up and listen to her aunt, she shuddered again at the thought of the scene she just witnessed.

Finally, when she was calmer she moaned, "Now we'll have to give up the whole thing, Aunt Hannah. We can't have people getting drunk." She shuddered again.

"Now, child! Don't get into your cellar of despair again. It's like some people's cyclone cellars out west, always there ready for you. You fly down the stairs at the first little cloud that appears in your sky. Can't you remember we have a heavenly Father who's looking out for us? Get a little more trust, dear. No, of course we'll not have to give up, just for one boarder who's gone wrong. We're not obliged to keep him, if he makes a disturbance. But I'd not be the first one to turn him out without another trial. What are we here for but to try to help someone like him?

"Maybe he was never really drunk before. He's young and doesn't look bad. He'll be sorry enough for it all tomorrow, I'm sure, or I've mistaken his mother's face in that picture on his bureau. A boy who's had a mother like that can't go wrong all at once. We'll do what we can for him. You have some work to do for him, dear, and you must try and forget tonight for Christ's sake!"

"Oh, Aunt Hannah!" groaned Celia. "How can I ever speak to him again, after his talking that way to me. The idea of his taking the liberty of speaking that way. Oh, I feel as if I never could try to help anybody again."

"Now, Celia!" said Aunt Hannah, speaking rather sharply. "You must *not* talk that way. That wasn't Harry Knowles that spoke to you tonight. He swallowed a demon that took entire possession and put out the light of reason in him for a time. You told me yourself that he's always been respectful, and he's nothing but a boy in years, much younger than you. And, Celia, he's very dear to your Savior."

Aunt Hannah's heart had gone out to the poor motherless boy, and she longed to save him from the awful destruction she saw yawning in front of his path. Celia knew her aunt was right and by degrees regained her composure. She began to mount up into the first story at least of her faith and believe everything wasn't ruined yet.

But she went to the store the next morning with a heavy heart. She had a great horror of drunkards and drunkenness and a strong belief in the power of appetite. Thus she felt little or no hope in trying to save anyone from the awful end of a drunkard, who had once started on that downward path. She went about all day, feeling as deep a sadness as if she'd witnessed the terrible death of a friend.

Hannah spent a long time in prayer that night, after she knew Celia was asleep. She asked God's grace to help her do what was best for this poor homeless boy. If He honored her with bearing the message of salvation to his soul, she would give God all the glory. Her soul longed for the soul of the boy whose feet went astray, and she was filled with compassion for him, such as Jesus would have us feel, such as He felt, for those for whom He died.

The minister, meanwhile, had put the poor boy to bed. He was docile and almost grateful, in a maudlin sort of way, for the help given him, and he sank at once into a deep sleep. Horace Stafford turned the gas low and sat by the bedside for some time, until he felt certain nothing else was the matter with the slumberer. Then he knelt beside the boy and asked God's mercy for him and went to his own room.

Not until far into the afternoon did the sleeper rouse. Horace Stafford found out by judicious questioning and without revealing his condition to the other boarders (who fortunately hadn't heard the disturbance in the night) where the young man worked. He then went to the store and asked for the head of the firm, giving his own card and explaining that the young salesman was ill and unable to come to work that day.

The head of the firm was very kind. He recognized the minister's name as well as that of the mission chapel which he mentioned in introducing himself, doubtless thinking a minister's word might go further toward excusing the young man's absence. The man asked how the work was getting on. He said he'd meant to send in a contribution, but he let it slip by without attention. Then he handed the minister a crisp ten-dollar bill. He promised to see that young Knowles's place for the day was supplied; he also asked to be notified if the illness should prove serious and if he could do anything for him. He said he liked the young man, though of course he knew little about him. But he feared he didn't have good health, since he looked frail.

On leaving the store, Horace Stafford had a better opinion of employers than he'd received from some reading he'd done recently.

When Harry Knowles awoke that afternoon, he was conscious first of his physical condition. His head ached miserably, and he couldn't bear to move. His throat burned, and everything seemed ghastly and distorted. Opening his eyes, the first thing he saw was his mother's picture. It stood on the bureau opposite his bed. Hannah had gone softly about the room that morning, putting things to rights and putting a touch of home here and there where she could do it in a few minutes. She wiped the dust from the velvet and polished the glass in the frame with a damp cloth.

So the clear sweet eyes of Harry's mother looked straight into his, so full of love and compassion and motherly tenderness, that Harry felt it and suddenly realized his present condition and what had caused it. He couldn't bear his mother's tender love. She seemed to be looking into his very soul. He closed his eyes to shut hers out. As he did so, the previous night's experiences came to him one by one and then passed before his mother's eyes. He seemed to know at every instant what she would feel about it all.

He recalled his determination to stay in and how the boys coaxed him away from his determination and interested him in their evening plans. They planned an evening at the theater and a supper afterward. They said they thought him mean not to join in and help with the expenses; they'd presumed he was coming and ordered a seat and plate for him. They teased him unmercifully and said they believed he was going to Sunday school again and promised his nice little teacher he'd be good. They called him a "dear little fellow" and said they wouldn't bother him anymore.

He declared he had no intention of not joining them and bearing his share of expenses.

They seemed glad. "We didn't really believe you were getting to be a weak little boy," they said.

His conscience had no time to reproach him. They hadn't mentioned going to any of their favorite haunts for a game—that game he feared because it reduced his always scanty funds. They only seemed bent on having an innocent good time. Oh, they knew how to get him into it. They knew they could touch what he called his sense of honor, when they said he left them in a tight place; if he didn't pay for the supper they'd ordered, they'd have to.

And they took him to a play that was *very* funny. But one or two things toward the end brought a warm flush to his cheeks; he couldn't help thinking how ashamed his mother would be to know he was listening to and laughing at such things. But he wouldn't have the fellows know that. He went to the supper and was as jolly as any of them after it.

But he had determined, when he gave in to them, that he wouldn't drink. That was the main reason he declined. When people offered him a drink, he could always hear his mother's voice saying, "Harry, dear, I hope you'll always have the courage to say no, if you're ever asked to drink wine or any strong drink." He tried to make it right with his conscience when he turned to go with the boys, by saying he wouldn't drink a drop. He knew they'd ask him, and it would be uncomfortable to refuse. But he'd done it before, and he would do it tonight.

After tonight, he would try to drift away from that set. It wouldn't do to break off all of a sudden, but he'd try to do it gradually. Of course he could. Didn't he stay home that evening when Miss Murray fixed the lamp and again last night? Both times he'd promised to go with the boys. He felt strong with having conquered once before. He didn't remember a Bible verse then that his mother often quoted, "Let him that thinketh he standeth take heed lest he fall." He only told himself he'd proved he was fully able to break off going with those boys whenever he chose. Therefore he had a right to go with them for a little innocent fun just once more.

Ah, but he didn't know even now, as he lay in his bed with shame in his heart and tears of repentance in his eyes, that Satan had allied against him last night; that those boys had vowed to conquer his foolish protests once and for all and get him gloriously drunk. Let him break down that silliness, they said, and he'd be a jolly fellow, for Harry was bright and quick-witted.

Why they wanted to do it isn't quite certain. Perhaps some of them were fiendish enough to want to drag him down as low as they were, just for very love of deviltry. Others, perhaps, felt rebuked by his shrinking back from daring ideas; still others, older in their sin, liked him for his lively words and witty sayings and wanted to make him a thoroughly bad fellow they could enjoy. Their experience had taught them that when one like that goes astray, he'll dare more than some who never had scruples.

Harry only knew they'd passed some cider first. They declared they ordered it for his sake since they knew his temperance principles. As it was passed they laughed, nudged one another and winked, and Harry felt goaded to do almost anything to prove he was just as good, or as bad, as they were.

Now Harry wasn't fond of sweet cider. The few times he tasted it, it seemed insipid to him. He knew, indeed, that some people went so far as to object to cider drinking. In a general way, he knew there was a difference between sweet cider and hard cider; it would have been better for him that night if he'd formed a few definite opinions on the subject.

He hesitated and then took some. But the boys noticed his hesitation and asked him if he was afraid of that, too. He flushed crimson and declared he wasn't, and they unmercifully passed his glass for more and watched to see if he drank that.

Then something else was brought on—Harry didn't just know what, whether wine or beer or something else. The cider was by no means sweet and must have gone to his head. When they passed by his chair with the wine glasses, he caught the whispered words and laughs of his companions around him. Turning quick with only a thought to prove his—what, cowardice?—he ordered the waiter to give him some. A tremendous cheer rose from the boys, so loud it almost brought him to his senses. He drank that glass and another, and then he felt a feverish desire to swallow more. They filled his glass again and again, with him not asking or caring what it contained.

That was the story. He didn't know how he got here, to what he called home. He supposed it was in the same shameful way others were taken—the way that had before this provided a strong barrier to his joining in their drinking festivities. Whether anyone saw or knew, he didn't dare to ask. He only knew that he lay here, and his mother's eyes were over there; that God always seemed to be near his mother, and he didn't dare open his eyes again.

He heard the soft movement of a woman's dress and a light step. It seemed like his mother's. He could almost think as he lay here that this was his home and his mother was nursing him from some dreadful illness. Only this bed was hard. Oh, the shame and horror if this had happened at his dear old home with his mother in it. It would have killed her. He groaned aloud; then he heard that soft step again and wondered. Was he dead? Was this the—where? The judgment seat? For his mother surely was there and God! Oh—!

Chapter 15

Someone stood beside him and put a large cool hand on his aching brow. Then a woman's quiet, gentle voice said, "Drink this."

The thought of eating or drinking anything disgusted him, but he let himself be raised from the pillow and swallowed the hot steaming coffee held for him. Hannah Grant fluffed his pillows, and he settled back again with his eyes closed. He didn't care for the coffee; he wondered that he could have drunk it. Yet he knew by the aroma it was unlike any coffee he ever drank in that house. Gradually he felt relief from drinking it. The throbbing in his temples wasn't any less, but perhaps he could bear it a little better.

Hannah brought a clean linen cloth and a large soft towel and washed his hot face and hands, just as his mother had when he was sick. He didn't look at her. His eyes were closed tight, and he was trying with all his might to force back the hot tears burning their way out beneath his eyelashes. The tears came, and Hannah saw them.

She stooped and kissed him softly on his forehead and said in that gentle pitying voice again, "Poor boy!" Then she slipped away and left him alone.

If Hiram Bartlett were there he would have said Hannah was encouraging drunkenness by giving the young man so much attention; that pity wasn't what the fellow needed. Rather he should be soundly thrashed. He'd get an idea coming home drunk was fine, if he were petted and taken care of for it. But Hiram Bartlett wasn't there, and Hannah was glad. She did what she felt in her inmost soul Jesus Christ would have her do, if she could hear His voice telling her.

When she slipped away and left Harry alone, it was to tap lightly on the minister's door and tell him Harry was awake.

It wasn't the first time that day she'd gone to the minister's room. She'd resolved during the night to discover what sort of man she took in her first night. He seemed to be all right, and he'd helped nobly in this emergency. Now, if only he were a Christian, how much help he might be with this young man. She thought she could find out for herself without asking him; so instead of letting Molly clean his room the next morning, she did it herself.

She knew, if he were a Christian, she'd likely find evidence somewhere about his room. She was greatly pleased and somewhat surprised, therefore, when she saw not only the Bible in full view, but also a number of theological books. She glanced at the row of old familiar ones in rusty bindings, *Barnes's Notes* and other commentaries, standing against the wall on the floor. A soap box beside them contained other volumes still unpacked, and at the top lay two by F. B. Meyer and Andrew Murray's *With Christ in the School of Prayer*.

These were dear favorites and friends of hers, and she began to hope that perhaps she was entertaining a minister.

This hope was confirmed a few minutes later when the postman came and brought several letters for the Rev. Horace Stafford.

She made his bed and set the room in order with a light in her face then, for wasn't she serving one of the Master's messengers? When Mr. Stafford came in later, she had a short conference with him about young Mr. Knowles. They agreed he should go to the store and, after the young man awoke, talk with him.

Harry lay still, reviewing his miserable existence and the last few months of mistakes and sins. Suddenly it occurred to him it must be late and he ought to get up and go to work. With a moan he tried to get out of bed, but he was dizzy and sick and had to sit still and cover his eyes. He wasn't so used to dissipation that he could rise and go about like anyone else the next day, and the dissipation was deeper than he realized. What mixed or drugged glasses were given him, after he began to drink, he didn't remember. Thus he could scarcely account for the effect.

Just then he heard a knock at his door, and Horace Stafford entered. He'd been listening for some sound and was ready. He wanted to help the boy when he came to his senses and realized his condition, and try to keep him from rushing out to drink again. Of course, he knew nothing about Harry's past life, but he judged from his appearance and from what little he could learn of his character that this was probably his first experience, or if not the first, at least he wasn't a hardened sinner yet.

"Do you feel any better?" asked Horace in a pleasant, everyday tone.

Harry looked up, his bloodshot eyes and white face making a pitiful picture of wretchedness.

"I feel worse than I ever felt in my life," he answered, with his usual brightness gone entirely from his voice.

"Better lie down again," said the visitor. "You're hardly able to get up yet."

"But I must get up," said Harry in a despairing tone. "What time is it? It must be late. I'll get fired if I'm not on time. They're terribly particular down there."

"Never mind the time. You're not to go to the store today," answered the other quietly, in a tone that seemed used to commanding obedience.

"Why not?" asked Harry sharply, with sudden apprehension in his eyes. "Have they found out and sent me my walking papers already? What time is it? How long have I been here? Let me up. But it's no use if they've found out. I'm done for. I might as well go to destruction first as last." He sank back with a groan and turned his face to the wall.

"Listen, my boy," said the young minister, bending over him and placing a kind hand on his shoulder. "Don't say that. You're not going to destruction. We won't let you. And you don't need to feel like that. You haven't been dismissed. Your place is waiting for you when you can go back. The firm knows only that you're too ill to be at your work today. It's afternoon, and you've slept all day. Lie still now until you can get up. Is there anything you'd like to have?"

Harry turned over and opened his eyes in astonishment.

"How do you know I'm not to be dismissed? Has anyone been there?"

"Yes, I went this morning and had a good long talk with Mr. Prescott. He seemed very sympathetic and asked me to send him word if you weren't better tomorrow."

Harry closed his eyes and swallowed hard. He was almost overcome by this kindness. Suddenly, he remembered dimly the previous night's scene.

"Say," he said huskily, "where was I, that is—how, what did I—do? Who was down there last night when I came in? How did I get here?"

"I brought you up here," answered Horace quietly, in a matter-of-fact tone. "Miss Grant was present." He thought it was better for Harry not to know Celia was there; it would do no good and only add to his embarrassment. "You've slept ever since," he finished briefly.

"Were the boarders around? Do they know?"

"No."

There was silence a moment. Harry was trying to recall some faint memory. At last he spoke. "Didn't I—wasn't Miss Murray there too? Did I talk nonsense to her?"

The minister turned about and faced the young man. "Yes, she was there," he said truthfully, "and you didn't speak very respectfully to her, I must admit."

Harry groaned again. "Oh, she's been so kind to me." After a pause he added, "But they didn't turn me out of the house. If they turned me out I could stand it, but I can't stand being treated this way. I haven't been treated kindly since Mother died." Then his weakened nerves gave way, and he wept.

Horace Stafford let him cry for a few minutes. He thought it might do him good. He had no mind to minimize the offense. It was serious and must be realized.

Presently he talked in quiet tones, and the young man on the bed ceased moaning and showed he was listening. When he was calmer, Horace drew from him as much of the story of the evening before as he could remember. He talked with him seriously about life and the true meaning of it, about the wonderful trust God gave each one, when He put him upon the earth and gave him the responsibility of doing his best. He drew him on to speak of his mother and his boyhood life.

He didn't talk too long. This fisher of men was gifted with rare tact. He seemed to know what to say and when to say it and, what is sometimes more important, when to keep still. He gave just the right note of warning to the young man before him, but he knew enough of human nature to see at once that here was true repentance and deep humiliation and that the lesson didn't need to be impressed further this time. What he needed now was kind sympathy and help to get on his feet again.

Harry, in a pause, reverted to Celia. What should he do? He never could look her in the face again, and she'd been so kind to him.

"Tell her so," said Horace promptly, as if it were the easiest thing in the world. "Just beg her pardon as manfully as you can, and then look out that you'll never do so again."

The slender frame of the young man on the bed shook involuntarily as he said fiercely, "I should hope not."

There came Miss Grant's light tap at the door, and a tray was handed in. Harry thought to himself that he couldn't eat, that he could never eat again. But when the tray was placed in front of him, and the minister said in his quiet, commanding voice, "Now eat every bit of that," he found that he could.

Miss Grant knew by instinct just what to prepare for the invalid. Not pastries and jellies and confectionery. Just a small, thin, white china bowl of very strong soup, containing much nutrition in a small space and sending forth a delicious odor. She included some thin beautifully toasted slices of bread, a ball of sweet butter and more of that black aromatic coffee. The minister mentally decided that Miss Grant must be an expert in culinary art. Many women would have brought sour bread, muddy coffee, and a piece of dyspeptic pudding or pie or cake, or perhaps tried more substantial foods where there was no appetite.

He noted also the fine napkin covering the tray, the transparent china bowl and the silver spoon. The spoon looked old and thin as if it were an heirloom, but it was bright and unmistakably of aristocratic origin and pleasant to use.

He noticed these things because they were part of his former existence before he gave up his life to saving souls. Since he'd lived in boardinghouses, he sometimes missed them in a vague, undefined way. He didn't know he cared about these little refined accessories, but he was conscious of a friendly look in the spoon and bowl and fine linen. He didn't know these were among the very few bits of home Miss Grant brought with her and that she carefully hunted them out of an unpacked trunk; she felt that perhaps these dishes might help in saving that soul.

Nor was she wrong. Harry knew silver when he saw it. This supper seemed like one his mother would have prepared for him.

"Now, sir," said Horace. He lighted the gas and prepared to be cheerful while the young man ate his supper. "You must forget everything about this for awhile and just eat your supper and enjoy it." He laughed pleasantly.

Harry looked up with a wan smile and thanked him in his heart for lifting the heavy burden for a few minutes. Horace Stafford could talk, even if Harry just then could not. He showed he had no trouble in speaking the right thing at the right time. He told in detail the story of a young man he was interested in, who had a wife and young family dependent upon him; he was out of work and couldn't find a position. The minister had spent some time that day describing the different employers so well that once Harry forgot his own troubles and was beguiled into a laugh.

Passing the door, Celia heard them laughing, and one more wrinkle crept into her brow. She thought Mr. Stafford must be an odd minister to laugh with a young man who recently committed such a grave offense against the laws of God and society.

Poor Celia, she'd had a hard day, what with doing her own work and carrying in her heart the thought of Harry Knowles drunk. She didn't care more for that boy than she would have for any other. But it was the shock to her faith in human nature to find someone she believed to be at least tolerably good and interesting, suddenly appear in that condition. Young people are often prone to look upon their faith in human nature as something akin to their faith in God, something holy and religious, which if broken almost outrages their belief in the kindness of their God.

Perhaps this is why some sweet honest souls must pass through the fiery trial of believing in, even loving, some human brother or sister, only to find them utterly false. Such ones need to learn the lesson of George Herbert, that

> Even the greatest griefs
>> May be reliefs,
> Could he but take them right, and in their ways.
>> Happy is he whose heart
> Hath found the art
>> To turn his double pains to double praise.

Chapter 16

I t's my opinion," said Molly Poppleton, standing with her arms akimbo and facing Miss Hannah as she entered the kitchen one morning shortly after breakfast, "that them three-cent girls need tendin' to." She set her lips firmly and then returned to the polishing of her range.

Miss Hannah went on with her work. She was rubbing pumpkin through a colander and reducing it to the velvety texture she required in her pies. She waited calmly for Molly to go on with her reasons, as she knew she would. Molly finished the oven door and stood up again.

"Yes, they need tendin' to bad. If you'd just go up to their room once you'd find out. There's a stack of paper novels in their closet knee deep, an' there's pictures round that room of women from the-ay-ters, without much clo'es on, that are perfickly scand'lous. Besides, they've got a picture of them two took in a tintype down to Atlantic City with bathing suits on, an' two young fellers alongside of 'em without much on but a little underclo'es. They're grinning fit to kill and look real silly. No decent girls would have a picture took like that, let alone keep it round in sight afterward."

"Well, Molly, you know all girls haven't been brought up alike," said Miss Hannah, as she measured out the cinnamon and ginger. "Molly, bring me the big yellow bowl and the molasses jug."

"I should hope not," said Molly, as she put the jug down on the table with a thump and went back to her range. "Not like them, anyways. You don't know all. They have any amount of little pink and blue tickets lying round droppin' out of pockets and the like, an' I give that one they call Mamie one I picked up in the hall, thinkin' it was something valuable, an' she laughed an' said it was no good, just an old the-ay-ter ticket, been used. 'My land!' says I, not being able to keep still. 'If all them round your room is the-ay-ter tickets, you must've been an awful lot!' Then she giggled an' got red an' says, 'Yes, most every night now,' an' the one they call Carrie spoke up and says, 'Yes, she's got plenty of gentlemen friends, Molly, an' so have I,' an' then they both laughed and went out.

"Now I s'pose it ain't none of my business, but I must say them girls ought to be back with their mothers. They can't be over fifteen a day, or sixteen anyway. They ought to be in bed every night by nine o'clock. They ain't fit to sit at the same table with Miss Celia with their messy hair and dirty teeth and fingernails. The fact is, I'd like to give 'em both a good bath anyway."

Molly slammed out of the kitchen, and Miss Hannah heard her sweeping the dining room with all her might and main.

She went on measuring the milk, beating the eggs, fashioning the flaky crust in the pie pans and thinking. She was troubled about those two girls herself. She felt they needed a great deal of help and so far she couldn't approach them. They seemed shy and uncomfortable when she came near them, and they grew silent at the table, too, unless the tenor brakeman was present. Then the three carried on a bantering conversation in suppressed tones, with glances toward the others.

Hannah wondered why she couldn't reach the hearts of some people around her. It was just so with Nettie; she never could make any headway in training that child. As a little girl, she was sullen and silent when her aunt corrected a fault, and as a young woman she was impertinent and cold for days after any attempt by Aunt Hannah to change her plans. With Hiram, too, she felt the same repellent influence. She wondered why she couldn't reach their hearts in any way, though she prayerfully and conscientiously longed to be to these people what God wanted her to be.

Now these two girls weighed heavily upon her. She'd watched them for days and determined to make some move pretty soon. She felt sure they needed help urgently, far beyond what Molly had bluntly expressed. And while Aunt Hannah weighed and measured and baked and thought, she was developing a plan for the salvation of Mamie Williams and Carrie Simmons.

She'd noticed Mamie several times lately when Celia came to the table, and she knew she watched Celia intently and admired her from a distance—at least she admired her as far as outward appearance was concerned. Even during the few weeks since Aunt Hannah had come to Philadelphia, she noticed the gradual change in Mamie's dress, from fussy and frivolous, to more subdued and neat. She reduced the baggy bunches of frizzy hair that used to project over her forehead and loop far down over her ears, till they were more like Celia's graceful braids with a stray curl slipping out here and there. Other little changes about her showed she was to a certain extent making Celia a model.

Aunt Hannah's brow cleared. She thought she knew a way to Mamie's heart and perhaps through hers to Carrie's. Celia had an influence, and she could help. But how to bring that about in the wisest way was her puzzle, for Celia was disgusted with the actions of the two "three-centers," as she called them. She never acknowledged them, and her dignified bearing at the table was always meant to rebuke them. Celia didn't like the two girls. She was willing for their lives to be more comfortable by the good food her aunt gave Mrs. Morris's old boarders. But Celia wouldn't have felt badly if they left, so their places might be occupied by more interesting people.

Celia was getting to be a puzzle anyway. She didn't enter into some things as her aunt thought she would. Instead she remained aloof and seemed troubled about something. She didn't even make friends with the young minister, though Aunt Hannah saw growing possibilities of a valued friendship for them all. They talked together on topics of mutual interest, and he'd shown he was a man of culture and education.

Aunt Hannah wasn't a matchmaker and didn't immediately think of every young man in the light of a possible husband for her niece. But she did have ambitions that Celia might have friends who'd be helpful to her, both spiritually and mentally. She felt that such a friendship, though nothing more than occasional conversation on some literary theme, would be excellent for the young girl whose ambitions and abilities were so far beyond her opportunities.

But Celia only smiled and remained quiet and distant. She told her aunt that the young minister belonged to her, and she mustn't expect her niece to take him on faith. Nevertheless, she knew that Horace Stafford's slightest movement or word at the table didn't escape Celia. She was evidently measuring him.

Celia didn't enter heartily into the plans made for Harry Knowles. She did what she was told, but she didn't make plans herself. She seemed to have received a setback on the night when Harry came home drunk.

There was much to do in the evening, however, and her aunt hadn't had time to have a good long talk with her. She felt it should come at once. She put the pies in the oven and closed the oven door carefully. Then, glancing at the clock, she went to her own room to kneel, as was her custom when perplexed, and lay her trouble at her Master's feet.

She returned to her work around the house with a calm brow and an untroubled heart, feeling sure the way would be opened and words given her, if she must speak. She bent her sweet, thoughtful face to her work, her mind busy with the problems of souls, while she worked with her hands to feed their bodies. It was like a revelation of what God can do in a human soul through sorrow, to look at Hannah Grant and think of her past life and its buried and risen joys.

Methinks we do as fretful children do,
    Leaning their faces on the windowpane
To sigh the glass dim with their own breath's stain,
    And shut the sky and landscape from their view.
And thus, alas! since God, the Maker, drew
    A mystic separation 'twixt those twain,
The life beyond us, and our souls in pain,
    We miss the prospect which we're called unto
By grief we're fools to use. Be still and strong,
    O man, my brother! hold thy sobbing breath
And keep thy soul's large window pure from wrong,
    That so, as life's appointment issueth,
Thy vision may be clear to watch along
    The sunset consummation-lights of death.

"Auntie, who's the young man in the parlor smelling so of Hoyt's German cologne and cigarette smoke?" asked Celia cheerfully, coming into her aunt's room just after dinner that night. "You opened the door for him. I hope he's not a new boarder, for I'm certain he wouldn't be any help. I think we have enough heathen to work for at present, don't you? Now don't tell me you called me up to ask my permission to take in that oily-looking fellow, Aunt Hannah."

Aunt Hannah laughed and then grew serious.

"No, dear, not that," she said. Then she drew the little rocker close beside her own and said, "Sit down, dear. I want to talk to you."

"Why, Aunt Hannah, what have I done that's naughty?" asked Celia, pretending to be scared. "This sounds like old times." But she settled herself comfortably and nestled her head lovingly on her aunt's shoulder.

"Well, then, first of all, Celia, why do you act so strange sometimes, and what's the matter with Mr. Stafford? You and he ought to be friends, and he could help much in the work you planned for us to do together. You seem to have lost your interest in the house and everything in it, and I don't understand it. You could do a great deal and should at once, and you don't seem to care to do it."

"Why, Aunt Hannah, what does the minister have to do with it all? I'm afraid you're mistaken about him as a helper. In fact I know you are. I'd just come home that night—the night after Harry was drinking, you know—and was passing the door. I heard Mr. Stafford's laugh, and then I heard Harry laugh, too. I couldn't help hearing Mr. Stafford telling a funny story to Harry as I went on up the hall. Now just think of that after what happened. A fine minister he is. He should have been preaching a sermon."

"Celia! Take care how you judge without knowing. You can't tell what the moral of the funny story was or if the Lord could use a laugh just then to help that young man better than anything else. He doubtless put it into His servant's heart to know that. I believe that man has rare tact in winning souls. Be careful, and be slow to criticize a minister's actions. Some think his office brings him nearer to God than most men."

Celia's cheeks flushed a little. She was slightly annoyed to have her aunt speak in that way, but she respected the older woman's opinion too much to resent the words or refuse the lesson.

After a moment she said, "Well, Aunt Hannah, maybe I've been wrong. I'll try to be good."

Celia had another reason in her heart for her dignified coldness toward the minister. After a few days, she recognized he was a man of unusual education and refinement. She immediately wondered whether he looked down on her, a saleswoman in a store, a poor girl who had to earn her own living. She decided he probably did in a certain undefined way, though he probably didn't confess such things to himself; it might have conflicted with certain Christian theories he felt himself bound to abide by.

She'd show him she never expected anything in the way of courtesy even from him and that she was one girl who wasn't ready to fling herself at any desirable young man who was thrown into her neighborhood. She was strengthened further in her determination by a little occurrence one evening a few days before this talk with her aunt.

The minister had gone to prayer meeting, after being engaged in his room all day. Aunt Hannah couldn't finish dusting and straightening things as thoroughly as she desired. In the evening she was busy with kitchen work and asked Celia to slip up there when the halls were quiet and finish the dusting.

Celia turned up the gas and worked in earnest, glancing with interest at the books over the little table against the wall. She wished she had an opportunity to look at them, but she wouldn't even touch them, except to do her necessary work, in their owner's absence. When she came to the bureau she had to remove some things to wipe the dust beneath them. A Bible was lying there open before a painted miniature of a lovely young woman. The pictured face was so beautiful that she could only look at it again as she carefully wiped the dust from the velvet and gold case. The blue eyes and golden hair and the sweet intellectual face stayed in her memory. Because the miniature stood open before his Bible, she judged it was someone quite near and dear.

Celia didn't reason it out in words, but she thought she should maintain a womanly dignity. As her aunt talked, however, she saw she carried this feeling to an extreme. What was it to her what the young man thought or how many velvet-framed girls he carried in his pocket next to his heart? She was in the same house with him and must treat him with Christian courtesy, nor did she need to make herself prominent before his eyes. She would try to do differently. After this he'd be like the other boarders to her.

"What else, auntie?" she asked, after a minute.

"Harry, next," her aunt said. "You ought to interest him in something occasionally, as you once told me you did with the lamp. He's struggling to keep away from those companions who are after him every day now, Mr. Stafford says. He does all he can for him. But his meetings occupy so many evenings that he can do very little, and he hasn't thought it wise to try to take him to church yet. You know he's nothing but a boy. He wants to be interested in something."

"Yes," said Celia, "I know. I'll try. But, auntie, I can't forget how he looked that night." She shuddered. "But I'll try to get up something to help and that right away. Now what else? You always save the worst till last. Which is it? Miss Burns or the tenor brakeman? Or—oh, *auntie*, now it *isn't* those three-centers! Don't tell me to try to do something for them, for I can't." The girl put up her hands in mock horror.

Aunt Hannah detailed to her what she knew of them, including an account of Molly's moralizing on the subject. Celia laughed and then grew serious.

A call to the kitchen came for Miss Hannah then, and she left Celia thinking. When she returned a few minutes later she was greeted with: "Aunt Hannah, are those boards still in the cellar? Are they any use there? Because if they're not I'm going to make a cozy corner in the parlor if you don't object. I've thought of a beautiful way. Harry will help, I'm sure. He sat in the parlor looking glum when I came up. Do you suppose I must get the three-centers to help? Would they come, do you think? And, by the way, who did you say that oily youth in the parlor was?"

"His name, he said, was Clarence Jones, and he asked for Miss Simmons. I called her, and I think she went out with him, for I don't see either of them around. I don't know whether Mamie Williams is in her room or not. I think it would be good to see. By all means make as many cozy corners as you please, dear, and the boards are of no use to me."

Celia departed to find her helpers, and Hannah locked the door and prayed for them before she set to darning some tablecloths.

Chapter 17

Now, Harry, where are you going?" said Celia, with dismay in her voice. She was running down the stairs and saw the young man with his overcoat on and his hat in his hand just opening the door.

He started and looked guilty as she spoke. He'd been sitting in the parlor for an hour trying to keep himself in the house and away from an especially alluring evening the boys had held out as bait. It was one, too, which seemed, from their account of it, to be perfectly harmless.

He hesitated and stammered out, "Nowhere, I guess." Then he laughed and sat down in the hall chair. "Is there anything I can do for you, Miss Murray? For some reason, I don't quite know what to do with myself tonight."

Celia's heart filled with pity for the lonely fellow and with remorse that she hadn't attempted to do something sooner to cheer him up.

"Oh, I'm so sorry," she said earnestly, with a ring of truth in her voice which he recognized at once. "But if you're lonesome and really have nothing pressing to do, why, come and help me carry out a plan. I'm going to make a cozy corner in the parlor. In fact, I think I'll make two, one in the bay window and one over there by the organ. Will you help? You're such a good carpenter, and this parlor looks so bare and desolate."

"All right, I'm with you," answered the young man. "Just tell me what to do. I don't know the first thing about cozy corners, but if you know as much as you did about lamps, they'll be a success. Let's have a half dozen of 'em. What'll I do first?"

"Bring that lamp and come down into the cellar. Wait, I don't know whether you can do it alone; they're pretty heavy and are a good many. Perhaps Mr. Hartley or Mr. Osborn would help a minute in bringing up the boards. I'll show you what we want first, and then you can pick out the right boards. I want a good firm seat here in the bay window to fill the whole place to the edge of the window frames either side, just a foot from the floor. Then I want another over here, to reach from here to here, so wide, and the same height from the floor. Here's my tape measure. Now you can pick out your lumber."

Celia moved about the dull parlor, furnishing it with gesture and imagination, till the young carpenter was quite interested. He called the two young men upstairs, who came willingly and helped for a few minutes, showing not a little interest and curiosity in the undertaking. They all lingered with advice and offers to help. When Celia saw the carpentry work well started, she ran upstairs and knocked at the door of the two young girls.

"Come in," drawled the voice of someone chewing.

Celia hesitated, then entered.

Mamie Williams lay across the foot of the bed, with the two pillows and a comforter under her head, the gas turned as high as it would go and a paper-covered volume in her hand. She was chewing gum. When she saw Celia, her tone of indifference changed to one of pleased surprise. She sat up quickly and hid her book under the pillows. Then she put her hand up to straighten her hair.

"Why, it's you!" she exclaimed.

From the evident pleasure her visit gave, Celia knew her aunt's conjecture that this girl admired her was true. This unbent Celia still more, and she tried to be winning.

"We're having some fun downstairs fixing up that old barn of a parlor," she explained, still standing by the door, though her hostess had slipped from the bed and cleared a chair from a pile of clothing thrown upon it. "I thought maybe you'd like to help. Is your friend here?"

"No, she ain't; she's gone out with a gentleman friend," said Mamie, with a conscious giggle. "It's a wonder you found me in. I'm mostly out when she is. Sit down, can't you? I'm really glad you come up. I was lonesome. The book I had wasn't any account either. What did you say you were doing?"

Celia explained and succeeded in interesting Mamie so that she hunted out her thimble from a mass of ribbons and collars tumbled into a bureau drawer and went downstairs to see what was going on. She confessed, though, that she wasn't much used to doing things like that.

They went to work in earnest. Celia had some printed burlap she brought home from the store one night to make curtains for an improvised clothespress in her room. It was cheap, and there was plenty of it. The clothespress could wait. Those cozy corners must be finished tonight, at least as far as possible. She gave the tick of the cushions to Mamie to run the seams, while she sewed the burlap cover for it.

Meanwhile, the hammering and sawing and directing went forward. By half past nine when Horace Stafford opened the front door and came in, two very solid-looking rough wooden shelves stood a foot from the floor in the parlor. One occupied the entire bay window space in the front of the room, and the other one was at the further end of the room. To the sides of this Harry Knowles was just nailing some more boards to serve as ends, under the supervision of the other two young men. Celia and Mamie were on their knees in front of the bay window tacking the dark blue burlap printed in a heraldic design, in a pleated valance. A nearly completed cushion lay beside them on the floor.

Mr. Stafford was attracted by the unusual noises and, entering the room, surveyed the work a moment. Celia turned from the valance then and was trying to thread a large needle with a cord. She vainly endeavored to pull its short proportions through the thick cushion, which had been stuffed with excelsior and a layer of cotton on the top.

"You need an upholsterer's needle for that, Miss Murray," he said quietly.

"I think I have one upstairs that we used in fixing up the pulpit chairs at the mission. I'll go and get it."

Celia was pleased he offered to help and thanked him. As he turned toward Harry, he said, "Knowles, why don't you put springs in? It would be twice as comfortable."

"Springs!" said Harry, jumping up and turning around. "Do you expect us to turn into upholsterers the first night?" He laughed good-naturedly.

"No, but it isn't difficult," explained the minister. "You just have to tie them down firmly. I'll show you if you don't mind running out with me to that little upholsterer's around the corner. I think it's still open. It was when I came by. The people live over the store, and they don't close early."

"Yes, let's do have springs," answered Celia to Harry's look of enquiry. "I didn't hope for that much luxury, but we'll take what we can get." Her cheeks had grown red with excitement, and her eyes were shining.

The minister, as he turned to go on his self-appointed errand, was reminded of the first evening he came. He and Harry soon returned with several sets of springs, and the three young men, with Celia quietly in the background, took a lesson in putting in springs. They found it wasn't so difficult after all. The minister didn't forget to get some small dark blue cotton upholstery buttons when he was out, and Mamie and Celia soon learned how to use the odd double-pointed needle and tie the cushion with the little buttons. Altogether it looked very pretty and quite like real upholsterer's work when it was finished.

In spite of the proverbial "many hands" and "light work," it was nearly eleven o'clock when the two seats were finished and a light framework over the seat in the back end of the parlor erected. Aunt Hannah came down to send them all to bed and found them enthusiastic to see their work completed.

Celia had remembered she had two or three pieces of plain and printed denim and some turkey red calico. Mounted on the stepladder beside the canopy frame, she deftly draped the rough wood. Horace Stafford seemed to understand what she wanted to do and could drape a graceful fold of cloth, if he *was* only a man and that a minister. He contributed a Chinese sword made of coins and hung it above the drapery. This roused the others to emulate his example.

The university student thought he knew where he could get a couple of Arabic spears to help out the canopy drapery, and Harry Knowles declared he'd hunt around and find one of those dull old filigree bull's-eye lanterns that hang by long chains from the center. Mamie said her contribution should be a couple of sofa pillows, and Celia promised to make some more.

Miss Burns walked in just then looking weary and worn. She brightened as she entered the parlor and exclaimed over the new furnishings. "They're simply—*fine*—aren't they, Miss Grant? Indeed they *are!* What wonderful taste and skill here! I declare it's simply marvelous! Indeed it is!" she giggled wearily. She asked permission to contribute a pillow also.

"Now we need a low bookcase running along that wall and turning that corner," said the minister, as they turned to go to their rooms. "Can't you manage that, Knowles?"

Celia's eyes sparkled over the idea. The minister evidently understood esthetics anyway. The bookcase would be a great addition.

She'd almost forgotten her three-cent protegee, till Mamie squeezed her hand over the stair railing and said, "Good night, Miss Murray. I've enjoyed myself ever so much. And say, would you mind coming to my room a few minutes tomorrow night? I want to ask you some very particular questions."

Celia promised readily enough, though the prospect wasn't a pleasant one. She'd made up her mind to try to help this girl, however, so she might as well accept the situation and the opportunity together.

But Aunt Hannah sat up that night till nearly one o'clock and looked over the stair railing till she heard the night key click and saw the befeathered hat of Carrie Simmons as she came airily in.

"Poor child!" murmured the watcher, as she turned out the hall light and went to bed. "Something must be done! Out till one o'clock and with that kind of young man!"

The next morning she noticed that Carrie had dark rings under her eyes and was developing thin, sharp lines about her nose and mouth, which didn't add beauty to her pert, weak face.

The next evening Celia started for Mamie Williams's room. Carrie had again left with the same youth.

Aunt Hannah called to her. "Celia, dear, two things," she said, with her hand on Celia's arm. "Don't forget to pray before you go, and if you get a chance mention soap and water."

Celia laughed and said, "All right, auntie," and returned to her room to take the first advice.

Reinforced by turning her heart to her heavenly Father for guidance, she went to her unpleasant task, with her mind nearly full of the new bookcase and some other plans she had for adorning the parlor. The minister and Harry Knowles left immediately after dinner, so she had no one to help her carry out any parlor schemes at present. She couldn't help being disappointed she must turn aside to another piece of work.

Mamie was evidently expecting her this time. She'd given the room some semblance of order—that is, she picked up Carrie's store dress from the floor where she left it and tumbled everything that was out of place on the bureau and table into a drawer.

She seemed to be in earnest and plunged at once into her subject after she seated Celia.

"Say, I thought maybe you wouldn't mind telling me how you do it. You're not any prettier than I am, and you haven't got expensive clo'es, but you manage somehow to look awful stylish and pretty in spite of it. I know it takes a knack, but don't you think I could learn? I've tried ever since you came here to do my hair the way you do, but I can't make it act right. Maybe you wouldn't mind doing it a few times for me to get me started, and perhaps you could tell me what the difference is between you and me. I know it ain't very polite to ask you things like this, but I thought you was so kind last night asking me to help that I'd just be bold and ask you. You ain't mad, are you?"

Celia ignored the doubtful compliments and tried to smile, although her soul shrank within her. Handle the coarse greasy hair of that girl who seemed actually dirty to her? How could she? Surely the Lord didn't require that sacrifice. Why did she undertake this task anyway? It was *dreadful*. She half rose from her chair, as she foresaw the magnitude of this proposition. What mightn't she be asked to do? Then she remembered whose she was and whom she served and sank back in her chair, sending up a petition for help to her heavenly Father.

What is prayer? . . .
    'Tis the telegraphic cord,
Holding converse with the Lord;
    'Tis the key of promise given
Turning in the lock of heaven.

Chapter 18

D o you think I'm too homely to fix up?" asked Mamie anxiously, since her visitor didn't respond at once.

"Oh, no, indeed!" said Celia, laughing. "I was only trying to think how to answer you, and it's so funny for you to want to copy me. I've never tried to be 'pretty' as you call it. I only tried to be clean and neat and have things look as nice as I could without spending much money. But now that you've asked me, if you really want to know how you could improve your appearance, in my eyes at least, I'll try to tell you a few things. What troubles you most? We'll start with that."

"Oh, my sakes!" Mamie said with a giggle. "There's so many things. Well, my hands and my feet. They're so big and in the way. My hands are red and rough and bony, and my face is always breaking out in little ugly black pimples, and my hair won't get into any shape I want it to. My teeth aren't pretty, and then of course my clothes, and I just *wish* I could walk across a room like you," she finished with a sigh.

Celia smiled cheerfully. "Your hands," she said, "let me see them."

She turned up the gas and surveyed them a moment, while Mamie waited in breathless anxiety comparing her red, beringed fingers to Celia's small white ones.

"Well, if I were you I'd take all those rings off first," said Celia. "They look gaudy and out of place, except perhaps on a woman in society, and even then I'd prefer to see just one or two at a time, and not a whole jewelry store at once."

Mamie looked disappointed. She pulled them off slowly. "I thought they were pretty," she said, with dismay in her voice. "Don't you like any rings?"

"Not for young girls—unless they mean something. Do you have any with tender associations?"

"Some," Mamie said, looking self-conscious.

"Which one?" she asked, ignoring or not understanding the girl's answer. "Did your mother or father or brother or sister give it to you?"

Mamie blushed. "Well, yes, I've got one Ma give me, but it isn't any of them. It's a little plain gold thing, looks kind of out of style now. I don't wear it anymore."

"I'd wear that one," said Celia, "and put the others away. You're too young for strangers to give you rings to wear. Now about training those hands, I can give you some little exercises they gave me when I was taking music lessons, which I think help the hands to be graceful. First, if I were you, I'd go into the bathroom and give them a good washing in hot soapsuds, finishing off with cold water. That'll make them more pliable. Do you have a nailbrush? You ought to have one. There's nothing like it for making the nails look rosy. I suppose you have a hard time keeping them clean, with working all day, don't you? I do. But a nailbrush makes the work much easier. I'd cut the nails more in this shape if I were you, see?" Celia held out one seashell-tipped hand to be inspected.

When the hands were duly scrubbed, Celia gave her a short lesson in Delsarte, an exercise for each joint of the finger and hand. Mamie's eyes sparkled, and she proved herself an apt pupil.

"Now," said Celia, "practice that, but be sure you never do it where anyone can see you. It'll have its effect on your movements in time, but never practice in public. Don't think about your hands. That's best. If they're clean they'll take care of themselves, and the more you think about them and think how awkward they are, the more awkward they become.

"Didn't you ever try to make people on streetcars stop staring at you by looking at their feet? Well, you ought to try it some time. It's very funny. I've been annoyed once or twice by somebody staring at me till I was very uncomfortable. I remembered what I read somewhere and looked down at their feet as if I was very interested in them. They soon took their eyes from me and began to draw their feet back out of sight and to fidget around and wonder what was the matter with their shoes."

Mamie laughed and looked at her new teacher with admiration. She decided she was mistaken in saying Celia wasn't pretty.

"Now the complexion," began Celia again in a businesslike tone. "Your general health will affect that. You shouldn't eat much fat or sweets for one thing, and you ought to bathe all over every day and rub your skin till it's glowing. That'll make a great difference in the complexion. How often do you bathe?"

"Oh, my!" gasped Mamie. "I do hate to take a bath. Why, Ma used to scrub us children all around once a week, and I s'pose I'd ought to keep that up. But sometimes I skip a week; it's so dreadful cold in the morning."

"Well, if I were you I'd bathe every day, for awhile anyway. You don't know what good it'll do you, and after a while you'll get to love it. Once a week you ought to wash thoroughly with warm water and plenty of soap and finish off with a cold dash and a good hard rub. Then every morning sponge off in cold water and rub your skin well. That'll make your complexion very different. Then I'd give the face some treatment of hot and cold water. Wash it in water just as hot as you can stand it every morning and then in very cold. That'll give your cheeks some color, too, I think. As for your teeth, let me see them. Oh, Mamie, it's too bad to let such nice even teeth get into such a condition. They're hopelessly black, and you can't get them white yourself. Do you brush them every day after every meal?"

"My land, no!" exclaimed Mamie. "What an awful nuisance that would be! I only had a toothbrush once, and Carrie used it to scrub the ink off her fingers when she was going to the theater."

Celia could scarcely repress the exclamation of disgust that rose to her lips on this announcement, but Mamie was too interested in her own words to hear.

"Don't you think I could ever do anything with my teeth?"

"Why, yes, you must go to a dentist at once and have them attended to. They need a good cleaning. While you're there you should have him go over your teeth and put them in first-class order. It doesn't pay to let your teeth go before you're a woman yet. He'll tell you how to take care of them. You shouldn't eat much candy or chew gum. That injures the teeth."

"Oh!" said Mamie, in despair. "You don't have much fun, do you, if you try to do all them things? But I don't mind, for I want to look pretty, an' I'm willin' for it all, if it'll do any good."

Celia's pulses quickened. If this girl would do so much for outward adorning, perhaps she might persuade her sometime to do as much for the beautiful inward adorning of a meek and quiet spirit which in God's sight is worth much.

"Then your hair," Celia continued, "needs to be washed often. I'd wash it first with powdered borax in the water. It isn't good to use borax often, for it makes the hair so brittle it breaks. But it'll take out the extra oil now, and that's what you need. Then it'll need to be thoroughly rinsed and dried and combed. After that you can do almost anything you want to with it. I'll let you watch me do mine once, and then you'll see how it's done. That's the best way to learn.

"And then about your dress—why, that's a long subject. You'll need to take a lot of time for that. You'll have to decide things one at a time. One rule I go by, in buying. I never buy a thing that's in the very extreme of fashion. For one reason it'll look odd very soon, and for another it's sure to be poor material or else very expensive. It's always best to get good material. The plainer things are, the better, you can be sure, as a general rule. Then you should study your complexion and eyes and buy things to become you. You'll excuse me, if I mention the necktie you have on. I don't think you should ever wear that color. Cerise may be becoming to some people with dark eyes and very brown hair. Dark blue would be more becoming to you. Then, too, I think a necktie is an unbecoming thing on you anyway. You'd look much better in a close, round collar."

Mamie looked down at her cherished silk scarf; she went without new stockings for some time to buy it. Her mind was like the maiden's our grandmothers used to tell about, who said: "I ken wear my palm leaf and go barefooted, but I *must* have a buzzom pin."

Celia's zeal was perhaps about to get the better of her wisdom. She was growing interested in making over this girl as her aunt was interested in making over Mrs. Morris's boardinghouse. She forgot that a long line of prejudices must be overcome before the girl would be willing to walk in a different way, even though she asked to be directed in that path. It would look thorny to her at first.

"Mamie," she said, seeing the downcast expression on the young girl's face, "don't get discouraged with all these new things. You can't do them all right at first. But, do you know, I think it makes a great difference when people try to be and look the best that's in them. You mustn't think you're a homely looking girl. You're not. You were meant to be pretty, and I think you can make yourself look ever so much prettier—I do indeed. Now I wonder if you'd be willing to do something just to please me."

"Why, of course I would!" said Mamie, readily enough and brightening up at the encouraging words. "What is it? You've been awful kind to me, and I won't forget it, Miss Murray."

"Well, then, it's this. Out in Cloverdale, where I used to live, I belonged to a little society. We each promised to try and get up another band where we were going, even if we could get only one other person to join it. Now I was wondering if you wouldn't join it to start my new circle? We called ourselves the Bible Band. I believe there are a good many such bands all over the country. We have this little gold badge. Isn't it pretty?" Celia held out a tiny scarf pin with a pendant gold heart, on which the letters *B.B.* were engraved. "If you'll join us, I'll give you my pin, and I can send and get another."

Mamie grew interested as soon as she saw the pin. Jewelry of all sort was attractive to her. It would be quite delightful to appear in the store with a new pin on, engraved with mysterious letters, and let the girls and young men try to guess what they meant. Of course she didn't need to tell them if she didn't want to.

She asked again what would be required of her. Mamie belonged to the group, however, from which come so many untrue members of the Christian Endeavor societies and, sad to say, of the church. They're eager and willing to join anything and don't care what obligations or solemn vows they take—or break. To such, indeed, might apply the many and various arguments against making promises or taking pledges, not because promise making or pledge taking is bad, but because those who do so don't understand the solemnity of their vows.

Mamie cared very little what pledge she took, so long as she might perform it in private and at her own discretion. She didn't stop to think long but accepted the card and donned the pin with pride, thanking Celia.

"I ain't much of a hand at prayin', Miss Murray. I never could think of anything to say when I was a little girl, and Ma used to make us say our prayers every Saturday night. I guess I could learn a prayer and say the same one every time, if that would do. You write me out one, can't you? 'Course I'll do it to please you; you've been so good to me, and I'm awfully obliged for this pin.

It's a beauty, and won't I have fun tomorrow at the store with it?

"Say, I don't mind telling you why I want all this fixin' up to be pretty. You won't tell Carrie, will you? I wouldn't have her know, 'cause before you know it you'd see her settin' up to the same thing. Why, there's a new boss at the store. The head of the firm's going out to Chicago, and he's put this feller, Mr. Adams, Harold Adams his name is, in at the head. He's only just nineteen or twenty, though he made them think he was twenty-one; but he's dreadful smart. His father's been at the head of a three-cent store in Baltimore for a long time, and he kind of growed up in the business. He's handsome, too, and everybody likes him, and the girls will just stand on their heads to please him. He's been payin' me attention for four weeks now, takin' me to theaters and gettin' me flowers and candy.

"All the other girls was hoppin' mad. They've just done everything they could to get him to look at them, but he never did till a new girl came to the china teacup counter. She has gold hair and must paint her cheeks. She's awful stylish and has the littlest mite of a waist, and he's just gone clean crazy over her. He's still nice to me, but she gets half the flowers now, and I want to get him back. I don't mind telling you I'm in love with him myself, and of course I ain't willin' to just give him up without tryin'. So I made up my mind if I could get to be good-lookin' an' stylish, maybe I could do something."

Before Celia had time to collect her thoughts and say something in response to this startling disclosure, she heard a hurried knock at the door and Molly Poppleton's strong voice demanding, "Is Miss Celia there? Miss Hannah wants her right away bad. That old lady upstairs's got a fainting spell. She says to come right away."

Celia dropped everything and ran. She wondered afterward if the heavenly Father arranged that call at just that moment to prevent her from saying anything to Mamie. She felt sure if she'd said what was on her mind then, it might have proved, for the sake of her influence on the girl, the wrong words.

Blind unbelief is sure to err,
    And scan his work in vain;
God is His own interpreter,
    And He will make it plain.

Chapter 19

Old Mrs. Belden was made comfortable at last. She'd apparently worked too hard for the last three weeks, sitting up far into the night to finish an order. She knitted fancy hoods, sacques, socks, and mittens. Miss Grant, while she ministered to her, heard a feeble account of the poor soul's life. Her husband and children were dead, except one boy who was a sailor and might be dead, too, for she hadn't heard from him for over four years. She resorted to the only thing she knew how to do to earn her living. It was hard work sometimes, though, perhaps, no harder than many other women had to do.

She was very thankful for the good food that came with Miss Grant's arrival. She murmured her gratitude in an apologetic way for everything that was done for her and said she didn't see why they made so much trouble; they might just as well have let her slip quietly away, if it had been the Lord's will. Her life wasn't worth much anyway, and she was only making a lot of trouble that may have to be done over again soon.

Aunt Hannah and Celia looked around the room and resolved to bring in more comforts before another night. When she was at last ready for sleep, and they felt sure she only needed a good rest to be restored to her usual health, they left her. Molly's room was next to Mrs. Belden's, so she promised to sleep with one ear open and step in occasionally to check on the older lady.

After she and her aunt went to their room for the night, Celia sat down on the bed and rested her forehead on the footboard.

"Aunt Hannah," she said, "I'm discouraged. I have so many things to worry about in the world and don't see how I can keep from it."

"Celia! Celia!" said her aunt, laying her hand on the brown head bent on the footboard. "Is my little girl questioning God's wisdom? You sound like a little child who thinks his parents cruel because they won't give him fire to play with. Remember that God knows all and does everything for good. That old lady may need the kind of thing she's going through now to fit her for heaven. I don't know whether she's getting ready for heaven or not. Maybe God had to call her to Himself by taking all her dear ones first, or maybe she's set to help someone else—perhaps you. Does my little girl doubt Him because she can't see and understand? Oh, Celia, don't grieve Him."

"Well, auntie, I didn't mean all that, of course; but I'm so tired and disheartened. I meant to try to plan a grill work for the parlor tonight, and I couldn't find Harry at all. I'm afraid he's gone out again with those dreadful fellows. What's the use in trying to do anything with setbacks all the time?"

"But your heavenly Father had another plan for you tonight, and the parlor can wait. As for Harry, I think he's safe in his room by this time. He went out with the minister. And while you were up with Mrs. Belden they came in with a lot of boards and screws and a saw and hammer and a pot of varnish, and then worked hard. The other young men went down and helped, and in the morning I think you'll find something new in the parlor. Didn't you smell new varnish? They asked for you before they began, but I told them how you were occupied and said I was sure you'd want them to go ahead and not wait for you."

Celia sat up and smiled through her tears. "Did they really, auntie? How nice! What did they make? A bookcase? I'm sure it must have been that, for Mr. Stafford spoke of it and asked me if I didn't like the low kind running around the room. I'm so glad. And Harry stayed in! I was so afraid for him."

She brushed away the tears and began to take down her hair, when she remembered another discouragement.

"Oh, Aunt Hannah," she said, "you don't know what an utter failure my three-cent enterprise was." She gave a detailed account of her visit with Mamie Williams.

Aunt Hannah listened intently, sometimes laughing with Celia and sometimes looking grave over possible danger for the girl, which perhaps the younger woman hardly understood. When Celia finished, her aunt's face was serious.

"Celia, dear, you've made a good beginning. Your first trial was by no means a failure, and I don't believe you half understand that young girl's great need. She revealed volumes in her few frank sentences. Be careful to keep her confidence, and ask to be guided in what you say, so you can be wise as a serpent and harmless as a dove. That's one of the greatest gifts God gives to His workers, and it needs to be carefully watched and tended daily to keep it fit for work—that mixture of wisdom and gentleness."

"But, auntie," said Celia doubtfully, "do you believe I can ever accomplish anything? What's the good of getting such a girl to read a verse every day in the Bible? As likely as not, she'll choose one among the minor prophets, and it won't mean anything to her. As for praying, she said she didn't know how. What good will it do her to pray, 'Now I lay me down to sleep,' for instance, every night, not meaning a word of it or scarcely knowing what she's saying?"

"Remember, Celia, that it's His work. You have nothing to do with the end of it, and the results aren't in your hand. Don't you know He says, 'Ye have not chosen me, but *I* have chosen *you,* and ordained you, that ye should go and bring forth fruit, and that your fruit should *remain:* that whatsoever ye shall ask of the Father in my name, he may give it you.' After I read that I always feel comforted to do the work without seeing the results, knowing God has planned all that out from the beginning. All I have to do is execute the little part of the plan He's entrusted to my hand.

"As for saying that such a girl won't get any good out of the Bible, you talk as if you don't believe in the Holy Spirit, Celia. Won't He guide her to the right words that will help her? And don't you remember the Bible says it's written so plainly that 'he who runs may read' and that the way of life is made so plain that the 'wayfaring men, though fools, shall not err therein'? Then even if her heart and her lips don't know how to pray, if she truly tries to kneel and present herself every day before her Maker, don't you believe He can find ways and means to speak to her heart and teach her lips the right phrases? It's a great thing to have a habit of prayer, even though your heart isn't always in it, for you at least bring your body to the meeting place with God and give Him a chance to call the inattentive heart. Do you recall that Daniel had a habit three times a day of praying with his face toward Jerusalem?"

"Oh, yes, Aunt Hannah, I see it plainly. You always have a Bible verse ready for all my doubts and complaints. I wish I had the Bible labeled and put away in the cabinets of my brain the way you have, ready to put my hand on the verse I need at the right time," interrupted Celia, laughing and putting her arms around her aunt's neck to kiss her. "Come now. It's late, and you look tired. I'll be good and go to bed without fretting anymore, and tomorrow I'll try to think up some ways of helping that feather-headed girl."

Meanwhile, up in the third-story room of the "three-cent" girls, quiet and darkness reigned. Carrie Simmons had come in a few moments before, tired and cross. Her mind was wrought up by a play she'd witnessed, and she'd quarreled with her escort about something she didn't wish to explain to her roommate. They went to bed at last without the usual giggling confidences, and Mamie lay there in the darkness thinking over her evening and the advice given her. She wondered what the adorable Harold Adams would think of her changes when she was fully made over to suit her new guide.

Suddenly she sat straight up in bed, throwing the covers off Carrie's shoulders, and exclaimed: "My land alive! If I didn't forget the very first night." With that she flung herself out of bed and, striking a match, relit the gas.

"What in the world's the matter with you, Mamie?" Carrie said, jerking the covers up. "I was fast asleep, and you woke me up! Turn that gas out and come back to bed! Come! We won't be fit to get up in the morning, if you keep rampaging around all night."

But Mamie proceeded with what she was doing. She tumbled two great piles of paper-covered books over in the closet, searched among a motley collection of boxes, old hats, and odds and ends on the closet shelf, and then hunted in the bottom of her trunk. It was some minutes before she found what she wanted, and by that time her roommate was asleep. Mamie drew forth from an entanglement of soiled ribbons and worn-out garments a small, fine-print red Bible with an old-fashioned gilt clasp. It was stained on one side and blistered as if a tumbler of water had been left standing wet on it.

She remained seated on the floor beside her trunk while she turned the pages rapidly, intent upon keeping her promise in as short a time as possible, for the furnace fire was low for the night and she was cold. She opened near the beginning of the book and chanced upon a list of long, hard names she couldn't pronounce. Perhaps her conscience would have been eased by any verse, but it was too much trouble for her unaccustomed mind to pronounce the words to herself. She opened again at random toward the end of the book and let her eye run down the page in search of something attractive and brief. She was caught by this verse: "And to her was granted that she should be arrayed in fine linen, clean and white: for the fine linen is the righteousness of saints."

"Well, now, ain't that funny!" she said to herself, as she paused to read it over before she turned out the gas again. "That seems kind of like her talk. Dressed in fine linen! It would be kind of nice and pretty, and real stylish, too, if it was tailor-made. I saw a girl on Chestnut Street last summer in a tailor-made white linen that was awful pretty. It sort of rustled as if there was silk underneath, and her hair was all gold and fluffy under a big white hat with chiffon on it. She looked real elegant. It would take an awful lot of washing though, to keep her in fine fine linen 'clean and white.' "

She glanced at the verse again with her hand stretched out to turn out the gas and read it over once more, then got into bed. " 'For the fine linen is the righteousness of the saints!' Well, it does seem sort o' saintlike dress, now that's so," she thought. "Come to think of it, Miss Murray's got a sort of saint-like face. I knew it was something kind o' strikin', and I couldn't think what. You wouldn't exactly call her pretty, and yet she ain't the other thing, and some folks—most folks maybe—would like it better than to have her pretty. Maybe it's because she's got what this talks about. Anyway, she'll look like a saint for sure when she's as old as Miss Grant. Miss Grant, now, is a saint sure! And she'd look nice in a fine white linen dress, too.

"How funny it is to have the Bible talk about dress. I supposed the Bible thought clo'es was wicked. I'm sure the Sunday school teachers always say you mustn't think about 'em. Well, that's a pretty verse anyhow. I wonder who had the fine linen dress granted to her, and if she wore it all the time, that is, clean ones every day, all fresh and crisp! My! I wish 'twas me! Wouldn't I be happy though! I guess this reading's going to be real interesting, maybe. I never thought there could be any verse in it like that. Most things I've read before was about sinning and dying and heaven and scary things like that. Anyhow, I've kept my promise," she told herself.

"Why, no, I haven't either!" she exclaimed aloud and suddenly bounced out of bed again, to the detriment of her roommate's temper.

She knelt down beside the bed, and her thoughts paused while she tried to put her mind in praying frame. She tried to think how to pray right. She wanted to feel the satisfaction of having performed this duty that she felt in her Bible reading. She must ask for something. She was conscious of a vague wish in her heart to be good enough and have friends great enough that what she read might be granted to her—to be arrayed in spotless, beautiful apparel given by the love of someone who cared for her above others. How to put such a thought into a fitting phrase, or even if it would be proper to express it in prayer, she didn't know. At last she whispered, "Oh, God—" paused, waited and tried to collect some better words, then murmured again, "Oh, God"—and then—"Amen."

When she lay down to rest again, a sense of awe was upon her that wouldn't let her sleep for some time. She'd been near the great God and touched, as it were, the hem of His garment with curious perfunctory fingers. She was like a child who was dared to do a certain thing and coming, curious and unthinking, touched and suddenly felt the power and greatness and beauty of that which she touched and thus stole away ashamed.

Altogether Mamie Williams wasn't as satisfied with her first effort at prayer as she had been with her Bible reading. Yet in heaven it was recorded, "Behold, she prayeth!"

Chapter 20

The next day was Sunday.

Celia woke up early, although she was up late the night before. She lay thinking over the changes that had come into her life and wondered how things were going to work out. Somehow a cloud hung over what she was trying to do. She hadn't accomplished much with Harry. She kept him in the house a few evenings and interested him in a few good books, but nothing really to much purpose after all. To be safe from the temptations that crossed his path every day, he needed to be anchored on the Rock of Christ. She didn't think she knew how to help him in that way; he was such a bright fellow, so ready to laugh.

She thought of the minister and his apparent influence over the young man; she felt half indignant at him for not exercising it in a religious way, instead of merely a personal one. Then she realized she knew nothing at all about what influences he was using and shouldn't judge him. For all she knew, he'd spoken to him many times. How unjust she'd been! Then she remembered what her aunt told her about the improvements made last evening in the parlor and jumped up to dress and run down to see them.

Aunt Hannah had already dressed and gone down to the kitchen to help Molly and direct the new waitress who'd been in the house only three days.

Celia was delighted with the bookcase. Somebody had an artistic eye and building ability. The bookcase was exactly the right height and filled the long bare wall on one side of the room beautifully. It was finished with a neat molding of natural wood and the whole piece nicely oiled. A few books were piled on the floor beside it, waiting till the shelves should be perfectly dry. She stooped to read their titles and was astonished and pleased to find several new books by best authors, which she'd wanted to read but hadn't seen yet. They were nearly all in new bindings as if fresh from the bookstore, though one or two had the name *Horace L. Stafford* written inside in fine, strong handwriting.

Celia drew back, a slight flush creeping over her face. She was grateful for the books to be there. The newcomer was evidently bound to help and knew how to do so. Now if they could have a few games under the lighted lamp on the table, perhaps some of the young people might stay in evenings. Would such things reach Mamie Williams and her friend? She sighed and feared that Mamie was too much interested in other things to be reached so simply. She remembered Mamie was reading the other night. Perhaps some of these delightful stories would touch her.

One or two religious books, small and carefully bound, looked attractive. Celia picked one up and turned the pages, her face expressing a thought she read here and there. Then she walked to the small cozy corner by the organ and sat down. She looked about her at the few changes they'd made and remembered the night she looked around in that parlor waiting for the postman. How much difference a few little things made! She could see other changes that might improve matters and resolved to try them as soon as possible.

Celia sat down at the organ. She'd never tried that whining instrument, since coming to the house. It pained her sometimes to hear it groan and wheeze under the tenor brakeman's bold touch as he ground out an accompaniment to his solos. Celia didn't like a cabinet organ. She longed for a piano; but there was no piano, and here was this organ. What could be made of it? Perhaps it might be tuned and encourage singing occasionally. Certainly, if it was to stay there and be used, it would add to her own comfort to have it put in order. She touched the keys softly to see how bad it was and went on playing chords gently. She wasn't a finished musician, but she had learned to play a little for pleasure at home. Instinctively her fingers sought out some of the old favorite tunes.

Safely through another week,
 God has brought us on our way,
Let us now a blessing seek,
 Waiting in His courts today.

Her conscience pricked her, as the words ran through her mind. She hadn't gone to church regularly since coming to the city. She'd wandered around from one church to another, feeling forlorn and lonely at all. She hadn't gone often enough to one place to become noticed as a stranger and welcomed, even if the people were inclined to welcome her.

Since Aunt Hannah had come, she'd made an excuse to stay at home with her if she couldn't go out. When her aunt could go, she took her to the different churches nearby in rotation, so she might choose where they should go. The older lady hadn't chosen yet or even expressed her opinion about the worship places they'd visited.

Celia thought of it now and wished their dear old church from Cloverdale could be transplanted bodily. It was so desolate to go among strangers and not have any place or work in the church home. She sighed and decided to go more regularly and perhaps offer to take a class in Sunday school or something of the sort. Of course it wasn't right to live this way; but her heart wasn't in her decision. She played on, not realizing what tune she'd started till she hummed the words in a low sweet voice.

"The day of rest once more comes around,
 A day to all believers dear;
The silver trumpets seem to sound,

> That call the tribes of Israel near;
> Ye people all,
> Obey the call,
> And in Jehovah's courts appear—"

She broke off suddenly and played a few stray chords. She knew that the next verse began:

> Obedient to Thy summons, Lord,
> We to Thy sanctuary come.

It was strange that all the words were on that subject. She'd have chosen something else. She thought a moment, her fingers lingering on the keys. Then she began to sing:

> "Father in Thy mysterious presence kneeling,
> Fain would our souls feel all Thy kindling love;
> For we are weak, and need some deep revealing
> Of trust, and strength, and calmness from above."

She felt the beauty of the words and the depth of meaning and sang with her heart, each word as a prayer. Her voice grew fuller and sweeter as she went on.

> "Lord! We have wandered forth through doubt and sorrow,
> And Thou hast made each step an onward one;
> And we will ever trust each unknown morrow;
> Thou wilt sustain us till its work is done.

She didn't hear the step on the stairs or know someone entered the parlor and sat down on the divan nearby. But as she started the third verse, a rich, sweet tenor, cultivated and with feeling, joined her.

> "Now, Father, now in Thy dear presence kneeling,
> Our spirits yearned to feel Thy kindling love;
> Now make us strong; we need Thy deep revealing
> Of trust, and strength, and calmness from above."

Celia's voice trembled at first, but the stronger one sustained the tune, and she continued, the pink color stealing up her cheeks and to the tips of her ears. If the other singer saw her embarrassment, he didn't notice it. The last note died slowly away, and Celia wondered what to do and how to get away from the room.

Then he said in a matter-of-fact voice, as if they were accustomed to singing together early on Sabbath mornings: "Will you play 'Lead Kindly Light,' please?"

She played it, glad she knew it well enough to do so, and they sang together.

"Thank you!" he said simply, when the last verse was finished. "That's helped me for my work today. In fact that song always helps me. Do you ever come to a place where you want to look ahead and see whether things are coming out the way you'd like? Isn't it good to think He leads the way and makes the gloom for us so we won't be afraid for what's to come. If we could look sometimes—in disguise—and see the blessings, we might turn and run. You belong to Him, don't you, Miss Murray? I thought I couldn't be mistaken. Thank you for this pleasant morning praise. It's been like home."

Celia raised her eyes in one swift glad glance of recognition of their kindred discipleship, when he asked her if she was a Christian, and answered softly yet earnestly, "Yes, I do." She felt in her heart how wrong she was to call this man unspiritual. She longed to reach that high plane of trustful living where he seemed to move.

"Do you think it's possible," she asked, "for everyone to feel that perfect assurance where they can't see the way? I wish I knew how to trust that way and not worry about things."

"It's hard sometimes, isn't it, to lay down our burdens at the Father's feet and realize we don't need to carry them? But isn't it strange that it's hard?" He looked at her with that peculiarly bright smile she noticed the first night he came to the house. "One would think we'd be only too glad to get rid of the burden and the worry, when He offers to take it. Perhaps that's one reason I like that hymn. It helps me remember whose I am and who my Savior is. When I think, for instance, of some dear one who's fading day by day and can't be long on this earth, I'm prone to forget the night will ever be gone.

"And with the morn, those angel faces smile
    Which I have loved long since, and lost awhile!"

A deep sadness settled over his face, as he looked up to her and repeated the lines of the hymn they'd just sung. Her heart was filled with pity for some sorrow she felt he was bearing. Instinctively she remembered the sweet beautiful face in the velvet case. While she thought of him in his sorrow as set apart and sacred, she let a shade of her old dignity creep back into her voice, though it had fallen from it for a few moments.

The breakfast bell sounded, and the boarders were coming downstairs. With one accord the two rose and walked toward the dining room, feeling they didn't wish the quiet confidences of their few moments together intruded upon or misunderstood. Celia thanked Horace Stafford for his words a little stiffly, as someone might thank any strange minister for a good sermon. And perhaps the young man wondered a little at her seemingly variable moods.

After breakfast, the church bells sent their various calls to worship through the city's clear cold air. Celia stood dressed for church, waiting for her aunt in the front hall. Molly had called to Aunt Hannah, just as they were starting out the door, and Celia tapped her foot impatiently on the hall oilcloth and wished her aunt would hurry. Not that she was anxious to go to church, but she wanted to get the duty over with and come back. Mr. Stafford had slipped an inviting little book into her hand, as he passed her in the upper hall after breakfast, saying, "Have you read Daniel Quorm? If not, it might interest you. It's along the line of our talk this morning, and it's helped me trust Him where I couldn't trace Him."

She read a few pages while her aunt tied her bonnet and put on her gloves and was already deeply interested in the quaint phrases in the story of the little maid. She wanted to get back to it. She quieted her conscience when it pricked her for not caring to go to church, by telling it the book would probably do her more good than a sermon in a strange church. But her conscience was too well trained to let her forget that God had promised to meet her in the church.

Someone was standing in the shadow of the parlor curtains, but Celia didn't know who. She thought it might be the brakeman. He'd returned the night before and was off duty for the day. She unfastened the door and breathed in the clear sunny air with delight, then glanced up the stairs to see if her aunt was coming. Just then she heard her voice, as she leaned over the stair railing, and Celia saw that her gloves were off and her bonnet untied again.

"Celia, don't wait for me. I'm not going this morning. My duty is with Mrs. Belden. She's feeling very despondent. Go on without me. Isn't there someone else you can go with?" she asked, as she saw the look of dismay on Celia's face and heard her exclaim, "Oh, auntie!"

Then Harry Knowles stepped out of the shadow of the window curtain in the parlor.

"Miss Murray, would I do?" he asked humbly. "Or—would you rather not go with me?" He had a hesitancy and shamefacedness that wasn't like his usual manner, and he seemed anxious she accept.

While Celia hesitated, her aunt said, "Why, yes, Celia, that's very nice. You and Mr. Knowles go together. I'm so glad he's going." Then she slipped away from the stairs pleased, for Celia that she wouldn't be alone, and for the young man that he was willing to go to the house of the Lord!

As Celia turned to go with him, she thought about how she'd wished he would go to church or that she might say some word to help him, and now he opened the way by inviting her to go. She felt reproached for not inviting him before.

But Harry seemed uncomfortable. After closing the door, he stopped on the top step and asked again, "You're sure you're willing to go with me? You aren't afraid or anything?"

Celia looked up in surprise and saw the eager face and said, "Why, surely, Harry, I'm willing. Why should I be afraid?"

"Well, I thought—I was afraid you—after that night—you know—," he said, growing red and grinding his heel into the stone step. "I can't forgive myself, Miss Murray—that's all. And I thought you didn't like me asking you." He looked up bravely through his embarrassment with his sorry, boyish eyes asking forgiveness.

"Harry," said Celia, turning her clear, honest gaze upon him, "I was truly glad and was only being ashamed myself because *I* hadn't asked *you* before. I've been wishing you'd go to church, and—I've been praying for you."

She spoke the words quietly and with some discomfort, for she wasn't used to talking much about such things to strangers.

But the young man's eyes filled with moisture. "Thank you," he said in such hearty tones that she knew he meant it. Then he added, "So is the minister, and maybe I'll amount to something, after all."

Celia was surprised she suddenly felt a sense of satisfaction in what he told her about the minister. She didn't understand all her feelings today. She must sit down and analyze them when she returned home.

"But where are we to go, Harry?" she asked, pausing on the sidewalk. "Do you have any choice? I haven't put my letter into any church yet, though I should have done so before this."

She tried to remember which church she'd attended would most likely help the young man but couldn't remember any of them definitely. She thus concluded she'd taken her body to church and left her soul at home or wandering in fields of other thoughts than those presented at the sanctuary.

Harry's face grew eager again. "Well, that's nice. Maybe you wouldn't mind going to hear Mr. Stafford, because I half promised him I'd come there this morning."

"Oh, of course we will," said Celia, wondering why she'd never thought to go and hear him before, and why the thought of hearing him preach suddenly was so pleasant.

She wondered again as she listened to his opening prayer. Every word seemed to be prayed for her and to fit her needs exactly. She pulled herself up sharply when she found herself imagining he remembered their talk before breakfast and was praying thus for her.

The hymn just before the sermon was wonderful. Again she reprimanded herself severely, for thinking he looked at her while he read that last verse, so perfectly did it appeal to her need. He read it exquisitely and tenderly, and as he reached the last line he looked at her again. It gave her a strange pleasure to feel those words spoken so to her, as if the Father Himself sent her a special message that morning by a noble messenger.

"Take my soul, thy full salvation!
    Rise from sin, and fear, and care.
Joy to find in every station,
    Something still to do or dare.
Think what Spirit dwells within thee.
    Think what Father's smiles are thine!
Think what Savior died to win thee!
    Child of heaven, shouldst thou repine?"

Chapter 21

That Sabbath afternoon was one of deep thought and soul-searching for Celia. The sermon she heard, the hymns she sang, the prayer she listened to, the book she partly read—all seemed to bring her the one thought of the possibility of a life beyond anything she'd known before, a life whose every breath was trust and whose joy was unalloyed because it had no care to break the deep, sweet peace. The longing for some change of this sort in her own heart didn't take her interest from the work she'd just begun around her. Instead it deepened her interest in everyone in the house and made her heart throb anew with love to her Savior.

With the little book Horace Stafford loaned her, she passed through the hall that afternoon on some errand for her aunt. Returning, she saw Harry Knowles hovering restlessly about the parlor. She thought perhaps she might say something to help him, but what could it be? She felt hardly ready yet without more thought and preparation. She might do more harm than good. Following an impulse she offered him the book to read awhile and then went back to her room, half sorry she deprived herself of the pleasure of finishing it. But she'd read enough to remember, and her Bible was here.

Somehow the words seemed to fit all the other circumstances of the day and help her to the one great desire that was growing deeper in her heart, that she might stop fretting and worrying and learn to trust Jesus entirely for all that was to come. She read a chapter and part of another. The words seemed fresh and new to her. She wondered if she'd given her whole mind to her Bible reading lately.

Then suddenly from out of the printed page a command came. It wasn't marked more than other verses she'd read; yet it seemed to have a special significance for her. It reminded her of a young girl nearly her own age upstairs, whom she could influence and who was perhaps needing her help at this very moment. She felt she must go, though she could scarcely tell why, and laid aside her Bible and knelt to ask God's help before she went.

As she knocked at Mamie Williams's door she wondered at herself for coming and how she'd explain her visit. She decided that if anyone answered she'd say she came to ask them to go to church with her that evening, though she hadn't decided to go herself. She felt embarrassed right after she knocked and wished she were back in her own room.

But she didn't have long to wait. The door was thrown open after a moment of what sounded like scuffling inside. Mamie appeared, this time without gum in her mouth, but with rather red cheeks and her hair floating in wet strings down her back over a towel. Her face and hands were a brilliant, soft pink, evidently from a severe scrubbing Celia had recommended the night before. She instantly recognized what it meant, and her heart sank that the girl was spending her Sunday afternoon this way from her advice.

The other roommate occupied a comfortable lounging spot on the bed. Her hair was tumbled and her dress loosened, and in her hand was a paper-covered book. Celia observed afterward that it was the same one Mamie was reading the day before.

Carrie Simmons didn't rise from the bed. But she greeted the intruder with surprise and a general show of pleasure that made Celia feel she wasn't unwelcome. She was munching cheap candy from a box beside her on the bed and held it out at once to the guest.

"Sit down. Have some candy, do. I had it give to me last night." She said this with a giggle interpolated into her natural drawl. Then looking at her roommate, she said apologetically, "You must excuse Mamie. She's took an awful fit of cleanin' up. I don't know what she's getting ready for, but she's made herself a sight. Her nose's as red's a beet. Did you want something, or did you just come in to kill time?"

Celia accepted the chair, declining the candy as graciously as possible, saying she seldom ate it. Then she asked if they would go with her that evening to the meeting. She spoke of the service she attended that morning and that it might interest these two to go and hear the minister who lived under the same roof with them. As an incentive, she described the pleasant room, good singing, and genuine friendliness with an enthusiasm that surprised her.

"I can't go," Carrie Simmons said. "I'm expecting company."

She said this with the same conscious drawing in of the breath, evidently meant to express a certain and special company, that Celia noticed in Mamie's talk the night before. It made her heart sink with the uselessness of trying to work against such odds, till she remembered her new resolution not to look ahead for results, but to do the work and trust the rest to God.

Mamie's cheeks had grown redder, if that was possible. She was sitting on the edge of a chair with the hairbrush in her hand. She seemed a bit shy.

"It's awful nice of you to ask us," she said, "but I might be havin' company, too. It wouldn't do to be away, though I ain't just positive."

"Couldn't you bring them along?" Celia asked, as if it would be the most natural thing in the world to do. Her heart misgave her at the idea of taking the oily youth she saw in the parlor waiting for Carrie not long before.

"Oh, no, indeed!" snickered Carrie. "He wouldn't go a step. He ain't that kind. And besides he'd be mad, for he said he might be going to bring another fellow along he wants me to meet. He wants to see me very particular tonight anyway, so I couldn't think of going out," she said, then retired behind her book.

Meanwhile Mamie was puzzling over how to please herself and her new object of adoration at the same time, and seemed to arrive at a solution.

"I don't know but I *might* go after all," she said slowly, looking down at the toe of her shoes. "Say, Carrie, if he comes would you be sure to tell him I went out with somebody *else?* You could tell him it was a *very special* friend who invited me, and he'd think it was another fellah. That might have a good effect on him, you know. I believe I'll try it this time anyway. I'll go, Miss Murray, if you want it so much. It's a good thing to get people jealous once in awhile, don't you think?

"Say, was that you down in the parlor singing this morning early? It was awful sweet! Who else was there? It didn't sound like Mr. Yates, but I didn't know any of the others sang. It wasn't Harry Knowles, was it? He's too young for you anyway. You don't say it was the minister! My! He's awful talented, ain't he? Wouldn't it be romantic if it should turn out you was to marry him sometime? Did you ever know him before? I've heard of stories like that lots of times."

Celia's cheeks rivaled Mamie's in hue, and her anger had risen rapidly. She didn't dare trust herself to rebuke this girl, for her desire to do her good was still strong. She quickly sought to turn the conversation.

"Are you fond of singing? Then come downstairs and let's sing now. I think some of the others are down there. We can have a pleasant time. I have some gospel songbooks. Put up your hair and come."

She walked to the door trying to steady her fluttering nerves and still that strange beating of her heart, half indignation, half something else she didn't understand and didn't wish to condone.

"My land!" said Mamie, beaming. "I'd come in a minute, but what'll I do with my hair? It's about dry, but it'll take me an hour to do it up after washing; it's so tangled and slippery. Perhaps you'll fix it for me. Do, that'll be nice. Then you can show me how to do it like yours."

Celia was dismayed. She'd scarcely have chosen Sunday afternoon for a lesson in hairdressing. But how could she refuse, since the request was made in answer to her own? To handle another person's hair anytime was a sore trial to her. She shrank from contact with anyone except her nearest and dearest. But how would she influence Mamie if she let her see she was unwilling to do what she asked? For a minute her repugnance of the coarse girl, with her coarse hair, red face, and loud, grating words, was so intense she almost yielded to her desire to turn and flee from the room and shake the dust from her feet; she'd tell her aunt to take her away from the horrible boarders and never let her see any of them again.

Then she gained control of herself, and though her cheeks were still red at the memory of the girl's careless words, she consented to fix her hair. Even the deeply absorbed Carrie on the bed, who had been furtively watching the stranger, never suspected what a trial she'd quietly taken upon herself.

After taking on the task, she did it well; she had a naturally artistic eye and hand. She even took some pleasure, after overcoming the dislike, in making Mamie's hair look as she often thought it should. Quickly and deftly she twisted it, smoothed it here and there, and fastened it. Afterward Mamie surveyed herself.

"It looks awful plain," she said hesitantly, "and it makes me seem strange, 'cause I ain't used to it. But I guess I like it. Don't you, Carrie?"

"It looks real stylish," that young woman answered enviously, mentally resolving to try her own that way as soon as the others left the room.

Celia went to wash her hands with a heavy heart. She must certainly have mistaken the voice she thought called her to go to that room. What had she accomplished by teaching the fashions this afternoon? How would she ever know whether a thing was a duty or not?

She brought her songbooks down to the parlor and found Mamie there before her, looking pretty and a little shy in her new coiffure. She was talking to the tenor brakeman who was lost in admiring her charms.

Celia crossed at once to the organ and started the singing. But the brakeman's tenor wasn't as pleasant as the voice that had blended with her own earlier in the day. The other boarders heard the music and one by one dropped in, all joining in the words when they were familiar until even Miss Burns was there.

The minister also came in and joined in the singing, though he sat in a shaded corner of the room and sang softly, as if he were weary. Celia found her thoughts wandering to him and wondered what was the matter. She grew very annoyed at this when she remembered Mamie Williams's careless words a little while before. She was glad when the tea bell rang and called them from the organ.

The church party was larger than she expected. Mamie wheedled Mr. Yates into being one of the number. She was the kind of girl who always wants a young man along when she goes anywhere. The other three young men joined the group also, perhaps at Harry's solicitation, or it might have been out of interest in the minister who was singing with them.

They were starting out the door. Aunt Hannah was behind with Harry Knowles. Miss Burns had volunteered to stay with Mrs. Belden during the evening. Celia stepped down to the pavement beside Mamie and walked on.

"Say, he's awful nice. I like him. I wish he *would* marry you, 'cause I like you both," said Mamie in a confidential whisper.

"What do you mean? Who?" asked Celia startled, vaguely thinking she meant the tenor brakeman.

"Why, Mr. Stafford, the minister!" said the other girl.

"You must never say anything like that again," she said in a chilling tone that almost froze Mamie's enthusiasm for a minute. "It's utterly absurd and ridiculous."

She wished afterward she could have turned it off with a laugh and let the girl see she had no idea of such a thing, without making such a tragedy of it. But she felt so annoyed at the second bold intimacy of the girl; it seemed as if clumsy, unknowing hands had mixed up sacred things. She almost stopped in her walk and went back to the house. But she steadied her voice and her steps and kept on.

"Why?" asked Mamie timidly. "Don't you like him?"

"Certainly, I don't dislike him. But neither of us has any idea of such a thing. It's very annoying to have it suggested. He's simply a boarder," she said in a freezing voice.

"Oh," said Mamie, frightened, "I didn't mean any harm. I just thought it would be nice—that's all." After that she dropped behind with Bob Yates who'd come up, and Celia walked with Aunt Hannah and Harry Knowles.

"She's an awful odd girl in some ways," confided Mamie to her escort a few minutes later. "I just said she and the minister would make a nice match, and she got as mad as a hornet. My! She scared me so I thought I'd cry!" Then she giggled in a way Bob Yates much admired.

Celia sat in the meeting too much annoyed to rally her spirits and enjoy what was going on. She scarcely heard the hymns or the sermon. The voice of the minister, cultured, earnest, tender, loving toward his people, awakened in her the knowledge that she was more interested in this man than she wanted to be. She didn't wish to hear his voice and like it. Therefore she tormented herself with her annoyance, so that she didn't hear it and saw between the lines in her hymnbook a sweet pictured face in a velvet frame. She called herself a fool and wondered how a man she hadn't even heard of until recently could make her feel so uncomfortable.

Then she turned to watch Mamie's face, and her heart sank again as she reflected how useless it was to try to do anything for her. True, her hair was becoming and neatly arranged, and the black eyes of the young man beside her were admiringly turned toward her occasionally. But perhaps that was only another source of harm to the poor girl. After all Celia's resolves, her day seemed to be ending miserably.

How could she know that at that very moment the young girl beside her was listening to the minister with undisguised awe, as he read the words of his text, "And to her was granted that she should be arrayed in fine linen, clean and white: for the fine linen is the righteousness of saints." She didn't know about the girl's hurried getting out of bed to read the promised verse the night before or how the verse impressed itself upon her mind, perhaps more because it was about dress and the one great theme of interest to her mind—except perhaps those of love, courtship, and marriage. If Celia knew this, it might only have discouraged her more that the Bible itself meant no more to Mamie than a fashion book. So it was wise that Celia couldn't see and know until God's plan was worked out to the finish and she was given eyes perfected through His teaching to understand the whys and wherefores.

The sermon was simplicity itself. If Celia hadn't been so taken up with her own uneasy heart, she would have recognized the preacher's skill. He explained the meaning clearly of what to others might have been an empty and meaningless passage. Even feather-headed Mamie could understand and carry away with her the few facts she wished to know when she first read the words, together with their deep spiritual meaning. She felt disappointed when she heard that this incomparable person was the church, Christ's bride. And she told herself, enviously, that she had nothing to do with the verse at all, of course.

But immediately the preacher made it plain that each one in the house did individually belong, ought to belong, by right were, members of that church for whom Christ died. Only through their own wills did they deliberately put themselves outside its pale. Indeed, to everyone present it had been granted as a privilege, and it was their own fault if they didn't accept and wear it. He spoke of the challenge of keeping such garments white and pure in the midst of a world of work and constant contact with that which would soil, how only children of the rich could afford to dress in a color that would so easily soil, and how only those whose garments were washed in the blood of the Lamb would remain pure and white.

Then he talked about that righteousness of the saints until even Bob Yates dropped his eyes from the earnest, eloquent face of the speaker. He searched his own heart and wished he might somehow be different.

Mamie's cheeks glowed, and her heart beat fast. She forgot Harold Adams and the admiring glances of her escort to church that night. She even forgot her new hair arrangement and stopped touching the back of her head to discover how it might be affecting those who saw her from the rear. She determined to discover how she might wear this fine linen. When the closing hymn was announced, she stood up with the others and sang the words loudly, meaning them in her heart more than any words she'd ever sung before. She felt a strange, sweet longing, new and faint, but real, as the hymn continued.

> "O Jesus Christ the righteous! live in me,
>   That, when in glory I Thy face shall see,
> Within the Father's house, my glorious dress
>   May be the garment of Thy righteousness."

That night, for the first time, Mamie felt a strong determination to go to heaven when she died. The white linen could be worn then, if not before. The minister said it might be worn now also. Well, perhaps—

Her heart was softened. On the way home she confided the coincidence of her verse the night before and the minister's text to Bob Yates, who was deeply interested and impressed. Celia would have been surprised if she could have heard the brakeman telling Mamie at the door that she helped him, that he wanted to be better and was glad she was that kind of girl.

As for Celia, the minister walked home with her. She hoped Mamie didn't see, for her cheeks burned red and her embarrassment didn't lessen during the entire walk. He asked her to help him in his Sunday school work, and, after much hesitation, she accepted the class he offered. But she was stiff and unlike herself.

Aunt Hannah wondered why Celia seemed so cold and uninterested in things. She sighed as she went about preparing for the night and wished Celia's mother had lived; nobody could understand a girl like her own mother, she thought. Then she knelt as she always did and, laying her care at her Master's feet, rested with an unburdened heart for the next day's work.

Chapter 22

One morning, about eleven o'clock, Molly Poppleton was up in the third-story hall attending to the rooms on that floor. The chambermaid wasn't well, and Molly was set back in her work a good deal; so it was late, and she was in a hurry. She thumped the water pitchers down, slammed the doors, and punched the pillows into shape with extra vigor.

Suddenly, in the midst of making up the university student's bed, she stopped and straightened up to listen. She wasn't mistaken. She heard sounds of distress. They grew clearer now as she went to the hall door and quickly located them. They were low, half-suppressed sobs, one right after the other.

After listening, she marched down the hall and without ceremony threw open the door of the room. There lay Mamie Williams across the foot of her unmade bed crying bitterly and shaking with sobs. Molly was a straightforward person and believed in coming to the point at once; she was brought up that way. So, without apology for intruding into the young girl's trouble, she demanded to know what was the matter.

Mamie raised her head long enough to show a red nose and blurred eyes and see who came in without knocking. Then she cried harder than ever.

Molly shut the door with a bang. "For mercy's sake, tell me what's the matter. Are you hurt? Do you want a doctor? Or are some of your friends dead?"

Mamie shook her head and finally controlled herself enough to sob, "No, M–m–molly. It's my heart! It's broken!"

"Oh, well, if that's all, you'll get over it! They always do! I've been there myself, and I know that state don't last long. You better get up and wash your face while I make the bed." Molly proceeded to throw open the window and shake the pillows.

"Oh, Molly! You don't know. You never was crossed in love!" wailed the miserable girl, without stirring, and then she sobbed harder.

Molly turned irately from the bureau where she'd begun to dust.

"Crossed in fiddlesticks!" she said sharply. "You ain't near so hurt as you think. As for me, I've had my chances in my time like other girls, and plenty of 'em at that, an' I preferred to live single. It's much more independent. It's my opinion you ain't old enough to be away from home anyway. You better go back to your ma if you've got one."

But as this only set Mamie to crying harder, the perplexed Molly marched down to find Miss Hannah and report the case.

"Miss Hannah, you're needed up there in that three-cent room. That silly thing is actin' like a fool over some poor sickly fellow that couldn't support her if she got him, I s'pose. She says she's been crossed in love an' her heart's broke, an' she's cryin' fer dear life. It's my opinion she better be crossed with a good spankin', an' I wouldn't feel sorry to be the one to give it to her neither."

But the latter part of this sentiment was lost upon her hearer who had already started for the third story.

A moment later Mamie felt a cool hand on her hot forehead, and Miss Grant stooped down and took her in her arms and kissed her. She was so surprised to be kissed that she stopped crying for a minute. Then the sympathy of the eyes that met hers started her tears afresh, and she buried her head in the motherly arms held out to her and cried like a hurt child who had found a comforter. After she cried a few minutes and was soothed by the woman who seemed to have the gift of soothing from above, as others have a gift for music or painting, she told her little sad, commonplace story.

"It was Harold Adams at the store. And he was awful handsome. The girls all thought so. I fell in love with him the first time I saw him. Yes, ma'am, he was the head clerk; all this winter he had charge. The owner went to New York and left him here to run the business. He was awful smart, they said. He paid me lots of attention at first and told me many times he loved me better than anyone else." Here she broke into fresh sobs.

"When that ugly girl with bleached hair and a pretty face came, he got to going with her. Now I'd planned a way to look nicer than her and get him back. He's been real nice to me for a whole week—she was away—and they all said she was sick. But now it turns out she was getting ready to be married. And he's to have full charge of a three-cent store up in Ohio, and they say she's going along.

"The girls had it all ready to tell me this morning when I went in to the store, and they just couldn't laugh enough at me, till I nearly sank through the floor. They was always jealous of me. First one twitted me an' then another, till I got so mad and felt so bad I just come home. He's goin' to marry her, they say, an' it's all been no use after all, an', oh, my heart's just broke!"

It's commonly supposed that women who don't marry and have no children cannot enter into young people's feelings or sympathize with them. But God somehow gave this woman sweet insight into natures in distress, which helped her give comfort wherever she went and say the right word and do the right action. She bent down now and kissed the tear-wet face.

"You're awful kind," moaned poor Mamie. "But you don't know how it is yourself. You ain't never been crossed in love."

The shadow of a dark cloud, tipped with brilliant light, passed over Hannah Grant's face, leaving the light reflected there, before she spoke again.

"Listen, Mamie," she said. Her voice was sweet and tender, and her eyes looked dewy, as though she saw things beyond the range of human vision. "I want to tell you a story about myself."

Yes, she went back to those bright days so long ago, when she found a kindred spirit and lived in a sweet elysium of hope and dreamed those rose-colored visions of youth. Some women would have counted it a desecration to the memory of her dead hopes and sacred love to tell the story to a vulgar girl who wept over a man a hundredfold more vulgar; they would have thought it lacking in good taste and delicacy to do so.

Not so this woman. Hadn't she sent swift petitions to the throne as she came up the stairs, asking for guidance? She felt in her heart that her story, which had never passed her lips to mortal ear, told here might help this poor, friendless, untaught girl. It might help her see life in a different way and begin to live it for God above, instead of for her own selfish pleasure. And she knew the man she'd loved, who'd been in heaven these years, would be glad also for her to tell the story, if it could help a soul find comfort.

And so she told it, simply and eloquently. She even dwelt on the tender passages, the little things that make such a story beautiful in a girl's eyes. She spoke about the flowers he sent her, the simple pretty gowns he admired, and the ribbon he stooped and kissed as it floated from her throat that last time he parted from her, saying she would soon be with him now to stay. And how she treasured it yet.

Before she was halfway through the story, Mamie had dried her eyes and sat up on the bed, her face expressing intense interest. She forgot her own troubles in another's. Her tears, dried on her own sorrows, soon flowed silently for Miss Grant. She wondered at that peaceful face. It shone bright even through the mist that gathered in her eyes, as she told of the dark days when her hopes were taken from her and of the time when she wandered about forlorn, until the Lord spoke to her and comforted her. When the story was finished, Mamie found she could look up and talk. She seemed to have risen above her recent grief. She sensed a longing in her heart, but she scarcely knew for what.

"I always thought it would be awful to be an old maid," she said bluntly. "But if I could look like you and be like you, I wouldn't mind it—not much!" There was a look of admiration on her face.

It wasn't much encouragement, but Hannah Grant didn't let her work depend on results. She talked, cheered, advised, and drew out the girl, until she understood pretty thoroughly her life before this. She didn't wonder that the heart seemed broken or the poor girl freely gave to an unworthy object what she felt was the love of her life. What better example was set before the girl? She was untaught and unguided.

Before Hannah left her, Mamie confided to her the story of her Bible reading and her thoughts about the fine linen garments. And this missionary of the Most High sifted out from the chaff of foolish talk and worldly longings the grain of earnest desire after better things and found the joy of encouragement in it. She even knelt beside the girl with her arm about her waist and prayed for her as Mamie had never heard herself prayed for before.

Then, instead of sending her back to the atmosphere of selfish longings and foolish thoughts of what should be noble things, she advised her to stay away from the three-cent store, at least for that day, and come down in the kitchen. She had some work for her there which might take her mind off her trouble for a little while.

Molly sniffed when she saw her come into the kitchen with her red eyes washed and a white apron on. But Hannah wisely sent Molly to work in another part of the house. She herself introduced the awkward novice into the mysteries of baking a delicious cake, for celebrating Miss Burns's birthday that evening. It spoke well for Hannah's ability to read human nature, that she chose cake to teach Mamie. If it had been bread or potatoes, the girl doubtless wouldn't have been interested. Cake, though, seemed "sort of stylish" and belonged to the festive side of eating.

So she enjoyed learning how to make it and came to the dinner table that evening beaming over the cake she'd iced and decorated with smilax and candles. She told everyone she made the cake, and it received much praise, especially from Bob Yates. He asked for a second piece and said quiet words of commendation that brought a smile and bright flush to the girl's face, just as Molly passed the ice cream.

"H'm!" said that woman coming out to the kitchen to converse with herself better. "I thought so! She's got over it sooner than most of 'em. It generally takes overnight at least to let the glue dry, but she must have used some lightnin' stuff. Her heart ain't more'n skin deep anyway."

Chapter 23

The days following were filled with new things for Mamie Williams. However shallow her hurt had been, it was deep enough to make her shrink from returning to the store. The young man whose charms had fascinated her wasn't gone, and Carrie Simmons brought word from day to day of a delay in sending him away. The yellow-haired girl seemed to have returned to her place behind the candy counter.

After this report continued for about a week, Mamie suddenly expressed a desire to return to her position and hoped she might still win her lover back. But Hannah, feeling this might be the turning point in her life, had a long talk with her. An hour later she appeared in the kitchen with red eyes, a meek air, and a clean gingham apron and made herself generally useful. Molly, who'd kept herself informed, nodded approval and announced to Miss Hannah at the first opportunity that she thought that girl might grow a little sense after all.

Mamie's resolution might not have outlasted the next day, however, if several things hadn't occurred to strengthen what Hannah said to her during that long earnest talk. The first was the announcement that the charming Harold Adams had departed from the city to parts unknown, taking with him a goodly portion of the profits of the three-cent business. This he had, by careful bookkeeping, been laying up for himself for this day. Nor did the yellow-haired girl share in his booty. She seemed to be as happy as ever and, as the days passed, was reported to be "making up" to the new head of the business, who came to straighten out affairs.

On hearing this news, Mamie spent a whole morning in her room, where she cried and was angry alternately. From it she came out a wiser and meeker girl, ready to do what Miss Grant asked and to look for another position. But that lady was in no hurry to urge the girl to apply for another position. Life in such a store, as Mamie would likely get into in her present stage of development, was too dangerous and risky for the unformed girl, who seemed on the brink of better things.

After careful thought and discussion with Celia, Hannah told Mamie she'd like it very much if she'd help her for two or three weeks with upstairs work, sweeping and table setting, until she could find another second girl who suited her. She'd give her what she paid the girl who had just left, and she'd of course have her board. She could then look for the right place and still lose nothing by being out of work.

After struggling with her pride and reiterating many times to her roommate that she only did this for a few days as a favor to Miss Grant, Mamie finally accepted. She was somewhat surprised Carrie didn't scoff at her for "doing housework," which to both girls was always menial service quite beneath them.

But Carrie had other things to think of than her roommate's affairs. Scarcely three weeks after Mamie left the three-cent store, Miss Carrie Simmons "eloped" with the friend of the oily youth who had visited her. She left a note in Mamie's Sunday dress pocket stating she eloped and bidding an affectionate farewell.

It was no more than could be expected, Hannah thought after the young girl's departure, as she turned over pile after pile of romantic, third-class, sensational novels in the closet. But she sighed and brushed away a tear, sad that she wasn't able to help this girl also. By this time she had some hopes of Mamie. Her roommate's affair, she feared, might upset her and stir her desire for romance herself. But happily it worked the other way, rather frightening her and causing her to cling to Miss Grant, asking her advice daily and almost hourly. This effect became still more salutary when some days later it was learned the young man Miss Simmons eloped with already had a wife in another state.

During these events Mamie cried a good deal. But growing in her face was the shadow of a sweet womanliness for what might be in the future if all things went well. She didn't even have the brakeman to brighten this hard time for her, for he was out west on some special work for one of the heads of the road and wouldn't return for a month. Mamie learned to efface herself somewhat and seemed to be cultivating some of Celia's quiet, reserved manner.

Celia was very interested in the girl. She kept her in mind daily and was always trying to help her and praying for her.

"She may, after all, develop enough to become a ribbon girl sometime," she said one night to her aunt, when Mamie had left them.

Aunt Hannah smiled. She had much hope for her young protegee herself.

"Yes," she said, with her faraway look in her eyes, "she may wear the white linen dress someday. Who knows?"

"You mean the tailor-made one?" asked Celia mischievously.

"The heaven-made one, dear. She told me tonight that she's beginning to feel as if she prays like other people now."

Other influences were at work also. Horace Stafford was holding meetings every night in the new chapel, and the boarders had as a family adopted that church as their own. Now everyone who could usually attended Sunday services morning and evening, and several of them dropped in to the special meetings. Miss Hannah, Celia, and Mamie Williams were there every night. Harry Knowles joined the choir, and his friends rejoiced that at last all his evenings were securely filled. His face was bright and interested. He was enthusiastic in sounding the praises of Mr. Stafford and ready to do anything to help in the church work. As yet, though, he didn't seem to have made any move to number himself among the Christians.

Celia was deeply interested in a class of big boys who were beginning to attend the services. She kept herself in the background with them as much as possible. No one could say she was trying to get the minister's attention. She tried to keep away from him so much at times that he noticed it and was puzzled and troubled.

He sometimes sat in his room with his hand shading his eyes, weary with his work, and thought about it. Did she dislike him? Or did someone else fill her life so she didn't want other friends? More and more her sweet, womanly face and her pleasant ways were impressing his mind. Eventually he confessed it to himself and thought of what his friend Roger Houston said about finding a wife, that night he met him while searching for a boarding place. His heart told him such a thing was more possible than he cared to confess to his friend just yet.

In fact, his friend had visited him several times and once remained to dinner with him. Since then he voted unreservedly for the new boardinghouse and declared the cooking as good as they had at his own home, though perhaps not quite so stylishly served. He laughed, it's true, at Bob Yates, who that evening favored the house with one of his high-keyed solos, while Roger and Horace tried to talk in the latter's room directly over the organ. And he mimicked Miss Burns's laugh—for he was a born mimic—and called Mamie Williams and Carrie Simmons "giggling kids."

But he admired Miss Grant and declared Celia to be artistic in the extreme. He kept talking about her after they came upstairs. He was an artist by profession and begged his friend to ask her to sit as a model for him. He was surprised at the prompt way the suggestion was squelched. He asked if Celia's character was as fine as her face and pondered afterward his host's slow, thoughtful answer: "Yes, I think it is." He was so possessed of catching Celia's expression on canvas for a picture he planned to paint that he asked again as he was leaving, "And you don't think you can ask that girl to sit for me, Horace? I like that style of face and don't know where else to look for it."

"I don't think there *is* another face anywhere just like hers," answered the minister slowly again.

"Now look here, Horace, you talk as if you were personally interested in her. Don't go so far as that, I beg of you. You ought to marry a rich girl, for you never will allow yourself to get money any other way, unless you fall dead in love with it. Well, I suppose I may ask her myself. It won't hurt my feelings if she refuses. Where can I find her?"

A firm line came around the minister's mouth as he said, "I would rather you not do that, Roger. She's not that kind of girl."

Afterward the young artist remembered his friend's face and whistled on his way home as he thought it over.

But though Horace Stafford had watched Celia for several months, saw her under varying and trying circumstances, and showed her little attentions, the outcome of a frank talk he had within himself in which he confessed a deep interest in her, she still remained aloof from him. Her aunt gave up trying to understand. Celia was too deep for her.

Meanwhile Bob Yates came home from the West. He'd worked hard and was glad to get back again. He'd been promoted to engineer and was off duty every evening now. He seemed struck with the change in Mamie Williams. Miss Grant noticed it the first evening at dinner. He showed deference in his manner when he addressed her. She also noticed its effect on Mamie. Did she take a lesson from Celia's reserve, or were the influences of prayer and daily life and her new hopes and resolves making the change? Miss Grant wondered.

Mamie flushed a little, but she dropped her eyes modestly and was unobtrusive during the entire meal, a thing so unlike the old Mamie Williams that the contrast was marked. Bob Yates admired it evidently, for he cast many glances across the table at her, and his own loud, jolly voice seemed somewhat toned down, in harmony.

Celia passed through the hall behind them after dinner and heard Mamie shyly decline an invitation to the theater.

"I'd like awful well to go, but we all go to meetin' every night now," she was saying. "I promised in the meeting last night I'd bring somebody along tonight, and I don't just like to break my promise. Mebbe you'd just as soon go to meetin' as the theater tonight, then I could keep my promise. The minister's awful good, and the singin' is fine. They'd like your voice in the choir."

And so Bob Yates willingly gave up the theater to go to the meeting. He wasn't greatly concerned where he took his amusement. The theater had no special attraction for him, but he thought of it because Mamie once told him she'd rather go to the theater than anywhere else in the world. In fact, the prospect of a "good sing" was rather more enticing in itself than sitting still and listening to other people singing.

That night the minister preached a soul-searching sermon. Some of Celia's boys arose at the close when the invitation was given during the hymn for all who'd like to belong to Christ to stand with those who were Christians.

Mamie sat quite still, her cheeks pink and her eyes downcast during the singing of the first verse and part of the second. She held one side of the hymnbook with Bob Yates, and her hand trembled a little. He was singing the deep, heart-stirring words with his usual fervor, but Mamie didn't sing. Just as the second verse was nearly finished, she suddenly rose with a jerk and an embarrassed expression, leaving the book in his hands.

He looked up astonished and continued singing, but not as loud as before, and his words were getting mixed up. He fidgeted on his chair, and when they began to sing the next verse, he rose also and stood beside Mamie, offering her the book again. She took it, looking down, her heart fluttering gladly that he rose too and kept her company, and so they stood until the benediction was pronounced.

"Say," said Mamie softly, when they'd walked halfway home in an embarrassed silence, "what did you mean by that? Did you mean what the minister said? What made you do it?"

"Mean it? 'Course I did!" answered Bob heartily. "My mother used to be a good woman, an' I've always meant to turn that way sometime myself. The first time I heard Mr. Stafford, I made out he was more'n halfway right, an' tonight I thought so again. I don't know as I'd 'a' said so out 'n out fer folks to see, if you hadn't, but I calculated I wanted to be on that side if you was, so I stood up. Why?"

"Well, I didn't know," said Mamie embarrassedly. "I was afraid mebbe you just did it out o' politeness. But I'm real glad you meant it."

"Are you? Sure?" He looked at her searchingly by the light of the next streetlight, then added, "Well, I don't mind tellin' you 'twas you that did it. That what you said about wearin' a white dress got me to thinkin'. You seem most 's if you was wearin' it yourself since I come home. I thought 'twas my 'magination, but when I see you get up in meetin', I knew it was that there white dress in the Bible you was wearin'. I mostly made up my mind while I was out to Ohio, I wanted to be fit to walk alongside o' you."

Mamie's heart stood fairly still with joy she hadn't known before and only half understood—the joy of helping another immortal soul to find the Light.

"I'm only just startin' myself," she murmured low. "I ain't half fit for that white dress yet, but I'm goin' to try, an' I'm awful glad you think I helped you."

"Well, then, let's start out together, and mebbe we can help each other," he said.

And she murmured with downcast eyes, "All right," as he grasped her hand in a hearty clasp, then helped her up the steps into the house.

Other young men had clasped Mamie's hand in a more or less hearty grasp on the way home from amusements. But no hand ever touched in her the chord of such true, heartfelt, honest friendship and purpose to do right. She felt as though she'd been lifted up in some way, and yet she didn't know how or why.

A little later Harry Knowles sat in Miss Grant's private sitting room, his head leaning on his hand and his whole attitude indicating deep thoughts.

"I tell you, Miss Grant," he was saying, "it was that three-cent girl. When I saw her stand up there all by herself, right in the middle of a hymn when no one else was standing up, it made me ashamed. Here I was sitting still, and I was brought up to pray and read the Bible and know how to be good and had a good mother. And that girl, who never had any upbringing to amount to much, I guess, standing right away as soon as she was asked. I can't take it any longer, and I wanted to talk to somebody about it, so I came to you. I knew you'd help me, and it would seem a little like having Mother to tell it to. I've made up my mind to be a Christian. Yes, I'll tell the minister soon, but I wanted to talk to you first, and he was busy anyway. But I don't think I'd ever have done it, if it hadn't been for Mamie Williams tonight."

The mysteries of influence in this world are great and past understanding. We cannot tell if our actions may affect the eternal welfare of someone we've never seen.

Certainly, Mamie Williams, as she sat reading her Bible that night, didn't dream she helped bring Harry Knowles to Christ.

Hast thou not garnered many fruits
    Of other's sowing, whom then knowest not?
Canst tell how many struggles, sufferings, tears,
    All unrecorded, unremembered all,
Have gone to build up what thou has of good?

Chapter 24

C elia Murray went to her room and locked the door. It was just after church, and Aunt Hannah was busy in the kitchen. It was the only time during the day when she might hope to be undisturbed in the room she shared with her aunt. She couldn't remember a time in her life when she would have cared whether her aunt came in upon her or came to the door and found it locked, but this time she did. She wanted to be entirely alone and face her own heart.

Winter had passed, and they were well into spring. The meetings in the little chapel continued for several weeks, and during that time Harry Knowles, Mamie Williams, and Bob Yates professed publicly their faith in Jesus Christ. The university student took his church letter out of its hiding place in his trunk and put it into Mr. Stafford's church, and the schoolteacher sent to his faraway home for his; and both were working hard for the salvation of others.

Family worship was established daily in the boardinghouse, not in the morning, because the coming and going of the boarders was at such different hours, but in the early evening, just after dinner, while they still sat around the table. No one was obliged to stay, but all chose to, unless called away by something urgent. Horace Stafford conducted it and read a few verses and prayed. Once or twice, when he was absent for a day, Miss Grant read part of a chapter and asked Harry Knowles once and the brakeman once to pray. They'd each done so, stumblingly and with few words. But she was glad and went about her daily work feeling joy where the Lord had placed her.

They'd grown to be a pleasant family, in spite of the various types of character and upbringing they represented. They talked about their abiding place as HOME, and each one felt it to be that in the true sense of the word. Miss Grant observed each birthday with some little festivity in the way of food, and at Christmas and other holidays they made merry enough to forget, most of them, that they were away from their own families.

Horace Stafford grew to be part of the household so fully that the thought of his leaving would have dismayed everyone. Even Celia unbent, and they became good comrades in a way. She always kept up a dignified barrier, though, which prevented his showing her the ordinary attentions young men like to show the young women they admire. She quieted her conscience by keeping up this wall of conventionality and excusing herself from anything of a social nature he offered her. Thus she shut her eyes to consequences and enjoyed his presence in the house. How could she do otherwise? She read the books he loaned her and conversed about them with him afterward, and she visited the poor and sick for him sometimes and took them little delicacies.

At times, it troubled her that she enjoyed his company as much as she did, but she'd been learning during the winter months to put this aside and think no more about it. Occasionally she prayed to be delivered from a trouble which she sometimes saw hovering like a shadowy cloud over her own life. Looking at Aunt Hannah she resolved to trust the Lord to make her what He wanted her to be, even if it must be in spite of sorrow, as He had with her aunt.

But now the time came when Celia must face her heart and understand. If she must come out of the ordeal bowed in spirit, then she must face it and accept it, but she must understand herself now.

It came to a sudden crisis in this way.

Horace Stafford had been away for nearly two weeks. A telegram had come to him, when Miss Grant was out. Molly took it up to him and a little while afterward was surprised to see him standing in the kitchen door, his grip and umbrella in hand and a drawn, anxious look upon his face. He told Molly to tell Miss Grant he was called away by news of sudden illness and didn't know how long he'd be gone. They heard nothing from him until Saturday evening of that week, when his friend Roger Houston called to get some church notices from Mr. Stafford's room to give the visiting minister.

Celia opened the door for him and showed him to the second-story front room. With a thought of petitioning her to give him a sitting sometime, he lingered a moment.

"It's very sad indeed," he remarked to Celia, as though she knew all about the matter. "You knew there was no hope of her life? Oh, haven't you heard? Well, I suppose Stafford has his hands too full of other things to write. He gave me no particulars, only said all hope was gone and she could linger a few days longer at most. He asked me to get this man to preach and arrange everything for him. It'll be very hard for him, for he depended on her so much. They had a peculiarly close relationship. He never missed writing to her regularly, and some of her letters were wonderful. He read bits of them to me once or twice. She was a wonderful character. He'll miss her immeasurably."

Then Mr. Houston looked up from the papers he selected from the minister's table, to the face of the girl who stood silent in the doorway. He wondered whether he dared ask her to let him sketch her face sometime. But when he looked at her he remembered his friend's words, "She's not that kind of girl," and concluded his friend was right; it would be better not to ask her this time. He wondered what made it seem impossible to speak to her about it, as he would to other pretty girls just as nice and refined as she was. He thought as he looked again that she was white about the mouth, but, of course, that must have been his imagination.

Late the next Saturday night, after everyone retired, Horace Stafford returned to Philadelphia. Letting himself quietly in with his latchkey, he went to his room. They didn't know he'd returned the next morning at breakfast time, for one and another were wondering who'd preach. They said they wished their own minister was back and didn't know whether they cared to go to church or not. And they added all those other things people say when they love a minister, just as if he were their God and they went to church to worship him; and when he was absent they had no object for worship.

He called to Molly, as she passed through the hall early in the morning, and asked her for a cup of coffee. He told her not to mind if he didn't come to breakfast; he needed all his time for preparation since he was away so long. He went to church early, while those who were going out were dressing.

So not until Celia was seated in church and saw the little study door open and the minister walk out and into the pulpit, did she know Horace Stafford was back with them again.

She'd experienced many changes of feelings since the night Roger Houston spoke those few words to her. She didn't ask him then what he meant or who was lying so low and was so dear to Mr. Stafford. Instinctively she knew. It was the young woman of the pictured face, so sweet and lovely, within that velvet frame. Something rose in her throat while she listened and froze the words she would have spoken, an expression of sympathy for him, and her heart was filled with conflicting emotions.

She'd dreaded his return. It was as if her convictions were verified now, and knowing his heart was engaged she wished to put him entirely from her thoughts. It seemed impossible, though, for constantly the boarders would conjecture why Mr. Stafford was away, when he would return, and so forth.

She repeated a few of Mr. Houston's sentences, so few that boarders were left in doubt as to whether the one who was keeping the minister away was man, woman, or child. When Miss Burns asked if she knew whether it was one of the family, his mother perhaps, Celia answered briefly, "He didn't say." Then she wondered if she did wrong by not telling what she was certain of; but she silenced her conscience by saying he might not want them to know he was engaged at all.

Celia then tried to fill the week with hard work. She persuaded Dobson & Co. to let her introduce Mamie Williams into the ribbon business, with a view to possibly succeeding her in the future, and she found she could keep busy. Mamie was teachable enough and grew quick to appreciate the fine distinctions in manner and actions Celia strove to inculcate. But there was still room for improvement, and Celia worked steadily at her chosen task, molding the young woman's character as carefully as though she were an artist making a model for some marvelous statue.

"When you finish with her, Celia, dear, I'm afraid she'll be too good for the engineer. And I can see he wants her," said Aunt Hannah with a quiet smile.

"Well, that's all right, auntie," said Celia with a thoughtful sigh. "He'll make her a good husband, and I don't believe she'll be too good for him. It seems to me her influence on him has been wonderful. He seems to change as fast as she does. I never would have dreamed it last fall."

"I thought so, dear. Do you remember the talk we had about him some time ago? Most people have more good than we suspect. You have to live with them awhile to find it out," said Aunt Hannah.

"You mean *you* have to live with them, auntie, and *I* have to live with *you* to find out about them. I never would have found out all these boarders, if you hadn't been here with your 'saint's eyes' to read them."

Aunt Hannah smiled. But she watched Celia furtively and wished she could read *her* and understand what caused the little cloud to settle down upon her usually bright girl and make her heavyhearted these days.

But to return to church. Celia's heart throbbed painfully when she saw the minister walk into the pulpit. She knew by his face that his dear one was dead. His face didn't wear a look of bitter grief; rather one of chastened exaltation. He preached a sermon about heaven that morning that seemed written by one who'd stood very near its portals, seen them open, and caught glimpses of friends and of Jesus inside. Celia forgot her throbbing heart and listened, forgetting too who was preaching, absorbed in his words. She struggled to keep back the tears during the closing hymn, when they sang:

"And with the morn those angels' faces smile,
    Which I have loved long since, and lost awhile."

She knew why he selected it. He sat during the singing with shaded brow and bowed head. Celia couldn't sing. She felt as if she were choking. As soon as the benediction was pronounced and the solemn hush after it was broken, she bent down to hide her tears by searching for her umbrella which had rolled under the seat. When she rose again and turned around, the minister was standing in the aisle beside her.

He put out his hand and clasped hers, and a light of joy lit up his pale, worn face. "I'm so glad to see you again," he said.

They were ordinary words. He might have used them to any member of his congregation, with the same tone and look too, perhaps, she told herself as she hurried home. But they sent a thrill of mingled joy and sorrow through the girl which she didn't understand and couldn't control. One minute she was fiercely glad, and the next she was plunged in a whirl of shame and despair because it affected her so.

And now she was locked in her room. She took off her hat and coat and sat down, but she couldn't think. She could only feel the joy—and the certainty it wasn't hers. She tried to face herself and shame herself with saying plainly to her heart, "Celia Murray, you have fallen in love with Horace Stafford. Yes, and you did it when you knew he belonged to another woman, though you wanted to pretend it wasn't so because no one told you. But now you love him, and he *does not love you!* He's just buried his heart, and you know you wouldn't consider him the noble gentleman you think he is, if he forgot that love was 'so peculiarly close in its relationship.' And you love him in the face of that! Aren't you ashamed! He doesn't love you, and he never will, and you mustn't *let* him, and oh—what shall I do?"

The poor girl threw herself upon her knees and begged for forgiveness and help. She felt she did wrong to let her heart grow interested so easily. She tried to remember some of God's gracious promises for help and that He would bear her trouble for her. But her head seemed in a whirl of excitement, and she couldn't think clearly. She heard the dinner bell ring and rose to wash her face, but she decided she wouldn't go down. She wanted to be by herself. Molly came up soon and asked what was the matter. She told Molly to tell Aunt Hannah she had a headache and wouldn't come down now. Then she bathed her throbbing temples and lay down to calm herself before Aunt Hannah came, as she felt sure she would.

Wise Aunt Hannah! She knew something was amiss. She hadn't watched her girl in vain. She saw the start and the change of color when the minister came into the pulpit and again when he took her hand. She noticed other things during the months past. Just what the trouble was she didn't understand and wouldn't ask Celia yet. If Celia needed counsel, she'd confide in her sooner or later. In the meantime she could pray.

Aunt Hannah didn't go up to her room for some time. Instead, she arranged a lovely tray with a tempting lunch and fragrant cup of tea. Under the corner of the napkin she slipped a note that was merely a scrap of poetry with the words "Dear child" pencilled above it. It read:

Dear child:
God's plans for thee are graciously unfolding,
    And leaf by leaf they blossom perfectly,
As yon fair rose from its soft enfolding,
    In marvelous beauty open fragrantly.
Oh, wait in patience for thy dear Lord's coming,
    For sure deliverance He'll bring to thee;
Then, how thou shalt rejoice at the fair dawning
    Of that sweet morn which ends thy long captivity.

Then she laid beside it a lovely rosebud Harry Knowles brought her the night before and sent the tray up by Molly. She herself went to the third story and read to Mrs. Belden nearly all afternoon.

Chapter 25

Celia roused herself from her unhappiness in time to hurry to her Sunday school class. She purposely went late to avoid walking with anyone and intended to hurry home before others from their house left the chapel. But it so happened that one of her students had a sad tale to tell her of trouble and need, and she was obliged to linger and get the particulars—an address and information she'd need to help him find work.

When she finished and glanced hurriedly around to see if the others were gone, she noticed one of her boys lingering with an embarrassed expression, as though he wished to talk with her. Something told her this heart was ready for a quiet personal word, and here was the time. The other boarders were gone; the minister with hat in hand was standing by the front door talking with a man. He was evidently about to leave also. One or two groups were in earnest conversation, a teacher with two of her class, three women in a corner, and a young man and a young girl talking.

"Ben," she said, "can you sit down and talk with me a few minutes?"

A hunger for souls was awakened in the young teacher. Her own unrest and sadness increased her interest, and she put her whole soul into her words. The young man listened intently. There was no doubt she reached his heart and he was on the point of yielding to the Holy Spirit. Celia prayed as she talked and forgot herself, forgot everything but her desire for this soul's salvation. She listened with bated breath to his hesitant, quiet words in answer to her earnest questions. She could almost hear her own heart beating while she waited for his final decision. Minute after minute he stared at the toe of his rough, unblackened shoe, trying to fit it between two nails in the floor where the boards were worn away by many feet tramping over them.

The decision was made at last. The boy, with a furtive glance around him, wiped his coat sleeve hurriedly across his eyes and murmured an incoherent good-bye as he walked out of the room.

Celia stooped to pick up her rubber boots under the seat and then looked about the deserted room. The sexton was doing something to a refractory window, which refused to go up and down right. He was used to busying himself while lingerers kept the church open. Celia thought everybody else gone. As she neared the door, however, the minister rose from one of the back seats and walked toward her.

"Would you mind sitting down a few minutes longer?" he said. "I want to tell you something, and I think I can tell it better here than anywhere else."

Celia felt her heart throbbing, and her knees suddenly grew weak. She sat down then more to keep from tottering than because Mr. Stafford asked her to.

The day had been exciting for her, and her emotions were stirred deeply by the wonderful talk she'd just had with Ben. What could be coming now? She didn't understand, and yet she felt in some way it would have to do with what had hurt her all day and would probably hurt her more. She passed her hand across her forehead wearily, bracing herself to bear whatever might be said. Perhaps he'd ask for sympathy in his sorrow, and how could she give it? She sent up a prayer for help.

Horace Stafford noticed the weary expression and baffled look in her face. A troubled one crossed his own, as he took a seat in a chair near her.

"Are you too tired now? Perhaps I should wait. You've been working hard, and your work is telling, too. I could see by that boy's face as he left that he'll be different from now on. So if you'd rather go right home, please say so."

But a note of longing in his voice to be heard now caused Celia to push aside her desire to leave on the plea of weariness. She asserted, a little coolly perhaps, that she could hear him now as well as wait.

Her manner made his heart sink, but he began with a frank, "Well, then I'll try not to keep you long.

"Miss Celia"—it was the first time he'd ever called her that, though other boarders had adopted it from hearing Molly address her that way—"I don't know whether you know I've passed through deep waters during the past week. I've been by the deathbed and then the grave of someone who was very dear to me. I felt as though I wanted to tell you about her, not only because I need the sympathy which I know you can give, but because she knew all about you and your work and was deeply interested in you."

If the minister hadn't been looking down and struggling to control his voice in his deep emotion, he would have noticed Celia's face pale. It was worse than she feared. Not only was she asked to give sympathy, but this other woman knew all about her. They'd talked about her together. Why this was so dreadful to the girl she didn't understand, but at the time it was more than she could bear. It was well he didn't pause for her reply, for Celia couldn't have given any just then.

"She was ill for a long time," he went on, his voice breaking a little. "We knew she couldn't stay with us much longer, but it was so hard to part with her."

He told of her beautiful life of sweet patience and cheerfulness in the face of pain that endured for years, till Celia felt ashamed of her selfish jealousy and longed to shut herself away so she might cry. Tears filled her eyes and fell unnoticed on her hands. She felt like the meanest, smallest mortal and this other one beautiful and bright enough to be, as she was, with the angels. She longed to speak a word of sympathy but knew she couldn't and blamed herself for it.

"I want to show you her face," he said, pulling from his breast pocket a velvet case Celia knew even through her blinding tears. He opened and placed it in her hands, the lovely face with its soft blue eyes looking into hers. "She was my only sister, and she was *so good* to me." Then the man bowed his head on his hand and covered his eyes.

He didn't see Celia start, as he said this, but he heard the difference in her startled exclamation. "Your sister? Why! I thought—!"

He glanced up at once. Her cheeks had turned from white to rosy red. In her face, lovely behind its tears and blushes, he read the dawning sympathy and was glad, even in his sorrow.

"You thought what—may I know?"

"Why, I—," said Celia, blushing deeply. "I—I didn't know you had only one sister!" she finished desperately.

"But what was it you thought? May I not know?" he asked again, with a searching look at her face.

"No," said Celia, dropping her eyes to the picture and trying to hide her embarrassment by wiping away the tears with her handkerchief.

"Then may I tell you and you'll say whether I'm right?" asked the minister, a daring light coming into his eyes. "You thought she was even nearer and dearer than a sister?"

He looked at her long and earnestly and seemed satisfied with the answer of her silent, bowed face.

"Oh, Celia, didn't you know you were the only one who ever did or would occupy that place in my heart? Haven't you seen that I love you? Don't you know it? And don't you care just a little, Celia?"

The front chapel door stood open, and the afternoon spring sunshine was flickering fitfully across the floor. They could see the people on the street passing, loitering and talking, some looking curiously in as they passed, but none seeming to notice them. Celia felt it all as she sat there in the whirl of joy and sorrow and shame and what else, she didn't know. She couldn't answer, couldn't look up. The minister's eyes were upon her, and she felt what the look in them would be and knew she couldn't bear the joy of seeing it.

The silence was long and could almost be heard. The sexton, growing hungry, came back from the alcove where the primary class was held and where he'd been straightening chairs for the evening service and distributing hymnbooks. He drew closer to them now and slammed books and closed windows significantly.

Feeling she must say something, with her eyes still downcast, Celia murmured quietly, "How would I know it?"

The minister laughed and then grew serious. "That's true," he said. "I never could tell you, because you wouldn't let me. But *she* knew it, and she was glad of it. And she loved you and left her blessing for you."

Then he turned suddenly to the sexton, a new tone in his voice. Something about Celia no longer discouraged him.

"Thomas," he said, "I'm going now. Will you kindly see if I left my Bible in the primary room?"

Thomas went with alacrity to search the primary room.

The minister watched the sexton until he disappeared, and then he bent and picked up Celia's gloves which had fallen unnoticed to the floor. He handed them to her, reverently touching his lips to one of her little, cold, ungloved hands. She lifted her face for a moment, and in that moment he got his answer from her eyes.

The sexton was coming back without the Bible, which the minister suddenly discovered to be lying on the floor under his chair, and the two stood decorously apart. Celia tried to keep her cheeks from growing redder, as she walked to the open door and looked out into the glad spring sunshine, gladder than any sunshine her eyes had looked upon.

Some little child, perhaps, had dropped a flower upon the steps. As she waited for the minister, she saw it. Then she remembered the rose on her lunch tray and its sweet message of hope.

> God's plans for thee are graciously unfolding,
> And leaf by leaf they blossom perfectly.

Her heart thrilled with delight that this had come true. She realized her happiness was only budding, yet she saw the promise of its opening day by day. Oh, why did she doubt? Why couldn't she trust Him perfectly? She lifted her heart in one swift breath of penitence and thanksgiving. She felt in that first gush of ecstasy that she would never doubt her Lord again.

Then she turned to walk down the glorified street and gaze on the familiar surroundings under a halo of joy.

Chapter 26

It was noon and it was June, and a wedding was about to be in Mrs. Morris's former boardinghouse. It was not *the* wedding, the one nearest and dearest to Aunt Hannah's heart; that was to be later in the new chapel, and most of the boarders hadn't even heard about it yet. Later, when they knew, the bridegroom of the first wedding said it was a pity they didn't fix things up sooner, so they could've had a double wedding; that would have been "real nice."

Celia and Horace Stafford had looked meaningfully at one another and never hinted that such an arrangement would have been anything other than entirely satisfactory to them, provided "things had been fixed up" in time. They laughed quietly over it, of course, and kept their secret.

Meanwhile, the present wedding was a source of deep interest to every member of the household. Each one contributed something to the general plans. The once-dismal parlor was itself in bridal array.

The organ at the further end was smothered in palms. Roger Houston contributed the palms and flowers. He wasn't a boarder, but he'd become a frequent visitor at the house and was as much interested as anyone in the event.

Celia arranged the palms and was to sit behind them and play the wedding march in the softest, sweetest tones she could coax from the old organ. They made a lovely background for the bride and groom and hid the organ and player. Under and above the mantelpiece, where the crayoned visage of the deceased Mr. Morris used to hang, were more palms. The imitation-marble mantelpiece, which Celia always said looked as mottled as if it were made of slices of Bologna sausage, was covered with a bank of lovely roses, white, pink, yellow, and crimson. If the wedding were Celia's, she'd have preferred all white roses, but the bride in this case was extravagantly fond of color.

She'd declared herself in favor of "lots of roses all colors" so longingly that Roger Houston said, "Let's please her for once if she wants *green* roses, even if the white would be in better taste, Miss Murray. It's her first wedding, and, after all, a rose is a rose."

But Celia arranged the colors with skill, and no two colors dared but harmonize.

Out in the dining room the long white table was dressed in trailing vines of smilax and roses, and the largest and most traditional wedding cake available occupied the place of honor. All around it were evidences of Molly Poppleton's art, and everything was ready for the ceremony to begin.

Up in her room the bride was being dressed. The gown was a simple white muslin, but she was to wear a veil. It might have been more sensible to wear a traveling dress, since she was to go away at once. But Mamie (for of course you know the bride was Mamie Williams and the groom Bob Yates) cried and said she wouldn't feel really married if she didn't wear white, when Miss Grant counseled economy and good sense. Seeing her heart so set, they didn't try to persuade her. But they did convince her not to purchase a flimsy white silk, which would never be any use to her afterward, and take the simple white lawn instead. She had demurred but finally consented. She was never reconciled to the change, however, but was somewhat consoled that it was white and she would have a veil.

Celia arranged her hair and the soft folds of the veil, and kissed her, and she told her aunt afterward that Mamie Williams looked lovely in her pretty attire. Aunt Hannah thought so too as she came up to give the girl a few last words, as her mother might have done if she'd been there. She found Mamie standing by her bureau with her open Bible before her. Aunt Hannah didn't know that seeing herself all in white in the glass prompted her to turn to that first Bible verse: "And to her was granted that she should be arrayed in fine linen, clean and white; for the fine linen is the righteousness of the saints." Nor could she know that the soft, glorified look on her face came from her thought that now even she might wear that pure heavenly dress of clean white linen, the garment of Christ's own righteousness.

Bob Yates had saved up a nice little sum, and now, not many blocks away, a new house of four or five rooms, neatly furnished, awaited them. There Mamie was to practice the culinary arts she learned from Miss Grant and Molly Poppleton and entertain her friends and some of the young girls she'd grown intimate with when she sold ribbons with Dobson and Co. She'd attained to that and taken Celia's place, and now in turn she was giving it up to a young girl from the minister's Sunday school class.

And they'd take a real wedding trip, too, like the girls in the stories Mamie had read when she imagined Harold Adams held the key to all delights for her. They were going to Atlantic City to a hotel for a whole wonderful week, and they were going to see Mamie's mother, her little brothers and sisters, and her gruff, hardworking father. After that Bob Yates would take his bride to visit his married brother and sister out in Indiana—the far west, Mamie called it—and then they'd come back to their little house and their new furniture, and their dear church and respective Sunday school classes.

Mamie felt very happy, and all the boarders felt happy for her. She remembered when Mrs. Morris was there and felt, rather than thought, how different her life was now. In fact everything was different, and she thanked God for the change. She thought of Carrie Simpson with a pang and wished she could have done something for her. Perhaps, if Miss Grant had come sooner, Carrie might have been saved. As it was, she'd heard her old roommate was living in misery and shame.

Miss Grant went down to the kitchen to watch things while Molly put on her best gown for the ceremony, and everything was progressing toward the last exciting minute when the doorbell rang. The second girl who was arranging chairs in the dining room walked quietly to the door. Her neat blue and white striped gingham and white apron and cap contrasted sharply with the slatternly Maggie who used to answer the door in Mrs. Morris's time.

The large, old woman and the tall, grizzled man, unmistakably a farmer, standing on the step stared at the girl in amazement.

"Why!" said the woman at last, looking up at the number over the door. "Isn't this—at least—isn't this a boardinghouse?"

"Yes, it is," responded the maid. "Won't you come in? Miss Grant is busy just now—that is, she will be in a minute—but I guess she can see you first. Did you want board?"

She ushered them into the parlor, which at the moment was empty, since the boarders were all in their rooms donning their festive attire.

But they evidently didn't hear her question. Telling them to be seated, she then went for Miss Grant.

The strangers, however, didn't sit down. Instead, they stood staring around the parlor.

"For the land sake!" exclaimed the woman at last, looking more and more bewildered.

"Wal, it's pretty nice, 'pon honor, M'ria. I wonder now you ever give it up fer an ole fellow like me," he said and looked at her quizzically.

But the look was lost this time. She was taking in the familiar pattern of the carpet, which looked strangely bright, and noting everything new and old about the room.

Then Hannah Grant entered in her soft gray cashmere, made lovelier by the white tulle about her neck, which blended so well with her creamy white hair. She looked doubtfully at the visitors, noticing something familiar about the woman's face, but for an instant not recognizing her.

"Miss Grant, don't you know me? I'm Mrs. Morris—leastways that used to be me name. I'm Mrs. Sparks now. I married out there in Ohio, and I'm real comfortably fixed. He"—nodding her head toward the man—"has a farm and a nice house and owns several houses in the town besides. But I couldn't rest comfortably noways, a-thinkin' of you an' the hole I left you in. At last me husband found out what was the matter, an' he just brought me on to see how you was gettin' along. He said he'd help you out of it, if you got badly stuck, and pay some of the bills I left behind. But when we got here everything looked so different that I couldn't think 'twas me own house. You don't look as if you was hard up. What's the mean' of it all anyway, an' what's goin' on? Are you expectin' company?"

Miss Grant's face shone with welcome and her greeting was cordial, even in the midst of this busy time.

"We're going to have a wedding in half an hour," she said cordially, her face shining, "and you're just in time. They'll both be delighted to have you here—they're two of your old boarders. And you can relieve your mind about me, for I'm not in any hole at all, and coming here was the best thing that ever happened to me in some ways. I'm grateful to you for giving me a full-fledged boardinghouse. Every month I'm getting on a little more financially. It isn't great riches, but it's sure."

"A wedding! For the land sake!" said Mrs. Morris-Sparks.

After Miss Grant excused herself quickly to answer a call from Molly, the guest called after her.

"It must be that nice niece of yours, Miss Murray, but I didn't never think she'd take Bob Yates. She used to be so awful stiff with him, but, land alive, you never can tell!"

Miss Grant smiled to herself as she hurried down the hall. She wouldn't explain now, as the visitor would soon see for herself.

That evening, after the guests were gone and the bridal pair departed, Miss Grant took Mrs. Morris-Sparks and slipped out the front door. She let her in by a latchkey to the adjoining house which had for months been closed, with a "For Rent" sign in the window. This, however, had disappeared. She carefully locked the door behind her and, turning up the gas, pointed out the place where wide, double doors were roughly drafted on the wall between the two houses. She also enlarged upon other improvements, among them a wide bay window to be added in both first and second stories of the front of the houses. Then she took her upstairs, showed her a suite of beautifully furnished rooms and told the story of how the minister bought this house and furnished these rooms for himself and Celia. The houses were to be connected, and the remainder of the room used to enlarge the boardinghouse, in which scheme their hearts were deeply interested.

She told her, too, that with careful looking to the little details she'd not only made both ends meet but had a little over. And she hoped in the coming year with the expansion and her present experience to make it a paying business.

And Mrs. Morris-Sparks looked and listened and shook her head. But all she could say was, "For the land sake! Who'd 'a' thought it!"

Chapter 27

Hiram and Nettie Bartlett had talked a good deal lately about running down to Philadelphia to see Aunt Hannah and Celia. Hiram felt a little ready money in his business would enable him to get through a hard time he saw ahead. Nettie was missing Aunt Hannah dreadfully, as the hot days grew longer. They decided it would be good to forget and forgive, and open their home and as much of their hearts as was necessary to their relatives.

Aunt Hannah would manage the kitchen, and Celia the children, and Hiram would manage Celia's money. After deciding matters thus and arranging the rooms to suit the new order of things, they felt sure it was to be. Of course Aunt Hannah and Celia were thoroughly tired of living in a boardinghouse by this time and would welcome the change, and they had only to speak the word and they'd fly back to Cloverdale. But before they came, it would be a pleasant change to take the children to Philadelphia for a visit.

No sooner had they decided this than Nettie wrote to Aunt Hannah.

The letter reached Philadelphia in the midst of Celia's wedding plans. Celia and Aunt Hannah read it together and looked at one another in dismay. Somehow, in the joy of the life they were living, they forgot to write Nettie about Celia's proposed marriage. Perhaps it was natural, since Nettie seldom answered Aunt Hannah's long letters which she wrote at regular intervals at first, until she felt they weren't desired. But now they both thought Nettie must be invited.

Celia summoned all the cousinly feeling she'd ever possessed for Nettie and wrote her a nice letter, adding a little touch of her sweet girlish joy over her new happiness. She finished with a cordial invitation to them all to come on, though the addition to the family at this time would be extremely inconvenient.

Celia fretted a little over their coming. Hiram would be disagreeable, and Nettie would want to manage everything, and the children would be always about when they weren't wanted.

She was sitting one evening with her brow wrinkled when Horace Stafford entered. He watched her a moment and then, placing his hands on her brow, smoothed the wrinkles out. Then he bent and kissed her forehead gently.

"What's the matter, dear?" he said. "I mean to make it my business to keep that troubled look away from your sweet face."

"Oh, Horace! How can I help it? I've tried and tried, but I don't seem able to conquer the habit. Indeed, I'm ashamed of it. Can't you tell me how to conquer it?"

"Only by casting all your care upon Him who cares for you. Listen, Celia, have you ever heard this?" he asked.

"Wherefore should we do ourselves this wrong,
    Or others, that we are not always strong;
That we are ever overborne with care,
    That we should ever weak or heartless be,
Anxious or troubled, when with us is prayer,
    And joy and strength and courage are with Thee?"

Then Celia opened her heart to him and told him the story of her winter, beginning with her birthday and the little bookmark Aunt Hannah sent.

"And I thought then, Horace," she went on, "after that money came to me, my 'daily rate' for 'all the days of my life,' that I'd never doubt anymore because I had money. With that I could relieve most of the other anxieties. But I found it wasn't so. I began to fret about other things. Then after I got money, I wanted love. And now that I have that, I find I'm still fretting."

"It's because you don't remember that it's 'for every day,' and that means for every need of every day. You trust from one set of things, but you think you have to worry along and look out for another set. Here's an old poem I cut out the other day and saved to read to you. It fits in right here. Let me read it," he said, pulling the paper from his pocket.

"I have a never-failing bank,
    My more than golden store;
No earthly bank is half so rich,
    How, then, can I be poor?

" 'Tis when my stock is spent and gone,
    And I not worth a groat;
I'm glad to hasten to my bank,
    And beg a little note.

"Sometimes my banker smiling says,
    Why don't you oftener come?
And when you draw a little note,
    Why not a larger sum?

"Why live so niggardly and poor,
    My bank contains a plenty;
Why come and take a one-pound note,
    When you can have a twenty?

"Nay, twenty thousand ten times told
    Is but a trifling sum,

To what my Father has laid up
  For me in God and Son.

"Since, then, my banker is so rich,
  I have no need to borrow,
But live upon my notes today,
  And draw again tomorrow."

∽

Nettie Barlett settled herself for the homeward trip from Philadelphia with a discontented look. She slapped Johnny when he went to get a drink—which he did in the first fifteen minutes of the journey—because he stepped on her toes. She jerked the baby, who was endeavoring to pick orange peel out of a pool of tobacco juice on the floor, and then settled into her discontented silence again. She was thinking about the fall sewing, the housecleaning, and the endless darning and baking, with no Aunt Hannah to fall back on.

Occasionally, she reflected upon the bride's pretty dress or had visions of Celia in her cloudlike veil looking up with happy eyes into her husband's face, and a half-jealous feeling shot through her heart. She knew how Celia felt—or thought she did. She'd felt so herself, but of course all such nonsense was passed. She looked gloomily across at Hiram, who was staring stolidly out of the window, with his inevitable newspaper lying across his knees. Then she curled her lip and told herself Celia would soon have the sentiment taken out of her by the prose of everyday life.

"You made a great mistake by not cultivating that minister cousin-in-law, Nettie," remarked Hiram snappily. "I talked to him every chance I got. But it takes women and compliments and that sort of thing to work on men, especially ministers, I guess. You ought to have invited them to our house for part of their wedding trip. I'm dead certain he's rich. Did you see all that furniture he's fixed out for Celia? He'll spoil her first thing."

"You made a great mistake yourself when you let Aunt Hannah, and Celia, too, leave our house, and you can't ever undo it. Yes, I saw the furniture, but his mother sent it, for Celia said so. We might have had a few blessings, and our children would have been brought up right, if Aunt Hannah had been with us. She always brings a blessing wherever she goes, and we've had nothing but ill luck since she left us."

Nettie put her handkerchief to her eyes and wept while the train sped rapidly through the darkness.

∽

Some weeks later Celia was seated in the pleasant study of her new home, and yet her old home. She was engaged in the delightful task of classifying and placing in a cabinet the various clippings her minister husband gathered about him during his bachelor years. She came upon this poem and, pausing to read it, smiled with an echo of the peace it spoke in her heart. Then she bent her head to thank her Father it was true.

> The child leans on its parent's breast,
>   Leaves there its cares and is at rest;
> The bird sits singing by his nest,
>   And tells aloud
> His trust in God, and so is blest
>   'Neath every cloud.
> He has no store, he sows no seed;
>   Yet sings aloud, and doth not heed;
> By flowing stream of grassy mead,
>   He sings to shame
> Men, who forget, in fear of need,
>   A Father's name.
> The heart that trusts, forever sings,
>   And feels as light as it had wings;
> A well of peace within its springs;
>   Come good or ill,
> Whate'er today, tomorrow brings,
>   It is His will.

The Girl
From Montana

Chapter 1

T he late afternoon sun streamed in across the cabin floor as the girl stole around the corner and peered cautiously in at the door.

She had a duty to perform and was resolved to do it without delay. She shaded her eyes from the glare of the sun and stepped firmly onto the threshold. With one glance around to see whether all was as she left it, the girl entered her home and stood for a moment shuddering in the middle of the floor.

Memories of a long procession of funerals journeyed out of the past as she looked upon the signs of the primitive, unhallowed funeral just gone out from there.

The girl closed her eyes, pressing the hot, dry lids with her cold fingers. But the vision was clearer than with her eyes open.

She could see the tiny baby sister lying there in the middle of the room. Her handsome father sat at the head of the rude homemade coffin, sober for the moment, with her mother, faded before her time, beside him. But that was long ago, almost at the beginning.

There had been other funerals: the little brother, drowned while playing in a forbidden stream, and the older brother, set off in search of gold or his own way, crawling back parched with fever to die in his mother's arms. But those, too, seemed long ago to the girl as she stood in the empty cabin and looked fearfully about her. They seemed almost blotted out by the last three that had crowded so close within the year. The father, who even at his worst had a kind word for her and her mother, had been brought home mortally hurt—and never roused to consciousness.

At all these funerals a solemn service was conducted by a traveling preacher when one happened to be within reach or by the determined, untaught lips of the mother. The mother had always insisted upon it, especially a prayer. It had seemed like a charm to help the departed one into a pitiful heaven.

And then, a few months after the father, the mother grew pale, till one day she clutched at her heart and lay down. "Good-bye, Bess! Mother's good girl! Don't forget!" she said and was gone from her burdened life. The girl prepared that funeral with the aid of the one remaining brother. Her voice had uttered the prayer, "Our Father," just as her mother had taught her. There was no one else to do it, and she was afraid to send the wild young brother for a preacher, lest he not return in time.

Six months had passed since the funeral train wound its way among sage-brush and greasewood, and the mother's body laid to rest beside her husband. For six months the girl kept the cabin in order and, when possible, the brother to his work and home. But in the last few weeks he often left her alone, for a day and sometimes longer. Then he'd come home in a sad condition with rowdy companions who terrorized her. Now, two short days ago, they brought his body lying across his horse, with two shots through his heart. They told her it was a drunken quarrel, and they were sorry; but no one seemed responsible.

Her brother's companions were kind in their rough way. They dug the grave and stood around their comrade in good-natured grimness, marching about him to give a last look. But when the girl tried to utter the prayer her mother would have spoken, her throat refused to let out a sound. She took refuge in her room in the shed and stayed there till the rough companions took away the still form of the only one left in the family circle.

In silence the funeral procession wound its way to the spot where the others were buried. The wild young men respected the sister's tearless grief. They withheld their rude jokes and looked back now and then to the slim girl who followed them with a stony face. They thought someone should do something, but no one knew what; so they walked on silently.

Only one, the ringleader, ventured back to ask if he could do anything for her. But she answered coldly with a "No!" that cut him; he'd forced himself to be gentle. He turned sharply away from her with a wicked expression in his eyes, but she didn't see it.

The crude ceremony was over, the last clod heaped on the mound and the relentless words "dust to dust" murmured by one who dared. The men turned and looked at the girl, who had stood on a mound of earth and watched them as a statue might. They couldn't figure out the silent, marble girl. They hoped she would change now that it was over. They felt relieved because their comrade was no longer lying cold and still among them. He must settle his own account with the hereafter now; they had enough in their own lives without the burden of his.

One glimmer of life crossed the girl's face, making her beautiful for an instant. She bowed her head to them and spread out her hands.

"I thank you—all!"

She hesitated before the last word, as her eyes rested upon the ringleader, and then, as if she must be just, uttered it. Turning, she fled to her cabin alone.

Those men who feared nothing in the wild, primitive West were taken by surprise, and for a moment they watched her go in silence. Had the girl heard the words that broke the air, she would have sped away much faster.

But the ringleader said nothing. His brows darkened, and the wicked look returned to his eyes. He walked on ahead of the others and reached the horses first. He took his and rode alone to the cabin.

The girl in the cabin worked quickly. She took the boxes that had lain under the coffin, threw them out the back door and moved the furniture around, as if to erase the scenes just passed. Then she took her brother's coat from its peg on the wall and an old pipe from the mantel and hid them in her room.

Suddenly a shadow darkened the sunny doorway. Looking up, the girl saw the man she believed to be her brother's murderer.

"I came back, Bess, to see if I could do anything for you."

His tone was kind enough. The girl caught her breath. She wanted to tell him what she thought, but she didn't dare; nor did she let her thought appear in her eyes. The dull look she wore at the grave crossed her face, and the man thought it was grief.

"I told you I didn't want any help," she said, trying to speak in the same tone she used when she thanked the men.

"Yes, but you're alone," said the man, "and I feel sorry for you!"

She felt the menace in his words.

He came closer. Instinctively she glanced at the cupboard door; behind it lay her brother's belt with two pistols.

"You're very kind," she forced herself to say, "but I'd rather be alone now."

It took all of her strength to speak calmly when she wanted to strike out at him and call down curses for the death of her brother. But she looked at his face, and a fear for herself worse than death stole into her heart.

He took encouragement from her gentle dignity. Where did she get such a manner when she was born in a mountain cabin and bred in the wilds? How could she speak with an accent so different from those about her? The brother wasn't that way, and the mother had been plain and quiet. He hadn't known her father, since he'd recently come to this state in hiding from another. Despite his knowledge of the world, he was awed by her wild, haughty beauty and gloated over it. Here she was, a prize for the taking, alone, unprotected.

"But it ain't good for you to be alone. I'll protect you. Besides, you need cheering up, little girl." He came nearer. "I love you, Bess, you know, and I'm going to take care of you now."

She almost felt his breath on her cheek. She faced him, growing white to the lips. Was there nothing on earth or in heaven to save her? Mother, father, brother—gone! If she'd known the quarrel that ended her wild brother's life had been about her, pride in him might have assuaged her grief and choked her horror.

She watched the glint in his eyes but calmed herself. She mustn't shrink from him. Instead she drew back gently, as a woman with wide experience and fine breeding might have done.

"Remember—my brother was just lying there dead!" she said, pointing to the center of the room.

Her dramatic gesture and tone almost convicted the man. He drew himself together.

The girl caught her breath and took courage. She held him for a minute.

"Think about it!" she said. "He was just lying in this room, and now he's buried. It isn't right to talk about love here. You must leave me alone for awhile. I can't talk or think now. We must respect the dead, you know." In desperation she appealed to him.

He had half a mind to humor her. When she spoke of the dead he could see the look in her brother's eyes just before he shot him. Wooing her may hold promise after all. He wouldn't win her easily, for she could hold her own. She might be the better for getting her way a little. At any rate, he liked the excitement of such a game.

She saw she was gaining and breathed more easily.

"Go!" she said with a faint smile. "Go for a little while."

He tried to take her in his arms and kiss her, but she held up her hands to stop him.

"I tell you—you mustn't now. Go! Or I'll never speak to you again."

He looked in her eyes and sensed some power he must obey. Sullenly he drew back toward the door.

"But, Bess, this ain't the way to treat a fellow," he said. "I came back here to take care of you. I love you, and I'm going to have you. No other fellow's going to run off with you—"

"Stop!" she cried. "Don't you see this is wrong? My brother has just died. I need time to mourn. It's only decent."

By now she stood with her back to the little cupboard where the two pistols lay. Her hand was behind her on the wooden latch.

"You have no respect for my troubles!" she said, putting her hand to her eyes. "You don't care for me if you won't do as I say."

The man was almost overcome by her tears. He'd never seen her weak and found it charming.

"How long—must I stay away?" he asked, faltering.

"Forever!" she wanted to shout, if only she dared, but she could scarcely speak.

She was desperate enough to shoot him if she had the pistols and was sure they were loaded. And that would be a desperate chance, indeed, against the best shot on the Pacific Coast and a desperado at that.

She pressed her hands to her throbbing temples and tried to think. At last she said, "Three days!"

He swore under his breath and frowned.

She shuddered to think what it would be like to be in his power forever. He'd play with her and toss her aside—or kill her when he tired of her! Life on the mountain had taught her about evil.

He took a step toward her.

She was losing ground, she thought. Straightening up, she said coolly, "You must go away at once and not think of coming back at least until tomorrow night. Go!" She smiled at him, one frantic smile. To her amazement he pulled back. At the door he paused, a softened expression on his face.

"May I kiss you before I go?"

She shuddered without thinking but held up her hands in protest again.

"Not tonight!" she said, shaking her head and forcing a smile.

He thought he understood her and turned away half satisfied.

Then she heard his step coming back to the door and went to meet him. He mustn't come in again. She'd gained the advantage in sending him out and wished she could close the door quickly. She confronted him in the doorway as he stood ready to enter. In the sunlight she could see the scheming look upon his face.

"You'll be alone tonight."

"I'm not afraid," she said calmly, "and no one will trouble me. Don't you know what they say about the spirit of a man—" She stopped; she'd almost said, "who is murdered." She continued, "—coming back to his home the first night after he's buried?"

The man looked around nervously. "You better come away tonight with me," he said, edging away from the door.

"See, the sun's setting! You must go now," she said with authority.

Reluctantly the man mounted his horse and rode down the mountain.

She watched his silhouette against the blood-red globe of the sun as it sank lower. She could see the outline of his slouched hat and muscular shoulders.

Now and then he turned and saw her standing alone at her cabin door. Why he was going he didn't know. But he rode away, frowning, with the gleam in his eye; he meant to return. At last he disappeared.

The girl looked up. The white ghost of the moon rode overhead. She was alone.

Chapter 2

F ear settled upon the girl as she realized she was alone and, for a few hours at least, free. Her escape was miraculous. Even now she could hear the echo of the man's last words and see his malicious smile as he waved and promised to come back for her tomorrow.

She was sure he wouldn't wait until then. He might backtrack even now. She looked down the darkening road again and listened carefully. She could no longer hear hoofbeats, but she must hurry. He paled at her suggestion of walking spirits, but his courage might rise up after all. She shuddered to think of his returning later in the night. She must flee.

She stepped inside the cabin, barring the door. She hadn't an instant to spare. He might even return before dark. Her one chance of safety was to get away hastily; where, mattered little—only that she was away and hidden.

She pulled the belt from the cupboard and buckled it around her waist. Her throat tightened when she discovered the barrels empty. Even if she could have reached them, the weapons would have done her no good. She loaded the pistols.

Tucking her brother's small, sharp knife into her belt, she gathered up every bit of food she could carry—dried beef, cheese, cornmeal, pork, coffee berries and a few pieces of hard corn bread. She hesitated over half a pan of baked beans and finally added them. She had no desire for food and now realized she hadn't eaten all day. While she worked, she forced herself to eat a few pieces of dry corn bread and swallow some coffee that stood cold in the coffeepot.

Next she found some old flour sacks in the cabin and packed the food into two of them, with the pan of beans on top, adding a tin cup and tieing them together securely. Then she went into her shed room and put on the few extra garments from her wardrobe; it was the easiest way to carry them. From a box she took her mother's wedding ring and slipped it on her finger. She had kept it as a sacred treasure since her death, and now it seemed to be the closing act of her life in the cabin. The girl paused and bent her head as if to ask her mother's permission to wear the ring. Perhaps it would protect her in her lonely situation.

The box also held some papers and an old letter or two yellowed with the years, which the mother had guarded carefully. One was her mother's marriage certificate, but the girl didn't know what the others were. She'd never looked at them closely, but she knew her mother had counted them as precious. She pinned these into the bosom of her calico dress.

The girl gave one glance of farewell about the cabin. She'd spent nearly all of her life there, at least what she could remember. She gathered up the two flour sacks and her father's old coat that hung on the wall, remembering at the last minute to put in its pockets the few matches and the single candle from the table. Then she left the cabin, closing the door behind her.

The girl paused, looking down the road, and listened again. No sound came to her but the distant howl of a wolf. The moon rode high and clear by this time. It didn't seem so lonely outside, with everything bathed in soft silver, as it had in the darkening cabin with its flickering candle.

She stole away from the cabin across the patch of moonlight into the shadow of the weathered barn. The faithful horse on which her brother rode to his death stood there stamping, as though he too were ready to go.

She laid the coat over the horse's back and swung her brother's saddle into place. She had no saddle of her own and could as easily use his—or none, for that matter, for she was at home on horseback. Her fingers ice cold with excitement, she strapped the girths and hung the two flour sacks across the saddlebows.

As an added measure, she tied some old burlap about each of the horse's feet; she must make no sound and leave no track. The horse looked down curiously and whinnied at her.

"Hush!" she murmured, laying her cold hands across his nostrils. He put his muzzle softly into her palm.

She led the horse out into the clear moonlight and once more looked down the road that led away in front of the cabin. No one was coming yet, though her heart beat fast as she listened, imagining every falling bough or rolling stone to be a horse's hoofbeat.

Three trails led away from the cabin: one down the mountain toward the west, to the nearest clearing five or six miles away and the supply store some three miles farther; a second, less traveled, to the east and into the world; and a third behind the cabin, deserted and barren under the moon. That third trail led back to desolation, where five graves lay stark and ugly at the end. It was the way they took that afternoon.

She hesitated, not sure which trail to take. Not the one to the west—any but that! To the east? Yes, that must be the trail she would eventually strike, but she had a duty to perform. That prayer was still unsaid. Before she could seek safety—if there was such a thing for her in the world—she must make her way down the lonely path. She walked in front of the horse, holding the reins, as he followed with muffled steps. Slowly, silently, she moved into the river of moonlight and dreariness. The moonlight here seemed cold, and the girl, as she walked with bowed head, almost imagined she saw strange misty forms flit past her in the night.

As they came in view of the graves, something dark and wild with a plumy tail slunk into the shadows. The girl stopped to gather her courage when she saw the graves. The horse snorted and stopped, too, his ears twitching and his eyes darting back and forth over the scene.

She patted his neck and soothed him, mumbling, as she buried her face in his mane and let the first tears fall. Then, leaving the horse to watch her, she went down to the head of the new mound. She tried to kneel, but a shudder passed through her. She felt as if she were descending into the place of the dead herself; so she stood and lifted her eyes to the night and the moon riding high and far away.

"Our Father," she said in a voice that sounded miles off. Was there a Father, she wondered, and could He hear her? And did He care? "Which art in heaven"—but heaven was so far away and looked so cruelly serene to her in her danger and desolation. "Hallowed be thy name. Thy kingdom come"— whatever that might mean. "Thy will be done in earth, as it is in heaven."

It was a long prayer to pray, alone with the pale moon rain, the graves, and a distant wolf; but it was her mother's wish. Her will being done here over the dead—was that anything like the will of the Father being done in heaven? Her untrained thoughts hovered on the verge of asking deep questions and then slipped back behind her fear, while her tongue hurried on through the words of the prayer.

Once the horse stirred and breathed a soft protest. He had looked at the shapeless mound before which the girl was standing but saw no sign of his lost master, and his instincts warned him wild animals were about.

A few loose stones rattled from the horse's motion. The girl started, glancing around and listening for a possible pursuer, but she saw only bleak space in the white sea of moonlight. She finished with the "amen" and, with one last look at the lonely graves, turned to the horse. Now they might go, the duty done, with no time to lose.

Somewhere to the east was the trail that led from the cabin to the world beyond. She dared not return to the cabin to take it, lest she find herself followed. Neither she nor the horse knew the way across the plain. In fact, there was no way. The arid plain was so situated that human travelers seldom came near it. It was so large and barren that one might wander there for hours and go nowhere, and so dry that nothing would grow.

With another glance over her shoulder, the girl mounted the horse and urged him down into the valley. He stepped cautiously onto the sandy plain, as if he were entering a river and must test its depth. The girl was light; he didn't mind her weight. But he couldn't get a sure footing and stumbled here and there. He preferred the high mountain trails, where he could step firmly and hear the twigs crackle under his feet.

The girl's heart sank as they trudged on, for the sand was deep and drifted in places. She was losing time. The way ahead appeared endless. It was like the valley of the dead, and she longed to escape it. Sudden fear seized her lest the moon go down and leave her in this dark valley alone. She must get higher. She turned the horse a little more to the right. He paused, surveying the new direction, then stepped more briskly. At last they were rewarded with shallower sand and now and then a bit of rock.

The young rider dismounted and untied the burlap from the horse's feet. He nosed about her neck as if to thank her. Perhaps their mission was over, and they could head home. But she remounted and continued their eastward direction.

The ground rose steadily before them and at times grew steep. But the horse was still fresh and clambered upward with a stout heart, while the rider was used to rough places and felt no discomfort. For now, the fear of being followed had given way to the fear of being lost; instead of listening closely to the track behind, she watched the wilderness ahead. The sagebrush was dense now, and trees lay ahead.

After that she grew fearful that she couldn't climb the sheer incline and find the trail that must lie somewhere in that direction, though she'd never taken it far. That it led straight east into the great cities she never doubted, and she must reach it soon. The man would be enraged when he found her gone! He wasn't beyond shooting her for giving him the slip.

The more she thought about it, the more frightened she became, till every obstacle seemed treacherous to her. A bobcat shot across her path. She caught her breath when she saw its green eyes staring sharply at the intruders and put her hand on a pistol.

They climbed for what seemed like hours to the girl, when at last they reached a spot where she could get a better view. The land was high and sloped away on three sides. In the clear night she could make out the outline of a mountain ahead, but the lay of the land was not what she'd expected. It gave her a curious sense of being lost. Over to one side ought to be the familiar direction of the cabin, but she recognized no landmarks. The course she'd chosen, which seemed to be the only one, would take her straight up over the mountain, but it was nearly impossible.

She must change her course, but which way? After all, one might be as good as another, as long as it didn't lead to the cabin. Why not give the horse his lead and let him pick out a safe path? Would he carry her back to the cabin? Horses did that sometimes. But at least he could guide them through this maze until some surer place was reached. She signalled him, and he nimbly found a path for his feet.

They entered a forest where scraggly branches let the pale moon through in patches, and grim figures seemed to chase them from every shadowy tree trunk. Sometimes the girl shut her eyes and held on to the saddle to keep from seeing these creatures, real or imagined, living or dead, following her. Other times a black specter crept alive across the path and slipped into the darkness of the undergrowth to stare with yellow eyes upon the strangers.

But the forest didn't last forever, and the moon wasn't gone yet when they emerged upon the rough mountainside. The girl studied the moon and knew by the way it was setting that they were heading in the right direction.

At every turn, however, some new horror presented itself. Once she had to cross a wild stream with slippery, precipitous banks. Then twice, in climbing a steep incline, she came suddenly upon sheer precipices that dropped down into a rocky gorge, where the moonlight seemed repelled by dark, bristling evergreen trees growing halfway up the sides. She could hear the rush of a tumbling mountain stream in the depths below. Once she fancied she heard a distant shot, and the horse pricked up his ears and started forward nervously.

But at last the dawn contended with the night, and in the east a faint pink flush crept up. Down in the valley a mist like a white feather rose gently into a white cloud and obscured the scene. She wished she might carry the wall of white with her to shield her. She had longed for the dawn. Now, as it brought the light and a revelation of the things about her, it was almost worse than night, so dreadful were the dangers clearly seen, so deep the chasms, so angry the mountain torrents.

With the dawn came the terror of being followed. The man would have no fear of approaching her in the morning; murdered men weren't thought to haunt their homes after the sun rose, and murderers always took courage in the day. He might arrive sooner, find her gone, and follow. He wasn't one to relinquish easily an object he coveted, nor could she forget the evil in his eyes.

As the day grew clearer, she studied her surroundings. There was no sign anyone had ever passed that way. Yet, at that moment, the horse stopped and snorted; in the rocks before them lay a man's hat riddled with shot. Then, clutching the reins with icy hands, the girl walked her horse to the edge, leaned over, and saw a man lying facedown at the bottom of the incline. He may have fallen off his horse and rolled down there, she thought.

For an instant fear held her riveted to the horse like a statue; the next, panic seized her. From the rigid attitude of the figure she was certain he'd been dead some time. But how did he die? Scarcely by his own hand. Who killed him? Were fiends lurking in the thick mountain growth above her?

She urged her horse forward with caution, and for miles the horse scrambled with great breaths. The girl held on with her eyes shut, not daring to see what fearful sights lay ahead or behind.

At last the way sloped downward, and they reached more level ground, with wide stretches of open plain, dotted here and there with sagebrush and greasewood.

She was hungry before stumbling upon the dead man. But the hunger had left her, and she felt only faintness. She dared not stop long enough to eat. She must make as much time as possible in the open space, especially since someone could spot her more easily here.

But the horse decided it was time for breakfast. He'd had a drink or two of water on the mountain, and the plain before him offered nothing to eat. He halted and neighed, shaking his head around at his mistress. She roused herself, realizing she must tend to his needs, at least.

She must sacrifice some of her own supply of food. In time they might happen upon a good pasture, but now there was nothing.

She had more cornmeal than anything else and poured a scanty portion onto a paper. The beast lapped it up greedily, licking every grain from the paper, while the girl guarded it lest his breath should blow any away. He snuffed hungrily at the empty paper, and she gave him a little more meal, while she ate some of the cold beans and scanned the horizon anxiously. Nothing but sagebrush lay ahead and more hills farther on where dim outlines of trees were visible. She wanted to get higher where she could see farther and find a bench with grass and shelter.

The girl rested briefly. Then she put some corn bread in her pocket, packed her supplies, mounted, and rode on.

The sun shone hot on the stony ground overgrown with cactus. Despair possessed her. She felt as if she were in an endless flight from an unseen pursuer, who would never give up until he had her.

At high noon, with the sun glaring overhead, she saw what might be another human. It was only a speck. But it inched toward her, separated by a wide valley that stretched for miles, along the skyline on a high bench on one side of the valley. She prodded her weary beast on to the top of another bench, hoping to find a grassy stretch and a chance to rest.

But the sight of the moving speck startled her. She watched it breathlessly as they neared each other. Then she saw a puff of smoke as if a rifle had been discharged, followed by the distant echo of the shot. It was a man on a horse, but they were still a great way off. Should she turn and run before she was discovered? Go back? No! Her enemy was there. This couldn't be that man. He was coming from the opposite direction, but he might be as wicked. Her experience taught her to shun men. Even fathers and brothers were hurtful.

She couldn't go back to the place where the dead man lay, or back at all. In going forward she was pursuing the only course that seemed possible through the natural obstructions of the region. She shrank onto her saddle and urged the patient horse on. Perhaps she could reach the bench and hide before the newcomer saw her.

But the way was longer to the top and steeper than it seemed at first, and the horse was tired. Sometimes he stopped of his own accord and snorted, craning his head toward her as if to ask how long and how far this strange ride would continue. Then the man in the distance seemed to ride faster. The valley between them had narrowed. He was distinctly a man now, and his horse was galloping. Once it seemed as if he waved his arms; but she turned her head and nudged her horse quickly on. They were almost to the top. She dismounted and clambered alongside the animal up the steep incline. Her breath came in quick gasps, with the horse's breath hot upon her cheek as they climbed together.

At last they reached the top! Ten feet more and they would be on a level, where they might disappear from view. She turned to look across the valley, and the man was directly opposite them. He must have ridden hard to get there so soon. He was waving his hands and calling. A chill swept over her. The man she fled might have sent him to foil her attempt for safety.

She clutched the bridle wildly and urged the horse up with one last effort. At the moment they reached high ground, she heard him cry wildly, "Hello! Hello!" Then she heard something that sounded like "Help!" Was he trying to deceive her, pretending he needed help or would help her?

She flung herself into the saddle and signalled the horse to run. The animal broke into his prairie run, as she cast one fearful glance behind her. The man was pursuing her at a gallop! He was crossing the valley. There was a stream to cross, but he would cross it. He had determination in every line of his flying figure. His voice pursued her, too. The sound seemed to reach out and clutch at her heart, trying to draw her back as she fled. And now she had three pursuers: her enemy, the dead man upon the mountain, and the voice.

Chapter 3

Straight across the prairie she galloped with the voice pursuing her. For hours it seemed to ring in her ears. Even after she was out of range, she thought she could still hear a faint echo ringing hello, like some strange bird amid the silence of the world.

Cattle and sheep grazed on the bench, and the horse would have stopped to dine with them; but the girl pushed him on.

Hours passed before she dared to stop for rest. Her mind was bewildered with fright and weariness. She couldn't stay in the saddle much longer for fear of falling asleep. The afternoon sun would soon be slipping down behind the mountains. She didn't dare rest during the night, for that would mean almost certain death with the wild beasts about.

A little group of greasewood shrubs offered a scanty shelter. As if he understood her thoughts the horse stopped with a neigh and looked around at her. She scanned the area. Cattle were scattered around; they had looked up as the horse flew by but were now grazing quietly. They would serve as a screen if anyone was still pursuing her. One horse among the other animals in a landscape would not be so noticeable as one alone against the sky. The greasewood wasn't far from sloping ground where she might easily hide if danger approached.

The horse was already cropping the tender grass at his feet. The girl took a few beans from her pack and ate them, though she wasn't hungry and her dry throat almost refused to swallow. Against her will her eyes kept closing. Finally she folded the old coat into a pillow and, fastening the horse's bridle in her belt, lay down.

The sun set, the horse ate his supper, and the girl slept. After a time the horse drowsed off, too. The bleating of the sheep, the lowing of the cattle, and the sound of night birds were heard in the distance. But the girl slept on. The moon rose full and round, shining with flickering light through the cottonwoods. And the girl stirred in a dream and thought someone was pursuing her, but slept on again. Then out through the night rang a clear human voice, "Hello! Hello!" The horse roused from his sleep and stamped his feet, twitching at his bridle. And the girl slept on. The horse thought he heard a good sound. He neighed again, but the girl slept on.

The first rays of the rising sun shot at last through the dawning gray and touched the girl full in the face as they slid under the branches of her sheltering tree. The light woke her, but before she opened her eyes she sensed that she had missed much during her sleep. With another flash her eyes opened, almost involuntarily.

She shrank from the new day and the memory of the old one. Then, suddenly, the blood in her veins all but froze. Her breath stopped, and for a moment she thought she was paralyzed. Before her, not ten feet away, stood a man! Beyond him, near her horse, stood his. She couldn't see it without turning her head and dared not do so. But she knew it was there, felt it even before she heard the double stamping and breathing of the animals. Her keen senses allowed her to see the surrounding landscape without moving a muscle. She knew exactly how her pistols lay and what movement would bring her hand to the trigger; yet she didn't stir.

Gradually she grew calm enough to study the man in front of her. He stood almost with his back to her, his face turned so that one cheek and part of his brow were visible. His shoulders were broad, and strength ran through every line of his body. How powerless she would be in his grasp! Her only hope was to take him unaware; yet she lay still.

He wore a brown flannel shirt, open at the throat, a brown leather belt and boots, all brand-new. His soft felt hat was rolled back from his face, and the young red sun tinged the short brown curls to a ruddy gold. He was gazing toward the rising sun. The gleam of it shot across the pistols in his belt and flashed twin rays into her eyes. Then all at once the man turned and looked at her.

Instantly the girl sprang to her feet, her hands on her pistol. With calm defiance her eyes met the blue ones fixed on her. She was braced against a tree and quickly measured the distance between her horse and her to see if she could escape.

"Good morning," said the man politely. "I hope I haven't disturbed your nap."

The girl eyed him in silence. This was a new kind of man. He wasn't like the one she had fled or any she'd ever seen, but he might be worse. She'd heard the world was full of wickedness.

"You see," continued the man with an apologetic smile, "you led me on such a desperate race nearly all day yesterday that I was obliged to keep you in sight when I finally caught you."

He looked for an answering smile, but there was none. Instead, the girl's dark eyes grew wide with fear. He was the same one she saw in the afternoon—the voice that cried to her—and he had pursued her. He was an enemy, perhaps, sent by the other man. She gripped her pistol with trembling fingers and tried to think what to say or do.

The young man wondered at the formalities of the plains. Were all western maidens so reserved?

"Why did you follow me? Who did you think I was?" she asked breathlessly at last.

"Well, I thought you were a man," he said. "At least you appeared to be a human being and not a wild animal. I hadn't seen anything but wild animals for six hours, and very few of those; so I followed you."

The girl said nothing. He hadn't answered her question directly. The young man was playing with her.

"What right did you have to follow me?" she demanded.

"Well, now that you put it that way, I'm not sure I had any right at all, unless it may be the claim that every human being has upon all creation."

His arms were folded across his broad brown flannel chest, and the pistols gleamed in his belt below like fine ornaments. He wore a thoughtful expression and looked at the girl as if she were a new specimen of humankind. He was studying her impersonally, it is true, but with interest. But something in his look angered the girl.

"What do you want?" She'd never heard of the divine claims of the whole human family. Her one instinct at present was fear.

An almost bitter expression flitted across the young man's face, as if an unpleasant memory forgotten for an instant had been recalled.

"It really wasn't of much consequence when you think of it," he said with a shrug of his shoulders. "I was merely lost and wanted to inquire where I was—and possibly the way to somewhere. But I don't know that it was worth the trouble."

The girl was puzzled. She had never seen a man like this before. He wasn't like her wild brother or any of his associates.

"This is Montana," she said, "or was when I started," she added with a sudden thought.

"Yes? Well, it was Montana when I started, too. But it's as likely to be the Sahara Desert as anything else. I'm sure I've come far enough and found it barren enough."

"I never heard of that place," said the girl seriously. "Is it in Canada?"

"I don't believe so," said the man with seriousness; "at least, not that I know of. When I went to school, it was generally located somewhere in Africa."

"I never went to school," said the girl wistfully. "But," she said with sudden resolve, "I'll go now."

"Do!" said the man. "I'll go with you. Let's start at once. Now that I think about it, I haven't had a thing to eat for over a day, and we might find something near a schoolhouse. Do you know the way?"

"No," said the girl, studying him; she wondered if he was making fun of her. "But I can give you something to eat."

"Thank you!" said the man. "I assure you I shall appreciate anything from hardtack to bisque ice cream."

"I haven't any of those," said the girl, "but there're plenty of beans left. And if you'll get some wood for a fire, I'll make some coffee."

"Agreed," said the man. "That sounds better than anything I've heard for two days."

The girl watched him as he strode away to find wood, frowning for an instant. But his face was sober, so she set to getting breakfast. For a little her fears were allayed. At least he would do her no immediate harm. Of course, she might flee from him now while his back was turned. But, of course, he'd pursue her again, and she had little chance of getting away. Besides, he was hungry. She couldn't leave him with nothing to eat.

"We can't make coffee without water," she said when he returned with a bundle of sticks.

He whistled.

"Can you tell me where to look for water?" he asked.

She saw how worn and gray he was about his eyes, and sudden compassion filled her.

"You'd better eat something first," she said, "and then we'll hunt for water. There's sure to be some in the valley. We'll cook some meat."

She took the sticks from him and made the fire in an orderly fashion. He wondered at her grace. Who was she, and how did she wander out into this waste place? Her face was both beautiful and interesting. She would make a fine study if he were not so weary of all human nature, especially women. He sighed as he thought again of himself.

The girl caught the sound and, wheeling around with the quickness of a wild creature, caught the sadness of his face. It drove away much of her fear and resentment. A half-flicker of a smile crossed her lips as their eyes met. They seemed to recognize comrades in sorrow. But her face hardened at once when he answered her look.

The man felt a fleeting disappointment. After a minute, during which the girl dropped her eyes to her work again, he asked, "Now why did you look at me that way? Should I be helping you? I'm awkward, but I can do what you say if you tell me how."

The girl was puzzled, then she replied somberly, "There's nothing more to do. It's ready to eat."

She gave him a piece of the meat and the last of the corn bread in the tin cup and placed the pan of beans beside him. But she didn't eat anything.

He took a hungry bite or two and looked furtively at her.

"I insist upon knowing why you looked"—he paused and eyed her—"why you look at me in that way. I'm not a wolf if I'm hungry, and I'm not going to eat you up."

The look of displeasure deepened on the girl's brow. In spite of his hunger the man was compelled to watch her. She was looking at a flock of birds in the sky. Her hand rested lightly at her belt. The birds were coming toward them, flying almost over their heads.

The girl raised her hand in one quick motion, and something flashed in the sun across his sight. He heard a loud report, and a bird fell inches from his feet, dead. It was a sage hen. Then the girl turned and walked toward him with as haughty a carriage as a society belle could boast.

"You were laughing at me," she said quietly.

It happened so suddenly the man had no time to think. Surprise passed over his countenance. Then the meaning of the girl's act dawned upon him, along with the full intention of her rebuke, and the color mounted in his tanned face. He set down the tin cup, balanced the bit of corn bread on the rim and arose.

"I beg your pardon," he said. "I'll never do it again. I couldn't have shot that bird to save my life." He touched it with the tip of his boot as if making sure it was real.

The girl was sitting on the ground, eating a portion of the cooked pork. She didn't answer. Somehow the young man felt uncomfortable. He sat down, picked up his tin cup, and tried to finish his breakfast; but he'd lost his appetite.

"I've been trying to learn to shoot during the last week," he began. "I haven't hit anything yet except the side of a bush. Say, I'm wondering—suppose I'd shot at those birds just now and missed? Would you have laughed at me—quietly, to yourself?"

The girl looked up at him, without saying a word for a full minute.

"Was what I said as bad as that?" she asked slowly.

"I'm afraid it was," he answered thoughtfully; "but I was a blamed idiot for laughing at you. A girl that shoots like that may locate the Sahara Desert in Canada if she likes, and Canada ought to be proud of the honor."

She glanced into his face and noted his earnestness. All at once she broke into a clear ripple of laughter. The young man was astonished that she understood him enough to laugh. She must be unusually sharp-witted, this lady of the desert.

"If 'twas as bad as that," she said in quite another tone, "you can laugh."

They looked at each other then in mutual understanding, and each fell to eating his portion in silence. Suddenly the man spoke.

"I'm eating the food you prepared for your journey, and I haven't even said, 'Thank you,' yet, nor asked if you have enough to carry you to a place where there's more. Where are you going?"

At first the girl didn't answer. But, when she did, she spoke thoughtfully, as if the words were a new vow from an impulse she just received.

"I am going to school," she said in her slow way, "to learn to 'sight' the Sahara Desert."

He said nothing, but his eyes gave her the homage he felt was her due. Here evidently was an indomitable spirit, but how did she get into the wilderness, and why was she alone? He'd heard of the freedom of western women, but surely girls like this didn't frequent such a wasteland of uninhabited territory as he believed this was. He studied her.

The brow was sweet and thoughtful, with a certain inquisitiveness about the eyes. The mouth was firm, yet it had gentle lines about it. In spite of her coarse, dark calico garb, styled to cover her with the least fuss, she was graceful. Every movement was alert and clean-cut. When she looked full in his face, he decided she had almost beautiful eyes.

She had stood up while he was watching her and was gazing into the distance with sudden apprehension. He followed her gaze and saw several dark figures moving against the sky.

"It's a herd of antelope," she said with relief; "but it's time we hit the trail." She collected her things with speed, giving him little opportunity to help, and mounted her horse without more words.

For an hour he followed her at high speed as she rode full tilt over rough and smooth terrain, casting furtive glances behind her now and then, only half including him in her glance. She seemed to know he was there and following; that was all.

The young man was amused. Most women he knew would have ridden by his side and tried to make him talk. But this girl of the wilderness rode straight ahead as if her life depended on it. She had nothing to say to him; she wasn't eager to impart her own history or to know his.

Well, that suited his mood. He came to the wilderness to think and forget. Here was ample opportunity. He had a little too much of it yesterday; he'd wandered from the rest of his party that had come out to hunt. For a time he felt he'd rather be back in his native city with a good breakfast and his troubles than to be alone in the vast waste forever. But now he had human company and might get somewhere sometime. He was content.

The lithe, slender figure of the girl ahead seemed one with the horse. He tried to imagine what this ride would be like if another woman were riding on that horse, but he found small satisfaction in that. He couldn't imagine the haughty beauty in a brown calico riding a high-spirited horse of the wilds. There was one parallel. If she'd been there, she would, in her present state of mind, likely be riding imperiously and indifferently ahead instead of by his side where he wanted her. Besides, he came out to the plains to forget her. Why think about her?

The sky was bright and expansive. Why hadn't he ever noticed this in skies at home? Another flock of birds flew overhead. What if he tried to shoot one? Idle thinking. He'd probably hit anything but a bird. Why did the girl shoot that bird, anyway? Was it just because she might need it for food? She'd picked it up carefully with the other things and fastened it to her saddlebow without a word. He was too ignorant to know if it was edible or not—or was she merely carrying it to remind him of her skill?

And what sort of girl was she? Perhaps she was escaping from justice. She ran from him yesterday and apparently stopped only when exhausted. She seemed anxious when the antelopes came into view. He had no way of knowing whether her company meant safety, after all. Yet his interest was so thoroughly aroused in her that he was willing to risk it.

Of course he might go more slowly, let her get ahead, and then slip out of sight. He probably hadn't wandered so many miles from human habitation that he wouldn't reach it sometime. And now that he was reinforced by food, it might be wise to separate from this strange girl. While he was thinking, he unconsciously slackened his horse's pace. The girl was several yards ahead and just vanishing behind a clump of sagebrush. She disappeared, and he stopped for a moment and gazed about him on the desolation. A great loneliness settled upon him like a mist. He was glad to see the girl riding back toward him with a friendly smile.

"What's the matter?" she called. "Come on! There's water in the valley."

The word *water* sounded good to him. Life was suddenly good for no reason except that the morning was bright, the sky was vast, and there was water in the valley. He rode forward, keeping close beside her now, and in a few minutes they saw the sunlight sparkling on a gushing stream.

"You seem to be running away from someone," he said. "I thought you wanted to get rid of me, so I was giving you a chance."

She looked at him, surprised.

"I am running away," she said, "but not from you."

"From whom, then, may I ask? It might be convenient to know, if we're to travel in the same company."

She looked at him sharply. "Who are you, and where do you belong?"

Chapter 4

I'm not anyone in particular," he answered, "and I'm not sure where I belong. I live in Pennsylvania, but I don't seem to belong there, not right now anyway. So I came out here to see if I belonged anywhere else. Yesterday I concluded I didn't. At least, not until I came in sight of you. I suspect I'm partly running away from myself. But that's just it—I'm actually running away from a woman!"

He looked at her with his honest hazel eyes. She liked him. She felt he was telling her the truth, but it seemed to be a truth he was just discovering for himself as he talked.

"Why are you running away from a woman? How could a woman hurt you? Can she shoot?"

He glanced at her with amusement and pain mingled.

"She uses other weapons," he said. "Her words are darts, and her looks are swords."

"What a strange lady! Does she ride well?"

"Yes, in an automobile!"

"What's that?" she asked shyly as if she feared he might laugh again.

He realized then that he was talking above her. In fact, he was talking to himself more than to the girl.

He felt some pleasure in speaking of his lost woman to this wild creature who seemed more like an intelligent bird or flower than the humans he was used to.

"An automobile is a carriage that moves about without horses," he answered her seriously. "It moves by machinery."

"I shouldn't like it," said the girl decidedly. "Horses are better than machines. I saw a machine once that cut wheat. It made a noise and went slowly, and it frightened me."

"Automobiles go fast, faster than any horses. And they don't all make a noise."

The girl looked around apprehensively.

"My horse can go very fast—you don't know how fast. If you see the lady coming, I'll change horses with you. Ride to the nearest bench and over, and then turn backward on your tracks. She'll never find you that way. I'm not afraid of a lady."

The man broke into a hearty laugh, loud and long, and laughed until the tears rolled down his cheeks. The girl, offended, rode haughtily beside him. Then all at once he sobered.

"Excuse me," he said. "I'm not laughing at you now. It looks that way, but

I'm not. It's because of the picture you put before me. I'm running away from the lady, but she won't come out in her automobile to look for me. She doesn't want me!"

"She doesn't want you? And yet you ran away from her?"

"That's exactly it," he said. "You see, *I* wanted *her!*"

"Oh!" She gave a quick gasp of understanding and fell silent. After a minute she rode close to his horse and laid her small brown hand on the animal's mane.

"I'm sorry," she said simply.

"Thank you," he answered. "I don't know why I told you. I've never told anyone."

There was a long silence between them. The man seemed to have forgotten her as he rode with his eyes upon his horse's neck and his thoughts apparently far away.

At last the girl said softly, as if she were returning his confidence, "I ran away from a man."

The man lifted his eyes courteously, with a question, and waited.

"He's dark and good-looking, but I hate him. He shoots to kill—he killed my brother. I frightened him away, though, because he's afraid of dead men he's killed. After my brother's funeral, he came after me. He said he wanted me, so I ran away from him."

The young man gave his attention now to the extraordinary story the girl told as if it were a common occurrence.

"But where are your people, your family and friends? Why don't they get rid of the man?"

"They're all back there in the sand," she said with a sad little smile and a gesture that spoke of tragedy. "I said the prayer over them. Mother always wanted it when we died, and nobody was left but me. I said it, and then I left. The moonlight was cold, and I heard noises. And the horse was afraid. But I said it. Do you suppose it will do any good?"

She fastened her eyes on the young man with her last words as if demanding an answer. The color rose to his cheeks. He felt embarrassed at such a question in light of her trouble.

"Why, I should think it ought to," he stammered. "Of course it will," he added with more confidence.

"Did you ever say the prayer?"

"Why, I—yes, I believe I have," he answered uncertainly.

"Did it do any good?" She was hanging onto his words.

"Why, I believe—yes, I suppose it did. That is, praying is always a good thing. The fact is, it's a long time since I've tried it. But of course it's all right."

It was a curious topic for conversation between a young man and a young woman on a ride through the wilderness. The man had never thought about prayer for so many minutes consecutively in his whole life—at least, not since the days when his nurse taught him to pray, "Now I lay me. . ."

"Why don't you try it about the lady?" asked the girl suddenly.

"Well, the fact is, I never thought of it."

"Don't you believe it will do any good?"

"Well, I suppose it might."

"Then let's try it. Let's get off now, quickly, and both say it. Maybe it will help us both. Do you know it all the way through? Can't you say it?" This last she asked anxiously, when he hesitated and looked doubtful.

The color crept into the man's face. Somehow this girl had put him in a bad light. He couldn't shoot, and if he couldn't pray, what would she think of him?

"Why, I think I could manage to say it with help," he answered uneasily. "But what if that man suddenly appears?"

"You don't think the prayer is any good or you wouldn't say that," she said with a sad, hopeless tone in her voice.

"Oh, why certainly," he said, "only I thought there might be a better time to try it. But, if you say so, we'll stop right here." He sprang to the ground and offered to help her, but she was beside him before he could get around his horse's head.

Down she dropped, clasping her hands as a little child, and closed her eyes.

"Our Father," she repeated slowly, precisely, as if every word belonged to a charm and must be repeated just right or it wouldn't work. The man's mumbling words halted after hers. He was reflecting upon the curious scene they would make to a chance passerby on the desert, if any passersby ventured that way. It was strange, this aloneness. There was a wideness here that made praying seem more natural than at home.

The prayer, because of the unaccustomed lips, proceeded slowly. But when it was finished, the girl sprang to her saddle again with a businesslike expression.

"I feel better," she said with a pleasant smile. "Don't you? Don't you think He heard?"

"Who heard?"

"Why, 'our Father.' "

"Oh, certainly! That is, I've always been taught to presume He did. I haven't experimented much with it, but I daresay it'll do some good somewhere. Now do you suppose we could get some of that sparkling water? I'm thirsty."

They spurred their horses and were soon beside the stream, refreshing themselves.

"Did you ride all night?" asked the girl.

"Pretty much," answered the man. "I stopped once to rest a few minutes, but a sound in the distance stirred me up again. I was afraid I wouldn't catch you, and then I'd have been hopelessly lost. You see, I went out with a hunting party, and I sulked behind. They took off up a steep incline, and I told them I'd wander around below till they returned or perhaps ride back to camp. But when I tried to find the camp, it wasn't where I'd left it."

"Well, you've got to lie down and sleep awhile," said the girl. "You can't keep going like that, or it'll kill you. You lie down, and I'll watch and get dinner. I'm going to cook that bird."

He demurred, but in the end she had her way; he was weary, and she saw it. So he let her spread the old coat down for him while he gathered wood for a fire, and then he lay down and watched her simple preparations for the meal. Before he knew it he was asleep.

When he started to awaken, he found himself in that curious blending of dream and reality. He thought his lady was coming to him across the rough plains in an automobile, with gray wings like those of the bird the girl had shot. His prayer when he knelt in the sand was drawing her, while overhead the air was filled with wild, sweet music from strange birds that mocked and called and trilled. But when the automobile reached him and stopped, the lady withered into a little, old, dried-up creature of ashes; and the girl of the plains was sitting in her place radiant and beautiful.

He opened his eyes, saw the crude dinner set, and smelled the delicious odor of the roasted bird. The girl was standing on the other side of the fire, intently whistling an extraordinary song, like all the birds of the air at once.

She'd made a little cake out of the cornmeal, and they ate heartily.

"I caught two fish in the brook. We can take them along for supper," she said as they packed the things again for travel.

He tried to convince her to rest also and let him watch. But she insisted they must keep going and promised to rest just before dark.

"We must travel hard at night, you know," she added with an anxious tone in her voice.

He questioned her more about the man who might be pursuing and then understood her fears.

"The scoundrel!" he muttered, observing the delicate features and clear profile of the girl. He felt a strong desire to strangle the man.

He asked about her life and wondered at the flowerlike girl who had blossomed in the wilderness with no hand to cultivate her except a lazy, clever, drunken father and a kind but naive mother. How did she escape being coarse amid such surroundings? In fact, how did she, growing up with her brothers, come forth as lovely and unhurt as she seemed? He felt a great anxiety for her lonely future and wanted to find protection for her. But they were still in the wilderness. He was glad he was here now so he could protect her, if the need arose.

Evening drew near, and they discovered a grassy spot in a gully where the horses might rest and eat. Here they stopped. The girl threw herself under a shelter of trees, with the old coat for a pillow, and rested, while the man paced up and down at a distance, gathering wood for a fire and watching the horizon.

As night fell, the city-bred man longed for shelter. He was by no means a coward where known quantities were concerned. But to face wild animals and drunken brigands in a strange plain with no help near was not an enlivening prospect. He couldn't understand why they hadn't found any human habitation by this time. He'd never realized how vast this country was. He didn't recall crossing such long, uncivilized stretches of country on the train west. Of course, a train traveled so much faster than a horse that he had no adequate means of judging. Besides, they weren't on a trail now and had probably wandered around in a circle.

In reality, unbeknownst to them, they'd twice come within five miles of small homesteads, tucked away beside a stream in a fertile spot. A mile farther to the right would have put them on the trail and made their way easier and shorter, but they didn't know that either.

The girl didn't rest long. She felt the pursuit more as darkness crept on, and she looked anxiously for the moon.

"We must head toward the moon," she said, watching the bright spot in the east.

They ate their supper of fish and corn bread with the appetite that grows on horseback. By the time they started on their way again, the moon spread a path of silver before them, and they went forward feeling as if they'd known each other a long time. For a while their fears and hopes were blended in one.

Meanwhile, as the sun sank and the moon rose, a traveler rode up the steep ascent to the lonely cabin the girl had left. He was handsome and dark and strong, with a scarlet kerchief knotted at his throat. He rode slowly, looking furtively about. His pistols gleamed in the moonlight, while an ugly knife nestled in a hidden sheath.

He scowled, and his face became ugly. A coward, he started at the flutter of a night bird scurrying to its home in a rock by the wayside. The mist rising from the valley in wreaths of silver gauze startled him as he rounded the trail to the cabin. For an instant he stopped and drew his dagger, thinking the ghost he feared was walking early. He took a draught from the bottle in his pocket to steady his nerves and continued. Then, in front of the dark cabin, he stopped again, for another horse stood there, and in the doorway stood a figure! His curses rang through the still air and smote the moonlight, and his pistol flashed forth a volley of fire.

He demanded to know who was there, and another torrent of profanity poured forth in response. It was one of his comrades from the day before. He explained that he and two others had come to pay a visit to the pretty girl. They wagered as to who would win her, but she wasn't there. The door was fastened. They'd forced it, but there was no sign of her. The other two went to look for her where her brother was buried. He agreed to wait at the cabin, but he was getting uneasy. If the other two found her, they might not be fair.

The last to arrive explained with a loud oath that the girl belonged to him and no one else had a right to her. He demanded that the other one accompany him to the grave and see what had become of the girl. Then they'd all go and drink together—but the girl belonged to him.

They rode toward the graves and met the other two returning. There was no sign of the girl. The three men taunted the one, saying the girl had given him the slip. Amidst much arguing over where and whose she was, they rode on, cursing through God's beauty. They passed the bottle among them that their nerves might be steadier. When they returned to the deserted cabin, they discussed what to do.

At last they agreed to set out after the girl. And with oaths and coarse jokes and drinking, they started down the trail the girl had searched for by her round-about way.

Chapter 5

It was a wonderful night that the two spent together wading the sea of moonlight on the plain. The almost unearthly beauty of the scene grew upon them. Neither felt the loneliness that had possessed each the night before, so they might now discover the marvels along the way.

Early they happened upon a prairie dogs' village. The man would have lingered to watch with curiosity, but the girl urged him on. It was the time of night when she'd first left the cabin, and the same apprehension that filled her then haunted her with the evening. She longed to be out of the land that held the man she feared. She'd rather bury herself in the earth and smother to death than be caught by him.

They rode on, and the girl told her companion about the habits of the curious little creatures they'd seen. Then, as the night settled down upon them, she pointed out the dark creatures that stole from their way now and then or gleamed with a fearsome green eye from some temporary refuge.

At first the cold shivers ran up and down the spine of the young man. Here before him in the sagebrush was a real live animal he'd read so much about and one he'd come out bravely to hunt. He kept his hand on his revolver and was constantly on the alert, glancing in back of him lest a troop of coyotes or wolves should be stalking him. But the girl talked about them in much the same manner we talk about a neighbor's fierce dog, until at last he grew calm and could watch a dark, velvet-footed object slink by without starting.

After a time he pointed to the heavens and talked of the stars. Did she know that constellation? No? Then he explained. Such and such stars were so many miles from the earth. He recited their names and a bit of mythology connected with each name and then spoke of the moon and the possibility it had once been inhabited.

The girl listened, amazed. She knew certain stars as landmarks, telling east from west and north from south, and had often watched them coming out one by one. She considered them to be her friends. She'd never heard they were worlds or that the inhabitants of this earth knew anything about the heavenly bodies. With question after question she plied him, showing extraordinary intelligence and thought in some and greater ignorance than a child in kindergarten in others.

He grew more amazed as their discussion continued and was thrilled with unfolding the wonders of the heavens to her. As he studied her pure profile in the moonlight with an eager, wistful gaze, her beauty impressed him more and more. In the East he had a friend, an artist. He thought this scene would make a wonderful theme for a painting—the girl in a picturesque hat of soft felt, riding with careless ease and grace: horse, maiden, and plain, bathed in a sea of silver.

The more she talked, the more the man wondered how this girl reared in the wilds had acquired a speech so free from grammatical errors. She was apparently ignorant of the world, and yet with a few exceptions she made no serious errors in English. How was that possible?

He pressed her with questions about herself but couldn't find that she'd ever come into contact with educated people. She hadn't lived in any of the small towns that flourished in the wildest of the West and not within several hundred miles of a city. Their nearest neighbors in one direction had lived forty miles away, she said, as if that were an everyday distance from a neighbor.

Mail? They received a letter once that she could remember, when she was a little girl. It was just a few lines in pencil to say that her mother's father had died. He'd been killed in an accident of some sort, working in the city where he lived. Her mother had kept the letter and cried over it till almost all the pencil marks were gone.

No, they had no mail on the mountain where their homestead was.

Yes, her father went there first. He thought he discovered gold, but it turned out to be a mistake. Since they had no other place to go, and no money to go with, they stayed there. Her father and brothers had been cowpunchers, but she and her mother had scarcely ever left home. They cared for the little children. When they died, her mother didn't want to go and wouldn't let her go far alone.

Oh, yes, she rode a great deal, sometimes with her brothers, but not often. They rode with rough men, and her mother was afraid for her to go. The men all drank. Her brothers drank. Her father drank, too. She stated it as if it were a sad fact common to all mankind and ended with a statement that was almost, but not quite, a question: "I guess you drink, too."

"Well," said the young man, hesitating, "not that way. I take a glass of wine now and then in company, you know—"

"Yes, I know," sighed the girl. "Men are all alike. Mother used to say so. She said men were different from women. They had to drink. She said they all did it. But she said her father never did; he was very good, though he had to work hard."

"Indeed," said the young man, his color rising, "you're mistaken. I don't drink at all, not that way. I—why, I only—well, the fact is, I don't care a red cent about the stuff anyway, and I don't want you to think I'm like them. If it'll do you any good, I'll never touch it again, not a drop."

He said it earnestly. He was trying to vindicate himself. Just why he cared to do so he didn't know—just that all at once he wanted to appear different in the girl's eyes from the other men she'd known.

"Will you really?" she asked, turning to look in his face. "Will you promise that?"

"Why, certainly I will," he said, a bit embarrassed she'd taken him at his word. "Of course I will. It's nothing to me. I only took a glass at the club occasionally when the other men were drinking, and sometimes when I went to class banquets and dinners—"

Now the girl had never heard of class banquets, but to take a glass occasionally when the other men were drinking was what her brothers did. She sighed. "Yes, you may promise, but I know you won't keep it. Father promised too. But when he got with the other men, it did no good. Men are all alike."

"But I'm not," he insisted. "I tell you I'm not. I don't drink, and I won't drink. I promise you solemnly here under God's sky that I'll never drink another drop of intoxicating liquor again if I know it as long as I live."

He put out his hand toward her, and she put her own into it with a quick grasp for just an instant.

"Then you're not like other men, after all," she said with a glad ring in her voice. "That must be why I wasn't so afraid of you when I woke up and found you standing there."

A distinct sense of pleasure came over him at her words. Why he was glad she wasn't afraid of him when she first saw him in the wilderness he didn't know. But he forgot his own troubles, and he forgot the lady in the automobile. Then and there he dropped her out of his thoughts. He didn't know it, but something erased her. He didn't think about her anymore during the journey. He ran away from her and succeeded most effectually, more so than he knew.

There in the desert the man took his first temperance pledge, too, urged to it by a girl who'd never heard of a temperance pledge, never joined a women's temperance society, and knew nothing about women's crusades. Her own heart taught her out of a bitter experience how to use her God-given influence.

They reached a long stretch of level ground then, smooth and hard. The horses, of one accord, took off at a gallop shoulder-to-shoulder in a wild race across the plain. Talking was impossible. But the man reflected on his experiences—first a prayer and then a pledge, all in the wilderness. If anyone had told him he was going into the West for this, he would have laughed scornfully.

Toward morning they rode more slowly. Their horses were jaded. They talked in lower tones while they looked toward the east—as if they feared they might awaken someone too soon. There is something awesome about the dawning of a new day, especially when one has been sailing on a sea of silver all night. It's like returning from an unreal world into a sad, real one. Each one was almost sorry the night was over. The new day might hold hardship or relief, trouble or surprise, while the night had been perfect, a jewel set in memory with every facet flashing in the light. They didn't like to get back to reality from the conversation they'd held together. It was an experience each would never forget.

Once there came the distant sound of shots and shouts. The two drew closer to each other, and the man laid his hand on the mane of the girl's horse. But he didn't touch her hand. The other woman had sometimes let him hold her jewelled hand and smiled with drooping lashes when he caressed it. When she tired of him, other admirers might claim the same privilege. But this woman of the wilderness—he wouldn't even in his thoughts presume to touch her small firm brown hand. Somehow she commanded his honor from the first minute, even before she shot the bird.

Once a bobcat dashed across their path a few feet in front of them, and later a kit fox ran growling up with ruffled fur. The girl's quick shot soon put it to flight, however, and they passed on through the dawning morning of the first real Sabbath the girl had ever known.

"It's Sunday morning at home," said the man, watching the sun lift its rosy head from the mist of mountain and valley spread out before them. "Do you have such an institution out here?"

The color drained from the girl's face. "Awful things happen on Sunday," she said with a shudder.

Pity rose in his heart for her, and he strove to turn her thoughts in other directions. Evidently a recent sorrow was connected with the Sabbath.

"You're tired," he said, "and the horses are tired. We need to rest. Daylight has come, and nothing can hurt us now. Here's some shelter. We can fasten the horses behind these bushes, and no one will guess we're here."

She assented, and they dismounted. With his knife the man cut an opening into a clump of thick brush, and they fastened the weary horses there, concealed from view if anyone chanced by. The girl lay down a few feet away in a spot almost surrounded by sagebrush that had reached an unusual height and made a fine hiding place. Outside the entrance to this natural chamber the man lay down on a bed of sagebrush. He gathered enough for the girl first and spread the old coat over it, and she dropped asleep almost as soon as she lay down. His own bed of sagebrush was comfortable enough, even to one accustomed to the finest springs and hair mattress that money could buy. The girl insisted that he must rest, too, for he was weary and there was no need to watch. But sleep didn't come to him.

He lay there resting and thinking. He wondered if a wealthy, college-bred, society man had encountered anything like this. What did it mean—his being lost and wandering for a day, the sight of the girl and his pursuit, the prayer under the open sky, and that night of splendor under the moonlight riding side by side?

And this girl! Where was she going, and what would become of her? Out in the world where he came from, she'd be nothing. Her station in life was so far beneath his that the only recognition she could have would degrade her. This solitary journey they were taking—the world would raise its hands in horror at it! A girl without a chaperone! Yet it seemed right and good, and the girl was evidently recognized by the angels. How else had she escaped from degradation thus far?

Ah! How did he know she had? But he smiled at that. No one could look into that pure, sweet face and doubt that she was as good as she was beautiful. If it wasn't so, he hoped he'd never find out. She seemed to him a woman unspoiled, and he shrank from the thought of what the world might do to her— the world and its cultivation. It wouldn't be for her because she was without friends, money, or home. The world would give her nothing but toil, with a meager living.

What did she propose to do? Mustn't he try to help her in some way? Didn't the fact that she saved his life demand so much from him? If he hadn't found her, he would have starved before he found a way out of this desolate place. Starvation was still a possibility. They hadn't reached any signs of habitation yet, and only a little cornmeal and coffee remained. They had two matches left and hadn't come upon any more flights of birds or brooks with fish.

In fact, the man found a great deal to worry about as he lay there, too worn out with the unaccustomed exercise and experiences to sleep.

The girl had told him little about her plans. He must ask her. He wished he knew more about her family. If he were only older and she younger, or if he had the right kind of woman friend to whom he might take her or send her! How horrible that scoundrel was after her! Such men were beasts, not men, and should be shot.

Far off in the distance, perhaps in the air or in his imagination, a sound of faint voices or shouts floated by. It came and went, and he listened; but by and by he heard no more. The horses breathed heavily behind their sagebrush stable, and the sun rose higher and hotter. At last sleep came, troubled, but sleep. This time there was no lady in an automobile.

It was high noon when he awoke. The sun had reached around the sagebrush and was pouring full into his face. He was uncomfortable, and an uneasy sense of something wrong pervaded his mind. Did he hear a strange, sibilant, writhing sound just as he came to consciousness? Why did he feel that something or someone had passed by him a moment earlier?

He rubbed his eyes open and fanned himself with his hat. He heard no sound except a distant hawk in the sky and the breathing of the horses. He stepped over to make sure they were all right. Was the girl still sleeping? Should he call her? But what would he call her? She had no name to him as yet. He couldn't say "my dear madam" in the wilderness or even "mademoiselle."

Perhaps she'd passed him—looking for water or firewood. He glanced around, but the thick growth of sagebrush prevented his seeing much. He stepped to the right and then to the left of the little enclosure where she'd gone to sleep, but there was no sign of life.

At last the sense of uneasiness grew upon him until he spoke.

"Are you awake yet?" he asked. But the words stuck in his throat and wouldn't sound out clearly. He ventured the question again, but it seemed to go no further than the gray-green foliage in front of him. Did he detect movement? Had he frightened her?

His flesh grew creepy, and he was angry with himself for standing there actually trembling for no reason. But he sensed danger. What did it mean? He'd never believed in premonitions or superstitions. But the thought came to him that perhaps that evil man came softly while he slept and stole the girl away. Suddenly a horror seized him, and he decided to end this suspense and venture in to see if she was safe.

Chapter 6

He stepped boldly around the green barrier. She was still asleep. But the awareness of another presence held him. There, coiled on the ground beside her, with fangs extended and eyes glittering like slimy jewels, lay a rattlesnake.

For a second he stared in fascinated horror, and his brain refused to work. Suddenly he knew he must act at once. He'd read of snakes and travelers' encounters with them, but he didn't remember what to do. Shoot? He'd probably kill the girl, not the snake. He couldn't wake up the girl and drag her from danger, either, for the slightest movement on her part would unleash the poisoned fangs upon her.

He looked about for some weapon, but no stick or stone was in sight. He played golf well. If he had a loaded stick, he could easily take off the serpent's head, he thought—but there was no stick. He had only one hope—to attract the creature to himself. He scarcely dared to move lest the deadly gaze should close upon the victim where she lay sleeping, unaware of her peril.

All at once he knew what to do. He slipped quietly back out of sight, tore off his coat and cautiously approached the snake again, holding the coat in front of him. He paused for an instant, calculating whether the coat could drop between the snake and the smooth brown arm in front before the fangs pierced it. Then the coat dropped, with the man holding one end of it like a wall between the serpent and the girl and crying out to her to wake up and run.

In one terrible moment he realized the girl was safe and he himself was in danger of death, while he held on to the coat till she escaped. Then he saw the writhing coil at his feet turn and fasten its eyes of fury upon him. He didn't know if his fingers could let go of the coat or whether his shaking knees could carry him away before the serpent struck. Then it was all over. He and the girl were standing outside the sagebrush, with the sound of the pistol dying away among the echoes. He felt the fine ache of his arm where her fingers had grasped him to drag him from danger.

The serpent was dead. She shot it—as coolly as she'd taken the bird in its flight. She stood looking at him with round eyes of gratitude, and he looked at her amazed they were both alive and barely understanding what had happened.

The girl broke the stillness.

"You're what they call a 'tenderfoot,' " she said.

"Yes," he agreed, "I guess I am. I couldn't have shot it to save anybody's life."

"You're a tenderfoot, and you couldn't shoot," she continued, as if she must state it plainly. "But you—you are what my brother used to call 'a white man.' You couldn't shoot, but you could risk your life, hold that coat, and look death in the face. *You* are no tenderfoot."

Her eyes were eloquent, and her voice held tears. She turned away to hide any tears that might be in her eyes. But the man reached out and placed his hand on her sure little brown one. He took it firmly in his own, gazing down upon her, unashamed, with his own eyes filled with tears.

"And what am I to say to you for saving my life?" he said.

"I? Oh, that was easy," said the girl, shrugging off his question. "I can always shoot. But you were hard to drag away. You seemed to want to stay there and die with your coat."

"They laughed at me for wearing that coat. They said a hunter never bothered himself with extra clothing," he said thoughtfully.

"Do you think it was the prayer?" asked the girl.

"It may be!" the man said.

They mounted quietly and rode on. The path, due east, took them around the shoulder of a hill. They were obliged to go single file and talked very little.

Near the middle of the afternoon they heard a new sound. The two riders stopped their horses and looked at each other. It was the faint sound of singing drifting toward them, then away, on the light breeze. They guided their horses around the hill, staying close together now. They were approaching some human being or beings. No bird could sing like that. They could hear indistinct words to the music.

They rounded the hillside and stopped again side by side. Below them lay the trail they'd been searching for, and just beneath them, nestled against the hill, stood a log schoolhouse, weatherboarded, its windows open. Around it horses waited, some tied and some hitched to wagons, but most of them with saddles.

The singing was clear now. They could hear the words. "O that will be glory for me, glory for me—"

"What is it?" she whispered.

"Why, I suspect it's a Sunday school or something of the kind."

"Oh! A school! Could we go in?"

"If you like," said the man, enjoying her simplicity. "We can tie our horses here behind the building so they can rest. And there's fresh grass in this sheltered place."

He led her down behind the schoolhouse to a spot where the horses couldn't be seen from the trail. The girl peered around the corner into the window. Two girls about her age were sitting there; one smiled at her in what seemed like an invitation. She smiled back and walked to the door with assurance. When she entered the room, they pointed to a seat near a window, behind a small desk.

Desks were placed all over the room at regular intervals, with a larger desk in front. Almost all the people sat at them.

A curious wooden box stood in front of the room at one side of the larger desk. A girl sat in front of it pressing down with her fingers some black and white strips that looked like sticks, working her feet and singing heartily. The curious box made music, the same music the people were singing. Was it a piano? she wondered. She'd heard of pianos. Her father used to talk about them. And what was that her mother used to want? A "cab'net-organ." Perhaps this was a cab'net-organ. At any rate, she was entranced with the music.

On the wall behind the man at the front desk was a large dark board with white marks on it. The sunlight glinted across it at first, so she couldn't tell what they were. When she moved to one side a little, though, she saw a large cross with words under it—"He will hide me."

The girl glanced around shyly and felt immersed in the songs that rolled around her, from untrained voices, perhaps, but sincere hearts. It was how she might have imagined heavenly music to sound: "Glory," "glory," "glory!" The words seemed to fit the day, the sunshine, and her recent deliverance. She looked for her companion and deliverer to enjoy it with him, but he hadn't come in yet.

The two girls were handing her a book now and pointing to the place. She could read. Her mother had taught her a little before the other children were born, but not much literature had come her way. She grasped the book eagerly and noticed where the finger pointed. Yes, there were the words: "Glory for me!" "Glory for me!" Did that mean her? Was there glory for her somewhere in the world? She sighed with the joy of the possibility, as the "Glory Song" rolled along.

The singing stopped, and the man at the front desk said, "Let's have the verses."

" 'The eternal God is thy refuge, and underneath are the everlasting arms,' " said a woman in the front seat.

" 'He shall cover thee with his feathers, and under his wings shalt thou trust,' " said a young man next.

" 'In the time of trouble he shall hide me in his pavilion: in the secret of his tabernacle shall he hide me,' " read the girl sitting nearby. The slip of paper she'd written it on fluttered to the floor at the feet of the newcomer, who stooped and picked it up, offering it back. But the other girl shook her head, and the newcomer kept it, wondering at the words and trying to figure out their meaning.

Other verses were repeated, but just then the girl heard a sound that deadened all others. In spite of herself she trembled. She looked up and saw the man coming toward the door. But her eyes blurred, and she felt faint.

Up the trail on horseback, with shouts and ribald songs, rode four men, too drunk to know where they were going. The schoolhouse attracted their attention as they passed, and just for devilry they let out a volley of oaths and vile talk to the worshippers inside. One in particular, the leader, looked straight at the young man, who had tied the horses and was about to enter the schoolhouse. The leader pretended to point his pistol at him, then discharged it into the air. This signalled the other men to fire off their guns as they rode past the schoolhouse. They left behind a train of curses to haunt the air and confuse the "Glory Song" in the memories of those who heard.

From her seat beside the window the girl saw the face of the evil man who shot her brother. For one terrible minute she thought she was cornered. She looked about helplessly on the people in the schoolhouse and wondered if they would help her. Could they fight and prevail against those four men mad with liquor?

Suppose he said she was his—his wife, or sister, who ran away. Would they believe her? Would the man who saved her life believe her?

The party passed, and the man came in and sat down beside her quietly. Without a word or a look he knew who the man was he'd just seen. His soul shook for the girl, and his anger flared. He felt like gathering her in his arms and hiding her himself. Her courage for shooting the snake was gone now. He saw that she was trembling and ready to cry. Then he smiled upon her—in a way he'd never smiled on anyone before, except his mother when he was a baby and looked up into her face with confidence. His deep smile fell like sunshine on a nervous chill.

The girl felt its comfort. Her eyes dropped to the paper in her shaking hands. Then gradually, letter by letter, word by word, the verse spoke to her. She didn't understand the whole meaning, for *pavilion* and *tabernacle* were unknown words to her, but the hiding she understood. She had been hidden in her time of trouble. Someone had done it. *He*—the word would fit the man by her side, for he'd helped to hide her and save her more than once. But she perceived dimly that it was another He, Someone greater, who worked this miracle and saved her once more to go on perhaps to better things.

Many good, wise, and true things were said in that meeting. They might have helped the girl if she'd understood. But one grain of truth she saved for future use. There was a "hiding" somewhere in this world, and she'd had it in a time of trouble. One moment more in the open, and the wicked man might have seen her.

During a time of prayer all heads were bowed, and a voice here and there murmured a few low words she couldn't distinguish. But at the close they all joined in "the prayer." When she heard them say, "Our Father," she closed her eyes—she had been watching curiously—and joined her voice softly with the rest. Somehow it connected her safety with "our Father," and she felt a stronger faith than ever in her prayer.

The young man listened intently to all he heard. He was strangely impressed by this simple worship in what to him was a vast wilderness. He felt more of the true spirit of worship here; at home he would be sitting in the handsomely upholstered pew beside his mother and sister while the choirboys chanted the processional and the light filtered through costly windows of many colors over the large, sophisticated congregation. The words of these people went straight to the heart more than all the intonings of the cultured voices he'd heard. They meant what they said, and God had been a reality to them in many times of trouble. The theme of the afternoon seemed to be the saving power of the eternal God, made perfect through the need and the trust of His people. He was reminded more than once of the morning's incident and the miraculous saving of his own and his companion's life.

When the meeting was over, the people gathered in groups and talked with one another. The girl who shared the book walked over and spoke to the strangers, putting out her hand pleasantly. She was the missionary speaker's daughter.

"What is this? A school?" asked the stranger eagerly.

"Yes, this is the schoolhouse," said the missionary's daughter. "But this meeting is Christian Endeavor. Do you live near here? Can you come every time?"

"No, I live far away," said the girl sadly. "That is, I did. I don't live anywhere right now, and I'm going away."

"I wish you lived here. Then you could come to our meeting. Did you have a Christian Endeavor where you lived?"

"No, I've never seen one before. It's nice, though. I like it."

Another girl came up now and put out her hand in greeting. "You must come again," she said politely.

"I don't know," said the visitor. "I won't be coming back soon."

"Are you going far?"

"As far as I can. I'm going east."

"Oh," said the inquirer. Then she whispered, nodding toward the man, "Is he your husband?"

The girl looked startled, while a slow color mounted into her cheeks.

"No," she said thoughtfully, "but he saved my life a little while ago."

"Oh!" said the other, awestruck. "My! And isn't he handsome? How did he do it?"

The girl shuddered. "It was a dreadful snake, and I was—it was awful! I can't talk about it."

"My!" said the girl. "How terrible!"

The people were leaving the schoolhouse now. The man was talking with the missionary, asking directions. The girl realized the precious hour was over, and life must be faced again. The men! She recognized the others as having been among her brother's funeral train. Why did they come through here? Were they tracking her? Had they any clue to her whereabouts? Would they turn back soon and catch her when the people had gone home?

The nearest town appeared to be Malta, sixteen miles away, in the direction where the men had passed. Only four houses were near the schoolhouse, and they were scattered in different directions along the stream in the valley. The two stood still by the door after the congregation left. The girl shivered. As she peered down the road, she seemed to see the man's face and hear his coarse laughter and oaths. What if he came back?

"I can't go that way!" she said, pointing down the trail toward Malta. "I'd rather die with wild beasts."

"No!" said the man firmly. "We definitely won't go that way. Was that the man you ran away from?"

"Yes." She looked up at him in awe over how he'd coupled his lot with hers.

"Poor girl!" he said with deep feeling. "You'd be better off with the beasts. Come on—let's get away from here!"

They turned sharply from the trail and followed a family that was almost out of sight around the hill. They'd have a chance to get some provisions, the man thought. The girl thought of nothing except getting away. They rode hard, soon came within hailing distance of the family ahead of them and asked a few questions.

No, there were no houses to the north until you crossed the Canadian line, and the trail was hard to follow. Few people traveled that way. Most went to Malta. Why didn't they go to Malta? A road and stores were there. It was, by all means, the best way. Yes, there was another house about twenty miles farther on this trail. It was a large ranch near another town with a railroad. The trail was seldom used and might be hard to find in some places. But if they kept the Cottonwood Creek in sight, followed on to the end of the valley, and then crossed the bench to the right, they couldn't miss it. It was a good twenty miles beyond their house. But if the travelers didn't miss the way, they might reach it before dark. Yes, the people could supply a few provisions at their home if the strangers didn't mind taking what was at hand.

The man in the wagon tried his best to find out where the two were going and why. But the man from the East baffled his curiosity in a most skillful manner. When the two rode away from the two-roomed log house, they left no clue to their identity or mission beyond the fact that they were making quite a journey, got a little off their trail, and ran out of provisions.

They felt relatively safe from pursuit for a few hours at least, for the men could scarcely return and trace them very soon. They hadn't stopped to eat anything; but they'd been given as much milk as they could drink and felt refreshed by it. They started on their long ride enjoying the pleasure of their companionship.

After a long gallop across a smooth level place they settled into a steady gait.

"What was it all about?" asked the girl.

He looked at her questioningly.

"The school. What did it mean? She said it was a Christian Endeavor. What's that?"

"Why, some sort of a religious meeting, I suppose," he answered. "Did you enjoy it?"

"Yes," she said, "I did. I've never been to such a thing before. The girl said they had them all over the world. What do you think she meant?"

"Why, I don't know, I'm sure, unless it's some kind of a society. But it looked to me like a prayer meeting. I've heard about prayer meetings, but I've never gone to one, though I never guessed they were so interesting. That was a remarkable story that old man told of how he was taken care of that night among the Indians. He evidently believes prayer helps people."

"Don't you?" she asked quickly.

"Oh, certainly!" he said. "But there was something so genuine about how the old man told it that made you feel it in a new way."

"It's all new to me," said the girl. "But Mother used to go to Sunday school and church and prayer meeting. She's often told me about it. She used to sing sometimes. One song was 'Rock of Ages.' Did you ever hear it?"

She said the words slowly and in a singsong voice, as if she were measuring off the words to imaginary notes: " 'Rock of Ages, cleft for me. Let me hide myself in Thee.' I thought about that the night I started. I wish I knew where that rock was. Is there a rock somewhere called Rock of Ages?"

The young man was visibly embarrassed. He started to laugh, but he didn't want to hurt her again. He wasn't used to talking about religion. Yet here by this strange girl's side it seemed natural that he, who knew so little about it, should be trying to explain the Rock of Ages to a soul in need. All at once he realized that it was for just such souls in need that the Rock of Ages came into the world.

"I've heard the song. Yes, I think they sing it in churches. It's quite common. No, there isn't any place called Rock of Ages. It refers—that is, I believe—why, you see the thing is figurative—that is, a kind of picture of things. It refers to the Deity."

"Oh! What's that?" asked the girl.

"Why—God." He tried to say it as if he'd been telling her it was Mr. Smith or Mr. Jones, but the sound of the word on his lips shocked him. He didn't know how to go on. "It just means God will take care of people."

"Oh!" she said, and a light of understanding spread over her face. "But," she added, "I wish I knew what it meant, the meeting, and why they did it. There must be some reason. And how do you know it's all so? Where did they find it out?"

The man felt he was beyond his limits, so he changed the subject. "I wish you'd tell me about yourself," he said gently. "I'd like to understand you better. We've traveled together for a good many hours now, and we ought to know more about each other."

"What do you want to know?" she asked seriously. "There isn't much more to tell. I've lived on a mountain all my life and helped Mother. The rest all died. The baby first and my two brothers, then Father, Mother, and now John. I said the prayer for John, then ran away."

"Yes, but I want to know about your life. I live in the East where everything is different. It's all new to me out here. I want to know, for instance, how you learned to talk so well. You talk like a girl who went to school and read and studied. You make so few mistakes in your English and speak quite correctly. That's unusual when people live their whole lives away from school. You don't talk like the girls I've met since I came out here."

"Father always made me speak right. He kept at every one of us children when we said words wrong and made us say them over again. It made him angry to hear words said wrong. He made Mother cry once when she said 'done' when she ought to have said 'did.' Father went to school once, but Mother only went a little while. He knew a great deal, and when he was sober he used to teach us things sometimes. He taught me to read. I can read anything I've ever seen."

"Did you have many books and magazines?" he asked innocently.

"We had three books!" she answered proudly. "One was a grammar. Father bought it for Mother before they were married, and she always kept it wrapped up in paper carefully. She used to get it out for me to read sometimes. But she was very careful with it, and when she died I put it in her hands. I thought she'd like to have it close to her because it always seemed to mean so much to her. You see, Father bought it. Then there was an almanac and a book about stones and earth. A man who was hunting for gold left that. He stopped overnight at our house and asked for something to eat. He had no money to pay for it; so he left that book with us and said when he found the gold he would come and buy it back again. But he never came back."

"Is that all you've ever read?" he asked gently.

"Oh, no! We got papers sometimes. Father would come home with a whole paper wrapped around some bundle. Once there was a beautiful story about a girl. But the paper was torn in the middle, and I never knew how it came out."

Her voice sounded wistful. She'd always regretted not knowing how the girl in the story fared. All at once she turned to him.

"Now tell me about your life," she said. "I'm sure you have a great deal to tell."

His face darkened in a way that made her wish she hadn't asked.

"Oh, well," he said, as if it mattered little about his life, "I had a nice home—have yet, for that matter. Father died when I was little, and Mother let me do just about as I pleased. I went to school because the other fellows did and that was the thing to do. After I grew up I liked it. That is, I liked some studies, so I went to a university."

250—GRACE LIVINGSTON HILL, COLLECTION NO. 1

"What's that?"

"Oh, just a higher school where you learn more difficult things. Then I traveled. When I came home, I went into society a good deal. But"—and his face darkened again—"I got tired of it and thought I'd come out here for awhile and hunt. Then I got lost and found you!" He smiled into her face. "Now you know the rest."

Something passed between them in that smile and glance, a recognition of souls and a gladness in each other's company, that warmed their hearts. They said no more for some time but rode quietly side by side.

They reached the end of the valley and, crossing the bench, could see the distant ranch. The silver moon had risen, for they weren't hurrying, and a great beauty pervaded everything. They almost shrank from approaching the buildings and people. They had enjoyed the ride and the companionship. Every step brought them closer to what they knew all along would come: an uncertain future they were joyously shut away from till they might know each other.

Chapter 7

They found rest for the night at the ranch house. The place was warm and spacious, and the girl admired the comfortable work area. If only her mother had had such a kitchen to work in and such a pleasant, happy home, she might still be living. A cheerful, gray-haired woman the men called Mother gave the girl a kind welcome and urged her to sit down to a nice hot supper. Afterward, she led her to her own room and told her she might sleep with her. Amazed at all this, the girl lay down; but she was too weary to stay awake and think about it.

The two travelers slept, a sound and dreamless sleep, and forgot their sorrows.

Early the next morning the girl awoke. The woman was already stirring beside her. She must get breakfast for the men. The woman asked her a few questions about her journey and then about the man.

"He's your brother, ain't he, dearie?" she asked as she was leaving the room.

"No," said the girl.

"Oh," said the woman, puzzled, "then you and he's goin' to be married in the town."

"Oh, no!" said the girl with scarlet cheeks, thinking of the woman in the automobile.

"Not goin' to be married, dearie? Now that's too bad. Ain't he any relation to you? Not an uncle or cousin or nothin'?"

"No."

"Then how is it you're travelin' 'lone with him? It don't seem right. You's a sweet, good girl, an' he's a fine man. But harm's come to more'n one. Where'd you take up with each other? Is he a neighbor? He looks like a man from way off, not hereabouts. You sure he ain't deceivin' you, dearie?"

The girl flashed her eyes in answer.

"Yes, I'm sure. He's a good man. He prays to our Father. No, he's not a neighbor or an uncle or a cousin; he's just a man who got lost. We were both lost on the prairie in the night. He's from the East and got lost from his party. He had nothing to eat, but I did, so I gave him some. Then he saved my life when a snake almost bit me. He's been good to me."

The woman looked relieved.

"And where you goin', dearie, all 'lone? What your folks thinkin' 'bout to let you go 'lone this way?"

"They're dead," said the girl with tears in her eyes.

"Dearie me! And you so young! Say, dearie, s'pose you stay here with me.

I'm lonesome, an' there's no women nearby here. You could help me and be comp'ny. The men would like to have a girl round. There's plenty likely men on this ranch could make a good home for a girl sometime. Stay here with me, dearie."

Had this refuge been offered the girl during her first night in the wilderness, with what joy and thankfulness she would have accepted! Now it was impossible to stay. She must go on. She had a pleasant ride before her and delightful companionship, and she was going to school. She had entered the vast world and wasn't inclined to pause on the threshold and never see more than Montana. Furthermore, the woman's last words didn't please her.

"I can't stay," she said decidedly. "I'm going to school. And I don't want a man. I've just run away from a man, a dreadful one. I'm going to school in the East. I have some relations there, and perhaps I can find them."

"You don't say so!" said the woman with disappointment. She'd taken a liking to the sweet young face. "Well, dearie, why not stay here a little while, write to your folks, and then go with someone who is heading your way? I don't like to see you go off with that man. It ain't proper. He knows it himself. I'm afraid he's deceivin' you. I can see by his clo'es he's one of the fine young fellows that does as they please. He won't think any good of you if you keep travelin' 'lone with him. It's all well 'nough when you get lost, an' he was nice to help you out and save you from snakes. But he knows he ain't no business travelin' 'lone with you. You're a pretty little creature."

"You mustn't talk that way!" said the girl, rising and looking sharply at the woman. "He's a good man. He's what my brother called 'a white man all through.' Besides, he's got a lady, a beautiful lady, in the East. She rides in a grand carriage that goes by itself, and he thinks a great deal of her."

The woman looked only half convinced.

"It may seem all right to you, dearie," she said sadly, "but I'm old, and I've seen things happen. His fine lady wouldn't go jauntin' round the world 'lone with him unless she's married. I've lived East, and I know. And he knows it too. He may mean right, but you never can trust folks."

The woman walked out of the room to prepare breakfast and left the girl feeling as if the whole world were against her, trying to hold her. She was glad when the man suggested they hurry their breakfast and get away as quickly as possible. She didn't smile when the old woman came out to bid her good-bye and put a detaining hand on the horse's bridle.

"You better stay with me, after all, hadn't you, dearie?"

The man looked at the two women. He understood at once the older woman's suspicion and read the trust and anger in the beautiful younger face. Then he smiled at the old woman whose hospitality spared them from the terrors of the open night.

"Don't you worry about her, ma'am. I'll take good care of her. Perhaps she'll write you a letter someday and tell you where she is and what she's doing."

Half reassured, the old woman gave him her name and address, and he wrote them down in a small red notebook.

When they were well on their journey, the man explained why he had hurried. From conversation with the men he learned that the ranch lay on the direct trail from Malta to another town. The pursuers might go farther than Malta. Did she think they'd go so far? They must have come almost a hundred miles already. Wouldn't they be discouraged?

But the girl looked surprised. A hundred miles on horseback wasn't far. Her brother often rode a hundred miles just to see a fight or have a good time. She felt sure the men wouldn't hesitate to follow a long distance if something else didn't turn them aside.

The man's face appeared stern under his hat. He felt a great responsibility for the girl since he'd seen the face of the man who was pursuing her.

Their horses were fresh, and the day was fine. They rode hard as long as the road was smooth, and did little talking. The girl was thinking about the woman's words. What troubled her most was, "And he knows it is so."

Was she doing something for which the man by her side would not respect her? Was she overstepping some unwritten law she'd never heard? Did he know it and still encourage her in it?

She would never believe she needed to fear him. Hadn't she seen the deep respect on his face as he waited quietly for her to awaken that first morning? Didn't he have an opportunity again and again to dishonor her with his words or his looks? Yet he was only gentle and courteous to her. She didn't call things by these names, but she sensed the gentleman in him.

Besides, there was the lady. He talked about her at the beginning. He evidently honored her. The old woman had said the lady wouldn't ride with him alone. Was it true? Was his thought of the lady different from his thought of her? It must be because he loved the lady, but he shouldn't think less honorably of her than of any lady in the land.

She sat straight and proud in her man's saddle to show him she was worthy of respect. She had tried to show him this when she shot the bird. Now she recognized that there was something finer than shooting or prowess of any kind that would command respect. She felt she had it, yet she wasn't sure she commanded it. What did she lack, and how could she secure it?

He watched her quiet, thoughtful face, and the lady of his troubled thoughts was utterly forgotten by him. He was unconsciously absorbed in studying her eyes and lips and brows. He was growing used to the form and feature of this girl and took pleasure in watching her.

They stopped for lunch in a gully under a cluster of cedar trees a little back from the trail, where they might survey the territory they'd covered and be warned against pursuers. About three o'clock they reached a town. Here the railroad came directly from Malta, but only one train a day stopped each way.

The man found the public stopping place and asked for a room, demanding a private place for his "sister" to rest for awhile. "She's my little sister," he told himself in excuse for the word. "She's my sister to care for. That is, if she were my sister, this is what I'd want some good man to do for her."

He smiled after leaving the girl to rest. The thought of a sister pleased him. The old woman at the ranch had made him careful about the girl who was thrown into his company.

He rode through the rough town to the railway station, only a short distance from the crude stopping place. There he inquired about roads and towns in the neighboring locality and sent a telegram to the friends he'd been hunting with when he got lost. He said he'd be at the next town about twenty miles away. He knew they'd be back home by now and anxious about him, if they weren't already sending out search parties for him. His message read: "Hit the trail all right. Am taking a trip for my health. Send mail to me at—"

Then, after asking for specific directions and learning that more than one route led to the town he'd mentioned in his telegram, he returned to his companion. She was ready to go, for the presence of other people made her uneasy. She feared that others would object to their traveling together, for the old woman's words had cast a shadow over her. She mounted her horse gladly, and they left the town. He told her what he'd done and that he expected to get his mail the next morning when they reached the next town. He explained there was a ranch halfway where they might stop all night.

The thought of another ranch troubled her—more questions and perhaps other disagreeable words. But she held her peace, listening to his plans. She was filled with wonder over the telegram. She knew little or nothing about modern discoveries. It was a mystery to her how he could receive word by morning from a place a two-day journey away. And how did he send a message over a wire? Yes, she'd heard of telegrams, but she was never sure they were true. When he saw her interest, he told her about other triumphs of science: the telephone, the electric light, gas, and the modern system of waterworks. She listened as if it were a fairy tale and sometimes studied him to see if it was true or if he was making fun of her. But his earnest eyes permitted no doubt.

At the ranch they found two women, a mother and her daughter. The man asked frankly whether they could take care of his young friend overnight, adding that she was going on to the town in the morning and was in his care for the journey. This relieved any suspicion. The two women eyed each other and smiled.

"I'm Myrtle Baker," said the ranch owner's daughter. "Come—I'll take you where you can wash your hands and face, and then we'll have supper."

Myrtle Baker was a chatterer by nature. She talked incessantly, and, though she asked many questions, she didn't wait for half to be answered. Besides, the traveler had grown wary. She didn't intend to talk about the relationship between her and her traveling companion. She was charmed so much by Myrtle's company, however, that she half regretted leaving the next morning. But they left quite early, amid protests from the two women who liked having a visitor in their isolated home.

The ride that morning was strained. Each felt in some subtle way that their pleasant companionship was reaching a crisis. Ahead in that town would be letters, communications from the outside world of friends, people who didn't know or care what these two had gone through together and wouldn't hesitate to separate them. Neither put this thought into words, but it was in their hearts, in some vague fear. They talked very little, but each felt how enjoyable the journey had been and dreaded what might lie ahead.

They wanted to stay in this Utopia of the plains, journeying together forever, never reaching a troublesome future with laws and opinions they must follow.

But the morning grew bright, and the road wasn't long enough. At the end they walked their horses and still reached the town before the daily train passed through. They headed straight for the station and found that the train was an hour late. But a telegram had arrived for the man.

The girl sat on her horse by the platform and watched him through the open station door where he stood tearing open the envelope. She saw a deathly pallor spread over his face. She felt as if the same arrow piercing his heart, pierced hers as well. Then she waited. It seemed like hours before he glanced up.

The message read: "Your mother seriously ill. Want you immediately. Will send your baggage on morning train. Have wired you are coming."

His cousin signed the telegram. He'd gone with him on the hunting trip, and now the cousin was bound by business to go farther west in a few days.

The young man almost collapsed under this sudden shock. His mother was very dear to him, and he'd left her well and happy. He must go home at once. But what should he do with the girl who in the last two days had taken so strong a hold upon his—he hesitated, then called it "protection." That word would do for the present.

Then he looked, saw her own face pale under the tan, and stepped out to the platform to tell her.

Chapter 8

She took the news like a Spartan. She expressed her gentle pity simply, and then she held her peace. He must go. She knew the train would carry him to his mother's bedside quicker than a horse could go. By the look in his eyes and the set of his mouth she knew he'd already decided that. Of course he must go. And the lady was there too! His mother and the lady! The lady would regret things by this time and love him. Well, it was all right. He was a strong, bright angel God sent to help her out of the wilderness. Now that she was safe the angel must return to his heaven. He had only an hour before the train arrived. He had very little money with him since men don't usually carry a fortune when they go into the wilderness for a day's shooting. Fortunately he had his railroad return ticket to Philadelphia. That would carry him safely. But the girl had no money. And where was she going? He realized he'd failed to ask her many important questions. He hurried out and explained to her.

"The train's an hour late. We must sell our horses and try to get money enough to take us to the East. It's the only way. Where do you intend to go?"

But the girl stiffened in her seat. She knew it was her opportunity to show that she was worthy of his honor and respect.

"I can't go with you," she said very quietly.

"But you must," he said impatiently. "Don't you see there's no other way? I have to take this train and get to my mother as soon as possible. She may not be alive when I reach her if I don't." Something caught in his throat as he uttered the thought that kept coming to his mind.

"I know," said the girl. "You have to go, but I must keep riding."

"And why? I'd like to know. I can't leave you here alone. Those men may come on us at any minute. In fact, it's a good thing to get on the train and out of their miserable country as fast as steam can carry us. I'm sorry you have to part with your horse; I know you're attached to it. Maybe we can sell it to someone who'll let us redeem it when we send the money out. You see, I don't have enough money with me to buy you a ticket. I couldn't go home myself if I didn't have my return ticket. But surely selling both horses will bring enough to pay your way."

"You're very kind, but I mustn't go." The red lips were firm, and the girl was sitting up straight. She looked as she did after she shot the bird.

"But why?"

"I can't travel alone with you. It's not your custom where you come from. The woman at the ranch told me. She said you knew girls didn't do that and that you didn't respect me for going alone with you. She said it wasn't right and you knew it."

He looked at her impatient, angry, and half ashamed that she would face him with these words.

"Nonsense!" he said. "This is a case of necessity. You're to be taken care of, and I'm the one to do it."

"But it's not the custom among people where you live, is it?"

The clear eyes confronted him, and he had to admit that it wasn't.

"Then I can't go," she said decidedly.

"But you must. If you don't, I won't go."

"But you must," said the girl, "and I mustn't. If you talk that way, I'll run away from you. I've run away from one man, and I guess I can from another. Besides, you're forgetting the lady."

"What lady?"

"Your lady. The lady who rides in a carriage without horses."

"Hang the lady!" he said. "Do you know the train will be along here in less than an hour, and we have a lot to do before we can get on board? There's no use stopping to talk about this matter. We haven't time. If you'll just trust things to me, I'll attend to them all, and I'll answer your questions when we get safely on the train. Every instant is precious. Those men might come around that corner any minute. That's all bosh about respect. I respect you more than any woman I ever met. And it's my business to take care of you."

"No, it's not your business," said the girl bravely, "and I can't let you. I'm nothing to you, you know."

"You're every—that is—why, you surely know you're a great deal to me. Why, you saved my life, you know!"

"Yes, and you saved mine. That was beautiful, but that's all."

"Isn't that enough? What are you made of, anyway, to sit there when there's so much to be done, and those villains on our track, and insist that you won't be saved? Respect you! Why a lion in the wilderness would have to respect you. You're made of iron and steel and precious stones. You have the courage of a—a—I was going to say man, but I mean an angel. You're pure as snow and true as the heavenly blue and firm as a rock. And if I'd never respected you before, I would have to now. I respect, I honor, I—I—I pray for you!" he finished fiercely.

He turned his back to hide his emotions.

She lifted her eyes to his when he turned back, and her own were full of tears.

"Thank you!" she said very simply. "That makes me—very—glad! But I can't go with you."

"Do you mean that?" he asked her desperately.

"Yes," she said.

"Then I shall have to stay, too."

"But you can't! You must go to your mother. I won't be stayed with. And what would she think? Mothers are—everything!" she finished. "You must go quick and get ready. What can I do to help?"

He gave her a look which she remembered long years afterward. It burned its way into her soul. How was it that a stranger had the power to scorch her with anguish this way? And she him?

He turned, still with desperation in his face, and accosted two men who stood at the other end of the platform. They didn't need a horse at present, but they were always ready to look at a bargain. They walked down the uneven boards of the platform to where his horse stood and inspected it.

The girl watched the proceeding with eyes that saw only into the future. She put in a word about the worth of the saddle once when she saw it was going lower than it should. Three other men gathered about before the bargain was concluded, and the horse and its equipment sold for about half its value.

That done, the man turned toward the girl and motioned to her to lead her horse away to a more quiet place. He sat down to plead steadily against her decision, but the girl was more determined than ever not to go with him. She spoke of the lady again. She spoke of his mother and mothers in general and reminded him that God would take care of her and of him, too.

They heard the whistle of the train and saw it growing from a speck to a large black object across the plain. To the girl, the sight of the strange machine horrified her; it seemed more like a creature rushing at her to snatch beauty and hope and safety from her. To the man it seemed like a dreaded fate tearing him apart. He barely had time to divest himself of his powder horn and a few things that might help the girl in her journey, before the train halted at the station. Then he took out of his pocket the money for his horse. Selecting a five-dollar bill for himself, he wrapped the rest in an envelope bearing his name and address. The envelope was one addressed by the lady at home. It had contained some gracefully worded refusal of a request. But he didn't notice what envelope he gave her.

"Take this," he said. "It'll help a little. Yes, you must! I cannot leave you— I *will* not—unless you do," he added when he saw that she hesitated. "I owe you all and more for saving my life. I can never repay you. Take it. You may return it sometime when you get plenty more of your own, if it hurts your pride to keep it. Take it, please. Yes, I have plenty for myself. You'll need it, and you must stay at nice places overnight. You'll be very careful, won't you? My name is on that envelope. You must write to me and let me know you're safe."

"Someone is calling you, and that thing is moving again," said the girl, with awe in her face. "You'll be left behind! Oh, hurry! Quick! Your mother!"

He turned toward the train and then came back.

"You haven't told me your name!" he gasped. "Tell me quick!"

She caught her breath.

"Elizabeth!" she answered and waved him away.

The conductor of the train was shouting to him, and two men shoved him toward the platform. He swung himself aboard with the ease of a man who has traveled. But he stood on the platform and shouted, "Where are you going?" as the train clattered noisily off.

She didn't hear him but waved her hand and gave him a bright smile brimming with unshed tears. It seemed like instant suicide for him to stand on the swaying box as it moved off down the plane of vision. She watched him till he was out of sight, a mere speck on the horizon of the prairie. Then she turned her horse slowly into the road and went her way into the world alone.

The man stood on the platform and watched her as he whirled away—a little brown girl on a brown horse, so staunch and firm and good. Her eyes were dear, and her lips as she smiled, and her hand was beautiful as it waved him good-bye. She was dear, very dear! Why hadn't he known it? Why did he leave her? Yet how could he stay? His mother may be dying. He mustn't fail her in what might be her last summons. Life and death were tugging at his heart.

The vision of the little brown girl and the brown horse blurred and faded. He tried to focus on something closer so he could look for her again, and straight before him in his line of vision came a shackly old saloon. Its rough character was apparent from the men grouped about its doorway and from the barrels and kegs outside. From the doorway spilled four men, wiping their mouths and shouting raucously. Four horses stood tied to a nearby fence. The train sped by so fast that he couldn't be sure, but those four men reminded him sharply of the four who had passed the schoolhouse on Sunday.

He shuddered and looked back. The brown horse and the brown girl were one with the station far away, and presently the saloon and the men were blotted out in one blur of green and brown and yellow.

He looked to the ground in despair. He *must* go back. He couldn't leave her in such danger. She was his to care for by all the rights of manhood and womanhood. She had been put in his way. It was his duty.

But the ground whirled by under his madness and showed him plainly that to jump off would be instant death. Then the thought of his mother came again and the girl's words, "I am nothing to you, you know."

The train made its way between two mountains and the valley, and the green and brown and yellow blur was gone from sight. He felt as if he had just seen the coffin close over the girl's sweet face, and he'd done it.

By and by he crawled into the car, pulled his slouched hat down over his eyes, and settled down in a seat. All the time he was trying to see again the old saloon and those four men and make out their passing identity. The agony of thinking about it and trying to figure out if those men were the pursuers panicked him. More than once he almost pulled the bell cord to stop the train and get off to walk back. Then the utter hopelessness of finding her would sweep over him, and he would settle back in his seat again and try to sleep. But the least drowsiness would bring a vision of the girl galloping alone over the prairie with the four men in full pursuit. "Elizabeth, Elizabeth!" the car wheels seemed to say.

Elizabeth—that was all he had. He didn't know the rest of her name or where she was going. He didn't even know where she came from, just "Elizabeth" and "Montana." If anything happened to her, he'd never know. Why did he leave her? Why didn't he *make* her go with him? In a case like that a man should assert his authority. But, then, it was true he had none, and she said she'd run away. She would have, too. If it had been anything but sickness and possible death at the other end—and his mother! Nothing else would have kept him from staying to protect Elizabeth.

What a fool he'd been! He might have asked questions and made plans during all those beautiful sunlit days and moon-silvered nights. How could he know that modern improvements would steal him away from her in the midst of a prairie waste, when he had just started to know her and prize her company as a most precious gift from heaven?

By degrees he returned to a more normal state of mind. He convinced himself that those men were not like the men he'd seen Sunday. He knew that one could not recognize one's own brother at that distance and speed. He tried to think Elizabeth would be cared for. She'd come through many dangers. Wasn't it likely that the God she trusted, who had guarded her so many times in her great peril, would not desert her now in her dire need? Wouldn't He raise up help for her somewhere? Perhaps another man as trustworthy as he'd tried to be would help her.

But that thought wasn't pleasant. He put it away impatiently. Why did she talk so much about the lady? The lady! Ah! Why didn't he think about her anymore? The memory of her haughty face no longer made his heart beat faster. Was he so fickle that he could lose what he thought was a lifelong passion in a few days?

The darkness crept on. Where was Elizabeth? Did she find refuge for the night? Or was she wandering on an unknown trail, hearing voices and oaths through the darkness, seeing wild eyes gleam in the bushes ahead? How could he leave her? He must go back!

And so it went on through the long night.

The train stopped at several places to take on water, but he saw no human habitation nearby. Once, when they stopped longer than the other times, he stood up, walked the length of the car and stepped down to the ground. He even stood there and let the train start jerkily on till his car had passed him. The steps were sliding by, while he tried to think whether he shouldn't stay and go back to find her. Then the impossibility of the search and of getting back in time to do any good helped him spring on board just before it was too late. He walked back to his seat saying to himself, "Fool! Fool!"

Not till morning did he remember his baggage and go in search of it. There he found a letter from his cousin, with other letters and telegrams explaining the state of affairs at home. He returned to his seat laden with a large leather grip and a suitcase. He sat down to read his letters, and these took his mind off his troubled thoughts for awhile. There was a letter from his mother, sweet, graceful, offering her sympathy. She guessed the reason he left her and went to this far place. His dear mother! What would she say if she knew his trouble now? And then his frenzy over Elizabeth's peril would return. Oh, to know that she was protected, hidden!

Fumbling in his pocket, he came upon the slip of paper the girl had given Elizabeth in the schoolhouse on Sunday afternoon. "For in the time of trouble he shall hide me in his pavilion: in the secret of his tabernacle shall he hide me."

Ah! God had hidden her then. Why not again? And what was it he said to her when he was searching for a word to cover his emotion? "I pray for you!" Why couldn't he pray? She'd made him pray in the wilderness. Shouldn't he pray for her now?

He leaned back in the hot, uncomfortable seat, pulling his hat down further over his eyes, and prayed as he never had before. He stumbled through "Our Father" and tried to recall how her sweet voice had filled in the places where he didn't know it. Then, when he was finished, he waited and prayed, "Our Father, care for Elizabeth," and added, "for Jesus' sake, amen." Through the rest of his journey, and for days and weeks to come, he prayed that prayer. Sometimes he found in it his only solace from the fear that some harm had befallen the girl, whom it seemed to him now he had deserted in cold blood.

Chapter 9

Elizabeth rode straight out to the east, crossing the town as rapidly as possible. On the edge of town she crossed another trail running back the way they'd come. Without swerving she turned out toward the world and soon passed into a thick growth of trees around a hill.

Not three minutes elapsed after she passed the junction before the four men rode across from the other direction. They paused and looked both ways.

"What d'ye think, Bill? Shall we risk the right hand 'r the left?"

"Take the left hand fer luck," answered Bill. "Let's go over t' the ranch and ask. If she's been hereabouts, she's likely there. The old woman'll know. Come on, boys!"

And who shall say that the angel of the Lord did not stand within the crossing of the ways and turn aside the evil men?

Elizabeth didn't stop her fierce ride until about noon. Her fear of pursuit had returned with renewed force. Now that she was alone she dared not look behind her. She was strong enough as she smiled farewell. But when the train had dwindled into a mere speck in the distance, tears fell thick and fast upon the horse's mane. Thus in her loneliness now she rode as if enemies nearby were pursuing her.

But the horse must rest if she didn't, for he was her only support now. So she sat down under a shady tree and tried to eat some dinner. The tears came again as she opened the pack the man's hands had wrapped for her. How little she'd thought at breakfast that she would eat the next meal alone!

It was one thing to tell him he must go and say she was nothing to him. But it was another to face the world without a single friend when she'd learned how good a friend could be. She almost wished he'd never found her, never saved her from the snake, and never ridden beside her and talked of marvelous new things to her. The emptiness was so much harder to bear, and she longed for things that couldn't be hers.

It was well he'd gone so soon and she had no longer to be charmed by his company. He belonged to the lady and wasn't hers. Thus she ate her dinner with the indifference of sorrow.

Then she took out the envelope and counted the money. He'd given her forty dollars, keeping only five for himself. How wonderful of him to do that for her! It seemed to be a great wealth in her possession. Well, she would use it sparingly so she could return it all to him sooner. She must use some, she supposed, to buy food, but she could shoot a bird or catch a fish or find berries to eat. She promised to stop at a respectable house at night. Awful things might happen to her, he said, if she slept in the wilderness alone. Her lodging may cost something; yet some people might take her in for nothing. She'd be careful with the money.

She studied the name on the envelope: George Trescott Benedict, 2 Walnut Street, Philadelphia, Penn. The letters were large and angular, not easy to read, but she figured them out. It didn't look like his writing. She'd watched him as he wrote the old woman's address in his red book. He wrote small round letters, slanting backward, plain as print, pleasant to read. Now the old woman's address would never be of any use, and her wish that Elizabeth should travel alone was fulfilled.

From the envelope she breathed in a faint perfume like wildwood flowers. Was it perfume from something he carried in his pocket, some flower his lady gave him? That wasn't a pleasant thought. She slipped the envelope into her bosom, after studying it until she knew the words by heart.

Then she drew out her mother's papers she'd brought from home and for the first time read them over.

The first was the marriage certificate. She'd seen that before and studied it with awe, but her mother had kept the others in a box the children never opened.

The largest paper she couldn't understand. It was something about a mine and contained a great many "herebys" and "whereases" and "agreements" in it. She put it back into the wrapper, thinking it was probably her father's and her mother had treasured it for old time's sake.

Then came a paper regarding the claim where their log cabin stood and on the extreme edge where the graves lay. That, too, she laid reverently in its wrapper.

Next she read a card with "Mrs. Merrill Wilton Bailey, Rittenhouse Square, Tuesdays" inscribed on it. That was the name of her grandmother—her father's mother—though she'd never seen the card before. She looked at it in wonder, as if she were getting a distant glimpse of that woman. What kind of place was Rittenhouse Square, and where was it? There was no telling. She laid it down with a sigh.

One paper remained, and that was a letter written in pale pencil lines:

My dear Bessie,

Your pa died last week. He was killed falling off a scaffold. He was buried on Monday with five carriages and everything nice. He was buried on Monday with five carriages and everything nice. We all got new black dresses and have enough for a stone. If it don't cost too much, we'll have an angel on the top. I always thought an angel pointing to heaven was nice. We wish you was here. We miss you very much. I hope your husband is good to you. Why don't you write to us? You haven't wrote since your little girl was born. I s'pose you call her Bessie like you. If anything ever happens to

you, you can send her to me. I'd kind of like her to fill your place.
Your sister has got a baby girl too. She calls her Lizzie. We couldn't
somehow have it natural to call her 'Lizabeth, and Nan wanted her
called for me. I was always Lizzie, you know. Now you must write
soon.

> *Your loving mother,*
> *Elizabeth Brady.*

The letter carried no date or address, but an address had been pencilled on the outside in her mother's cramped schoolgirl hand. It was dim but still readable: "Mrs. Elizabeth Brady, 18 Flora Street, Philadelphia."

Elizabeth studied the last word, then drew out the envelope again. Yes, the two names were the same. Maybe she would see him again sometime, though of course he belonged to the lady. If she went to school and learned fast, she might meet him at church—he attended church, she was sure. Then he might smile and not be ashamed of his friend who'd saved his life. Nonsense! She hadn't done much. He wouldn't feel any ridiculous indebtedness to her when he returned home to friends and safety. He saved her much more than she had saved him.

She put the papers back into safety and, after packing her few things, knelt down. She would say the prayer before she started. It might keep the pursuers away.

She said it once, then waited with her eyes closed. Might she say it for him? Perhaps it would help him and keep him from falling off that terrible machine he was riding on. In her mind prayers had always been for the dead, but now they seemed to belong also to all who were in danger or trouble. She said the prayer over again, then paused and added: "Our Father, hide him from trouble. Hide George Trescott Benedict. And hide me, please, too."

Then she mounted her horse and set out. The long way reached over mountains and through valleys, across winding, turbulent streams and broad rivers with few bridges. Twice the rivers led her farther south than she meant to go. She'd always felt that Philadelphia was due east, as straight as one could go to the heart of the sun.

Night after night she lay down in strange homes, some poorer and more forlorn than others, and day after day she took up her lonely travel again.

Gradually, as the days lengthened, and mountains piled themselves behind her and rivers stretched like barriers in between, she dreaded her pursuers less and looked forward to the future more. But it seemed so long a way!

Once she asked a man where Philadelphia was. She'd been traveling for weeks and thought she must be almost there. But he said, "Philadelphia? Oh, Philadelphia is in the East. That's a long way off. Once I saw a man from there."

She set her firm little chin then and traveled on. Her clothes were worn, her skin brown as a berry. The horse plodded on, too. He would have stopped at a number of places they passed; instead he walked on over any old road and solaced himself with whatever bite the roadside afforded. He was becoming a much-traveled horse. He knew a threshing machine by sight now and thought it was about the same as a prairie bobcat.

At one place a good woman advised Elizabeth to rest on Sundays. She told her God didn't like for people to do the same on His day as on other days, and it would bring her bad luck if she kept up her incessant riding. It was bad for the horse, too. Since it was Saturday night, Elizabeth stayed with the woman over Sunday and heard the fourteenth chapter of John read aloud. It was a wonderful revelation to her, though she didn't altogether understand it. In fact, the Bible was unknown. She'd never known it was different from other books. She'd heard her mother speak of it, but only as a book. She didn't know it was a book of books.

Elizabeth pondered the beautiful thoughts on the way and wished she had the Book. She remembered it was called the Bible, the Book of God. Then God had written a book! Someday she would try to find it and read it.

"Let not your heart be troubled"—so much of the message drifted into her lonely, unlearned soul and settled down to stay. She said it during nights when she found shelter in some unpleasant place. She remembered it on days when the road was rough or a storm came up and she was compelled to seek shelter by the roadside under a haystack or in a friendly but deserted shack. She thought of it the day she found no shelter and was drenched to the skin. She wondered afterward when the sun came out and dried her whether God had really been speaking the words to her troubled heart, "Let not your heart be troubled."

Every night and every morning she said "Our Father" twice, once for herself and once for the friend out in the world.

One day she crossed a railroad track. Her heart beat wildly. Railroads belonged to the East and civilization. But the lonely days continued, until she crossed more and more railroads and came upon the line of towns that stretched along the snakelike tracks.

She stayed overnight in a town and rode on to the next in the morning. But her clothes were becoming so dirty and ragged that she felt ashamed to go to nice-looking places lest they turn her out; so she sought shelter in barns and smaller houses. But the people in these houses were distressingly dirty, and she found no place to wash.

She had lost track of the weeks or months when she finally reached her first great city. Into the outskirts of Chicago she rode, her head erect, with the carriage of a queen. She had passed Indians and cowboys in her journey; why should she mind this city? Miles and miles of houses and people—surely this must be Philadelphia.

A large, beautiful building attracted her attention. Handsome grounds surrounded it, and girls played a game with a ball and curious webbed implements across a net of cords. She drew her horse to the side of the road and watched a few minutes. One girl was skilled and hit the ball back every time. Elizabeth almost exclaimed out loud once when a particularly fine ball was played. The game finished, she rode reluctantly on a little ways, noticing over the arched gate the words "Janeway School for Girls."

Ah! This was Philadelphia at last, and here was her school. She would go in now before she went to her grandmother's.

She dismounted and tied the horse to an iron ring in a post by the sidewalk. Then she moved slowly, shyly up the steps. She was shabby, but her long journey would explain that. Would they be kind and let her study?

She stood by the door, with a group of girls not far away laughing and whispering about her. She smiled at them, but they didn't return her greeting; their actions made her more shy. At last she stepped into the open door, and a maid in cap and apron came forward. "You mustn't come in here, miss," she said haughtily. "This is a school."

"Yes," Elizabeth said, smiling. "I want to see the teacher."

"She's busy. You can't see her," snapped the maid.

"Then I'll wait till she is ready. I've come many miles, and I must see her."

The maid retreated at this, and an elegant woman in trailing black silk and gold-rimmed glasses approached. This was a new kind of beggar, of course, and must be dealt with at once.

"What do you want?" she asked frigidly.

"I've come to school," Elizabeth said. "I know I don't look very nice, but I've come all the way from Montana on horseback. If you could let me have some water and a needle and thread, I can make myself look better."

The woman eyed the girl incredulously.

"You've come to school!" she said. Her voice was loud and frightened Elizabeth. "You've come all the way from Montana! Impossible! You must be crazy."

"No, ma'am, I'm not crazy," said Elizabeth. "I just want to go to school."

The woman thought this might make an interesting case for benevolent people, but it was an annoyance to her. "My dear girl"—her tone was bland and disagreeable now—"are you aware it takes money to come to school?"

"Does it?" asked Elizabeth. "No, I didn't know, but I have some money. I can give you ten dollars now. If that isn't enough, I can work and earn more."

The woman laughed sharply.

"It's impossible," she said. "The yearly tuition here is five hundred dollars. Besides, we don't take girls of your class. This is a finishing school for young ladies. You'll have to inquire further."

Then the woman swept away to laugh with her colleagues over the new kind of tramp she'd just interviewed.

The maid came pertly forward and told Elizabeth she could no longer stand where she was.

Bewildered and disappointed, Elizabeth went to her horse, with tears welling up in her eyes. As she rode away, she kept looking back at the school. She didn't notice the passersby commenting on her appearance. She made a striking picture in her rough garments with her wealth of hair, her tanned skin and her tear-filled eyes. An artist noticed it and watched her ride down the street, thinking he would follow and secure her as a model for his next picture.

A woman, dressed in soiled finery and heavily rouged, also watched her and followed. At last she called out, "My dear, my dear, wait a minute." She spoke several times before Elizabeth realized she was talking to her and stopped the horse by the sidewalk.

"My dear," said the woman, "you look tired and discouraged. Don't you want to come home with me and rest?"

"Thank you," Elizabeth said, "but I must go on. I only stop on Sundays."

"Come home with me for a little while," coaxed the woman. "You look so tired, and I've some girls of my own. I know you'd enjoy resting and talking with them."

The kindness in her voice touched the weary girl. Her pride had been stung by the haughty woman in the school. Surely this woman would soothe her with kindness.

"Do you live far from here?" asked Elizabeth.

"Only two or three blocks," said the woman. "You ride along by the sidewalk, and we can talk. Where're you going? You look as if you've come a long distance."

"Yes," the girl said, "from Montana. I'm going to go to school. Is this Philadelphia?"

"This is Chicago," said the woman. "There are finer schools here than in Philadelphia. If you'd like to come and stay at my house awhile, I'll see about getting you into a school."

"Is it hard work to get into a school?" asked the girl. "I thought they wanted people to teach."

"No, it's very hard," said the woman. "But I think I know a school I can get you in. Where are your folks? Are they in Montana?"

"They're all dead," said Elizabeth, "and I've come to go to school."

"Poor child!" the woman said too easily. "Come right home with me, and I'll take care of you. I know a nice way you can earn your living, and then you can study if you like. But you're quite big to go to school. It seems to me you could have a good time without that. You're a pretty girl—did you know that? You only need pretty clothes to make you a beauty. If you come with me, I'll let you earn some beautiful new clothes."

"You're very kind," said the girl. "I do need new clothes. If I could earn them, that would be all the better."

Elizabeth wasn't quite certain she liked the woman, but she decided that was foolish.

After a few more turns they stopped in front of a tall brick building with a number of windows. It looked like every other building up and down the street. She tied her horse in front of the door and entered with the woman. The woman told her to sit down until she called the lady of the house, who would tell her more about the school. Several pretty girls were sitting about in the room and talked freely with her. They twitted her about her clothes and reminded Elizabeth of the girls in the school.

Suddenly an idea occurred to her. This was the school, and the woman hadn't wanted to say so until she spoke to the leader about her.

"Is this a school?" she asked shyly.

Her question was met with shouts and laughter.

"School?" cried the boldest, prettiest one. "School for scandal! School for morals!"

One—a thin, pale girl with dark circles under her eyes, a sad droop about her mouth, and bright scarlet spots in her cheeks—walked over to Elizabeth and whispered something to her. Elizabeth stood up instantly with horror on her face.

She fled to the door but found it fastened. Then she turned as if she had been brought to bay by a pack of lions.

Chapter 10

O pen this door!" she commanded. "Let me out of here at once."

The pale girl started to do so, but the pretty one held her back. "No, Nellie. Madam will be angry with us all if you open that door."

Then she turned to Elizabeth. "Whoever enters that door never goes out again. You are nicely caught, my dear."

The taunt at the end of the words held a sting of bitterness and self-pity. Elizabeth felt it as she seized her pistol from her belt and pointed it at the astonished group. They weren't used to girls with pistols.

"Open that door, or I'll shoot you all!" she cried.

As she heard someone descending the stairs, she rushed into the room where she remembered the windows were open. They were guarded by wire screens. She grabbed a chair, smashed it through one and plunged out into the street. At that moment hands reached out to detain her; they were hindered at first by the glint of the pistol and fear that it might go off in their midst.

She wrenched the bridle from its fastening and mounted her horse, then rode through the city at a pace only millionaires and automobiles were allowed to take. She met and passed her first automobile without a quiver. Her eyes stared ahead, and her lips were set; angry, frightened tears streamed down her cheeks. She urged her poor horse forward until a policeman here and there thought it his duty to try to restrain her. But nothing impeded her. She fled through a maze of wagons, carriages, automobiles, and trolley cars, until she passed the whirl of the big city. At last she was free again and out in the open country.

Toward evening she neared a little cottage on the edge of a pretty suburb. The cottage was covered with roses, and the front yard was full of great old-fashioned flowers. On the porch sat an old woman in a rocking chair, knitting. A path led from a gate up to the door, and at the side another gate opened to a path leading around to the back of the cottage.

Elizabeth murmured, "Oh, 'our Father,' please hide me," and dashed into the driveway and up to the side of the porch at a full gallop. She jumped off her horse and left him panting with his nose to the fence and a strip of clover in front of him where he could graze when he caught his breath. Then she ran up the steps and flung herself at the feet of the astonished old woman.

"Oh, please won't you let me stay here a few minutes? I'm so tired, and I've had such a dreadful time!"

"Why, dear me!" said the old woman. "Of course I will. Sit right down in this rocking chair and have a good cry. I'll get you a glass of water and something to eat. Then tell me all about it."

She brought the water and a tray with thick slices of brown bread and butter, a generous piece of apple pie, some cheese, and a glass pitcher of creamy milk.

Elizabeth drank the water, but before she could eat she told the terrible tale of her last adventure. She'd heard there were bad people. In fact, she'd seen bad men, and once a woman had passed their ranch whose character was said to be questionable. She wore a hard face and could drink and swear like the men. But that sin should appear in this form, with pretty girls and pleasant, wheedling women for agents, she never dreamed—and this in the great civilized East! She almost wished she'd stayed in the desert alone and risked the pursuit of that awful man than to come this far and find the world gone wrong.

The old woman was horrified, too. She'd heard more than the girl of licensed evil; but she had read it in the paper as she'd read about the evils of the slave traffic in Africa, and it never seemed true to her. Now she lifted up her hands in horror and looked at the beautiful girl who'd been trapped in a den of iniquity and escaped. She made the girl repeat over and over what was said, how it looked, how she pointed her pistol, and how she got out. Then she called her escape a miracle.

They were both weary from excitement when the tale was told. Elizabeth ate her lunch; then the old woman showed her where to put the horse and where she could sleep. It was only a little room with a snow-white cot; but the roses peeped in at the window, and the box covered with an old white curtain held a large pitcher of fresh water and a bowl and soap and towels. The woman brought her a clean white nightgown, coarse and mended in many places, but smelling of rose leaves. In the morning she tapped on the door before the girl was up and carried in an armful of clothes.

"I had some boarders last summer," she explained, "who left these things and said I might put them in the home-mission box. But I was sick when they sent it off this winter. Besides, if you aren't a home mission, I never saw one. You put 'em on. I guess they'll fit. They may be a mite large, but she was about your size. I guess your clothes are about worn-out, so you just leave 'em here for the next one and use these. You can pack a couple of extra shirtwaists in a bundle for a change. I guess folks won't dare fool with you if you have some clean, nice clothes on."

Elizabeth looked at her gratefully and counted her a saint with the woman who read the fourteenth chapter of John.

Bathed and clothed in fresh garments, with a white shirtwaist and a dark-blue serge skirt and coat, Elizabeth looked like a different girl. She surveyed herself in the little glass over the washstand. All at once vanity was born in her, with an ambition to be always thus clothed, for she remembered the woman from the day before, who had promised to show her how to earn some pretty clothes. But pretty clothes might be a snare; perhaps they'd been to those girls in the house.

With much good advice and blessings from the old woman, Elizabeth set out on her journey again, more worldly-wise and less sweetly credulous than before, but better fitted to fight her way.

The story of her journey from Chicago to Philadelphia would fill a volume, but it might pall upon the reader from the variety of its experiences. It was slow and painful, with many stops and a great drop in the money that had seemed so much. The horse went lame, and on the advice of a farmer she took him to a veterinary surgeon. He doctored him for a week before he finally said it was safe to let him hobble on again. After that the girl took more care of the horse. If he should die, what would she do?

One dismal morning late in November, wearing the old overcoat to keep from freezing, Elizabeth rode into Philadelphia.

Armed with instructions from the old woman in Chicago, she rode up to a policeman and showed him the address of her grandmother, her mother's mother, to whom she had decided to go first. He sent her in the right direction, and in due time, with the help of other policemen, she reached the right number on Flora Street.

It was a narrow street, banked on either side by small, narrow brick houses. Here and there a white marble doorstep sparkled, but most of the houses were approached by steps of dull stone or painted wood. The place had a dejected and dreary air about it, and the street was swarming with soiled children.

Elizabeth knocked timidly at the door. Mrs. Brady was washing when the knock sounded throughout the house. She was a broad woman, with a face unmarked by the cares and sorrows of the years. She still enjoyed life, even though she spent a good part of it at the washtub, washing other people's fine clothes. She had fine ones of her own, tucked away in her clothespress upstairs and brought out for special occasions.

The perspiration formed little beads on her forehead and trickled down the creases in her well-cushioned neck toward her ample bosom. Her gray hair was combed neatly, and her calico wrapper stood open at the throat even on this cold day. She wiped the soapsuds from her plump arms on her apron and walked to the door.

Mrs. Brady looked disapprovingly at the peculiar person on the doorstep attired in a man's overcoat. She was prepared to refuse the Salvation Army's demands for a nickel for Christmas dinners; to silence the banana man, the fish man, or the man selling shoestrings and pencils; or to send the photograph agent away, and even the man who sold postcard albums. She had no time to bother with anybody this morning.

But the young person in the rusty overcoat, wearing a dark-blue serge Eton jacket, which might have come from Wanamaker's two years ago, and a leather belt with pistols under the jacket, was a new species. Mrs. Brady was caught off guard; otherwise Elizabeth might have found entrance to her grandmother's home as difficult as Madame Janeway's finishing school.

"Are you Mrs. Brady?" asked the girl. She searched the forbidding face for some likeness to her mother, but found none. The cares of Elizabeth Brady's daughter had outweighed those of the mother, or else they sat upon a more sensitive nature.

"I am," said Mrs. Brady, imposingly.

"Grandmother, I'm the baby you talked about in this letter," she announced, handing Mrs. Brady the letter she'd written nearly eighteen years before.

The woman took the envelope gingerly in the wet thumb and finger that still grasped a bit of the gingham apron. She held it at arm's length and squinted up her eyes, trying to read it without her glasses. It was a new kind of beggar, of course. She hated to touch these dirty envelopes, and this one looked old and worn. She stepped back to the parlor table where her glasses were lying and, adjusting them, began to read the letter.

"For the land sakes! Where'd you find this?" she asked, eyeing the girl suspiciously. "It's against the law to open letters that ain't your own. Didn't me daughter ever get it? I wrote it to her meself. How come you by it?"

"Mother read it to me long ago when I was little," answered the girl, the slow hope fading. Was everyone, even her grandmother, going to be cold and harsh with her? *Our Father, hide me!* her heart murmured, because it had become a habit.

And her listening thought caught the answer, *Let not your heart be troubled.*

"Well, who are you?" snapped the grandmother, still puzzled. "You ain't Bessie, me Bessie. For one thing, you're 'bout as young as she was when she ran off 'n' got married, against me 'dvice, to that drunken, lazy dude." Her brow puckered, and she finished the letter.

"I am Elizabeth," said the girl with a trembling voice, "the baby you talked about in that letter. But please don't call Father that. He was never bad to us. He was always good to Mother, even when he was drunk. If you talk like that about him, I'll leave."

"For the land sakes! You don't say," said Mrs. Brady, sitting down hard in astonishment on the biscuit upholstery of her best parlor chair. "Now you ain't Bessie's child! Well, I *am clear* beat. And growed up so big! You look strong, but you're kind of thin. What makes your skin so black? Your ma never was dark, ner your pa, neither."

"I've been riding a long way in the wind and sun and rain."

"For the land sakes!" as she looked through the window to the street. "Not on a horse?"

"Yes."

"H'm! What was your ma thinkin' about to let you do that?"

"My mother is dead. There was no one left to care what I did. I had to come. There were dreadful people out there, and I was afraid."

"For the land sakes!" That seemed to be the only remark Mrs. Brady could make. She looked at her new granddaughter in bewilderment, as if a strange sort of creature had suddenly laid claim to relationship.

"Well, I'm right glad to see you," she said stiffly, wiping her hand again on her apron and extending it formally for a greeting.

Elizabeth accepted her reception soberly. She sat down, and her head fell suddenly back against the wall. A gray look spread over her face.

"You're tired," said the grandmother. "Come far this morning?"

"No," said Elizabeth, "not many miles. But I used up all the bread yesterday, and there wasn't much money left. I thought I could wait till I got here, but I guess I'm hungry."

"For the land sakes!" exclaimed Mrs. Brady as she hustled out to the kitchen, clattering the frying pan onto the stove and shoving the boiler aside. She came in presently with a steaming cup of tea for the girl. Then she settled her in the rocking chair in the kitchen with a plate of appetizing things to eat and went on with her washing, punctuating every rub with a question.

Elizabeth felt better after eating and offered to help, but the grandmother wouldn't hear of it.

"You must rest first," she said. "It beats me how you ever got here. I'd sooner crawl on me hands and knees than ride a big, scary horse."

Elizabeth sprang to her feet.

"The horse!" she said. "He needs something to eat worse than I did. He hasn't had a bite of grass all morning. There was nothing but hard roads and pavements. The grass is all brown now anyway. I found some cornstalks by the road, and once a man dropped a big bundle of hay out of his load. If it hadn't been for Robin, I'd never have gotten here. Here I've sat enjoying my breakfast, and Robin out there hungry!"

"For the land sakes!" said the grandmother, taking her arms out of the suds. "Poor fellow! What would he like? I don't have any hay, just some mashed potatoes, and what else is there? Why, there's some excelsior the lampshade came packed in. You don't suppose he'd think it was hay, do you? No, I guess it wouldn't taste very good."

"Where can I put him, Grandmother?"

"For land sakes! I don't know," said the grandmother, glancing around the room in alarm. "We don't have any place for horses. Perhaps you might get him into the backyard for awhile till we think what to do. There's a stable, but they charge high to board horses. Lizzie knows one of the fellers that works there. Maybe he'll tell us what to do. Anyway, you lead him round to the alley, and we'll see if we can't get him in the little ash gate. You don't suppose he'd try to get in the house, do you? I shouldn't like him to come in the kitchen when I was getting supper."

"Oh, no!" said Elizabeth. "He's very good. Where's the backyard?"

This arrangement was finally made, and the two women stood in the kitchen door, watching Robin drink a bucketful of water and eat heartily of the various provisions Mrs. Brady set forth for him, with the exception of the excelsior, which he sniffed at in disgust.

"Now ain't he smart?" said Mrs. Brady, watching from the doorstep, where she might retreat if the animal stepped near the kitchen. "But don't you think he's cold? Wouldn't he like a—a—shawl or something?"

The girl drew the old coat from her shoulders and threw it over him, while her grandmother watched her fearless handling of the horse with pride and awe.

"We're used to sharing this together," said the girl simply.

"Nan sews in an uptown dressmaker's place," explained Mrs. Brady later. The wash had been hung out in fearsome proximity to the weary horse's heels, and the two had returned to the warm kitchen to clean up and get supper. "Nan's your ma's sister, you know, older'n her by two years. Lizzie—that's her girl—she's about as old as you. She's got a good place in the ten-cent store. Nan's husband died four years ago, and her and me've been livin' together ever since. It'll be nice for you and Lizzie to be together. She'll make it lively for you right away. Prob'ly she can get you a place at the same store. She'll be here at half past six tonight. This is her week to get out early."

The aunt came in first. She was a tall, thin woman with faded brown hair and a faint resemblance to Elizabeth's mother. Her shoulders stooped slightly, and her voice was nasal. She was the kind who always found a rocking chair to sew in if she could and rock as she sewed. She was skillful in her way and commanded good wages.

She welcomed the new niece reluctantly—more excited than pleased by her remarkable appearance among her relatives after so long a silence, Elizabeth felt. But after satisfying her curiosity she was kind and talked about Lizzie, mentally comparing this thin, brown girl with rough hair and dowdy clothes to her own stylish daughter.

Then Lizzie burst in. They could hear her calling to a young man who had walked home with her, even before she entered the house.

"It's just fierce out, Ma!" she exclaimed. "Grandma, ain't supper ready yet? I never was so hungry in all my life. I could eat a house afire."

She stopped short when she saw Elizabeth. She was chewing gum—Lizzie always chewed gum—but her jaws ceased their action in sheer astonishment.

"This is your cousin Bessie, come all the way from Montana on horseback, Lizzie. She's your aunt Bessie's child. Her folks is dead now, and she's come to live with us. You must see if you can't get her a place in the ten-cent store along with you," said the grandmother.

Lizzie came airily forward and grasped her cousin's hand, shaking it laterally in a way that bewildered Elizabeth.

"Pleased to meet you," she said glibly, setting her jaws to work again. One could not embarrass Lizzie long. But she kept her eyes on the stranger and let them wander disapprovingly over her apparel. At the same time she removed the long pins from the bulky hat she wore and adjusted her pompadour.

"Lizzie'll help fix you up," said the aunt, noting her daughter's glance. "You're all out of style. I suppose they get behind times out in Montana. Lizzie, can't you show her how to fix her hair in a pompadour?"

Lizzie brightened. She was not averse to a cousin of her own age, if she could change things. But she could never take such a dowdy-looking girl into society, not the society of the ten-cent store.

"Oh, cert!" answered Lizzie affably. "I'll fix you fine. Don't you worry. How'd you get so awful tanned? I s'pose riding. You look like you'd been to the seashore and lay out on the beach in the sun. But it ain't the right time o' year quite. It must be great to ride horseback!"

"I'll teach you how if you want to learn," said Elizabeth, trying to return the kind offer.

"Me? What would I ride? Have to ride a counter, I guess. I guess you won't find much to ride here in the city 'cept trolley cars."

"Bessie's got a horse. He's out in the yard now," said the grandmother with pride.

"A horse! All your own? Gee whiz! Won't the girls stare when I tell them? Say, we can borrow a rig at the livery some night and take a ride. Dan'll go with us and get the rig for us. Won't that be great?"

Elizabeth smiled. She felt the glow of at last contributing something to the family pleasure. She didn't wish her coming to be the wet blanket it seemed at first. To tell the truth, she saw blank dismay on the face of each separate relative as her identity was revealed. Her heart was lonely, and she hungered for someone who "belonged" and loved her.

Supper was put on the table, and the two girls got a little acquainted, chattering over clothes and hairstyles.

"Do you know if there is anything in Philadelphia called 'Christian Endeavor'?" asked Elizabeth after the supper table was cleared.

"Oh, Chrishun 'deavor! Yes, I used t' belong," answered Lizzie. She had removed the gum while she ate supper, but now it was busy again between sentences. "Yes, we have one down to our church. It was real interesting, too. But I got mad at one of the members and quit. She was a stuck-up old maid, anyway. She was always turning round and scowling at us girls if we just whispered the least little bit or smiled. One night she was leading the meeting, and Jim Forbes got in a corner behind a post and made faces at her behind his book. It was something fierce the way she always screwed her face up when she sang, and he looked just like her. We girls, Hetty and Em'line and me, got to laughing and couldn't stop.

"And didn't that old thing stop the singing after one verse, look right at us, and say she thought Christian Endeavor members should remember whose

house they were in and that the owner was there and all that rot. I nearly died—
I was so mad. Everybody looked around, and we girls got up and left. I haven't
been down since. The lookout committee came to see us 'bout it. But I said I
wouldn't go back where I'd been insulted, and I've never been inside since.
She's moved away now. I wouldn't mind going back if you want to go."

"Whose house did she mean it was? Was it her house?"

"Oh, no, it wasn't her house," laughed Lizzie. "It was the church. She
meant it was God's house, I s'pose, but she didn't need to be so persnickety.
We weren't doing any harm."

"Does God have a house?"

"Why, yes, didn't you know that? Why, you talk like a heathen, Bessie.
Didn't you have churches in Montana?"

"Yes, there was a church fifty miles away. I heard about it once, but I never
saw it," answered Elizabeth. "But what did the woman mean? Who did she say
was there? God? Did you see Him and know He was there when you laughed?"

"Oh, you silly!" giggled Lizzie. "Wouldn't the girls laugh at you, though,
if they could hear you talk? Why, of course God was there. He's everywhere,
you know," she said with superior knowledge. "But I didn't see Him. You can't
see God."

"Why not?"

"Why, because you can't!" answered her cousin with the final word. "Say,
haven't you got any other clothes with you at all? I'd take you down with me
in the morning if you was fixed up."

Chapter 11

When Elizabeth lay down to rest that night, with Lizzie still chattering by her side, she found that one source gave her intense pleasure in its anticipation. That was the prospect of going to God's house to Christian Endeavor. Now perhaps she would find out what it meant and whether it was true that God took care of people and hid them in troubled times. She felt almost certain in her experience that He had cared for her, and she wanted to be sure so she might grasp this precious truth to her heart and keep it forever. No one could be quite alone in the world if there was a God who cared and loved and hid.

The aunt and the grandmother were up early the next morning, looking over some old clothing. They found an old dress they thought could be refurbished for Elizabeth. They were hardworking people with little money to spare, and everything had to be utilized. But they made a great deal of appearance, and Lizzie was proud as a young peacock. She wouldn't take Elizabeth to the store to face the head man without fixing her up according to the most accepted style.

So the aunt cut and fitted before she left for the day, and Elizabeth was ordered to sew while she was gone. The grandmother presided at the rattling old sewing machine, and in two or three days Elizabeth was declared fixed up enough till she could earn some new clothes. Her fine hair was snarled into a cushion and puffed out into an enormous pompadour that didn't suit her face in the least. Then with an old hat and jacket of Lizzie's which didn't fit her exactly, she started out to make her way in the world as a saleswoman. Lizzie had already secured her a place if she worked out.

The store amazed the girl from the mountains—so many bright, bewildering things, ribbons and tin pans, glassware and toys, cheap jewelry and candies. She looked about in a daze.

But the manager was used to judging faces and regarded her favorably. He saw that she was alert and as yet unspoiled, with a refined face far beyond the girls who generally applied to him for positions. And he didn't mind a friendly flirtation with a pretty new girl himself; so she was hired at once for duty at the notions counter.

The girls flocked around her during breaks. Lizzie had told of her cousin's long ride, embellished, wherever her knowledge failed, by her wild notions of western life. She'd told how Elizabeth arrived wearing a belt with two pistols; this gave Elizabeth standing at once among the people in the store. A girl who could shoot and wore pistols in a belt like a real cowboy possessed a social distinction of her own.

The novel-reading, theater-going girls rallied around her, and the young men in the store were not far behind. Elizabeth was popular from the first. Moreover, as she settled into the routine of life and ate three meals a day, her cheeks rounded out just a little. It became apparent that she was unusually beautiful in spite of her dark skin, which lightened gradually under the electric light and high-pressure life of the store.

Elizabeth and her cousin attended Christian Endeavor, and Elizabeth felt as if heaven had opened before her. She lived from week to week for that Christian Endeavor.

The store, a novelty at first, became a trial to her. It wore upon her nerves. The air was bad, and the crowds large. Christmas was approaching, and the store was crammed to bursting day after day and night after night since they stayed open evenings until Christmas. Elizabeth longed for the mountain air and grew paler. Sometimes she felt as if she must break away from it all, take Robin, and ride into the wilderness. If it weren't for the Christian Endeavor, she might have.

Robin, poor beast, was well-housed and well-fed, but he worked for his living as his mistress did. He was a grocer's delivery horse, working from early Monday morning till late Saturday night and subject to curses and kicks from the grocery boy. He was expected to stand meekly at the curbstones, snuffing the dusty brick pavements while the boy delivered a box of goods. Meanwhile trolleys and beer wagons and automobiles slammed and rumbled and tooted by him. Then he had to start on the double to the next delivery place.

To be thus under the rod when he had trod the plains with a free foot and snuffed the mountain air was a great comedown, and his life became a burden to him. But he earned his mistress a dollar a week besides his board and, had he known it, would have been consoled. And she would have gladly gone without the dollar if Robin could be free and happy.

One day, the manager of the ten-cent store approached Elizabeth with a look in his eyes that reminded her of the man in Montana from whom she fled. He smiled and said some overly pleasant words. He wanted her to go with him to the theater that evening and complimented her on her appearance. He admired her, he said, and wanted to show her a good time.

But ever since she left the prairies Elizabeth compared all men with George Trescott Benedict. And this man, although he dressed neatly and was every bit as handsome, did not compare well. His eyes held a sinister, selfish glitter that reminded Elizabeth of the serpent on the plain just before she shot it.

A missionary meeting was also being held at the church that evening. All the Christian endeavorers had been urged to attend. Elizabeth gave this as an excuse. But the manager dismissed it, saying she could go to church any night, but she couldn't go to this particular play with him any night.

The girl eyed him calmly, as though she were pointing a pistol at his head, and said, "But I don't want to go with you."

After that the manager despised her, as he did every girl who resisted him, and wanted to hurt her. So he persecuted her to receive attention. He was a young fellow to occupy such a responsible position and no doubt had business ability. He demonstrated it in his management of Elizabeth. The girl's life became a torment to her. In proportion to how she appeared to be the manager's favorite, the other girls became jealous of her. They taunted her on every possible occasion. When they found anything wrong, they blamed her; so she was kept going constantly to the manager, which was perhaps just what he wanted.

She grew paler and more desperate. She ran away from one man; she ran away from a woman; but here was a man she could not run away from unless she gave up her position. If it hadn't been for her grandmother, she would have done so at once. But if she gave up her position, she must turn to her grandmother for support, and that must not be. From the family talk she understood they were having trouble making both ends meet and keeping the all-important god of Fashion satisfied. This god Fashion seemed to Elizabeth an enemy of the living God. It seemed to occupy everyone's thoughts, and everything else had to be sacrificed to meet its demands.

She had broached the subject of school one evening soon after she arrived but was instantly squelched by her aunt and cousin.

"You're too old!" sneered Lizzie. "School is for children."

"Lizzie went through grammar school, and we talked about high for her," said the grandmother proudly.

"But I just hated school," grinned Lizzie. "It ain't so nice as it's cracked up to be. Just sit and study all day long. Why, they always kept me after school for talking or laughing. I was glad enough when I got through. You may thank your stars you didn't have to go, Bess."

"People who have to earn their bread can't lie around and go to school," remarked Aunt Nan dryly, and Elizabeth said no more.

But later she heard of a night school and took up the subject once more. Lizzie scoffed at this, saying night school was only for very poor people, and it was a disgrace to go. But Elizabeth stuck to her point, until one day Lizzie came home with a tale about Temple College. She heard it was very cheap. You could go for ten cents a night or something like that.

She heard it was quite respectable to go there, and they had classes in the evening. You could study gymnastics, and it would make you graceful. She wanted to be graceful. And she heard they had a course in millinery. If it was so, she believed she would go herself and learn to make the new bows they were wearing on hats this winter.

Elizabeth wanted to study geography. At least, that was the course Lizzie said would tell her where the Sahara Desert was. She wanted to know all kinds of things. But Lizzie said such things were only for children, and she didn't believe they taught such baby studies in a college. But she would inquire. It was silly of Bessie to want to know, she thought, and she was ashamed to ask. But she would find out.

It was about this time that Elizabeth's life at the store grew intolerable.

One morning, little more than a week before Christmas, Elizabeth was sent to the cellar to get seven small red tin pails and shovels. A woman wanted them for Christmas gifts for a Sunday school class. She had counted out seven and turned to go upstairs when she heard someone step near her. She looked up in the dim light and saw the manager.

"At last I've got you alone, Bessie!" he said, catching Elizabeth by the wrists. Before she could wrench herself free he kissed her.

With a scream Elizabeth dropped the pails and shovels, and with one mighty twist pulled her hands from his grasp. Instinctively her hand slipped to her belt, where no pistols were now. Had one been there she would have shot him in her horror and fury. But, since she had no other weapon, she grabbed a little shovel and struck him in the face. Then with the frenzy of the desert back upon her she rushed up the stairs, out through the crowded store, and into the street, hatless and coatless in the cold December air. The passersby made way for her, thinking she'd been sent out on some hurried errand.

She left her pocketbook, with its few nickels for carfare and lunch, in the cloakroom with her coat and hat. But she didn't stop to think of that. She was fleeing again, this time on foot, from a man. She half expected him to pursue her and force her to return to the dreaded work in the stifling store with his wicked face moving above the crowds. But she didn't look back. She ran on over the slushy pavements, under the leaden sky, with a few white flakes floating above her.

The day seemed as pitiless as the world. Where could she go? There seemed to be no refuge for her in the whole world. Instinctively she felt that her grandmother would think a calamity had befallen them in losing the patronage of the manager of the ten-cent store. Perhaps Lizzie would get into trouble.

She reached the corner where she and Lizzie usually took the car home. The car was coming, but she had no hat or coat and no money to pay for a ride. She must walk. She didn't pause but kept up a steady run, for which her years on the mountain had given her breath. It was three miles to Flora Street, and she scarcely slowed her pace after settling into a half-run, half-walk. Only at the corner of Flora Street did she pause and glance back. No, the manager had not pursued her. She was safe to go in and tell her grandmother without fearing he'd come up behind her as soon as her back was turned.

Chapter 12

Mrs. Brady was at the washtub again when her most uncommon and unexpected grandchild burst into the room.

She wiped her hands on her apron and sat down with her usual exclamation. "For the land sakes! What's happened, Bessie? Tell me quick. Is anything the matter with Lizzie? Where is she?"

But Elizabeth was on the floor at her feet in tears. She was shaking and scarcely managed to stammer out that Lizzie was all right. Mrs. Brady settled back with a relieved sigh. Lizzie was the first grandchild and therefore the idol of her heart. If Lizzie was all right, she could be patient and find out by degrees.

"It's that awful man, Grandmother!" Elizabeth cried.

"What man? That feller in Montana you run away from?" She wasn't afraid of a man, even if he did shoot people. She would call in the police and protect her own flesh and blood. Let him come. Mrs. Brady was ready for him.

"No, no, Grandmother, the man–man–manager at the ten-cent store," sobbed the girl. "He kissed me! Oh!" She shuddered at the memory.

"For the land sakes! Is that all?" the woman said with relief and some satisfaction. "Why, that's nothing. You ought to be proud. Many girls would boast about that. What are you crying for? He didn't hurt you, did he? Why, Lizzie seems to think he's fine. She wouldn't cry if he was to kiss her, I'm sure. She'd just laugh and ask him for a holiday. Here, sit up, child—wash your face and go back to work. You've evidently struck the manager on the right side, and you're bound to get a raise in your wages. Every girl he takes a notion to gets up and does well. Perhaps you'll get enough money to go to school. Goodness knows what you want to go for. I s'pose it's in the blood, though Bess used to say our pa wa'n't any good at study. But if you've struck the manager the right way, no telling what he might do. He might even want to marry you."

"Grandmother!"

Mrs. Brady was favored with the flash of the Bailey eyes. She viewed it in astonishment mixed with admiration.

"Well, you certainly have spirit," she said. "I don't wonder he liked you. I didn't know you was so pretty, Bessie. You look like your mother when she was eighteen—you really do. I never saw the resemblance before. I believe you'll get on all right. Don't you be afraid. I wish you had your chance if you're so anxious to go to school. I shouldn't wonder if you'd turn out to be something and marry rich. Well, I must be getting back to me tub. Land sakes, but you did give me a turn. I thought Lizzie had been run over. I couldn't think what else'd make you run here without your coat. Come, get up, child, and go back to your work. It's too bad you don't like to be kissed, but don't let that worry you. You'll have lots worse than that to come up against. When you've lived as long as I have and worked as hard, you'll be pleased to have someone admire you. You better wash your face, eat a bite of lunch, and hustle back. You needn't be afraid. If he's fond of you, he won't bother about your running away a little. He'll excuse you if 'tis busy times and not dock your pay neither."

"Grandmother!" said Elizabeth. "Don't! I can never go back to that awful place and that man. I would rather go back to Montana. I'd rather be dead."

"Hoity-toity!" said the grandmother, sitting down to her task, for she perceived some wholesome discipline was necessary. "You can't talk that way, Bess. You got to go to work. We ain't got money to keep you in idleness, and land knows where you'd get another place as good's this one. If you stay home all day, you might make him awful mad. And then there'd be no use goin' back, and you might lose Lizzie her place, too."

But though the grandmother talked and argued and soothed by turns, Elizabeth was firm. She would never go back. She would go to Montana if her grandmother said anymore about it.

With a sigh Mrs. Brady gave up. She'd given up once before nearly twenty years ago. Bessie, her oldest daughter, had a will like that and tastes far above her station. Mrs. Brady wondered where she got them.

"You're for all the world like yer ma," she said as she thumped the clothes in the washtub. "She was just that way, when she would marry your pa. She could 'a' had Jim Stokes, the groceryman, or Lodge, the milkman, or her choice of three railroad men, all of 'em doing well and ready to let her walk over 'em. But she *would have* your pa, the drunken, good-for-nothing, slippery dude. The only thing I'm surprised at was that he ever married her. I never expected it. I s'posed they'd run off, and he'd leave her when he got tired of her. But it seems he stuck to her. It's the only good thing he ever done, and I'm not sure but she'd 'a' been better off if he hadn't 'a' done that."

"Grandmother!" Elizabeth's face blazed.

"Yes, *gran*'mother!" snapped Mrs. Brady. "It's all true, and you might's well face it. He met her in church. She used to go reg'lar. Some boys used to come and set in the backseat behind the girls and then go home with them. They was all nice enough boys 'cept him. I never had a bit a use for him. He belonged to the swells and the stuck-ups, and he knowed it and presumed upon it. He thought he could wind Bessie round his finger, and he did. If he said, 'Go,' she went, no matter what I'd do. So when his ma found it out, she was hoppin' mad. She came driving round here to me house and presumed to talk to me. She said Bessie was a designing snip, a bad girl, and a whole lot of things. Said she was leading her son astray and would come to no good end and a whole lot of stuff and told me to look after her. It wasn't so. Bess got John Bailey to quit smoking for a whole week at a time, and he said if she'd marry him he'd quit drinking, too. His ma couldn't 'a' got him to promise that.

She wouldn't even believe he got drunk. I told her a few things about her precious son, but she curled up her fine, aristocratic lip and said, 'Gentlemen never get drunk.' Humph! Gentlemen! That's all she knowed about it. He got drunk all right and stayed drunk. So after that, when I tried to keep Bess at home, she slipped away at night. Said she was going to church. She did, too— went to the minister's study in a strange church and got married, her and John. Then they up and ran off to the West. John, he'd sold his watch and his fine diamond stud his ma give him. He borrowed some money from some friends of his father's and went off with three hundred dollars and Bess. And that's all I ever saw of me Bessie."

The poor woman sat down in her chair and wept into her apron, regardless for once of the soapsuds that rolled down her red, wet arms.

"Is my grandmother still living?" asked Elizabeth. She felt sorry for this grandmother but didn't know what to say. She was afraid to comfort her lest she take it for yielding.

"Yes, they say she is," said Mrs. Brady, sitting up with interest. She was always ready for a bit of gossip. "Her husband's dead and her other son's dead, and she's all alone. She lives in a big house on Rittenhouse Square. If she was any 'count, she'd ought to provide for you. I never thought about it. But I don't suppose it would be any use to try. You might ask her. Perhaps she'd help you go to school. You've got a claim on her. She ought to give you her son's share of his father's property, though I've heard she disowned him when he married our Bess. You might fix up in some of Lizzie's best things and go up there and try. She might give you some money."

"I don't want her money," said Elizabeth stiffly. "I guess there's work I can do somewhere in the world without begging even from grandmothers. But I think I ought to go and see her. She might want to know about Father."

Mrs. Brady looked at her granddaughter with awe. She'd never taken this view of things.

"Well," she said, "go your own gait. I don't know where you'll come up at. All I say is, if you're going through the world with such high-and-mighty notions, you'll have a hard time. You can't pick out roses and cream and a bed of down every day. You have to put up with life as you find it."

Elizabeth went to the room she shared with Lizzie. She wanted to get away from her grandmother's disapproval. It lay on her heart like lead. If grandmothers were not refuges, where would one flee? The old woman in Chicago understood. Why didn't Grandmother Brady?

Then came the sweet old words, "Let not your heart be troubled" and, "In the time of trouble he shall hide me in his pavilion: in the secret of his tabernacle shall he hide me." She knelt down by the bed and said, "Our Father." She was beginning to add some words of her own now. She'd heard them say sentence prayers in Christian Endeavor. She wished she knew more about God and His book. She'd had so little time to ask or think about it. Life seemed to be one rush for clothes and position.

At supper Lizzie came home excited. She was in hot water all afternoon. The girls said at lunchtime that the manager was angry with Bessie and discharged her. She found her coat and hat and brought them home. The pocketbook was missing. There was only fifteen cents in it. But Lizzie was disturbed, and so was the grandmother. They consulted quietly in the kitchen. When the aunt came, the three held another whispered conversation.

Aunt Nan sat down beside Elizabeth and talked coldly about expenses and being dependent upon one's relatives; she could not sit around and do nothing. Elizabeth answered by telling her how the manager treated her. The aunt then gave her a dose of worldly wisdom, which made the girl withdraw inside herself. Lizzie's loud exhortations only added to her misery. Supper was an unpleasant meal. At last the grandmother spoke up.

"Well, Bessie," she said firmly, "we've all decided that, if you're going to be stubborn about this, something will have to be done. I think the best thing is for you to go to Mrs. Bailey and see what she'll do for you. It's her business, anyway."

Elizabeth's cheeks blushed red. She said nothing. She let them go on with the arrangements. Lizzie got her best hat and tried it on Elizabeth to see how she'd look. Then she produced a silk waist from her closet and a spring jacket. It wasn't warm, but the occasion demanded strenuous measures, Lizzie explained. The jacket was stylish, and that was the main thing. One could be cold if one was stylish.

Lizzie was up early the next morning. She'd agreed to dress Elizabeth in battle array for her visit to Rittenhouse Square. Elizabeth submitted meekly to her cousin's attempts. Her hair was brushed over her face, curled on a hot iron, brushed backward in a perfect mat and then puffed out in a bigger pompadour than usual. She put on the silk waist with Lizzie's best skirt and was adjured not to let it drag. Then the best hat with the cheap pink plumes was set atop the elaborate coiffure. Finally she slipped into the jacket and struggled into a pair of Lizzie's long silk gloves. They were a trifle large, but to the hands unaccustomed to gloves they were like being run into a mold.

Elizabeth endured it all until she was pronounced complete. Then she came and stood in front of the cheap little glass and surveyed herself. Blisters in the glass twisted her head into a grotesque shape. The hairpins stuck into her head. Lizzie had tied a spotted veil tight over her nose and eyes. The collar of the silk waist was frayed and cut her neck. The shirt band was too tight, and the gloves were torture. Elizabeth turned slowly and went downstairs, past the admiring aunt and grandmother. They exclaimed at the girl's beauty, now that she was attired to their satisfaction, and said they were sure her grandmother would want to do something for so pretty a girl.

After Lizzie dashed out to catch the car for work, Elizabeth walked a few steps in the direction she'd been told to go, turned around, and came back. The watching grandmother felt her heart sink. What was this headstrong girl going to do next?

"What's the matter, Bessie?" she asked, meeting her at the door. "It's bad luck to turn back when you've started."

"I can't go this way," said the girl excitedly. "It's not right. I'm not like this. It isn't mine, and I'm not going in it. I must have my own clothes and be myself when I go to see her. If she doesn't like me and want me, then I can take Robin and go back." And like another David burdened with Saul's armor she returned for her little sling and stones.

She tore off the veil and the sticky gloves from her cold hands and all the silk finery, and donned her old plain blue coat and skirt in which she'd arrived in Philadelphia. They'd been cleaned for a working dress. They belonged to her. Under the jacket, long enough to hide her waist, she buckled her belt with the two pistols. Then she took the battered old felt hat from the closet and tried to fasten it on, but the pompadour interfered. Relentlessly she pulled down Lizzie's work of art, brushed out her long, thick hair, and braided it down her back. Her grandmother should see her just as she was. She should know what kind of girl belonged to her. Then, if she chose to be a real grandmother, well and good.

Mrs. Brady was quite disturbed when Elizabeth came downstairs. She tried to force the girl to go back, telling her it was a disgrace to go in such garments into the sacred precincts of Rittenhouse Square; but the girl was not to be turned back. She would not even wait till her aunt and Lizzie came home. She would go at once.

Mrs. Brady sat down in her rocking chair in despair for a full five minutes after she'd watched the reprehensible girl go down the street. She hadn't been so completely beaten since the day her own Bessie left the house and moved away to the Wild West to die in her own time and way. The grandmother shed a few tears. The girl was like her daughter, and she couldn't help loving her. But a streak of something else made her seem above them all, and that was hard to bear. It must be the Bailey streak, of course. Mrs. Brady did not admire the Baileys, but she was obliged to reverence them.

If she'd watched or followed Elizabeth, she'd have been more horrified. The girl headed straight to the corner grocery and demanded her own horse, handing back to the man the dollar he'd paid her last Saturday night and saying she needed the horse at once. After some parley, in which Elizabeth showed her ability to stand her ground, the boy unhitched the horse from the wagon and got her old saddle from the stable. Then she mounted her horse and rode away to Rittenhouse Square.

Chapter 13

Elizabeth took her horse with her in order to have all her armor on, as a warrior goes out to meet his foe. If this grandmother proved impossible, why then, so long as she had life and a horse, she could flee. The world was vast, and the West was still open to her. She could return to the wilderness that gave her breath.

The old horse stopped before the tall, aristocratic house in Rittenhouse Square, and his mistress fastened the halter to a ring in the sidewalk. He looked up questioningly at the house, but saw no reason why his mistress should go in there. It was not familiar ground. Coffee and Sons never came up this way.

Elizabeth crossed the sidewalk and mounted the steps before the formidable carved doors. Here was the last hope of finding an earthly habitation. If this failed her, the desert, starvation, and a long, long sleep remained. But while the bell still echoed through the high-ceilinged hall the words came to her: "Let not your heart be troubled. . . . In my Father's house are many mansions: if it were not so, I would have told you. I go to prepare a place for you. . . . I will come again, and receive you." How sweet that was! Then, even if she died on the desert, a home was prepared for her. She had learned that in Christian Endeavor meetings.

The butler let her in. He eyed her questioningly and said Madam was not up yet. Elizabeth told him she would wait.

"Is she sick?" asked Elizabeth with a tightness about her heart.

"Oh, no, she is not up yet, miss," said the kind old butler. "She never gets up before this. You're from Mrs. Sands, I suppose." For once his butler eyes were mistaken. He thought she was the errand girl from the dressmaker's.

"No, I'm just Elizabeth," said the girl, smiling. She felt that this man, whoever he was, was not against her. He was old and had a kind look.

He still thought she meant she wasn't the dressmaker, just her errand girl. Her quaint dress and long braid made her look like a child.

"I'll tell her you've come. Be seated," said the butler.

He gave her a chair in the dim hall just opposite the parlor door, where she glimpsed elegance she never dreamed existed. She tried to think how it must be to live in such a room and walk on velvet. The carpet was deep and rich. She didn't know it was a rug or that it was woven in some poor peasant home and brought here years afterward at a fabulous price. She only knew it was beautiful in its silvery sheen, with colors glimmering through it like jewels in the dew.

Through another open doorway she caught a glimpse of a painting on the wall. It was a man as large as life, sitting in a chair. The face and demeanor were her father's—her father at his best. She was startled. Could it be her father? And how had they made this picture of him? He must have changed in those twenty years he'd been gone from home.

Then the butler came back, and before he could speak she pointed toward the picture. "Who is it?" she asked.

"That, miss? That's Mr. John, Madam's husband, who's dead a good many years now. But I remember him well."

"Could I look at it? He is so much like my father." She walked quickly over the ancient rug, ignoring its beauty, while the butler followed a bit anxiously. This was unprecedented. Mrs. Sands's errand girls usually knew their place.

"Madam said you are to come right up to her room," said the butler.

But Elizabeth stood there, studying the picture. The butler had to repeat his message. She smiled and turned to follow him. As she did so she saw on a side wall the portraits of two boys.

"Who are they?" she asked, pointing. They looked like her own two brothers.

"They are Mr. John and Mr. James, Madam's two sons. They're both dead now. At least, Mr. James is, I'm sure. He died two years ago. But you better come right up. Madam will be wondering."

She followed the old man up the velvety stairs. Then that was her father, the boy with the beautiful face and the heavy wavy hair tossed back from his forehead and the haughty, don't-care look. And he had lived here—amid all this luxury.

In an instant came the contrast of the home in which he died, and a wave of reverence for her father rolled over her. It wouldn't have been strange if, having grown up in such surroundings, he had tired of the rough life out west and deserted his wife, who was beneath him in station. True, much of the time he was a burden to her and caused her great anxiety. But he stayed and loved her—when he was sober. She forgave her father for his trying ways and his finding fault with her mother's little blunders—no wonder, when he came from this place.

The butler tapped on a door at the head of the stairs, and a maid opened it.

"Why, you're not the girl Mrs. Sands sent the other day," said a voice from a mass of lace-ruffled pillows on the great bed.

"I'm Elizabeth," said the girl, as if that were full explanation.

"Elizabeth? Elizabeth who? I don't see why she sent another girl. Are you sure you'll understand the directions? They're very particular, for I want my dress ready for tonight without fail." The woman sat up, leaning on one elbow. The sleeve of her pale-blue silk robe fell away from a round white arm that didn't look as if it belonged to a very old lady. Her gray hair was becomingly arranged, and she was extremely pretty, with small features.

Elizabeth marveled. The vision of the other grandmother at the washtub flashed across her mind. The contrast was startling.

"I am Elizabeth Bailey," said the girl gently. "My father was your son John."

"The idea!" said the new grandmother, and promptly fell back upon her pillows with her hand upon her heart. "John, John, my little John. No one has mentioned his name to me for years. He never writes to me." She held up a lace-trimmed handkerchief and cried.

"Father died five years ago," said Elizabeth.

"You wicked girl!" said the maid. "Can't you see that Madam can't bear such talk? Go right out of the room!" The maid rushed up with smelling salts and a glass of water, and Elizabeth in distress came and stood by the bed.

"I'm sorry I made you feel bad, Grandmother," she said when she saw that the fragile, childish creature on the bed was recovering.

"What right have you to call me that? Grandmother, indeed! I'm not so old as that. Besides, how do I know you belong to me? If John is dead, your mother better look after you. I'm not responsible for you. It's her business. She wheedled John away from his home, carried him off to that awful West and never let him write to me. She did it all, and now she must bear the consequences. I suppose she has sent you here to beg, but she made a mistake. I won't have a thing to do with her or her children."

"Grandmother!" Elizabeth's eyes flashed as they had to the other grandmother a few hours earlier. "You mustn't talk so. I won't hear it. I wouldn't let Grandmother Brady talk about my father, and you can't talk so about Mother. She was my mother, and I loved her, and Father loved her also. She worked hard to take care of him when he drank for years and she had no money to help her. Mother was only eighteen when she married Father, and you shouldn't blame her. She didn't have a nice home like this. But she was good and dear, and now she is dead. Father and Mother are both dead, and all the other children. A man killed my brother, and as soon as he was buried the man wanted me to go with him. He was an awful man, and I was afraid, so I took my brother's horse and ran away.

"I rode all this long way because I was afraid of that man. I wanted to get to some of my own folks, who would love me and let me work for them and go to school. But I wish now I'd stayed out there and died. I could have lain down in the sagebrush, and a wild beast might have killed me. That would be a great deal better than this. Grandmother Brady doesn't understand, and you don't want me. But in my Father's house in heaven are many mansions, and He went to prepare a place for me. So I guess I'll go back to the desert, and perhaps He'll send for me. Good-bye, Grandmother."

Before the astonished woman in bed could recover her senses from this remarkable speech, Elizabeth turned and walked from the room. She was petite, but in the strength of her pride and purity she seemed almost majestic to the awestruck maid and bewildered woman.

Down the stairs walked the girl. She'd never again try to get a friend. Only in the desert had she found a friend. One man was good to her, and she had let him go away. But he belonged to another woman. There was something to be thankful for, though. She had knowledge of her Father in heaven, and she knew what Christian Endeavor meant. She could take that with her into the desert, and no one could take it from her. She had one wish—to have a Bible of her own! She had no money left. Nothing but her mother's wedding ring, the papers, and the envelope with the money from the man. She couldn't part with them, unless someone might take the ring and keep it until she could buy it back. But she would wait and hope.

She walked by the old butler with her hand on her pistol. She didn't intend to let anyone stop her now. He bowed pleasantly and opened the door for her, however, and she marched down the steps to her horse. But just as she was about to mount and ride off into the unknown where no grandmother, Brady or Bailey, could ever search her out, the door suddenly opened again with a great commotion. The maid and the old butler both hurried out and grasped hold of her. She dropped the bridle and grabbed her pistol, covering them both with its black, forbidding nozzle.

They stopped, trembling, but the butler stood his ground. He didn't know why he was to detain this extraordinary young person, but he felt sure something was wrong. Probably she was a thief and had taken some of Madam's jewels. He could call the police. He opened his mouth to do so when the maid explained.

"Madam wants you to come back. She didn't understand. She wants to ask about her son. You must come, or you'll kill her. She has heart trouble, and you mustn't excite her."

Elizabeth put the pistol back into its holster and, picking up the bridle again, fastened it in the ring, saying simply, "I'll come back."

"What do you want?" she asked abruptly when she returned to the bedroom.

"Don't you know that's a disrespectful way to speak?" asked the woman. "Why did you have to get upset and go off without telling me anything about my son? Sit down, and tell me all about it."

"I'm sorry, Grandmother," said Elizabeth, sitting down. "I thought you didn't want me and I better go."

"Well, the next time wait until I send you. What do you have on, anyway? That's an odd hat for a girl to wear. Take it off. You look like a rough boy. You remind me of John when he'd been out disobeying me."

Elizabeth took off the offending headgear and revealed her smoothly parted, thick brown hair in its long braid.

"Why, you're rather a pretty girl if you were fixed up," said the woman, sitting up with interest now. "I can't remember your mother, but I don't think she had fine features like that."

"They said I look like Father," said Elizabeth.

"Did they? Well, I believe it's true," she said with satisfaction. "I couldn't bear it if you looked like those low-down—"

"Grandmother!" Elizabeth stood up and flashed her Bailey eyes.

"You needn't 'Grandmother' me all the time," said the woman. "But you look quite handsome when you say it. Take off that ill-fitting coat. It isn't thick enough for winter, anyway. What in the world are you wearing around your waist? A belt? Why, that's a man's belt! And what's on it? Pistols? Horrors! Marie, take them away at once! I'll faint! I never could bear to be in a room with one. My husband used to have one on his closet shelf. I never went near it and always locked the room when he was out. You must put them out in the hall. I can't breathe where pistols are. Now sit down and tell me how old you are and how you got here."

Elizabeth surrendered her pistols with hesitation. She felt that she must obey her grandmother but wasn't sure this was friendly ground or that she should be weaponless.

Beginning as far back as she could remember, she told the story of her life, simply, without a single claim to pity. Yet she told it so earnestly and vividly that the grandmother, lying with her eyes closed, forgot herself and let the tears trickle unbidden down her cheeks.

When Elizabeth came to the graves in the moonlight, she gasped, "Oh, Johnny, my little Johnny! Why were you always such a bad boy?" When she described the ride in the desert and the man who pursued her, the grandmother caught her breath and said, "Oh, how frightening!" Her interest in the girl was growing and kept at white heat during the whole story.

Elizabeth passed over one part of her experience lightly, however, and that was the meeting with George Trescott Benedict. Instinctively she felt that this experience would not find a sympathetic listener. She said merely that she'd met a kind gentleman from the East who was lost and they'd ridden together for a few miles until they reached a town. He'd telegraphed to his friends and gone on his way. She said nothing about the money he had lent her, for she shrank from speaking about him more than was necessary. She thought her grandmother might feel as the old woman of the ranch had about their traveling together. She let it be inferred she might have had a little money with her from home. At least, the older woman asked no questions about how she secured provisions for the trip.

When Elizabeth came to her Chicago experience, her grandmother clasped her hands as if a serpent had been mentioned. "How degrading! You certainly would have been justified in shooting the whole company. I wonder such places are allowed to exist!"

But Marie sat in amazement and repeated the story in the kitchen later for the benefit of the cook and the butler, so that Elizabeth became a heroine among them.

Elizabeth passed on to her Philadelphia experience and found that here her grandmother was roused to blazing indignation. But what roused her was that a Bailey should serve behind a counter in a ten-cent store. She lifted her hands and uttered such a moan of real pain that the smelling salts were required again.

When Elizabeth told of her encounter with the manager in the cellar, the grandmother said, "How disgusting! The impertinent creature! He ought to be sued. I'll consult the lawyer about the matter. What did you say his name was? Marie, write that down. And so, dear, you did quite right to come to me. I've been looking at you while you talked, and I believe you'll be a pretty girl if you fix up. Marie, go to the telephone and call up Blandeaux. Tell him to send up a hairdresser at once. I want to see how Miss Elizabeth will look with her hair done low in one of those new coils. I think it'll be becoming. I'd have tried it long ago myself, but it seems too youthful for hair that is turning gray."

Elizabeth watched her grandmother in wonder. Here truly was a new kind of woman. She didn't care about great facts—only about little things. Her life consisted of the pursuit of fashion, just like Lizzie's. Were all people in cities alike? No, the man she met in the wilderness didn't seem to care. Maybe, though, when he returned to the city he cared. She sighed and turned toward the new grandmother.

"Now I've told you everything, Grandmother. Shall I go away? I wanted to go to school. But it costs a great deal of money, and I don't want to burden anyone. I didn't come here to ask you to take me in because I didn't want to trouble you. But I thought before I went away I ought to see you once because—because you are my grandmother."

"I've never been a grandmother," said the little woman reflectively, "but it might be rather nice. I'd like to make you into a pretty girl and take you out into society. That would be something new to live for. I'm not very pretty myself anymore, but I can see that you'll be. Do you wear blue or pink? I used to wear pink myself, but I believe you could wear either when you get your complexion in shape. You've tanned it horribly, but it may come out all right. I think you'll take. You say you want to go to school. Why, certainly, I suppose that will be necessary. Living out in that barbarous, uncivilized region, you don't know much, of course. You seem to speak correctly, but John always was particular about his speech. When he was little, he had a tutor who tripped him up every mistake he made. That was the only thing that tutor was good for; he was a linguist. We found out later he was wild and drank. He did John more harm than good.

"Marie, I shall want Elizabeth to have the rooms next to mine. Ring for

Martha to see that everything is in order. Elizabeth, did you ever have your hands manicured? You have a pretty-shaped hand. I'll have the woman attend to it when she comes to shampoo your hair and put it up. Did you bring any clothes along? Of course not. You couldn't on horseback. I suppose you had your trunk sent by express. No trunk? No express? No railroad? How barbarous! How John must have suffered, poor fellow! And he was used to every luxury! Well, I don't see that it was my fault. I gave him everything he wanted except his wife, and he took her without my leave. Poor fellow!"

Mrs. Bailey in due time sent Elizabeth off to the suite of rooms she said were to be hers exclusively and arose to dress herself for another day. Elizabeth was a new toy, and she anticipated playing with her. It put new zest into a life that had grown monotonous.

Elizabeth, meanwhile, surveyed her quarters and wondered what Lizzie would think if she could see her. According to orders, the coachman had taken Robin to the stable. He was already rolling in the luxuries of a horse of the aristocracy and congratulating himself on the good taste of his mistress to select such a stopping place. He was now satisfied not to move further. This was better than the wilderness any day. Oats like these and hay such as this were not to be found on the plains.

Toward evening the butler, with many a glance at the neighborhood, arrived at the door of Mrs. Brady. He delivered the following message to that astonished lady, backed by her daughter and her granddaughter, with their ears stretched to hear every syllable: "Mrs. Merrill Wilton Bailey sends word that her granddaughter, Miss Elizabeth, has reached her home safely and will remain with her. Miss Elizabeth will come sometime to see Mrs. Brady and thank her for her kindness during her stay with her."

The butler bowed and turned away with relief. His dignity hadn't been taxed so by the family demands in years. He was glad he might shake off the dust of Flora Street forever. He felt for the coachman. He'd probably have to drive the young lady down here sometime, according to that message.

Mrs. Brady, her daughter, and Lizzie stuck their heads out into the lamplit street and watched the butler till he was out of sight. Then they went inside and sat down in three separate stages of relief and astonishment.

"For the land sakes!" exclaimed the grandmother. "Well, now, if that don't beat all!" Then after a minute she added: "The impertinent fellow! And the impudence of the woman! Thank me for my kindness to me own grandchild! I'd thank her to mind her business, but then that's just like her."

"Her nest is certainly well-feathered," said Aunt Nan enviously. "I only wish Lizzie had such a chance."

Said Lizzie: "It's awful odd, her looking like that, too, in that crazy rig! Well, I'm glad she's gone, for she was so awful odd it was fierce. She talked religion a lot to the girls, and they laughed at her behind her back. They kep' a telling me I'd be a missionary 'fore long if she stayed with us. I went to Mr. Wray, the manager, and told him my cousin was awfully shy and sent word she wanted to be excused for running away like that. He kind of colored up and said 'twas all right; she might come back and have her old place if she wanted, and he'd say no more about it. I told him I'd tell her. But I guess her acting up won't harm me. The girls say he'll make up to *me* now. Wish he would. I'd have a fine time. It's me turn to have me wages raised, anyway. He said if Bess and I would come tomorrow ready to stay in the evening, he'd take us to a show that beat everything he ever saw in Philadelphia. I mean to make him take me, anyway. I'm just glad she's out of the way. She wasn't like the rest of us."

Said Mrs. Brady: "It's the Bailey in her. But she said she'd come back and see me, didn't she?" And the grandmother in her meditated on that for several minutes.

Chapter 14

Meanwhile, Elizabeth's life passed into more peaceful scenes. By means of the telephone and the maid new and beautiful garments were provided for her. They fit perfectly and bewildered her not a little until Marie explained them. Elizabeth ate her meals upstairs until the things arrived and she was wearing them. The texture of the garments was fine and soft, and they were rich with embroidery and lace. The flannels were as soft as the down in a milkweed pod, and everything was of the best quality.

Elizabeth found herself wishing she might share them with Lizzie—who adored rich and beautiful things and had shared her meager outfit with her. She mentioned this wistfully to her grandmother.

In a fit of childish generosity that woman said: "Certainly, get her what you wish. I'll take you downtown someday, and you can pick out some nice things for them all. I hate to be under obligations."

A dozen ready-made dresses were sent out to the Bailey house before the first afternoon was over, and Elizabeth spent the rest of the day trying on and walking back and forth in front of her grandmother. At last two or three were selected that would "do" until the dressmaker could come, and Elizabeth was clothed and allowed to enter into the life of the household.

It was not a large household—only the grandmother, her dog, and the servants. Elizabeth fit into it better than she feared. It was more pleasant than the house on Flora Street, with more room, more air, and more quiet. With her mountain breeding she couldn't catch her breath in a crowd.

She was soon taken in a luxurious carriage, drawn by two beautiful horses, to a large department store, where she sat by the hour and watched her grandmother choose things for her. Another girl might have gone wild over being able to have anything in the shops. Not so Elizabeth. She watched it all with apathy, as if the goods displayed were the leaves on the trees set forth for her admiration. She could wear only one dress and one hat at a time. Why were so many necessary? Her main hope lay in the words her grandmother spoke about sending her to school.

On the third day of her stay in Rittenhouse Square, Elizabeth reminded her of it, and the grandmother said impatiently: "Yes, yes, child, you shall go of course to a finishing school. That will be necessary. But first I must get you fixed up. You have scarcely anything to wear." So Elizabeth relented.

At last a beautiful Sabbath dawned when, the wardrobe seeming complete, Elizabeth was told to dress for church, since they were going that morning. With delight and thanksgiving she put on what she was told. When she gazed in the French plate mirror after Marie added the finishing touches, she was astonished at herself. It was true, after all. She was a pretty girl.

She looked down in awe at the lovely gown of finest broadcloth, with the exquisite finish that only the best tailors can put on a garment. The folds of dark-green cloth brought grace to her movements. The green velvet hat with its long curling plumes of green and cream color rested above the beautiful hair that was arranged naturally and becomingly.

Elizabeth wore her lovely ermine collar and muff without knowing they were costly. They seemed so fitting and quiet and simple, so much less obtrusive than Lizzie's pink silk waist and cheap pink plumes. Elizabeth liked it and walked to church beside her grandmother with a happy heart.

The church stood just across the square. Its tall brown stone spire and arched doorways attracted Elizabeth when she first arrived at the place. Now she entered with joy.

It was the first time she had attended a regular Sabbath morning service in church. The Christian Endeavor had been as much as Lizzie could stand. She said she had to work too hard during the week to waste so much time on Sunday in church. "The Sabbath was made for man" and "for rest," she had quoted glibly. For the first time since she left Montana, Elizabeth felt as if she had a real home and was like other people. She looked around shyly to see if her desert friend might be sitting near, but no familiar face met her gaze. Then she settled back to enjoy the service.

The organ was playing soft, tender music. She learned afterward that the music was Handel's "Largo." She didn't know the organ was one of the finest in the city or that the organist was one of the most skilled; she knew only that the music lifted her soul above the earth so that heaven surrounded her and the clouds seemed to sing to her. Then came the processional, with the wonderful voices of the choirboys sounding far away, then near. No one used to these things all his life could know how they affected Elizabeth.

It seemed as though the Lord Himself was leading the girl in a very special way. At scarcely any other church in a fashionable quarter of the great city would Elizabeth have heard preaching so exactly suited to her needs. The minister was one of those rare men who lived with God and talked with Him daily. He had one peculiarity that marked him from all other preachers, Elizabeth heard later. He would turn and talk with God in a gentle, sweet, conversational tone right in the midst of his sermon. It made the Lord seem very real and near.

If he hadn't been the brilliant preacher of an old established church and revered by all denominations as well as his own, the minister would have been called eccentric and asked to resign. His religion was so personal that it embarrassed some. His rare gifts and remarkable consecration and independence in doing what he thought right, however, had produced a most unusual church for a fashionable neighborhood.

Most of his church members were in sympathy with him, and a wonderful work was going forward right in the heart of Sodom, unhampered by fashion, form, or class distinctions. Of course, some, like Madam Bailey, sat calmly in their seats and let the minister preach without ever thinking about what he was saying. It was the same to them whether he prayed three times or once, just so the service ended at the usual hour. But most were being led to see that there is such a thing as a close and intimate walk with God upon this earth.

Into this church came Elizabeth, the sweet heathen, eager to learn all she could about the things of the soul. She sat beside her grandmother, drank in the sermon, and bowed her head when she realized God was in the room and was being spoken to by His servant. After the last echo of the recessional had faded, and the hush of the congregation had grown into a quiet, well-bred commotion of putting on coats and greeting one another, Elizabeth turned to her grandmother.

"Grandmother, may I please ask that man some questions? He said just what I've been longing to know, and I must ask him more. Nobody else ever told me these things. Who is he? How does he know it's true?"

The elder woman watched the eager, flushed face of the girl. Her heart throbbed with pride that this beautiful young thing belonged to her. She smiled indulgently.

"You mean the rector? Why, I'll invite him to dinner if you wish to talk with him. It's perfectly proper that a young girl should understand about religion. It has a most refining influence, and the doctor is a charming man. I'll invite his wife and daughter too. They move in the best circles, and I've been meaning to ask them for a long time. You might like to be confirmed. Some do. It's a pretty service. I was confirmed myself when I was about your age. My mother thought it a good thing for a girl before she entered society. Now, just as you are a schoolgirl, is the proper time. I'll send for him this week. He'll be pleased to know you're interested in these things. He has some kind of a young people's club that meets on Sunday. 'Christian Something,' he calls it. I don't know just what, but he talks a great deal about it and wants every young person to join. You might pay the dues, whatever they are, anyway. I suppose it's for charity. It wouldn't be necessary for you to attend the meetings, but it would please the doctor."

"Is it Christian Endeavor?" asked Elizabeth, her eyes sparkling.

"Something like that, I believe. Good morning, Mrs. Schuyler. Lovely day, isn't it? For December. No, I haven't been well. No, I haven't been out for several weeks. Charming service, wasn't it? The doctor grows more brilliant. Mrs. Schuyler, this is my granddaughter, Elizabeth. She has just come from the West to live with me and complete her education. I want her to know your daughter."

Elizabeth passed through the introduction as a necessary interruption to her train of thought. As soon as they were outside on the street she began again.

"Grandmother, was God in that church?"

"Dear me, child! What strange questions you ask! Why, yes, I suppose He was, in a way. God is everywhere, they say. Elizabeth, you'd better wait until you can talk these things over with a person whose business it is. I never understood much about such questions. You look very nice in that shade of green, and your hat is most becoming."

The question was closed for the time, but not shut out of the girl's thoughts.

Christmas came and passed without much notice by Elizabeth, to whom it was an unfamiliar festival. Mrs. Bailey suggested she select some gifts for her "relatives on her mother's side," as she always spoke of the Bradys. Elizabeth did so with alacrity, showing good sense and taste, as well as deference to the wishes of the recipients. Lizzie, it's true, was a bit disappointed that her present wasn't a gold watch or a diamond ring; but on the whole she was pleased.

A new world opened to Elizabeth. School filled her with wonder and delight. She absorbed knowledge like a sponge in water and rushed eagerly from one study to another, showing marvelous aptitude and bringing enthusiasm to every task.

Her growing intimacy with Jesus Christ through the influence of the pastor who knew Him so well caused her joy in life to blossom into loveliness.

She studied the Bible with the zest of a novel reader, for it was a novel to her. Daily, as she rode in the park on Robin, now sleek and wearing a saddle of the latest style, she marveled over God's wonderful goodness to her, just a maid of the wilderness.

So passed three beautiful years in peace and quiet. Every month Elizabeth visited her grandmother Brady and took some charming little gifts, and every summer she and her grandmother Bailey stayed at some fashionable waterside resort or in the Catskills. The girl was always dressed in exquisite taste and was as sweetly indifferent to her clothes as a bird of the air or a flower of the field.

She saved the first pocket money she was given and before long had enough to send the forty dollars to the address of the man in the wilderness. But she sent no word with it, thinking she had no right.

She went out more and more with her grandmother among the fashionable old families in Philadelphia society, though as yet she was not supposed to be "out," since she was still in school. But in all her goings she saw and heard nothing of George Trescott Benedict.

Often she looked at the beautiful women who came to her grandmother's house and smiled and talked to her and wondered which one might be the lady to whom his heart was bound. She imagined she must be sweet and lovely in every way, otherwise he couldn't care for her; so she picked out this one and that one. Then, as some glaring fault appeared, she dropped that one for another. Only a few did she think were good enough for the man who had become her ideal.

But sometimes in her dreams he would come and talk with her. He smiled as he did when they rode together, laying his hand on the mane of her horse—horses were always in her dreams. She liked to think of it when she rode in the park and how pleasant it would be if he could ride beside her. They might talk of the things that had happened since he left her alone. She wanted to tell him she'd found a friend in Jesus Christ. He'd be glad to know about it, she was sure. He seemed to be interested in such things, not like other people who were engaged in the world.

Sometimes she felt afraid something had happened to him. He might have been thrown from the train and killed, and no one knew anything about it. But as her experience broadened, and she traveled on trains, this fear lessened. She came to understand that the world was vast, and many things might have taken him away from home.

Perhaps the money she sent reached him safely, but she put in no address. She didn't want to draw his attention to her and felt "the lady" wouldn't like it. Perhaps they were married by this time and lived in some charmed land far away. Perhaps—a great many things. Only this fact remained: He never came into the horizon of her life anymore. Therefore she must try to forget him and be glad God had given him to her for a friend in her time of need. Someday in the eternal home she might meet him and thank him for his kindness to her. Then they might tell each other about their journey through life's wilderness after they parted. The links in Elizabeth's theology were well supplied by now, and her belief in the hereafter was strong and simple like a child's.

She had one great longing, however—that her friend, who had in a sense first helped her to higher things and saved her from the wilderness, might know Jesus Christ as he hadn't known Him when they were together. And so in her daily prayer she often talked to her heavenly Father about him, until she had an abiding faith that someday, somehow, he would learn the truth about his Christ.

During the third season of Elizabeth's life in Philadelphia her grandmother decided it was high time to bring out this bud of promise, who was developing into a more beautiful girl than even her fondest hopes had pictured.

So Elizabeth "came out," and Grandmother Brady read her doings and sayings in the society columns with her morning coffee and an air of deep satisfaction. Aunt Nan listened with her nose in the air. She could never understand why Elizabeth should have privileges beyond her Lizzie. It was the Bailey in her, of course, and Mother oughtn't to think well of it. But Grandmother Brady felt that, while Elizabeth's success was doubtless due in large part to the Bailey in her, still, she was a Brady, and the Brady had not hindered her. It was a step upward for the Bradys.

Lizzie listened and with pride related at the ten-cent store the doings of "my cousin, Elizabeth Bailey," while the other girls listened in awe.

And so arrived the springtime of the third year Elizabeth had spent in Philadelphia.

Chapter 15

I t was summer and it was June. There was to be a picnic, and Elizabeth was going.

Grandmother Brady had arranged it. If Elizabeth could go, her cup of pride would overflow. So after arguing pro and con with her daughter and Lizzie, she sat down to write the invitation. Aunt Nan was against it. She didn't wish to have Lizzie outshone. She'd worked nights for two weeks on an organdie with pink roses for Lizzie to wear. It had yards of cheap lace and a whole bolt of pink ribbons of various widths. The hat was a marvel of impossible roses, calculated for a wreck if a thundershower came up at a Sunday school picnic. Lizzie's mother was even thinking of getting her a pink chiffon parasol to carry, but the family treasury was nearly depleted. After all that, it didn't seem pleasant to have Lizzie overshadowed by a cousin in silks and jewels.

But Grandmother Brady had waited long for her triumph. Above all else, she wanted to walk among her friends and introduce her granddaughter, Elizabeth Bailey, with the remark: "You must have seen me granddaughter's name in the paper often, Mrs. Babcock. She was giving a party in Rittenhouse Square the other day."

Elizabeth would likely marry soon and move from Philadelphia to New York or Europe—there was no telling what fortune might come to her. Now the time was ripe for triumph, and when things are ripe they must be picked. Mrs. Brady proceeded to pick.

She sat down when Nan and Lizzie had left for their day's work and constructed her sentences with great care.

"*Dear Bessie*"—Elizabeth had never asked her not to call her that, although she fairly detested the name. But still it was her mother's name and dear to her grandmother. It seemed disloyal to her mother to suggest she be called "Elizabeth." So Grandmother Brady called her "Bessie" to the end of her days. Elizabeth decided that to care a lot about such little things, in a world with so many great things, would be as bad as to pursue fashion.

The letter proceeded laboriously:

> *Our Sunday school is going to have a picnic out to Willow Grove. It's on Tuesday. We're going in the trolley. I'd be pleased if you would go 'long with us. We'll spend the day and take our dinner and supper along and won't get home till late, so you could stay overnight here with us and not go back home till after breakfast. You needn't bring no lunch, for we have a lot of things planned, and it ain't worthwhile. But if you wanted to bring some*

*candy, you might. I ain't got time to make any and what you buy at
our grocery might not be fine enough for you.*

*I want you to go real bad. I've never took my two granddaugh-
ters off to anything yet, and your Grandmother Bailey has you to
things all the time. I hope you can manage to come. I am going to
pay all the expenses. Your old Christian Deaver you used to 'tend is
going to be there, so you'll have a good time. Lizzie has a new pink
organdie, with roses on her hat, and we're thinking of getting her a
pink umbreller if it don't cost too much. The kind with chiffon
flounces on it.*

*You'll have a good time, for there's lots of sideshows out to
Willow Grove, and we're going to see everything there is to see.
There's going to be some music too. A man with a name that sounds
like swearing is going to make it. I don't remember it just now, but
you can see it advertised round on trolley cars. He comes to Willow
Grove every year. Now please let me hear if you will go at once, as
I want to know how much cake to make.*

*Your loving grandmother,
Elizabeth Brady.*

Elizabeth laughed and cried over this note. It pleased her for her grandmother to show kindness to her. And she felt that whatever she did for Grandmother Brady was in a sense showing love to her own mother. So she brushed
aside several engagements, much to the annoyance of her Grandmother Bailey,
who couldn't understand why she wanted to go down to Flora Street for two days
and a night at the beginning of warm weather.

True, not much was going on between seasons, and Elizabeth could go as she
pleased, but she might get a fever in such a crowded neighborhood. It wasn't at all
wise. But if she must, she must. Grandmother Bailey was lenient overall. Elizabeth
was too successful and willing to please her for Mrs. Bailey to cross her wishes.

So Elizabeth wrote on her fine notepaper bearing the Bailey crest in silver:

Dear Grandmother,

*I shall be delighted to go to the picnic with you, and I'll bring
a nice box of candy, Huyler's best. I'm sure you'll think it's the best
you ever tasted. Don't get Lizzie a parasol; I'm going to bring her
one to surprise her. I'll be at the house by eight o'clock.*

*Your loving granddaughter,
Elizabeth.*

Mrs. Brady read this note with satisfaction and handed it to her daughter
to read with a glow of triumph in her eyes at the supper table. She knew the

pink parasol would go far toward reconciling Aunt Nan to the addition to their party. Elizabeth never did things by halves, and the parasol would be all that could be desired.

So Elizabeth went to the picnic in a cool white dimity, plainly made, with tiny frills of itself, edged with narrow lace that didn't shout to the unknowing multitude, "I'm real," but was content to be so. And she wore a white Panama hat adorned with only a white silken scarf, but whose texture was possible only at a high price. The shape reminded Elizabeth of her brother's old felt hat she'd worn on her long trip across the continent. She'd tried it on in the milliner's shop one day. When her grandmother discovered how exquisitely the hat was woven, she purchased it for her. It was stylish to wear those soft hats in all sorts of odd shapes. Madam Bailey thought it would be just the thing for the seashore.

Elizabeth fixed her hair in a low coil on her neck, making the general appearance and contour of her head much as it was three years before. She wore no jewelry, except the unobtrusive gold buckle at her belt and the plain gold pin fastening her hat. She didn't even wear her gloves but carried them in her hand and tossed them carelessly upon the table when she arrived in Flora Street. Soft white ones, they lay there all day in their costly elegance while Elizabeth was at Willow Grove, and Lizzie sweltered around under her pink parasol in long white silk gloves.

Grandmother Brady surveyed Elizabeth with disapproval. It seemed too bad on this her day of triumph, and after she hinted, as it were, about Lizzie's fine clothes, that the girl should be so blind or stubborn or both as to come in that plain rig. Just a common white dress and an old hat that might have been worn about a livery stable. It was mortifying. She expected a light silk, kid gloves, and a flowered hat. Why, Lizzie looked a great deal finer. Did Mrs. Bailey fix her up this way for spite? she wondered.

Since it was too late to send Elizabeth back for more suitable garments, the woman resigned herself. The pink parasol was lovely, and Lizzie was wild over it. Even Aunt Nan seemed mollified. It gave her great satisfaction to look the two girls over. Her own outshone the one from Rittenhouse Square by many counts, thought the mother. But all day long, as she walked behind them or viewed them from afar, she couldn't understand why passersby looked twice at Elizabeth and once at Lizzie. It seemed, after all, that clothes did not make the girl. It was disappointing.

The box of candy satisfied everyone. In fact, she brought two boxes, one of the most delectable chocolates of all imaginable kinds, and the other of mixed candies and candied fruit. Both boxes bore the magic name "Huyler's" on the covers. Lizzie often passed Huyler's, taking her noon walk on Chestnut Street, and looked enviously at the girls who walked out with white square bundles tied with gold cord. And now she was eating all she pleased of those renowned candies.

The day was long and pleasant. Elizabeth had never been to Willow Grove before, and the strange blending of sweet nature and Vanity Fair charmed her. It was a rest after the winter's round of monotonous engagements.

Two youths from the livery stable attached themselves to the party in the early morning and gave most of their attention to Lizzie, much to Aunt Nan's satisfaction.

They mounted the horses in the merry-go-rounds, though Elizabeth didn't understand the amusement derived from this, and tried each one several times, till Lizzie declared it was time to go to something else.

They went into the Old Mill and down into the Mimic Mine and sailed through the painted Venice, eating candy and chewing gum and shouting. All but Elizabeth. Elizabeth would not chew gum or talk loud. But she smiled on the rest and didn't let it worry her that someone might recognize the popular Miss Bailey in so ill-bred a crowd. She knew it was their way, and they could have no other. They were having a good time, and she was part of it today. They weighed one another on the scales with jokes and laughter and saw all the moving pictures in the place. They ate their lunch under the trees, and then at last the music began.

They seated themselves on the outskirts of the company, for Lizzie declared that was the only pleasant place to be. She didn't want to go "way up front." She had a boy on either side of her, and she kept the seat shaking with laughter. Now and then a weary guard would look down the line and motion for less noise, but they giggled on. Elizabeth was glad they were too far back to annoy more people.

The music was good, and she watched the leader with pleasure and the many people absorbed in it. The melody reached her soul. She hadn't heard much good music in her life. The last three years, of course, she'd visited the Academy of Music; but, though her grandmother had a box there, she seldom attended concerts. When Melba or Caruso or some world-renowned favorite was performing, she would take Elizabeth for an hour, usually slipping out after the favorite solo. So Elizabeth had scarcely known the delight of a whole concert of fine orchestral music.

She heard Lizzie talking.

"Yes, that's Walter Damrosh! Ain't that name fierce? Grandmother thinks it's kind of wicked to pronounce it that way. They say he's fine, but I must say I liked the band they had last year better. It played a whole lot of lively things, and once they had a rattlebox and a squeaking thing that cried like a baby right out in the music, and everybody just roared laughing. I tell you that was great. I don't care much for this kind of music myself. Do you?"

Jim and Joe both agreed that they didn't, either. Elizabeth smiled and kept on enjoying it.

Peanuts were the order of the day, and their assertive crackle broke in upon the finest passages. Elizabeth wished her cousin would take a walk. Soon she did, politely inviting Elizabeth to go along. But she declined, and she was left to sit through the remainder of the afternoon concert.

After supper they watched the lights come out. Elizabeth thought about the description of the heavenly city as one after another the buildings blazed against the darkening blue of the June night. The music was about to begin. Indeed, it could be heard already in the distance and drew the girl irresistibly. For the first time that day she made a move, and the others followed, half weary of the amusements and not knowing exactly what to do next.

They stood the first half of the concert well, but at the intermission they wandered out to view the electric fountain with its changing colors and to take a row on the tiny sheet of water. Elizabeth remained sitting where she was and watched the fountain. Even her grandmother and aunt grew restless and wanted to walk again. They said they'd heard enough music and could hear it well enough, anyway, from further off. They would get some ice cream. Didn't Elizabeth want some?

She smiled sweetly. Would Grandmother mind if she sat there and heard the second part of the concert? She loved music and didn't feel like eating another thing tonight. So the two ladies, thinking the girl odd that she didn't want ice cream, left to enjoy theirs with a clear conscience. Elizabeth sat back with her eyes closed, to rest and breath in the sweet sounds.

Just at the close of this wonderful music, which the program said was Mendelssohn's "Spring Song," Elizabeth glanced up to meet the eyes of someone near in the aisle watching her, and there stood the man of the wilderness!

He was studying her face, drinking in the beauty of the profile and wondering: Could this be his little brown friend, the maid of the wilderness? This girl with a lovely, refined face, an intellectual brow, a dainty manner? She looked like some pure white angel dropped down into that motley company of Sunday school picnickers and city pleasure-seekers. The noise and clatter of the place seemed far away from her. She was absorbed in the sweet sounds.

When she glanced up and saw him, the smile that spread over her face was like sunshine on a day that had been still and almost sad. "You are come at last!" the eyes said. "I am glad you are here!" the curve of the lips said.

He went to her as one hungry for the sight of her for a long time. After he grasped her hand they stood thus for a moment while the hum and gentle talk that always starts between numbers seethed around them and hid the first few words they spoke.

"Oh, I have so longed to know if you were safe!" said the man as soon as he could speak.

Then the girl forgot her three years of training and her success as a debutante, and became as serious and shy as she'd been when he first saw her. She looked up with awed delight into the face she had seen in her dreams and yet dared not long for.

The orchestra began again, and they sat in silence listening. Yet their souls seemed to speak to each other through the medium of the music, as if the intervening years were being bridged and brought together in the space of those few waves of melody.

"I have found out," said Elizabeth, glancing up shyly with eyes sparkling. "I've found what it all means. Have you? Oh, I've wanted so much to know whether you found out, too!"

"Found out what?" he asked half sadly that he didn't understand.

"Found out how God hides us. Found what a friend Jesus Christ can be."

"You're just the same," said the man with satisfaction in his eyes. "You haven't been changed or spoiled. They couldn't spoil you."

"Have you found out, too?" she asked softly. She looked into his eyes with wistful longing. She wanted this so much and had prayed for it for so long.

He couldn't withdraw his own glance, nor did he wish to. He wanted to answer as she hoped.

"A little, perhaps," he said doubtfully. "Not as much as I'd like to. Will you help me?"

"*He* will help you. You'll find Him if you search for Him with all your heart," she said earnestly. "It says so in His book."

Then came more music, delicate, searching, tender. Did it speak of heavenly things to other souls there than those two?

He bent over and said in a quiet tone that seemed to blend with the music like the words that fit it: "I will try with all my heart if you'll help me."

She smiled her answer, brimming with deep delight.

Into the final lingering notes of an andante from one of Beethoven's sublime symphonies clashed the loud voice of Lizzie. "Oh, Bess! B-es-see! I say, Bessie! Ma says we'll have to go over by the cars now if we want to get a seat. The concert's most out, and there'll be a fierce rush. Come on! And Grandma says, bring your friend along if you want." This last was said with a smirking acknowledgment of the man, who turned around to see who was speaking.

With a glance that took in bedraggled organdie, rose hat, and pink parasol, and recognized their worth, George Benedict observed and classified Lizzie.

"Will you excuse yourself and let me take you home a little later?" he asked in a low voice. "The crowd will be large, and I have my automobile here."

She looked at him gratefully and assented. She had much to tell him. She leaned across the seats and spoke clearly to her cousin.

"I will come a little later," she said, smiling with her Rittenhouse Square look that always made Lizzie a little afraid of her. "Tell Grandmother I've found an old friend I haven't seen for a long time. I'll be there almost as soon as you are."

They waited while Lizzie explained, and the grandmother and aunt nodded reluctantly. Aunt Nan frowned. Elizabeth might have introduced her friend to Lizzie. Did Elizabeth think Lizzie wasn't good enough to be introduced?

He wrapped her in a great soft blanket in the automobile and tucked her in beside him. She felt as if the long, hard days since they met were all forgotten and erased in this delightful night. Not all the attentions of all the fine men she'd met in society were ever like his, so gentle, so perfect. She'd forgotten the woman as completely as if she'd never heard of her. She wanted now to tell her friend about her heavenly Father.

He let her talk and watched her glowing, earnest face by the dim light of the sky. The moon had come out to crown the night with beauty, and the unnatural brilliance of electric blaze, with all the glitter and noise of Willow Grove, died into the dim, sweet night as those two sped onward toward the city. The heart of the man kept singing: "I've found her at last! She's safe!"

"I've prayed for you always," he said in one of the pauses. They were coming into Flora Street then, and the urchins ran hooting after the car and gathered about as it slowed up at the door. "I'm sure He hid you safely, and I shall thank Him for answering my prayer. And now I'm coming to see you. May I come tomorrow?"

"Yes," she said, with gladness in her eyes.

The Bradys had arrived from the corner trolley and were hovering about the door. An onlooker would have said this was a good opportunity for an introduction, but the two people were entirely oblivious. The man touched his hat solemnly, with a look of admiration, and said, "Good night," like a benediction.

The girl turned and went into the plain little home and to her belligerent relatives with a light in her eyes and a joy in her steps not present earlier in the day. The dreams that visited her hard pillow that night were heavenly and sweet.

Chapter 16

Now we're goin' to see if the paper says anythin' about our Bessie," said Grandmother Brady the next morning. She settled her spectacles on her nose and crossed one gingham knee over the other. "I always read the society notes, Bess."

Elizabeth smiled, and her grandmother read down the column. "Mr. George Trescott Benedict and his mother, Mrs. Vincent Benedict, have arrived home after an extended tour of Europe. Mrs. Benedict is much improved in health. It is rumored they will spend the summer in their country home at Wissahickon Heights."

"My!" interrupted Lizzie with her mouth full of fried potatoes. "That's the fellow that was engaged to that Miss What's-her-name Loring. Don't you 'member? They had his picture in the papers, and hers. Then all at once she threw him over for some dook or something, and this feller went off. I heard about it from Mame. Her sister works in a department store, and she knows Miss Loring. She says she's an awfully handsome girl, and George Benedict was just gone on her. He had a fearful case. Mame says Miss Loring—what *is* her name?—oh, Geraldine—Geraldine Loring bought some lace from her. She heard her say it was for the gown she was going to wear at the horse show. They had her picture in the paper just after the horse show, and it was lace all over. I saw it. It cost a whole lot. I forget how many dollars a yard. But there was something the matter with the dook. She didn't marry him, after all. In her picture she was driving four horses. Don't you remember it, Grandma? She sat up tall and high on a seat, holding a whole lot of ribbons and whips and things. She has an elegant figger. I guess mebbe the dook wasn't rich enough. She hasn't been engaged to anybody else, and I shouldn't wonder now but she'd take George Benedict back. He was so awful struck on her!"

Lizzie rattled on, and the grandmother read more society notes. But Elizabeth heard no more. Her heart froze and dropped down like lead into her soul. She felt as if she could never raise it again. The lady! She had forgotten the lady. But Geraldine Loring! Of all women! Could it be? Geraldine Loring was almost—well, fast, at least, as much as someone from a fine old family could be and still hold her own in society. She was beautiful as a picture, but her face, in Elizabeth's opinion, lacked fine feeling and intellect. Her heart extended pity to the man whose fate rested in that doll-girl's hands. True, she'd heard Miss Loring's family was unquestionable, and she knew her mother was charming. Perhaps she'd misjudged her, for it couldn't be otherwise.

The joy had gone out of the morning when Elizabeth went home. She saw her grandmother at once. After she read her letters for her and performed the little services that were her habit, she said: "Grandmother, I'm expecting a man to call on me today. I thought I'd better tell you."

"A man!" said Madam Bailey, at once alarmed. She wanted to pick out the right man when the time came. "What man?"

"Why, a man I met in Montana," said Elizabeth, wondering how much to tell.

"A man you met in Montana! Horrors!" exclaimed the now thoroughly aroused grandmother. "Not that dreadful creature you ran away from?"

"Oh, no!" said Elizabeth, smiling. "Not that man. A man who was very kind to me and whom I like very much."

So much the worse. Immediate action was necessary.

"Well, Elizabeth," said Madam Bailey stiffly, "I really don't care to have any of your Montana friends visit you. You'll have to excuse yourself. It will lead to embarrassing entanglements. You don't in the least realize your position in society. It is all well enough to please your relatives, although I think you often overdo that. You could just as well send them a present now and then and please them more than to go yourself. But as for any outsiders, it is impossible. I draw the line there."

"But, Grandmother—"

"Don't interrupt me, Elizabeth. I have something more to say. I received word this morning from the steamship company. They can give us our staterooms on the *Deutschland* on Saturday, and I've decided to take them. I've telegraphed, and we'll leave here today for New York. I have one or two matters of business I wish to attend to in New York. We'll stay at the Waldorf for a few days, and you'll have more opportunity to see New York than you have yet. It won't be too warm to enjoy going about a little, and a number of our friends are going to be at the Waldorf, too. The Craigs sail on Saturday with us. You'll have young company on the voyage."

Elizabeth's heart sank lower than she knew it could go, and she grew white to the lips. The observant grandmother decided she had done well to be so prompt. The man from Montana was by no means to be admitted. She gave orders to that effect, unknown to Elizabeth.

The girl went slowly to her room. All at once it dawned upon her that she hadn't given her address to the man the night before or told him by so much as a word about her circumstances. An hour's meditation brought her to the unpleasant decision that perhaps even now in this hard spot God was only hiding her from worse trouble. Mr. George Benedict belonged to Geraldine Loring. He had declared as much when he was in Montana. It was better for her not to renew the acquaintance. The ache in her heart told her she would be crushed under a friendship that could not last.

Very sadly she sat down to write a note.

"My dear Friend," she wrote on plain paper with no crest. She would not

flaunt her good fortune to his face. She was a plain Montana girl to him, and so she would remain.

> *My grandmother has been very ill and is obliged to go away for her health. Unexpectedly I find that we are to go today. I supposed it would not be for a week yet. I am so sorry not to see you again, but I send you a little book that has helped me to get acquainted with Jesus Christ. Perhaps it will help you too. It is called 'My Best Friend.' I shall not forget to pray always that you may find Him. He is so precious to me! I must thank you in words, though I never can say it as it should be said, for your very great kindness to me when I was in trouble. God sent you to me, I am sure.*
>
> > *Always gratefully your friend,*
> > *Elizabeth.*

That was all, no date, no address. He wasn't hers, and she would hang out no clues for him to find her, even if he wished. It was better that way. She sent the note and the little book to his address on Walnut Street. Then after writing a note to her grandmother Brady, saying that she was going away for a long trip with Grandmother Bailey, she gave herself into the hands of the future like a submissive but weary child.

The noon train to New York carried in its drawing-room car Madam Bailey, her granddaughter, her maid, and her dog, bound for Europe. The society columns stated it thus, and Grandmother Brady read it a few days later. George Benedict also read it, but it meant nothing to him.

When he received the note, he was almost as agitated as when he saw the little brown girl on the brown horse vanishing behind the brown station on the prairie. He went to the telephone and realized he knew no names. He called up his automobile and tore up to Flora Street. But in his bewilderment the night before, he hadn't noticed which block the house was in or which number. He thought he knew where to find it, but in broad daylight the houses looked alike for three blocks. For the life of him he couldn't remember whether he turned to the right or the left on Flora Street. He tried both but saw no sign of the people he noticed only casually at Willow Grove.

He couldn't ask where she lived, for he didn't know her name. Nothing but Elizabeth, and they had called her Bessie. He couldn't go from house to house asking for a girl named Bessie. They'd think him a fool, as he was, for not finding out her name, her precious name, at once. How could he let her slip from him again when he'd just found her?

At last he hit upon a bright idea. He asked some children along the street whether they knew of any young woman named Bessie or Elizabeth living there; but they all with one accord shook their heads, though one volunteered the information that "Lizzie Smith lives here." It was most disturbing. He could only go home and wait in patience for her return. She would come back sometime probably. She hadn't said she would, but she also hadn't said she would not. He found her once; he might find her again. And he could pray. She found comfort in that; so would he. He would learn what her secret was. He would get acquainted with her "best Friend." He studied that little book diligently. Then he hunted up the man of God who wrote it and led Elizabeth into the path of light by his earnest preaching every Sabbath, though he didn't know this.

The days passed, and Saturday came. Elizabeth, heavy-hearted, stood on the deck of the *Deutschland* and watched her native land disappear from view. So again George Benedict had lost her from sight.

It struck Elizabeth, as she strained her eyes to see the last of the shore through tears that burned and fell on her pale cheeks, that she was running away from a man again, only this time not of her own free will. She was being taken away. But perhaps it was better.

And it never once entered her mind that, if she had told her grandmother who the friend in Montana was and where he lived in Philadelphia, it would have made all the difference in the world.

From the first of the voyage Grandmother Bailey grew steadily worse, and when they landed on the other side they traveled from one place to another seeking health. Carlsbad waters did not agree with her, so they journeyed to the south of France to try the climate. At each move the little old woman grew weaker and more querulous. She finally resigned herself to the role of invalid. Then Elizabeth had to be at her side constantly. Madam Bailey demanded reading, and no voice was as soothing as Elizabeth's.

Gradually Elizabeth substituted books of her own choice since her grandmother didn't seem to mind, and now and then she'd read a page of some book that told of her best Friend. At first, because the dear pastor at home had written the book, it commanded her attention. Finally, because some dormant chord in her heart had been touched, she allowed Elizabeth to speak of these things. But not until they were away from home for three months, and she'd grown weaker by the day, did she allow Elizabeth to read in the Bible.

The girl chose the fourteenth chapter of John. Over and over again, whenever the restless nerves tormented their victim, she read those words, "Let not your heart be troubled." At last, the selfish soul, who had lived her life to please the world and seek her own pleasure, heard the words. And she felt that perhaps she did believe in God and might accept that invitation, "Believe also in me."

One day Elizabeth had been reading a psalm and thought her grandmother was asleep. She was sitting back with a weary heart, wondering what would happen if her grandmother should not get well. The old woman opened her eyes.

"Elizabeth," she said abruptly, just as when she was well, "you've been a good girl. I'm glad you came. I couldn't have died right without you. I never thought much about these things before, but it really is worthwhile. In my Father's house. He is my Father, Elizabeth."

She went to sleep then, and Elizabeth tiptoed out and left her with the nurse. By and by Marie came in crying and told her the madam was dead.

Elizabeth was used to people dying. She wasn't shocked. It just seemed lonely again to find herself confronting the world, in a foreign land. And when she faced the arrangements that had to be made, which, after all, money and servants made easy, she found herself dreading her own land. What must she do after her grandmother was laid to rest? She couldn't live in the great house in Rittenhouse Square, nor could she live in Flora Street. Oh, well, her Father would hide her. She needn't plan; He would plan for her. The mansions on the earth were His, too, as well as those in heaven.

And so resting she passed through the weary voyage and the day when the body was laid to rest in the Bailey lot in the cemetery, and she returned to the empty house alone. Not until after the funeral did she go to see Grandmother Brady. She hadn't thought it wise or fitting to invite the hostile grandmother to the other one's funeral. She thought Grandmother Bailey would not like it.

Too weary to walk or take the trolley, she rode to Flora Street in the carriage. She was thinking about friends and which ones she cared to see. One of the first bits of news she heard on arriving in this country was that Miss Loring's wedding was to take place in a few days. It struck her like a thunderbolt, and she was criticizing herself for this as she rode along.

It didn't help her state of mind, therefore, for her grandmother to remark grimly: "That feller o' yurs 'n his aughtymobble has been goin' up an' down this street, day in, day out, this whole blessed summer. Ain't been a day he didn't pass, sometimes once, sometimes twicet. I felt sorry for him sometimes. If he hadn't been so high an' mighty stuck-up that he couldn't recognize me, I'd 'a' spoke to him. It was plain as the nose on your face he was lookin' for you. Don't he know where you live?"

"I don't believe he does," said Elizabeth languidly. "Say, Grandmother, would you care to come up to Rittenhouse Square and live?"

"Me? In Rittenhouse Square? For the land sakes, child, no. That's flat. I've lived me days out in me own sp'ere, and I don't intend to change now at me time o' life. If you want to do somethin' nice for me, child, now you've got all that money, I'd like real well to live in a house with white marble steps. It's been me one aim all me life. There's some round on the next street that don't come high. There'd be plenty of room for us all, an' a nice place for Lizzie to get married when the time comes. The parlor's real big, and you could send her some roses, couldn't you?"

"All right, Grandmother. You shall have it," said Elizabeth with a relieved sigh, and in a few minutes she went home. Someday soon she must think what to do, but there was no immediate hurry. She was glad Grandmother Brady didn't want to come to Rittenhouse Square. Things would be more congenial without her.

But the house seemed vast and empty when she entered, and she was glad to hear the friendly telephone ringing. It was the wife of her pastor, inviting her to their home for a quiet dinner.

This was the one home in the city where she felt like going in her loneliness. There would be no form or ceremony. Just a friend with them. It was good. The doctor would give her some helpful words. She was glad they asked her.

Chapter 17

G eorge," said Mrs. Vincent Benedict, "I want you to do something for me."

"Certainly, Mother, anything I can."

"Well, it's only to go to dinner with me tonight. Our pastor's wife has telephoned me that she wants us very much. She said she especially needed you. It's a case of charity, and she'd be so grateful if you'd come. She has a young friend with her who is very sad and wants to cheer her up. Now don't frown. I won't bother you again this week. I know you hate dinners and girls. But really, George, this is an unusual case. The girl is just home from Europe and buried her grandmother yesterday. She hasn't a soul in the world belonging to her that can be with her, and the pastor's wife has invited her to dinner quietly. Of course she isn't going out. She must be in mourning. And you know you're fond of the doctor."

"Yes, I'm fond of the doctor," said George, frowning. "But I'd rather take him alone and not with a girl flung at me. I'm tired of it. I didn't think it of Christian people, though. I thought she was above such things."

"Now, George," said his mother severely, "that's an insult to the girl and to our friend, too. She hasn't an idea of doing any such thing. It seems this girl is quite unusual, very religious, and our friend thought you'd be just the one to cheer her. She apologized several times for presuming to ask you to help her. You really must go."

"Well, who is this paragon, anyway? Anyone I know? I suppose I've got to go."

"Why, she's a Miss Bailey," said the mother, relieved. "Mrs. Wilton Merrill Bailey's granddaughter. Did you ever meet her? I never did."

"Never heard of her," growled George. "Wish I hadn't now."

"George!"

"Well, Mother, go on. I'll be good. What does she do? Dance and play bridge and sing?"

"I haven't heard anything she does," said his mother, laughing.

"Well, of course she's a paragon. They all are, Mother. I'll be ready in half an hour. Let's go and get it done. We can come home early, can't we?"

Mrs. Benedict sighed. If only George would settle down with some suitable girl of good family! But he was so odd and restless. Ever since she took him to Europe, when she was so ill, she'd been afraid for him. He seemed so moody and absentminded then and later. Now this Miss Bailey was said to be as beautiful as she was good. If only George would take a notion to her!

Elizabeth was sitting in a great armchair by the open fire when he came in the room. He hadn't expected to find anyone there. He heard voices upstairs and supposed Miss Bailey was talking with her hostess. His mother followed the servant to remove her wraps, and he entered the drawing room alone. She stirred, looked up and saw him.

"Elizabeth!" he said, walking forward to grasp her hand. "I've found you again. Why are you here?"

But she had no opportunity to answer, for the ladies entered almost at once, and there stood the two smiling at each other.

"Why, you've met before!" exclaimed the hostess. "How delighted I am! I knew you two would enjoy meeting. Elizabeth, child, you never told me you knew George."

George Benedict kept looking around for Miss Bailey to enter the room. To his relief she didn't come, and he found no place set for her in the dining room. She must have remained at home. He forgot her and settled down to the joy of having Elizabeth by his side. His mother watched his face blossom into the old-time joy as he handed this new girl the olives and had eyes for no one else.

It was a blessed evening to Elizabeth. They conversed sweetly with one another as children of the King. For a little while, under the influence of the restful talk, she forgot "the lady" and all the questions that had vexed her soul. She knew only that she had entered into an atmosphere of peace and love and joy.

Not until the evening was over and the guests were about to leave, did Mrs. Benedict address Elizabeth as Miss Bailey. Up to that moment it hadn't entered her son's mind that Miss Bailey was present at all. He turned with a start and looked into Elizabeth's eyes. She smiled back at him as if to acknowledge the name. Could she read his thoughts? he wondered.

It was only a few steps across the square, and Mrs. Benedict and her son walked to Elizabeth's door with her. He had no opportunity to speak to Elizabeth alone, but he said as he bid her good night, "I shall see you tomorrow, then, in the morning."

The inflection was almost a question. But Elizabeth only said, "Good night," and vanished into the house.

"Then you have met her before, George?" asked his mother wonderingly.

"Yes," he answered hurriedly, as if to stop her further question. "Yes, I've met her before. She is very beautiful, Mother."

And because the mother was afraid she might say too much she held her peace. It was the first time in years that George had called a girl beautiful.

Meanwhile Elizabeth went to her own room and locked the door. She hardly knew what to think—her heart was so happy. Yet beneath it all was the troubled thought of the lady, the haunting lady they'd prayed for on the prairie. Then, as if to add to the thought, she noticed a bit of newspaper lying on the floor beside her dressing table. Marie must have dropped it as she came in to turn up the lights. It was only the corner torn from a newspaper and should be consigned to the wastebasket. As she picked it up idly, her eye caught the words in large headlines: "Miss Geraldine Loring's Wedding to Be an Elaborate Affair." Nothing else was readable. The paper was torn in a zigzag line below it. Yet that was enough. It reminded her of her duty.

Down beside the bed she knelt and prayed: "Oh, my Father, hide me now! I'm in trouble. Hide me!" Over and over she prayed till her heart grew calm and she could think.

Then she sat down quietly and put the matter before her.

This man whom she loved with her whole soul was to be married in a few days. All of society would be at the wedding. He was pledged to another, and he was not hers. Yet he was her old friend and was coming to see her. If he came and looked into her face with his clear eyes, he might read in hers that she loved him. How dreadful that would be!

Yes, she must search yet deeper. She heard the glad ring in his voice when he met her and said, "Elizabeth!" She saw his eyes. He was in danger himself. She must help him be true to the woman he was pledged to, whom now he would have to marry.

She must go away—at once. It seemed she was always running from someone. She could return to the mountains where she started. She wasn't afraid now of the man who had pursued her. Culture and education had done their work. Religion had set her upon a rock. She could go back with the protection of her money, with the companionship of some good, elderly woman, and be safe from harm. But she couldn't stay here and meet George Benedict in the morning, or face Geraldine Loring on her wedding day. It would be all the same whether she were in attendance or not. Her days of mourning for her grandmother would of course protect her from this public encounter. It was the thought she couldn't bear. She must get away from it all forever.

Her lawyers should arrange the business. They would purchase the house Grandmother Brady desired and then give her her money to build a church. She would go back and teach among the lonely wastes of mountain and prairie what Jesus Christ longed to be to the people made in His image. She would go back and place stones above the graves of her father and mother and brothers, bearing the words of life to passersby in that desolate region. And that would be her excuse to the world for going, if she needed any excuse—she went to see about placing a monument over her father's grave. But the monument should be a church somewhere where it was most needed. She was resolved about that.

That was a busy night. Marie was called upon to pack a few things for a hurried journey. The telephone rang, and the sleepy night-operator answered crossly. But Elizabeth found out all she wanted to know about the early Chicago trains and then lay down to rest.

Early the next morning George Benedict telephoned for some flowers from the florist. When they arrived, he pleased himself by taking them to

Elizabeth's door.

He didn't expect to find her up, but it would be a pleasure for the flowers to reach her by his hand. They would be sent up to her room, and she would know in her first waking thought that he remembered her. He smiled as he touched the bell and waited.

The old butler opened the door. He looked as if he hadn't finished his night's sleep. He listened mechanically to the message, "For Miss Bailey with Mr. Benedict's good morning," and then his face took on an apologetic expression.

"I'm sorry, Mr. Benedict," he said, as if he were personally to blame. "But she's just gone. Miss Elizabeth's mighty quick in her ways, and last night after she came home she decided to go to Chicago on the early train. She went to the station not ten minutes ago. They were late and had to hurry. I'm expecting the footman back any minute."

"Gone?" said George Benedict, standing on the doorstep and staring down the street as if that would bring her. "Gone? To Chicago, did you say?"

"Yes, sir, she's gone to Chicago. That is, she's going further, but she took the Chicago Limited. She's gone to see about a monument for Madam's son John, Miss 'Lizabuth's father. She said she must go at once, and she went."

"What time does the train leave?" asked the young man. It was a thread of hope. He was stung into making a superhuman effort as he had on the prairie when he caught the flying vision of the girl and horse, and he shouted, and she wouldn't stop for him.

"Nine-fifty, sir," said the butler. He wished this excited young man would go after her. She needed someone. His heart had often stirred against fate that this pearl among young mistresses should have no intimate friend or lover now in her loneliness.

"Nine-fifty!" He looked at his watch. No chance! "Broad Street?" he asked sharply.

"Yes, sir."

Would he have a chance with his automobile? Possibly, but only if the train was late. He'd have slightly more chance of catching the train in West Philadelphia. Oh, for his automobile! He turned to the butler in despair.

"Telephone her!" he said. "Stop her if you can on board the train, and I'll try to get there. I must see her. It's important."

He started down the steps, his mind in a whirl. How should he go? The trolley was the only available way, but it was useless; it would take too long. Nevertheless, he rushed down toward Chestnut Street blindly, and in his despair his new habit came to him. "Oh, my Father, help me! Save her for me!"

Up Walnut Street a flaming red automobile raced, sounding its taunting menace, "Honk honk! Honk honk!" But George Benedict didn't stop for automobiles. He dashed straight into the jaws of death and was saved only by the timely grasp of a policeman, who rolled him over on the ground.

The machine halted, and a familiar voice shouted, "Conscience alive, George, is that you? What're you trying to do? Say, but that was a close shave. Where you going in such a hurry, anyway? Hustle in, and I'll take you there."

The young man sprang into the seat and gasped: "West Philadelphia station, Chicago Limited! Hurry! Train leaves Broad Street station at nine-fifty. Get me there if you can, Billy. I'll be your friend forever."

By this time they were speeding. Neither one had time to consider which station was easier to make. As the machine was headed toward West Philadelphia, on they flew, regardless of laws or policemen shouting in vain.

George Benedict sprang from the car before it stopped and nearly fell again. His nerves weren't steady from his other fall yet. He tore into the station and out through the passageway past the beckoning hand of the ticket man who sat in the booth at the staircase and up three steps at a time. The guard shouted: "Hurry! You may catch it. She's just starting!" And a friendly hand reached out and hauled him up on the platform of the last car.

For an instant after he was safely in the car he was too dazed to think. He thought he must keep rushing blindly through the train all the way to Chicago, or she'd get away from him. He sat down in an empty seat for a minute to collect his thoughts. He was on the train! It hadn't left without him!

Now the next question was, Was she on it herself, or had she slipped from his grasp even yet? The old butler might have caught her by telephone. He doubted it. He knew her stubborn determination. All at once he began to suspect she was running away from him intentionally and may have before! It was an astonishing thought and a sobering one. Yet, if it were true, what did she mean by that welcoming smile that shone like sunshine on his heart?

He had no time to consider such questions now. He had started on this quest, and he must find her. Then she must explain fully once and for all. He would live through no more torturing separations without understanding the matter. He stood up shakily and started to hunt for Elizabeth.

Suddenly he realized he was still carrying the box of flowers. It was battered and out of shape, but he clutched it as if it held the very hope of life for him. He smiled grimly as he tottered down the aisle, grasping his floral offering with determination. This wasn't the morning call he'd planned, nor the way he'd expected to present his flowers. But it was the best he could do. Then, at last, in the furthest car from the end, he found her in the drawing room, sorrowful, watching the landscape fly by.

"Elizabeth!"

He stood in the open door and called to her, and she started as from a deep sleep. Her face glowed with sunshine at the sight of him. She put her hand to her heart and smiled.

"I've brought you some flowers," he said grimly. "I'm afraid there isn't much left of them now. But, such as they are, they're here. I hope you'll accept them."

"Oh!" gasped Elizabeth, reaching out for the poor crushed roses. She drew them from the battered box into her arms, as if to caress them for all they'd come through. He watched her, half pleased, half wild. Why should she waste all that tenderness on fading flowers?

At last he spoke, interrupting her brooding over his roses.

"You are running away from me!" he charged.

"Well, and what if I am?" She looked at him with loving defiance.

"Don't you know I love you?" he asked, sitting down beside her and speaking quietly but almost fiercely. "Don't you know I've been torn away from you, or you from me, twice before now and that I can't stand it anymore? Say, don't you know it? Answer, please!" The demand was kind, but peremptory.

"I was afraid so," she murmured with downcast eyes and cheeks from which all color had fled.

"Well, why do you do it? Why did you run away? Don't you care for me? Tell me that. If you can't ever love me, you're excused. But I must know it now."

"Yes, I care as much as you," she faltered, "but—"

"But what?" he said sharply.

"But you are going to be married this week," she said in desperation, raising her miserable eyes to his.

He looked at her in astonishment.

"Am I?" said he. "Well, that's news to me. But it's the best news I've heard in a long time. When does the ceremony come off? I wish it was this morning. Make it this morning, will you? Let's stop this blessed old train and go back to the doctor. He'll fix it so we can't ever run away from each other again. Elizabeth, look at me!"

But Elizabeth hid her eyes now. They were full of tears.

"But the lady—," she gasped out between sobs. She was so weary, and the thought of what he suggested was so precious.

"What lady? There is no lady but you, Elizabeth, and never has been. Haven't you known that for a long time? I have. That was all an hallucination of my foolish brain. I had to go out on the plains to get rid of it, but I left it there forever. She was nothing to me after I saw you."

"But—but people said—and it was in the paper. I saw it. You can't desert her now. It would be dishonorable."

"Thunder!" exclaimed the distracted young man. "In the paper! What lady?"

"Why, Miss Loring! Geraldine Loring. I saw that the preparations were all made for her wedding, and I was told she was to marry you."

In sheer relief he began to laugh.

At last he stopped, as the old hurt look spread over her face.

"Excuse me, dear," he said gently. "Miss Loring and I had a little acquaintance. It only amounted to a flirtation on her part, one of many. It was a great distress to my mother, and I went out west, as you know, to get away from her. I knew she would only bring me unhappiness, and she wasn't willing to give up some of her impossible ways. I'm glad and thankful God saved me from her. I believe she's going to marry a distant relative of mine by the name of Benedict, but I thank the kind Father that *I* am not going to marry *her*. There is only one woman in the whole world I am willing to marry, or ever will be, and she's sitting beside me now."

The train was moving rapidly now. It wouldn't be long before the conductor would reach them. The man leaned over and clasped the little gloved hand that lay in the girl's lap. Elizabeth felt the great joy that had tantalized her these three years in dreams and visions settle down about her in beautiful reality. She was his forever. She needn't ever run away again.

The conductor reached them, and the matter-of-fact world had to be faced once more. The young man produced his card and said a few words to the conductor, mentioning the name of his uncle, who, by the way, happened to be a director of the road. Then he explained the situation. The young lady must be recalled at once to her home because of a change in the circumstances. He caught the train at West Philadelphia by automobile, coming as he was in his morning clothes, without baggage and with little money. Would the conductor be so kind as to put them off so they might return to the city by the shortest route?

The conductor glared at them and said people "didn't know their own minds" and "wanted to move the earth." Then he eyed Elizabeth, and she smiled. He let a slight glimmer of what might have been a sour smile years ago peep out for an instant, and—he let them off.

They wandered delightedly about from one trolley to another until they found an automobile garage and soon were speeding back to Philadelphia.

They waited for no ceremony, those two who met and loved by the way in the wilderness. They went straight to Mrs. Benedict for her blessing and then to the minister to arrange for his services. Within a week a quiet wedding party entered the arched doors of the placid brown church with the lofty spire, and Elizabeth Bailey and George Benedict were united in the sacred bonds of matrimony.

Mrs. Benedict was present, and one or two intimate friends of the family, besides Grandmother Brady, Aunt Nan, and Lizzie.

Lizzie brought a dozen bread-and-butter plates from the ten-cent store. They were adorned with cupids and roses and gilt. But Lizzie was disappointed. No display, no pomp and ceremony. Just a simple white dress and veil. Lizzie didn't understand that the veil had been in the Bailey family for generations and the dress was an heirloom also. Elizabeth wore it because Grandmother Bailey had given it to her and told her she wanted her to wear it on her wedding day. Sweet and beautiful she looked as she turned to walk down the aisle on her husband's arm, and she smiled at Grandmother Brady in a way that filled the grandmother's heart with pride and triumph. Elizabeth was not ashamed of the Bradys even among her fine friends. But Lizzie grumbled all the way home at the plainness of the ceremony and the lack of bridesmaids and fuss and feathers.

The social column of the daily papers stated that young Mr. and Mrs. George Benedict were honeymooning in an extended tour of the West, and Grandmother Brady read it aloud at the breakfast table to the admiring family. Only Lizzie looked discontented.

"She just wore a dark blue tricotine one-piece dress and a little plain dark hat. She ain't got a bit of taste. Oh, *boy!* If I just had her pocketbook wouldn't I show the world? But anyhow I'm glad she went in a private car. There was a *little* class to her, though if 't had been mine I'd uv preferred ridin' in the parlor coach an' havin' folks see me and my fine husband. He's some looker, George Benedict is! Everybody turns to watch 'em as they go by, and they sail along and never seem to notice. It's all perfectly throwed away on 'em. Gosh! I'd hate to be such a nut!"

"Now, Lizzie, you know you oughtn't to talk like that!" reproved her grandmother. "After her giving you all that money for your own wedding. A thousand dollars just to spend as you please on your clothes and a blowout and house linens. Just because she don't care for gewgaws like you do, you think she's a fool. But she's no fool. She's got a good head on her, and she'll get more in the long run out of life than you will. She's been real loving and kind to us all, and she didn't have any reason to neither. We never did much for her. And look at how nice and common she's been with us all, not a bit high-headed. I declare, Lizzie—I should think you'd be ashamed!"

"Oh, well," said Lizzie, shrugging her shoulders. "She's all right in her way, only 'taint my way. I'm thankful t' goodness I had the nerve to speak up when she offered to give me my trousseau. She asked me would I rather have her buy it for me, or have the money to pick it out m'self, and I spoke up right quick and says, 'Oh, Cousin Bessie, I wouldn't *think* of givin' ya all that trouble. I'd take the *money* if it's all the same t' you,' and she just smiled and said all right; she expected I knew what I wanted better'n she did. So yes'teddy when I went down to the station to see her off she handed me a bank book. And—oh, say, I forgot! She said there was a good-bye note inside. I ain't had time to look at it since. I went right to the movies on the run to get there 'fore the first show begun, and it's in my coat pocket. Wait till I get it. I s'pose it's some of her old *religion!* She's always preaching at me. It ain't that she says so much as that she's always *meanin'* it underneath everything, that gets my goat! It's sorta like having a piece of God round with you all the time watching you. You kinda hate to be enjoyin' yourself for fear she won't think you're doin' it accordin' to the Bible."

Lizzie dashed into the hall and brought back her coat, fumbling in the pocket.

"Yes, here 'tis, Ma! Wanta see the figgers? You never had a whole thousand dollars in the bank t'woncet yourself, did ya?"

Mrs. Brady put on her spectacles and reached for the book, while Lizzie's mother got up and came behind her mother's chair to look at the magic figures. Lizzie stooped for the little white note that had fluttered to her feet as she opened the book, but she had little interest to see what it said. She was more intent upon the new bank book.

It was Grandmother Brady who discovered it. "Why, Lizzie! It ain't *one* thousand; it's *five* thousand, the book says! You don't s'pose she's made a mistake, do you?"

Lizzie seized the book, and her mouth dropped open.

"Let me have it!" demanded Lizzie's mother, reaching for the book.

"Where's your note, Lizzie? Mebbe it will explain," said the excited grandmother.

Lizzie recovered the note which had fluttered to the floor again in the confusion and, opening it, read:

Dear Lizzie,

I've made it five thousand so you'll have extra for furnishing your home. If you still think you want the little bungalow out on the Pike you'll find the deed at my lawyer's, all made out in your name. It's my wedding gift to you, so you can go to work and buy your furniture at once and not wait till Dan gets a raise. And here's wishing you a great deal of happiness.

Your loving cousin,
Elizabeth.

"There!" said Grandmother Brady, sitting back with satisfaction and holding her hands calmly. "Whadd' I tell you?"

"Mercy!" said Lizzie's mother. "Let me see that note! The idea of her *giving* all that money when she didn't have to!"

But Lizzie's face was a picture of joy. For once she lost her hard little worldly screwed-up expression and was wreathed in smiles of genuine eagerness.

"Oh, *boy!*" she exclaimed, dancing around the room. "Now we can have a victrola an' a player piano, and Dan'll get a Ford, one o' those limousine kind! Won't I be some swell? What'll the girls at the store think now?"

"H'm! You'd much better get a washing machine and a 'lectric iron!" grumbled Grandmother Brady.

"Well, all I got to say about it is, she was an awful fool to trust *you* with so much money," said Lizzie's mother with discontent. But with a pleased pride she watched her giddy daughter fling on her hat and coat to go down and tell Dan.

"I sh'll work in the store for the rest of the week, just to 'commodate 'em," she announced, putting her head back in the door as she went out, "but not a day longer. I got a lot t' do. Say, won't I be some lady in the five-an'-ten the rest o' the week? Oh, *boy! I'll tell the world!*"

Meanwhile in their own private car the bride and groom were whirling on their way to the West. But they saw little of the scenery, absorbed as they were in talking about each other's lives since they'd parted.

And one bright morning they stepped down from the train at Malta and gazed about them.

The sun was shining clear, and the little brown station stood drearily against the brightness of the day like a picture that has long hung on the wall of one's memory and is suddenly brought out and the dust wiped away.

They purchased a couple of horses and with camp accoutrements following began their real wedding trip, over the road they had traveled together when they first met. Elizabeth showed her husband where she hid while the men went by, and he drew her close in his arms and thanked God she escaped so miraculously.

It was so wonderful to be in the same places again, for nothing out here in the wilderness changed much. Yet they two were so changed that the people they met didn't recognize them as having been there before.

They dined sumptuously in the same gully and recalled little things they said and did. Elizabeth, now worldly-wise, laughed at her former ignorance as her husband reminded her of questions she had asked him. And ever through the beautiful journey he told her how wonderful she was to him, both then and now.

Not until they reached the old ranch house, however, where the woman had tried to persuade her to stay, did they stop for long.

Elizabeth held a tender feeling in her heart for the motherly woman who sought to protect her; she longed to let her know how safely she was kept through the long journey and how good the Lord had been to her through the years. Also they both desired to reward these kind people for their hospitality. So in the early evening they rode up just as they did before to the old log house. But no door was flung open as they came near. At first they thought the cabin deserted, till a candle flare suddenly shone forth in the bedroom. Then George dismounted and knocked.

After some waiting the old man came to the door holding a candle high above his head. His face was haggard and worn, and the whole place looked dishevelled. He peered into the night warily, without recognizing them.

"I can't do much for ya, strangers," he said, his voice sounding tired and discouraged. "If it's a woman ye have with ye, ye better ride on to the next ranch. My woman is sick. Very sick. There's nobody here with her but me, and I have all I can tend to. The house ain't kept very tidy. It's six weeks since she took to bed."

Elizabeth had sprung lightly to the ground and was now at the threshold. "Oh, is she sick? I'm so sorry. Couldn't I do something for her? She was good to me once several years ago!"

The old man stared at her, blinking, noting her slender beauty, the exquisite eager face, the dress that showed her of another world. He shook his head. "I guess you made a mistake, lady. I don't remember ever seeing you before—"

"But I remember you," she said, stepping eagerly into the room. "Won't you please let me go to her?"

"Why, sure, lady, go right in if you want to. She's layin' there in the bed. She ain't likely to get out of it again, I'm feared. The doctor says nothin' but an operation will ever get her up, and we can't pay for no operations. It's a long ways to the hospital in Chicago where he wants her sent, and M'ria and I, we ain't allowin' to part. It can't be many years—"

But Elizabeth didn't wait to hear. She slipped into the old bedroom she remembered so well and knelt beside the bed of the woman.

"Don't you remember me?" she asked. "I'm the girl you tried to get to stay with you once. The girl who came here with a man she met in the wilderness. You told me things I didn't know, and you were kind and wanted me to stay here with you. Don't you remember me? I'm Elizabeth!"

The woman reached out a bony hand and touched the fair young face she could see only dimly in the flare of the candle that the old man brought into the room.

"Why, yes, I remember," the woman said, her voice sounded alive in spite of her illness. "Yes, I remember you. You were a dear little girl, and I was so worried about you. I would have kept you for my own—but you wouldn't stay. And he was a nice-looking young man, but I was afraid for you—you can't always tell about them—you *mostly* can't—!"

"But he was all right!" Elizabeth's voice rang joyously through the cabin. "He took care of me and got me safely started toward my people, and now he's my husband. I want you to see him. George, come here!"

The old woman raised herself from the pillow and looked toward the young man in the doorway. "You don't say! He's your *husband!* Well, now isn't that grand! Well, I certainly am glad! I was that worried—!"

They sat around the bed talking, Elizabeth telling briefly of her experiences and the wedding trip they were taking back over the old trail. The older couple spoke of their trouble, the woman's breakdown, and how the doctor at Malta said she had a chance of getting well if she saw a certain doctor in Chicago; but they had no money unless they sold the ranch, and nobody wanted to buy it.

"Oh, but we have money," laughed Elizabeth joyfully, "and it's our turn to help you. You helped us when we were in trouble. How soon can you start? I'm going to pretend you're my own father and mother. We can send them both, can't we, George?"

They settled down to sleep sometime later that night, what with all the planning to be done. And Elizabeth and her husband had taken out their supplies and cooked a good supper for the two old people who had lived mostly on cornmeal mush for several weeks.

And after the others were asleep the old woman thanked God for the two angels who had dropped down to help them in their distress.

The next morning George Benedict, with one of the men who looked after their camping outfit, rode into Malta and got in touch with the Chicago doctor and hospital. Before he returned to the ranch that night everything was arranged for the couple to start at once. He even planned for an automobile and the Malta doctor to attend to getting the invalid to the station in a few days.

Meanwhile Elizabeth went through the woman's coarse wardrobe and selected garments from her own baggage that would do for the journey.

The old woman looked glorified as she touched the delicate white garments with their embroidery and ribbons.

"Oh, dear child! Why, I couldn't wear a thing like that on my old worn-out body. Those look like angels' clothes." She traced a work-worn finger over the embroidery and smoothed a pink satin ribbon bow.

But Elizabeth overruled her. It was nothing but a plain little garment she'd bought for the trip. If the friend thought it was pretty she was glad, but nothing was too pretty for the woman who took her in in her distress and tried to help her.

The invalid was thin from her illness and could easily wear the girl's simple dress of dark blue and small dark hat. Elizabeth donned a khaki shirt, brown cap, and sweater, and gladly dressed her old friend in her own bridal traveling gown for the journey. She hadn't brought a lot of things and could get more when she reached a large city. Besides, what was money for but to clothe the naked and feed the hungry? She rejoiced in her ability to help this woman of the wilderness.

On the third day, garbed in Elizabeth's clothes and her husband fitted out for the East in some of George's extra things, they started. They carried a bag containing necessary changes, a silk robe of Elizabeth's, and toiletry accessories with silver monograms, enough to puzzle the most snobbish nurse. The two old people were settled in the Benedict private car and in due time were hitched onto the Chicago Express and hurried on their way. Before the younger pair returned to their pilgrimage they sent telegrams arranging for every detail for the old couple's journey, so they would be met with cars and nurses and looked after most carefully.

The thanksgiving and praise of the old people seemed to follow them like music as they rode happily on their way.

They paused at the old schoolhouse where they'd attended the Christian Endeavor meeting, and Elizabeth looked up the road her pursuers had taken. She moved her horse closer to her husband's. So they traveled along the way as nearly as Elizabeth could remember, telling her husband all the details of the journey.

That night they camped in the little shelter where George had come upon the girl that first time they met, and under the clear stars they knelt together and thanked God for His leading.

Then they rode on to the lonely cabin on the mountain, shut up and going to ruin now. George gazed at the surroundings and then at the delicate face of his lovely wife. She reminded him of a white flower he once saw growing out of the blackness down in a coal mine, pure and clean without a smirch of soil.

They visited the seven graves in the wilderness. Standing reverently beside the sand-blown mounds she told him much of her early life she'd never told him. She introduced him to her family, telling a bit about each to show him their loveable side. They chose to have seven simple white stones set up, bearing words from the book they both loved. Over the careworn mother was to be written, "Come unto me, all ye that labour and are heavy laden, and I will give you rest."

On that trip they planned what came to pass in due time. The little cabin was made over into a modest, pretty home, with vines planted about the garden and a garage with a sturdy little car. Not far away a church nestled into the side of the hill, built out of native stones, with many sunny windows and a belfry in which bells rang out to the whole region.

At first it seemed impractical to build a church out there away from the town, but Elizabeth said it was centrally located and high up where settlers in the valleys could see it. Moreover it was on a well-traveled trail. She longed to have some such spot in the wilderness as a refuge for anyone who hoped for better things.

When they went home they sent out two consecrated missionaries to occupy the new house and use the car. They were to ring the bells, preach the gospel, and play the organ and piano in the church.

Over the pulpit was a beautiful window bearing a picture of Christ, the Good Shepherd. And in clear letters above were the words: "And thou shalt remember all the way which the Lord thy God led thee these forty years in the wilderness, to humble thee, and to prove thee, to know what was in thine heart, whether thou wouldest keep his commandments, or no."

And underneath the picture were the words, " 'In the time of trouble he shall hide me in his pavilion: in the secret of his tabernacle shall he hide me.' In memory of His hidings, *George and Elizabeth Benedict.*"

But in the beautiful home in Philadelphia, in an inner intimate room these words were beautifully engraved and hung on the wall, "Let not your heart be troubled."

Mara

by Isabella Alden

Chapter 1

"So runs the round of life."

Naomi sat on the bed, as she nearly always did. When the three chairs were occupied, as they generally were, it became, by common consent, her place.

"Young ladies," she said, as she plumped herself into the middle of it, "beds were made for people to recline upon when resting and should never be used as substitutes for chairs." The tone was primness itself and evidently not Naomi's own.

The others laughed, as they had dozens of times before and as each knew they would soon not have opportunity to do again. Even their worn jokes carried an echo of last things.

"This particular bed was evidently designed for students in geography," said Gertrude, laying her hand tenderly upon one of its many humps. "Poor old Nebo! We'll give up a regretful sigh now and then, even for you."

That particular hump, the largest, had been named "Nebo" because, when perched on it, the best view of the outside world could be secured from the one window.

Nobody laughed at Gertrude's words; her tone was too distinctly sad.

"Let's not be dismal," Naomi hurried to say. "If there's anything I hate, it's looking back, regretting, sighing, and being generally dismal. What if our school days are over? We have other days in store, quite as good. And what have we been looking forward to all these years but getting through? Now that we've done it, why not enjoy it? I do wonder when we four will be together again, where we'll meet, and what will have happened in the meantime. Oh, girls, think of all the fun we've had!"

They all laughed now, little bursts of laughter that are near neighbors to tears.

"You're an excellent person to preach!" said Bernice, an attempt at reproof in her tone. "Who's 'looking back' now?"

"We're not to do it!" said Gertrude, with decision.

" 'Look ahead, young ladies—look ahead! Ignore your limited horizons and insist upon being lifted up and beyond.' " It was the prim tone again, well imitated, but the girl broke off to say in her natural voice: "I wonder if we'll sigh with regret occasionally for even Madame Nordhoff?"

Barbara rose from her seat under the window and crossed the room to her trunk. It was packed so full that the four agreed it was impossible to lock it; yet it was being left open for certain "last things" which must be added in the morning.

"You're all alike," she said, as she bent over the tray in search of a fresh handkerchief. "You resolve not to look back and be dismal, and then you end every sentence in dismal suggestions. I think we'd better go to bed. We'll feel cheerier in the morning."

A general protest arose.

"Oh, not yet, Bab! Why, the moon is just rising! Look at it, dear, and think where we'll be when it rises next."

"We'll be asleep, I hope," said Barbara, amid the general laugh at Gertrude's success in making cheerful suggestions. "It rises an hour later than this tomorrow night—remember."

"But we're not a bit sleepy," said Bernice. "I admit it seems rather hard to go to bed, as usual, at reasonable hours, on the first night of our lives when we've been given unlimited freedom. We might as well visit a little longer, since it's the very last night. When we're a thousand miles apart, we'll think of a thousand things we meant to say to one another and didn't."

"A thousand miles!" echoed Gertrude. "That's putting it well below the facts. Think what distant regions of the earth we represent. Barbara stands for New England, Bernice for the Midwest, while little Naomi is almost as far toward the setting sun as she can get."

"And you represent the center of things," said Bernice. "Or, no, Boston is the center of the earth, isn't it, Bab?"

Then Naomi, who was silent longer than usual and was by turns their hoyden and their sentimentalist, suddenly changed the subject.

"Girls, you won't forget our pledge to get together on our wedding days, no matter how separated we may be? I wonder which of us will issue the first call? Isn't it interesting to have it all so shrouded in mystery? Yet when you think about it, it really seems strange that not one of us has any plans along those lines."

They laughed then, merrily, as Bernice, leaning over to pat Naomi's shoulder, said, "It's strange and sad, my dear. Advanced as we all are in age, especially you! It looks as if we were designed by the fates for four old maids, doesn't it? If there should be no weddings for us to attend, what would become of us?"

"Well, nonsense aside," said Naomi, "I mean it seems unusual that not one of us has an intimate friend she thinks of occasionally as a possible lover. Schoolgirls nearly always have at least their daydreams. I don't believe you could find four more in our three hundred who haven't. It's odd that just we four got together."

" 'Birds of a feather flock together,' " quoted Gertrude. "Only that doesn't describe us; there isn't a 'feather' among us like any other. It's rather remarkable we've become such close friends. Madame Nordhoff would say it was due to propinquity rather than affinity, but I don't believe it. People can be like and unlike at the same time. Naomi, my dear, you're to be the first to give us a wedding. We expect it of you and shall depend upon you. See that you don't disappoint us."

"I!" echoed Naomi. "Why, I'm *years* the youngest."

"That's not of the slightest consequence, my child. I'm surprised you remembered we 'count time by heartthrobs, not by figures on a dial.' It's written in the annals of fate that Naomi Newland shall be the first to change her name. And do insist, dear, that his name shall commence with 'N.' I'm so fond of alliteration."

"I don't even know by name a person I'd think of a second time," said Naomi.

"That's dreadful," Gertrude answered, "and you so old! What about that Richard T something, I don't remember what, that I've watched you write on envelopes in your best style?"

"Oh, Dick!" she said with a toss of her head. "I'd as soon marry my brother. We're more intimate than many brothers and sisters are. Dick is my own first cousin, and don't you think we're twins! He was born on my birthday. But it's a singular thing, now that I think of it, that I've never even laid eyes on a person I could be persuaded under any circumstances to marry."

"I have," said Gertrude. "There was a nice old man in the village where we used to live. He must have been about sixty when I was six, and he was a wood sawyer by profession. But he had a head shaped exactly like Judge Holworthy, who was the very biggest man in the village in every way. Everybody noticed the resemblance. For years I never saw Judge Holworthy without thinking of dear old father Brandt the wood sawyer. The same kind eyes and pleasant mouth. He used to give me red-cheeked apples and hazelnuts— the wood sawyer did, not the judge. I used to say that when I grew to be a woman I was going to be father Brandt's wife. I still think I might have made a worse choice; his type of men are rare. Environment is a strange matter. If he'd grown up among cultured people and been given opportunities, he'd have developed into a college president or something of the sort. As it was, with as fine a head as any of them, he became a wood sawyer."

"Moralizing not allowed," said Bernice.

But Naomi paid no attention. "Life is strange. How we go on, generation after generation! Meeting strangers, falling in love with them, marrying them, growing old, and in time dying, leaving children behind us to go through the same round."

"Tennyson in prose," said Bernice.

" 'So runs the round of life from hour to hour,' you know. The pity is that none of us grows any wiser but makes the same mistakes our grandmothers did before us. I think I'll vary the program and be a fine old maid."

Barbara was looking at her watch. "Now we've had enough," she said firmly.

"It sounds inhospitable, I know, but you two girls must go home. Naomi, remember, has to make an early start and should have been sleeping for an hour. And we can't be sensible tonight if we try, so we might as well give it up and go to bed. Come, Namie, dear, your charming future is waiting for you, no doubt, just a little ahead. And Gertrude will be sure to find another wood sawyer in due time. Hug us good night and go, both of you."

"There isn't a speck of sentiment in your composition, Barbara Dennison," pouted Naomi as she slid down from the hump on the bed and shook out her skirts. "Not a speck! Turning us out in cold blood on the last night we'll ever be together, and the first night we've been allowed to stay as late as we pleased!"

Shouts of laughter greeted this contradiction, but Naomi held her ground.

"She knows what I mean," she said, with a toss of her head toward Barbara. "She doesn't need to state she's never had any romance in her life—that's obvious. She never saw a man yet to whom she wouldn't say—if he were calling on her and the clock struck ten—'Come, it's time you were at home. I have a busy day tomorrow, and I want to go to bed.' If it were the last evening he had to spend with her, it wouldn't make the least difference to Barbara."

She wrapped her arms around Barbara's neck, as soon as the last word was spoken, and the hug she received in turn was tender. The laughter they joined in at Barbara's expense died out suddenly, and for a moment no one trusted her voice.

Then Barbara came to the rescue. "Don't leave your west window open tonight, dear. There's a keen wind from that direction. Don't let her, Gertrude. If she does, you'll both take cold."

"We'll be good, Grandmother," said Gertrude. "Dear old Bab! I—there! Good night." She pulled herself suddenly from Barbara's embrace and ran after Naomi, who had slipped away. The "two B's," as the others called them, were left together.

"Poor little Namie," said Bernice, trying to smile. "I hope that mysterious future she dreams so much about has something bright in store for her. I don't think I could endure it if trouble touched her life."

Barbara made no answer but busied herself in putting the room in order.

When Bernice was in her robe she pushed aside the curtain and exclaimed, "Oh, look! The moon is in her glory. I'm glad we'll have a full moon for traveling. I'll watch it rise tomorrow night. Will you, Barbara, and think of me?"

"That would do for Naomi," said Barbara. But her smile was tender, and she came and smoothed Bernice's hair.

Bernice broke the silence that fell upon them again. "Naomi was quite certain none of us had ever felt a heartthrob, wasn't she?"

"Does that mean there's some deep secret that's never been revealed even to me?"

"No," said Bernice, with a frantic little laugh, "it doesn't mean anything. If there were anything in the world to tell, of course I should have told you, but—"

"Well, dear," said Barbara, after waiting a few minutes, " 'but' what?" She slipped an arm about her friend.

"I'm not like Naomi or even Gertrude. I've seen him, and he isn't a wood sawyer."

"My dear child! And you never even showed his shadow to me?"

"I have nothing to show," said Bernice, trying to laugh. "I mean, there's no 'shadow' in which I have a proprietary right. He's simply one of my friends. Perhaps we might be called intimate friends, but we're equally intimate with a half dozen others, and I have no reason to think I'm more to him, or ever will be, than those others are. So, you see, there's nothing to tell."

"Not even his name? Am I not to know that?"

"Why should you, dear? So long as it is as it is, what right have I to use his name in this talk?"

"But I may tell it to you if I can?"

And then Bernice laughed outright. "Oh, yes," she said. "You may if you can. I know you can't."

"Isn't it George? George Wilbur?"

She felt the start in the girl's frame and in the moonlight flooding their room could see that Bernice was distressed.

"Barbara," she said, "how do you know? It's possible that—but, no, that's too absurd. I'm sure you've never met him. It seems equally impossible that I've ever, ever—"

"You've never said or done anything, dear friend, that wasn't sweet and womanly. How can you imagine such foolishness? I know, or I mean I guessed, the name because—I hardly know how to tell even myself how it was. There's the very slightest shade of difference in your tone when you speak that name, from what you have for other friends—and just a touch of difference in the way you handle the papers that come with those initials on the corner, or the cards bearing that name. Not perceptible, of course, to anybody else in the world, but how could you have a thought that wouldn't insist upon sharing itself with me?"

Chapter 2

"The glories of the possible are ours."

S o you knew all the time!"

Barbara laughed. "I know very little, Bernice. I've imagined sometimes that you liked him a little better than your other friends and that
someday you might even like him better still. But I didn't know, of course, and
I would never have spoken my thought if you hadn't permitted me."

"It humiliates me to think I may have told others in the same way," said
poor Bernice. Her friend had to turn comforter and go over the ground again
and again, assuring her that such a thought was absurd, when she herself had
only dimly surmised possibilities. Bernice was to remember how close they'd
been for four years—so that their very thoughts seemed to flow together.

"I know it," said Bernice, comforted. "And I'm sure I ought to understand
it. If you had a special thought for anyone in your heart, however remote, I'd
certainly know it. We couldn't deceive each other if we wanted to, could we?
I know I'm freer with you than with any other person in this world. If there'd
been the least thing to tell, I couldn't have helped telling you. But he never
said a word to me in his life that couldn't have been said before all the world.
And yet—there are intonations and words that are ordinary enough in themselves but—" She broke off in such pitiable confusion that Barbara hastened
to help her.

"I understand you perfectly, and I hope and believe he's all and more than
you think him to be."

"He's all that is grand and noble, you may be sure of that. Now that I've
begun I may as well complete my confession and say he's the only man on
earth I could ever marry. I'm sure of it. So I was much more sincere than the
girls thought tonight in saying I'd never marry, because I don't believe he'll
choose me, and I won't be chosen by anybody else."

Barbara smiled. She had it in her heart to remind her friend she was still
young and that perhaps—but she held her lips from the words. What use was
there to argue about such matters? Time must show all of them what time
could do for them.

On the following evening at that same hour Barbara Dennison stood alone
by the moonlit window. Instead of being two hundred miles away, as she expected, she was still there, though the others had gone their ways. A telegram
from her father, announcing twenty-four hours' delay, with directions for her to
join him a day later where they were to meet, had come just in time to hold her.

"That means a double dose of desolation for you," Naomi said when she
kissed her good-bye. "Poor Bab, I wouldn't be left alone in these rooms for

anything in the world—they're haunted. Bab, dear, memories will stare at you from every hump on the bed."

Barbara thought of these words as she turned off the gas and gave herself to moonlight and melancholy. How still the old house was! And how dark! Not a room lit on the south side, where literally hundreds of girls had swarmed the day before.

Barbara had never before in her college years been left until last. This was the last in more senses than one. The four years she'd looked forward to as an all but endless period of time were in the past. School days for her were over, and real life was at the threshold. She shivered a little and told herself the night air was chilly, June though it was. But she hunted for a wrap and placed herself in the window seat for a deliberate survey of the years. Sleeping, at present, was out of the question.

Very prominent figures in her recent past were her three friends—Bernice, Gertrude, and Naomi. Bernice, her roommate and inseparable companion, and the other two, next door—they were so entirely in accord with one another that out of study and sleeping hours one room was sure to hold the four. How steadily close they were! Just they four, out of the hundreds who swarmed the halls. Not certainly because of similarity in appearance or tastes or former environment. Gertrude was right when she said, "Not a feather about them was alike."

But there must have been similarity in some direction, Barbara told her thoughts. They were drawn to one another from the very first, and the interest, whatever it was, grew steadily through the years. They were like sisters. Oh, more intimate than sisters, and she thought of Elinor. Yet there could hardly have been greater contrasts than their home environments represented, or must represent. They had never visited at one another's homes and knew only what chance references or perhaps, on occasion, marked silences had revealed. At last, Barbara gave up trying to think of reasons for their friendship and let herself enjoy the sweetness of the fact. They were friends, fast-bound for life.

"For more than life," she said. She looked straight through the path of glory the moonlight was making in the shimmering lake over toward what seemed radiant enough for the entrance into the celestial city.

This little earth life doesn't limit friendship. As surely as I know heaven is beyond it, I know I'll love our little Naomi there as here. Still, short as this life is, by comparison, I want it bright for Naomi. The rest of us can endure trials if we must, but dear little Namie we instinctively shelter. Not one of us wouldn't give up much to make her happy. I wonder if the wretch lives who could be other than good to her? Her thoughts had reverted to the last night's talk.

"Sentimental little dear," she said, with a smile and a sigh, as she seemed to hear Naomi's voice planning for their reunion at a wedding. Danger to the child might lie in that very direction. If some designing man wooed her for the sake of her father's millions and then broke her heart, Barbara felt as though their hearts would break in sympathy.

Appearing next before her were Bernice and her last night's confidences. She smiled to think how carefully the girl had guarded her secret, which was no secret to her. Numberless times she'd seen those expressive eyes off guard while looking at one photograph. The case on Bernice's table held a dozen photographs, among them pictures of her brothers and several of their college chums. But this special one was constantly at the top of the case, even though it was left underneath only an hour before. Yet it never occupied the place of honor on the little easel, where first one brother and then another, or a brother's friend, was placed "for company."

Bernice would never openly seek George Wilbur's company. By these and a hundred other hints her closest friend had come to know her story nearly as well as she knew it herself. Sometimes she felt almost hurt because it wasn't told to her. Yet Bernice was far more frank than she herself was. She blushed in the moonlight over this thought and then promptly justified herself.

I had no occasion for frankness. I have absolutely nothing to tell. I should despise myself if I even mentioned his name.

She didn't mention it; yet the image of a tall young man with fine blue eyes and a wide forehead crowned with masses of brown hair arose distinctly before her. She had no photograph of his face, yet she compared it dozens of times with the pictured face of George Wilbur, to the great disparagement of the latter. She wondered whether Bernice could, if given the opportunity, not see the infinite stretch of difference between them. George Wilbur's face to represent the noblest type of manhood, indeed! Didn't she know better? She admitted to her secret self that she didn't quite like his face. Not for the world would she have hinted such a thought to Bernice. It was unfair and foolish to judge character merely from a shadow which might or might not do the substance justice. Yet she was unable to put from her the notion that lurking behind that pictured mouth, yes, even in the eyes themselves, was a suggestion, or at least a suspicion, of insincerity. Instinctively she felt that she would hesitate to trust him utterly. But this other face, no one who was the least judge of character could look into those singularly penetrative eyes without feeling they belonged to a man to be trusted.

"There is no human being whose word I would trust for a moment if it contradicted his." She said the words aloud, with only the moonlight for witness, but it gave her pleasure to put the thought into words. She wasn't often quite alone. She would perhaps be even less so in the future, for Elinor was there to share her room—Elinor who was more assertive in all ways than Bernice and had none of her fine delicacy of feeling. Barbara's face shadowed a little at the thought of her. This was by no means a remark to be made in Elinor's hearing; but for once, just once, she would give voice to her thought and hear how it sounded.

"No truer, nobler, stronger human being walks the earth than Ellis Carpenter," she said. "Someday I'd like to tell him that he, more than any other person, has illustrated to me the kind of man Jesus Christ may have been when He lived on earth. He would think that irreverent, but it isn't; it is the truth."

The name Ellis Carpenter startled her, absolutely alone though she knew she was. She'd never spoken it in that room before. Through the year she'd spent in it since she came to know him well she never mentioned his name. In their chatter together, when Bernice and Gertrude and Naomi and she herself were detailing vacation experiences and describing for one another's enjoyment new acquaintances, never, even incidentally, did his name come to the surface. The reason for this she hadn't chosen to explain even to herself.

She wasn't young; she came late to college, as girls count time, and now was twenty-four. She wasn't sentimental; she had no schoolgirl escapades of the common kind and had indulged in no frantic friendships or heartbreaking experiences of any sort. She had considered herself to be above such foolishness and was glad to know she wasn't cast in that sort of mold.

Her sister Elinor's frantic friendships with young men had by turns frightened and irritated her. Elinor was twenty-six, but she neither looked nor acted it, nor wished to. Indeed she was more than willing to pose in public as younger sister of the quiet, dignified girl who, for what seemed to her half a lifetime, had been embarrassed and humiliated by Elinor's way of doing and talking. Not for anything would she have stooped to think and speak of Ellis Carpenter as Elinor spoke of half a dozen of her friends. As for mentioning his name before Elinor, that was never to be done.

Truth to tell, it surprised and at first humiliated her to discover she couldn't think of Ellis Carpenter as she thought of other friends nor could she, had she wished to do so, mention his name indifferently. The humiliation was keen for a time. Was she, after despising such girls all her life, now that she'd passed her twenty-third birthday, all at once to become like them? She never would, she told herself, with firmly set lips.

At least, no other should ever know she'd fallen from her ideal of young womanhood. With a strong will and outwardly quiet nature, she'd succeeded in hiding her secret within her own heart. She filled her life with work, becoming a better student during that last year of school than ever before.

Nor did she allow herself to brood in secret over her discovery. As a matter of fact this moonlit evening was the first time she deliberately took out her own heart and looked at it. Bernice's confidences had brought this about. Her conscience was asking her if she had been as true to Bernice as Bernice was to her. This made it necessary for her to find just where she stood.

Her conscience acquitted her; she was wise to keep silence. Had she spoken, it must have been to say she had a friend who never by word or tone or glance hinted that she was more to him than any of his other friends; yet he was consciously more to her at that moment than any other human being. It was surely wise for a self-respecting young woman to keep such knowledge to herself. Yet the time had passed when she felt humiliated by it.

There's no disgrace, she told herself, *in discovering you have a friend you respect and admire above others. The disgrace lies in letting such a discovery spoil one's life. That I won't do.*

On the whole it was not an unprofitable hour Barbara Dennison spent with her secret self that night. She was frank with herself or thought she was. She admitted gravely that, given the opportunity, she could live a brave, true, helpful life with and for Ellis Carpenter. But she added with equal gravity that she hadn't the slightest reason for believing the opportunity would ever be hers and that her business was to live her true, brave life without him.

Yet, behind all this, was an undertone she was hardly aware of—a secret voice entering its protest. Why was it necessary to settle possibilities now and make them impossibilities? What if Ellis Carpenter had never by word or look hinted a special interest in her? Neither had he, so far as she knew, to any other woman. Yet he was a young man, with his lifework fairly planned and entered. It was natural, certainly, to suppose that in due time he would single out one woman from all others—why shouldn't that one be Barbara Dennison? The thought didn't present itself so badly as that, but it lingered subtly about her.

She couldn't help recalling the number of afternoons Ellis Carpenter spent at the farm last summer and the plainly written complaints of Elinor as to the infrequency of his calls during the winter. Then, recognizing the trend of her thought, she drew herself up sharply and told herself that even little Naomi wouldn't be so silly.

At once her heart took up the interests of this young, tenderly loved friend, dear little Namie. The vigil ended in a prayer for Naomi, that the world opening so brightly before her might be all to her that this world should be and yet might not dim the prospects of that other world. And then this young woman, who was usually practical, subdued the moonlight with blinds and shades, and went to bed.

Chapter 3

"Thus are my blossoms blasted in the bud."

For pity's sake, Gertrude Fenton, what are you willing to do? If you can't wait on tables or take the tickets or do anything I plan, what are you good for? You might as well go back to school and stay there. It's just as I said. I told your father that four more years of schooling would spoil you, and it's done it. You're too fine for our kind of living, and I can't afford to dress you up and let you sit in the parlor and play on the piano—I know that. The rest of us have to work for our living. And unless you caught a rich husband out in that college where you've been for so long, I guess you'll have to do the same."

Annie Fenton laughed good-naturedly. She was nearly four years younger than her sister, Gertrude, and as unlike her in every respect as a girl could be. Blue-eyed, fair-haired, and freckled, like her mother, large-boned, with plenty of flesh, her plump figure and round good-natured face were pleasant enough to see. Annie was nearly always good-natured. She was a favorite with boarders she could joke and laugh with. She would cheerfully do her best for them, taking extra trips from dining room to kitchen to indulge their whims. In fact it was the fashion in this popular boardinghouse of the second class, for the informed to make a dash for Annie's tables.

This house Mrs. Fenton ruled with energy and success was, in fact, a semi-restaurant. Besides caring for a large class of boarders who were more or less regular, it was a house where meals of some sort could be had at all hours, and transients were almost as numerous as the regular boarders.

From being a comparatively modest little venture, when Gertrude first went away to school, it had grown to startling dimensions. And the girl fresh from college life, with her diploma in her trunk setting forth in excellent Latin, for all who could read it, that she completed her studies with satisfaction, was expected to fit into these surroundings and assume her share of the work. Nothing more utterly distasteful to her could be imagined. It wasn't simply that four years spent in a different world had unfit her for it; she was unfit for it by nature.

"She don't take after neither of us," was an explanation she'd heard her mother give many times.

"If she favors anybody, it's her pa's gentleman brother. Goodness knows, I hope she won't be like him. He's too fine for this world: everlastingly at books; spending every cent he could earn or get on 'em; and looking down on common folks who earned their living and didn't know anything about Greek and Latin and such things."

The tones Mrs. Fenton used to explain this were always peculiar. She was professedly expressing strong disapproval, and that was without doubt in her mind. But there was also a curious little undercurrent of family pride. It might be inconvenient, and on some occasions it was disagreeable to have this scholar intimately connected with their family. But at the same time she couldn't quite overlook the distinction in it. The same curious mixture of feeling had been evident in her treatment of the daughter, who was unlike the others.

"You are as like your Uncle Edward as two peas in a pod." This often repeated statement conveyed, and was meant to convey, strong objection; yet that thread of pride was woven through it. It was strange and vexatious, but also interesting, that her oldest daughter should be "bookish."

The Fentons believed life had treated them badly. The father, an excellent mechanic, with good prospects for rising to a master builder or contractor, was suddenly stopped in his prosperous career by an accident that resulted in two years of helplessness. After that, "about half of him," as he sometimes jocosely expressed it, got well. Head and arms and hands were able to resume their duties, but the lower limbs were paralyzed; the poor feet would never walk again.

During the two years Mrs. Fenton had struggled bravely, making the small sum laid aside for emergencies go as far as most women would have done and adding to it by work of all sorts as she had opportunity. But when she realized fully her husband's condition, she arose in strength and declared her determination to open a boardinghouse.

"I can cook," she affirmed, "as well as anybody. And I believe there's a living to be made in that business if a body knows how to manage. Anyhow, I'm going to try it. We can't sit around and starve because *he* is laid by."

She tried it and was eminently successful. In less than two months from the day of her first venture it began to be noised abroad: Over at that little corner house with its modest sign that read, "Board by the day, week or meal; prices reasonable," better bread and cake and coffee could be had than anywhere else in that part of town.

Mrs. Fenton's girls were small then. She kept them in school because she understood in these days that the place for children was the schoolroom. But when at fifteen Gertrude was ready for high school, her mother argued the question vigorously. She needed the child's help in the dining room; work was growing heavier there every day. And what more schooling did Gertrude need? She could write now as pretty as engraving, and there wasn't a word in the dictionary she couldn't spell. As for figures, she was quicker at them than her father. Why should she go to high school?

But the girl's heart was set upon going, and her father in his invalid chair, brisk of brain if not of feet, was on her side. "We may as well have another scholar in the family, Mother," he said, and there was undisguised pride in his tone. "Her Uncle Edward went across the water to study, and they say he's making his mark there, too. It'll be a fine thing to have a girl of ours who can match him at his books."

The mother grumbled; but that hidden pride in education she couldn't quite get rid of added its force, and she yielded. Annie took her place, very willingly, in the increasingly popular dining room, and Gertrude went to high school. She easily led her class.

The winter before her graduation her Uncle Edward came home. He was a pale, frail, scholarly man, with scarcely an idea in common with his brother or, especially, with his brother's wife. But, as the former had prophesied, he "took to" his niece. The two spent much time together, talking of books and studies. Uncle Edward spoke of the girl's acquirements and evident talent in flattering terms. He fed her ambitions and urged her not to be content with a mere high school education but to aim for a college course. When she sorrowfully told him of the difficulties before she reached the high school and of the impossibility of going farther, he looked wise.

"Don't you worry—only determine to go to college. A great deal can be accomplished if one has determination. I've proved it. When you're through with high school, we'll see what can be done."

What was done was not in accord with his plans at that time. He secured a good position as teacher, and his salary was fair. He taught for some years before he went abroad; and while in Oxford, what with writing frequent acceptable articles for the home papers and magazines, he lived his modest life without drawing very much on his savings account. He planned to set up a quiet little home and install his niece Gertrude as housekeeper, or at least as nominal head, giving her spare time to study, under his supervision, until he was ready for her to enter an advanced class in college. Instead of that, he died.

The will he left made Mrs. Fenton for a time almost too indignant to express her mind. All his savings through the years, and they looked to her like a small fortune, he left to his niece Gertrude. Mrs. Fenton admitted that since he didn't see fit to leave it to his only brother, which would have been more natural, the least he could do was to remember his own nieces. But why should he pick out one of them to have it all? And worse than all the rest, why should he tie it up in a way to be of no use to anybody? Such was Mrs. Fenton's point of view.

What he did was plan in his will that every penny of his savings should be spent for Gertrude's education. She was to go to a certain college, enter at a given time, and remain through the entire college course, the funds being carefully divided for each year and apportioned: so much for clothing and traveling, so much for college and incidental expenses. There was, he calculated, enough money to take her through the college course and support her for possibly six months afterward. He planned as wisely as he could and provided for possible obstacles in the student's way. Any deviation from the terms of the will, not caused by disability on Gertrude's part, and the money passed to a third cousin, a boy not yet in high school.

"There's no help for it, Mother," the father said from his invalid chair, in a pitiful attempt to be merry. "The girl has to have either an education or an accident that will perch her up here along with me, or else lose the money."

"Such a fool will!" said Mrs. Fenton severely.

But she said no more, and Gertrude went to college. Her uncle had reasoned that, with an education such as a girl like Gertrude Fenton would secure, six months would give her ample time to get settled into her lifework, which he was sure ought to be teaching.

But thirty girls graduated with her, and hundreds of colleges and high grade schools sent out their graduates at about the same time, and fully two-thirds of them were seeking positions as teachers. Moreover, it seemed to Gertrude that hundreds of thousands of girls and young women, without higher education or special training of any sort, were eager to teach school until they could marry and were willing to take low salaries and stoop in many ways to secure positions. Competition was everywhere. And the scholarly uncle was gone; she had no special friend to watch out for her interest.

Some days she gave in to the terror of thinking she must spend her life in that restaurant, where she was expected not only to wait on tables, but to be friendly and cheerful with those customers who liked that way of being served. Why not? Annie could do it, and Gertrude was no better than Annie. Poor Gertrude looked at her mother in perplexed silence, unable to explain to her why she shrank with inexpressible horror from a life that her sister, Annie, admitted she liked.

"There's such a lot of them to feed," explained the red-cheeked, good-natured girl, "and some of them are so full of ideas, and their ideas are all so different. It's as good as a circus, Gert, to hear them go on."

Why couldn't Gertrude take life in that way? Such was the mother's thought.

"She's all *books,* spoiled for anything useful, just as I told you she'd be." Mrs. Fenton was complaining to the father of Gertrude's revolt from the functions of the dining room. He laughed a little, sympathetically. Many days of sitting alone in his little room had given him clearer vision than some had. He was sympathetic with both currents of feeling in his wife's makeup. He distinctly felt that undercurrent of pride and heard it in the half-contemptuous emphasis she placed upon that word *books*. The pity of it was that Gertrude never understood this part.

She'd been at home for nearly three months, and they seemed to her, at times, as long as a full year at school. She was earnestly trying to fit into the home life and shoulder faithfully her share of the work. It wasn't work she shrank from. She believed she could have spent the entire days in the kitchen, baking, boiling, or frying. She was ready to scrub, wash dishes, do anything, so she might be saved from the horrors of the dining room service when the guests crowded in.

And it was in the dining room that her mother wanted her especially. The brawny-armed Irish and German workers at her command in the kitchen were stronger and also, in their way, more capable than her school-trained daughter. At times she was even in the way there, with her "fine" ideas and her temptation to "wash a dish three times" before she used it.

The mother's first plan was for her educated daughter to "dress up fine and stan' round as a sort of headwaiter; just keepin' her eyes open and puttin' in a hand here and there where it's needed, and havin' a word with this one and that one, kind of as if she was interested in makin' 'em comfortable. Easy work, enough—sight easier than schoolteachin' and a chance to keep fixed up all the time.

"If you'll do that," she said, "and take the tickets from the regulars and the pay from the others, and keep that part of the accounts straight for your father, why"—rising to the heights of magnanimity—"I'll excuse you from *work* altogether. You don't seem to be cut out for that."

So Gertrude, hiding her dismay and her reluctance as much as she could, did her best. She was prompt in her attendance in the dining room and vigilant in her attentions to the customers. They weren't compelled to ask twice for her service or to wait unduly; but she was far from giving satisfaction.

The mother tried to explain the difficulty to her bookkeeper, who never left his invalid chair and who waited each night for a history of the day's doings, while he made up the day's accounts.

Chapter 4

*"Alight with vanished faces,
And days forever done."*

She tries, Joseph. I believe the girl tries as well as she knows how. But it ain't in her. To begin with, she looks like the Queen of Sheba the whole time. I don't know how she does it. She don't wear nothing but a plain black dress and a white collar, but she looks for all the world as if she's dressed for a party. And the boys are afraid of her. She doesn't ever say a pleasant word to them, you know, as Annie does, or laugh a little and make them feel at home and satisfied with themselves. She's just as serious as if it was a meetinghouse and she was the preacher. They look at one another when she comes down the room, and they nudge each other's elbows and stop their chatter and act half scared. She'll thin out the room for us as sure as the world, and I'm at my wits' ends."

So was Gertrude. The day she rebelled and begged to stay in the pantry and cut pie and fill up bread plates, or go to the kitchen and scrub the floor, or do anything but serve in that terrible dining room, was the day Mr. Perkins from the variety store, and the acknowledged wag at his table, attempted a weak joke with her. The way she looked at him in reply made him color to the roots of his hair. After that dinner was over, she fled to her mother with the result described.

The sense of aloneness was never stronger upon the girl than when she sat that afternoon in the upper back room she and Annie shared. While Annie, downstairs in the kitchen, sang cheerily at her work, Gertrude went over in detail her woeful present and contrasted it with her recent beautiful past. She let a few tears drop on her folded hands in the hope that their fall might ease the pain of disappointment and humiliation at her heart. What a failure she was! Her poor uncle, who saved and sacrificed for her, would be disappointed if he could know what she was doing with her life.

As the days went by her hope of getting a situation as a teacher sank lower. The schools had all opened now. She must wait for another year, at least. But how was she to live for a whole year the life that now hedged her in?

It was impossible to make her mother understand how she hated the role that was planned for her with the belief she was being given the easy place in which she could be "fixed up" all the time. The girl's lip curled as she recalled the phrase that seemed to mean so much to her mother and Annie. She hated the neat dress she wore, since it must be put on for the purpose of entertaining the "guests"; that, in her mother's mind, meant listening to their puns and laughing and bantering with those who chose to notice her. If she could serve real men and real women, who would know enough not to notice her at all, she told herself, except by way of business, she wouldn't mind. But to be stared at and even complimented to her face and to be expected to laugh and respond—she loathed it.

Oh, the contrast between this life and the four beautiful years standing in the near background! What would Barbara and Bernice and dear little Naomi think if they could glimpse her home life? She had been very reticent about home matters. Oh, they knew; she hadn't kept silence over the fact that they were poor, that her father was an invalid and that her mother supported the family by keeping boarders. They knew how strong her ambitions were to make life easier for her father and mother by her salary. But there are various ways of keeping boarders. Gertrude didn't consider it necessary to enter into details as to her mother's way, nor did she say very much about Annie.

Although she was reticent about her own environment, she knew, or thought she knew, all about the others' home life. She felt a pang of something like jealousy as she recalled those friends and told herself how much they had to make life blessed.

There was Barbara Dennison, living among the grand hills of New England, on a farm of wide stretching acres in the quaint old farmhouse to which her mother had come as a bride. Every window of the rambling old house, Gertrude was sure from the photograph she had seen, commanded views that must remind them all the time of the wonders of the eternal city.

She believed that life on a farm in daily communion with nature led one closer, of necessity, to nature's God. It was the most interesting, as well as the most independent, way of making a living—just to plant seed, in soil that God's rain and sunshine prepared and into whose heart He Himself had hidden the life principle, and then to stand aside and see Him work His miracle of growth and development and maturity. People so living could hardly be coarse, she thought, or sordid. It was *very* different from living where one's outlook was rows of tall chimneys or more brick houses, and the sounds that greeted the ear were the endless clatter of dishes and the endless chatter of silly tongues.

Barbara didn't even need to teach school for a living. Her family wanted her at home, were looking forward to her coming. The blessed earth furnished them with food enough and to spare. They took no boarders and could live as they would and be happy in one another. Barbara was going to teach for the love of it, as people should, and not because she must.

Then there was Bernice, who lived in that lovely town too small to be called a city, yet large enough to have the advantages and escape the discomforts of city life. Gertrude gazed a long time at the picture of their large stone house set in a square of greenery, its stone seeming to speak to her of dignity and repose.

"Oh, no, we're not rich," Bernice told them, with complacency in her tone. And she told of brothers who idolized her and who considered it foolish for her to think of teaching. They spared her from home for her college course, and that was enough. They would see to it that she and her mother had every comfort money and love could furnish.

As for Naomi, dear little Namie! She lived in California, and her father was chief owner in a gold mine and heavily interested in a copper mine, and was a bank director and a railroad magnate, and Gertrude didn't know how many other vast interests he represented. But she knew that Naomi, the only child, had more money even now than she knew how to spend and that she had only to hint at a wish to have it gratified.

Would they love her less, those three dear girls, if they could look in upon her in her stuffy little room, dominated everywhere by Annie's belongings and Annie's tastes, and scented at that moment by the ham being boiled for the next day's needs? Would they care just as much for her, if they knew? Gertrude repelled indignantly the thought that they wouldn't; she was loyal to her friends. Nevertheless, her sensitive face flushed over her surroundings. For now she was glad they were so far away from her, and living such different lives, that a visit from any of them in the near future was unlikely.

She recalled Naomi's cherished scheme that wedding bells from any quarter should summon them all from far, and she smiled in dreary sarcasm over the impossibility of her journeying to California, for instance, to see little Namie married.

"I'll write to her," she said, "that she must try to get me a situation in Washington or Oregon and then wait for her wedding day until I've earned enough to buy me a gown, or I can't come."

And then her mother's voice broke in upon her unprofitable thoughts, and her mother, without knocking, pushed open her door almost in time to see the tears.

"Where are you, Gertie? What you doing? I wonder if you can't go over to Mathers' a little while in my place? They've sent for me to come and stay while the doctor is there, and I'm that tuckered out with the canning and the extra things that it doesn't seem as if I can go yet. I've got to have a little let-up before I pitch into the dinner. All they want is somebody with a head on her shoulders to tend to that doctor. He knows all there is to know in life, that doctor does, and more too, he thinks. They want somebody to obey his orders and take his directions. Mrs. Mather is so scared and worried over the baby that she hasn't got more than half her wits about her, and that Mamie who's helping 'em isn't worth a piece of tissue paper. Do you s'pose you could go for a spell?"

Gertrude stood up when her mother entered and changed her dress, as soon as she understood the nature of her call. She was more than willing to give the needed help. The Mathers had become their neighbors a few weeks earlier. They were in moderate—now that illness had come upon them, almost in straitened—circumstances, and the little child was very ill. Gertrude had wished more than once, during her last year in college, that she had turned her attention and training toward nursing. She was "a born nurse," the girls at school assured her, and she herself believed she had native talents of worth in that line. To escape from getting dinner for no one ever knew just how many people, would be a distinct relief to Gertrude, even though the escape was by way of a sickroom.

"I'll go, Mother, and be glad to do it," she said cheerfully. "Don't you want to lie down on our bed and get a little rest while I'm away?"

"Me lie down in the daytime!" exclaimed the burdened mother. "When I do that, you may send for the lordly doctor to tend me, for I'll be sick, sure. I'll get my rest peeling the apples and sorting over the beans for tomorrow. But I can sit down to that, thank goodness." Nevertheless, she liked the touch of consideration in her daughter's words and manner.

"Education didn't spoil her heart, anyhow," she said to herself, as the door closed after Gertrude. The thought had in it a hint that in all other respects the girl had been spoiled; and yet it was tinged with motherly tenderness and pride.

Dr. Adams gave one swift glance to the strange young woman who stood at his elbow, waiting for orders, then he issued them. "A dish of boiling water, please. Boiling, remember, not merely hot. Be as quick as possible. I shall want ice water, also, a bowlful. Let me have that vial, Mrs. Mather, please, and the flannel compress I used yesterday."

His manner was courteous and his voice evenly pitched, but it held a masterful note that made Gertrude understand what her mother meant by saying he "owned the earth." The child was desperately ill—that was evident even to one unskilled—and the doctor was fighting for a bit of hope, but he fought well. The frightened mother watched for his words, for his glance, with an eagerness pitiful to see, and he didn't forget her. He smiled when the child swallowed the drops of liquid he gave her and said cheerfully, "She swallows better than she did this morning; that's quite encouraging."

When he received the water from Gertrude, he asked, "Are you the one who's to help me? Are you a trained nurse? No? Then take hold of the sheet at this end, and do just as I tell you."

An anxious and busy half hour followed. When the physician's skill and care had accomplished all they could, and he was preparing to leave, he turned to Gertrude, who had obeyed him as silently as an automaton, and asked, "Are you to watch here tonight? Can you? Do so, please, if you can; it will be a critical night. Trained service is needed, but so far we've been unable to secure it. You'll answer, however, for I see you can do as you're told. If you can be here tonight, I'll come in later and give you explicit directions."

When Gertrude went home, the house still smelled of ham, with the odor of onions added. She caught her breath as she entered the hall from the outside air, thinking even the odor of disinfectants was preferable to this. Her mother received her deprecatingly. She'd meant to get over there long ago, but one thing after another hindered her. Yes, she "sort of" promised to sit up that night; the doctor hadn't found anyone else he thought would do. She was astonished to learn that Gertrude was willing to take her place.

"Are you sure you can keep awake?" she asked. "Annie can't; she goes right off to sleep as soon as she sits down and keeps still. I think the baby is right sick. I ain't had any hope of her from the first, and she may die in the night. Hadn't I better go? It'll be hard on you if she does."

Gertrude looked at the worn face of her mother who had been hard at work since an hour before daybreak. She suddenly felt respect for a woman who, freighted with her own cares and responsibilities, could so patiently shoulder the burdens of others. She was glad to take her mother's place, giving her the night's rest she needed.

Two days afterward, while Gertrude was piling generous slices of home-made bread on the plates for the midday meal, Annie dashed in from the dining room. Her voice was louder and more excited than usual.

"Mother! Don't you think that swell doctor has come here for his lunch! He's taken a seat at that middle table on the left, and he looks as if he meant to order turkey and lobster salad. Gert, you'll have to go right in and wait on him. Just looking at him scares me—he's so awful swell!"

"Dear me!" said the mother in a flurry. "I hope he'll get what he likes. If them kind of folks would come oftener, we could afford to raise our prices. Gertie, you'll see to him and fix him up nice, won't you? That's a good girl."

But Gertrude was unaccountably irritated and spoke in her haughtiest tone. "I shall treat him exactly as I do others, of course."

The color flamed into her face as she spoke, and knowing this increased her annoyance. For a night and a day she had served under Dr. Adams's orders, obeying them carefully, but to serve him lunch in her mother's house, for pay, was quite another matter. She shrank from the ordeal and was ashamed she did so. But he'd seated himself at a table she was serving, so without more words she went to her task.

Dr. Adams didn't even look up. He was absorbed in a letter and gave his order mechanically, pausing in the midst of it with his mind evidently on the page before him. After waiting a reasonable time, Gertrude felt compelled to recall him to the business at hand with a question. Then he glanced at her in surprise and immediately spoke of their common interest.

"Why, good morning! The child is distinctly better. I may almost say, past the danger line."

"I'm glad," said Gertrude, putting into her voice the joy she felt. It was good to have this battle with a common enemy end in unexpected victory. Others besides her mother were hopeless.

"Yes," he said genially, "so am I. That poor little mother needs her baby. She has many burdens. It was good of you to give her your timely and skillful help; she owes much to you."

Gertrude's face flushed, but she explained quickly. "I merely took my mother's place for a little while. I know nothing about nursing. Will you have coffee, Dr. Adams?"

"One wouldn't have suspected it by the way you handled the case. I wouldn't care for better help than you gave me. No coffee, thank you; cold water, please."

Behind the glass doors Annie was watching and giggling. "What an age you were taking his order!" she began. "And he talked all the while! I guess he came here in search of you instead of lunch. Say, Ma, look at her cheeks."

Gertrude was even more angry to know they flamed.

"I wish you wouldn't be coarse, at least." The words seemed to say themselves; she hadn't meant to make them audible.

"Hoity-toity!" said the mother, instantly jealous for her younger daughter. "Annie didn't mean any harm. Don't you go to putting on too many airs, even if you have caught a beau. You had just as many as her and me could stan' before."

Annie laughed good-naturedly.

"Never mind, Ma," she said. "We ain't college educated, you and me, and I s'pose we do bother her some. I don't mind, Gert. I ain't thin-skinned."

This last was in reply to Gertrude's soft-spoken "I beg your pardon, Annie." At that moment the college-bred girl felt distinctly inferior to her sister. She, under provocation, kept her temper.

Chapter 5

"Let's love a season,
But let that season be only spring."

T he lawn looked like a flower garden. Its carpet of thick, velvety grass was dotted over with bright color: pinks and blues, and lavender and white, with here and there a touch of vivid yellow. The girls were out in summer glory.

Conspicuous among them, distinctly the queen of the hour in the eyes of more than her fond mother, was Bernice Halsted.

It had been a tennis, and was now a garden, party. The young women, flushed from exercise, reclined on cushions and brightly colored afghans in lovely pretense of fatigue. Attentive young men were serving them ices and wafers.

From a shaded window that overlooked the scene and protected her from view Mrs. Halsted watched her daughter's every movement with appreciative eyes. How pretty she was, and how graceful! That last year at school had added just the touch of womanliness the child needed. It made her more fascinating than ever, while suggesting to her acquaintances that she was no longer a child to be played with but was grown-up.

The young men seemed to realize it. They hovered about her. They served the guests courteously enough, but they were eager to serve the young hostess. Mrs. Halsted watched especially "that artist youth," as she called young Davenport. From being a boy in their midst, he had recently returned from a four-year stay in Europe, an artist "of decided talent," the local newspapers said when they heralded his coming.

As Mrs. Halsted observed his marked attentions to her daughter, her face, shielded as it was by the network of climbing vines, gathered in a disapproving frown. Frank Davenport might be well enough; he came from a good family and had always been respected in the community. But he was poor and would of course remain so. The phrase "a struggling young artist" had a certain distinction of its own. But how would it sound when that ugly word *old* took the place of *young,* and the struggle continued? Mrs. Halsted knew that such was the rule and the exceptions were not many.

She wasn't mercenary. She often expressed herself as "truly thankful" that she cared very little about money. She asked only that they had enough to be comfortable. Of course, her ideas of what was required to make one comfortable would have differed from many.

Neither was she a matchmaker. Heaven knew the last thing she desired was to give up Bernice, now that she had her again after a sacrifice of four years. But girls married generally. Since Bernice would probably be like the rest, it was a matter of ordinary common sense to watch her associates and choose her friends with discrimination.

And this careful mother, as she watched the groups in the garden, almost settled it that her visiting list was already long enough and need not be enlarged to take in the name of Frank Davenport's mother. That good woman, though eminently respectable, had never been classed among those who received and paid formal calls; why should she be now that her son had returned?

George Wilbur probably brought the young man with him today, without any formal invitation. George often took liberties with her; probably he felt he had a right to do so, since his friendship with them was of such long standing. She didn't pause to reflect that she'd known Frank Davenport even longer; that wouldn't have been to the point.

Of all the young men who moved about her spacious grounds that afternoon Mrs. Halsted knew that George Wilbur was her favorite. The others were well enough; in fact, unexceptionable, of course, as became her daughter's friends. But George was—there was really nothing left to be desired for George.

Most of the other young men had their way to make in the world. For a number of them the way ahead looked prosperous enough. They were established in good positions or professions, with every prospect of advancement before them. If one excepted Frank Davenport, there really wasn't another who needed to awaken anxiety on that ground. But George's place in the world was already made by his father. George didn't need to lift his finger unless he chose; his father's millions were sure to become his eventually and were lavished freely upon him now. It spoke volumes for the young man's character, she thought, that he chose to be a lawyer; it proved he had no intention of living an idler's life.

George and Bernice had been intimate friends from their childhood. Since he'd grown to manhood he had many intimate friends among the ladies. He didn't hesitate to say that he enjoyed the ladies' society and found them more interesting than men. Certainly with none had he been more intimate than with Bernice.

The mother, behind her screening vines, watched the two and reflected over the years. Was there a touch of difference in his manner to her this afternoon? Did he, too, see plainly that when Bernice was at home last she had been one of "the girls" and now she had blossomed into young womanhood?

He was certainly watching young Davenport with eyes that didn't express a high opinion of that rising artist. She wondered if he felt he was foolish in bringing the large-eyed youth into paradise with him that afternoon. It would be curious and interesting if George should really be growing jealous. But it wouldn't do for Bernice to be careless. He was too popular, and too much given to having his will, to brook interference.

The garden party was breaking up. One after another of the bright bits of color flitted away with black-coated attendants. One or two carriages rolled up and carried away others. Young Davenport lingered as long as he could, until someone called to take him reluctantly to another engagement. At last, to Mrs. Halsted's quiet satisfaction, only Bernice and George Wilbur were left on the lawn. He had his hat in his hand and might be making his adieux. She waited until the last other guest was out of sight, then parted the vines and glanced out.

"Daughter, won't some of your friends stay to dinner with us? I think I might have my share of this garden party. Why, have they all gone?"

"No, Mother, one tardy guest hears your hospitable intent."

"And he was waiting in the hope of getting an invitation to stay," said the young man quickly. "I'm the sole representative, Mrs. Halsted. Will I do, or is such an insignificant part of the brilliant scene worse than nothing?"

Mrs. Halsted laughed indulgently.

"It's you, is it, George? Stay to dinner, by all means. I'm sorry I was so tardy with my invitation that no others are here to keep you company. But Bernice and I evidently need you. The train is in, and my boys haven't come. They told me they were afraid of being kept in town until late. If you don't take pity on us, Bernice and I will be forced to a tete-a-tete dinner."

He needed no urging, he assured her, and put aside his hat and arranged an afghan and five sofa pillows under the great oak with such alacrity that the mother's heart was glad. She pushed open the casement and stepped out on the lawn to enjoy a closer view of her daughter. Mrs. Halsted was very fond of her three grown sons, but she couldn't help being glad they were kept in town that evening. There was something very cozy and interesting in sitting down to a table set for three, with George Wilbur at her right and her beautiful daughter opposite her.

George's table manners were like all things about him—perfect. He did the honors which fell to him with more ease and grace than many hosts. Mrs. Halsted's satisfaction in the occasion was so evident that she felt she must explain it.

"You don't know what it is to me to have her again," she said, turning her beaming glance from daughter to guest.

"Don't I? I know what it is to the rest of us who've been shut away from the light of her countenance for—how long is it? Two years?"

"Just nine months and two days," said Bernice, with smiling composure.

"Is that possible? I will appeal to your mother to know if it isn't almost two years since we had our last lawn party together."

"It's only nine months," said Mrs. Halsted. "I know by the calendar; I marked the date on it. But I agree with you that it seems more like two years. Children have no idea what their absence means to their mothers, and I have only the one daughter."

"I know something about it," the guest said heartily. "It's wonderful how mothers reach out after their children, even when the child is nothing but a son. In his mother's eyes he is beyond rubies. I'm my mother's only son, you know. But Bernice has no idea of the large space she leaves desolate. I thought of that on Sunday. To hear her voice again in the music is something she can't appreciate. If she could come invisibly to this town, at the same time she's absent in body, she'd have some idea of what we've sacrificed through these years. But I'm afraid she doesn't care. If this whole town were in mourning for her, so that she could be with those three friends I'm distinctly jealous of, I don't think she'd give us a thought."

Bernice laughed easily, despite a heightened color on her face.

"I care very little for the town," she said, "as compared with my dear girls." And she thought she was speaking truth. So long as George Wilbur made himself merely one of her acquaintances and spoke of them in masses, she might affirm that her school friends were dearer to her than any others.

"There! What did I tell you?" he said triumphantly. "Mrs. Halsted, I hope you won't aid and abet your daughter's scheme to get those three young women to this part of the world. I feel that I shall disapprove of them all."

"I'm afraid Barbara and Gertrude are hopeless," said Bernice. "They have home duties that I imagine will hold them, but little Naomi flits about wherever she chooses. I shouldn't be surprised to see her anytime. I'd like you to know her," she added, with sudden earnestness.

She looked thoughtfully at the face of their guest and tried to guess what effect little Naomi's dainty beauty and winsome ways would have on him. There was a sudden thrill in her heart that was almost like jealousy. Would she be afraid to have those two meet? But she answered her thought instantly. Afraid! Of what? If there was a woman living for whom he could care more than for her, did she want his love? He might be the one man on earth for whom she could ever care very much—she was afraid he was—but unless he were equally sure of himself, she wanted none of him.

He was prompt to reply.

"I haven't the least desire to know her. What a disagreeable name she has, by the way. 'Naomi.' I once had an old aunt who bore that name, and it fit her well. She was fully as lugubrious as it sounds."

"There's nothing lugubrious about my Naomi," said Bernice, with emphasis. "She's charming, and everybody who comes in contact with her feels the charm. Mama, will you write and invite her to spend the winter with us, so George can see for himself how lovely she is?"

"Don't, please," said George. "I'm entirely satisfied with the prospects of my winter as it opens before me. I want no other charm than I already have, and I have a feeling that this Naomi would be distinctly in the way."

"That's a Bible name," said Mrs. Halsted. "Why didn't they call her 'Mara'? That's prettier."

"And that would have relieved her of the alliteration," George added. "Isn't her last name Newland? Naomi Newland, think of it! I detest alliterations."

" 'Mara' wouldn't have suited her," said Bernice. "Doesn't it mean bitterness or trouble or something like that? No shadow of trouble ought to touch her bright nature. We were always planning happiness for Naomi; she seems made for it."

"Then I predict she'll wade through seas of trouble," George Wilbur said confidently. "She'll marry some wretch, probably. These butterfly creatures made for sunshine always get their wings injured early."

"Naomi is no butterfly," said Bernice, half indignantly. "And I don't believe the wretch lives who is mean enough to cause her an hour of unnecessary sorrow. Wait until you know her, and you'll understand."

He didn't want to know her, he protested. He already knew ladies enough to keep him constantly distracted. He returned to the subject when they were left together on the porch, while Mrs. Halsted received a caller. He asked many questions about her friend, with the air of one who thought he was gratifying his companion. Suddenly he broke in on one of her replies.

"Do you realize, Bernice, the reason why I don't care to know her or any other young woman? It's because I'm more than satisfied with one. I wonder if you know her name. If you had a spark of vanity in your composition, you'd have guessed it long ago. Don't you really know, dear girl, the name of the one woman in the world for me?"

Chapter 6

"We know not what we do when we speak words."

Gertrude Fenton's somewhat romantic ideas as to farm life would have received a setback had she shared her friend Barbara Dennison's home for a few weeks. Mr. Dennison's acres were far-reaching enough and highly cultivated. The barns and outbuildings were ample, and the stock generally was all that could be desired.

But the rambling old house, with all its picturesqueness and its many charming views of river and hill and valley, could have been improved in numberless ways. It was built when people's ideas of comfort differed materially from the present ones, and it hadn't kept up, as the stables had, for instance, with the march of improvement. The dairy had running water, but for the kitchen it had to be pumped in the old-fashioned way. This one item will illustrate many others.

Mr. Dennison had that curious mixture of narrowness and broadness that a certain kind of farm life often develops. He mingled with men and affairs enough to have advanced ideas as to farming and intelligent views regarding many questions of the day. In public he was spoken of as a prosperous man and a worthy citizen, with reasonably progressive ideas. In his home life he remained narrow.

The small economies necessary in his youth became habits by the time he prospered so well he might have given them up. He still considered it wasteful to use cream freely at the family table; even milk, at certain seasons, should be dealt out sparingly. When his wife's excellent butter brought forty cents a pound in the market, it seemed wanton extravagance to this man to use many pounds of it at home. It was the same with eggs when prices were high. As for fruits, only the unmarketable should ever appear on the home table.

By similar reasoning he thought it foolish to pay out money for hired help in the kitchen, when he had two grown daughters to share the work with his capable wife. When Barbara went away to school, economy was needed more, with heavy school bills twice a year. Moreover, of course, there was less work with one family member away. So the mother and the older daughter, Elinor, shouldered the burdens between them and didn't complain; at least the mother didn't, for a lifetime's habits were upon her.

This family lived much as their farmer neighbors about them did, regardless of the fact that no such highly cultivated fields and blooded stock and secure bank accounts were connected with any other farms in the neighborhood. Mr. Dennison's curious mixture of character showed plainly in his ideas about education. He associated with the outside world and read enough to believe reasonably in the higher education not only of men, but of women, if they wanted it.

"I should never oblige a boy of mine to go to college," he was fond of explaining. "But if he really wanted to go and had brains enough for it, I'd open the way. And I don't know why I shouldn't do the same for my girls, since I haven't anybody."

When Barbara showed early not only the brains, but an intense desire for a college course, her father was proud of her and bravely planned for the necessary expenditures. Since the expense seemed very great, he was heartily glad his daughter Elinor wasn't so inclined and was content with the education in the common school.

He impressed it upon Barbara that she'd be having more than her share during those royal four years and that she must come back prepared to make up for it. A college education ought to command a good salary as a teacher. They paid forty dollars a month in the upper district, and the young woman who taught there wasn't college-bred either. Mr. Dennison's farm education led him to believe that forty dollars, in what he called "hard money," meant a great deal. Counted in stock or land it was a mere nothing.

To such a home Barbara returned from her college life. Because of the pressure she felt, compelling her to work as soon as possible, she had, without waiting for better opportunities, accepted the vacant school in their own district, which before this was taught by a man and paid fifty dollars a month. She was to be boarded at home for three dollars a week and to be carried to and from the school each day.

To Mr. Dennison's mind this was a liberal offer, and viewed from some standpoints it was. The three dollars a week rather more than paid the wages of the stout girl who was hired to take Barbara's place in the farm kitchen; for the mother was ailing and didn't seem able to get along any longer without more help. Barbara's indignation over the fact that her small overworked mother was compelled to work at all these days, was growing with her years and her powerlessness to change the conditions.

But for one obstacle she would have refused the school with its generous salary and stayed in the kitchen, using her trained mind to make the day's toil easier. She believed she could influence her mother and manage her father so that, in time, the old kitchen stove would be exchanged for a modern range; the whole house would be piped to bring them water from the excellent spring which now supplied the cattle; and a dozen other much-needed improvements would be a question of short time. The obstacle was Elinor.

Barbara, with her logical mind and pleasant ways, might manage her mother and coax her father, but she could neither coax nor manage Elinor. That young woman, who was in her twenty-seventh year, had a mind of her own and a sharp tongue with which to express it; and her ways were never Barbara's ways.

It may almost be said that she didn't believe in Barbara. In secret she resented the idea of her sister's superior education as being in some sense a reflection upon her, although she had by no means desired it for herself. She had a way of doing everything in the kitchen and out of it exactly opposite to Barbara's ways. She was given to tossing her head and sneering at Barbara's opinions regarding practical life, assuring her that such ideas belonged in books and wouldn't apply elsewhere.

Nor were household matters the only things in which they differed. Elinor was popular in a way in the society she gathered about her, and her manner of entertaining guests didn't always agree with Barbara's ideas of propriety. These ideas were invariably sneered at as "educated whims."

Barbara discovered the adverse atmosphere of the home during her long vacations and would have tried to secure a school in another district, so she might board away from home. Two objections, however, offered themselves to this course.

In the first place, she longed to try to put a little more brightness into her weary, fading mother's life. They were so used to seeing her at work, that none of them, least of all the father, realized she'd worked too hard. The father and Elinor didn't realize it now, but Barbara's eyes were open. She thought she saw ways in which, despite Elinor's antagonism, she could be helpful.

The other reason was that another district would have meant another church, and Barbara wanted, more than anything else, to attend her home church. So failing to find at once a better opening elsewhere, she withdrew her application, giving up a hopeful outlook for the near future, to take charge of the school in the home district.

"There!" said Elinor Dennison one evening as the family rose from the supper table. "Mr. Carpenter is tying his horse at the gate. That's what I expected now. Twice in one week; it seems natural, though he came every day last summer. Wasn't it every day, Barbara? We had no trouble keeping count of his calls after you left, I know. I'm going to congratulate him on discovering again that we live in this neighborhood."

Fortunately the guest was at the door, leaving no time for reply; otherwise Barbara, in her haste and annoyance, might have said words needing repentance. As it was, fear of what her outspoken sister might say and awareness that she was being closely watched made Barbara's greeting extremely formal and kept her restrained and unnatural during the visit. She was taken to task for it as soon as the guest went his way.

"I wouldn't think a college-bred young lady needs to be so embarrassed over having a call from a man—that would be enough for an ignorant country girl like me. You blushed till your face looked like a peony, and you were as stiff as if you'd been put into splints and were afraid to bend. Didn't you notice, Mother, how absurd she was? I wouldn't want to let a man know I thought so much of him."

The flash in Barbara's eyes led her usually quiet mother to speak with unwonted spirit.

"Nonsense, Elinor! Why do you want to nag at Barbara? I didn't notice that she acted any different from usual. Of course Mr. Carpenter will come oftener now that she's home. She takes an interest in the Sunday school and the young people and is ready to help—and that you'd never do."

"No," said Elinor, "I don't have Barbara's reasons for being devoted to church work. And I don't see what she admires in Mr. Carpenter. But she's quite welcome to him; he's too proper for me."

Elinor Dennison liked to torture in this way. As the days passed, Barbara often found it nothing less than torture. The young pastor, enthusiastic in his work, had immediately involved Barbara in plans for developing his young people, and he found such obvious reasons for consulting with her that they didn't need to be named "excuses," as Elinor called them. Some of the many schemes would have heartily included Elinor, and more than one effort was made to enlist her.

But she remained aloof from church work with caustic dignity, assuring the pastor she wasn't good enough to "pose" in that line, and contented herself with being alert to "tease" Barbara. That was what their father called it, and he saw in it only the kind of "fun" prevalent in the neighborhood. Neither the father nor the mother had any idea of the suffering their younger daughter was enduring at her sister's hands. For that matter, Elinor herself likely didn't understand what she was doing.

For the most part Barbara suffered in silence. First, because she realized that whatever she might say could be twisted in a way to add fuel to her sister's "fun." The second reason of forbearance—Barbara admitted with humiliation that it was second—grew out of her honest effort to control her naturally sarcastic tongue and to establish more sisterly relations between Elinor and her.

But life was by no means all discomfort to her. School duties were demanding, and before the winter was well under way she became certain she should fully earn even the fifty dollars a month that seemed so much to the board of trustees. As the weeks passed, she got control of the turbulent element in the schoolroom and aroused in some of her students an interest in and enthusiasm for their studies to which they were strangers before. The work became so fascinating then that she found herself saying one day to that inner self of hers with whom she often talked: "I believe I was designed to be a teacher. What if, after all, I make it my lifework?"

She was instantly glad that Elinor's keen eyes weren't there to note the flush this thought brought to her face. What did that phrase "after all" cover?

But Barbara was growing more frank with herself. It seemed reasonable to her that the minister, who was deeply interested in her pupils and who almost daily expressed his joy that she was their teacher, should have some interest in her, for her own sake.

He never called at the schoolhouse or the farmhouse without having in mind some plan connected with their work together that he was eager to discuss, but that was as it should be. She wanted nothing better of life than to be able to work with and for him in his chosen field. Was there anything better in the world than that?

By degrees, as her school and church duties multiplied, and her friendship with Mr. Carpenter grew, Elinor's tongue hurt her sister less and less. Even the broad hints, that it was high time for details, didn't stab Barbara as she once supposed such talk must. When Elinor said, "For my part, I think it would be much more sensible for him to say out and out that he wanted to marry you, and set the day, than it is to set all the tongues in the congregation talking, with nothing definite to talk about," Barbara was able to reply with a semblance of indifference.

"I think Mr. Carpenter gives his congregation a great deal to talk about! And so much to do that one would think they'd have no time for idle gossip. He came last night to plan the new committee for Christmas. I wish you'd let us put you on that committee, Elinor. You could be such a help to us. You do just the kind of work that's needed better than anyone else in the congregation."

"Thank you for nothing!" said Elinor with unusual brusqueness. "When you're actually the pastor's wife will be quite time enough for you to go around hunting humdrum roles for your ordinary members to fit into. You can remember then, what I'm telling you now, that I refuse to be fit in anywhere, and I'm not one bit hoodwinked by all this parade of church work and school interests. I'd think more of him, and of you too, if you did your courting in a commonsense way like other people, without forever inventing excuses for it."

Chapter 7

"I, too, was sorely hurt this day,
But no one knows."

Others in Mr. Carpenter's congregation evidently thought as Elinor Dennison did. One evening Mrs. Barbour, with whom the minister boarded, spoke her mind. Her opportunity was a rare one. Mr. Carpenter was so late that the other boarders had left, and Mrs. Barbour served him herself. Then she sat down to enjoy this unusual chance while he ate his supper. She was nerved for the occasion by a conversation at the Ladies' Aid that afternoon. As a matter of fact, she'd promised to secure certain much-desired information the first chance she had. So she went straight to the point.

"Well, Mr. Carpenter, when's it to be? I think you might let us ladies know a good while beforehand, because—I don't mind telling you there're a good many little things we'd like to do for your comfort, and hers too, if you give us time enough."

Mr. Carpenter's face flushed slightly as he showed his astonishment for a moment, but he spoke in his usual congenial manner. "That sounds friendly and pleasant, Mrs. Barbour, though mysterious. You leave me quite in the dark as to the 'it' that I'm supposed to be guarding in secret. Won't you speak plainly?"

"Oh, well, now! Mr. Carpenter, of course you know just as well as I do that I'm talking about your getting married. Even though you haven't confided in any of us, we can't help having eyes in our heads. It's plain enough that sometime or other, and before long I'd say, you mean to get married. We were thinking it seemed foolish to keep the date a secret any longer. Nothing else about it is secret. And if you once spoke out, you and she wouldn't have to keep busy inventing excuses for being together."

The sentence closed with a little half-apologetic laugh. But the minister's face was serious, and the flush had faded from it. Indeed, Mrs. Barbour saw with uneasiness that it had grown pale and troubled. He had a bit of cold chicken on his fork, and he held it poised and looked at Mrs. Barbour like a man startled out of a calm.

"Perhaps you're right," he said at last. "I may not have made my private affairs as plain to the congregation in general as would have been wise. I'll consider your advice, Mrs. Barbour. Thank you."

He left the chicken uneaten, drained his glass of milk, and arose from the table, declining her eager offer to make him a bit of nice toast if he didn't feel like eating the bread and to bring two other kinds of cake if he didn't want that on the table.

"He acted real odd," Mrs. Barbour explained to a member of the Ladies' Aid, who dropped in to see her a little later. "I was taken aback. If he'd told me I was meddling with what didn't concern me, I'd feel better than I do now. He wasn't disagreeable a bit, but he seemed startled and kind of hurt. I told Joel he acted for all the world like a boy surprised into something he didn't mean to do."

"He didn't mean folks should know about it, not till he got ready to tell 'em," explained her neighbor. "Them kind of make-believe frank folks are always closemouthed about their own affairs."

"But good land!" said Mrs. Barbour. "What did the man expect? Hasn't he been running there steady ever since she got home? He's talking about selling his horse to the milkman and getting a new one. Joel heard he wanted a carriage horse. That sounds like getting ready for two, doesn't it? What should he want of a carriage, a man all alone and so fond of horseback riding? I told the milkman if he bought the minister's horse there would be two places he could be trusted to deliver milk all by himself: the Dennison farm and the schoolhouse in that district. He's gone there this minute, I guess. He saddled his horse within half an hour of the supper that he didn't eat and galloped off in that direction. I s'pose he'll go and tell her all I said, and she'll think I'm a meddlesome old woman. I wish I'd held my tongue."

Did the minister wish so? He didn't go directly to the Dennison farm. Instead, he took the roughest road he could find and galloped hard and fast, paying no attention to his horse's suggestions to stop at certain places for calls. It was eight o'clock when a horse who bore the marks of having been ridden hard succeeded in doing what he thought was the only sensible thing done that evening; namely, stopping before a familiar post at the Dennison gateway.

Mr. Carpenter knew there was a party in the neighborhood to which Barbara had declined and Elinor accepted an invitation. So, although he'd made no engagement with her for the evening, he hoped to find Barbara alone. Elinor's fondness for neighborhood evening gatherings had enabled him thus far to talk over with Barbara their many plans for church work, without being trammeled by her sister's mocking tongue. Mr. Dennison was an early riser and a hard worker, and he and his wife liked to retire early. The minister, as he thought of these details during his ride that evening, set his lips once or twice and told himself he'd been a fool.

The stout girl installed in the kitchen in Barbara's stead was on her way upstairs to bed when Mr. Carpenter's ring intercepted her. She smiled warmly at him and, without waiting for a question, said, "She's home. She's in the settin' room all alone. Walk right in."

Something in her tone made the color flame for the second time that evening into the minister's sensitive face.

"I'm glad to find you alone," he said abruptly. "I was hoping to because there's something I want to tell you. Something I've looked forward to telling you, when a convenient hour should come. I'd like to tell it now. May I?"

The book Barbara still held in her lap trembled visibly, and her eyes held a look that might have troubled the minister had he seen it. He didn't wait for her murmured word that she'd be glad to hear whatever he had to tell but dashed into the center of things.

"You may wonder that I haven't told you before, since we've been so closely associated in church work. I've had the story almost on my lips a number of times, but something else intervened."

Barbara knew at once what Elinor would say could she hear the manner in which this young man was wooing her sister. She could almost hear Elinor's sneer that he was far too certain of his answer to suit her tastes. But their tastes were different, and this was something Elinor would never hear.

The minister hurried on.

"First, I want to show you a picture." He drew a small photograph from his breast pocket. "It's a shadow, and not at all a satisfactory shadow, of a face that is dearer to me than any other."

Could he be speaking of his mother? Barbara reached for the picture and studied the face. It was that of a woman, young and beautiful. The dress was modern; it could hardly be a picture of his mother in her youth. Barbara felt herself trembling and felt an instinct that made her want to hide the fact.

"It's a beautiful face," she said, struggling to speak in her usual tone.

"Does it impress you so? What else do you see in the face? It belongs to one who's beautiful in character as well as in feature. It's a joy to me to believe you'll know and love her one day."

A sudden light glowed in Barbara's face, and a strange tightness about her heart gave way.

It's his sister! she told herself eagerly. *That's why the face looks familiar to me; it resembles him. It's his only sister, and he means to make a home for her someday.*

"I think it would be easy to love her," she said out loud, and the minister noted the sweetness of her voice.

"I'm sure you'll find it is," he said heartily. "You're my first confidante, Barbara. I have no home friends to talk to, you know."

"Will you tell me all about her?" said Barbara, full sympathy in her voice.

He laughed congenially. "It might not be safe to start me with such a promise. I'll enjoy very much talking about her to an appreciative listener. We've been engaged for nearly three years, and yet it may be years before we can be married. She's held at home by the helpless invalidism of her mother, who can't be moved and from whom she can't be separated. So my future, as far as setting up a home of my own is concerned, is very uncertain. This is why I thought it best to be silent to the church about my affairs. There's a great deal one doesn't care to share with a congregation. But I felt I'd like to tell my story to you and claim a share of your friendship for my Lilian."

Barbara said the correct words. In thinking it over long afterward she felt sure she must have done so, though what she said could never be recalled.

He was evidently satisfied with her sympathy, for he stayed longer than usual and talked freely about the woman of his choice. She couldn't imagine, he told her with one of his winsome smiles, how delightful it was to sit talking with her of Lilian. He'd pictured himself doing it, and yet he hesitated lest he might be expecting too much for her to be interested in a stranger merely for his sake. He went away in the best of spirits. To talk about Lilian to her, he said, was the next best thing to a visit with Lilian herself.

He would go home now and write to her about the evening they had and the friend awaiting her. Oh, he'd told her often about his good right hand in the church and what a helper she was to his girls and boys in the school. But now it would hold a special interest because *she* had been admitted into the circle.

He gave Barbara's hand a cordial clasp, holding it a second longer than usual as he said, "Good friend, you've met my confidences tonight as I felt sure you would, and I thank you. You can't know how much I thank you."

When he was well away from the house, he drew rein and let Selim walk a few paces while he bared his head to the night. Then he said a few grateful words to God for having saved him from the humiliations that had become possibilities an hour or two earlier. If that well-intentioned but hopelessly coarse woman had had a shadow of truth on which to base her words, he felt he could never look into Lilian's eyes again without a blush of shame.

He, by his heedlessness, to have implanted false ideas and awakened false hopes in the mind of any woman, worst of all such a noble woman as Barbara Dennison! Could he have borne his own company if such had been the case? Thank God, there was nothing like it. How rich and full her voice had been, how free from the suspicion of petty jealousies when she said, "It would be easy to love her."

The minister was jubilant; he'd been saved from a great sorrow and shame. Not by his own good sense, for he must have been culpably careless; otherwise that woman who was honest and good-intentioned, if she was coarse, would never have dared to speak such words to him. It was a merciful preservation. His mind and heart were so filled with Lilian that he'd never thought of gossip. It must be a lesson to him in the future.

Perhaps the gossips had been busy for weeks. Yet if they were going to talk, why wasn't it about Lilian? Hadn't a thick letter found its way, with the regularity of the sunrise, twice each week to the village post office, bearing the same feminine name? And then he laughed to think how he unwittingly outwitted the talkers. The name misled them: "Miss Lilian Carpenter," his own name. Lilian was a cousin so far removed that it seems even he forgot it, and the people evidently believed her to be his sister.

"I must be posing as a devoted brother," he said and laughed joyously.

Barbara sat quite still in the chair she returned to when the door closed after her caller sat there motionless for a space of time she didn't reckon by the clock.

"We count time by heartthrobs." The trite quotation, which Gertrude was fond of saying when she felt melodramatic, persisted in repeating itself to Barbara's dazed brain. Her hands were dropped loosely in her lap, not clasped. No tears were shed. She sometimes cried, like other women. But, with her, tears were always about relatively trivial matters that would bear being brought to the surface. She had no tears for this experience. But there was no bitterness in it to shadow her face with hard lines.

Ellis Carpenter hadn't disappointed her. He was a true, strong man. He was all she believed him to be; he was more. He held enshrined in his heart of hearts one who was young and lovely and loving; hard duty separated him from her and might separate him for weary years to come. Yet he was brave and bright, and he threw himself heart and soul into his work with such self-abandonment that he deceived even her into thinking that—

She would finish no such sentence; she left it abruptly. She was a good woman with a strong, true heart. In her pain—and there was pain—and in her humiliation—and for a time there was humiliation—there was also a touch of comfort. She didn't have to reconstruct her friendships. Her model of true manhood didn't fall, wasn't even marred; in nothing was her nobility of soul more plainly revealed than in the fact that this gave her comfort at once.

She heard the sound of feet crunching the snow and the chatter of tongues in good nights, and Elinor rushed in from the outside world.

"Mercy! How cold it is! I'm half frozen, and you sat here mooning and let the fire go out. Mr. Carpenter has been here as usual, I suppose? I saw Selim's tracks at the gate. That's the reason you didn't have brains for even the fire. Well, I do hope you settled things and set the day."

"I'm sorry I let the fire go down," said Barbara, rising. "I didn't realize it was cold. I'll see if there isn't fire enough in the kitchen to warm your feet."

"Oh, never mind my feet. Answer my question. I'm so worn-out trying to evade the questions hinted to me about you and Mr. Carpenter. The girls think I know all about it, of course, and won't tell. I think you're treating me meanly. Why can't you be honest with me, at least? If it has to be such an awful secret, I'll keep it as well as I do now, perhaps better."

Barbara turned back from the door out of which she was slipping and spoke steadily: "Elinor, I'll be honest with you once for all. I am never going to be married to Mr. Carpenter or to any other person."

"Goodness!" said Elinor. "You don't tell me you've refused him, after all? Well, of all the flirts!"

Chapter 8

"I meant to have but common needs,
Such as content, and heaven."

Midwinter was everywhere. What happened on this particular morning in Barbara Dennison's home was announced in the parlance of the farm by the succinct and startling statement that the pump had frozen! Mrs. Dennison, with an old shawl pinned over her gray head, her teeth chattering with the cold, struggled with the icy pump handle. Her daughter Elinor stood wrathfully by, feeding its mouth with dippers full of boiling water and expressing her mind about pumps in general and that one in particular.

At the Fenton boardinghouse, several hundred miles from the Dennison farm, the same general conditions of weather prevailed. The boarders rushed in from the biting outside air, hidden in heavy overcoats and mufflers. Conversation at the tables was sure to begin with, "Well, is this cold enough for you?" or, "I tell you what—this is weather!" or some of the other original and brilliant remarks that are kept in stock for such occasions. The snow lay thick on the ground in both these regions, and Elinor Dennison and Annie Fenton, unknown to each other, bemoaned the fact that with such "splendid sleighing" it was too cold and "blustery" to enjoy it.

In Bernice Halsted's home, rain, slush, and slipperiness varied the program.

"It's an awfully treacherous world," George Wilbur told them as he removed his outer wraps. "I all but lost my footing several times between here and the corner. If I'd been on skates, I could have done better. But there's a sleety rain falling at this minute that will spoil even the skating. Dreadful weather! I believe I'll try another one before I'm much older. How would you like to go a good deal farther west, Bernice? Far enough to reach civilized weather?"

Could they have seen Naomi at that moment, they would have been sure she'd accomplished it. Midwinter still, by the calendar, yet earth and air were combining to make a scene fair enough for another world than this. Naomi, dressed in white, as was her pleasure at all seasons of the year, stood bathed in sunlight, with a spray of yellow roses in her belt and a mass of blooms, just gathered, in her arms.

She was thinking at the moment of the snows and frosts and stormy winds described to her in recent letters from the girls and wondering why they lived there. Why were people content to live in uncomfortable, disagreeable weather? Such an easy thing to manage, it seemed to her. Surely there was enough room on the great sunny, flower-strewn earth for them all.

From the spot where Naomi stood, the splendid hills of the San Bernardino range, with their heads crowned in snow, were distinctly visible. That was as it should be. Snow enough to cap those glorious hills and help make an added glory in the sunsets: that was what snow was for and where it should stay.

More than hills held one's gaze, though these were so varied in their lights and shadows the eye never wearied of them. Naomi knew the faint, purply gray line in the near distance was the lovely bay, the most beautiful piece of water, she believed, to be found on this beautiful earth.

Yet she didn't need to look away to distant hill or bay for beauty; it surrounded her. The fine old house which was her home was set in the midst of it. The lawn that stretched away from it on either side was a vivid green seen only in wintertime in semitropical climates. It was velvety rich and smooth, unmarred by a stray weed or even a dead leaf. Dotting the lawn at convenient distances were fountains that tossed up and sent out in fine sprays the blessed water responsible for all the freshness and greenery.

Luxuriant pepper trees also in vivid green and aglow with scarlet berries vied with the grand old live oaks in furnishing wide stretches of shade. Below the trees rustic chairs, bamboo settees, and brightly colored hassocks invited the weary or the indolent to rest and dream.

As for flowers, viewed from her standpoint, the world looked to be what Naomi thought for the most part it was—made of flowers. Roses everywhere, climbing the trees, wandering over the fences, clambering the lattices to the very tops of second-story windows ready to shower bloom and perfume upon whatever hand stretched out to gather them. All shades and grades of roses, from the lovely "gold of Ophir," with their sunset tints and their faint sweet breath, to the tiny "seven sisters," who huddled together in their shy beauty and made Naomi more fond of them than any of their brilliant rivals.

Nor was it roses alone. Blossoming vines in gold and crimson rioted over the latticework of the wide porches in such a reckless display of bloom and sweetness that almost took one's breath. Down below were calla lilies, of the same variety that Naomi knew from letters Barbara and Bernice were nursing as houseplants, each rejoicing over a single promising bud, and hoping and praying for them to bloom for Easter. She thought of them as she stood counting hers.

"The callas on this side are doing fairly well, Mama. I can count eighty-three large blooms from where I stand."

Yet roses and heliotrope, even when they bloom as they did about Naomi in reckless masses, do not make up the whole of life. The golden sunshine flowed unceasingly about her that winter morning, and the balmy air, just crisp enough to bring out the pink and white wool trailing from her shoulders, was laden with the perfumes of literally a thousand flowers. Yet a slight shadow was reflected on her fair face which would have been new to her school friends. Life was beginning to touch even Naomi in a way that jarred.

"It's so tiresome," she told herself, in a discontented, rather than sorrowful tone. "It will make no end of disagreeableness."

Presently she turned from the beauty spread with such a lavish hand and went in with her masses of flowers, only to come upon beauty of a different kind—that which cultured taste and unlimited means can cause to appear, even inside walls of brick and stone. The sunlight's softer hues had been imitated in the furnishings. Carpets, cushions, even the walls lent themselves to the impression that the sun was setting in glory and sending its rays into the room. Rare furniture that showed its costliness in fitting its surroundings and bestowing comfort, rather than in the glory of its finish, filled every suitable niche, yet left an impression of ample room.

A lady with a delicate face and a general air of fragility was ensconced in the soft pillows of an easy chair, toying with a dish of fruit on a small table by her side.

She smiled gently on Naomi and her flowers, and asked, "Did you try some of these oranges this morning, darling? They're not as sweet as they were last year."

"Nothing is, Mama," said Naomi, the shadow on her face gathering strength as she went about the room disposing of her flowers.

"Even these roses that used to have the sweetest breath in the world don't smell as sweet this morning as the poor little bud Gertrude and I nursed last winter to make it bloom for the first day of spring."

"You have the blues, child," said the lady, gently chiding. "And there can be no one in the world with less reason. If you were an invalid like your poor mother, there would be some excuse for the roses not smelling sweet."

"But, Mama, don't I have reason? Think how very trying this matter about Dick is! How can I make roses or any other flowers satisfy me when he's gone off in a huff and thinks himself mistreated?"

Mrs. Newland laughed softly. "You're overly sensitive, child," she said. "If you have no heavier trial in life than poor Dick, I'll be thankful. What did you expect? You were away for a year. Dick thought of you as a child and expected you to remain one. Instead you burst in upon him a lovely young woman instead of his child playmate. What should he do then, being Dick, but fall desperately in love with you and rush to tell you so. It's the common lot, dear, of womanhood. You can't expect to be exempt."

"But, Mama, it's a great deal worse than you make it seem. Dick thinks I'm to blame; that I understood his feeling and even—even led him on." The pure face flushed with indignation. "As though I would do such a thing! I could never look Barbara Dennison in the face again if I harbored a thought like that even for a moment. He insulted me by suggesting it. Yet he went away so hurt and grieved that I can't be as indignant with him as I ought. Do you think, Mama—I mean, have you thought at all—that Dick and I have been any different this time from what we've always been, just like brother and sister?"

"Well, dear, to be honest, I never had as much faith in Dick's brotherliness as you did and lately no faith in it at all."

The indignant color flowed over Naomi's face, and there was reproach in her voice. "Mother! Why didn't you tell me?"

Mrs. Newland laughed again, still softly.

"Why, dear child, I didn't realize I needed to. I must ask you again what you expected. You've blossomed into lovely young womanhood, and of course young men will find it out. Poor Dick is the first, but I'm afraid he won't be the last. You can't help being loved, daughter."

"I can help encouraging people to think I have a feeling for them that I never dreamed of having. At least, I always thought I could, and said so, and I'm humiliated that I failed. It hurts me to think what Barbara would say if she knew I had. It does seem to me, Mama, that if you understood, you might have given me a hint and saved me some of this. Dick and I have been together so constantly from our babyhood that I never dreamed of his having any different feeling for me from what I had for him and what we always had. But I can see now that it's as he said: I must have appeared to be leading him on. I don't know what to do."

Her voice held such evident distress that her mother pushed away her fruit and gave herself to the task of being comforter.

"Nonsense, darling. I won't have you growing morbid. There's no need for you to worry about Dick. He'll recover. Young men his age aren't crushed by such experiences. If they were, I'd have to send you to a convent. You're fortunate not to have had this lesson earlier. Why, bless you, at your age I'd broken at least three hearts which were thought never to be mended. But they were, some of them in a single season, and I lived to see them all happily married."

"But, Mother, conditions must have changed since you were a girl. Self-respecting people don't talk that way now. We all believe that a girl who conducts herself as she should, has no need to make a man she doesn't intend to marry go through the humiliation of a refusal. I certainly thought I was that kind of girl, and it hurts me more than I can tell you to find I'm not."

Mrs. Newland leaned back among the cushions with a somewhat bored though indulgent smile. "A 'Daniel come to judgment,' " she murmured. "My dear little Namie, those strong-minded women you're so fond of have all but spoiled you. That Barbara, especially, whom you quote so often, could never have been a girl. She must have been born an old woman. It isn't good to force life, daughter. You'll be a woman soon enough. Be a carefree girl as long as you can. Take my advice, and don't torture your heart over Dick. Your mother is glad you don't care for him the way he thinks he wants you to—so glad that if she'd seen the slightest indication of it, she would have interfered long ago. Dick is a dear boy, and I love him well enough to be his auntie forever. But I don't want him for a son. I look higher than that for you, my darling."

"Mother, I have no such feeling. There's no man living I'd sooner marry than Dick Holwell if I wanted to marry anybody. I mean if—in plain English, Mama—if I loved him, or ever could, in any such way, there would be nothing else to prevent my marrying him. But I—oh! *Don't* you understand?"

"Certainly I do, dear. Dick was premature and foolish, but it's just as well to have it over early. It was bound to come. As for your marrying, child, it's the last thing your father and I are anxious about. You may wait and welcome, until you find that perfect being who was created from all eternity for just you. I know your romantic nature, darling, better than you think I do. It's my duty to hint that the ideal creature who must alone claim you is not as common as girls of your friend Barbara's type would have you believe. But wait for him, by all means, as long as you please."

"Then, Mama, if the one I can love and honor with my whole being doesn't come for me, I'll never marry. We all said that, we girls, and meant it. It shall be the right one or no one."

"Very well, daughter, I'm content, I assure you. Your father will be quite able to support you as long as you give him the chance, without the aid of a husband. But suppose just now you ring for Maida. I must lie down for a while; our conversation has exhausted me."

The girl's eyes followed the delicate form being half carried from the room in her attendant's arms, and she smiled back in answer to the kiss thrown to her from her mother's fingers. She realized more fully than usual that this dainty little mother was from another world than Barbara, for instance, and there were things she didn't understand.

Chapter 9

"I've none to smile when I am free,
And when I sigh, to sigh with me."

L eft to herself, Naomi wandered out again among the roses and gathered great masses because it seemed natural to pick flowers, and they needed to be gathered. Then she wondered what she could do with them and wished she knew someone to send a basketful to. If she could only send them to Gertrude, who had written about nursing a single tea rose.

For more than one reason this child of luxury was not as happy in her lovely home as she might have been, nor as she'd expected to be. She missed, and at times longed for, the wholesome atmosphere of her school days; the systematic division of her time into periods with duties and responsibilities belonging to each; the feeling that she was one with the busy world and had her portion with the workers. Then, aside from routine work, some interest had always held her and her chosen friends to eager plans and activities, and kept the sense of comradeship and usefulness alert inside her.

Now that she was stranded in a luxurious home, with servants to anticipate every want, and horses and carriage at her bidding, she was dismayed to discover that even driving, under such circumstances, wasn't the delight it had been at school. There she took her turn in driving old Dolly to town with half a dozen girls in the carryall and errands to do for a dozen others. How sweet the memory of those homely errands was. A paper of pins for one, the careful matching of a spool of silk for another, and perhaps a pair of shoes to be left for mending, in the interest of a third.

That Naomi Newland, the petted darling of a millionaire, should need to look longingly back to such homely memories as these, might well afford food for thought to others besides her. She didn't like to think of it. Too young and untrained for close introspection, her regretful longings for the dear past seemed to her like ingratitude, and she struggled to rise above the loneliness and actual weariness that sometimes possessed her.

It was well enough during her vacations. She enjoyed the flowers and horses and servants and other trifles that represented ease and luxury with a zest that deceived her. She knew now that always in her mind was the thought of returning to those third-floor rooms and meeting the girls and telling them eagerly about the lovely holiday. That word expresses it: Home was holiday; school and study and the girls were life. To shut down upon life, all at once, by turning it into perpetual holiday was to make it pall upon the girl without her understanding why.

She left her flowers at last for Maida to arrange and went to her room and an unfinished letter to Barbara.

You dear Bab, I must flee to you for comfort this morning. That was the sentence with which she began the day's record.

> *I'm lonesome. What will you think of me if I tell you I am most of the time? Yes, I know it's dreadful when I'm at home with my own beloved ones for the first time in years. But you must take in the situation fully before you look at me with those reproachful eyes and suspect something wrong in poor little Namie.*
>
> *We live a mile or so out of town, and while any number of girls in town are pleasant enough and would be neighborly perhaps if we lived closer together, there isn't one among them whose neighborliness stretches over the mile. Nor, to be frank, is there one I sadly miss when she doesn't come. So I'm very much alone.*
>
> *I even have to drive alone, which you know we never had a chance to do with Dolly—dear old Dolly! I wonder who drives her now? A big carriage and two horses who step on the ground as though they hardly considered it good enough for their feet, and me on the backseat alone. Does it sound very cheery when you remember that I was used to five girls at once, and there was no backseat to speak of?*
>
> *Yes, ma'am, I hear you. And there's reproach in your dear gray eyes, too. You're sure I might find people, if I chose, who'd delight in taking drives with me and would be helped by them. You'd do it, and I'd delight to go along and help entertain them. I mean to try all by myself someday, just for the sake of your approval, but, the truth is, your poor little Naomi doesn't know how to do such things. She isn't you and never can be, no matter how hard she may try. It's all in her heart—you know it is—but it won't come to the surface, somehow, without seeming like patronage or goody-goodiness.*
>
> *Oh, I'm not always alone. Mama rides with me occasionally, but it is very occasionally. She's an invalid, you know, and the weather is generally too bright, or too cool, or too something for her comfort. And poor Papa never has time.*
>
> *Barbara, do you know who the worst drudges in the world are? The businessmen. Our man Rogers who takes care of the horses and carriages has a great deal more leisure and a pleasanter time in life than Papa has. Really, I never before realized the downright drudgery of it all. Papa goes to town in the morning before Mama or I have thought of breakfast, and as a rule he can't get home until*

after Mama has retired. Even then there are papers to sign and letters to be read that require the sending of telegrams, and all sorts of
what he calls "tag ends of business" that have followed him home.
It's really dreadful. I'd like to get real well acquainted with my
father, but I don't know how I'm ever to do it.

Still, I'm not fretting, dear. I'm only talking. Imagine me perched
on dear old Nebo, and let me go on. (Do you suppose they have a
new mattress on that bed this year?) I don't want you to think I've
forgotten there are lovely things in life. I know there are in mine—for
instance, flowers. Our gardens are simply intoxicated with bloom. If
you were here I could literally smother you in roses.

Speaking of roses reminds me of Gertrude (not that I've forgotten
her for a minute since I heard her great news). How fond she was of
them! If the wedding were to be in March, instead of June, I would
express a barrel of them to her. But by June I suppose even that bleak
world in which she lives will have its own roses.

Two peals of wedding bells—think of it! And you and I not in
them. I thought you would be the first one, Bab, dear. Don't ask me
why. It was just a presentiment I had, and I might have known then
that it wasn't correct—my presentiments never are. I certainly
never dreamed of Gertrude as the first to break our ranks. Bernice
seemed much more likely. She, however, appears to be content with
'him' just as he is.

Do you know, those convenient pronouns he and him are all
the knowledge I have of Bernice's friend even yet. I presume he has
a name, two of them indeed, but I'm none the wiser. "My wood
sawyer" she called him in her first letter after the engagement. You
remember, don't you, what Gertrude told us that last night about
the wood sawyer of her childhood? Since then pronouns have done
duty entirely. Not that Bernice has wasted many of them on me. I
haven't had many letters from her, and I expect fewer now than
ever. I don't believe I like her choice utterly, without reserve. Now
isn't that supremely silly when I know nothing about him, not even
his name? Can't help it. I suppose it's presentiment again. We'll
consider him angelic and drop him.

I'll go back to Gertrude. Isn't it lovely she's so happy? I know
Dr. Adams must be a good man; I like him. Gertrude sent me a tiny
little photograph of him; wasn't she nice? I wish she were to be married next month instead of waiting until June. Not that I'm hungering
and thirsting for a wedding. Instead, I have my melancholy hours
over the fact that our ranks are to be broken so soon. But I can never
tell you how my heart leaps at the thought of seeing you all again.

Barbara and Bernice and Gertrude and Naomi—think of it! How can I wait?

Bab, dear, I'm going to tell you something: I've decided to be an old maid. I used to think it wouldn't be nice, you remember, but I've concluded it will. I like some people a little and a few people very much, but I don't really love anybody, not in that way, you understand. And I would never marry a man simply because I liked him quite well. I've been too long under your influence to believe in such things.

Barbara, dear, don't get engaged, please, not just yet. I'm so lonesome with Bernice and Gertrude gone that if I were to lose you too, I couldn't endure it. I know I'm being silly, but if you were here you would be very gentle with me and tell me I was indulging in a sentimental streak. It's more than sentiment, Barbara—what I've been telling you about not ever being married. There are reasons why I'm quite sure of it.

Before Naomi wrote that last phrase she held her pen and thought. She wanted to confess to Barbara about poor Dick and tell her she hadn't meant to lead him astray—hadn't dreamed of such a thing until the mischief was done—and assure her the experience made her realize she wasn't like other girls. Dick told her that. He said that any girl with sense would have known she was either willing to marry him or else she was flirting.

"I wasn't flirting," Naomi would like to say to Barbara, "and I'm not willing to marry him, therefore"—but she would say none of it. Much as she longed to exonerate herself in Barbara's eyes, she would keep silence. It was poor Dick's secret, not hers. She wouldn't spread it out on paper for other eyes to read, even for the pleasure of having Barbara write, "I know you didn't mean to do wrong, dear child." It was, perhaps, the first time in her life that she had held herself deliberately and resolutely from sympathy. It was an indication that the woman was stirring within the heart of the child when she determined to bear this trouble alone.

Not quite alone, it's true. Dick rushed away in such high wrath, making it apparent something was terribly wrong, that silence was impossible, even if Naomi's sense of filial duty allowed her to keep a secret from her mother. *But*—the girl paused in her thinking with that word and wouldn't finish the thought coherently.

It may be said for her, however, that she was studying mothers. She spent short vacations at different times with school friends and saw other mothers; she knew there were varying types. Some, for instance, were not invalids and were strong in many ways; their daughters leaned on them and were guided by them in both small and great things.

There are mothers, said this homesick child to herself, *of the kind that Barbara would make*, and then she sighed. For whom and for what was the sigh? Her loyal, loving heart would not for the world have admitted—mothers were sacred; but some of them stayed young while their daughters grew up and grew old.

"Mama has stayed young," said Naomi one day. She said it aloud and with deliberation, and from then on she felt more alone than before.

Barbara was the one with whom she thought aloud—with certain reservations. She read her letter over carefully before she wrote another line, after that one given, then began a sort of running commentary on part of her text.

Dear Barbara,

Let me warn you. You'll be greatly dissatisfied with this letter. I won't wonder—I am myself.

I do consider my mercies, and they're many. Indeed, I consider it a privilege to be with Mama, and she tells me a dozen times a day that I'm a comfort to her. In a sense I know I am, and yet I can't help knowing Maida is even more so. She knows how to arrange the pillows and the footrest and the carriage robes and, oh, a hundred things. She knows just how warm the broth ought to be and just how cool, and at just what hour it's needed without being told. You must see that all this is a comfort.

She's been at Mama's elbow for four years while I've been— with you, for instance. It's reasonable that Maida should know more about everything than I do, and I appreciate Mama's feelings when she kisses me and pats my hair and calls me her darling and says I'd better ring for Maida. I do it cheerfully, and I'm not jealous. I'm even fond of Maida in a way. But I'm lonesome.

I'm planning, however, for the future. In that good time coming, when I've become a neat and well-preserved old maid, and Papa has wound up his business affairs and retired—he promised me he will—my blessed days will begin. Papa, you see, has no 'Maida' and has no time for being waited on except by office boys and telegraph boys and the like. He doesn't know how to be pampered, and it will be my duty to teach him. I'll have his easy chair in just the right corner, and his slippers—don't you know they always have slippers?—I'll put them on his dear old feet if he'll let me. I'll find out his favorite flower as soon as he has time to like any of them, and his newspaper—they always have newspapers read to them—I'll find out somehow just what ought to be read. While Maida is pampering Mama, I'll make a scientific business of pampering Papa. I think he'll like it, and I'm sure

I shall—somebody just for me.

Oh, dear! Now your big gray eyes look bigger and a bit grayer than usual, and your mouth has two puckers in the corners that mean disapproval. "She's inherently selfish, I'm afraid," you murmur, meaning me—and I'm afraid so too. I discover an element of self in every thought.

It seems strange too, when we four were together I never thought of such a thing. I even imagined at times that I had streaks of genuine unselfishness. I know now that it must have been simply the reflex influence of the other three. I'm going to be unselfish now. You won't be burdened with me another minute.

I'll go down at once and order the carriage and drive to town and match Mama's worsteds, a task nobody can ever perform. And I'll call on her friend Mrs. Bertrand, whom I don't like, and take her to the studio of a disagreeable young artist where I don't like to go. Then I'll wait while they pretend to make plans for a picture which neither of them intends to carry out and take her back on the boulevard where I don't like to drive, and she does. And I'll bring her home for a five o'clock tea with Mama, which function I detest.

There! Isn't that an exciting day's program? And haven't I put enough unselfishness into it to spread over several days? Oh, dear Bab! Your poor little Naomi! I believe there's something to her in spite of appearances.

"She needs the discipline of life in order to her true development." How many times did Madame Nordhoff repeat that striking statement with special reference to poor me? Put your ear close until I whisper. Barbara, dear, it's true; I feel it. What will the discipline be?

Under all circumstances and disciplines I am as ever,
Your little Namie.

Chapter 10

"What I thought was a flower,
Is only a weed, and is worthless."

T he height of Mrs. Halsted's ambition had been reached: Her daughter was formally engaged to Mr. Wilbur. This was what the good mother had expected for years as the natural and only reasonable conclusion of the intimacy.

Yet here was, with the expectation, an element of uneasiness. George was so careless about it all; so leisurely in his efforts to settle his happiness on a secure foundation. He had been silent through years in which he might have had everything comfortable arranged.

Even now he was leisurely. Instead of hastening the marriage, as an eager lover might do, especially with no conceivable obstacle in the way, he hadn't even asked that the day be fixed but seemed quite content with his present happiness.

Mrs. Halsted assured herself she was glad; the longer George was content without having Bernice all to himself, the better it would be for her mother. Nevertheless she was glad with just a shade of anxiety. Why shouldn't a man who had chosen a wife and was abundantly able to set up a home, be eager to set it up?

If Bernice had any such questionings in her heart, she kept them hidden, as a loyal nature was bound to do. It's doubtful she questioned. She believed so entirely in the man she singled out long before as the embodiment of all manly virtues that it ruled out anxiety.

Gertrude Fenton was to be married in June, and she and George were invited to the wedding. Mrs. Halsted remarked casually that it was a wonder George wasn't begging to be married just before Gertrude's date, thus making the journey part of his own wedding trip.

Bernice smiled peacefully as she replied, "Not yet, Mama. You won't get rid of your daughter as easily as that."

She wouldn't for the world have admitted that she, too, wondered why some such plan hadn't occurred to George. But there was no anxiety in the wondering. Of course George had good reasons for not hastening his marriage; she wouldn't sully her absolute trust in him by letting herself linger over the wonder as to what they were.

Matters were in this state when their first separation since the engagement came to them. The law firm Mr. Wilbur was connected with wanted him to take a trip to the West in the interests of certain clients. The plan would involve an absence of at least two months. He grumbled over it a little, assuring Mrs. Halsted that if he'd foreseen such an extended trip he would have carried Bernice off with him. He added that if Satan had upset the original Eden with mining interests and a scheme for a new railroad instead of with a paltry bit of fruit, it would have been more in keeping with the trend of modern history.

It occurred to the mother that, in view of such an extended trip to the West, including the California her daughter desired so much to visit, it wouldn't have been unreasonable to have pressed for an immediate marriage. But she didn't say it, of course, and George Wilbur went his way, leaving Bernice to learn by his absence how necessary he'd become to her happiness.

It was a lesson that came to her forcefully. The unrest she felt during those early days of loneliness almost frightened her and vexed her mother. It was very well for Bernice to be devoted to the man she was to marry; Mrs. Halsted wouldn't have it otherwise. Nevertheless it was trying that the girl she'd lived twenty years and more for, and whose brothers were devoted to her, should seem to have no interest in life because one person was gone.

"It isn't wise to center everything on one human being," she said to her daughter, reproof in her tone. "What would become of you if you lost him?"

"Mother, don't!" said the girl sharply. Then she laughed apologetically. "I beg your pardon, Mama. But why put unnecessary horrors into my life? I provoked that naughty speech of yours, though, by wearing such a long face. I don't mean to be miserable, Mama. I'll get used to being without George in a few days, I suppose. But I've seen him every day for months and can't help missing him at every turn."

Soon afterward came an invitation from a school acquaintance who was spending the summer with an aunt living only a half day's ride by rail from Bernice's home. She missed George so much and was so long and slow to rally that she suddenly decided, with her mother's approval, to accept it.

She wasn't extremely fond of Celia Archer during her school days, but at least she was one of the girls. All the dear old times could be talked over with her, and it would help to wear away another week of George's absence.

With Mrs. Halsted's approval, she also smothered a sigh. In accomplishing her plans for her daughter's happiness she was only too successful. It was plain that every nook and corner of the lovely home was distasteful to her now that George wasn't there.

When her daughter left for the week's visit, the mother said to her sons: "Of course it's lonely without Bernice; yet it's a positive relief to have the child away for awhile. She hasn't done much but mope since George went. I hate to think what would become of her if anything happened to him on this trip. I don't think I ever saw a girl so absorbed in someone as she is in him. I must say I'm surprised and a bit annoyed. She's been so intimate with him all her life that I thought she'd have grown used to him and not have cared so excessively."

While one son laughed over his mother's ideas about a life-friendship, the other attempted to lessen her anxieties.

"No danger of anything happening to George Wilbur, Mother. He's a good traveler and used to himself and can look out for No. 1 better than any man I know."

∽

Celia Archer and her friend Bernice talked for several hours and reached at last a point where something besides old school days could be mentioned. They then discovered that the afternoon had waned and neither of them was dressed for the day.

"Well, never mind," said Celia, "there's no one here but us and Louise. Perhaps not even Louise; sometimes she doesn't feel well enough to come down to tea. Oh, I haven't told you about her. I'm anxious to have you meet her; she's a study. It's quite romantic, her being here. Her mother's an old friend of Aunt Kate's, a school friend of forty years' standing. Think of it, Bernice! Do you suppose any of us girls will keep up a friendship for forty years?

"She married unhappily, I believe. At least Aunt Kate is grim whenever she mentions the husband. This daughter is the only child, and she's declining. Aunt Kate invited her here for her health. They live in town on one of the narrow streets and on a narrow income, and Aunt Kate is trying to build this girl up on country air and cream and things. But she can't; the poor thing fails every day.

"She's very interesting though. She has a history—I don't know what it is. Aunt Kate is darkly mysterious when she refers to it. She despises all mankind, I believe, for Louise's sake, but she keeps the girl's secret. I hope she'll appear tonight so you can meet her. Now that I think of it, she probably will, just to see you. For some reason she's especially interested in you. As a rule, she shrinks from meeting strangers. I was here nearly two days before I glimpsed her. But the only bit of color I've seen on her face since I came was at the mention of your name."

"What does she know of me?" Bernice asked with an amused laugh.

"Goodness knows! Perhaps she's heard of some of your conquests and wants to see a girl who's succeeded when she's failed. That sounds rather heartless, doesn't it? But I don't mean it that way. I'm wonderfully interested in Louise."

Within two days Bernice could have said the same. The pale-faced, sad-eyed girl, who was evidently fading from life, had a peculiar fascination for the one aglow with health and radiant with hope for a blissful future. Her naturally kind heart was touched by the girl's physical weakness; she helped make the hours pass less wearily and thus won Aunt Kate's unqualified approval.

Only a day or two before the end of her visit, Bernice spent an evening alone with her hostess. Celia had gone to a society function that seemed necessary to observe.

After making her invalid comfortable for the night, Aunt Kate entered the sitting room where Bernice had set out the little round table with its white cover, lit the shining Rochester burner, and was seated comfortably in an easy chair. Aunt Kate's favorite rocker was drawn to just the right position and waiting for her. Bernice held a book in her hand, but a bit of work lay in the basket at her feet if their mood was to talk. She smiled warmly at her hostess, but that lady's face was gloomy.

She dropped into the waiting chair with a deep sigh. "That child is growing thinner all the time. Her poor body would make you shiver; it's nothing but skin and bone. Her little mother has another heavy sorrow right at the door. It does beat all how much some people have to bear."

"Has she had a hard life?" Bernice asked, her voice tender with sympathy.

"Which, the girl or her mother?"

"Both. If the life of one were hard, the other's would be also, wouldn't it?"

"Yes, it would. You're right there. You understand something about life, I see. They've lived for each other, Louise and her mother, and now she's slipping away. Soon her mother will have nothing."

"Is it consumption, do you think?"

"No," said Aunt Kate fiercely. "It's murder—that's what I call it. The doctor's name for it is consumption, I suppose. Oh, it's the old story—a trusting girl and a brute of a man. I haven't told Celia anything about it. She's such a flighty girl that I was afraid she'd let on to Louise that we were talking about her. But sometimes I get so angry thinking about it that I feel as if I must talk to somebody.

"The courting was going on for nearly a year. Louise left home; she went to Brandon to learn millinery. There happened to be an opening there, and after she learned the trade she had a chance to stay and work at good wages. They were so pleased with her. The woman in charge said she was a genius.

"She wanted to stay there, poor thing. His office was only a block or so from her shop. From all the mother has told me—and I've heard it from others, too—he was about as attentive to her as he could be. We all thought it was a sure thing and very fine for Louise. He was rich and educated and all that. Louise is a perfect lady, and so is her mother, but she stepped down a good deal when she married. I suppose she thought Louise was getting back to the place where she naturally belonged. Her mother used to talk everything over with me, because we've been the same as sisters ever since we were girls at school.

"One thing I never liked. I kept asking when the wedding was to be, and it troubled me that, as near as I could make out, nothing was said about it. The others seemed to think it was all right. Louise thought some business trouble stood in the way of his being married, perhaps, and he didn't want to plan until he knew just what he could do. But I didn't like it; it seemed unnatural.

"Well, all of a sudden the man stopped coming. Louise came home, to her own city, and he came to see her several times, although it's a good hundred miles. One night he stayed for a later train than usual. Louise told her mother he said he couldn't bear to leave her, and he laughed about having a presentiment of something coming between them. Sure enough, something did. That fellow never came near her again."

"Why not?" asked the horror-stricken listener.

"That's what it took us all a good while to find out. As near as can be discovered it was because he didn't want to. He had another interest, or maybe he had it all the while and only took Louise up to play with between times. All we're sure of is that he never came near her again."

"And it was this trouble that made her ill?"

"Well, it helped. Louise was never very strong, and she took a hard cold just about that time and didn't have strength to shake it off. The doctor prates about a 'lack of vitality.' It's a lack of inclination; the poor child doesn't want to get well. You can see she doesn't have a strong will. But she was a lovely girl and just as bright and sunny as a bird before her life was spoiled. Hanging is too good for such men."

"But wasn't any effort made to clear up the mystery?" persisted Bernice. "How do you know there wasn't some third person, some unprincipled gossip who made trouble? Similar things have happened."

"Oh, bless you! Effort enough—trust her father for that. He's kind of a scamp himself. He was very pleased about Louise's 'catch,' as he called it, and more eager than I was to have the day set. It was all they could do to keep him from meddling. And when the break came, he nearly killed Louise outright with his investigations.

"Louise sent back the man's notes and some little trinkets he gave her. She had enough spirit for that, though no doubt he'd have sent for them if she hadn't. He wasn't the kind of man to leave any evidence he could get rid of. But he forgot a few scraps with 'My darling' and 'My own' and lies of that kind on them, and his name signed. There was a little photograph, too, with some dangerous stuff written on it.

"The poor child's father got hold of them, and as soon as report came that the fellow was planning to be married, he threatened him with a breach of promise suit. You can see what kind of creatures they both were when I tell you the fellow tried to hush him with money and was willing to pay well for it. I suppose the only reason he couldn't buy his man was because he expected a suit to bring him more. It's no wonder the poor child is dying, considering what she's endured between them."

"And did the man marry?"

"No, hasn't yet. They say he's afraid to while she lives. Pleasant, isn't it, to think of a villain watching out for one victim to die so he can marry another? If I knew the name of the girl, I'd write and tell her the whole story. They say he's playing sharp all the time, paying attention to half a dozen girls at once so that outsiders can't be sure which it is. Maybe he doesn't know himself."

"Do you know the man's name?"

"Oh, yes, I've heard it often enough! I heard only this week that his old home is in the town where you live, though he now lives in the city. I thought I'd tell you something about it and ask if you knew anything about him. It isn't likely you do; you wouldn't be his type. But his name is Wilbur, George Wilbur, and he's a lawyer himself and probably knows how to manage."

Chapter 11

*"His honor rooted in dishonor stood,
And faith unfaithful kept him falsely true."*

Mrs. Halsted's usually placid face was shadowed. The plans she'd congratulated herself on making were in mortal peril. The daughter she believed she trained herself had suddenly developed ideas which the mother thought untenable, along with a degree of obstinacy that was alarming. They sat together that spring morning in the luxurious room Mrs. Halsted had delighted in refurnishing, just before Bernice's final return from school, with special consideration for her tastes and colors.

But the girl wasn't concerned with luxury that morning, for she sat bolt upright in the only straight-backed chair the room contained. Her face was pale except for small pink spots that flowed on either cheek, and her mouth was drawn in firm lines that lent a shade of sternness to her face. Her mother was regarding her with a look of dismay. She broke in on the silence that had fallen between them, with disapproval in her tones.

"I must say, Bernice, that I don't understand you. I never imagined you had a spark of jealousy in you. Don't you know it won't do to look for perfection in any man? I might have expected this when you set poor George up on a pedestal and tried to worship him. He's human, like the rest of the world, and you were determined to make him into a saint. That's just the trouble. I'm sure he's given you proof if ever a man did that you're the only girl he has a thought for now. If he had his friendships while you were away at school and he was in no sense bound to you, I don't see why a reasonable person should blame him."

A spasm of pain, perhaps, but certainly mingled with indignation, crossed Bernice's face. She answered quickly.

"Mother! Haven't I told you enough? The girl was as much engaged to him in God's sight as ever a woman can be. It's true that no marriage day was set. Do you remember, Mother, that none has been set for me? It's too evident that he's waiting for his victim to die in the hope of escaping public disgrace. Do you think I'm one to wait patiently for a woman to die, so that I may comfortably marry her murderer?"

"Bernice, you're too excited to talk. You've allowed your jealous passions to get such control that you're simply insane now. I can't listen to such talk. Why, you're almost coarse, and I never expected a daughter of mine to be that. It's certainly good that George can't see you at present. As deeply in love as he is, he might be repelled.

"My daughter, listen to me and not to your wild ideas. George can't help being a fascinating young man, and he's undoubtedly what people who use such language would call a 'catch,' especially for one struggling with poverty. Why, I could point out several girls to you who've made frantic efforts to win the prize. Must he be held responsible because one person has chosen to fall so deeply ill by it? Do try to be reasonable, and remember you've heard only one side of this remarkable story. And you heard it from those anxious to put the worst possible light on acts that were probably merely kindhearted efforts to cheer a girl who was lonesome and homesick.

"George is very kindhearted naturally. He's very free, too, from petty suspicion and so deeply in love with you that he'll bear almost anything. Nevertheless I feel it my duty to remind you that you're insulting him by these doubts and no man will bear everything. It's quite beneath you, Bernice, to go on this way. I must say I'm ashamed of you."

The young girl arose and moved across the room toward the door. The crimson spots on her cheeks were deepening, and they emphasized the pallor of her face. But her voice was low and controlled.

"Mother, it's useless for us to talk anymore about this. We don't understand each other. It seems impossible to make you understand how slow I was to give up my faith in the man I believed I could trust utterly. You won't consider that I spent days in sifting this story to its depths; that I went to the girl's mother and heard the minutest details of the acquaintance. And I saw with my own eyes words written by a hand I couldn't be mistaken about, words he had no right to use with any woman but the one to whom he'd given all there is of him to give. Mother, some of those words were written less than one week before the day he told me I was the one girl in the world of interest to him. Do you think I'd marry a man like that? Can you want me to, even if I were homeless and friendless and he were the last man left on earth?"

Mrs. Halsted was thoroughly alarmed. What she called obstinacy in her daughter's disposition wasn't new to her. "She's like her father," was a phrase often on this mother's lips regarding her daughter, and she had had more than one occasion in her life to think Judge Halsted was obstinate. She regretted it as a blunder, rousing his daughter to speak words to which she might obstinately adhere. She made what effort she could to repair her blunder.

"Poor child," she said soothingly, "you've been through an ordeal. I should have remembered it and not forced you into going over offensive details. It's evident you're making mountains out of molehills. But I should have recalled what provocation you've had. You're right, dear. We shouldn't talk about it anymore. We both feel too deeply to be quite fair to each other.

"Of course there must be investigations. Gossip of this sort has to be looked after, and your brothers will attend to that. You mustn't imagine that your experience is peculiar or startling. If you were older and more familiar with the world, you'd know how easy it is for unprincipled people to get up a fair-sounding story out of meager material, especially when a wealthy man and the possibility of extorting money are involved. I'm not saying anything against the girl, Bernice. You don't need to look so indignant. Probably the worst that can be said about her is that she was too softhearted and that she's the victim of an unprincipled father who has led her on. But of course your brothers will do what should be done and will know how to manage.

"Meanwhile, daughter, I beg you not to do anything rash, that you'd regret the rest of your life. Men, especially those of such honorable connection as George Wilbur, like to be trusted and find it hard to forgive unnecessary prying into their affairs. Everything should be managed discreetly. I deplore the fact that you've evidently fallen in with a set of sharpers, of whom this 'Aunt Kate,' who knew so much, must be one." Mrs. Halstead was growing excited again; the thought of an investigation frightened her.

Bernice opened her lips to reply, then closed them. What use was there to say more? Her mother didn't and wouldn't understand. They belonged, it seemed, to different worlds. After what she had learned from the following-up of Aunt Kate's story, she was still willing, even anxious, that her daughter should marry George Wilbur. It seemed incredible to Bernice. Why should her point of view be so unlike her mother's?

When she puzzled over questions like these, the girl thought of Barbara, the high-principled, strong-souled friend, whose views of honor and truth had dominated her own life for four years. Barbara, who was clear-eyed and open-hearted, would have leisure from herself to help one in sore need of help. Bernice thought with a sick longing of the miles stretching between them and felt at times as though she must fly to her friend at once.

Her brothers would "investigate." She, too, turned sick at heart over that word. Hadn't there already been almost enough investigation to undermine her faith in mankind? How would she live through more of it and withstand them all, even her mother?

Bernice could never look back upon the days that immediately followed without a distinct sense of pain, as well as humiliation. Much had to be endured—among others, the varying opinions of her brothers, two of them businessmen accustomed to dealing with and weighing other men.

"It's undeniable," said the oldest brother in confidence to his mother, "that he's done some tall flirting. If the girl's father can't be bought, and she doesn't die before long, there will be some intensely disagreeable revelations. But the probabilities are that the man can be bought; most men of that class have their price. George must make up his mind to pay well for entertainment, that's all. A man is a fool to get himself into such a scrape as that; I thought George had more sense."

"It's a wretched business," said the second son when the anxious mother interviewed him in the hope of some encouragement. "I don't wonder Bernice is angry. She'll forgive him, I suppose. But I think she'll find it hard work. What the fellow meant by running with that girl, writing her notes, and sending her presents, and professing at the same time to be devoted to Bernice, I can't imagine. He deserves a lesson he'll remember for life. But it's going to be disagreeable giving it to him. Everybody knows he's engaged to Bernice, and there'll be no end of gossip if it's broken off. Fact is, I don't see how it decently can be—it's gone so far. You better urge Bernice, if it's necessary, to make peace somehow for appearance' sake."

Only the youngest brother, hardly considered a man yet, boldly agreed that Bernice was right in her judgment and ought to be supported in her resolve to have nothing to do with an unprincipled man. He knew he'd feel just as she did if he were a girl, and he admired her for standing up to it.

The others laughed at him for being a boy who didn't know the world. He might admire his sister as much as he pleased, they said; they were willing to join him so far, but that was far from making agreeable the disgrace that such action on her part would involve. Wilbur hadn't done anything so very new or strange. Society fellows were always getting into similar scrapes. But George had been abominably careless.

They were sure they didn't know what to advise for immediate action. It might be good for Bernice to leave home for awhile. She might even take a position as a teacher for a few months, if she still wanted to. That would occupy her mind and give her anger a chance to cool.

In the meantime the girl would probably die. One of the brothers had seen her and opined that she wouldn't live out the year. Wilbur had evidently been waiting for affairs to smooth themselves out that way. If Bernice had been kept from people like that Archer girl and her gossiping aunt, who were distinctly not of her set, the affair probably would never have reached her ears. The more they thought about it the more sure they were that the best thing was to let Bernice go away before Wilbur returned from the West. It would keep her from a personal interview with him, which was of all things to be avoided just now. She might be prevented then from making a break that would be difficult to mend.

But what could be done about that wedding? the distressed mother asked. All their friends knew Bernice was to attend her classmate's wedding in the East and serve as maid of honor, and George was to go with her. All sorts of questions would be asked if arrangements were changed, and there would be no end to the embarrassment.

Oh, well, the brothers said, the details must be managed in the best way possible. It was a disagreeable business, of course, and there would be talk. But they couldn't force or even expect Bernice to act as if nothing had happened, at least not right away, and this plan was simply making the best of a bad matter.

It was finally settled that Bernice was to be hurried to an uncle's in Colorado, whose family had been requesting a visit from her for a long time. The mother heard herself explaining to inquiring friends that the child was really quite rundown with the spring weather and needed an invigorating climate. Her uncle lived close to the mountains, and she had finally persuaded the young people not to go off to that warm little New York town and experience the fatigues of a country wedding. It sounded good, and she began to take courage.

But they were reckoning without regard to that vein of obstinacy the mother had discovered in Bernice. The girl refused to leave before George Wilbur's return. It wasn't she, she declared, who needed to be ashamed of her conduct and hide in Colorado. Nor would she give him a chance to say she condemned him unheard. If he could tell her that the words she read in his handwriting were base forgeries; that he knew no such person as Louise Webster, or knowing her hadn't spoken those words or performed those acts which marked him in the eyes of all respectable people as her suitor, why, then, she would kneel before him and beg his forgiveness and feel that he would be justified in having nothing more to do with her.

But here the much-talked-at and suffering girl made a distinct pause and drooped her eyes with a sense of shame that was not for herself. Then she began again, her cheeks aflame.

Chapter 12

"There be many kinds of partings—yes, I know
Some with brave hands that strengthen as they go.
Ah yes, I know, I know.
But there be partings harder still to tell,
That fall in silence, like an evil spell,
Ah yes—too hard to tell."

Mother, his own mother knows it all. She's gone to beg the girl to use her influence with the father, that he won't ruin her son's name. Could anyone ruin his name if he hadn't done so first?"

"Child!" said Mrs. Halsted, with new dismay in her voice. "What foolishness is this? How do you know what his mother has heard or done?"

"I know it from her. I went to her. On my way home I stopped over one train and went to the hotel where she's staying and heard from her lips what confirmed my worst fears. I was told things that made me sure she knew all about it, and I had a feeling she would tell me the truth. I think she did.

"But she's like all of you, consumed with posing before the world as honorable, no matter who's sacrificed. Both Louise and I were expected to contribute to this. She can't do her part, poor thing, though I believe she would if she could. But I won't. No one needs to plan and urge and lay before me the complications of misery—don't I know them? I realize it all as the rest of you can't.

"I'll tell you again what I've said before: I will never marry George Wilbur, never! He's deceived me. If he'd met me later in his life, after he unwittingly or heedlessly compromised himself with another girl, and if he'd told me the truth—owned that he had no right to ask what he wanted to ask; that he was bound in honor where his heart was not—I might have thought him weak. But I could have pitied and, in time, forgiven him.

"But he *lied* to me! His deceit was premeditated and uncalled for. I trusted him completely and asked no questions. Yet he took pains to repeat to me the lie that from my childhood up to now he'd thought of and cared for no other girl. He said that he—but I won't humiliate myself by repeating what he said. Isn't it enough that I know he's taken pains to repeat and emphasize a series of lies, without even the poor excuse of being called upon for explanations?"

For once in her life Mrs. Halsted was speechless. It wasn't the deceit of the man she trusted that overwhelmed her, but the thought that the whole miserable business had been talked over between her daughter and Mrs. Wilbur—the woman who represented in its most august form that potent word *society*. How could Mrs. Wilbur be expected to look with favor upon her prospective daughter after such a scene? Poor Mrs. Halsted couldn't stop hoping that however much incensed her daughter might be at the moment, time would furnish a healing balm. But this wasn't so sure, if the all-powerful mother had become prejudiced against Bernice.

Viewed in any light much had to be endured. Bernice could talk resolutely before her mother and brothers, with her vein of obstinacy standing her in good stead. But alone in her room, hidden by darkness from even her own observation, she sank into the depths of self-abandonment, when it seemed impossible to her that anyone else's pain and humiliation could be like hers.

Among many minor questions she must consider were those concerning Gertrude Fenton's fast-approaching wedding. Could she keep her pledge and pass through the tortures connected with the great event? If so, how? If she went alone, after writing George Wilbur such a letter that he wouldn't dare attempt to accompany her, how would she account to formal inquirers for the absence of the guest whose name had been so closely linked with hers?

What would she say to Gertrude herself and to Naomi, who would have a right to question closely? To Barbara she thought she could lay bare her heart; it would be a relief to do so. But would it be possible, so soon, to go over her humiliations to the others? This was one phase of her feeling.

At times the longing to see Barbara, and to hear her say while her arms were about the stricken girl, "You could do no less, dear. You couldn't respect yourself and do less than you've done," so possessed her that she felt she could brave all the others for the sake of this. Barbara was the one friend who, she felt, would understand her moral revulsion and at the same time her pitiful desolation in losing the one she'd given herself to unreservedly. But there were other hours when she shrank and cowered and was sure she couldn't meet even Barbara.

The days didn't wait for her decision. They moved steadily on until it was within two weeks of the wedding.

During this time, in the always bustling boardinghouse or restaurant where Mrs. Fenton carried on her brave work, life was more pressured than usual. Both Mrs. Fenton and her daughter Annie were determined to bring about as fine a wedding as they could for the one who was to bring them honor. That it was a distinct honor to be allied with a physician so universally respected as Dr. Adams, both mother and daughter heartily conceded.

"It isn't that we aren't as good as any of them," Mrs. Fenton affirmed as she and Annie worked and talked. "Your father and me both came from first-rate families as far back as you've a mind to go, and some of them were real well-to-do and smart, too. But they weren't doctors and lawyers and things of that kind. Still, Gertie is every bit as good as he is, and educated, too. It's a fine thing, after all, that she went to college. It wouldn't be quite the thing, I s'pose, for a doctor's wife not to know how to talk books with her husband. He seems pleased enough to think she can do it. But he isn't a bit stuck-up, and he's helping your father right along. I'm dreadful glad she's got him."

The unselfish Annie agreed to it all and worked early and late to help carry out the preparations that, despite Gertrude's constant protest, were in danger of being elaborate.

To Gertrude herself life was golden-hued. Nothing about the wedding dresses or the wedding breakfast troubled her. Indeed, her mother, half in pride and half in vexation, accused her of being willing to be "married in her old brown serge, and to have johnnycake and warmed-up potatoes for refreshments, so that she had a chance to go off with 'him' and no one to interrupt."

Gertrude laughed and blushed over the charge and admitted to herself that there was truth in it. Why should commonplaces interest her now? The very best life has for mortals had come to her in the exclusive love of a good man— a man in whose nobility of soul and integrity of life others as well as she placed perfect confidence.

What hadn't the year brought to her—the single winter that opened so drearily and whose daily ordeal she shrank from so abjectly! How rebellious she'd been because no escape came to her! What if she'd secured one of the teaching situations, for which she tried so hard, and missed knowing Dr. Adams? How good her Father in heaven had been to her, even when she was living in indifference to His claims!

That time, too, was past for Gertrude. The beautiful winter through which she just passed brought her much more than a cupful of earthly bliss. Early in her acquaintance with Dr. Adams she discovered he had one Master and his highest aim in life was to follow in his Master's footsteps. It was easy and delightful to lead Gertrude Fenton's awakened heart to recognize in Jesus Christ a stronger claimant for her love and service.

"It seems strange," she wrote to Barbara, "that I never understood before. I thought becoming a Christian was a solemn, gloomy thing to do, and yet it's so simple and beautiful. I realize now what made you so different from other girls. Why didn't you tell me, dear, more plainly—so plainly that a girl as stupid as I could understand—how your love for the Lord Jesus Christ colored all your life?"

Barbara looked serious at those words. They told her plainly that her following of Christ hadn't been as it should; otherwise she would have won to fellowship those friends who seemed so willing to be led. But she was glad for Gertrude, and the coming wedding festivities were eagerly looked forward to. The occasion would mark their first reunion.

"Isn't it strange," wrote Gertrude, "that I, the least likely of the four, should have been the one to ring the first wedding bells? I surely thought it would be our little Naomi. And isn't it wonderful that nothing has occurred to prevent the reunion? So many things might have happened in a year. I don't believe school-girl notions as a rule work out this way."

Suddenly out of a clear June sky a thunderbolt struck this rose-tinted time. One morning Mrs. Fenton was boasting to a caller, with her usual complacency, "Yes, it's nice for me to keep my girl right here in town. The doctor's house is in as good a neighborhood as there is, and he's furnished it as well as the best of them. Gertrude will be about as well fixed as any girl in this town, and she'll make a real nice housekeeper, too, if I do say so. I used to think she was too fond of her books to amount to much in other ways, but they ain't spoiled her a bit as I can see. Anyhow, the doctor thinks she's about right. And he—"

Then she heard herself called loudly and ran to see what happened.

Through the years Gertrude Fenton never forgot the spot where she stood in her room and the size and shape of the tiny hole she discovered in the sleeve of the dress she was folding away. Her face reflected the pleasant thought that she wouldn't need the garment again until she was working in her own kitchen. These minute details burned themselves into her memory of the morning and belong with Annie's scared face and anxious voice as she burst in with her message.

"Oh, Gertie! Dick Foster run into the doctor's carriage, and he's hurt. They hope he ain't bad, but they want you to come right away. They took him into the drugstore at the corner. Mother's there helping."

Annie called this after the girl, who asked no questions, waited for no further word, but seized the hat that Annie, who was crying, thrust at her. She ran in her morning wrapper as she was down the stairs, down the street, and across the road to the drugstore, before whose closed doors a crowd of boys was gathered. As they drew back respectfully for her, she remembered afterward that their stillness struck her like a blow. What happened to hush that crowd of noisy boys?

Within three hours telegrams began to speed over the wires. Bernice Halsted's reached her on the evening George Wilbur was expected home. She held it a moment, trembling, in a curious mixture of indignation and wild hope. At first she thought it was from him. What right had he to send her telegrams? Unless, indeed—unless what? She didn't answer her thought, but controlled herself and read her message: "Dr. Adams, thrown from carriage this morning; died at noon."

Long afterward Gertrude Fenton told Bernice that hers were the first helpful words piercing through the midnight that fell upon her in the midst of that June day.

Bernice had just before that reached her decision. She couldn't go to the wedding, couldn't write, could never again write to any of them. She had lived what couldn't be told, and she had no other life about which to write. She, of all others, had been singled out for misery; she must keep to herself and not shadow by her presence or her words the joy of others. Then, after the first shock of the news was over, she wrote out of the depths of her soul to Gertrude. She didn't give the details of her story; as far as words are concerned, the story was brief. Yet she bared her heart for Gertrude to see what pain really was.

> *I know, dear friend, you think the words, "There is no sorrow like unto my sorrow," were written to describe you. But it isn't true! Let me, the one who has lived a lifetime in this little year and who KNOWS as you never can, assure you it isn't true. Gertrude, you have an honored grave that belongs to you and strong, sweet memories that no one can steal from you, while I–I cannot tell my story. I have lived it, but some things which have to be lived cannot be told in words. Dear friend, there is no grave for me to cry beside, save the grave of my buried faith in one whom I trusted utterly and vainly. Forgive me for thrusting my pain upon you. My only reason is the belief that it will help you to see how sweet and holy is your sorrow beside mine.*

There was no reunion of the four friends. The illness of Barbara's mother prevented her from going to Gertrude in the early days of her sorrow, as she would otherwise have done. And Naomi, who shrank from sorrow and couldn't endure the thought of meeting poor Gertrude, gave up her Eastern trip altogether and accompanied her father on one of his mountain mining tours.

As for Bernice, she agreed with her brother's views about going away from home. To teach school for a few years had been her ambition in early girlhood and was set aside only because her mother and brothers wouldn't listen to such a thought. Most opportunely an unexpected opening occurred in a school of good standing where Bernice had several friends. So by October of that eventful year she was hundreds of miles away from the scene of her happiness and her humiliation.

Before then, however, George Wilbur arrived home. He hurried to see if he couldn't in person satisfactorily answer Bernice's letter which had reached him two days before. Just what took place during that interview no one but those two ever fully knew.

Mrs. Halsted, who had hoped much from his presence, told her son sadly that she never saw a person look so crushed as poor George did when he walked through the hall after his hour with Bernice.

And the son replied that he was almost sorry for the puppy; that once his sister got up on stilts, there was no woman living he wouldn't rather meet.

Chapter 13

"Weary of the weary way
We have come, from Yesterday."

Her hand rested on one of the great stone pillars in the corridor, not for support, but because it was natural for Naomi to put out a hand toward whatever was nearest. The years had changed her in some respects, or else it was the deep mourning she wore that accentuated the pallor of her face. Her eyes, too, seemed to have grown larger; they were certainly sadder. Naomi believed life had dealt hardly by her. The girl graduate of nineteen and the young woman of twenty-five seemed to belong to different worlds. None of her plans matured as she intended.

Certain letters of Barbara's awakened a desire to be much more to her mother than a pretty darling to be kissed and chatted with on pleasant mornings when the invalid felt equal to it. Reading the twelve-page letter over carefully for the third time, studying the rugged farm life, as Barbara laid it bare for her to study, Naomi began to absorb what Barbara was becoming to her mother and to covet a like experience.

She began a systematic scheming to win her mother to herself. Had Mrs. Newland been stronger physically, the girl would have doubtless succeeded to a degree. As it was, the delicate lady, who had indulged herself and been indulged by others all her life, could not for even an hour rise to her young daughter's vigor. She loved her child with all the blind, unreasoning fondness of a self-indulgent mother, but the girl's fulness of life wearied her.

"I feel as if I'd walked miles," she said pathetically to Maida, as she languished among the pillows after a morning in which Naomi devoted herself to her mother. "The child is so full of energy and does everything with such vim, even her reading, that it exhausts me."

And Maida, whom her mistress had needed for six years and who had no desire either to relinquish her post or share it with a rival, skillfully fostered the sense of fatigue and discomfort.

"Miss Naomi is too young, ma'am, and too well and strong to accommodate an invalid's ways. She ought to stay out among young people where things are lively and not play at being nurse when she doesn't know how and just makes you worse. I can't have you being tired out in this way, ma'am. The doctor will scold me for it."

This illustrates the forces at work to make Naomi's efforts a failure. As her mother grew weaker, the girl, who didn't realize the growing weakness, couldn't help but realize the signs of failure in being a pleasing necessity; she couldn't see that she wasn't even an important addition to the invalid's train. It was humiliating to know that Maida was distinctly and constantly preferred to her. But she tried to quiet her disappointed heart with the thought that it was because her mother was used to Maida and that when she grew stronger it would be different.

But the hoped-for strength never came. Both father and daughter were used to seeing the wife and mother recline among the pillows and being waited upon. She accepted the invalid's role early and with relish, and it grew to be almost second nature. Even she herself didn't realize she was steadily slipping lower in the scale of life, and certainly none about her realized it, unless indeed Maida did. The busy man was distinctly shocked when his career was arrested one morning with news that his wife was sinking and the doctor feared she might not rally again. She didn't rally again, and both father and daughter were overwhelmed with astonishment and sorrow.

"I never thought she'd die," wailed the girl, held close in her father's arms. "She's always been ill. But I thought she'd stay here and grow into an old lady, and then she'd get used to having me near her waiting upon her and like it. I was waiting to have her grow used to me, and she never did."

The poor father couldn't comfort his darling; he was too surprised and bewildered. It seemed dreadful that the wife of his youth was no longer among the luxurious pillows he'd furnished. Despite the luxury in which he enveloped her, he had his regrets. At one time the delicate lady liked nothing better than a quiet drive with him or a slow walk about their own extensive grounds leaning on his arm. But in recent years he was so busy that those little pleasures slipped out of their world. In the rare moments when he allowed himself to daydream, he'd planned for a leisure time when he would give them back to her and teach her, as poor Naomi said, to grow used to him again. It was all over now; no rare, sweet leisure time would avail anything for her. The thought crushed him.

After Naomi's first prolonged outburst of grief passed, she came to understand something of her father's feeling and roused herself to minister to him. She succeeded so well that the memory of it afterward was sweet to both. It helped the man of business, who couldn't linger long even to respect death, to feel there was still something to look forward to. His child was growing into a woman and was companionable. When the coveted leisure came, he and she would enjoy it together.

But the sod was still fresh on the new grave when he was out again in the rushing world, meeting his committees and secretaries, receiving reports from all sorts of mammoth business operations, and receiving or seeking audience with persons important in the business world. The treadmill of life must go steadily on for him. He told his daughter so with a sigh and believed he regretted he had no time to spend with her in the great dreary house she called home.

For poor Naomi the dreariness continued. At times it seemed insupportable, when she felt she'd welcome any change. Yet she shrank from possible changes that presented themselves for consideration.

During those early years she unconsciously measured her acquaintances by her friend Barbara's standards, and they always fell short. She measured and dismissed more than one eager aspirant to the place of exclusive friend-ship her cousin Dick once occupied, when she felt Barbara's grave, gray eyes resting on her.

With no little anxiety her father watched some of these experiences develop, but the dismissals met with his unqualified approval. He'd found no one, as yet, upon whom he cared to bestow the title of son-in-law and the management of the millions he'd have to leave behind. As the years went by, he continued to be pleased. Naomi, womanly though she was growing in some respects, was still a child. She would mature late, like her mother. What a perfect child the mother was when he married her! And at such moments he took time for a single sigh over his lost youth.

In this way the years passed. Cousin Dick recovered from the sore wounds he declared were mortal and in time brought home a bride as unlike Naomi as a man's second choice is generally unlike his first. Naomi welcomed her new cousin with eagerness and for a time was quite close to her; it was so delight-ful to have someone near her age who belonged to them. The intensity of their friendship lessened, until they were simply civil to one another, seeing as lit-tle of each other as possible, to the evident comfort of both. In some respects it was unfortunate for Naomi that she'd acquired the habit of measuring every-body by that one girlhood friend.

Time and separation were, however, working their inevitable results with those early friendships. The solemn event that shut out the wedding bells and interrupted the proposed reunion brought other changes in its wake. Naomi hadn't ceased wondering over Bernice's sudden decision to become a teacher when her thoughts were turned into another channel by Gertrude Fenton's unexpected movements.

Gertrude, to everyone's surprise and her mother's vexation, had "gone back to school." At least, that was how the mother put it. Through Barbara's letters Naomi learned that Dr. Adams left his little property entirely to Gertrude: a pretty home and a few thousand dollars. Instead of investing the money securely and having what her mother called a "snug little income to depend upon," Gertrude determined to enter a training school for nurses and fit herself for a professional nurse, using what money she needed to bring that about.

To Naomi, who was used to conventional lines, this seemed almost as wide a departure as it had to Gertrude's mother. She wrote to Barbara that she didn't wonder Gertrude didn't want to write letters to her friends anymore; she'd done such an odd thing that it must be hard to explain her reasons. By degrees Naomi ceased to expect to hear directly from either Bernice or Gertrude.

Both young women shrank a little from writing to her. In their eyes she was still a child to be shielded. They didn't need to bare their hearts for her to weep over, and neither of them knew how to write to her in the old, half-playful strain. So they didn't write. From the first they were rather poor correspondents, as Naomi was herself. Her letters were creatures of her moods, and if the mood for writing didn't present itself, her friends suffered. She held on the longest to Barbara.

But that young woman was busy and had no time for long letters. As the months passed and her mother's illness continued, and the busy teacher felt she must give every possible moment to her mother, the letters grew less frequent. Naomi understood, and the habit of not writing, always easy for her to form, gained on her. Then came word that Barbara was motherless.

The girl shrank from writing other than the simplest word of immediate sympathy, because everything she tried to write sounded either cold or trivial. She didn't know how to talk to people in trouble, she told herself; it seemed impertinent to say anything. Within a few months her own bereavement came, and then she shrank from writing out her pain, even to Barbara. It was her first experience of sorrow, and it hurt her to touch it. Barbara's long, tender letter remained unanswered until she was all but ashamed to write at all. When she did, she found it hard to gather up the scattered threads.

"It's impossible to get back to where we left off," she said aloud to herself one day with a weary sigh, when she was trying to talk to Barbara. "*Living* has come in between somehow. If I could only see her for a little while." But that was still not easy to manage.

The time came when Barbara, too, left home. Bernice Halsted brought that about. There was a vacancy in the school where she was teaching, just the one she was sure Barbara could fill better than anyone else. So it came to pass that the "two B's" were together again within school walls, and Gertrude wasn't far from them, working hard in her chosen field. Only Naomi was at home, unoccupied and dreary—"left out," as she expressed it. This feeling of being "left out" may have helped her drop her school friends, not out of her thoughts, but out of her daily life. At last an entire year passed without writing to any of them. After that by tacit consent all attempt at correspondence ceased.

In the spring that marked Naomi's twenty-fifth birthday her father, warned by his physician, suddenly broke away from his pressing home cares and went abroad, taking his daughter with him. This was a long and eagerly anticipated pleasure, for Naomi believed that when the ocean rolled between her father and his place of business she could have him to herself. She knew nothing of the family physician's fears and thought the trip was taken largely for her sake.

The time had at last come when she could make herself so necessary to her father and so happy in his society that neither could, hereafter, do without the other and gradually she could coax him to give up business altogether. She almost succeeded.

Mr. Newland laid aside his business cares in a way that delighted his daughter's heart, and he liked nothing better than to have her beside him. In fact, he clung to her in a way that was an unmixed delight and later became a pathetic memory. For three months Naomi was happy.

Then, suddenly, without warning, night dropped down upon her, and she was alone in a strange land. Her father kissed her good night and said, with his arm around her, "We're having a happy time together, aren't we, daughter?"

She returned the kiss, assuring him she had no other wish in life than to be with him always. And in the gray of the next early morning a stranger, a physician, bent over her with grave, pitying face to tell her as gently as he could of her desolation. Her father's bell had rung vigorously and was promptly answered, but the father, even then, wasn't there.

She found friends, of course, as a suddenly stricken foreigner. They thronged about her and fairly oppressed her with their efforts to serve. Not foreigners alone, but her own countrymen: some she knew by reputation, some she never heard of. But they came, eager to help, to sympathize. It endeared her to that sunny land in which she was stranded and made her feel like lingering. It was more homelike there, she told herself, than that great, desolate house she called home could ever be again. So she stayed on, at first because she was too spent to undertake the journey; afterward because she didn't want to take it.

She was singularly alone in the world. The cousin Dick, whose marriage to an uncongenial wife had made her realize how little he really was to her, was the nearest relative. There were others, distant relatives of her father, scattered over the country somewhere; she didn't know and didn't care where. What did she want of relatives she'd never seen?

Then she thought sorrowfully of her school friends and told herself pitifully that if they knew how desolate their poor little Naomi was, they'd come to her aid. She resolved to write to them but shrank from the task. There was so much to explain, such a long chasm to bridge. And she let the days drag their slow length away without doing it.

Chapter 14

"The instruments of darkness tell us truths;
Win us with honest trifles, to betray us
In deepest consequence."

One day Naomi's seclusion was invaded by one who claimed relationship with her father. "I'm only a cousin by marriage, and twice removed at that," he said with a regretful smile on his face. "I don't think your father and mine ever met. Yet I've ventured to call upon you and claim the right to serve you in any way I can. You observed, I hope, that I bear the family name. I've been alone in a strange land myself and know something of the sense of loneliness. I hope you'll at least let me try to make some of your hours less weary."

Naomi looked again at his card, which she still held in her hand. "Volney Hermann Newland" was the name engraved on it—the family name, certainly. A faint color showed on her otherwise pale face as she read. It certainly was ludicrous that of all her thronging memories the one claiming her thought just then was frivolous in the extreme and was in Gertrude Fenton's voice: "It is written in the annals of fate that Naomi Newland shall be the first of the group to change her name. And do insist, my dear, that his name commence with N. I'm so fond of alliteration."

Mr. Volney Newland proved to be very pleasant. His first call was limited to the prescribed time, and he didn't intrude upon Naomi in any offensive way. He referred her to several prominent men among her father's acquaintances, whom she might consult if she chose to prove his right to the name of Newland and his claim to the family connection. Then he begged to serve her in any possible way, assuring her that for his mother's sake he was always glad to be of service to any woman. After that, his attentions were constant and delicately considerate.

Before a week passed Naomi felt she knew him better than anyone else in that land of strangers. When he told her the business that had called him to that part of the country would likely hold him there for weeks, possibly months, she felt distinctly glad and believed she couldn't do better than to carry out the original plan and remain where she was for the winter. Her father had engaged the rooms and made things comfortable, and there was not only nothing to call her home, but everything to make her shrink from going.

She grew to looking for Mr. Newland's coming and to feel disappointed when he failed to appear. As a rule, his mornings seemed to be given to business matters, and during those hours she wandered about a good deal in search of something to distract her from her loneliness.

One morning she wandered into a massive stone structure and stood in the vestibule leaning against a pillar lost in sorrowful thought. She was attracted inside the building by the grand sound of an organ. She found worshippers devoutly kneeling, bowing, crossing themselves at intervals, going through all manner of genuflections strange to her. But she was interested because the people seemed to be in earnest. Many were, like herself, in deep mourning. They had felt sorrow, then. Were they being helped by all these prayers—if they were prayers, as she judged by the attitude? She looked at them curiously, wistfully. Some of their faces brightened occasionally, as though they saw rays of hope through the gloom. Two or three peaceful faces were marked with the traces of storms outlived.

Most of the service was in Latin, and Naomi didn't remember her schoolgirl Latin well enough to understand much of it. But she caught here and there a phrase enough to discover, at least, that prayer was being said for some person or persons who had died. At first the idea startled her Protestant ears, then interested her strangely. She hadn't prayed for her father and mother while they were with her; she hadn't thought of such a thing. But if it were possible to pray for them now, she'd gladly learn to pray, simply for the privilege of speaking their dear names to God. Still, of course, Protestants had no such belief; and the thought left her profoundly saddened.

This girl, born and reared in a Christian land and educated in a nominally Christian school, knew very little about religious beliefs. Except for certain more or less vague ideas absorbed from the atmosphere, rather than learned, she held no beliefs and was almost as ready to embrace paganism as any other "ism," provided it looked attractive.

Barbara Dennison had often kept a Bible lying open on her desk, and the impression throughout the school halls was that she read in it at other times than during the responsive chapel service. Once Naomi burst heedlessly into her room, thinking no one heard her careless knock, and surprised Barbara on her knees. She went away on tiptoe with a curious feeling of both yearning and jealousy tugging at her heart, born of the thought that Barbara lived a life in which she wasn't included. The next time she saw her friend she watched her sympathetically for awhile, fearing bad news might have come to her that had driven her to prayer. That was about as much knowledge as the young woman of twenty-five had regarding practical religion.

She waited for the worshippers to pass by and was ostensibly studying the marbles within view. But she was really absorbed in her own sad thoughts and half wished she could speak to one of those white-robed priests and ask him what the service meant, when Volney Newland seemed to appear mysteriously from behind one of the marbles and in another minute was beside her.

"Listening to the music?" he asked. "I find myself often stopping at this corner for the same purpose. The organ is played by a master."

"The music lured me in," said Naomi, speaking at once from her deepest thought, as this man had a strange way of winning her to do. "But I stayed for something else. I was interested in the people. They seemed to be helped by the prayers; some of them looked that way, at least. I discovered, after awhile, that they were praying for their dead. I found myself almost wishing I was of their faith, or at least that somewhere I could go to a Protestant church for the same purpose. I believe I could pray then."

Mr. Newland gave her a quick, searching look. Here was a hungry soul evidently. Was she ready to be led? He hadn't hoped for it so soon. He resolved upon a bold effort.

"My dear Miss Newland, all Protestantism is not as cold as you think. Some people, not Romanists, don't teach that we must consign our beloved dead to silence and oblivion. On the contrary, they teach distinctly that we may still do for them; do far more, indeed, than we often could while they were with us."

She stepped toward him, lifting her eyes to his face with a sudden light in them that fairly dazzled him, as she said eagerly, "What do you mean? Do you mean there's such a church and that it teaches truth? Teaches what reasonable people can accept? You can't mean that, of course. But I believe I could join such a church today and promise to do all it could ask, for the sake of doing for my father and mother what I didn't know how to do nor think about at all when I had them. Are you a churchman, Mr. Newland?"

He met her interest with a smile that expressed deep sympathy.

"I trust I am, in the truest sense of the word, though I belong to none of the cold and formal churches you're probably familiar with. I may as well say frankly that I belong to one which some of your friends would probably sneer at, even brand as false. We're quite used to such treatment. It doesn't argue against the truth that its advocates are called upon to be martyrs. The greatest martyr who ever lived was Jesus Christ."

"That's true," she said, impressed. "But I know very little about churches. What is the name of yours?"

"It has, in one sense, an unpretentious name, and yet there can be no grander. We call ourselves simply the Church of Jesus Christ."

"But I shouldn't think that would be distinctive. Aren't all others the same? In what respects do you differ?"

"There are various points of difference. Some of them probably wouldn't interest you; others, I think, might. Do you mean you have no acquaintance whatever with the church I represent?"

"I don't think I have. As I said, I'm not very well acquainted with any church. My father was a liberal giver to all churches, but we weren't members, and I know nothing about their distinctive creeds. Still, I thought they were all able to claim the same name as yours. But of course what you said a few moments ago isn't taught in any of them—at least, I never heard it. I'd like to understand just what you mean."

He was fascinated by the light in her eyes. He spoke with infinite sympathy.

"Poor hungry soul being fed on husks! Believe me, I know all about it and am glad to explain. I meant all and more than my words conveyed. The church I'm honored to belong to teaches, as one of its most blessed truths, that we may think of, pray for, believe for, and do for our dead in a sense that, as I said, is often impossible while they're living. Shall we walk on? We can talk with less interruption than we can here."

The worshippers were still passing by, and the two foreigners were the center of some curious eyes. Naomi turned quickly and followed Mr. Newland's lead. She had forgotten the people; she must hear more of this wonderful talk. She heard more, much more. They walked slowly, and Mr. Newland talked as one who understood what he was explaining. He sat down with her in her little parlor and took her own Bible, to prove to her the truth of his words.

"I'll show you I'm not teaching heresy," he said, with one of his winning smiles. "What did you think these words meant when you read them? Listen: 'Else what shall they do which are baptized for the dead, if the dead rise not at all? Why then are they baptized for the dead?' Paul's argument here was to prove the doctrine of the resurrection, but he wouldn't have used a service that wasn't in existence to illustrate his truth."

She didn't know, she confessed to him, that the verse was there at all; she was afraid she wasn't much better acquainted with the Bible than she was with churches. These subjects hadn't interested her. Only since life became desolate did she feel she needed something that reached beyond this life.

"Poor heart," he said tenderly. "That's a confession that too many nursed by your cold creeds would have to make."

He found other verses equally new to Naomi and read and marked them for her to read. Then he promised to call again when he could give her more time.

After he was gone she read again and again the marked verses, especially that one about being baptized for the dead. It sounded so new to her that she told herself she'd hardly believe it was in the Bible if her own eyes didn't see it; but she lingered with it. Her desolate heart longed for some strong, tender link to bind her once more to her loved ones. She could never get away from the feeling that she might have been more, especially to her mother, if she'd known how. The possibility of atoning for it now, of being permitted some definite, tangible action in the name of her father and mother, at once thrilled and soothed her.

It was strange she hadn't heard of this. It must be true, must be right, this being baptized for the dead; otherwise it wouldn't be in the Bible. And there were the words before her eyes, and they must mean that and nothing else. So reasoned this young woman, who spent a quarter of a century in a Christian land and graduated from a nominally Christian school. Yet her very desire to believe in the new doctrine awakened doubts and anxieties she spread before Mr. Newland at her next opportunity, and he took care she shouldn't have long to wait.

"But why don't the churches generally observe such ceremonies?" she asked him. "I said I knew little about churches. But of course I've attended church more or less regularly all my life, and I never saw or heard of such a service as you describe."

"That's true," said Mr. Newland. His tones weren't bitter, but sad. "It's humiliating to admit it, but it's painfully true that this direction, like too many others, is simply ignored by the so-called orthodox churches. The only explanation I care to give is that they've grown away from the directness and simplicity of the gospel. It's an age when human intellect is greatly exalted and human theories and precepts are permitted to take the place of the divine. The fact that you, a fairly regular churchgoer, have never had your attention directed to those plain words marked in your Bible is a sad comment on the condition of things. The command is there, so plain that a child may read it."

Naomi protested faintly that the verse didn't really command anything, but he was ready for her. "My dear friend, isn't a reference to a manifest custom in a household almost, if not quite, equal to a command in the eyes of a dutiful child? By the same token, couldn't you say that the fourth commandment of the decalogue doesn't really command anything because it begins with the word *remember*?"

She was too unskilled in argument and too eager to accept the new doctrine to realize the absurdity of such words. She was intensely interested, and her teacher was sympathetic and gentle: patient with what she thought he must consider her dullness, gentle over her criticisms. It was quite natural, he assured her, that she should have her doubts and difficulties. She couldn't be expected to imbibe new phases of truth, some running counter to all her preconceived ideas, without much thought and study. What their church courted and coveted was people who would read and think and decide for themselves.

"To the law and to the testimony," he quoted, with one of his significant smiles. Did she remember how that quotation ended? And then he didn't smile as he repeated solemnly, "If they speak not according to this word, it is because there is no light in them." It became everybody, he said, to be careful. Then he borrowed her Bible and returned it with more verses marked and with pencilled explanations.

Chapter 15

"An evil soul, producing holy witness,
Is like a villain with a smiling cheek;
A goodly apple rotten at the heart;
Oh, what a goodly outside falsehood hath!"

I t was all new to Naomi, and it was very fascinating. Her new friend was indefatigable in his efforts to help her. At the same time he managed so skillfully to awaken her interest that it seemed to be she who was urging on the investigation. Besides her own marked and carefully annotated Bible, he left little leaflets and booklets, also carefully marked and with copious marginal notes, with her for study.

Among them were the Thirteen Articles of Faith, which represented, Mr. Newland told her, his church's belief. The first one read, "We believe in God the eternal Father, and in his Son Jesus Christ, and in the Holy Ghost." This had the ring of words Naomi had often murmured with great congregations. She read the articles through with utmost care and with her limited knowledge of religious terms and religious belief saw in them much to admire and nothing to disapprove.

But it was, after all, the living teacher who influenced her most. She was lonely and desolate, and he was uniformly thoughtful and tactful. He was interested evidently, not in her, as a young woman, but in her highest interests. He told her he wanted to be earnest, "in season and out of season," to save souls. He found the verse in her Bible for her where a disciple was ordered to be this and more. He found many verses for her that she hadn't known were in her Bible. She read it much during those days, but she confined her reading to the verses he marked and read no notes but those of his writing.

He talked a great deal to her of Jesus Christ, of His tenderness for humanity, of His abounding sympathy, of the joy of having Him for a personal Friend. Above all, he talked to her about her beloved dead—her father who had so recently left her, to whom she'd meant to be so much and didn't have time to carry out her plans.

Mr. Newland was an excellent reader. Even familiar words read by his sympathetic voice, with his impressive manner, sounded new and wonderful to her. One evening he drew from his pocket a small, daintily bound volume. Without any introduction, other than "Will you let me read some significant words to you?" he began: " 'And I saw the dead, small and great, stand before God; and the books were opened: and another book was opened, which is the book of life: and the dead were judged out of those things which were written in the books, according to their works.' "

He interrupted himself to rise and bring her own Bible to her, found the chapter and verse so she might follow closely, then read the verses again impressively. Without pausing he glided into an explanation of them, still reading from his own dainty volume.

"The books spoken of must be the books which contained the record of their works, and refer to the records which are kept on earth. And the book which was 'the book of life' is the record which is kept in heaven." He paused to make clearer to her just what this meant, then read again, " 'Whatsoever you record on earth shall be recorded in heaven, and whatsoever ye do not record on earth shall not be recorded in heaven; for out of the books shall your dead be judged.' "

It was all so simple, he told her, and so beautiful. God, in His infinite mercy, provided a way for the dead, who neglected the path of truth for themselves in life, to secure eternal salvation, by uniting with those still living who would obey for them and by being baptized not only for themselves, but for their beloved ones.

Then he read again: " 'Herein is glory and honor and immortality and eternal life. To be immersed in the water, and to come forth out of the water, is in the likeness of the resurrection of the dead in coming forth out of their graves.' "

At this point he leaned forward to turn the pages of her Bible and indicate the words as he read from his own volume: " 'Howbeit that was not first which is spiritual, but that which is natural; and afterwards that which is spiritual. The first man is of the earth, earthy: the second man is the Lord from heaven. As is the earthy, such are they also that are earthy: and as is the heavenly, such are they also that are heavenly—and as are the records on the earth in relation to your dead, which are truly made out, so also are the records in heaven.' "

Here again he stopped to emphasize to his eager pupil the wonderful love and grace of God as shown in this provision. What had he done but so link the destinies of the living and the dead that " 'that they without us should be made perfect' "—and he found that phrase for her in Hebrews— " 'neither can we without our dead be made perfect; for their salvation is necessary and essential to our salvation.'

"You see this is no new idea," he assured her. "Let me show you the words of the grand old prophet who had his eye fixed on the glories to be revealed in the last days, and especially this most glorious of all subjects—the baptism of the dead. Here it is in Malachi. Read it for yourself, please."

And Naomi read, " 'Behold, I will send you Elijah the prophet before the coming of the great and dreadful day of the Lord: and he shall turn the heart of the fathers to the children, and the heart of the children to their fathers, lest I come and smite the earth with a curse.' "

"Could anything be plainer?" he asked her with a reassuring smile, as she lifted her startled eyes to his—"plainer or more gracious? Let me read the inspired explanation: " 'The earth will be smitten with a curse unless there is a welding link of some kind or other between the fathers and the children, upon some subject or other, and behold, what is that subject? It is the baptism for the dead. For "we without them cannot be made perfect." ' "

"It sounds very plain," said Naomi, trembling with excitement, "and it seems simple and beautiful. I want to believe it. Such a little thing to do for my dear ones. And yet it seems so strange I haven't heard of it before and that all who recognize the claims of Christ don't practice it."

"My dear friend, that's as simple and beautiful as the rest of it. The world wasn't ready for the truth, wouldn't receive it. Why, only a handful is ready for it now. Only here and there is someone who'll listen to truth. But thank God for one here and there, and the Lord knew that, when He made this the fulness of time and ushered in a new dispensation.

"Notice how inspiration puts it: 'Those things which never have been revealed from the foundation of the world, but have been hid from the wise and prudent, shall be revealed unto babes and sucklings, in this, the dispensation of the fulness of times. Now what do we hear in the gospel which we have received? A voice of gladness, a voice of mercy from heaven, and a voice of truth out of the earth. A voice of gladness for the living and the dead. Glad tidings of great joy. How beautiful upon the mountains are the feet of those that bring glad tidings of good things, and that say unto Zion, behold, thy God reigneth. As the dews of Carmel, so shall the knowledge of God descend upon them.' "

Naomi had never been so moved. As the magnetic voice of the reader filled the room, growing jubilant with each added phrase, she felt her breath coming in quick throbs, and her soul shone in her eyes. For the first time since death robbed her of her father just as she was making herself indispensable to him, she felt she could continue to live and even be glad of life, for didn't she have a work to do, for him and for her mother, that was worthy of her?

By natural and reasonable steps the intimacy between her and her teacher flourished. The new disciple had much to learn, even after she frankly opened her heart to the truth in a way Mr. Newland told her was exhilarating beyond anything she could imagine. She hadn't been laboring for years to win people to these sublime truths of God, only to find the vast majority of them with vision so blinded by prejudice and ears so dulled by the superstitions of the past that they could neither see nor hear.

Naomi was a more than willing learner. She was eager, intense. She continued to study with the most painstaking care every verse her teacher marked for her in the Bible of which she'd known nothing. She read and reread them with ever-increasing satisfaction. In light of the copious explanations accompanying them they seemed beautifully clear and convincing.

She made great strides in the truth, Mr. Newland told her. On the day she announced herself ready to accept his faith as hers and to be baptized whenever he wished it, not only for herself, but for her father and mother, he bent over and lifted her hand to his lips with an emotion that for the moment seemed too deep for words.

"Dear child," he said at last, his voice tremulous with feeling. "Forgive me for using that word, but you seem so simple and childlike in your faith. I've been constantly thinking of the Master's words since I've come to know you intimately: 'Whosoever shall not receive the kingdom of God as a little child shall in no wise enter therein.' The trouble with many people is they're too wise; they want to argue instead of believe. The directness of your faith comforts me."

He had abundant ground for comfort. From the hour of her great decision a new life seemed to open before Naomi. She did nothing by halves—this girl of a strong though undisciplined nature. She became enthusiastic for the faith she had espoused. She attended the meetings where Mr. Newland spoke and took part as she could in the personal explanations arranged to follow the more formal talk. In this work her excellent knowledge of German was at last put to what she believed was good use.

Mr. Newland was very proud of his most distinguished proselyte. He accepted meekly her extravagant estimate of his service to her and was grateful for her help in the meetings. One evening he told her smilingly that he'd soon become quite jealous of her; that she was having better success with some of the inquirers than he had. All who came in contact with the girl recognized she was in earnest. All her past seemed to her as wasted years, in which she hadn't known how to live. Now opportunity was given her to atone, to make up as well as she might for lost time.

Her first disappointment was close at hand. Her desire to submit to baptism in the name of her precious dead burned with a fever that could ill brook delay. She couldn't understand why Mr. Newland allowed the subject to drop constantly into the background, treating it almost as though it were of minor importance. As last she compelled him to a direct statement.

"I confess I've avoided the subject lately," he said with a serious smile. "I saw a disappointment in store for you, and I don't like to have you disappointed in anything. Don't look so startled, my dear friend. It's just a little necessary delay."

"But why should there be delay in such an important service when I'm ready?"

"It's because of its very importance. When we first talked about it, I neglected to explain that we don't perform this solemn service everywhere or with ordinary surroundings. The ceremony must take place in one of our temples with unusual and very solemn accompaniments. Let me read you what our prophets say about it."

That daintily bound volume appeared from his pocket and seemed to open by itself to the right page: " 'To be immersed in the water and to come forth out of the water, is in the likeness of the resurrection of the dead in coming forth out of their graves; hence this ordinance was instituted to form a relationship with the ordinance of baptism for the dead, being in the likeness of the dead. Consequently the baptismal font was instituted as a simile of the grave, and was commanded to be in a place underneath where the living are wont to assemble, to show forth the living and the dead.' "

Naomi regarded the reader with wide-eyed wonder mixed with terror and interrupted him in a trembling voice. "That sounds very strange. It almost frightens me. Why are secrecy and mystery necessary? If it's right to be baptized for one's dead and is a merciful provision of God, why can't it be performed, as other church functions are, wherever there's a gathering of good people who wish it and a minister to do it? Why do you plan it to be done only in certain places that might be impossible for some to reach and hide the service from sight?"

He began very gently. "My dear friend, this is all so new and strange to you that I don't wonder at your questions. But consider what a solemn service it is, linking the living and the dead as closely as it does and as no other ceremony professes to do. Revelation has declared that the records of these ceremonies must be kept with utmost accuracy so as to accord in every particular with the records kept in heaven. Surely you see how dangerous it would be to multiply the places where the rite might be performed and perhaps leave the records in careless hands.

"But more than all that"—and here his voice grew serious and slightly stern—"do I need to remind you that men didn't make the laws which govern us? They were revealed to us through our prophet and are to us the voice of God. Who are we to question his ways?"

Chapter 16

"Suspicion sleeps
At Wisdom's gate, and to Simplicity
Resigns her charge, while Goodness thinks no ill
Where no ill seems."

F orgive me," said Naomi humbly. "I didn't think of that. If the minutest details of service have been revealed to you, of course you must obey." He promptly followed up his advantage, adding a touch of reproach to his gravity.

"After all, does that seem like such a hard condition to you, to gain such far-reaching and eternally important results? Just a journey by rail over an interesting country to our Mecca, which all true believers long to see, and personal greetings from the honored heads of our church. Still, I must remember that all these matters impress you very differently from what they do me. Your environment has been completely different, and you have only my poor word to set against a lifetime of preconceived ideas. I shouldn't think it strange you find it hard to trust me. I'm not at all offended by your doubts. I may be just a little hurt, but even that's foolish, and I'll rise above it after awhile."

Naomi was subdued. She begged him not to misunderstand her questions. She assured him her trust in him was complete and couldn't be shaken; she would have believed his teaching even if she hadn't read the same truths in her own Bible. What motive could he possibly have for deceiving her regarding such matters or any matters?

He smiled sadly over that question and said, "What, indeed!" Then he told her he desired nothing in life as much as her highest good.

Having yielded a point, it was like Naomi to yield wholly. Soon after that conversation she cheered her teacher with the statement that it seemed now to her not only appropriate but altogether beautiful that a sort of holy pilgrimage must be taken to perform her service of love for her dead. Such details lifted it above the common—set it apart as it should be. Of course the condition wasn't a hard one, not at least for her.

It was true, as he said, that one had a natural desire to visit the city which in a peculiar sense seemed to have been set apart for God's peculiar people, and to see that wondrous temple he'd told her about in all its massive beauty. She'd be very glad to go.

She didn't mean to be unreasonable again. She'd been acting like the undisciplined child she was. But she meant to curb her impatient spirit and wait whatever length of time he considered wise before starting on her journey.

More than that, she resolved to show her utter faith in him by not even asking why she must wait; she knew the reasons must be good, and she could trust him.

Mr. Newland was very touched by this exhibition of trust. His voice almost trembled when he said he hoped to prove himself worthy of such confidence. Then he walked the floor of her little parlor with a face so grave and suggesting trouble, or at least anxiety, that she grew sympathetic at once. She promised not to ask questions, but the promise applied only to her own affairs. Mightn't she ask about his? What was troubling him? Had anything gone wrong in his work? Couldn't she help him?

She succeeded in winning a solemn smile, and he came over and took a seat near her. Nothing had gone wrong, he told her. But he was puzzled about the right or wrong of a certain course and so sorely tempted in one direction that he feared it was biassing his judgment and making the wrong seem right, or at least the unwise seem wise.

Couldn't he tell her about it, she asked winsomely, and let her help decide? Papa used to say sometimes that two heads were better than one, even when one belonged to a silly little woman.

He shook his head and looked even more solemn as he said that if he were sure of her approval he could afford to laugh at others' views. It was what she would think, or rather what effect his thought would have upon her, that was troubling him. A great deal was at stake, and it was possible by making a careless move to lose all he'd dared to hope for. He looked steadily at her as he spoke, but she was innocently bewildered and begged him to confide in her if he could and let her help him in any possible way.

He let the silence fall between them until she grew flushed and embarrassed under it, though she couldn't have told why. Then he spoke in low, impassioned tones. Since she advised, he would take a chance and risk all. She was good enough to call him her teacher, but the truth was he had been a pupil and learned one lesson during these weeks, such as he never expected to learn. He realized he'd already gone too far for retreat, so he must tell her plainly that, as far as this world was concerned, his happiness depended upon her.

He knew only too well the infinite stretch between them: he a middle-aged man, and she a radiant young woman. And yet—and then he made good use of the other side of the question—he knew how to use words, and he poured them out upon her in an impassioned way, just enough tinged with hope to thrill her, just enough oppressed by fear of failure to enlist her sympathy. He watched her closely, and when at last he paused and waited for what he called his fate, he knew Naomi was ready to speak.

She looked at him with eyes that were swimming in tears but still had in them a slight smile.

"I'm overwhelmed," she said. "I've thought of you as my teacher, my guide. You seemed so far above me that to think of you as a friend I told myself was presumptuous. I'm all alone in the world. To find that you care for me is almost too much—"

She had no time to complete the sentence. She was gathered suddenly into a pair of eager arms, whose owner assured her he'd been longing for her while he waited and trembled over possibilities.

The next few weeks were like a dream of happiness to Naomi. It was much as she told her suitor: Surrounded by innumerable friends in the general understanding of that word, she'd lived her life, at least since her school days, chiefly alone and had looked forward to loneliness to the end.

Marriage and home, and the joys connected with those strong, pure words, she supposed weren't for her. Her early experience with her cousin, when she found herself astonished over the story of his love and unable to respond to it, gave her an impression she wasn't like other girls. The ease with which many of her acquaintances loved and married, choosing for life men whose company she wearied of in an hour, confirmed that impression; it further convinced her she was intended to create an earthly paradise for just her father and dwell in it with him.

Then, suddenly, in her deepest loneliness, a rich, new world opened for her, growing in interest and promise as the days passed. She hadn't realized what this new friend was becoming to her; she hadn't analyzed the sweetness of the companionship. So far as she thought at all, she told herself that her new peace and joy grew entirely out of her new faith and the hopes and opportunities it opened before her. There was enough genuine heart experience in this to hold good for her belief. But the moment she heard her new friend's confession of more than general interest in her as a human being with a soul to be saved, her heart met the confession and responded.

In the quiet of her room that first evening after they exchanged pledges, she went carefully over the way she was led, up to that supreme moment when her deepest self had been revealed to her. Then she said aloud and solemnly: "God has given me everything but heaven, and that is in store. I must give my life to His service."

Plans for the immediate or at least the near future, *their* future, were now in order. Naomi hadn't planned before, beyond an impression rather than decision she would remain in the lodgings her father secured until summer came.

"After that I suppose I'll go back to the place others call my home," she said once to Mr. Newland, with a sad tone. It thrilled her to realize she didn't need to make that desolate place home; her home now and forever was wherever Mr. Newland called home. She might even cease planning, which she told herself she hated. Someone else would plan, and her joy was simply to assent.

From the first, Mr. Newland dominated her, always in a gentle way that seemed to defer to her slightest wish and yet carried out his own. When she mentioned she was alone in the world, that no one living could claim the right of a relative to advise her or even had a right to inquire into her plans, Mr. Newland frankly said he was glad of it. It made her seem more entirely his own. It made him bold, perhaps, to urge swift movements. In reality he planned them carefully, but he let them appear to Naomi as if thrown upon him because of circumstances not under his control. Some of them weren't.

They were engaged only a few weeks when Mr. Newland came to Naomi's parlor one evening with an open letter in his hand and confusion on his face.

"Here is a complication, Naomi. I'm practically ordered home. At least, certain complications have arisen connected with our interests that seem to demand my presence earlier than I expected. I have a letter here from our president, which all but directs me to rearrange my plans and come home as soon as possible. It's rather disappointing to me, I must say. How do you feel about it, dear?"

What could she feel but dismay? She saw herself stranded again—alone in the great dreary world, as she was during those terrible days after her father left. To lose suddenly the prop she'd unconsciously leaned on since they first met, to be separated from one who for a few blessed weeks had practically thought for her, tenderly shouldering each responsibility as it loomed up to be considered, was to go back into the depths of desolation. She put her distress into her eyes and uttered no word.

"Poor child!" he said with infinite tenderness. "Poor little girl, it's too hard, after all you've endured. I wonder if the only other way would also be too hard for you?"

Of course he was asked to explain that other way, which he did with skill and a conviction of its advantages that grew upon him as he talked. What did they care, they two, about conventionalities? It wasn't as though she had home friends waiting for her. They were both sadly alone in the world. Why should custom hold them apart? What reasonable hindrance was there to their immediate marriage? Then they could take that long journey together with no weary separation to haunt their future.

Naomi was at first greatly startled, almost shocked. She had traditions and an inheritance of sentiment to overcome. She had dreamed—and a marriage of this sort did not fit the dreams. But all that belonged to her silly schoolgirl days—days when Barbara and Gertrude, and even Bernice, who was more romantic by nature than they, laughed at her for being sentimental. It was years since she dreamed, and she didn't need to anymore; blessed realities had come to her. As she grew used to the idea, she asked herself why she should make

Mr. Newland's life hard as well as her own because of a few conventionalities. What did they care about what people would say? What right had anybody to criticize their doings?

Mr. Newland prevailed, of course; he meant to when he began. Naomi and he were quietly married one sunny morning without other witnesses than a few of the stranger friends who gathered about the girl in her bereavement. There was no one who knew her before her trouble.

They said among themselves that it was rather unusual, this being married in a foreign country, away from all one's home friends. Still, the girl was unusually situated, being left alone unexpectedly. She probably knew Mr. Newland all her life, and he was certainly old enough to take care of her. For that matter, she wasn't a child herself.

Of course none of them talked to Naomi, which was, perhaps, quite as well. She would have resented all advice as intrusive. She had given her faith unreservedly with her heart, and the loyalty that made her place Mr. Newland's judgment above that of all others only echoed her heart's desire.

It's true she shed a few self-pitying tears on the eve of her marriage day, as she thought of her father and told herself how he would have admired and enjoyed Volney; as she thought of Barbara and the others and wished she could have gathered them about her. It was very unusual and sad for a girl to be alone at such a time in her life. Hadn't the girls promised to respond to wedding bells? And, behold, hers were the first to ring.

Who dreamed, at the time that sentimental promise was made, that the years and life's solemn events would stretch themselves between those four as they had. Poor Gertrude! It must be hard for her to go to weddings. And there was Bernice, whose life story Naomi had never understood, except she knew there was no wedding after all. Perhaps it was well she was so far removed from the girls as to make invitations out of the question.

But she didn't shed many tears; her heart was tender rather than sad. Chiming in with the loneliness was the blessed thought that her lonely days were over. Tomorrow they would be together, not for a precious hour or two, but forever. And nothing but death, no, not even death, could separate them again.

They made a rare holiday of the marriage day. After sitting down together at a wedding breakfast, as fine as the local resources permitted, they drove to one of the many wonderful views they had hoped to visit together sometime. They met many tourists and believed they acted just like the others and could in no way be distinguished as a bridal couple on their first outing. Yet to them it was a day set apart from all others.

Reliving it afterward, Naomi decided she wouldn't have changed one thing about it. It was eminently fitting they should have been quite alone together, with no outsider who had a right to intrude upon them. Didn't they each represent the other's world in an unusual manner? She felt she understood what her husband meant when he confessed he wasn't always sorry she was so entirely alone. If this really made her more fully his, she couldn't find it in her heart to be sorry either.

Chapter 17

"Master, go on, and I will follow thee
To the last gasp, with truth and loyalty."

M r. Newland had sounded the depths of loneliness for himself; so he told his wife. She agreed that his experience in this respect was far harder than hers. He couldn't remember his father, and his mother died when he was twelve. He had brothers but had been separated from them since childhood. His aunts, however, had been devoted to him. One was still living, and he told Naomi she'd find in her a woman to lean upon.

Early in their acquaintance Naomi learned that Mr. Newland married when quite young and lost his wife several years before. It was evidently hard for him to talk about that period of his life, and Naomi, out of sympathy for him, held herself from asking some questions she wanted to ask. She inferred, more from his silences than his words, that the marriage wasn't a happy one. She believed that his sense of honor, as well as his duty to the dead, kept him from speaking plainly, but he told her he was a mere boy when he chose his wife. Sometime afterward he said he was beginning to believe a man never understood his own heart or his capacity for loving until he was at least forty.

Naomi was too respectful of his honorable silence to let him suspect what these and several other statements revealed to her. She was his wife for a week before she made the astonishing discovery that he had children of his own.

"I suppose I should have told you," he said, with an embarrassed smile. "I'm going to confess to a weakness you don't suspect of me. My gray hairs never troubled me until I looked at your fair face. Now I seem too old for the prize I've won. I shrank from telling you about my daughter, for instance, who is sixteen, lest I seem a patriarch to you instead of a bridegroom. Since you've come into my life I like to forget I ever had any other life. In truth I'm in danger at times of forgetting it. I feel as if I'm a newly created being just starting to live. My shadowed past is so far in the background and so unlike this life that it seems to belong to some other creature."

After that he hurriedly explained to the serious woman who was regarding him with grave, anxious eyes: Of course he wouldn't have forgotten his honor and duty toward her as to be silent about such a matter if it made the slightest difference in their life together. His children hadn't been with him for years and weren't to be with him at all. Different arrangements were made for them so long before now that in a sense they had really gone out of his thoughts. Some experiences connected with these arrangements had been painful; he was glad to forget them as much as he could. Not that he really forgot his children, of course, or wasn't ready to do for them if he ever had opportunity. But the sweet life she led him into was so new and precious that for the time being everything else had dropped away.

Still, if she thought for a moment he hadn't been strictly honorable in his silence, he could never forgive himself. He looked so miserable as he said this and conveyed so well the impression of many painful scenes she'd shut away from his memory for a time, that Naomi felt her heart rise up in pity for him. She assured him that nothing he could tell her could shake her faith in his integrity and honor. Of course, since he was separated from his children and must be, she could understand how he felt she didn't need to know about them at once.

Then she asked certain questions as delicately as she could. He answered them with such hesitation and evident pain that she was sure he'd experienced a bitter chapter in his life, a wound that perhaps had healed over but mustn't be probed. She felt only pity for him and arranged, when by herself, a story fitting the situation. The children were with their mother's relatives, he admitted when she asked, and there was bitterness, probably, between their father and their mother's relatives. Perhaps his children were being taught to dishonor their father, and he was powerless to help it.

Having planned all the details in her mind, she sympathized so intensely that the chains of his influence were wound about her more tightly than before. She realized she must fill the place in his heart not only of wife, but of parents and children as well.

For several weeks following their marriage they were in a pleasant bustle preparing for a long journey; then came a change of plans. Mr. Newland entered Naomi's dressing room one morning with a telegram in his hand.

"Do you suppose, dearest, now that you've set your heart on an ocean voyage, you'll be disappointed by delaying? This telegram looks as if we won't reach home as soon as we planned."

The message was brief enough. It read simply: "Defer departure. Explanations by letter."

"Why, of course," said Naomi hesitantly, while studying the yellow paper for something that didn't appear on the surface. "I'm ready to do whatever you consider best, only—"

"Only you're disappointed over more delay. So am I, dearest. But it may not be for any length of time."

"No," said Naomi, "I wasn't thinking of my disappointment. But it seems very strange to me that a man like you should be so entirely controlled by others that they can order a complete change of plans without even consulting you. It must be very difficult for you to do your work or plan it. Why, Volney, even a trusted agent has responsibility laid upon him and goes and comes a great deal at his own discretion. And you're in business for yourself. Nobody ever ordered my father in this way. Why do they have a right to tell you what to do?"

His face clouded over a little. But it cleared under her anxious gaze, and he laughed pleasantly as he said, "You'd make a fierce little rebel, dearest, on occasion, meek as you seem. I suppose there is in our organization what looks to outsiders like despotism. Not that you're an outsider, darling, but I mean to one not brought up in our faith. You must constantly remember we have men among us who are directly taught of God, and to them we may defer without any loss of self-respect. If you had been with the Israelites in the wilderness, would you have thought it strange that the people were to obey Moses implicitly?"

"But there is no such disparity between you and these men as there was between Moses and the Israelites, is there? Or if there is, it's on your side. Judging from their letters they aren't as well educated as you. Why shouldn't you be the one to direct others? In other words, dear, why don't they trust you?"

The shadow of a frown passed over Mr. Newland's face; he spoke with deliberate emphasis. "My dear wife, can't you understand they direct me as the representatives of God Himself? Don't you know that in times past He chose some, not necessarily any better or wiser than others, to be His mouthpieces, speaking through them to the people? That time has come again, and our leaders simply quote to us what they receive from God. Would you have me superior to even His voice?"

Naomi's face cleared.

"No, Volney," she said earnestly, "a thousand times no. I must seem very stupid to you. I can't realize God speaks to men living today just as He did to the old prophets. Be patient with me, dear. It's all so new. I'll learn in time."

Since she was eager to go, it was she who needed patience. Apparently Mr. Newland was under dictation. The letters he received weren't shown to Naomi; it was merely revealed to her that they contained detailed explanations regarding matters she knew nothing about and would find dull, unintelligible reading. But they seemed to change his plans radically.

Instead of starting homeward they began an extended tour whose central object seemed to be sightseeing. Many meetings were held, however, and what Mr. Newland called good work was accomplished. Naomi was an indifferent traveler and had been sightseeing all her life. Sometimes she longed for the quiet of home. Moreover, the desire to carry out that new and blessed ceremony in the name of her father and mother remained as strong as ever. She referred to it so often that Mr. Newland told her once, smilingly, that she made as determined a little saint as the church could possibly desire. Still, sightseeing with Mr. Newland as guide and with his tender anticipation of every want was pleasant, and the months slipped away in a manner that surprised the woman on whose hands time had often hung heavily.

At various points, too, they settled down and "played home," as Mr. Newland said, for long periods. He played it with a relish that made Naomi think his home joys were few.

When they at last set sail for home, with great reluctance and Mr. Newland's outspoken criticisms as to the peremptory nature of his summons, nearly a year of their married life had passed—an eventful year to Naomi. Her husband watched her as she stood on deck catching her last view of the receding shore and determined, as he had a hundred times before, that she was a strikingly beautiful woman, and he was a man to be envied.

A tinge of sadness on her face did not detract from its beauty. Full of joy and hope as her present and future were, she couldn't forget that when she reached that foreign shore her father was beside her. Now that she was journeying homeward he wouldn't be there to greet her. Her husband knew what caused the tender shadow and kept his face decorously grave, in sympathy—despite the fact that he was distinctly glad of having Naomi to himself. Aside from his love for her, there were reasons why it was better no outsider should have the right to ask questions.

Their trip was swift and uneventful. Mr. Newland showed willingness to linger in New York and Philadelphia if Naomi wished and even proposed to take her to visit some of her school friends, but she promptly voted against all delays. She didn't care for New York and didn't know Philadelphia. As for the girls, the only ones she was eager to see had gone out west somewhere; she mourned forgetting or perhaps never knowing just where. But she was sure they weren't in their old homes, and what she desired above all was to be at home.

Mr. Newland laughed at her eagerness. He told her they had long years before them to stay at home, and it might be years before they could travel again.

"We'll travel whenever we wish," she said, with a willful little toss of her head that her husband rather admired when she didn't oppose his cherished plans. "You and I are going to do just as you and I please—and do let's please to get home as soon as we can. If you knew how much I think of having our own home together!"

He laughed indulgently, omitting the slight frown with which he generally greeted her rebellious hints that they should order their own lives. He himself criticized too recently to make reproof effective. Naomi enjoyed his criticism, and it made her bold.

"You may obey the church," she told him lightly one day, when he attempted to check her independent suggestions. "If you're expected to and you're willing, I'll try not to interfere. But I'll obey only you. I haven't promised to be subject to any other man."

He smiled and kissed her, calling her a beautiful little rebel. Wait until she saw some of the church dignitaries and heard their authoritative deliverances. Still, if she could obey him in her creed, he should be able to make it all right with the church.

Matronly dignity sat well upon Naomi. The year had rounded out her nature in many ways. Her exaggerated estimate of her husband's wisdom made her feel humble and ignorant in his presence. During her leisure hours, when he was employed with business concerning his mission abroad, she set herself to make herself more worthy of such a man's companionship.

Because the Bible was now the most interesting book in her possession, as well as because Mr. Newland seemed entirely at home with it, she chose it as her textbook. Earnest study of Christ's life led, as it inevitably must, to a yearning to draw closer to Him, to live in His atmosphere. This drew her to much prayer, and by degrees the loneliness that oppressed her later years slipped away. She grew to understand that Jesus Christ may become a potent factor in one's daily life and that His unseen presence is real and abiding.

The changes this experience brought about in her, though subtle, were distinct. Mr. Newland was conscious of a growing charm about the woman he won and thus exulted in her. Just what was causing this rapid development of her character he dimly understood, attributing a large part of it, as Naomi would have, to daily companionship with him. His life, he told himself, was broadened by contact with the world, by association with men and women of affairs. This was precisely what Naomi needed and to a degree missed. He hadn't realized she needed anything, but the changes in her were charming.

Yet at times he looked at her anxiously and told himself the child-nature so apparent when he first knew her was developing rapidly. Here might be a woman who would have a mind of her own and dare to differ radically even from him. But he put the thought away as far as he could. It would do no good to borrow trouble. He must try to plan so as to keep her from knowing anything she might not like, until his influence over her was still stronger. In the meantime he would enjoy the present.

Chapter 18

*"Where it concerns himself
Who's angry at a slander, makes it true."*

One episode of their journey given only passing attention at the time returned to Naomi with startling vividness afterward.

They had stopped, between trains, for Mr. Newland to attend to certain business and were obliged to travel for several hours on a crowded way train. During this time a woman seated just behind them entered into a friendly chat with Naomi when Mr. Newland visited another car.

"I reckon that ain't your husband?" she inquired, nodding her head toward Mr. Newland's retreating figure.

"Why do you reckon that?" Naomi asked, in an amused but kind tone.

The woman belonged decidedly to the uneducated common folk, but she was more than middle-aged and probably tired of her own company. The cultured woman had no objection to the diversion.

"Well, he looks too old for one thing and not like you, somehow. Though for that matter husbands and wives don't often look alike, do they? But there's somethin' about him, somehow, that makes me feel he don't belong."

"Nevertheless, he does," said Naomi with a happy little laugh. "I'm very glad to tell you he's my husband."

"Well, now," said the woman, "I didn't think it. I told Sarah he was twenty years older than you if he was a day, and maybe more. She thought so too; she even allowed he might be your father, though I told her he wa'n't old enough for that. Sarah's my girl—that one over there asleep. She ain't very well. I'm goin' out west for her sake. Are you goin' fur?"

"We're going to Utah," said Naomi absently, meanwhile studying Sarah's face with its telltale color high on the cheekbones. Did the mother realize, she wondered, what a futile journey she was taking?

Her questioner made a sound with her tongue for emphasis and said: "So am I, and I'm half scared about it. I wouldn't live there for anything. Sarah and me are only going for a few weeks, just to get past the nasty spring weather, but I dread even that. I don't want to breathe the same air with them Mormons for even a few weeks."

It was Naomi's turn to be startled, though she made no visible sign. Mormons! She hadn't thought of them for years. What were those schoolgirl stories that made her indignant for a few minutes until some local excitement crowded them out. It seemed strange she hadn't recalled even the existence of that sect in connection with her husband's home.

The voluble voice continued: "Still, they're everywhere nowadays. My sister lives in Iowa, and she says there's quite a settlement of them there. But Utah's kind of headquarters, you know. Horrid set, with their half a dozen wives apiece. It always makes me mad just to speak their names. I'll tell you what I think—every man of them ought to be sent to state prison. That would settle them."

The girl Sarah moved in her sleep, then roused herself and sat up and looked about her. She was a pretty girl, in spite of or perhaps partly because of, the hectic flush that helped make her eyes bright. She laughed a little at her mother, having caught her last words.

"You're on your hobby, ain't you?" she said.

The mother laughed also, in a shamefaced way. "Well, I dunno how I come to it. She said she was traveling to Utah," the mother said, nodding her head toward Naomi, "and I said we was too, but I wouldn't want to go there to live. And I wouldn't, not if I had a husband along anyhow, and goodness knows I wouldn't if I hadn't! Think of me being a second or third or fourth woman trotting along after a piece of a man! Faugh! It makes me feel creepy just to think of such things!"

"All the folks in Utah ain't Mormons by any means," volunteered Sarah, perhaps out of sympathy for the look of horror on the stranger's face. Her mother caught at the relief.

"No, they ain't; that's one comfort. Where we're going they say that more than half the folks are decent Christian people. If I was them I'd want to pull up and make my home where other decent folks lived. If I had to make my home there, I don't believe I could help being afraid that my husband, or my girl or boy, if I had one, would get roped in somehow with that set. They say they're as smart as snakes at getting around people."

"Oh, come, Mother," said Sarah. "You're getting too excited."

She spoke wearily, and the watchful mother's thoughts turned from all outside interests to center on her own little world again, leaving Naomi to her thoughts.

She hadn't thought much about either names or localities concerning her new home. She remembered only that it was *his* home and would therefore be hers from then on. With this blissful fact prominent, nothing else mattered. She didn't try to analyze why a vague unrest stirred within her by the talk of this ignorant woman who was distinctly disagreeable at the last. That suggestion about being afraid even of one's husband was awful! What sort of husband must a woman have to think such thoughts about him? But it couldn't be pleasant to live near people with such ideas as she remembered.

The talkative woman changed her seat, presently, to the farther end of the car, where the wind couldn't reach Sarah as well, but her words stayed with Naomi.

She began on some of her half-formed thoughts as soon as her husband returned to her. "Volney, it seems strange, but I never until just now thought of that singular sect called Mormons in connection with your home. Of course I knew they originally settled that region. Are many of them left? Do you ever come in contact with any in business, and are they as peculiar as they've been represented?"

Mr. Newland gave his wife a quick, startled look, but all he said was, "What an array of questions! Although not a Yankee, I'll follow one of their customs and ask another. What suggested the Mormons to you just now?"

She told him about their fellow travelers and repeated bits of the talk she heard.

An unmistakable frown gathered on his face. "That's a consequence of our missing the through train and having to travel with all sorts of people," he said loftily.

"She wasn't offensive, Volney—at least she had no thought of being so. She began talking to me simply to have a little human interest while her invalid daughter slept. You should see the girl; she has a pretty face that's quite refined in appearance. The mother is taking her west in search of health and is almost afraid to go to Utah because of the Mormons. She even hinted to me that it might be a dangerous place to live—not for me, of course, but for your sake."

The hint seemed sufficiently ridiculous to laugh over, but Mr. Newland didn't laugh. A deep red spread over his face as he said in his most reproving tone, "I should think the woman was insulting."

"Volney, she had no such intention. She's not that sort of person at all— not coarse, I mean. And she wasn't trying to be smart or funny. On the contrary, she was very much in earnest. Of course she's ignorant and misinformed and prejudiced; we don't need to notice what she said. But I want you to tell me about those people. I used to hear a good deal of them at one time, when I was in school. Was there any truth in the horrid things said about them? They don't really pretend to have two wives at once, do they?"

She had never heard his voice sound positively harsh.

"What utter nonsense you're talking! That woman is densely ignorant as well as coarse, but surely you know you're speaking of something that's directly contrary to the laws of our land! How can you ask if it's a practice among a law-abiding people?"

"I suppose I know very little about it," said Naomi meekly. "Papa never talked about laws and such matters much at home. Mama was an invalid, you know, and we shaped all our talk for her entertainment. Of course I heard about current events and understood them in a general way.

"I remember one time there was a good deal of excitement over the Mormons. We girls, especially Barbara, were quite wrought up over it, but nothing's very clear. I know there's a law against bigamy, but there was always that among civilized people. I mean there has been for hundreds of years, so that doesn't explain the excitement over the Mormons. Still, of course, one knows better than to believe half of what one hears. I suppose they've been slandered, and the lawless attempts of a few half-civilized persons made to stand for the morality of all."

Mr. Newland caught her words. "They've been fearfully slandered. No martyrs of old have endured more at the hands of an ignorant public. And yet there's no body of people more law-abiding and God-fearing and worthy of respect than they. Wait until you know them and can decide for yourself."

"Oh, shall I know some of them? Do you really know any Mormons personally? Volney, this is exciting! Did you ever know a man who tried to have two wives at once?"

Mr. Newland uttered an exclamation which was perhaps caused by a sudden bizarre movement of their seat. Some bolt or bar chose that instant for slipping out of place and with a thud let the seat down several inches below its proper level. Some bustle and confusion followed.

A brakeman appeared and one or two other trainmen, and an ineffectual effort was made to get the seat back into its place. It ended in a search through the crowded car for another seat, and after some waiting and much grumbling on the part of those who think that one ticket entitles them to two seats, Mr. and Mrs. Newland were reestablished. Half an hour later Mr. Newland returned to their interrupted talk quite as though no break occurred.

"The Mormons, my dear, are an inoffensive, maligned, sensitive people. It will be wise for you not to talk with anybody about them or their affairs. I mean after we reach home, as well. I want to guard you especially against the use of the word *Mormon*. It has sad associations to many of them. They've suffered, you understand, for their faith, and they've learned to be cautious about whom they trust. You'll come in contact with them, of course. They mingle with others on common ground as far as they can and just like other people. You won't know or need to know, for that matter, whether the people you meet casually are Mormons or not. The point is, don't talk about that matter."

"Then, Volney, you're really in sympathy with them as a people?"

"Certainly I am. So are all the people you'll come in contact with. They're victims of intolerance and prejudice and have endured enough to awaken the sympathies of all right-minded persons."

"Still, wasn't it their insane ideas regarding marriage that caused most of their troubles years ago?"

"By no means. It was political jealously and a concerted attempt by unprincipled politicians to make people throughout the country believe a mass of lies about them. But we don't need to unearth all that filth; it would be useless as well as disagreeable. You're right in saying you don't understand political questions, and I have no desire for you to. There's no reason for you to burden your mind and vex your conscience with such matters.

"As for that question of plural marriage that troubled your intelligent friend, I can assure you of my own knowledge that it never was the rampant thing sensational enmity tried to make it. And of course in any case it's a past issue and doesn't need to be discussed. What I want to impress upon you is how important it is for you to avoid any reference to your former ideas regarding this people. I mean, of course, in your conversation with others. I can explain certain facts concerning them later as the occasion arises, but don't, I beg of you, encourage others to talk with you along this line. You'll hurt somebody's feelings if you do, and I'm certain you want to avoid that."

Naomi believed she understood her husband thoroughly. He espoused the cause of those Mormons as she felt he would do for any oppressed or ill-treated people. Perhaps he'd suffered for it and been the victim at least of careless and hateful tongues. It might be that he dreaded a like experience for her.

She was sure of it when, after a moment of gloomy silence, he said, "I wish I could shield you always from coarse and irresponsible tongues."

Under cover of the heavy wrap thrown over the back of the seat she stole her hand into his; he pressed it instantly and smiled on her, though a moment before a frown was on his face. It gave her an exquisite sense of happiness to note that whatever annoyances he bore in the past, great enough for their memory to put gloom on his face, she had power to chase away the shadows and bring the smiles.

She resolved to be as wise as a serpent in her conversation with all classes of people. She would avoid hurting outsiders' feelings by her careless words, which was what her noble-hearted husband evidently thought of, and she would shield him. His sensitive nerves shouldn't be jarred by repeating careless words such as that ignorant and garrulous old woman, for instance, spoke. She could understand how their repetition might have awakened memories of unpleasant scenes. If she'd understood before, she wouldn't have repeated them for the world.

It was plain he couldn't quite get away from their memory. His annoyance showed in his next sentence: "We're nearing the junction where I hope we can connect with a through train. We've had enough of broken-down seats and low-bred tongues."

Chapter 19

"Beautiful as sweet!
And young as beautiful! And soft as young!
And blithe as soft! And innocent as blithe!"

Instead of frowning over the experience connected with the way train, Mr.
Newland should have rejoiced. He didn't realize how effectively it closed
Naomi's mouth to the word Mormon or to the many curious questions she
might have asked. Whether or not he intended it, he left the impression on his
wife that to talk might somehow injure him, which was, of course, enough to
seal her lips. She resolved to abide by his suggestions and ask questions even
about apparently commonplace matters of no one but him.

She entered upon her new duties as responsible head of a household with
some trepidation. She had never really ordered a house, the nearest approach
to it being to make tentative suggestions to the well-trained servants who were
for years in her mother's employ. To be the real as well as the nominal head of
a home, to interview "help" and direct the machinery of a new home in a new
country, was quite different from any former experience.

She expected trouble and friction. She remembered as a girl when her
mother had what she called "seas of trouble" with servants before she finally
gathered about her those who were willing to be trained and to stay when the
training process was over. Naomi wondered curiously and with more or less
anxiety whether or not she knew how to train servants.

Her husband's home had been rented, he told her, for a number of years.
But he gave directions to have it thoroughly renovated and put in perfect order,
so that all she had to do was "walk in and take charge." It sounded easy when
he said it, with a smile, but Naomi had enough life experience to tremble
sometimes over the thought of her responsibilities.

She needn't have worried. Before she was at home a week, she told her
husband that domestic service in this part of the world must be perfect, or was
it that perfect housekeeper of his who managed everything so that she wished
nothing different? Where did he find Mrs. Roper, and how was such a refined
and apparently cultured person willing to be a mere housekeeper in somebody
else's home?

Mr. Newland replied that he befriended Mrs. Roper at a time when she
needed friends, and he believed she was grateful to him. She chose the other
servants and was a woman who knew where to find good ones and keep them
in order. She seemed quite satisfied with her position. Why not? She had a
good home and was treated kindly by everybody. He was more than glad

Naomi was pleased. He'd been anxious lest she might not like Mrs. Roper for some reason; there was no accounting for women's whims about housekeeping. It was a great comfort to him that his borrowed trouble was unnecessary.

Truth to tell, Naomi saw relatively little of Mrs. Roper and was really only the nominal head of her household, although utmost deference was paid to her suggestions.

Despite the business cares Mr. Newland explained to his wife would be heavy, he contrived to give her a great deal of his time. He escorted her to all places of interest and devoted himself almost as exclusively to her entertainment as during the first few weeks of their marriage. This, of course, was delightful to Naomi, and she saw the beautiful city under the most favorable auspices; one who was thoroughly acquainted with the city and its suburbs took care that she saw only the beautiful portions. Thus guarded, there was continual pleasure in their almost daily rounds.

"Beautiful for situation, the joy of the whole earth, is mount Zion, the city of the great King." Naomi quoted the words as she stood one morning where she had a wonderful view of mountain and minaret and lovely vale. "It reminds me of it, Volney. I found that verse the morning after our first walk—just happened upon it. And I can't tell you how many times I've thought of it as we've walked or driven about the town.

"Can you think how glad I am that the great tabernacle as well as the beautiful temple will be mine in a sense that church never was before? I like, too, to think that the people I meet are consecrated in a peculiar sense to the Lord Jesus and live with His directions in mind as they say they do. It's what I've always thought religion should be—diffusive, you know, permeating the whole life."

He looked with admiration at her eager face and shining eyes and called her, as he often did, his "little fanatic." Then he added, with a seriousness she thought was growing on him: "Don't set your mark too high, Naomi. This is earth yet, remember, not heaven, and the people are, necessarily, of the earth. It won't do to expect too much of them."

She needed this caution as she began to make acquaintance with the people. She learned early what she suspected, that her husband stood very high among them, and his social circle was therefore of the choicest. But Naomi confessed disappointment in the women, who were, of course, the chief callers. They weren't in appearance or conversation what she'd imagined women who made their religion the center of their lives would become. She was attracted to an occasional face belonging to a woman of middle age: not because of its beauty or because it expressed happiness in the sense that Naomi had heretofore used that word; rather because it suggested a kind of peace that was born of pain.

"I'm sure she's been through deep trouble," Naomi said to her husband regarding a caller. "She shows it on her face. I wonder what her history is? Do you know it, Volney?"

He'd known her for years, he said, and wasn't aware she'd had more than her share of trouble. Some people made trouble out of what was intended for blessing; the woman might be like that. Still, he believed she'd lost a number of children; that might have shadowed her face.

His tone made Naomi think the caller in question wasn't one of his special friends and that he didn't care to see her often. She was sorry for this, for of her new acquaintances she was closest to feeling an interest in this one.

She was disappointed in the social talk she heard. It was bright enough, sparkling with airy nothings—some even suggested the word *reckless*—but there was an utter absence of the spiritual tone Naomi expected to lift her up into purer realms. The talk was of any subject under the sun other than the Lord Jesus Christ and His recognized claims.

Yet the very gateways of the city and supporting columns of the business houses proclaimed abroad their foundation and their faith. Afterward Naomi recalled with a sickening pain the impression those initial letters Z.C.M.I. made upon her when she saw them gleaming from tower and arch and learned they meant "Zion Cooperative Mercantile Institute." It seemed beautiful to her, as well as eminently appropriate, that the businessmen should thus proclaim whose they were and whom they served.

"If these should hold their peace, the stones would immediately cry out." Naomi quoted the verse to her husband one evening when she was telling him about calls from certain women and confessing to him that their talk disappointed her. "I couldn't help thinking of the letters on those stone columns on Broadway, Volney. They rebuke such talk as we had this afternoon."

But Mr. Newland answered her almost sternly, that she shouldn't judge so continually by mere externals. The very women she criticized lived their religion, which was far more important than talking about it continually. She was almost hurt by his words but comforted herself with the thought that her husband was evidently so fond of this people that he didn't like to have their failings pointed out. Thus she resolved to keep her future disappointments quite to herself.

One great disappointment, however, overshadowed all others. That vicarious baptism for her beloved dead was still being postponed. Mr. Newland was emphatic regarding it. He wondered why she didn't understand she wasn't strong enough for such an ordeal. The summer would soon be upon them, and she would need all her strength and nervous energy to carry her through. There was no reason for haste. When their beautiful autumn came and she was strong again, then would be the ideal time for such a service.

"But, Volney, what if, in the meantime, I should die?" she asked timidly.

He replied that he considered her a far too sensible woman to allow herself to grow nervous and brood over such matters. And then he added tenderly that in any event she might rest assured that the memory of her father and mother should be held sacred. If she wished, he would accept it as a trust, pledging his word of honor; in the event she was unable to take this sacred duty upon herself, he would see to it that proper persons were found to be buried in baptism in the name of her dear ones.

Mr. Newland didn't know it, but to Naomi this was the first jarring note in the beautiful provision that was explained to her as one linking her dead to her by an indissoluble tie. How could acceptable persons be found who could assume such a duty? Did he mean they were to be hired? But her husband's will was daily becoming more fully a law to her, and she felt she must hide this disappointment also and bide her time.

As the weeks passed, she grew more puzzled that she had nothing to do with her husband's relatives, near or remote. She asked often about the aunt, who lived not far away and whom she was to find especially congenial. And his children—wasn't she even to know them?

He smiled on her, called her an impatient little wife who wanted the world all at once, and assured her they would go, someday, to see his aunt, who never left her own home. Then he grew serious, with a gravity that always had a touch of annoyance in it, as he said there were reasons why it wouldn't be well at present for her to make the acquaintance of the children. Couldn't she trust him?

Of course she assured him that she could and did, and she felt her heart glow with sympathy for a man whose crosses were so heavy and so peculiar that they must separate him from his own children.

Matters were in this state when their first separation occurred. Mr. Newland announced the need for it with a clouded face and was evidently so reluctant that his wife had to turn comforter. He tried in vain to make different plans, he said, but the council was too much for him this time. They were determined he should go and no other.

Naomi was very helpful. She wasn't surprised he was the one chosen, she said, if there were important business matters to manage. They probably knew, as she did, that he could manage better than anyone else. He wasn't to worry about her; she could do very well for a little while. He grew cheerful under her soothing and repeated his assurance that he would make his stay as brief as possible. He was glad, at least, that he could leave her in such competent care. Mrs. Roper was thoroughly efficient and prepared to do everything possible for her comfort; she might trust her fully.

The parting was very tender, with Mr. Newland assuring his wife, as he came back for one more kiss, that he'd planned not to leave her, at least overnight, for a good many months yet. Naomi indulged herself in a few tears as she watched him from the window and received a final bow and smile. How dreary life would be without him! But she put her tears aside promptly and resolved to consider her blessings.

Suppose she were like the woman who called yesterday and said she was sure she didn't know how long her husband expected to be gone; the longer he stayed, the better she would like it. The words were spoken with a laugh, of course, but with a half-veiled sting in them that hadn't escaped Naomi. Some women doubtless regretted their marriage bonds. What awful living that must be!

Mr. Newland certainly didn't overrate Mrs. Roper. She was constant in her care and watchfulness of Naomi. At times it seemed to the wife almost like espionage. When, therefore, on the second day of Mr. Newland's absence, the housekeeper was summoned by telegram to the next town to attend to a dying relative, Naomi could have almost found it in her heart to be glad. She assured Mrs. Roper there was no reason whatever why she shouldn't remain away overnight and there wasn't the least need of having an outsider come in to fill her place. Mrs. Roper was thoroughly efficient, ladylike, eminently respectful to her and, indeed, what Mr. Newland considered a "treasure." Yet his wife couldn't help feeling relieved at the thought of being free from her guardianship for a few hours.

I'm not used to being treated like a child by anyone but Volney, she told herself, as she tried to account for the feeling of relief.

She was hardly alone for an hour when a gentle tap sounded at the door of her sewing room, and a clear voice asked, "May I come in?"

The voice was followed at once by a vision of loveliness—a young girl with a fluff of shining hair, a singularly beautiful face, and wonderful eyes. Naomi couldn't help exclaiming with pure delight at the sight of such beauty and gazed at her as she might have at a lovely picture suddenly unveiled before her.

"You want to see me, don't you?" the girl said, advancing and dropping among the cushions of Naomi's couch as though they'd been placed there expressly for her. She was dressed in exquisite taste and with careful attention to small details, so that the whole effect was faultless. Her voice was as silvery sweet as the face suggested and had in it a note of similarity which puzzled while charmed Naomi.

"Certainly I do," she said heartily. "You look as if you belonged on that couch. I find myself wondering how those cushions have done without you all this time. Now will you introduce yourself and tell me why you haven't come before?"

Chapter 20

"If I chance to talk a little while, forgive me,
I had it from my father."

H er guest gave a musical little laugh. "I should have rung the bell and been formally announced," she said, "but I was afraid. To be sure, I know the general manager is away. I waited until I was certain she was out of town before I ventured. I thought she might have assistants trained to consider me dangerous, and since I was simply dying to see you, I decided not to risk it. But I glimpsed you from the window and knew you were here alone."

Naomi looked both amused and puzzled. "For what do you take us," she asked merrily, "that you consider such diplomacy needed to call on the mistress of the house? Whom do you consider general manager?"

The girl tossed her pretty head with a wise and half-defiant air as she said, "Oh, I know Mrs. Roper. I knew her before you did." Then, without hinting in her tone or manner that she was saying anything unusual, added: "I heard you were beautiful, and it's quite true. I think you're perhaps the prettiest person I ever saw, and I expected to see a pretty one. Brother Newland may be trusted for that."

Naomi laughed almost as cheerfully as her guest had. "You're deliciously frank," she said, "or is it premeditated deception? I can imagine you a queen of the pixies come to cajole a poor mortal by flattering words that sound so real they almost deceive her. Do you come straight from the pixies, my dear?"

"I? No, indeed! I come from a land of plainest prose. Although I escaped somewhat after the fashion of a pixie—at least I made myself almost invisible. But I was nearly caught at the last moment. Don't you know who I am? Really? Or even surmise? Why, I am Mara."

"Mara," repeated Naomi, expressing only amused interest. "It has a rather queenly sound and a hint of unreality. I don't think I ever heard it applied to mortals, and it doesn't enlighten me in the least. What should it suggest to me?"

The girl's smiling face suddenly settled into seriousness as she said gravely, "It's a Bible name, I believe. My mother gave it to me. I've often suspected she had too good a reason for choosing it."

Her seriousness prevented Naomi from further questioning. Evidently some delicate family secret was hidden here that perhaps the girl shouldn't have even touched upon. She hesitated as to how to continue a conversation with this fascinating but peculiar guest.

But the girl began again, in her former light, almost reckless, tone: "Do you really mean the name doesn't tell you anything? Upon my word, I think my respected father might at least have mentioned me."

A sudden premonition of the truth broke upon Naomi. This must be—it would account for that bewildering reminder which she felt, rather than realized, at first.

"Is it possible you're Mr. Newland's daughter?"

"I have that honor," said the girl, with a whimsical toss of her head. "That is, I'm one of them—the one he likes the least, I think, which is disagreeable, since I'm the oldest. I trouble him sometimes, I guess, with my tongue and my ways generally. Hasn't he told you a thing about me?"

Naomi's face was serious now and her manner dignified. What way was this for a daughter to speak of such a father as hers? It gave her a hint of what the poor girl's home influence must be and of what her father might have had to suffer.

"He has spoken of his children, of course," she said, with a dignity she tried to make gentle. "But at this moment I don't recall his mentioning your names. Still, my memory for names is poor."

She was answered with an outburst of laughter.

"You might certainly be excused from remembering them all," the guest said cheerfully. "But I don't believe he spoke of me at all. As I told you, he likes me the least. The truth is, I see through a hundred little subterfuges he didn't mean for me to understand, and it's embarrassing at times."

"My dear, what a strange remark to make about your father!" Naomi couldn't keep reproach from her tone, strangers though they were. On her husband's behalf she resented such unfilial words.

"Is it?" said the girl lightly. "I don't know—I think fathers are odd creatures. They aren't a bit like mothers. When is the general manager coming back? I must be on guard. If Father has spells of not liking me, that woman absolutely hates me, I believe—which is ungracious of her, for at one time I took her part a little. Don't you dislike her? Or has she got you under her thumb mentally as well as bodily? I warn you that you want to watch out for her. She weaves just the meshes about people that Father chooses to have woven. Yet, strange to say, she has more influence over him than anyone else has. I believe she's a hypnotist."

This was certainly intolerable to Naomi. Yet she felt she must endure and for her husband's sake understand what extraordinary tales his enemies had poured into his daughter's ears.

"You haven't told me yet whom you're speaking of," she said coldly.

But the girl didn't seem to notice the changed tone. "I'm speaking of Mrs. Roper so called," she said brightly. "That's a convenient name for her at present, since she's right in town. But of course you understand."

The tone was too significant not to convey some disagreeable meaning. All the blood in Naomi's body seemed to rush in one indignant stream toward her face. She rose from her chair with an instinctive and overpowering desire to get further away from this unnatural child who could so carelessly insinuate suggestions against her father's good name. But the child regarded her with wide-eyed and apparently innocent wonder.

"What's the matter?" she asked. "What did I say? Why, I mean nothing new. Is it possible Father hasn't told you about her? I didn't think of that, and I think he ought to."

Naomi sat down again. The girl's ordinary tone and evident innocence of wrong intent recalled her to her senses. She began to feel she was foolish. This happy child, who talked at once older and younger than her years, was probably referring to gossip that low, ignorant people had indulged in concerning her father and his housekeeper. And she was silly enough to suppose the father magnified its importance by repeating it.

"Never mind," she said to the girl's repeated question as to what was the matter. "I misunderstood you at first. You mean nothing wrong evidently. I'm sorry you've taken a violent dislike to Mrs. Roper. She seems to be an admirable woman and is certainly very efficient in her position. I don't know how we could have a better housekeeper. But perhaps we don't need to talk about domestic matters. I wish you'd tell me about yourself, dear. I don't like to talk to your father about his children; it seems to make him sad. I think he misses you."

She answered with a mocking laugh. "I think he dreads us," said this unnatural daughter, "or rather me. I don't like some things my beloved father has done, and he knows it. Do you know, for instance, why he wants to keep me away from you? I think he's afraid you'll side with me in our dispute, and that would be very inconvenient and unpleasant. I've thought it out since I've seen you.

"He told me, you see, that I was on no account to come here, not even for a call, until he gave me formal permission. He was so positive about this and evidently so anxious we might meet that I knew there was some splendid reason why I ought to come at once. I'm acquainted with my father. So, under cover of going to Aunt Maria's for a couple of days, I skipped, took the train coming this way instead of the one going west, and here I am.

"After getting here it was great luck to find the general manager—I beg your pardon, I mean Mrs. Roper—gone for the afternoon, because I hadn't planned how I'd manage her. I suspected that my thoughtful father blockaded the house against me, and I daresay he did, but he didn't think of the windows. I came into the house by way of the dining room window. Why do you look so shocked? Are you sorry I came? I wanted very much to see you, and now that I have, I feel that you can help me."

"I'm glad to know you," said Naomi gently, feeling that the girl was dangerous and she must use her influence to try to save her. "But I don't like to think you had to act contrary to your father's wishes in order to come."

"Why, that's nothing," said the girl. "We all have to plan and contrive and use a little deception occasionally. We couldn't live our lives at all if we didn't. Don't they do such things where you came from? Is the world very different where you lived? Do girls, for instance, marry whom they please? If they do, I'd like to run away for good and live there.

"Since my respected father hasn't mentioned my name, it isn't likely he's told you why he especially disapproves of me. It's because he wants me to marry that creature he's picked out for me, and I won't. You needn't look reproachfully at me. I won't! I don't believe you would, if you were in my place. You don't look like that kind of woman. To be sure, you married my father, and he must be at least twenty years older than you. But that's different. My father is a handsome man who doesn't look his years, and you're not a young girl with life all before you.

"Wait 'til you see the man who's been chosen for me, and you'll understand. Why, he's over fifty, and I'm not even seventeen! Isn't that horrible? And he's loathsome in every way. There isn't a man anywhere that I detest as much as him. Would you marry a man you felt that way about? I won't; I'll run away and drown myself first.

"It isn't that I'm not willing to be married. Of course I know I should be ready for that. But I want to do my own choosing, especially when I've already chosen the person and he's willing to stand by me. Don't you think a girl of seventeen ought to be allowed to choose a husband for herself?"

Naomi was both shocked and puzzled. Her father's enemies must have been very busy and skillful to impress this young girl with the belief that a father like hers meant to force marriage upon her.

"My dear," she said gently, "what I think is that you're much too young to be troubling your brain with such matters. Aren't you still a schoolgirl? Young girls in school don't have any reason to think about love and marriage. As a matter of fact, I don't think a girl of seventeen has to decide whether or not she'll ever marry anybody. Let her wait until she's a woman and has a woman's judgment to help her."

The girl regarded her with surprise, perhaps also with curiosity, and spoke seriously. "I don't think that at all. I know it's my duty to marry, and I'm quite willing. I told you it wasn't marriage I was fighting against. I fully understand that we were made for just such a purpose. But when we have to live all the rest of our lives with that one person, it seems hard we can't pick and choose as the men do. If that old grandpa that Father picked out were the only one who wanted me, it would be different. But that isn't the case; there are three or four others. I told Father I was willing to marry George tomorrow if he wanted me to, and I'm sure George would like nothing better.

"Now when I tell you plainly that somebody else wants me and I hate the other man, won't you take my part? You're in high favor with Father just now;

I'm sure you can coax him to let me have my choice. You can tell him I don't object to getting married, if he insists upon that. I do think girls might have their freedom a little while longer than they do. I'm sure they have a hard enough life afterward. But I won't complain if I can only marry George. I'm sure he'd do almost anything for me, and I suppose I ought to take him while the mood lasts—they get over it soon enough.

"George isn't young; he's as much as thirty-five, I suppose, perhaps more. But he doesn't look it, and the other one does. Oh, the difference between them is like day and night. George is from the East. He isn't one of us exactly, not yet. But he says he likes our ideas and would as soon join us as not. I'll risk managing George if I can get Father to have anything to do with him. Look here—I've risked a great deal and run away here to get you to use your influence for me. Will you?"

Naomi was more than shocked, as well as bewildered. Where could a well-dressed young woman of today have acquired her extraordinary ideas of the marriage relationship? And her ideas of her father were almost equally bewildering. How could she have been even slightly associated with him all these years and not know him better?

"My child," she said, answering the eager look in the girl's eyes, "I'd do anything I could for your happiness, but I must admit I'm dismayed over some of your ideas. Of course you wouldn't marry any man unless you loved him with all your heart and believed marriage with him would be the best for both of you. And I must repeat that I can't understand why you should talk about marriage as a matter of course. You surely know there are good, noble women who don't marry at all. How can you tell at your age that you might not wish to be one of those? I can't imagine what has led you to think your father, of all fathers in the world, would force marriage upon you at any age."

Her guest regarded her with astonishment. "What odd talk!" she said. "Is that the way they feel about getting married where you came from? It isn't the way here, I can tell you. Everybody marries, and girls are expected to marry very early. We don't hear so very much about love, either. Of course it's nice if we can be in love, but we're expected to do our duty anyhow. Some of my folks think I should have been married a year ago. One old thing told my father he'd have had less trouble with me if he hadn't humored me so long. I guess there's some truth in that. I don't suppose I'd have made half as much fuss about it before I knew George. Still, I always disliked the man Father chose. But I know, of course, that it's my duty to marry."

Chapter 21

"O! many a shaft, at random sent,
Find mark the archer little meant."

W hat do you mean by that?" Naomi asked abruptly. She'd decided to lead this strange girl to state some of her false ideas definitely if she was to help her get rid of them.

"How did you discover it's your duty to marry? Marriage is a blessing when all the conditions are as they should be. But as I reminded you a moment ago, there are, as there've always been, unmarried women by the hundreds who are living noble lives and blessing the world by their daily ministries."

"But they're doing wrong," said the girl confidently. "They're being wicked, or else they're ignorant. I presume most of those you know are ignorant of the true way. You're speaking of people who are out of the true church. Every member of our church knows God made women for a work they can't do until they're married, and the work is waiting for them, and God wants it done. Why, aren't they wicked in refusing to do it? Didn't my father explain all that to you? He should have done so. How can you help others do their duty when you don't understand it yourself?"

She spoke with the air of a seer and was actually trying to teach—and what teaching! The fearful thought crossed Naomi's mind that she was entertaining an escaped lunatic. Surely, no young girl of sane mind seriously held such extraordinary views. Still, perhaps she didn't understand her; she must try again. What did such a strange, fascinating, and dangerous girl really mean?

"What work do you think is waiting for women that they can be fitted for only by marriage?" she asked, trying to speak lightly. She didn't want to attach much importance to what might be the vagaries of an overexcited brain.

"Don't you know?" the girl asked, regarding her as though she were a curious specimen from an unknown world. "Haven't you been taught that the air is filled with little immortal spirits waiting for bodies and that they'll be forever lost unless bodies are given to them, because God's plan of salvation is that it must be secured through tabernacles of clay? Besides, we all know that our only way of salvation, as women, is by being sealed to men. Those unmarried women you talk about will be lost forever if they stay unmarried, and the little bodiless souls they could help to save if they were married will be lost too. I think that's an awful responsibility for a woman to take just for the sake of escaping a little trouble here, don't you?"

Naomi's eyes fairly blazed, and her whole expression was that of indignant horror. It showed in her voice as well as words.

"What monstrous doctrine is this? Where did you get it? What human Satan has deceived you into thinking that ideas which belong only to the pit are actually teachings of the God of truth and purity?"

The girl stared at her in innocent wonder.

"I think you must be crazy," she said. "It can't be that you're so ignorant. Don't you really know these are revelations from God and that those who reject them are living only for this world and can never get to heaven? Could any other motive than their own salvation make women willing to give up their husbands to other wives instead of having them all to themselves? I'm not willing. I'm not one of the saints. If I marry George, I know I shall hate, HATE, mind you, any other woman who gets her salvation through him. But all the while I know I shouldn't feel that way, and perhaps when I'm old and gray and homely I'll get over it."

A sudden revelation came to Naomi. This girl was a Mormon; her mother's relatives were doubtless Mormons, and perhaps even her mother had been. It would account for many mysteries she felt were connected with her husband's life. It would explain why he felt it desirable to keep her from being acquainted with his children; he wanted to shield her from the disgrace of this as long as possible. Probably he still hoped to win his children—this girl—back to the true faith. Perhaps in his misery he even wanted the deluded child to marry a good man in the hope of thus winning her away from awful dangers.

These thoughts rushed through Naomi's mind, rather than presented themselves as reasonable deductions. They made her wish she could be very wise and gentle in dealing with this dangerous sinner, who had evidently been steeped in error from her childhood and who thought she was serving God by trampling upon even the instincts of purity. But she must be sure that her surmise was correct.

"Are you—have you been taught the Mormon beliefs?" she faltered. It seemed almost an insult to speak of such peculiar beliefs to such a young girl.

Again that astonished gaze was fixed on her. "How odd you are!" said the girl. "Of course I have. How else should I be taught?"

"And the other children? Are they being trained in the same way? How many children are there?"

"Father's children, do you mean? Why, I think there are thirteen. I have to stop and count. Yes, there are thirteen—unlucky number, isn't it? What's the matter? You look as if you might faint. What have I said to distress you—anything? I don't want to trouble you. I want you to like me and be my friend. I've had a feeling ever since you came that you could help me.

"Didn't you know before how many children Father had? You needn't mind. Father has enough money to take care of them all, and he's real good about that. He can't see much of us nowadays, scattered as we are, but each mother looks after her own, of course, and none of them will ever be allowed to trouble you. Brother Newland has always been master in his family. Really, there's nothing to make you look as white as a sheet. What if you'd been my mother when Father brought home his third wife? They used to live in the same house then—all the wives. I'm glad that can't be done anymore; I should hate it. Oh, dear! What have I done? What's the matter? Don't faint! Shall I get you some water? I didn't mean to say anything to hurt you, and I don't understand now."

Naomi clutched at the fair wrist within her reach and held it as in a vice.

"Girl," she said, "who are you? Where do you live?"

"Why, dear me," said the distressed girl, "haven't I told you? I'm Mara Newland, Mr. Volney Newland's oldest daughter, and I live with my mother, of course. Three of us belong to her, and we have a little home of our own. We lived in town with Father until the government made that awful fuss, you know. We don't anymore. It's all right; everybody understands. Mother told Father only last night that she'd never say a word to make you any trouble. Didn't Father explain to you? Oh, I think that was cruel! Oh, dear! What SHALL I do? She's fainted dead away."

The vicelike grasp had loosened at last. The girl ran frantically for water, poured it over the prostrate form, then dashed into the hall, crying: "Kate! Nannie! Where are you all? Come quick! I'm afraid she's dying."

When Mr. Volney Newland returned to his home on the evening of the following day, having been sought for by telegrams that failed to reach him, he found his wife lying at the point of death and a trained nurse on guard who firmly refused him admittance.

"It's no use, sir. The doctor's orders are imperative. He'll be here again in a few moments, and you can get them from him. It would be no comfort to you to see her. She's in a wild delirium and doesn't recognize anybody. But she notices the coming and going and grows frantic over every new face."

As far removed from the sickroom as the limits of the house would permit, in charge of another trained nurse, a little child who had opened its eyes too early on this sin-cursed world was wailing feebly. Mr. Newland, to whom the birth of a daughter had long been an ordinary event, turned from that door with no desire to enter and with a look of almost resentment on his face. What was that insignificant atom of humanity worth that she should peril the life of the only woman he ever truly loved?

Days, heavy with anxiety, were lengthening into weeks, and still the cloud of trouble didn't lift, and the door of the sickroom was still closed upon Mr. Newland.

"It's a peculiar case," said the doctor. "She's better certainly, at least as far as the physical is concerned. I begin to have hope now, as I told you, that she'll battle through. But her brain is still decidedly unbalanced, and the slightest move in the wrong direction might result fatally. She still refuses vehemently to see you, and that of course complicates matters very much. That's not an uncommon accompaniment of her mental state. Indeed, it's quite a common result of some forms of aberration that the patient goes back on his best friends. But you can see how carefully we must guard her on this account from any possible shock.

"No, Newland, I can't even admit you while she's sleeping. Who's sure she won't suddenly open her eyes and receive a shock that will settle the question for life? Be patient, my dear sir, and thankful it's a condition that won't last. She'll be all right as soon as reason resumes its seat."

So the man who was used to swaying his household with a motion of his authoritative hand was compelled to submit to orders and pass on tiptoe the closed chamber he knew held all his heart, lest his footstep should further excite his wife's unsettled brain.

Meanwhile, they puzzled together, doctor and trained nurse and husband, as to the nature of the shock which the doctor was sure had been sustained. Mr. Newland was able to surmise that his wife had heard certain facts sufficient to shock her, and he cursed the fate, almost the authority, which compelled him to leave her at a critical time. He was so fierce with Mrs. Roper for proving false to him and abandoning her trust for even a few hours that the devoted slave was well-nigh heartbroken.

But he couldn't discover who had been with Naomi or determine the character of the interview that helped bring her to the door of death. The two maids Mara in her haste and fright wildly summoned hadn't appeared. Kate was out for the afternoon, and Nannie had been dismissed from Mrs. Roper's service several weeks before. The stout German girl with only a few words of English at her command reigned in her stead and answered Mara's frantic call.

Not much information was to be had from her. It was a lady, and she'd never seen her before. She screamed and scared Hilda, and she ran and called out the window to Karl, who was in the back garden, to run for the doctor; the strange lady disappeared, and that was all Hilda knew. Her stern-faced master might question and cross-question her all he pleased; he could frighten her out of what little English she knew, but he could get nothing further.

As a matter of fact, Mara waited only to see that someone would care for the woman who fainted, then made all haste to the streetcar and the railroad station. Within an hour she boarded a train that took her at the rate of forty miles an hour to the "Aunt Maria's" where she was supposed to be.

Her father found her there when he called that evening on his way farther west. The telegrams that were searching for him had failed to penetrate to Aunt Maria's retreat. The girl was almost dying to know whether her poor victim had survived the shock she had unwittingly given. But she dared not mention her name, dared not stay long in her father's presence, lest she might, somehow, reveal what she knew. It wasn't difficult, however, to avoid her father. He hadn't seen "Aunt Maria" and her children—his children—in more than a year. So he naturally had enough to interest him during an overnight visit, without paying close attention to his oldest daughter, who had offended him by questioning his wisdom and almost disobeying his commands.

Mr. Newland could on occasion obey, even without question, those set in authority over him, and he expected at least the same from those under him. His daughter's attempt at rebellion was a surprise as well as an annoyance. She'd always been a singular girl. And he told himself when he looked again upon her lovely, half-defiant face that she was at times as disagreeable as she was beautiful and fascinating and that she must on no account come in contact with Naomi at present.

Naomi must learn certain truths from him, not from others, and she wasn't strong enough to bear them now. He repeated his prohibition to the girl with emphasis. But seeing her at her Aunt Maria's, where she was under appointment to go, attending her to the train the next morning and seeing her start homeward, he didn't in any way connect her with his wife's sudden illness.

There came a day, and it was the day on which her little daughter was six weeks old, that Naomi awakened at last from a sleep that was so long and quiet that the trained nurse twice reported its duration to the attending physician. Everyone in the house knew a great deal was hoped for from this long, unbroken rest. Their hopes were not disappointed.

Naomi awakened without the nervous start and the half-frightened roll of her restless eyes that had accompanied all recent awakenings. Instead, her eyes held that indescribable but easily recognized look that said reason had returned. She lay quite still and looked at the white-robed figure of the nurse, who sat over by the window, as still as a statue, with eyes purposely turned from the bed, while she awaited developments. She was pretending to be absorbed with a bit of soft white stuff belonging to the baby's wardrobe.

Her patient looked, and *looked,* and presently spoke in a quiet, though wondering tone: "Did I die, then, after all?"

The reply was quiet and cheerful. "No, my dear. You're very much alive. You've been quite ill, but you're getting well now, steadily."

"But you're Gertrude Fenton?"

The nurse glanced at the doctor who was waiting behind the screen. They'd planned for this and risked the possible shock in the hope of a counter interest that might keep the patient from other excitement. The doctor's look was reassuring, and the nurse went forward.

"Yes," she said cheerfully, as though it were the most ordinary occurrence. "I'm Gertrude, and you're our dear little Namie. And you're to swallow this liquid like the good girl you always were when you were ill and not talk at all until the doctor comes to say you may. You remember you always minded me when I took care of you at school?"

Naomi smiled, opened her mouth obediently and swallowed the potion, then closed her eyes again. She was too weak to wonder twice how her girlhood friend was at her side ministering to her wants. She opened her eyes after a few minutes to say softly, "When I had the fever you took care of me."

The nurse nodded, smiled, and laid her finger significantly on her lips. Naomi answered the smile and presently dropped back into sleep. Thus quietly was the chasm bridged between her present and her past, for the time being.

Chapter 22

"The shadow of a starless night was thrown
Over the world in which she moved alone."

The quietness didn't last. With the return of sanity and a degree of strength, memory asserted itself. Naomi didn't ask many questions and apparently didn't want to talk. The unquietness showed itself in an eager, almost frightened anxiety regarding the people who came and went in her sickroom. She begged excitedly that no one except the doctor and the assistant nurse should be admitted.

"Not anyone at all," she repeated, with so much earnestness that Gertrude hastened to promise and to add that the doctor had issued the same orders. She wasn't to see any of her friends until she was stronger. "Don't make *any* exceptions," Naomi said. "I don't want to see *anybody,* not yet."

Outside, the half-frantic husband was reaching the limit of his endurance and was almost ready to dismiss both nurse and doctor as imbeciles, or enemies conniving against his interests. Only the doctor's solemn warning that a single misstep now might make his wife a maniac for life held him in check as far as action was concerned. Nothing restrained his tongue.

"But, doctor, of course her ban doesn't include me. She would naturally shrink from others; they're almost strangers. But if she's sane, as you say she is, her first thought would be for me and her first desire to have me with her. Why, she hated even a day's separation. We've been more to each other, doctor, than husband and wife usually are. I can't think that she understands the situation. I was absent when she was taken ill, you remember, and you say she doesn't realize the length of time that's passed. She must still think I'm away. Why on earth don't you ask her if she doesn't want me?"

The doctor tried to explain and at the same time be reassuring. He was persuaded that Mrs. Newland knew of her husband's presence in the house. They'd taken pains to discover that. There was no accounting for a sick woman's whims. What did her husband think of a mother who asked no questions about her baby and didn't want to see even her? They must all wait and be patient. The case was peculiar, and one thing was clear: Her whims must be carefully deferred to, for more than her life now—her reason—was at stake.

But one day Naomi asked for her baby. She hadn't spoken for an hour and had lain so quiet that the watchful nurse thought her sleeping. Then suddenly she said, "I've decided I want my baby."

This event was looked forward to with mingled hope and fear. Thus far their patient had done nothing as other patients did, and they couldn't foretell the effect of this experience upon her. No sooner was the child placed in her arms than she burst into bitter weeping—the first tears she'd been known to shed—and the paroxysm lasted until the nurse was grave with fear.

But the doctor expressed relief and almost satisfaction. Some women cried naturally when under great nervous strain, and tears relieved them. He had no doubt they would do Mrs. Newland a world of good. In fact, he believed now that all the shoals were safely passed. He was mistaken.

Naomi did gain steadily in strength, and the interest she had at last manifested in her daughter increased with each passing day. Still, she not only declined to see her husband, but had fits of violent trembling, evidently from the sound of his voice in the hall. The puzzled doctor held a long conference with the nurse.

"There's some mystery here. This isn't, of course, a normal condition, and we can't consider Mrs. Newland on the high road to health. In fact, we must consider her distinctly in danger while it lasts. There must be something causing this reaction that we don't understand. I'm told they've been an unusually devoted couple, and the husband is certainly very distracted over the state of things. I can't hold him in check much longer. Can't your woman's wit plan a way to get at the secret, if there is a secret?"

Gertrude shook her head. She was more bewildered than the doctor. She knew, as he didn't, their confiding little Naomi. And unless the years had strangely changed her, as it didn't seem possible for years to do, this silent, reserved woman was not the friend of her youth. At times, despite her apparent sanity, Gertrude feared that the shock, whatever it was, had forever unbalanced the delicate brain. While she puzzled over how to win back the confidence that used to be so fully hers, Naomi met her halfway by a sudden question.

"Gertrude, tell me all about it. How is it you're here with me? I remember the faintness and my falling. Everything else is worse than a blank, a horrible nightmare, until I awakened and found you. Where did you come from, dear?"

"It was a 'happening,' Namie, darling. That's what some people would call it. I'm so glad to be with you that I know it's a Providence. I'm a nurse, you know. It's my business to attend the sick, and your promised nurse was out of town when you were taken ill. I had just reported at the office as off duty and was sent here to what we call an emergency case. When I found that the patient was our dear little Naomi, I begged to stay. I hadn't imagined that the same city held us both. I was silly enough to believe that even though you didn't recognize me, you might like to have me near you."

Naomi reached forth a trembling hand and said with an energy her friend knew the outward circumstances didn't explain: "Don't leave me, Gertrude. Promise me you won't."

"Not while you need me, dear. I've made arrangements to stay with you as long as I can be helpful. Don't you want to know about the others—Bernice and Barbara? I've been waiting for you to get strong enough to talk about them and see them."

Naomi raised herself up from the pillows, with an eager look in her eyes that hadn't been seen before, and spoke excitedly: "Gertrude, where are they? Where is Barbara? You don't mean she's here? Not in this city?"

"In this city, not three miles away from you. She's a teacher here; both of them are. Of course they had no idea you were within a thousand miles of this city until I wrote to them who my patient was. You can imagine their anxiety since then and their eagerness to see you, now that you're getting well enough to admit your friends. I try to send them daily messages. And fruit and flowers and love come almost daily from them. You're gaining so steadily now that we hope in a very short time to let them see you. Of course Mr. Newland must be the first one admitted, but I almost think you'll want Barbara for the second."

She was watching closely while she talked, speaking none of her words at random. She saw the eager light glowing on Naomi's face go suddenly out at the mention of her husband's name. The heart of the anxious woman sank within her. Here was trouble. How should she discover the nature? The wound must be probed and understood before they could hope to help heal it.

She began again, carefully: "You're a good deal stronger today than you were yesterday. Don't you think that by tomorrow you could admit Mr. Newland for a few minutes? He's very anxious, of course, and has been waiting a long time."

The words didn't seem to excite her patient; that much, at least, was gained. She had dropped back among the pillows and lay with closed eyes. The stillness lasted between them. Gertrude, perplexed and distressed, afraid to say more lest she should say the wrong word, waited.

At last Naomi spoke, in unnaturally quiet tones: "Gertrude, were you acquainted with Mr. Newland before you came here to take care of me?"

"Not personally, dear. I knew him by sight, as I know a large number of the city's businessmen. I passed him often on the street and never even dreamed he had a special interest for me. But of course I've met and talked with him daily during your illness—hourly, indeed, part of the time. I've never in my experience seen a more eager and devoted husband. Days and nights he simply haunted the halls for word from you. It has been a long, hard experience. We've all had deep sympathy for him."

"Gertrude, what do you know about him? I mean, what did you know before you came to this house? You say you saw him often; you must have heard things about him. Tell me what?"

"I heard nothing special, dear," said the sorely troubled nurse. "I knew of him as a businessman standing high in his own circle."

"What is his circle? Did you ever see him at church? Do you ever go to the same church he does, Gertrude?"

"My dear," said the distressed nurse, "what's in this to excite you? I'm afraid you shouldn't talk longer. Why, yes"—in answer to an almost imperious movement by Naomi—"I've been in the tabernacle. It's an interesting building, and the organ is of course very fine."

"Never mind the organ. What's the name of the church, of the organization?"

What was Gertrude to say? She'd had her hours of deep distress over the fact that this girlhood friend forgot her inheritance and environment so far as to marry a Mormon. She cried over it and prayed over it and wrote anxious letters to Barbara and Bernice about it, and received anxious ones from them in return. And all three determined to stand by poor little Namie and if possible help her through some of the trials of her new surroundings. Over some things they had in their ignorance rejoiced.

"At least," wrote Bernice, "she hasn't the slime of polygamy to wade through. We may thank God that the strong arm of law has reached after that and made it impossible for her to be menaced by it. Her husband is considered an honorable man, we're told. And he buried his first wife years before he sought Naomi. So we must just try to make the best of it and hold on to her. Perhaps she can win him from his errors. If she is as winsome as the dear girl Naomi, it will be hard to resist her. She CAN'T have accepted their absurd and blasphemous doctrines. I won't believe that. Her heart has simply run away with her judgment—that was to be expected, poor child."

These and kindred words flashed across Gertrude's memory while she waited and questioned how to answer the woman whose eyes were searching her. What did she mean? Was she using this means to learn whether or not her friends knew of her lapse from the world to which she belonged?

"Surely you don't need an answer to that question," she began in a soothing tone, "and I'm not going to let you talk anymore until you've rested. Your cheeks are getting too flushed."

"Gertrude, will you answer my question? Is there any reason why you shrink from naming the organization Mr. Newland belongs to?"

Naomi's tones were imperious and her intense excitement evident. This whim, if whim it was, must evidently be humored at once.

Her nurse spoke quickly: "There's no reason, my dear, since you wish it. I knew when I came to this house as nurse that it belonged to a prominent Mormon who had brought his wife home from abroad. But I didn't have the remotest idea that the wife was my dear friend."

She was watching closely, but her patient didn't start or pale. The momentary excitement was already dying out; she closed her eyes and lay quite still. The terrible suspicion she was deceived, which flashed across Gertrude, was put to rest. But this sudden stillness was perplexing and might indicate danger.

While she waited, trying to decide whether to speak or to hope her patient had exhausted herself and was dropping to sleep, Naomi spoke again: "I wanted to hear it in words. I knew it was so. I've thought it all out, lying here, but I HAD to hear you say it. Gertrude, do you understand? I've come to this knowledge recently. I knew his church was different from others, but I thought it was a holy and blessed difference. I knew no name for it except the Church of Jesus Christ, and I thought it was the earthly embodiment of His holy life. I never for a moment imagined that that other name could be associated with it, until—that day. Until then I believed in it and in him, utterly, as I did in God. Now—oh, Gertrude! I must be left alone. I cannot see him, not yet. I must think. I must pray."

Then a fear came to Gertrude, and with it a thought she hoped might bring some relief.

"Darling, you know—of course you know—that you're his honorably wedded wife? His first wife died years ago."

The woman who bore the name of wife recoiled as though a blow had been struck.

"Don't!" she said, crying out as one in pain. "Go away! I must be alone. Go to the other end of the room. Let me feel myself alone. Oh, Gertrude! Forgive me. I'm in sore trouble. I must pray. I haven't lost Jesus Christ."

In distress too deep for words, if she'd had wise words to speak, the helpless nurse moved slowly away. Here was something far beyond her skill—a case only the Great Physician knew how to handle.

Mr. Newland paced the room in a fever of anxiety and pain he couldn't control and tried to listen to the doctor's carefully chosen words.

"You see, Newland, your policy of secrecy hasn't worked well. Instead of waiting until you carefully prepared her to hear what you meant sometime to tell her carefully, she's heard from careless and probably malicious tongues what has shocked her terribly. Brought up as you say she was, and in total ignorance of facts, you can't wonder at it. The wonder is that she hasn't become a hopeless maniac. I know something about women, and I can tell you it was a marvelous and narrow escape.

"Moreover, I must warn you now that utmost caution must be used; otherwise in her weak state a fatal relapse should occur. Her whims must be humored at any sacrifice. She refuses for the present to see you; she mustn't be forced or urged. Of course, when she's really well again, with her mental powers fully balanced, all will be right. But she mustn't be hurried. Take yourself out of town, on any pretext you choose. Go down to the other house and let that pretty daughter of yours comfort you. She drives plenty of other men to distraction; she should balance it by comforting somebody. In any case, don't disturb this Mrs. Newland at present.

"Let her go to her friends as she wants to. They can't hurt your cause anymore than it's already hurt. They may even be able to help you. She's a legally married woman in their eyes as well as ours, and when that's established, their sense of what propriety, even respectability, demands will aid you. Anyhow, it's that or a raving maniac for life on your hands. You can take your choice." The last sentence was added with emphasis, as Mr. Newland paused before him, opposition in his eyes.

The doctor prevailed, and the troubled husband went his way without so much as glimpsing the woman who grew every day dearer to him. The outside world, that part of it that knew anything about them, knew only that Mrs. Newland was now well enough to be left in the care of her friends while her husband went away on important business.

On the morning following his departure a closed carriage conveyed Naomi and her baby and the baby's nurse to the house at the other end of the city where Barbara and Bernice were boarders. For an indefinite time Naomi took formal possession of the suite of rooms across the hall from her old-time friends. That evening the long-ago planned, long-deferred reunion of the four friends took place in Naomi's room.

Chapter 23

*"Thine to work, as well as pray,
Clearing thorny wrongs away."*

The following weeks stood out long afterward to Naomi as the ones that marked the real turning point in her life. Up to about that time she realized she'd remained a child in some respects; then she became a woman. She knew she must have appeared childish both to the doctor and the nurse in her determination to leave Mr. Newland's house and not see him for even a moment before she left. With the doctor she felt it must pass for a sick woman's whim and help mislead him as to her actual mental state. But to Gertrude she tried to explain.

"Gertrude, I can't talk, not yet. But there are reasons why I can't see Mr. Newland now and why I must see Barbara. I must have a long, long talk with her before I can decide some things which must be decided. That doesn't sound rational, does it? But I'm fully in my right mind. Perhaps I can make it plain to you afterward. Won't you trust me? I'm not a child anymore. I've lived, oh, an eternity in a few weeks, and I know I'm doing the best that's left for me. Won't you help me?"

And Gertrude helped, set her face like a flint against every other plan and argued the doctor into agreeing with her.

So Naomi sat, on that first evening, among the cushions like a young queen hovered over by three willing subjects, studying these girlhood friends the years had developed into women. They, too, had passed through the furnace, she reflected. At least Gertrude and Bernice had had their heavy sorrows, but they hadn't been crushed. Still, their trouble wasn't like hers; for in Naomi's heart was that old cry of the stricken soul, "There is no sorrow like unto my sorrow." She had no friend who wouldn't have instantly agreed with her; it was given to her to drink the dregs of a peculiarly bitter cup of misery.

As she watched Barbara's face the poor young woman told herself she wasn't mistaken; she came to the right source. Barbara could help her if any human being could. She'd grown into just the kind of woman Naomi's hungry soul often imagined her—a woman to be trusted. They were grand women, all of them—full of energy and purpose, doing a work in the world that was surely as great, yes, infinitely greater, than that of a multitude of mothers.

Yet that poor stunted soul, that girl with a face like an angel's and with thoughts like those from the pit, would look down upon them as women who were shirking their duties and living to please themselves and failing in that for which they were created. Hush! She mustn't think of Mara, not yet. She couldn't, without trembling.

The three friends talked incessantly that first evening. Not letting Naomi talk much, touching upon and moving away from topics that wouldn't bear analysis, and feeling cautiously for safe common ground—and feeling, each of them, keenly, that this reunion was not in the least like the one they planned. It seemed difficult to find common ground that wasn't too exciting; the three had lived such different lives from Naomi's.

It was Barbara who lingered latest, or who came back to give her another good night after nurse Gertrude saw to it that every possible task for her comfort was performed.

"Our little Naomi," she said, bending over to kiss her. "She doesn't know, she can't guess, how glad we all are to have her again." She promised Gertrude to say nothing more exciting than this and then slip away.

But Naomi caught her hand and drew her close and held her with arms that trembled as she said slowly, with the sort of solemnity that starts the tears: "Call me not Naomi—call me Mara; for the Almighty hath dealt very bitterly with me."

Work began in earnest for Naomi the next day. She had solemn work to do, a problem to solve and a new lesson to learn, which, turn it as she would, must be hard. But she was resolute. She must learn not only what she did with her life before this, but what to do with it now. She had come to Barbara for help, and her girlish intuitions did not fail her. Barbara, in her full, serene, strong womanhood, living her beautiful life of daily toil and helpfulness, was just the human help she needed.

Naomi laid bare her heart before her. She described the lonely years when school days were over—years she was at home and yet not at home. She told of the hope deferred regarding her mother and her; of the comfort at last of going away with her father; of the hope she'd cherished of blessing his life as soon as she got him away from the awful grind of the business world. She described her partial success and the emptiness when he died. Then she told of the friend who appeared to her suddenly out of the darkness as though he were an angel of light. She explained the dear hope he held out to her at once that she might redeem some of her lost opportunities and bless her beloved dead.

She dwelt on the fact that he spoke to her of that unseen, ever-present Friend in such a way that she was drawn to Him, and a new light and joy came into her life through fellowship with Him.

Then came the story of her surprise and her happiness in discovering this new earthly friend was not only friend, but lover. She told of her glad yielding of herself to him and of the year of wedded happiness that followed—a year in which he was all to her that human friend could be, until suddenly, out of the clear sky, swooped down upon her a horror of great darkness from which she felt she could never get away. It was a long story, with a lonely beginning, a dreary stretch of years, a single belt of light, and then a yawning cavern of blackness.

Barbara cowered inwardly before it and said to her conscience-stricken soul: *If I only had known! I could have helped her, led her, saved her. Intimate acquaintance with the perfect Life, the soul-satisfying Love, would have saved her, and I could have led her to Him.*

"Now," said Naomi, when she felt she'd made everything plain, "you can see, can't you, that I have work to do? I know now that much of the joy I thought I had in religious things was joy in one man's friendship; when I thought I loved God, it was love for man, instead, that was leading me on.

"And yet, Barbara, that's not all of it. After my marriage, when Mr. Newland was necessarily absent from me and I felt lonely, I turned to my Bible and to Jesus Christ as I found Him there. I studied His life and loved it, and loved Him and gave myself to Him anew. I know now that I belong to Him. In that, at least, I wasn't mistaken. The misery of my life hasn't separated me from Him. That's why I didn't die, Barbara, because He was left. Now I have a lesson to learn, and I've fled to you as my human helper. Do you understand what it is?

"Revelations have been made to me since I came to this place to live— doctrines hinted at, some of them spoken all too plainly, which seem to me monstrous, disgusting beyond belief. Yet I've learned that the man whose name I bear believes them and believes he's taught of God. And, Barbara, if it's of God, I'm bound to obey it, though it kill me. I found a verse this morning that expresses my thought, 'Though He slay me, yet will I trust in Him.' I feel utterly slain; yet I know that what He requires of me I'll try to do, even this.

"The awful question before me is, Does God require it? Are these horrible doctrines fresh revelations from Him? I must study; I must pray; I must think. Will you help me?

"I might have read their books; they were around me. But I couldn't get interested in them; I liked the Bible better. I thought since it was a first revelation it would be simpler, and I told myself I was too much of a child in the new life for strong meat. I would keep to the first Bible, especially to the New Testament, where my Lord's human life was made plain, until I was strong enough to read for myself those deeper truths. So I didn't know until it was sprung upon me what some of those beliefs were. I knew, of course, about Mormons, Barbara, something about them, at least. But I never for one moment imagined that the Church of Jesus Christ, as it was described to me, had anything to do with that."

By degrees Barbara understood the skillful way in which her girlfriend so utterly alone in her world was led and blinded and controlled. One blessed gleam of light shone out of the dark picture. Iniquity had overreached itself, if it was iniquity pure and simple. Given the Bible and the story of Jesus Christ and communion with Him, the inevitable result followed, and beyond and above all other loves stood His. What Naomi was convinced He taught, she would obey. In her sudden horror she had fled to Barbara simply for a chance to make sure what this supreme Leader asked of her. When her friend was convinced of this, she thanked God and took courage.

The next weeks were solemn weeks; great issues were at stake. Awful questions were considered, and on their answers hung the saving or the wreck of souls. The three friends felt the solemnity of the hour. As they sat together after Barbara explained to them as much as could be explained of Naomi's position and desire, a silence fell between them. It lasted until Bernice pushed her open Bible toward Gertrude, pointing with her pencil to a marked phrase.

"That's our part," she said. "Isn't it? Barbara can also help her personally. But I believe this is our stronghold."

The phrase was, "We will give ourselves continually to prayer." Barbara had many questions to answer during those days.

"I know," said Naomi at the beginning of the study, "that you don't believe in any of their doctrines. But why don't you? Have you reasons for the things you believe? Or did you simply believe them because the people about you did, and ordinary propriety seemed to call for some such form of belief? Barbara, do you know just what you believe? And more than that, do you know what these people believe and why they believe it?"

The clear-eyed woman she was searching with her singularly penetrative gaze didn't flinch. She not only knew what she believed and why she believed it, but she was thoroughly conversant with the early history and present teachings and practices of the strange people among whom she lived. Early in her experience as a teacher she discovered that in order to meet the insidious errors which were not only being drilled into the minds of the very babies, but pressed upon the inquiring at every point, she must understand the organization as thoroughly as possible. The result of four years of hard study and close watching she had put into a single sentence just the evening before, in reply to a remark of Gertrude's.

"I believe the most cunningly devised and, in this present day, the most dangerous of all the lies the 'father of lies' has used to deceive the earth since history began will be found here. The system has enough truth skillfully woven in with its monstrous falsehoods to accomplish exactly what it was designed from the first to do—deceive the ignorant and win the unthinking and the lonely and desolate.

"Our poor little Naomi! When we were girls together, if I hadn't been content with living my own selfish Christian life—if we girls had read and studied the Bible together as we studied our rhetoric and philosophy, and Naomi had come to know Jesus Christ in His purity and grandeur of character as a personal Savior, she wouldn't have fallen a sacrifice to this latter-day abomination. You and Bernice don't have as much to answer for, but I can never forgive myself."

"Haven't we?" said Gertrude, her face serious. "There's another way to look at that. At least you lived before us a life different from ours; we felt it. But I didn't have enough interest in the truth even to study it myself."

The studying and the praying went on steadily. All day, while the three women were busy with their regular duties, Naomi, with her child sleeping near her, went over with intense soul-interest the ground Barbara marked out for her. And Barbara's evenings were given to discussing step by step what was carefully studied. It wasn't the first time she'd had occasion to traverse the same ground for an inquiring soul. She was able swiftly and clearly to call attention to the misquotations, to point out the wresting of sacred words from their connection and obvious meaning, and to probe the false logic of the penciled annotations in Naomi's Bible.

Little by little there fell away from the poor new disciple the ground that seemed so solid when laid for her by Mr. Newland's fine voice and skillful interpretations. She had much to unlearn. She hadn't lived for more than a year in the daily companionship of such a man as Mr. Newland without unconsciously imbibing from him ideas not distinctly taught, and he carefully taught a great deal.

Yet they made rapid progress. Barbara told her fellow workers they must expect to move very slowly; that Naomi was under the power of a strong-willed teacher of error for so long, and with no background of early experience to rest upon, that their way would doubtless be plagued with many modern doubts. In that she reckoned without one potent Force. She forgot for a moment the crumbs of truth scattered through those monstrous falsehoods—crumbs at which the poor hungry soul had grasped and taken hold of forever.

Long afterward, Naomi realized the Shepherd was searching even then for His lost sheep and, through the dangerous paths her straying feet persisted in finding, was guiding her to Rock foundation. Through the maze of error one truth clung—the Lord Jesus Christ.

She couldn't read and study all day long, nor indeed so much as she believed was possible. The nurse who was still watching carefully over her body gave her stern orders. But while resting on her couch or walking daily about the grounds, she could pray. And pray she did, almost with every waking breath, and she hushed her tired brain to sleep each night surrounded by the atmosphere of prayer.

Under such nurturing her faith grew, and the fog of error cleared away. When she studied the lies on which the extraordinary doctrine of plural marriage was built and was being perpetuated, two forces helped her mightily—the innate purity of womanhood which had been her birthright, and her growing intimacy with Jesus Christ. It wasn't difficult to convince a soul who was living in hourly communion with God that, so far from its being her duty to live the life of duplicity and impurity such a doctrine demanded, it was her duty as a woman and a follower of Jesus Christ to enter her solemn protest against this lowest form of religious travesty. Yet so she might understand the rapid downward trend of the doctrine and the depths of blasphemy into which its advocates had sunk, she had to wade through what Barbara indignantly called a cesspool of filth.

"It's horrible," she told Gertrude, "to drag that pure-souled woman down into the slums of impurity as I've been forced to do in the name of religion. But somebody must wade in slime if victims are to be saved, and I believe she has a work to do for God in this very direction. There are depths connected with the past history of this horror that I don't dare so much as hint at, for fear of its effect upon her physically now. But I believe now that her eyes are opened she'll study the whole iniquity for herself."

Chapter 24

"Thou hast done evil and given place to the devil;
Yet so cunningly thou concealest
The thing which thou feelest,
That no eye espieth it,
Satan himself denieth it."

O ne morning, while this latest and most revolting of her studies was in progress, Naomi was interrupted by a caller. Since escaping to her retreat, the outside world had left her in peace; Mr. Newland's friends understood she wasn't strong enough to see people. The three friends who were watching over her interests had anxiously discussed what to do when they could no longer shield her. As yet nothing had been said to Naomi, nor had she hinted of any plan as to her future.

She remembered just what she was reading when the interruption came. It was a copy of a sermon delivered in the tabernacle where she had worshipped, by a man whose memory she knew was highly honored and whose teachings were quoted as authority in her husband's church. This was the paragraph she read three times, feeling unable at the first reading to trust her eyes or her senses.

"If He (Jesus Christ) was never married, his intimacy with Mary and Martha and the other Mary also, whom Jesus loved, must have been highly unbecoming and improper, to say the best of it. I will venture to say that if Jesus Christ were now to pass through the most pious countries in Christendom with a train of women such as used to follow Him, fondling about Him, combing His hair, anointing Him with precious ointments, washing His feet with tears, and wiping them with the hair of their heads, and unmarried, or even married, He would be mobbed, tarred and feathered, and rode, not on an ass, but on a rail."

Naomi caught her breath and trembled with the horror of it. She looked again to see if she could possibly have been mistaken in the source and read again to make sure her nerves weren't teasing her. Then she read once more with slow deliberation to compel herself to realize the fulness of the blasphemy, to make herself understand that it was actually the Lord Christ, the divine Redeemer, about whom this infinitely coarse pen was writing. Then she dropped the leaflet and bowed her head on the table before her, a great yearning in her heart to flee at once to Him for cleansing from contact with such a vile thought.

Just then Huldah came to her with a card. Only that morning Naomi explained to her maid that hereafter calls might be reported to her at once, leaving her to decide in each case whether she would or would not receive them. It was her first little step toward taking up the cross of living again and of getting used to people she knew she must meet.

She held the card for several minutes, not studying the name so much as staring at it with a face so pallid Huldah asked if she mightn't tell the lady her mistress was too ill to see people. Huldah's voice seemed to help her to a decision.

"No," she said, "you may show her up. And then, Huldah, close the door between these rooms, and don't let me be interrupted for anything less than a necessity."

The card she held read: "Mrs. Maria V. Newland." The lady was tall and stately in manner. She was stylishly dressed and quite at ease as she came forward and held for a moment Naomi's cold hand while she spoke in a cordial tone.

"I'm very glad to learn that you're able to receive your friends. What a long, weary time you've had! Illness is wearing upon one's courage, I think, as well as upon the body. The little daughter is doing nicely, I hear. I'm longing to see her. I'm so fond of all the children. I've been quite anxious to welcome you. I should have called before your illness if Brother Newland hadn't thought you weren't equal to meeting any of his people just then. I don't live in town, but I'd have been glad to make the trip if he'd considered it wise."

Naomi sat like one turned to stone. This wasn't the kind of interview she expected.

"Are you Mara's mother?" This was her first spoken word.

"Oh, dear, no! I'm only her Aunt Maria," said the guest, seating herself in an easy chair. "So it was Mara who made all the trouble, was it? I suspected it at the time and told Brother Newland so. I found that she left home for my place five or six hours before she reached there, although it's only an hour's ride from her house. I knew then that she'd been up to some mischief. That girl ought to be whipped, old as she is. If I had her in charge, I would tame her, but her mother spoils her and always has. You poor creature! What did she say to give you such a turn? I suppose it was the way she said it that shocked you.

"I told Brother Newland before your illness that it was a mistake for him to be so silent about our peculiar institutions. Of course you had general knowledge of affairs, and to talk them over frankly and have a perfect understanding in the families would be much more sensible than to act as if there was something to hide. We have to do some hiding in these days; but that's because of our enemies, and it shouldn't be carried on among us. But Brother Newland thought he knew best, as he generally does. You haven't lived with him for a year, I guess, without discovering he's a man who's fond of his own way."

Her tone was lightness itself. It helped somehow to increase Naomi's sense of shame. Her main feeling was that she must make an effort in behalf of her self-respect.

"When I married Mr. Newland," she said, in a voice that sounded unnatural, "I knew only that his wife was dead and that his children were living with their mother's relatives."

"Is that possible? You mean you didn't know of his living wives? You poor dear! I don't wonder you were shocked. It's a shock at first, of course— especially to those who haven't been educated among us. If it doesn't prove to have done you a lasting injury, I think we may all be thankful. At least it will be good for Brother Newland to discover he's not infallible."

"Will you tell me who you are?"

The guest looked her well-bred surprise at such a question.

"Why, my dear sister, didn't you receive my card? I am Mrs. Maria Newland, the mother of four young Newlands of whom you must have heard? I can't think that their father disowned his children, even though he had in a sense to disown his wives." The sentence closed with a sarcastic little laugh.

But without waiting for a reply the guest continued: "I'm surprised to hear this is new to you. You can't mean, of course, that the institution of plural marriage was unknown? At least I thought our affairs had been blazoned all over the United States, especially when Congress passed those infamous laws intended to separate families. I think the country has fearful crime to answer for, attempting to separate husbands and wives and bring distress into happy homes. The holiest institution of our land was touched when Congress tried to separate what God had joined together."

Mercifully for Naomi, she had in a way lost her personality. She was listening now with fascinated horror, much as a child might listen to a deadly serpent suddenly given power of speech. She didn't feel as if she belonged to a world where such conditions could exist and that she was looking down on some creature of another sphere, simply curious to understand her level.

"Do you mean you believe," she said in that strange impersonal tone, "that a man may honorably have two living wives?"

"My dear sister! I am myself a third choice, and the second one is living. That surely is a sufficient answer to your extraordinary question. I do more than believe it; I'm as sure the plan was ordained of God as I am that I exist. I believe the general practice of plural marriage would furnish the grand solution to the problem of a social evil—a problem the enlightened people of our land pretend to have been working at for years. Yet they're as blind as bats to the remedy the chosen people of God have tried to live before their eyes. Instead of accepting the God-revealed remedy, they've set to work to persecute the ones who've followed His voice. But that's simply history repeating itself. It was the way they treated Jesus Christ and the people of the early church. You read your Bible, I suppose?"

"And yet you're a woman!" It was the impersonal voice that spoke, and Naomi's gaze was still one that suggested fascinated horror.

Her caller went on briskly. "Certainly I'm a woman, my dear, and a mother, and glory in both. If you've given intelligent thought to this subject, as I hope you have, how would you plan otherwise? How else than by some such scheme as has been revealed in these latter days could woman fulfill her destiny and rescue from immaterialism immortal spirits who've been waiting for thousands of years?

"This leaves out altogether the question of personal salvation, although we believe, as you know, that no provision has been made for woman in the other world except as the wife of some good man. And of course you know there aren't enough men for each woman to have one all to herself. If there were, I have no desire to be so horribly selfish as that.

"Don't you understand human nature enough to know that no one woman is able to fill a man's heart? We women are constituted differently. We live chiefly in our children, anyway, and the love and care of one good man is all we would ask, if a wicked government would leave us our share of him in peace. We learn not to require exclusive attention. But men's natures have a wealth of love that no one heart will satisfy. The Creator made them so—that is, some men. There are small and sordid souls among them who profess to feel satisfied with one wife, just as there are mean and selfish women who want to claim sole right to the man whose name they bear. But these are the exceptions among us, we hope and believe."

"And you," said the fascinated victim, "you mean you went to live, as a wife, with a man whose wife was living, and you knew she was living, and you were willing to do it—you mean that?"

The guest drew herself up and spoke coldly. "Sister Newland, I trust you don't mean it, but you have a way of putting questions that makes them sound insulting. There are no first and second and third wives among us, when it comes to that. Once married, we're all wives and on a level. As Brother Newland's third choice I consider myself as much his wife in every respect as the woman he married first. She's dead now, but she wasn't when I was married. You'll notice I don't say 'third *wife*,' but 'third *choice*.' A man doesn't rate his wives in the order of their coming, anymore than he does his children."

"But the law," faltered the horror-stricken Naomi. "I thought that—"

"Oh, the law!" interrupted her guest with a defiant toss of her head. Then she laughed. "Of course we're law-abiding citizens and adhere strictly to even unjust and inhuman laws; everybody understands that. I suppose that lovely Congress and the good Christian people who urged them on believed that as soon as their infamous law was passed our men would hurry home and pitch their wives out-of-doors and toss their children after them. Chivalrous men they were, who enacted such laws, and charming wives and mothers who tramped about with petitions praying for it! We women owe our country a debt of gratitude, don't we? Oh, yes, of course we obey the laws—only among us we know God's law is higher than that of any man or set of men.

"But really, my dear, Brother Newland would be shocked beyond measure if he knew how long a call I'm making. I'm afraid I've wearied you. You're still deathly pale, aren't you? You need to get out into our nice bracing air.

"Well, I'm very glad you'll soon be among us. I told Brother Newland last week that I shouldn't wonder if you could help bring his oldest daughter to use common sense. Though between you and me, he'd have to get rid of her mother before he could expect her to have much. I assure you I don't feel flattered in being mistaken for Mara's mother. Brother Newland certainly has had his trials with us women. When do you expect him? I haven't seen him for nearly two weeks. Are you going to give me a peep at that wonderful baby? It seems rather hard that Brother Newland himself hasn't seen her yet, doesn't it? Still, he can afford to wait; he's used to babies."

She went away at last, talking volubly—offering graciously to come and help Naomi establish the nursery when she went back home, adding with a sarcastic laugh that "the Roper" might object. Then she spoke confidingly and admitted that Mrs. Roper was really like an outsider and obnoxious to all of them. But Brother Newland knew how to keep her in her place, and if Naomi would really like assistance, she had only to mention "Sister Maria's" name to Brother Newland. He was in the mood now to give her the moon if she asked for it.

Just how she got her caller outside the door, with the door closed and locked, Naomi never knew. But at last she was alone. She lay back in her invalid chair with closed eyes and hands clasped, making no sound, indicating only by her breathing that she was alive. Huldah came on tiptoe again and again to look anxiously at her and retire without speaking. The baby awakened and cooed and cried, was fed and comforted by her faithful nurse, and slept again. Still Naomi lay back in the chair almost as white as the pillow on which her head rested. Faithful Huldah whispered the story to Barbara and Bernice when they came to look after their charge.

"She's that pale, ma'am, that I'm sure she can't be whiter when she's dead. And she's all tuckered out. That woman—I could have choked her, ma'am, with a good heart—she stayed and *stayed!* But I haven't dared to wake her even for her tonic; she's that sound asleep."

Chapter 25

"There are no seas,
no mountains rising wide,
No centuries of absence to divide,
Just soul-space, standing side by side."

Yet Naomi wasn't sleeping. By degrees the numb horror of fascination that held her spellbound passed, only to be succeeded by an equally numbing horror of despair. What should she do? Where stay—or fly? How should she live at all and bear her agony of pain? These questions beat themselves against her brain, receiving no answer. The poor victim was under the spell that there was no answer for her in earth or heaven.

And then, just then, she thought of the Lord Christ, of that pure and perfect life revealed to us when the Son of God walked the earth, a man. She thought of the weight of pain He bore for humanity—pain and shame and blasphemy—and was bearing still. What were those awful words she read that morning—the blasphemy that paled her face and almost stopped her heart beating from terror? Who was she that she couldn't bear pain and shame when He, her Lord, was still being traduced in this vilest of human ways? And He wasn't simply a poor human creature like her; He was her Lord.

Her soul cried out to Him for help. This was why she lived through even such a morning as has been described. Though she had lost everything else that women and wives count dear and sacred, God lived and reigned, and the Lord Jesus Christ was her Redeemer.

Her friends asked no questions about her caller. Before this time Barbara was told all Naomi knew and much she feared regarding Mr. Newland's present position. She heard in minutest detail of the interview with the girl, Mara, and was charged with a trust. She was to learn, in ways she best would understand, how much or how little of the girl's story was to be believed. And Barbara in her investigations learned not only that Mara's statements were in the main correct, but that she might have told much more.

These revelations came as a shock to the three friends. Until then they believed Mr. Newland was married only twice and that his first wife was long dead. Not closely acquainted with men of his class, they never thought he could be personally involved in the offense against decency that had flourished under the name of plural marriage.

They were too long at the center of Mormon influence and too thoroughly in earnest in their desire to help the world upward, to have fallen into the trap in which many transient visitors have been caught. They hadn't been made to believe that the laws passed and the solemn pledges taken by the people against this crime had abolished it; they had abundant evidence to the contrary.

But instinctively they relegated all actual association with it to the lower classes and passed men like Mr. Newland on the streets of the city hundreds of times, knowing they were disciples of the strange religion, but not imagining for a moment they were personally associated with this sin. Therefore the condition of things revealed by this later investigation was a shock to them differing from Naomi's only in degree.

They read the caller's name on her card and imagined the rest. They scarcely talked of it even among themselves. Such a condition of things, coming so close as to enclose in its horrors the friend of their youth, seemed too appalling for words. And Naomi didn't talk about it in detail, not even to Barbara.

On that first evening, as Barbara was bidding her good night, she said in the steady monotone of one beyond emotion: "Barbara, I've gone down today into the lowest depths of degradation. I've come in contact with a woman who is passably educated and superficially refined. She not only accepts as a doctrine of her church this awful sin against womanhood and against God, but admires and exalts it as the most blessed of human institutions. I could almost respect an ignorant endurance of it as a curse from God, but to glory in it! Can humanity fall lower?"

Naomi's next caller, as expected, was Mr. Newland himself. She had spent hours of agony preparing a long letter which made as plain to him as words could her careful study of the past weeks and her solemn conclusions. But it seemed to make no impression upon him. He made no attempt to reply to her. His letters, received almost daily, were very brief; they simply expressed undying love for her, an apparently unalterable determination to see her as soon as he reached home, and his intent to reach there at the earliest possible moment.

She prepared for it as best she could. It was a midsummer Sunday morning when he came. Baby and nurse had just departed to the shade of the great tree at the farther end of the lawn, and Barbara and Bernice, dressed for church, were saying good-bye to Naomi when Huldah announced him. Barbara and Bernice exchanged glances as they heard the name, then Barbara quietly drew off her gloves as she passed into the next room. Naomi caught and understood her look as she passed. She couldn't at the moment trust herself to words. Their darling Naomi! To what a low estate the sins of others had reduced her when they felt that one of them must stay to watch over her because the man she'd given her heart to was coming to visit her.

He stepped forward eagerly with outstretched hands. But Naomi, who rose and stood with one hand resting on the back of her chair, motioned him back with the other and indicated a seat across the room from her. He stopped midway and looked at her, with his soul in his eyes.

"Naomi," he said, "my wife!"

Then a flash of Naomi's girlhood and the voice she had sometimes used, but never for him, were given to him.

"Not that name, that last. You have no right, and I do not want it."

He was awed and showed it, but he rallied and spoke sternly. "Naomi, this is worse than folly; it is sin. I won't try to tell you how cruel it is. I bore with it patiently while you weren't yourself, but now—it's hard. I tried to regard your letter to me as the ravings of a lunatic. Was I so utterly deceived in you, Naomi? Are the solemn vows you took worth nothing? Have you forgotten the words of the marriage service? Death hasn't parted us, and nothing else can. My heart is wholly yours. I've told you so again and again. I swear it to you by all you hold sacred. My poor little wife! Victim of fate and of tongues as cruel as death, let me take you in my arms and comfort you as only I can. I'll blot out the very memory of these awful weeks of separation. You remember, surely you remember, what we were to each other?"

It was a fearful ordeal. Naomi believed she'd drunk her cup of pain to its dregs already, but she discovered a still more awful potion remained. She was white to her lips, but her voice didn't falter.

She remembered everything, she told him; it was he who forgot. When she took those vows upon her lips at the marriage altar, she didn't know there was another woman living to whom such vows should be an insult. He knew it and kept silence and let her make them. God would forgive her ignorance; He had forgiven her and made her His child. But for him, the man who betrayed her trust, the least he could do for her now was to go away and leave her to her insulted womanhood.

He stared at her as one bewildered. She must still be insane, he told her. Didn't she remember he taught her a new religion, another revelation from God, and commands laid upon them they mustn't disregard?

She didn't understand these very commands, which were told to her hastily, unwisely, by heedless tongues; they worked on her nervous system to make her beside herself. He could have explained and made everything right; he could do it yet if she'd only trust him. It was his cursed folly in delaying that caused all the trouble; he could never forgive himself for the pain he inflicted. But he did it to shield her for awhile from revelations that, coming upon her suddenly, might hurt her. He made a mistake, but it was because of love to her; surely she could forgive him. Nothing should be hidden from her ever again. He didn't mean to hide, only delay. He would make all plain.

He had married wives to do his duty, to accomplish what God required at his hands. He married her because he loved her, and her alone, of all women in the world. All his heart was hers, and hers only, though he'd done his duty by other women; he was good to them and faithful. If Naomi would be true to him, would come home with him now, at once, away from her mistaken friends with their narrow ideas and false religion, he could make everything plain to her. He could show her the true way, the only safe way, and could promise her, swear to her, that no human being should ever come between them. Wouldn't she come with him? Didn't she owe it to her solemn vows to give him so much opportunity to explain?

He was terribly in earnest. At the same time he was consciously using all his power over her and watching every muscle of her face closely. He remembered the spell his voice and his views had woven about her in the past. If he only had an opportunity, he believed he could win her to his way of thinking, against all other influence in this world.

Perhaps he might have done so if all influences could be counted as of this world. Naomi had loved him with no common love. But during the weeks of separation she drank deeply at the fountain of eternal love, and the lines between that and the earthly and sensual were distinctly drawn. One result was that the very words Mr. Newland used to woo her, withdrew her from him. For this man to talk to her of going "home," as if the sacred place belonged jointly to those two, when within the very weeks of their separation he was in other "homes" as husband and father! And he did this in the name of religion and quoted God as his guide!

She answered quickly. The time was past, she told him, when such arguments could move her. She had been studying and praying. She was certain she was being led by the Lord her Savior, and she knew that what he was telling her in the name of God was a network of lies, the so-called revelations it was built on having sprung from the father of lies. She should have studied and prayed long ago, she told him, instead of submitting to human leading because the way was pleasant. But she hadn't, until the pit yawned before her and she found where her life was going.

Then indeed she fled to God, and He didn't spurn her. He made her sure that the new teaching she was leaning on had its foundation in falseness and impurity and was rotten through and through. She would have none of it, nor would she have fellowship with those who lived it.

He must not quote marriage vows to her. No woman had ever made them in better faith than she; no woman would ever have been truer to them than she, if he hadn't made it impossible. Another woman living had the right to claim a place beside him as wife. With such knowledge she was insulted that the name was applied to her. Her last word to him was to go to that other woman and be true to her.

Mr. Newland, experienced diplomat as he was, made one mistake. In his bitter pain and helpless rage over what he believed was caused by the interference of enemies, and wanting to make plain to Naomi the folly of her words, he said quickly, with the sound of a sneer in his voice: "Which of them?"

She understood him instantly, and the effect was the opposite of what he desired. The words recalled to her suddenly and terribly the depth of degradation into which this man had sunk. She visibly recoiled from him, with a cry like that of a wounded creature.

"Oh! WON'T you go?" she said. "You must do what you will—what you can—I don't know—I only know that I'm to keep myself as pure as I can from this latter-day curse. I'm not pure; I've helped others—other women and girls—into its depths, believing, in my folly, I was leading them toward God. I've given my life, what's left of it, to the task of trying to help someone out of the pit. Volney Newland, I am not the woman you knew. Sin and misery and grace have changed me. You might as well talk to a stone as to me when you talk of our past; it's dead and buried. It is beyond resurrection. I would not have it resurrected if I could; now go."

With that last word she turned and walked out of the room, closing the door behind her. And Barbara, her friend, received the stricken woman in her arms.

Mr. Newland did not, however, give her up easily. This man of many wives and numberless fantasies had met at last the woman who held what heart he had to give. He spoke truly when he said his first marriage was one of convenience, of advisement, with no feeling on his part more pronounced than indifference.

Naturally he was ready for the second venture when it was suggested to him, in accord with the peculiar views in which he was born and reared—far more ready than his wife. The poor young thing had loved, if he hadn't. She didn't "live her religion" well but took to heart her husband's indifference and almost desertion; she hated royally his "second choice," even though she went through the public farce of receiving her.

Much domestic infelicity resulted, and although Mr. Newland had been a "good man," judged by the standards about him, and had "done his duty by his wife," his home was anything but peaceful. It must have been a distinct relief to him when the poor victim of his youth gave up the struggle and was laid in the grave.

He made his "second choice" himself, but, in accord with the teachings of his religion, he found she didn't "fill" his heart. So he made more than one further effort to have that troublesome member filled, with more or less discord and discomfort and dissension as a result. Then, suddenly, when he was a middle-aged man, father of many children, without previous intention on his part—so much may be said in his favor—his heart was taken by storm and hopelessly filled. The man who had played with emotion and passion in the name of love, learned for himself the meaning of the word, as fully at least as a nature like his could learn such a lesson.

Chapter 26

"I have already
The bitter taste of death upon my lips;
I feel the pressure of the heavy weight;
But if a word could save me, and that word
Were not the Truth, nay, if it did but swerve
A hair's breadth from the Truth—I would not say it."

He left that morning, slowly, with bowed head, as one vanquished. But he was only rebuffed. He came again and again and between his visits wrote volumes to Naomi and interviewed her friends, beseeching their assistance, promising abjectly anything, everything she could ask, if she would only come back to him. For a time it seemed impossible for the man who had all his life secured whatever he greatly desired to believe that one small woman, over whom he thought he possessed unlimited influence, was proof against his power and that he couldn't move her from her solemn determination to separate her life from his forever.

By degrees, Naomi came to understand him and realize he wasn't the villain the first revelations seemed to unmask to her. He didn't plot deliberately to deceive her and ruin her happiness for life. Instead, she believed and, in a measure, understood he was a man who fully believed in himself and in the reasonableness of his course. He was convinced he could win her to his way of thinking in time and that then all would be well between them.

"He's a product of the religion he was reared in," Naomi said to Barbara, in the impersonal tone that meant she was stepping outside the scene and viewing it as if it were being acted by others. "He's an inevitable product of the system. I've studied it thoroughly, and I see he couldn't be other than as he is.

"Remember, Barbara, that he was born in an unholy atmosphere. His father subjected his mother to the awful torture—the thought fills us with horror—and she yielded and accepted it as part of her religion, her cross, to bear for Christ's sake, and reared her children in that faith. How can someone like that be expected to understand our moral recoil? Morality to Mr. Newland means something infinitely lower than it does to you and me. He doesn't have our foundation on which to build morality.

"Barbara, he has no God! Not such a God as you and I worship. He has many gods, manufactured ones, made out of such worthless material as human clay and fallen human nature. Even Jesus Christ, the perfect One, is made by this system into a creature of mere human impulse, His infinite love for humanity dragged in the mire and spoken of as human passion. What can one expect from such a source, a system that can drag down to earth, and lower than earth, the name of the divine Christ and pollute it with blasphemy?

"And that disgusting priesthood with its iron hand on every man, woman, and child is the rotten foundation of it all. Scorched as I am, *burnt* almost to death by this awful doctrine of plural marriage, even *I* believe Bishop Fowler was right when he said polygamy was the 'whitest bird in this infernal nest.' Those were his very words, and he showed by them that he'd studied the system and reached to its black heart. Because of this a man can't be a man; he's simply a tool. He must sink his reason, trample on his judgment, choke every uprising of his better nature, and blindly obey.

"You think you know this thing, Barbara, but you know it only as those who stand outside and look down at it. There's a deeper knowledge, and I have it. I'm in it, remember. Its curse is upon me, and I KNOW. I might have known before. I read its description and the warning against it this very day in my Bible: 'In the last times there should be mockers who should walk after their own ungodly lusts. These be they who separate themselves, sensual, having not the Spirit.' And 'this wisdom descendeth not from above, but is earthly, sensual, devilish.' Isn't that a moral photograph of the whole scheme?"

Barbara listened, amazed. Was this their "little Naomi," as they had delighted to call her—the "child" for whom they'd prayed life might be sweet and time should treat her tenderly? What strides she'd taken, not only in her study of the facts connected with this abnormal development of sin, but in her ability to grasp the moral issues involved and to see the inevitable trend of the whole. Bible words came to Barbara also. Instinctively in her thought she applied them, "From whence has this one wisdom, having never learned?" And instantly the inspired and fit answer came to mind, "They took knowledge of them that they had been with Jesus."

Eventually, fighting vigorously every step, Mr. Newland realized he'd lost his prize. The day was over when extreme measures could be applied; he was well aware his sect had resorted to them in the past to carry out the "designs of Providence." Now "Gentiles" were present in large force in the "City of the Saints," and many of them had keen eyes and were on the alert. The United States government had spoken in no uncertain voice, and United States artillery could be used on occasion. The advocates, not only of a new religion but a new morality, had to move carefully in cases where powerful and open-eyed Gentile enemies watched. Mr. Newland knew he must be careful.

In addition to that, perhaps above that—for Mr. Newland was in deed and in truth as good a man as his system of religious belief would permit—he loved Naomi. Loved her enough to sacrifice even himself to what he became at last convinced was the inevitable. In truth, he loved her enough to sacrifice his own soul, measured by standards. He made terrible propositions. He'd sacrifice his home, his business, yes, even his religion—he would be anything or nothing, as she wished. He would go away with her to the ends of the earth and never mention the old life to her again, or think of it, if she'd only come to him and let them live their lives together.

It was another of his terrible mistakes. He saw in Naomi's face that visible recoil from him which cut into his very soul.

"Your children," she said, "you would forsake them? Those other women you say you feel bound to in God's sight—you would desert them?"

Those questions were awful lessons in righteousness. They made him feel the yawning gulf he was constantly widening between himself and the woman he loved.

She broke only once before him, bowed herself in misery and stooped to abject pleading. It occurred after one of her solemn renunciations, in which she tried to make plain to his moral nature that the potent forces separating them forever were named RIGHT or WRONG and that no amount of love or desire could overcome them.

"And the child, Naomi, my child and yours, what of her?" he said.

Then a groan, such as he'd never heard from her, escaped her lips. She must acknowledge his rights here, and she did. She pleaded as for her life. He said he loved her, that he would do anything for her—would he do this great thing? Would he give her the child?

"And let you teach her to despise her father and hate his religion," he said sternly.

Naomi turned as white as the gown she wore and put her hand suddenly to her heart as though its strange beating hurt her. But her voice grew steady.

"I will be true," she said, "though it kill me. I will never speak one word to the child against her father. But that which he calls religion, and which has him in its awful toils, I will teach her by every means in my power to hate! *hate!* HATE! So help me God."

The perspiration stood like great beads upon the man's forehead. He clenched his hands until the flesh shrank at the print of his nails. He wanted to take that woman in his arms and fly to the ends of the earth and force her to be only his. And he couldn't touch her. She was haloed about with righteousness. After a moment he spoke in a low, hoarse tone. "You may have the child." Then he turned and went away.

Naomi had won. But she had another wish, and it grew upon her and oppressed her until she knew it was of God. She must have the girl, Mara; she must save her for the Lord Christ.

Mr. Newland didn't come again, but she wrote to him.

She had written him only one letter before this, and he practically ignored it. But she put her soul into her plea for Mara. The girl haunted her, she told him; day and night she thought of her. She was in peril, in deadly peril. He didn't know it. Since he was a man, perhaps he couldn't understand how a girl like his daughter might ruin her own life, would ruin it, if she weren't helped. Would he let her come for a little while? Just for a day or a few hours, perhaps, if he weren't willing for more?

It seemed foolish to her when she wrote it, this plea to a father to give her a chance to save his daughter from the very life he was pressing upon her, from beliefs on which his own soul rested. But she prevailed. Perhaps in part because Mr. Newland held no deep affection for his eldest daughter, he interposed no serious obstacles in her going to Naomi. He'd had ambitions regarding her marriage, and she'd succeeded in thwarting them so far—because of her perverse nature, he believed. He was somewhat irritated with her and at the same time puzzled over what step to take next. It was a relief to think of being rid of such a troublesome responsibility for a time.

But the main reason, after all, for yielding had to do with Naomi's power over him. He offered to peril his own soul for her sake, and it wasn't likely he'd hesitate over his daughter's soul. He hoped, rather forlornly, that the beautiful girl, who fascinated everybody she came in contact with, might accomplish with Naomi what he hadn't. The experiment should at least be tried.

He went down himself to bring Mara to town. He hadn't seen the girl since the evening of a certain very stormy domestic interview; in it he angrily accused Mara of wrecking her father's happiness for life. Her mother took the girl's part and told him with a new plainness that it was time he knew how wrecked lives felt. They parted in anger.

He was dignified when he returned. He told Mara coldly that despite the fact she brought heavy sorrow upon a father who'd been only good to her, he was still disposed to give her another trial. Few people in this world were offered an opportunity to undo some of their own mischief. She was one of those favored few. Her Aunt Naomi wanted her. If she chose even now to be true to her father, all might yet be well.

He found Mara eager to go, willing indeed to make all sorts of vague promises to be once more with the beautiful, intriguing woman whom she unwittingly brought close to death. On the way back to town Mr. Newland, after doing all he could to impress his daughter with the magnitude of her sin, changed his tactics and condescended in a dignified way to bribe. He led Mara to understand that if she succeeded in bringing about a different state of things between Naomi and him, nothing money could buy or his resources provide would be considered too great a reward. Poor man! He understood his daughter almost as little as the woman he persisted in calling wife.

Mara was charmed. She rejoiced with a young girl's joy in the sense of power. Rebellion against a man's will, especially when that man was "Brother Newland," as she spoke of him, was so new to the girl's environment that it gave her exquisite pleasure. Most women she knew intimately, however they might rave among themselves, were meek in the presence of the men who dominated them. Not so with Mara. She rebelled and knew, as a result, that many observed her in wonder. She hoped and believed she'd find in Naomi a kindred spirit. She was startled and shocked at first over the idea of a wife's rebelling against her husband; then she rejoiced in the daring spirit it indicated. What mightn't the two of them accomplish together?

In this mood, and not at all as the mediator her father hoped, she came again to Naomi. The first day or two of her stay resulted chiefly in a succession of shocks to Naomi and the earnest women who were to struggle with her for this periled soul.

"She's as beautiful as an angel," Bernice said to Gertrude, as she reported some of the talk that day. "But if that name applies, she must represent a fallen angel. Can you imagine such ideas being advanced by a young girl in her social position?"

"That would depend upon whether I'd lived in this part of the world long enough to be acquainted with it," Gertrude said calmly. "Why should we be astonished at the fruit, Bernice? We know how the children talk together in their play. We know what they see and hear at home. Why shouldn't they talk and why shouldn't each succeeding generation begin on a lower moral plane than the last? I think that's inevitable."

"Well," said Bernice, with a long sigh, "that's true. But isn't it awful? It's never come home to me so closely before. She's so beautiful and so winsome in many ways. Oh, Gertrude, we must save her!"

"We'll try," said Gertrude gravely. "But it's a hard problem we have to solve—nothing less than how to save a girl from her father and her religion."

Chapter 27

" 'Tis not a life;
'tis but a piece of childhood thrown away."

It wasn't difficult to learn Mara's views of life. She talked freely about her own affairs as well as others', having none of the reticence regarding personal matters which these women were used to finding in young people of culture. The girl admired Naomi very much and was eager to express the feeling.

"I just glory in her pluck," she said airily. "To think of her being able to withstand Brother Newland of all men in the world. That's good fun. I wish I could have seen him when he first took in the fact. But it didn't have a good effect upon his disposition. When he came out to us he was in a towering rage. I was really afraid for awhile that he'd order the earth to open and swallow poor me. Think of attributing all his troubles to me! I had such a time! I had to tell some skillful lies to escape immediate destruction."

"Does your religion allow you to tell lies?" It was the usually patient Gertrude who couldn't resist this thrust.

"Oh, well," she said with a graceful shrug of her pretty shoulders, "it was to save life this time—that makes a difference, doesn't it? Father was certainly angry enough for awhile to do some desperate deed. But we're on better terms now; he expects great things of me." She said this last with a shrewd, half-comical glance toward Naomi, who at that moment entered the room.

"What do I call you?" Mara asked abruptly. "It's awkward to talk about you and not have a name for you. But you don't seem to like me to say 'Aunt Naomi.' "

Naomi shrank from the words. She'd lived in the tainted atmosphere long enough to know this was how children addressed their fathers' plural wives. The phrase placed her irrevocably with that class.

"No," she said quickly, "don't call me that. I'm not your aunt."

"Well, then, shall I say Mrs. Newland?"

The victim shuddered as if the sound of the name caused physical pain. Mara laughed lightly.

"You see, you don't like any of your names," she said. "What am I to do?"

"Call me Naomi—nothing else," said that poor woman at last.

"Oh, shall I, really? I like that; it sounds so friendly and companionable. That's what your old friends call you, isn't it? And it makes an old friend of me? Good! I don't have any friends. I've even lost my poor old lover—the one I told you about that day, you remember? He was after me for months. Poor old grandfather! He lost a tooth, and it's dreadfully unbecoming. I don't mind gray hair; it makes one look rather distinguished. But yawning chasms where teeth ought to be are horrid. He got mad at me. I think it's because I made faces at him one night. He turned around at just the wrong moment and saw me as I was showing the girls how he looked when he told his experience. He found another girl. She isn't sixteen yet, and you ought to see the airs she puts on because she thinks she's cut me out—as if I cared!

"Oh, Mrs. Naomino? Well, then, just plain Naomi—if you plan it so I can marry my George, I'll do anything else in the world you want of me. I haven't seen him in five weeks. He's out of town, but I know he must be dying to get back to me. Couldn't I have him call here to see me when he comes back? Mother doesn't dare have him at our house except on the sly, because Father's set against him. The old grandfather put him up to that, and Father's wretched young ones are always looking for something to tell him against me. But away out here we could manage it. I'm under your care now anyway.

"You've made a splendid rebel once—couldn't you rebel again for me? Look! I'll kneel to you as a slave if you will. I can easily picture you as a queen with loyal subjects. You're queenly, you know, and pretty. I don't wonder Father adores you."

She dropped gracefully on one knee before Naomi and kissed a cold hand in mock humility, closing the farce with a little laugh.

"Who is 'George'?" asked Barbara, hoping to save Naomi from speaking just then.

"George is my willing slave. George is divine. I adore him. If he had seven wives already, I'd willingly be the eighth. But he hasn't, you understand. He doesn't approve of the plural marriage, not now. But very soon after we're married I'll take him East, because such disapprovals don't hold in this atmosphere.

"By the way, Miss Halsted, I wonder if George Wilbur was originally from your part of the country? I'm sure I've heard him mention the name I saw on the postmark of one of your letters this morning. Did you know such a man in the East? He isn't young. I suppose he's forty, perhaps more. But he's a handsome man, and he looks and acts young. I like him better than if he were a mere boy. In fact, I think little boys are as disagreeable out of their place as old men are out of theirs.

"I've always told Mama that since I have to be married, I thought I might at least have the freedom of choice and not be compelled to marry either a grandfather or a child in knee pants. That was when they wanted me to marry a silly boy about my own age. I've had oceans of trouble.

"Miss Halsted, wouldn't it be delicious if my George proved to be an old acquaintance of yours? You'd aid and abet me then, wouldn't you? He could come here all he chose under cover of visiting you. Wouldn't that pull the wool over Brother Newland's eyes in a most charming matter?"

Bernice replied in a calm tone that she once knew a George Wilbur and that he and Mara's friend might be one and the same; when she had more time, they would compare notes. Then she rose at once and broke up the circle. But from that moment her interest in the girl grew quickly. She interested herself in Mara's every movement, studied her tastes, and bore with her whims in a way that amazed Barbara and Gertrude, both of whom daily despaired over doing anything for her.

"There's more to the child than appears on the surface," Bernice would say emphatically. "She has great possibilities for good or evil. Naomi's right; she *must* be saved."

"She's so painfully frivolous," objected Gertrude.

"I know. But don't you think part of that is assumed—as a necessary outgrowth of her surroundings? The more I see of these girls, the more I realize they must make either comedy or tragedy of life. Poor Mara is in the comic stage or the pretense of it."

As the days passed and Bernice's interest in the strange young girl continued unabated, it looked as though she, not Naomi or Barbara, was to influence Mara. At least they grew hourly more intimate, until at last they spent every moment of Bernice's leisure together. Then, suddenly, a break came. For an entire day Mara held herself coldly away from her new friend, declining invitations to walk or drive, and showing by every means in her power that she was offended. In the evening she expressed her mind to Naomi.

"That Miss Halsted can be awfully disagreeable when she chooses. I've always heard that old maids were horrid creatures, and I think it must be true. Do you know why she never married? I do. Don't you think she was engaged to George Wilbur, my George. Isn't that strange? She threw him over, too—there's your honorable woman for you, who would die for the truth, all because he flirted with another girl and broke her heart. It was mean of him, of course. But I don't think he deserved such treatment as that, do you? Still, I should be glad. If she'd married him, he wouldn't be out here probably, dying to marry me. Perhaps he would. He might have come and joined us and taken me for his second choice. Isn't it interesting the way lives are mixed up?

"He told me a horrid fib, though. See if I don't pay him back for that one of these days, if I get a chance! He said he'd never married because he never met anybody he liked well enough until he saw me. But these men say pretty things like that. I presume they're all alike. Miss Halsted wants me to give George up, just because he cheated a girl years ago. I think that would be cruel, don't you? What do you think anyhow?"

What did Naomi think? She considered the question a long time that evening. Was this girl already hopeless? Had her terrible inheritance, together with her environment up to now, coarsened her nature beyond redemption? What foundation was there on which to build true womanhood? But Bernice was courageous.

"We must save her from that man," she said with emphasis. "It's strange, as she says, that his life and mine have crossed again, but I believe it's for a purpose. I've kept up on him somewhat, Naomi. He's less trustworthy than he was eight years ago; he'll not have Mara's life to ruin. The child doesn't love him; it'll help us to remember that. She doesn't love anybody but you, unless it's her mother, a little, with a protecting love. She loves you, Naomi, with a love that's almost idolatry, and it will save her. You can do what you will with her, after a little. Just now she's fascinated with the attentions of a man of the world who knows how to flatter her. George Wilbur can be very fascinating, but that's all there is. She's still a child, though the awful system she's been trained in has tried to force womanhood upon her. I don't think it's ingrained coarseness that leads her to talk as she does, it's atmosphere. You and I can't realize what that would do; it's so foreign to our experience.

"Imagine a girl reared in an atmosphere from which a child of twelve can come to school and chatter with her friends like this: 'We've had an awful fuss at our house, and Papa's gone to the other house to stay. He says he won't come back until Mama behaves herself. Mama can't endure Aunt Kate. Yesterday she shut the door in her face and told her never to come to our house again. But Aunt Kate just laughed; she knows Papa is sweet on her just now.'

"Forgive me, Naomi, for bringing such a picture before you"—Naomi was pallid and trembling—"I felt I must, so you might understand the environment of even the *children* and be encouraged for Mara. It's wonderful she's stayed as much of a child as she has. I could tell her more about George Wilbur. I shrank from it for her sake, and I hoped it mightn't be necessary. But I think it will be, and I think we can win her to protect herself from his influence. Don't be discouraged, dear. This child will be one of the stars in your crown someday."

They waited and were patient with the girl, who was so new a study to them. Her fascination for Naomi continued. She named her the queen, and Barbara the princess; but after nursing her dignity for a few days, she returned to Bernice as a companion.

"There's no use trying to quarrel with you," she said frankly. "You won't let me. I don't think you know how to quarrel. Being an old maid with peculiar views and no fear of being compelled to marry your grandfather, you can't understand how anxious I am to save myself from the worst by marrying poor George. I'm going to forgive you, even though you're hard on him. When he and I are married, you'll come and see us. Then you'll find how nice he's become and forgive him for those youthful follies."

"I'll have to tell her more," said this good woman to herself with a sigh.

But she resolved to wait and try to strengthen their influence over the girl. And their influence grew quickly. They'd opened a new world to Mara, and in some directions she flourished in the purer atmosphere. She asked shrewd questions from time to time, not always of Naomi, though she continued to be the "queen."

"She's grand!" the girl said to Bernice. "She's wonderful! Think of voluntarily giving up a man like my father to another woman. She ordered him to go back to my mother and be true to her. I heard him tell Aunt Maria so. It made Aunt Maria like a tiger—she wants him herself, you see. But the queen is ahead of them all in her influence over Father. I believe she could get him to do anything she wanted, and she has *given him up*.

"It's such an awful pity that Mother doesn't care—she doesn't anymore. She sneers at Father sometimes and says Mrs. Roper is the one who should have him because she can worship him in spite of everything. Mother can't. She thinks she's borne too much. She told me once that she wouldn't send for Father if she were dying; she wouldn't want to see him. I think she's foolish. It's different from the queen. Mother married Father with her eyes wide open, knowing then he'd had another wife. But she was very young, and she believed him when he told her he was marrying her for love and had never loved anybody else and never would. I'd never believe the creatures when they talk that way. I've heard too much of it."

When the girl dropped into talk like this, the three women who were trying to save her grew fainthearted. They reminded themselves of the conditions in which she was reared and comforted one another with the thought of the transforming power of real unadulterated religion. Mara's questions regarding the only religion she knew anything about were answered with perfect frankness and the strictest adherence to historic facts. And every day the girl's insight seemed to grow keener.

At last Bernice determined the time had come when she must present other facts concerning George Wilbur. Each day the man was expected, and it seemed important to diminish the effect of his personal presence. Bernice chose her time with care, giving up her Saturday to a long drive alone with Mara; she surrounded the susceptible child with the country's sweet and holy influences of earth and air.

During their return drive, after spending what Mara declared was a heavenly day, Bernice made the revelations she'd hoped to spare her. The young girl received them in startled silence. She was a creature of unpredictable moods, but Bernice was surprised and perplexed at this one. Apparently Mara wasn't angry; she didn't seem to have anything to say and didn't wish to be questioned. Her reticence and dignity included them all, though she hovered about Naomi and was still devoted to her.

"We've evidently reached a milestone," said Barbara, as Naomi's three helpers anxiously discussed the situation. "It remains to be seen just what it will mark in the future. We must wait."

Chapter 28

"I slept, and dreamed that life was Beauty,
I woke, and found that life was Duty."

"God did anoint thee with his odorous oil
To wrestle, not to reign."

Sunday was a day of restraint and general discomfort. Mara declined to go to church and gave most of her time to the baby. Later they were sitting together in the twilight, the four women and the restless spirit so unlike them she might have come from another world. She suddenly broke the silence that had fallen on them with a remark that had nothing to do with the subject they'd been discussing.

"I don't see that your boasted religion or morality or whatever you call it is any better than ours. It isn't as good as ours by your own showing. There's that girl you talked about yesterday, Miss Halsted, ruined soul and body. If George Wilbur had belonged to our sect instead of yours, he would have married her decently and taken care of her after a fashion, at least. She'd have been recognized as respectable and gone into society and all that, instead of skulking about as a wreck. Then George could have married his other wives when he got ready and didn't need to have anymore to do with the first one than he chose. But she'd have had her place, and there wouldn't have been any scandal. I don't see why that isn't a great deal better than the other way."

Naomi's breath came quickly, and she felt her face burn. They were all glad of the darkness. Starting from such a moral plane as that, what hope was there for the girl of seventeen? It was nurse Gertrude who first found voice.

"My dear, if you were reared in an atmosphere of ordinary purity, you couldn't raise such a question. Your whole soul would revolt against it. I don't think you're to blame for not seeing the matter in its true light; it's your misfortune. But I wonder if we can't explain what it is to us?

"To lift the poor victim of a bad man to the plane of supposed respectability by the road you propose is to take Sin, reeking with filth, and cover it over with white robes and label it Purity. What good would the label do? If you were trying to rescue a child from the slums, would you put the clean garments you prepared for her over the vile ones of the gutter and say to her, 'Now you are clean and pure—be happy'? If you would, that's not the way we do in a world where the Lord Jesus Christ sets the standard of living.

"There are such words as righteousness and purity, and there's such a word as sin. We lead no one into moral filth in the name of religion or respectability.

One who makes the descent, whether man or woman, does so with eyes wide open, being taught plainly what God and those who take God for their Guide will think of Him. Isn't that after all the safe way?"

But Mara had retired again into silence. She was obstinately uncommunicative; nothing could draw her out. The spell lasted for several days.

Then, as the girl laid the baby in Naomi's arms one morning, she burst forth again: "Do you know I believe those horrid things Miss Halsted said the other night are true? They were awful things—at least what they hinted at were. They made my blood boil with rage at first, but I believe them. There's such a thing as purity, and there's a veneer named purity that our people use, but it covers Sin. I feel it. I believe I've always felt it, without knowing what was the matter with me. It's what has made me odd. I hated to marry that old man. I felt it would be sin for me to do so, in spite of all they said. Queen Naomi, I'm not all bad. Won't you believe in me a little?"

She bent and kissed Naomi's forehead, then stamped her foot and added imperiously: "I won't be bad; they shan't make me! I won't live the life my mother has. She's had to lie; the system teaches it, requires it. I won't! I'll follow your example. I'll leave them! I hate it all! I believe I always have, though I'd never have dared but for you. Some streak of my great-great-grandmother must be in me. She was a Puritan; I will be, too. I don't want to get married; it was only that I knew I must. And I thought George Wilbur would—"

She stopped suddenly, then burst forth again. "I hate George Wilbur, too. The old man who was brought up in it is more decent than he is. Do you know what he's done? Did she tell you? And to think he could tell me he never cared for any human being until he saw me! Oh, lies! *Lies!* LIES! I'm sick to death of it all. I've lived in a lying atmosphere all my life, but I hate it. I've struggled and fought, yes, and prayed, against my hatred of this life, but I won't anymore. I'll pray to be delivered from it, and God sent you to answer my prayer."

Suddenly she dropped to her knees before Naomi and the baby. "Naomi, couldn't we go away somewhere, you and I, where the air is pure—miles and miles away from it all? Mother would be willing, would be glad. Poor Mother—she hates it, too. She told me once she'd rather go to my funeral than to my wedding. Think of that! Couldn't we do it somehow?"

Then Naomi leaned across her sleeping baby and kissed the kneeling girl, who was sobbing now, and knew God had given her this soul as a symbol of her martyrdom.

"We'll go away, dear," she said.

On the evening of that day Mr. George Wilbur's card was brought to Mara. She glanced at the name and tossed the card down scornfully. "I want nothing of him," she said, "except never to see or hear of him again. Will one of you go and tell him so for me?"

For this reason Bernice Halsted, bridging the years, moved once more down the stairs to an interview with George Wilbur. In her pocket at the moment lay a letter from her mother received the day before—her poor mother, who still had spasms of hopefulness for her daughter.

"Mrs. Wilbur is visiting here," so the letter ran, "for the first time in six years. She's much changed. Poor woman, she feels her separation from George keenly. He's never married, she tells me, and has lived what she calls a wrecked life, because of a bit of boyish folly. Those were her very words.

"Bernice, dear, you said I must never mention this to you again. But that was years ago, and time may have softened you. I've made the most exhaustive inquiries, and I'm sure now, as I was at first, that poor George was more sinned against than sinning. He wasn't to blame because girls lost their hearts to him. You're a dear daughter, and I'm blessed above most in my children. But I'm growing old and in a little while must go away and leave you. If I could only see you happily married first, to the man who was so long ago like a son to me!

"Poor George has been true to his first love; his mother told me so with tears in her eyes. He's living a roving life somewhere in the West. Wouldn't it be strange, most romantic indeed, if his path and yours should cross again? Daughter, if you should meet him, I trust you won't lose sight of the fact that it's a Christian's part to forgive. Whatever wrong you may imagine the poor fellow did in thought to you, must surely be amply atoned for by his years of martyrdom."

Bernice smiled as she read the letter, then sighed. The sigh was for her mother, who was trained in an environment that made it impossible for her to believe an unmarried life could be successful and happy.

George Wilbur was waiting for his latest charmer to arrive, ready to say, "My dear child, what an age it is since I've seen your beautiful face!" He was unprepared for the vision that was presently framed in the doorway. Bernice Halsted! He hadn't thought seriously of her in years, and the sweet faces and forms he consoled himself with in the interim were numerous. Yet here she stood before him—the girl who was once his ideal—a woman now, and he knew in an instant she was his ideal still.

He couldn't for his life have repeated what she said to him as she stood there in the doorway. He didn't remember, afterward, anything about Mara's message. He discovered somehow that he was dismissed. He found himself on the street and realized, not that he didn't see Mara, but that he saw Bernice Halsted.

He troubled Mara with no more letters, as they feared he might. But he wrote one letter to Bernice which in its way was a masterpiece. In it he assured his first love she was his only one. Through the years he couldn't tear her image from his heart. Only very recently did he let in a little hope that the years had made her—not less good, but less severe.

He sinned, but not to the extent she believed. That poor dead girl shouldn't be blamed for mistaking kind interest for a deeper feeling on his part. Let that pass; he was willing to bear all the blame and admit he was careless. But if he sinned, he also suffered. Wouldn't the past suffice? Hadn't the years atoned? Would she allow him to call her—friend? And might he visit her occasionally? Surely that wasn't much to ask of one who had been to him—but he wouldn't weary her with reminders.

She must allow him, though, a word of explanation regarding that lovely child, Mara. His interest in her had been extreme; and his desire and effort to save her from a cruel fate might have placed him in a false position. It seemed to be his fate to have his sympathies run away with his judgment. Now, however, that Mara had found wiser and more influential friends than he could be, he didn't need to think anymore about her except to be thankful she escaped.

This letter Bernice returned to the writer with these added lines: "I have acquaintances in Ardmore. I've been at the home of Mrs. Bennett Searles and have met several times the poor girl known in that region as Sarah Bateman. I've done what I could to help her in the 'cruel fate' which has fallen upon her. The 'false position' in which she's placed I fully understand. If you have any desire at this late day to unite 'judgment' and 'feeling,' the way is certainly open for you to make what tardy atonement you can.

"Bernice Halsted."

∽

In this way George Wilbur learned once more that in the souls of some women is a power that makes for righteousness and with them the name of sin is Sin and may not be disguised. To say he was disappointed is to put it mildly. When this man first engaged himself to Bernice Halsted, he purposed deep in his heart to marry her sometime. Through the years and his innumerable passing "fancies" he steadily nursed that idea. Sometime, somewhere, when he was tired of pretty faces and surfeited with adoration, he would look up Bernice Halsted, a good comfortable, sensible old maid, grown wiser with the years, and marry her, little as she deserved it.

He hadn't looked her up; he had blundered upon her, and the effect upon him of the meeting astonished him. But it wasn't until he read those lines appended to his long, carefully worded letter that he realized Bernice Halsted would never marry him.

Naomi and Mara were planning to go away. Barbara had urged it for several weeks; she was sure Naomi needed a change of scenery. She planned to send them to her friends in Colorado, Dr. Ellis Carpenter, pastor of the First Church of Glenmere, and his wife, Lilian. Barbara was sure two better friends than these for Naomi's sore heart and for the dangerous girl Mara couldn't be found this side of heaven. Moreover, she, Barbara, always spent a generous part of her summer vacations with them, and this would give her opportunity to be with Naomi. Much correspondence had ensued, and all arrangements were satisfactorily made. Mara even secured her father's consent without difficulty.

"Poor father," the girl remarked to Bernice as she folded the letter in which he wrote that his daughter was to do whatever her "Aunt Naomi" wished. "Poor father, he thinks I'm a connecting link. Strange, isn't it, how I can stand outside my life and appreciate it all? Father worships Naomi, and he thinks that sometime, somehow, he'll get her again, and he never will! I'm beginning to understand her, but Father never can. Father breathes tainted air, and it's in his lungs and is part of him."

Naomi had no financial struggles. Her keen-sighted father saw to it that the princely fortune he left his one child was so hedged about with trustees and provisions that even Naomi herself could dispose of only small portions of it for other than her personal use. Mr. Volney Newland had made no effort to change the business conditions surrounding her vast wealth. In truth, he was relatively indifferent to it; it wasn't Naomi's money he wanted, but Naomi.

It came to pass, then, that the four old-time friends were once more spending a last evening together. Not one of them but thought of that last evening years ago, in the third story south room of the old college; not one of them referred to it. The changes had been too solemn, and the sorrows that rested upon one of their number were too tense for words.

They tried to be cheery, or at least sensible and ordinary; but the conditions weren't ordinary. Naomi going away alone with her baby in her arms, widowed, yet not widowed. And always there was *Mara*. The conditions would not even bear thinking about.

Gertrude caught up the evening paper for relief. She glanced down the latest telegraphic news column, suppressed an exclamation, and glanced apprehensively toward Naomi, who was just then bending over her baby. She pushed the paper to Barbara with her finger on a paragraph, and Barbara read, "Just as we go to press we learn that our esteemed townsman Mr. Volney Newland has met with a terrible accident." The usual account of a belated and foolhardy man, a moving train, and a misstep followed.

The three friends left the room on some pretext and held an anxious consultation as to whether they should tell Naomi at once.

"And Mara," said Bernice. "After all, he's her father."

Still, no message came to them, and it was already late. They determined to wait until morning. Probably the account was exaggerated—first news of accidents generally were. In the gray of the early morning tidings came. Mr. Newland lay unconscious for several hours and then ceased to breathe.

Barbara went with her friend to the closed and darkened room where the body lay. "I want to see him," Naomi said, her face almost as white as the dead. "It can do no harm to anyone now."

At the door they met Mrs. Roper, her face swollen with weeping. She shot angry glances at Naomi and Mara and rushed away as if the sight of them were hateful. Poor slave of the man she'd lived for, she resented with all her ignorant power the arrival of those who didn't bend to that man's will. Mrs. Roper loved him as a dog might, fiercely, irrationally, and hated whatever caused him trouble.

Barbara went with Mara into the closed room and stood with an arm around her while the girl wept bitterly with regret that she was ever rude, disobedient, unfilial. She hadn't known her father very well or loved him much. Yet he was her *father,* and for a little while nature had its way.

Naomi went in alone, closing the door behind her. She wanted it so. What passed between the living and the dead in that quiet room only God knows. She didn't stay long. She made no scene; she shed no tears. As for color, she couldn't have been paler than she was when she went in. She spoke no word, and her friends respected her silence.

That evening, after Mara, still sobbing, said good night and left with Bernice, Barbara lingered to see to the comfort of mother and baby. Then she bent over to kiss Naomi and was held for a moment.

"Don't go, Barbara, not yet. He was the father of my baby, and once, I thought he was my husband. Stay and pray."

Not long after that they did what Naomi once thought she could never do—they went back to her girlhood home, she and Mara and the baby. The deserted house was opened and renovated and filled with sunshine and roses and all cheerful colors and odors and sounds. Naomi meant to surround the young life added to hers with all the brightness she could.

She also entered at once into the life of the nearby village. She took part in the church, the women's societies, the young people's gatherings, whatever invited cooperation; and the open doors, of course, were numberless. They gathered about her, the good friendly people who knew her mother a little and respected her father and remembered Naomi as a girl. They were glad to have her back and said so. They had reason to be glad; she made life richer for them in many ways.

They talked about her in a friendly manner when they met.

"What a beautiful woman Mrs. Newland is. She was a pretty girl, but as a woman she's charming. Isn't it strange she married without changing her name? She's still Naomi Newland."

"But isn't her stepdaughter lovely? She's the most beautiful girl I ever saw and so devoted to her stepmother. Naomi is certainly blessed in that respect."

"It's odd she calls her 'Naomi,' though, don't you think? To be sure, there isn't a great difference in their ages. I suppose it would be absurd for her to say 'Mother.' The baby must resemble the father; she doesn't look in the least like Naomi, nor like Mara."

"Naomi never mentions her husband, does she? I tried to think of something proper to say about him one day and couldn't. She silences a person—I don't know how."

An older voice took up the word: "Poor young widow, she worshipped him, I suppose. That was Naomi as a child. Silence is kinder to some natures than words. I wouldn't touch her sorrow if I were you."

So they kept merciful silence.

As the months passed, other talk was taken up in church circles.

"That lovely Mrs. Newland is an ardent missionary worker, isn't she?" said a newcomer. "Was she as a girl?"

There was a general laugh, in which one explained that neither Naomi nor her mother was apparently aware such a subject as missions existed.

"Nor a church either, for that matter," added another. "Naomi wasn't even a church member before she went abroad. It must have been her husband's influence that made her over."

"Mrs. Newland has a hobby," announced Mrs. Sinclair, the president of the missionary society. "She's intensely interested in the Mormons and is the best-informed woman on their peculiar beliefs that I've ever met."

"Speaking of Mormons," said one of the young women, "you should hear that girl, Mara Newland, talk. She's absolutely fierce. She's lived, she says, where she saw some of the fruits. It's wonderful to hear her—and terrible. It doesn't seem as if half she thinks can be true. I never heard such talk! I always thought the Mormons were a harmless set of fanatics, strange but honest."

"That's what too many of our people think," said the president with firmness. "I believe the United States will awaken someday to the fact that under the guise of that harmless fanaticism they've been harboring nests of poisonous serpents. My hope and prayer are that the government will open its eyes before irreparable mischief has been done."

"Dear me!" murmured a woman in the next room. "Our president is getting fanatical, too. There's no use in getting excited over it, I guess. The Mormons have a right to their religious notions, I suppose. It's a free country. If we let them alone, they'll probably do the same with us."

Naomi entered in time to hear that last remark. Her eyes flashed with a strange light. What would those people, those good, quiet, uninformed people, think if they knew her story? If she laid bare before them the way this religion they talked about so smoothly had let her "alone"—a girl reared in their midst, counted as one of their number?

What should she do to help open blind eyes? Victims? Why, the country was filled with them. Who might the next one be? And in the meantime what about the girls born and reared in the pestilent atmosphere—lovely innocent girls, as innocent as their awful environment permitted—being daily drawn downward by the hundreds, even as their mothers had been.

She rescued one, but what was one? Oh, why wouldn't the safe, sheltered people, wives and mothers in honored homes, fathers and sons and brothers whose lives were pledged to keep those homes pure—why wouldn't they understand this awful whirlpool of impurity? Why didn't they study the problem, watch it, pray, and ACT?

So once more in the depths of her desolated heart this one victim cried out, *Oh, Lord, how long?*